WHY
THIS BOOK
is a must for Chapter-wise study?

Class 10 (2022-23)

- **NEW PAPER PATTERN**
- **INFERENCE-BASED LEARNING**

Conceptual Learning

New Pattern

THEORY
- ✓ Topic-wise Notes
- ✓ Solved Examples
- ✓ ICSE Suggestions

QUESTIONS
- ✓ HOT (Most Asked) Questions
- ✓ Detailed Explanations
- ✓ Marking Scheme Answers

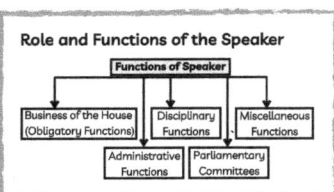

Example 5. Which types of cases are settled in the Lok Adalat?

Ans. The Lok Adalat mainly settles small civil cases, settlement of family feuds, minor cases of assault and injury which can be settled amicably.

1. Who is empowered to promulgate an Ordinance when the Parliament is not in session?
   (a) The Vice-President
   (b) The President
   (c) The Prime Minister
   (d) The Attorney General of India
   [ICSE Specimen Paper Sem-1, 2021]

Ans. (c) Germany, Italy, Austria-Hungary

Explanation: Germany entered into an alliance with Austria-Hungary. In 1882 Italy joined the alliance and it came to be known as Triple Alliance.

Lord Curzon's Reasons:
(1) That the province of Bengal was too big to be efficiently administered by a single provincial government. It was a mere readjustment of administrative boundaries to protect pockets of minorities both in West Bengal as well as East Bengal.
(2) To fetch more revenue through trade outlets.
(3) To protect pockets of minorities in East and West Bengal. [Any two]
[Marking Scheme]

Book Name	Educart ICSE Class 10 History and Civics 2 in 1 Guidebook 2022-23
Editor Name	Sonali Khosla
Edition	Latest
Published by	Agrawal Group Of Publications (AGP) © All Rights reserved.
ADDRESS (Head office)	28/115 Jyoti Block, Sanjay Place, Agra, U.P. 282002
CONTACT	quickreply@agpgroup.in We reply super fast
BUY BOOK	www.educart.co Cash on delivery available
WHATSAPP (Head office)	8937099777
PRINTED BY	Schoolcart
DESKTOP PUBLISHING	Agrawal Group Of Publications (AGP)
ISBN	978-93-5561-544-2
© COPYRIGHT	Agrawal Group Of Publications (AGP)

Disclaimer: This teaching material has been published pursuant to an undertaking given by the publisher that the content does not in any way whatsoever violate any existing copyright or intellectual property right. Extreme care is put into validating the veracity of the content in this book. However, if there is any error found, please do report to us on the below email and we will re-check; and if needed rectify the error immediately for the next print.

ATTENTION

No part of this publication may be re-produced, sold or distributed in any form or medium (electronic, printed, pdf, photocopying, web or otherwise) on Telegram, WhatsApp, Youtube, Amazon, Flipkart, Snapdeal or any online portal, without the explicit contractual agreement with the publisher. Anyone caught doing so will be punishable by Indian law.

इस प्रकाशन का कोई भी हिस्सा टेलीग्राम, व्हाट्सएप, यूट्यूब, अमेज़न, फ्लिपकार्ट, स्नैपडील या किसी भी ऑनलाइन पोर्टल पर किसी भी रूप या माध्यम (इलेक्ट्रॉनिक, मुद्रित, पीडीएफ, फोटोकॉपी, वेब या अन्य) में फिर से उत्पादित, बेचा या वितरित नहीं किया जा सकता है। जो कोई भी ऐसा करता हुआ पकड़ा जाएगा, वह भारतीय कानून द्वारा दंडनीय होगा।

AGP contributes Rupee One on every book purchased by you to the **Friends of Tribals Society** Organization for better education of tribal children.

INDEX

Syllabus 2022-23   viii

Civics

1. **The Union Legislature**   1-22
   - Chapter Notes   2
   - Objective Type Questions   8
   - Subjective Type Questions   11

2. **The President and The Vice-President**   23-38
   - Chapter Notes   24
   - Objective Questions   27
   - Subjective Type Questions   30

3. **Prime Minister and the Council of Ministers**   39-54
   - Chapter Notes   40
   - Objective Type Questions   43
   - Subjective Type Questions   45

4. **The Judiciary**   55-70
   - Chapter Notes   56
   - Objective Type Questions   60
   - Subjective Type Questions   62

5. **The High Courts and the Subordinate Courts**   71-80
   - Chapter Notes   72
   - Objective Type Questions   75
   - Subjective Type Questions   76

History

1. **The First War of Independence, 1857**   81-100
   - Chapter Notes   82
   - Objective Type Questions   87
   - Subjective Type Questions   93

2. **Growth of Nationalism**   101-112
   - Chapter Notes   102
   - Objective Type Questions   107
   - Subjective Type Questions   109

3. **First Phase of the Indian National Movement**   113-122
   - Chapter Notes   114
   - Objective Type Questions   118
   - Subjective Type Questions   120

4. **Second Phase of the Indian National Movement**   123-142
   - Chapter Notes   124
   - Objective Type Questions   129
   - Subjective Type Questions   132

5. **The Muslim League** 143-154
   Chapter Notes 144
   Objective Type Questions 149
   Subjective Type Questions 150

6. **Mahatma Gandhi and the National Movements** 155-176
   Chapter Notes 156
   Objective Type Questions 163
   Subjective Type Questions 171

7. **Quit India Movement** 177-186
   Chapter Notes 178
   Objective Type Questions 182
   Subjective Type Questions 183

8. **Forward Bloc and the INA** 187-196
   Chapter Notes 188
   Objective Type Questions 191
   Subjective Type Questions 193

9. **Independence and Partition Of India** 197-208
   Chapter Notes 198
   Objective Type Questions 201
   Subjective Type Questions 203

10. **The First World War** 209-220
    Chapter Notes 210
    Objective Type Questions 213
    Subjective Type Questions 215

11. **Rise of Dictatorship** 221-236
    Chapter Notes 222
    Objective Type Questions 228
    Subjective Type Questions 231

12. **The Second World War** 237-248
    Chapter Notes 238
    Objective Type Questions 241
    Subjective Type Questions 242

13. **United Nations** 249-260
    Chapter Notes 250
    Objective Type Questions 253
    Subjective Type Questions 255

14. **Major Agencies of the United Nations** 261-272
    Chapter Notes 262
    Objective Type Questions 264
    Subjective Type Questions 266

15. **Non- Allied Movement** 273-282
    Chapter Notes 274
    Objective Type Questions 275
    Subjective Type Questions 276

Sample Papers

Sample Paper 1 286
ICSE Specimen Paper 2022-23
(Solved)

Sample Paper 2 293
(Self-Assessment)

Sample Paper 3 297
(Self-Assessment)

Sample Paper 4 301
(Self-Assessment)

Sample Paper 5 305
(Self-Assessment)

FREE STUDY MATERIAL

Need some more assistance? Now get instant and FREE access to CISCE, NCERT and DIKSHA platform content on our website.

www.educart.co

- ✓ **News:** Latest happenings and updates from CISCE (simplified format)
- ✓ **NCERT:** Complete NCERT content (books, exemplars, other)
- ✓ **Specimen Papers:** Latest and past years ICSE Specimen Papers
- ✓ **Past Year Papers:** Previous year all ICSE papers available

and much more...

ICSE FUTURE ANNOUNCEMENTS

CISCE continues to provide updates pertaining to curriculum, official specimen papers, datesheets and more. With the help of the QR code given below, we will keep you updated with all such new changes.

Everyone who buys this book, benefits from this exclusive feature!

Scan this special QR code to Subscribe

TOPIC-WISE
CHAPTER NOTES
FOR BEST LEARNING OUTCOMES

Glossary
Difficult terminologies are explained in a simplified way at the end of chapter notes.

 Glossary
(1) **Impeachment:** Removal from office by a special trial conducted by the Parliament for violation of the Constitution.
(2) **Single Integrated Judicial System:** It means Supreme court is the apex court. Below it, there are High Courts in each State and below High Courts are Sub-ordinate District Courts.

ICSE Suggestions
→ The role of Gandhiji in the National Movement is very important and the Non-Cooperation Movement and Civil Disobedience are very significant movements, it should be studied event wise in details, by the students.
→ Students should write all Historical facts / clauses/ provisions correctly because they cannot be diluted or misquoted. Students should present their answers in factual manner.

ICSE Suggestions
Given points will help you have better understanding in answering questions..

Important
Critical examinable points are added in between theory to cover useful concepts regarding the topic..

 Important
→ The special session of the Indian Constituent Assembly was held in the midnight of 14-15 August, 1947. Lord Mountbatten was the first Governor-General of Independent India and Jawaharlal took the oath as the First Prime Minister of India.

NEW PATTERN QUESTIONS
COMPLETELY REFRESHED, INCLUDING REAL LIFE-BASED

Concept-based Questions
Our Subject Experts have prepared new types of questions based on the latest ICSE pattern.

36. In 1930 Mahatma Gandhi's demands were rejected by the British, as a result of which he launched the Civil Disobedience Movement. In this context, explain the following:

(A) Name the famous march undertaken by Gandhiji. Where did he begin this march? State *two* of its features.

38. With reference to the Supreme Court, explain its function stated below:
    (A) Original Jurisdiction
    (B) Advisory Function
    (C) As a guardian of Fundamental Rights
    [ICSE 2014]

Previous Year Questions
Many past year solved questions are inculcated in between the exercises along with marking scheme.

What Examiner Say
Tips and tricks have been given to explain how to answer a particular question and avoid silly mistakes.

What Examiners Say
→ (A) (a) *Most of the candidates were able to answer this question correctly. However, a few candidates instead of the President mentioned the Governor.*

(b) *A number of candidates gave the correct qualifications of a High Court Judge.*

Syllabus

Units	Unit Names	Marks
SECTION A : CIVICS		
The Union Legislature	• Lok Sabha • Rajya Sabha	40
The Union Executive	• The President • The Vice-President • Prime Minister and Council of Ministers	
The Judiciary	• The Supreme Court • The High Courts • Subordinate Courts	
SECTION B : HISTORY		
The Indian National Movement (1857 - 1917)	• The First War of Independence, 1857 • Factors leading to the growth of Nationalism • First Phase of the Indian National Movement (1885-1907)	40
Mass Phase of the National Movement (1915-1947)	• Mahatma Gandhi - Non-Cooperation Movement • Forward Bloc (objectives) and INA • Independence and Partition of India	
The Contemporary World	• The First World War • Rise of Dictatorships • The Second World War • United Nations • Non-Aligned Movement (NAM)	
INTERNAL ASSESSMENT Subject Teacher/ Internal Examiner (10) + External Examiner (10)		20
TOTAL		**80+20**

1 CIVICS
The Union Legislature

The Union Parliament of India operates as the highest legislative body in our country. It consists of the President and the two Houses—Rajya Sabha and Lok Sabha.

Chapter Notes

- The Union Parliament and the Federal Set-Up in India
- The Lok Sabha
- Speaker of the Lok Sabha
- The Rajya Sabha
- Powers and Functions of the Rajya Sabha and the Lok Sabha

TOPIC 1

THE UNION PARLIAMENT AND FEDERAL SET-UP IN INDIA

The Constitution of India has provided for a 'Federal System of Government'. In a federal system of government, all the administrative powers are divided between the Central and the State Governments by the Constitution and both are Supreme within their respective spheres – Executive, Legislative and Judiciary.

Federal Features of Our Constitution

In India, two sets of government exist – the government for the entire country or the Union Government and the governments for the states known as the State Government.

The Union as well as State governments derive their authorities from the Constitution. They have well defined and exclusive powers in the spheres of executive, legislature and judiciary.

The Supreme Court is the final interpreter and guardian of the Constitution. Only the Supreme Court can settle disputes between the Union Government and State Government or between the States themselves.

Important

→ Every Citizen of India obeys two sets of laws, i.e., The State Laws and the Union Laws.

→ Though normally the system of our government is federal but the Constitution enables the federation to transform itself from a unitary State (by the assumption of the powers of states by the union) only during emergencies.

→ The term 'Federation' is not mentioned anywhere in the Constitution.

→ Though India is a federation, it is not like other federal systems, for example the United States, because:
  (1) There is only one Citizenship.
  (2) One Flag
  (3) One Constitution

→ There is also single Judiciary (Unitary Government), which is not divided between the Union and the States. In fact, all powers and administrative divisions and authorities lies in the hands of Central Government.

Indian Parliament

India is a democratic country. In a democratic government, the Parliament acts as the law making organ of the government.

Example 1. Define 'Parliament'.

Ans. 'Parliament' may be defined as 'a representative body or the legislative organ of the government, whose permission is Constitutionally required in the process of making or changing the Country's laws'.

Example 2. What are the powers of the Parliament?

Ans. The two powers of the Parliament are:
(1) The Parliament has the power to control the executive, i.e., the Union Council of Ministers.
(2) Its control over the National Budget is a recognized principle of democratic government.

Example 3. What comprises the Union Parliament or the Central Legislature?

Ans. The Union Parliament or the Central Legislature consists of three Constituents – The Rajya Sabha (The Upper House), the Lok Sabha (The Lower House) and the President.

Important

→ India is 'the largest democracy of the world', and here:

→ The law-making wing or body is called the 'Legislature'.

→ The governing wing or body is called the 'Executive'.

→ The governing wing or body that dispenses justice is called the 'Judiciary'.

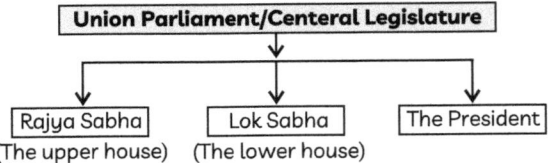

TOPIC 2

THE LOK SABHA

The Lower House of the Parliament of India is called House of the people or the 'Lok Sabha', which is the representative body of the people. The members of the Lok Sabha was directly elected by the adult voters of India on the basis of Universal Adult Franchise by the people.

Example 4. What do you mean by 'Universal Adult Franchise'?

Ans. It means that every citizen of India, not less than eighteen years of age who is not otherwise disqualified under any law, on grounds of unsound mind, crime or illegal practice, shall be registered as a voter for elections to the Legislative Assembly of a State or elections to the Lok Sabha, irrespective of gender caste, colour or religion, and has right to vote.

Example 5. What has the Principle of Universal Adult Franchise established?

Ans. The Principle of Universal Adult Frnachise has established a true democracy or government of the people, by the people and for the people in India.

Example 6. What is the importance of Secret Ballot in Lok Sabha elections?

Ans. The Lok Sabha elections are held by 'Secret Ballot,' which means the voters can cast their votes secretly, without any fear. They are saved from the pulls and pressures of the politicians. Moreover, no ill-feeling is created.

The Composition

The maximum strength of the Lok Sabha is 552 members. Out of this, 530 will represent the states and not more than 20 members will represent the Union Territories. Two Anglo-Indian members are nominated by the President to the Lok Sabha, if the President feels that the community is not adequately represented.

Term of the House

The term of the Lok Sabha is five years. It can be dissolved before the completion of five years by the President on the advice of the Prime Minister.

During the emergency period, the term of the Lok Sabha may be extended by the Parliament for one year.

Qualifications for the Members of the Lok Sabha

In order to seek membership of the Lok Sabha, a person must have some qualifications:

(1) He should be a citizen of India.
(2) He should be atleast 25 years old.
(3) He should not be a proclaimed criminal or offender.
(4) He should have his name in the electoral rolls in any part of the country.
(5) He or she should possess such other qualifications as specified by Parliament from time to time.
(6) He should not hold any office of profit under the State or Central Government.
(7) He should not be of unsound mind.
(8) He should not be an insolvent, i.e., he should not be in debt.

Presiding Officer

The speaker is the Presiding officer of the Lok Sabha.

Parliamentary Procedures and Sessions

Some formalities which the legislators have to observe in the Parliament as well as in State Legislatures are called Parliamentary Procedures.

Sessions

The President summons each House of the Parliament. Each House shall meet atleast twice a year and the interval between two consecutive sessions shall be less than six months.

Example 7. How many sessions are held in a year and When?

Ans. Normally there are three sessions in a year. They are:

(1) The Budget Session (February–May)
(2) The Monsoon Session (July–August)
(3) The Winter Session (November–December)

Quorum

The quorum means the minimum number of members required to the present in order to enable the House to transact its business.

As per rule, the quorum of the Lok Sabha and Rajya Sabha is one-tenth of the total membership of each House. The speaker may adjourn the House or suspend the meeting until there is a requisite quorum.

Question Hour

The fisrt hour on every working day of the Lok Sabha is reserved for questions unless otherwise decided by the speaker. This hour (which usually starts at 11 am) is known as the Question Hour.

Zero Hour

The Zero Hour refers to the period which begins at 12 O' clock soon after the Question hour and continues till lunch break which begins at 1 O'clock. During the Zero Hour members raise all types of questions, without any permission or prior notice.

Definition and Types of Motions

A 'motion' is a formal proposal made by a member that the House should do something regarding a matter of public importance.

The Adjournment Motion

An Adjournment motion means a proposal to buy all other business and take up definite matter of urgent importance. Such a motion leads to the interruption of normal business of the House.

Example 8. Who accepts the Adjournment motion in the Lok Sabha and how?

Ans. The speaker of the Lok Sabha accepts this motion if:

(1) The matter is definite.
(2) If he feels that the matter is so urgent that it should be discussed on the same day.
(3) If the subject is of Public importance.

The Union Legislature 3

Then only the normal routine work of the House will be suspended and the matter, which becomes urgent, will be discussed on the floor of the House.

Example 9. Adjournment motions are generally allowed on which subjects?

Ans. Adjournments motions are generally allowed on subjects such as a Railway accident resulting in the death of several persons, a daring decoity, Some natural calamities like a devastating flood or a tornado, communal tension, etc.

No-Confidence Motion

The No-confidence motion means expressing lack of confidence in the ministry. The Council of Ministers is collectively responsible to the Lok Sabha.

Example 10. Who can move the No-confidence motion and how?

Ans. The Council of Ministers in the Opposition can move the No-Confidence motion, if atleast 50 members support this motion, it is moved in the Lok Sabha.

Example 11. When can the motion be discussed?

Ans. The motion can be discussed within ten days from the day when the Lok Sabha grants leave to move the motion.

Example 12. What happens on the conclusion of the debate?

Ans. On Conclusion of the debate the Speaker puts the motion to vote and if it is passed then the government has to resign.

TOPIC 3

SPEAKER OF THE LOK SABHA

The speaker is the presiding officer of the Lok Sabha who conducts the business of the House. He/She occupies a position of great authority and responsibility. He/She has wide powers to maintain discipline in the House. He/She ranks higher then all Cabinet Ministers, other than the Prime Minister in the table of Precedence. With respect to the discharge of his/her powers and functions, the Speaker is not answerable to anyone except the House. No Court of Law can go into the merits of a ruling given by him/her.

 Related Theory
→ In the 12th Lok Sabha the government headed by Atal Bihari Vajpayee lost just by one vote.

Election of the Speaker

The speaker of the Lok Sabha is elected soon after the newly elected Lok Sabha meets for the first time. Till a new speaker is elected, the speaker of the preceding Lok Sabha presides over its session.

The Indian Constitution provides that when the House is dissolved the speaker shall not vacate his office. He remains in office till the new speaker is elected by the new Lok Sabha in its first meeting.

The Speaker as well as the Deputy Speaker are elected by the Lok Sabha from among its a members. Normally, the speaker is elected for five years. He can seek re-election for any number of times, if he is elected as a member of the Lok Sabha.

The speaker may resign from his/her post on health ground or on the other grounds by submitting a letter of resignation to the Deputy Speaker.

The Speaker can also be removed by the Lok Sabha, if the majority of the members pass a resolution to this effect.

Example 13. Who is the speaker of present Lok Sabha?

Ans. Mr. Om Birla is the speaker of present Lok Sabha.

Example 14. Who is the Deputy speaker of present Lok Sabha?

Ans. Thambi Durai is the Deputy speaker of present Lok Sabha.

Role and Functions of the Speaker

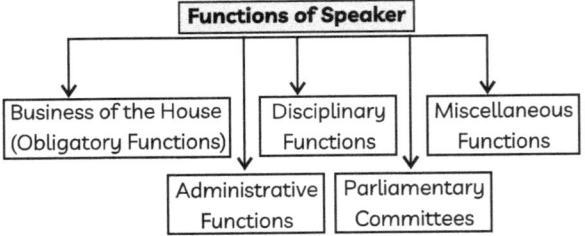

Obligatory Functions of the Speaker/ The Business of the House

(1) The Speaker presides over the meetings of the House. All speeches and remarks are addressed to the speaker. He/She allots time for discussion.

(2) The Speaker interprets the rules of procedures of the House. His/her decision in all Parliamentary matters is final.

(3) All Bills passed by the House are signed by him/her before they are sent to the Rajya Sabha for its consideration or to the President for assent.

(4) The Speaker decides the admissibility of all questions and resolutions. He/She decides the admissibility of a motion of adjournment.

(5) He/She puts the issues to vote and announces the results. The Speaker does not vote in the House, except when there are equal votes on both sides, i.e., the Treasury Benches and the Opposition.
(6) The Speaker decides whether a Bill is a money Bill or not.

Administrative Functions

(1) The Speaker receives all petitions and documents in the House.
(2) He/She communicates the decisions of the House to the concerned authorities.
(3) He/She regulates the admission of visitors and Press correspondents to the galleries of the House.

Disciplinary Functions

(1) The Speaker maintains order in the House. When members become unruly, he/she may order them to withdraw. He/she may suspend a member, if he/she disregards the authority of the Chair. In case of grave disorder, he/she can adjourn the House.
(2) In case the words used by a member are indecent or unparliamentary, the speaker may order that such words be expunged from the proceedings of the House.
(3) The Speaker decides whether there is a case for a matter relating to a breach of privilege or contempt of the House.

(4) In regard to a question whether a member of Lok Saba stands disqualified under Anti – Defection Law, the question shall be referred to the decision of the speaker. The Constitution says that speaker's decision shall be final and no court shall have any jurisdiction in this regard.

Parliamentary Committees

(1) The Speaker is the ex-officio Chairman of some of the Committees of the House, such as the Business Advisory Committee and the Rules Committee.
(2) He/she appoints Chairman of all the Committees of the House.
(3) He/She directions to the Chairman in all matters relating to their working and the Procedure to be followed.

Miscellaneous Functions

(1) The Speaker presides over the **Joint Sessions** of both the Houses of Parliament.
(2) In consultation with the Chairman of the Rajya Sabha, he/she nominates personnel for **Parliamentary Delegations** to various countries.
(3) He/She presides over the Conference of Presiding Officers of legislative bodies in India.

TOPIC 4

THE RAJYA SABHA

The Upper House or the Council of States is known as the 'Rajya Sabha' or 'Permanent House'. It represents the federation of states of the Indian Union.

Composition

The maximum strength of the Rajya Sabha can be 250 members. The members fall into two categories – Nominated and Elected.
Out of 250 members 238 are elected representatives of the states and the Union Territories.
And 12 members are nominated by the President from among persons having special knowledge or practical experience in matters such as Literatures, Science, Art and Social Service.

Election

The representatives of each State in the Rajya Sabha are elected by the elected members of the Legislative Assembly of each State in accordance with the system of proportional representation by means of a single transferable vote.

Term

The Rajya Sabha is a permanent House. It cannot be dissolved like the Lok Sabha. Each member of the Rajya Sabha is elected for a period of six years. One third of the total members of the house retire after every two years. Members can be re-elected if they so desire and if their electors support them.

Qualifications for the Membership

Conditions needed for a person to be a member of Lok Sabha are :

(1) He/She should be an Indian.
(2) He/She should be atleast 30 years of age.
(3) He/She should have his name in the electoral rolls in some part of the country.
(4) He/She should not be an insolvent, i.e. he/she should not be in debt and should have the ability to meet his/her financial commitments.
(5) He/She should not be a proclaimed criminal.
(6) He/She should not hold any office of profit under the government.
(7) He/She should not be of unsound mind.

Presiding Officer

The Vice-President of India is the ex–office Chairman of the Rajya Sabha. He/she presides over its meetings.

The Union Legislature 5

He/She cannot vote on any issue discussed in the House as he/she is not its member. However, in case of a tie, he/she exercises his/her casting vote.

The Rajya Sabha elects a Deputy Chairman from among its members. In the absence of the Chairman, he/she performs all functions and duties of the Chairman.

Example 15. Who is the present Vice-President of India?

Ans. M. Venkaiah Naidu the Present Vice-President of India.

 Related Theory
↳ *Dr. Servapalli Radhakrishnan was the first Vice President of India.*

Example 16. Who is our Present Deputy Chairman of Rajya Sabha?

Ans. Harivansh Narayan is our present Deputy Chairman of Rajya Sabha.

TOPIC 5

POWERS AND FUNCTIONS OF THE RAJYA SABHA AND THE LOK SABHA

The Parliament of India comprises the president, the Lok Sabha and the Rajya Sabha. The two Houses of Parliament are not competing centres of Power but are co-partners in the functioning of government. They enjoy equal power and status in all spheres except in financial matters and in terms of the responsibility of the Council of Ministers, which are exclusively in the domain of the Lok Sabha.

Rajya Sabha has equal powers with Lok Sabha in important matters like the impeachment of the President, removal of the Vice-President, Consitutional amendments and removal of the Judges of the Supreme Court and the High Courts.

Legislative Powers

The Parliament makes laws on following :
(1) Matters in the Union List
(2) Matters in the Concurrent List
(3) Residuary powers
(4) Matters in the State List
(5) Ordinances
(6) Powers during Emergency

Financial Powers

It controls the Union Finance, it takes care of the following :
(1) The Budget
(2) Permission for taxes
(3) Salaries
(4) Supplementary grants
(5) Vote on account

Judicial Powers

The Parliament has the power for :
(1) Impeachment of the President
(2) Removal of Judges of Supreme Court and High Courts
(3) Punishing a person obstructing the work of Parliament or showing disrespect to the House

Electroral Function

The parliament elects the President and the Vice-President of India and makes laws to regulate the conduct of elections in the country.

Amendment of the Constitution

Both Houses of the Parliament can amend the Constitution. The amendment must be passed but each House by a majority of total membership and by two-third majority of members present and voting.

Control Over the Executive

The Parliament exercises control over the government through Parliamentary procedure such as :
(1) Interpellation
(2) Vote of No-Confidence
(3) Adjournment Motion
(4) Other Motions of Censure
(5) Monetary Controls

Miscellaneous Powers

The Parliament can :
(1) Change the name of the States in the country.
(2) Amend some provisions of the Constitution.
(3) Alter the testimonial boundaries and divide and subdivide a State into two or more States.

Exclusive Powers of the Rajya Sabha

(1) The Rajya Sabha decides whether a particular subject in the State List has assumed national importance and it should be included in the Union List of subjects.
(2) The Rajya Sabha can decide to set up new all-India Services.
(3) The Proclamation of Emergency is approved alone by the Rajya Sabha.
(4) When a **state of national emergency** is declared, the Rajya Sabha looks after the responsibilities of the Union Legislature.

Relation Between the Two Houses of the Parliament

Common Powers
(1) Both the Houses enjoy equal rights in the election of the President and the Vice President.
(2) Both the Houses have equal rights in matter of impeachment of the President of India, the Chief Justice and the Judges of the Supreme Court or the High Courts.
(3) In case of Proclamation of a National Emergency and if the Lok Sabha is dissolved, it is the Rajya Sabha which shares all the responsibilities of the Union Legislature.

Difference in Powers
There is difference only on Legislative matters between the two Houses.
(1) In ordinary Bills
(2) Money Bills

Caution
→ Money bills can be introduced only in the lok sabha, The rajya sabha cannot reject or amend the money bill.

Important
→ The Rajya Sabha is a permanent House and not subject to dissolution. It is the Lok Sabha which is dissolved after every five years.
→ The Presiding officer of the lok sabha is not the Prime Minister, but the Speaker.
→ The Prime Minister presides over the meetings of the Council of Ministers.

ICSE Suggestions
→ Compartive study of Lok Sabha and the Rajya Sabha will ensure better clarity of the topic in the mind of students.
→ Different procedures of the Parliament could be classified by organizing a mock session in the class.
→ The meaning of Judicial and Electoral Powers must be clearly understood by the students.

Glossary

(1) **Amendment:** The term 'amendment' means, change or modification.
(2) **Adjournment motion:** It means a motion which seeks to suspend the work so that, some matters of urgent Public importance can be discussed.
(3) **Budget:** It is a statement of estimated revenue and expenditure for the coming financial year.
(4) **Money Bill:** It contains provision for imposition, alternation and abolition of taxes, regulations governing the borrowings and payment of money into or withdrawl of money from the Consolidated Fund or Contigency Fund of India, etc.
(5) **Residuary Powers:** In a Federal State, the Constitution divides the powers between the Central Government and the constituent Units. Matters, which are not included in the divisions of powers, are known as residuary powers.
(6) **Constituency:** Voters in a geographical area who elect a representative to the Legislative bodies.
(7) **Contempt of the House:** Disobedience to the authority of the Houses of the Parliament or other Legislative body.
(8) **Interpellation:** The formal right of a member of Parliament to ask questions as the floor of the House.
(9) **Progation:** To discontinue the meeting of the Parliament without dissolving it.
(10) **Resolution:** It is a motion through which the House expresses its majority opinion on any matter of Public interest. It is mandatory to give atleast 15 day notice before bringing any such motion.
(11) **Session:** It means a period during which the House meets to conduct its business. The maximum period that can intervene between the two sessions of parliament are summoned by the President.
(12) **Oath:** The members elected through general elections or by-elections need to take oath and affirm solemnly before participating in the affairs of the Parliament. Elected members are required to bear true faith and allegiance to the Constitution of India and uphold the dignity, integrity and sovereignty of the country while discharging their duties.

Chronology

January 25, 2020: The 104th Consitutional Amendment Act did away with the provision of nomination of Anglo-Indians to Lok Sabha and certain State assemblies. The reservation which was provided for last 70 years expired on this date.

January 26, 2020: The Union of Daman and Diu and Dadra and Nagar Haveli became a single union Territoty. The merged UT is named as Dadra and Nagar Haveli and Daman and Diu.

The Union Legislature

 **Who's Who?**

(1) **Shri G.V. Mavalankar** was the First speaker of Lok Sabha (Between 15. 05. 1952 to 27. 02. 1956)
(2) **Mrs. Meira Kumar** was the First women speaker of Lok Sabha (Between 04. 06. 2009 to 04. 06. 2014)
(3) **In the past, many eminent persons have been nominated by the President to the Rajya Sabha like—**
    Raja Ramanna (Nuclear Scientist)
    Mrinal Sen (Film Producer)
    Hema Malini (Actress)
    Kartar Singh Duggal (Writer)
    Nirmala Deshpande (Social Worker)

OBJECTIVE Type Questions

Multiple Choice Questions
[**1** mark each]

1. Who is empowered to promulgate an Ordinance when the Parliament is not in session?
   (a) The Vice-President
   (b) The President
   (c) The Prime Minister
   (d) The Attorney General of India
   [ICSE Specimen Paper Sem-1, 2021]

   Ans. (b) The President

   Explanation: The President is empowered to promulgate an ordinance at a time when the Parliament is not in session. It has the same effect as an Act. All Ordinances must be put up before both the Houses for their approval. Ordinance cease to operate after six weeks from the re-assembly of Parliament, unless they are approved by both the Houses.

   ⚠ **Caution**
   ↪ *Instead of President some students write Prime-Minister which is wrong, because under Article 123, the President is empowered to Promulgate an Ordinance.*

2. Lok Sabha : Speaker :: Rajya Sabha : ?
   (a) Vice President
   (b) Prime Minister
   (c) President
   (d) Chief Justice of India
   [ICSE Specimen Paper Sem-1, 2021]

   Ans. (a) Vice President

   Explanation: The Lok Sabha is presided over by the speaker. He or she is elected from among its own members soon after the newly elected House meets for the first time. The Rajya Sabha is presided over by the Vice-President. He or she is not the member of the House and is the ex-officio Chairman of the Rajya Sabha.

 Related Theory
↪ *The speaker is the presiding Officer of the Lok Sabha who conducts the business of the House.*

3. Which of these denotes the correct composition of the Rajya Sabha?
   (a) 232 elected + 12 nominated
   (b) 238 elected + 12 nominated
   (c) 238 elected + 8 nominated
   (d) 250 elected + 12 nominated
   [ICSE Sem-1, 2021]

   Ans. (b) 238 elected + 12 nominated

   Explanation: The maximum strength of the Rajya Sabha is 250 to 238 are elected members and 12 members are nominated by the president

4. What is the quorum of the Indian Parliament?
   (a) 1/3   (b) 1/2
   (c) 1/10   (d) 1/4
   [ICSE Sem-1, 2021]

   Ans. (c) 1/10

   Explanation: The quorum of the Lok Sabha and the Rajya Sabha is one tenth (1/10) of the total membership of each house.

5. Which of these is considered to be an exclusive power of the Rajya Sabha?
   (a) It can approve an ordinary bill.
   (b) It can make amendments to the constitution.
   (c) It can empower the Parliament to make laws on the state list.
   (d) It can make laws on subjects in the union list.
   [ICSE Sem-1, 2021]

   Ans. (b) It can make amendments to the constituion.

   Explanation: Rajya Sabha alone cannot make amendments to the constitution because both houses have to make it by majority of total membership and by a 2/3 majority of members present voting. Otherwise the amendment bill cannot be passed.

6. **Under what circumstances may the term of the Lok Sabha be extended by one year at a time?**
   (a) When the government resigns.
   (b) Proclamation of a National Emergency.
   (c) Economic instability
   (d) Rajya Sabha declares 1/4 majority.
   [ICSE Sem-1, 2021]

   Ans. (b) *Proclamation of a National Emergency.*

   Explanation: During the Proclamation of an Emergency the period of the Lok Sabha may be extended by Parliament for one year at a time. The new Lok Sabha must be elected within six months after the National Emergency is lifted.

7. **Which of these is not a qualification required to be a member of the Rajya Sabha?**
   (a) Should be a citizen of India.
   (b) Should not be an insolvent
   (c) Should be atleast 30 years of age.
   (d) Should be a graduate from any university in India.
   [ICSE Sem-1, 2021]

   Ans. (d) *Should be a graduate from any university in India.*

   Explanation: Points (a), (b) & (c) are requirements to become a member of the Rajya Sabha but point (d) is not mentioned in Constitution and it is not compulsary to be graduate from any university in India.

   Related Theory
   → Rajya sabha is also known as the Upper House or Permanent House.

8. **Which of these does not refer to the control of the Parliament over the Executive?**
   (a) No Confidence Motion
   (b) Amendement of Constitution
   (c) Monetory cuts
   (d) Rejection of a Government Bill.
   [ICSE Sem-1, 2021]

   Ans. (d) *Rejection of a Government Bill*

   Explanation: Parliament excercises control over the Executive in Interpellation, Vote of No-Confidence, Adjournment Motion, other Motions of Censure and Monetary cuts but not in Rejection of a Government Bill.

   Caution
   → Students should not get confused between Monetary cuts and Rejection of a Government Bill.
   A Government Bill cannot be rejected at all, it can be amended within fourteen days from the date of their receipt by Lok Sabha. Rajya Sabha has virtually no powers to reject or amend any money bill on its own.

9.
Questions Hour	10 days Notice
Zero Hour	?

   (a) 7 day notice (b) 14 day notice
   (c) 30 day notice (d) No notice [HOT]

   Ans. (d) *No notice*

   Explanation: Question Hour is the first hour of a lok Sabha sitting where the members ask questions from the government on matters of public interest. 'Zero Hour' is the session that is held just after the Question Hour'. During Zero hour members raise all types of questions, without any permission or prior notice.

   Caution
   → Students should not get confused between Question Hour and Zero hour. Because in Zero Hour all questions are answered randomely as members raise all types of questions without permission or prior notice.

10. **Complete the given analogy.**
    Election of Lok Sabha member: Citizen of India
    Election of Rajya Sabha member: ....
    (a) Members of the Legislative Assembly.
    (b) Members of the Legislative Council
    (c) Members of the Lok Sabha
    (d) Members of the Cabinet
    [ICSE Sem-1, 2021]

    Ans. (a) *Members of the Legislative Assembly.*

    Explanation: The representatives of each state in the Rajya Sabha are elected by the elected members of the Legislative Assembly of each state in accordance with the system of propotional representation by means of single transferable vote.

11. **The Lok Sabha Session which is conducted in the months of November and December is the:**
    (a) Summer Session
    (b) Monsoon Session
    (c) Winter Session
    (d) Budget Session [ICSE Sem-1, 2021]

    Ans. (c) *Winter Session*

    Explanation: Normally there are three sessions in a year.
    (1) The budget Session (feb - May)
    (2) The monsoon Session (July - Aug)
    (3) The winter Session (Nov - Dec)

12. **The .... Motion allows the House to take up a definite matter of urgent importance.**
    (a) no confidence (b) adjournment
    (c) censure (d) prorogation
    [ICSE Sem-1, 2021]

 The Union Legislature

Ans. (b) *adjournment*

Explanation: In Adjournment motion means a proposal to lay aside all other business and take up a 'definite' matter of urgent importance, such a motion leads to the interruption of normal business of the House.

 Related Theory
With the help of the motion, the members draw attention of the government of take suitable action on a particular matter.

13. The Rajya Sabha is called a Permanent House because 1/3 members retire every ....
   (a) Two years   (b) One years
   (c) Three years   (d) Six years
   [ICSE Sem-1, 2021]

Ans. (a) *Two years.*

Explanation: The Rajya Sabha cannot be disolved like the Lok Sabha. Each member of the Rajya Sabha is elected for a period of six years. One third of total members of the House retire after every two years.

14. In case of a conflict between the Centre and the State with reference to a subject in the concurrent list ....
   (a) each follow their own law
   (b) the State law will prevail
   (c) the president is empowered to decide
   (d) the union law will prevail
   [ICSE Sem-1, 2021]

Ans. (a) *the Union law will prevail.*

Explanation: If there is a conflict between the Union Parliament and the State Legislature on any law in the concurrent list, then the Union law will prevail.

15. The right of the members to .... is known as interpellation.
   (a) ask question
   (b) introduce Motion
   (c) adjourn the House
   (d) interrupt the preceedings
   [ICSE Sem-1, 2021]

Ans. (a) *Ask questions*

Explanation: The right of the members to ask questions from the government is known as interpellation.

16. Which of the statements regarding the speaker is false?
   (a) He/She is the presiding officer in the Lok Sabha.
   (b) Elected from among the members of the Lok Sabha.
   (c) Elected when the newly elected house meets for the first time.
   (d) The members of both the Houses vote to choose the Speaker. [ICSE Sem-1, 2021]

Ans. (a) *The members of both the Houses vote to choose the Speaker.*

Explanation: The Speaker of the Lok Sabha is elected from among its own members soon after the newly elected House meets for the first time and he is the presiding officer of the Lok Sabha who conducts the business of the House.

 Related Theory
The Speaker can seek re-election any number of times.

17. Who administers the Oath of office to the members of the Lok Sabha?
   (a) The President
   (b) The Prime Minister
   (c) The Speaker of Lok Sabha
   (d) The Chief Justice of India   [HOT]

Ans. (c) *The Speaker of Lok Sabha*

Explanation: The Oath of office is administered to the newly elected members of the Lok Sabha by the Protem Speaker, elected from among the members of the Lok Sabha.

 Caution
Some students write the answer as the president because they feel that the President is responsible to administer the oath of office to the Prime Minister and other members of the Lok Sabha as well.

18.

Lok Sabha members from States	530
Lok Sabha members from Union Territories	?

   (a) 25   (b) 22
   (c) 20   (d) 30
   [ICSE Sem-1, 2021]

Ans. (c) *20*

Explanation: The maximum strength of the Lok Sabha, as provided by the constitution is 552. Out of this 530 members represent the States and 20 members represent the Union Territories. (Two Anglo-Indian Members are nominated by the President to the Lok Sabha.)

19. What happens if a vote of No-confidence is passed against a minister?
   (a) The Minister has to resign.
   (b) The Prime Minister has to resign.
   (c) The whole Ministry has to resign.
   (d) The Lok Sabha is dissolved.

Ans. (c) *The whole Ministry has to resign.*

Explanation: A No-confidence Motion is a proposal expressing lack of confidence in the Ministry. The Council of Ministers is collectively responsible to the entire Lok Sabha including the member of the Opposition. If a Government acts against the Consitutional provisions, it can be voted out of office by passing a vote of no-confidence against the Prime Minister or the Ministry as a whole or any of its members. In case a vote of no-confidence is passed against a Minister, the whole Ministry has to resign.

20. Which of the following statement about ordinances is false?

(a) Promulgated by the President

(b) Issued when the Parliament is not in session.

(c) Has to be approved within six months from the re-assembly of the Parliament.

(d) Has to be approved by both the Houses of the Parliament. [ICSE Sem-1, 2021]

Ans. (c) Has to be approved within six months from the re-assembly of the Parliament.

Explanation: Ordinances cease to operate after **six weeks not six months** from the re-assembly of the Parliament, unless they are approved by the Houses.

SUBJECTIVE Type Questions

Short Answer Type Questions

[2 mark each]

21. (A) Name the two Houses of the Union Parliament.

(B) Name the bill that cannot originate in Rajya Sabha? [HOT🔥]
[ICSE 2018, 15, 12]

Ans.

(A) Lok Sabha, Rajya Sabha
(B) The bill that cannot originate in Rajya Sabha is Money Bill.
[Mod. Marking Scheme]

 What Examiners Say

→ Majority of the candidates named the bill that cannot originate in the Rajya Sabha Correctly.

 **Caution**

→ Students should know the difference between Money Bill and non-Money Bill and powers of the two Houses over these Bills in detail.

22. State any two federal feature of the Indian Constitution.

Ans. The federal feature of Indian Constitution is that it is a written Constitution and powers are divided between Centre and State.

They Are :
(1) A written constitution
(2) Bicameral Legislature
(3) An independent judiciary/(Suprme Court is the Final Interpreter of the Constitution)
(4) Division of powers/ (between the Union and the States) [Any two]

 **Caution**

→ Meaning of Federal is bicameral legislature, dual politics and written Constitution, etc., students should remember this.

23. What is meant by Residuary Powers of the Parliament? [ICSE 2016]

Ans. Apart from the powers mentioned in the three lists — Union list, Concurrent list and State list. The Parliament has the right to make laws on the list of miscellaneous functions, these are called Residuary Powers of the Parliament.

Residuary powers means that Parliament can make laws with respect to all those matters which are not mentioned in any of the three lists-the Union list, the State list and the Concurrent list. [Marking Scheme]

 What Examiners say

→ Most candidates lacked the knowledge of 'Residuary Powers' of the Parliament and wrote vague answers like Powers of Parliament to legislate on all subjects in the Union List, State List and Concurrent List.

24. Why is the Rajya Sabha called a 'Permanent House'? [HOT🔥]

Ans. The Rajya Sabha is a permanent House and is not subject to dissolution. One third of its members retire every two year. The members of the Rajya Sabha are elected for a term of six years. As such, the House is never empty. Hence, Rajya Sabha is called a Permanent House.

 Related Theory

→ The Union Territory of Delhi is represented in Rajya Sabha by three members.

25. What is meant by the term 'Session'?

Ans. 'Session' is the period during which the Houses of Parliament meet to conduct its business. Normally, there are three sessions in a year. They are Budget session, Monsoon session and Winter session.

26. State the meaning of the term 'Question Hour.' [ICSE 2019]

The Union Legislature  11

Ans. Question Hour is the first hour of every working day of both the Houses of Parliament. This hour is allotted for the questions of public interest asked by the members of the Parliament from the government and if admitted by the Chairperson, the government is obliged to answer them.

Question Hour representents:
(1) The first hour of every working day of the house (11:00 a.m. – 12:00 noon)
(2) The members can ask questions from the government.
(3) On matters of public interests (Scrutiny)
 [Marking Scheme]

 Related Theory
→ During Zero hours members raise all types of questions without any permission or prior notice.

27. What is meant by the term 'Quorum'?
 [ICSE 2018] [HOT]

Ans. **Quorum** refers to the minimum number of members of an assembly or society that must be present at any of its meetings to make the proceedings of that meeting valid.
The quorum has to constitute a sitting of House, which is one tenth of the total number of members of the House under Article 100(3) of the Constitution.

> A quorum is the minimum number of members required to be present before a meeting is allowed to being. The quorum to constitute a meeting of the House is one tenth of the total strength of the house.
> **[Marking Scheme]**

 What Examiners Say
→ Some candidates wrote incorrect interpretations of the term 'Quorum'.

28. How are the Rajya Sabha members elected?
 [ICSE 2017] [HOT]

Ans. The members of the Rajya Sabha are elected from different states. The representatives of state in the Rajya Sabha are elected by members of State Legislative Assemblies on the basis of proportional representation through a single transferable vote.

> They are elected indirectly by the elected members of the State Legislative Assemblies.
> **[Marking Scheme]**

 What Examiners Say
→ Most of the candidates answered the question correctly. A few made mistakes and wrote 'elected by the President' or 'elected indirectly'.

 Caution
→ Student should have complete knowledge about was elects whom, Rajya Sabha represents the States, hence elected members of the State Legislature elect the members of the Rajya Sabha.

29. What is the normal term of office of the Lok Sabha and who is the Presiding offiicer of the Lok Sabha. **[HOT] [Mod. ICSE 2019]**

Ans.

> Five years
> Speaker **[Mod. Marking Scheme]**

 What Examiners Say
→ A majority of candidates answered correctly, however, a few got confused with the term of Rajya Sabha.
→ Most of the candidates wrote the correct answer which was, the Speaker. However, a few candidates mentioned Prime Minister.

 Caution
→ The Rajya Sabha is a permanent Hosue and not subject to dissolution. It is the Lok Sabha which is disolved after every five year.

30. State the minimum number of times the Lok Sabha must meet in a year. **[HOT]**

Ans. The Lok Sabha must meet at least two times in a year. The interval between two consecutive sessions should not exceed six months. Normally, three sessions of Lok Sabha are held in a year.

31. What is meant by the term Universal Adult Franchise ? **[ICSE 2013]**

Ans. Every citizen of India who is minimum 18 years of use has the right to vote to elect the representative to the Parliament and State Legislatives. He/She possesses this right without any discrimination of sex, coste and creed.

32. How is the Speaker of the Lok Sabha elected?
 [ICSE 2020]

Ans. The speaker of the Lok Sabha is elected by the sitting members of the Lok Sabha, by a simple majority. He should be a member of the Lok Sabha.

> The speaker is elected by the members of the Lok Sabha/He should be one amongst the members/by simple majority of members present and voting. **[Marking Scheme]**

 What Examiners Say
→ Most condidates wrote the correct answer to this question.

⚠️ **Caution**
→ Student should know that the Speaker is elected from among the members of the House and by simple majority.

33. (A) What is the maximum gap allowed between the two Parliamentary Sessions?

(B) Who presides over the Joint Session of the two Houses of Parliament?

Ans. (A) The maximum gap allowed between the two Parliamentary Sessions is six months.

(B) The Speaker of the Lok Sabha.

💡 **Related Theory**
→ The Speaker does not vacate his/her office even when the House is dissolved. He/She remains in office till a new speaker is elected for a term of five years.

34. State any two subjects where in the Lok Sabha and the Rajya Sabha enjoy equal powers in legislation of laws

Ans. The Lok Sabha and Rajya Sabha enjoy co-equal powers in legislation of laws in the election and impeachment of the President of India.

💡 **Related Theory**
→ The two Houses are equal on most legislative powers except that Money Bills cannot be introduced in the Rajya Sabha nor it can pass a vote of no-confidence.

35. (A) State any one condition when the Parliament can legislate on subjects in the state list. [ICSE 2019]

(B) When can the speaker of the Lok Sabha cast his vote? [ICSE 2019] [HOT🔥]

Ans. (A) The Parliament can legislate on subject in the state list during President's rule in a state.

(B) When the votes for and against in the House on a proposal are equal, the speaker gives a casting vote. This vote decides whether or not the proposal will be passed.

36. Mention two provision of the Constitution. Which clearly establishes the supremacy of the Lok Sabha. with regard to Money Bills?

Ans.

> The Power of the Lok Sabha over the National income and expenditure is absolute/Rajya Sabha has no power over money matters/ Money Bills cannot originate in Rajya Sabha **(Any two point)** **[Marking Scheme]**

📋 **What Examiners Say**
→ Most candidates answered correctly. A few however failed to distinguish between a Money Bill and an Ordinary Bill.

37. What happens when a motion of 'No confidence is passed against a minister? [ICSE 2019]

Ans. If a Motion of 'No confidence' is passed against a minister, the Prime Minister along with his Council of ministers has to resign.

> The entire Ministry resigns en bloc (the government will resign) **[Marking Scheme]**

📋 **What Examiners Say**
→ Majority of the candidates were able to answer this question correctly. However, a few candidates, instead of resign wrote removed.

⚠️ **Caution**
→ Principle of collective responsibility should be studied in details by the student.

38. Under what condition can a Non-Member of Parliament be made a minister? [ICSE 2017]

Ans. In case a Non-Member of Parliament is made a minister, he must be elected or nominated to either House of Parliament within six months from the date of his appointment as a minister.

> If the Prime Minister so desires, however he/she must be elected/nominated to either House before six months. **[Marking Scheme]**

⚠️ **Caution**
→ There are exceptions in choosing the ministers. It need not always be elected member of the Parliament.

38. (A) What is the normal terms of office of the Lok Sabha? [ICSE 2019]

(B) What is the term of office of a Rajya Sabha member? [ICSE 2020]

Ans. (A)

> 5 Years **[Marking Scheme]**

📋 **What Examiners say**
→ Majority of the candidates were able to answer this question very well. However, a few candidates confused the term of office of the Lok Sabha with that of the Rajya Sabha and wrote, six years.

⚠️ **Caution**
→ A comparative study of the Lok Sabha and the Rajya Sabha to ensure clarity of the topic will help the students.

(B)

> 6 years. [One third of its members retire every two years.] **[Marking Scheme]**

📋 **What Examiners Say**
→ Many of the condidates have answered the question correctly. A few condidates either mentioned the term

The Union Legislature 13

of office of a Lok Sabha member instead of a Rajya Sabha member or wrote the Rajya Sabha being a permanent House, is not subjected to disolution.

⚠️ **Caution**
→ Students should remember that 5 years is the normal term of the Vice-President of India and the tenure of the Lok Sabha as well.

Structured Questions
[3+3+4= **10** marks each]

40. With reference to the Union Parliament, answer the following questions:
(A) Name the three types of authority in a federal set up in India. [ICSE 2013]
(B) What are the two advantages of the Rajya Sabha?
(C) State four important features of Federalism.

Ans. (A) The three types of authority in a federal set up in India are:
(1) Central or Union Govenment;
(2) State Government
(3) Panchayats and Municipilaties
(B) (1) The Rajya Sabha is a permanent chamber.
(2) It represents States
(3) It serves as a check upon hasty or rash legislation.
(C) Important features of federalism are :
(1) There are two or more levels of government and the different levels of government govern the some citizens, but each level has its own jurisdiction (legal authority) is specific matters of legalisation, administration and taxation.
(2) The jurisdiction of each level of government is Specified in the Constitution.
(3) The fundamental provision of the Constitution cannot be unilaterally changed by any are level of government. Such changes can be made by the consent of both the levels of government.
(4) The disputes between different levels of government which arise due to the exercise of their respective powers are settled by the courts.
(5) Sources of revenue for each level of government are clearly demarcated to ensure their financial autonomy.
[Any four]

41. With reference to the Indian Parliament, explain the following questions:
(A) What is the concurrent list of subjects ? Who can legislate on it? Whose law is final?
(B) Mention two ways in which the Rajya Sabha can control the executive ? Also explain any one of its limitations.
(C) State four disciplinary functions of the Speaker.

Ans. (A) The concurrent list contains all those subjects like Education, Forests, Trade union, etc. on which both State Legislature as well as the Union Parliament can make laws.
If there is a conflict between the union Parliament and State Legislature on any law in this list, the Union Law will prevail.
(B) The Rajya Sabha can control the executive in following ways :
(1) The members of the Rajya Sabha can question the executive in the Parliament to seek information from them regarding administration and criticise their policies.
(2) Adjournment Motions tabled by the Rajya Sabha on urgent matters bring for the inefficient handling by the government on any serious and urgent matter.
Limitation of Rajya Sabha—The Rajya Sabha cannot remove the Council of Ministers from office.
(C) (1) The Speaker maintains order in the house. When members become unruly, he/she may order them to withdraw. He many suspend a member, if he/she disregards the authority of the chair. In case of grave disorder, he/she can adjourn the house.
(2) In case the words used by a members are indecent or unparliamentarily, the Speaker may order that such words be expunged from the proceedings of the House.
(3) The Speaker decides whether there is a case for a matter relating to a breach of privilege or contempt of the House.
(4) In regard to a question whether a member of Lok Sabha stands disqualified under Anti-defection law, the question shall be referred to the decision of the Speaker. The Constitution says that Speaker's decision shall be final and no court shall have any jurisdiction in this regards.

42. With reference to the given picture, answer the following questions:
(A) Identify the person in given picture? He presides over which House of the Parliament? What is his designation?
(B) How is the Speaker of the Lok Sabha elected?
(C) What are the Speakers supervisory and administrative powers? [HOT🔥]

Ans. (A) The person shown in the picture is Shri OM Birla. He is then Speaker of Lok Sabha and is presiding office of the Lok Sabha.

(B) The Speaker of the Lok Sabha is elected from among its own members soon after the newly elected House meets for the first time. He/She ocupies a position even after disolving of the House, he/she does not vacate his/her office. He/She remains in office till a new Speaker is elected by the new Lok Sabha in its first meeting. The Speaker is elected for a term of five years.

(C) **The Speaker has a large number of Supervisory and Administrative Powers:**

 (1) He/She is the one who receives all petitions and documents in the House.
 (2) He/She communicates the decisions of the House to the concerned authorities.
 (3) The Speaker maintains order in the House.
 (4) He/She regulates the admission of visitors and press correspondents to the golleries of the House.
 (5) The speaker decides whether there is a case for a matter relating to a breach of privilege or contempt of the House.

43. The Powers and Functions of the Indian Parliament are wide ranging. In this context, answer the following:

(A) Explain *three* ways by which the legislature exercises control over the executive.

(B) Mention any three special powers of the Rajya Sabha that is usually not enjoyed by the other House.

(C) Mention any two Judicial powers and any two Electoral powers of the Indian Parliament. **[ICSE 2017]**

Ans. (A) **The ways by which the legislature exercises control over the executive are:**

 (1) **Question Hour:** The first hour of every sitting in both Houses of Parliament is known as question hour. During question hour, the members of parliament have the right to question any administrative and governmental policy related to the national as well as the international sphere.

 (2) **Vote of No-Confidence:** If a government flouts the Constitution and acts in contravention of the provisions thereof, the government can be voted out by passing a vote of 'No-Confidence' against the Council of ministers.

 (3) **Censure Motion:** A censure motion is a distinct type of a No Confidence motion. While a motion of No Confidence need not specify any grounds on which it is based, a censure motion must reveal the grounds on which it is based. This type of motion is moved for the specific purpose of censoring the government for certain policies and actions.

(B) **The special powers of the Rajya Sabha that is usually not enjoyed by the other House are:** **[Any three]**

 (1) The Rajya Sabha, under Article 249, may by a special majority of two-third votes adopt a resolution asking Parliament to make laws on subjects of the state list, in the national interest.
 (2) The Rajya Sabha can take steps to create All India Services by adopting resolutions supported by a special majority in national interest.
 (3) The Rajya Sabha has the exclusive right to initiate a resolution for removal of the Vice-President.
 (4) The Rajya Sabha is a permanent House. So during an emergency if the Lok Sabha is dissolved, it is the Rajya Sabha which handles all the responsibilities of the Union Legislature. **[Any three]**

(C) **The judicial powers of the Indian Parliament are:**

 (1) It has the power to impeach the President. The charges against the President can be initiated in either of the two Houses of Parliament by two-third of its total membership. If the charges are ratified by the other house too by two-third majority, the President stands impeached and he is removed from the office with immediate effect.

 (2) Parliament can remove the Vice President and the other High Federal officers like the Judges of the Supreme Court and High Courts,

Auditor-General, Members of the Public Service Commission *etc.*, if they are found guilty of violating any clause of the Constitution.

The electoral Powers of the Indian Parliament are:
(1) The Parliment of India along with the State Legislutuses elects the President of India.
(2) The Vice-President of India is elected by both the Houses of the Parliament.
(3) The Lok Sabha elects its own Speaker and Deputy Speaker from amongst its own Members while the Rajya Sabha elects its Deputy Chairman.

[Any two]

(A) Three ways are:
(1) **Interpellation:** Through the Question Hour, Calling attention notices and Half an Hour discussions, the members obtain information on a matter of public importance or grievance. It keeps the government on its toes.
(2) **Vote of No Confidence:** If the government (executive) acts in an unconstitutional manner, or against constitutional provision, then it can be voted out of office through the vote of No Cofidence.
(3) **Adjournment Motion:** Though, it allowed on occasions of natural/ national tragedies, etc, it is also aimed at censuring acts of omission and commission of the ministers.
(4) Censure Motion. **[Any three]**

(B) They are:
(1) It may by a resolution adopted by 2/3rd majority, empower the Parliament to make laws with respect to subjects in the State List.
(2) It may declare the creation of a new All India Service in the national interest.
(3) If lok Sabha is dissolved before or after the declaration of national emergency, Rajya Sabha takes over the functions of the Parliament.
(4) It is a parmanent House. **[Any three]**

(C) Judicial Powers:
(1) Impeachment of President.
(2) Removal of Judges of Supreme Court and High Courts.
(3) The Parliament may punish a person for obstructing the work of Parliament or showing disrespect for the House.

[Any two]

Elective Powers:
(1) Election of the President of India.
(2) Vice-President of India is elected by both Houses of Parliament.
(3) Electing the Speaker of the Lok Sabha only by its own members and the Deputy Chairperson of the Rajya Sabha only by the upper House. i

[Any two]
Marking Scheme]

What Examiners Say

→ (A) *Most of the candidates were able to write the correct answer. However, some were confused and wrote the legislative power of the Parliament.*

→ (B) *Most of the candidates wrote the correct answer. A few mentioned the powers of Lok Sabha.*

→ (C) *Candidates got confused between the Judicial and Electoral powers of the Parliament and some of them also confused it with the Legislative Powers.*

44. **The Rajya Sabha is the second chamber of the Indian Parliament and represents the interest of the states. In this context, explain the following:**
   (A) Its compositon
   (B) Qualification for membership
   (C) Term of the House and any two of its legislative powers. **[ICSE 2015]**

Ans. (A) The Rajya Sabha is the Upper House of the Parliament and is also known as the 'Council of States'. It consists of representatives of the states. The maximum strength of the Rajya Sabha is 250, of these 238 are elected from the States and Union Territories and the remaining 12 are nominated by the President for their distinguished contribution to the fields of literature, science, art, social service, *etc.*

(B) **The qualifications for membership of Rajya Sabha are:**
(1) He/She should be a citizen of India.
(2) He/She should be at least 30 years of age.
(3) He/She should be registered as a voter on the electoral rolls in any part of the country.
(4) He/She should not hold any office of profit under the government.
(5) He/She should not be a proclaimed offender.
(6) He/She should be of sound mind.
(7) He/She should not be insolvent, i.e., he/she should not be in debt and should be capable of meeting his/her financial commitments.

(C) The Rajya Sabha is a permanent body and is not subject to dissolution. The members of the Rajya Sabha are elected for a term of six years by the elected members of the State Legislative Assemblies. One-third of its members retire every two years.

The legislative powers of the Rajya Sabha are:

(1) An Ordinary Bill can be introduced in the Rajya Sabha and it cannot become a law unless passed by it.

(2) During National and State Emergency, the Rajya Sabha can pass a resolution with special majority asking to make the laws for subjects in the State List that have assumed National importance. Such laws can remain valid for one year.

(A) It consists of not more than 250 members (at present 245 members). The members fall in two categories – elected and nominated. Twelve members are nominated by the President from among persons having excelled in the fields of art. Literature, science and social service.

(B) Must be a citizen of India/must not be less than 30 years of age/must possess such qualifications as may be prescribed by law from time to time.

(C) (1) It is a permanent body not subject to dissolution/ one third members retire every two years / members of the Rajya Sabha have a six year term (any two points)

(2) All bills excepting Money Bills can originate in Rajya Sabha / Can approve ordinances / Rajya Sabha passes a resolution that a subject in the State List can assume National importance.

[Marking Scheme]

What Examiners Say

→ (A) Answered correctly by majority of candidates, however a few were confused in the number of elected and nominated members.

→ (B) Most candidates answered correctly. The age mentioned however was incorrectly written by few candidates and they instead of mentioning the qualifications explained the method of election.

→ (C) The first part of the question – the term of the House was correctly answered by most candidates. However, there was no clarity about the Legislative Powers of the Rajya Sabha as witnessed in the answers of a few candidates.

45. With reference to the Indian Parliament, explain the following:

(A) The tenure of the members of the Lok Sabha and the Rajya Sabha.

(B) The composition of the Lok Sabha and the Rajya Sabha.

(C) Its powers to make laws on subjects mentioned in the

(a) Union List

(b) Concurrent List   [HOT] [ICSE 2014]

Ans. (A) The tenure of the members of Lok Sabha is five years and the tenure of the members of the Rajya Sabha is six years.

(B) **Lok Sabha:** The maximum strength of the Lok Sabha is 552. Out of these 530 members are chosen directly from the territorial constituencies in 29 states, and 20 members shall represent the union territories. Besides this, two members from the Anglo-Indian community may be nominated to the Lok Sabha by the President of India, in case he feels that the community is not adequately represented.

Rajya Sabha: The maximum strength of the Rajya Sabha is 250. Of these 238 are elected from the states and union territories and the remaining 12 are nominated by the President for their distinguished contribution to the fields of literature, art, science, social service, *etc.*

(C) (a) **Union List:** The Union List consists of subjects on which the Central Government or the Indian Parliament can make laws. There are 97 subjects in the Union List which are of national importance and include subjects such as defence, foreign affairs, atomic energy, banking, post & telegraph, *etc.* The Central Government has the power to make laws on these subjects at all times, including National Emergencies.

(b) **Concurrent List:** The Concurrent List has 47 subjects on which both Parliament and State can make laws. These subjects include civil and criminal procedure, marriage and divorce, education, economic planning and trade unions. Yet, in case of conflict between a law made by the Central Govenment and a law made by the State Legislatures, the law made by the Central Governmnet shall prevail.

(A) The tenure of a member of the Lok Sabha is 5 years and the term for a Rajya Sabha member is 6 years.

(A) The composition of the **Lok Sabha** is
  (1) 530 members directly elected by the people of the various State. The allotment of members to the various states is made on a population basis.
  (2) not more than 20 members shall represent the Union Territories.
  (3) two members will be nominated by the President. The nominated members are to be from the Anglo Indian Community. The total strength is 552 members. It should not exceed this number.

In the Rajya Sabha:
  (1) 238 members are elected by the States in the Union. The seats are allocated to the States and Union Territories on the basis of their population.
  (2) twelve members are nominated by the President from among persons having special knowledge or practical experience in the field of Art, Literature, Science, and Social Service. The maximum strength of the Rajya Sabha is 250.

(C) The Union Parliament has **(1)** exclusive powers to make laws on 97 subjects in the Union list eg: defence, foreign policy, currency, etc., **(2)** in the Concurrent List the Union Parliament along with the State Legislative Assembly can make laws on 47 subjects. In case of a conflict the law passed by the Union Parliament will prevail **(3)** the Parliament can legislate even on the State List subjects **(a)** in case of emergency or **(b)** if the Rajya Sabha passes a resolution that a particular subject in the state list has assumed special importance or **(c)** when two or more states request the Parliament to legislate on a subject given in the state list. **(4)** any subject which is not mentioned in any of these lists come under the residuary powers of the Parliament. Only the Parliament can legislate on the subjects not mentioned in any of the three lists.

[Marking Scheme]

46. With reference to the Union Parliament, answer the following questions:
  (A) What is the maximum strength of the Lok Sabha provided by the Constitution? How many members does the President nominate to the Lok Sabha? How are members to the Lok Sabha elected?
  (B) **The two Houses of the Parliament enjoy co-equal powers in many spheres— explain it by giving any three examples.**
  (C) **Explain any four of the Rajya Sabha's powers in India's federal set up.**

Ans. (A) The maximum strength of Lok Sabha is 552. Out of these 530 members are chosen directly from the territorial constituencies in the States and 20 members shall represent the Union Territories.

The President may nominate two members from the Anglo-Indian Community to the Lok Sabha. The Lok Sabha is composed of representatives of the people chosen by direct election on the basis of Universal Adult Franchise (UAF). It means all citizens equal to or above 18 years of age have the right to vote without discrimination on the basis of sex, religion, caste, language, etc.

(B) The Lok Sabha and the Rajya Sabha enjoy equal powers and are partners in the functioning of the Government.
  (1) **Judicial Powers:** The Parliament has the power to impeach the President and the Vice-President. The charges against the President can be framed by either of the two Houses of Parliament by two-third of its total membership.
  (2) **Amendment to the Constitution:** The Parliament is the only constitutional body that can initiate any proposal for amendment to the Constitution of India. Such a proposal for amendment can be initiated in either House of Parliament.
  (3) **Formation of New States:** The Parliament may form a new state by seperating out the territory from any state or by uniting two or more states. The creation of a separate state Telangana in 2014 is such an example.

(C) **The powers of Rajya Sabha in India's federal set up are:**
  (1) The Rajya Sabha, under Article 249, may by a special majority of two-thirds votes adopt a resolution on the State List, in the National interest.
  (2) The Rajya Sabha can take steps to create All India Services by adopting resolutions supported by a special majority.
  (3) The Rajya Sabha has the exclusive right to initiate a resolution for the removal of the Vice-President.
  (4) The Rajya Sabha is a permanent House. So, during an emergency if the Lok Sabha is dissolved, it is the Rajya Sabha which handles all the responsibilities of the Union Legistature.

47. The Parliament is the body of people's representative who have Supreme power in a democracy. With reference to the Union Legislature answer the following:

(A) How are the members of the Rajya Sabha elected?

(B) Why is it called a Permanent House?

(C) State any two Financial and any two Legislative powers of the Indian Parliament. **[ICSE 2019]**

Ans. (A) The members of the Rajya Sabha are elected indirectly. The members, representing States, are elected by elected members of legislative assemblies of the States in accordance with the system of proportional representation by means of a single transferable vote, and those representing Union Territories are chosen in such manner as prescribed by the Parliament or law.

(B) The Rajya Sabha is a permanent House and it cannot be dissolved. The members of the Rajya Sabha are elected for a term of six years. One third of the members retire after every two years and the equal new members are elected to replace them. Hence, the House is never empty and thus, it is called a permanent House.

(C) **The financial powers of the Indian Parliament are:**

(1) **Annual Budget:** The Parliament is empowered to accept, reject or vote a cut in the annual budget.

(2) **Consolidated Fund of India:** The Parliament has the right to debate the propriety of items included in its fund. This central fund provides salaries of the President, the Chief Justice of the Supreme Court, and their respective establishments.

(3) **Salaries of the members of Parliament:** The Parliament decides the salaries and allowances of its members and other dignitaries.

(4) **Supplementary Demands:** The Parliament follows the same procedure to pass supplementary budget as it does for the annual budget. A supplementary budget might include some supplementary demands from the finance minister during the course of the financial year. **[Any two]**

The legistative power of the Indian Parliament are:

(1) **Union List:** The Union List consists of subjects on which the Indian Parliament can make laws. There are 97 subjects in the Union List which are of National importance and include subjects such as defense, foreign affairs, atomic energy, banking, etc. The Parliament has the power to make law on these subject all the times, including National Emergencies.

(2) **Concurrent List:** The Concurrent List has 47 subjects on which both Parliament and the State Legislatures can make laws. These subject include criminal and civil procedure, marriage and divorce, education, economic planning and trade unions. In case of conflict between a law made by the Central Government and the law made by the State Legislatures, the law made by the Central Government will prevail.

(3) **State List:** The State List contains 66 subjects of local or state importance. The State Governments have the authority to make laws on these subjects. These subjects include police, local governments, trade, commerce, and agriculture. However, during National and State Emergency, the power to make laws on these subjects is transferred to the Parliament.

(4) **Residuary Powers:** Apart from the powers mentioned in the three lists, there is also a list of miscellaneous functions which are not mentioned in any three lists and the right to make laws on these subjects is called Residuary Power. The Central Government has been given rights to legislate on these subjects. The Parliament can amend the Constitution, although in certain cases such amendments must be ratified by majority of the states. The states cannot nitiate any amendment to the Constitution. **[Any two]**

(A) Elected by the members of elected Legislative Assemblies.

Indirectly elected on the basis of proportional representation with a single transferable vote.

(B) 1/3 of its members retire every two years. The House is never dissolved as a whole.

(C) **Financial Powers**

(1) Passes the Budget of the Union Parliament,

(2) Determines the Salaries & Allowances of the members of Parliament,

(3) No taxes can be imposed unless approved by the Parliament,
(4) Passes the Supplement grants
(5) Vote on account,
(6) Passes the Money Bill. **[Any two]**

Legislative Powers
(1) Makes laws on subjects in the union List
(2) Makes laws on subjects in the State List (under certain conditions)
(3) Makes laws on subjects in the Concurrent list
(4) Possesses Residuary power
(5) Approves Ordinance.
(6) Power during an Emergency
(7) Makes amendments to the Constitution **[Any two]**
[Marking Scheme]

What Examiners Say

→ (A) Some candidates, instead of writing the manner of the election of the members of the Rajya Sabha, wrote about its composition. A few candidates were confused between the direct and indirect elections.

→ (B) Majority of the candidates answered this question very well by writing the required points.

→ (C) Some candidates could not distinguish between the Financial and Legislative powers of the Indian Parliament and mixed up the points in their answers.

Caution

→ (A) Students should have proper understanding about direct and indirect method of elections, emphasizing that the members of the Lok Sabha are elected by direct elections while Rajya sabha members are elected indirectly by members of the State Assemblies.

→ (B) Students should be aware of the fact that the Rajya Sabha is a Permanent House as it cannot be dissolved by the President. One third of the members retire every second year and new members are elected but the House is never dissolved.

48. With reference to the Union Legislature, answer the following questions:

(A) How is the Speaker of the Lok Sabha elected? State two Disciplinary Functions of the Speaker.

(B) Explain three conditions under which a member of Parliament can be disqualified under the Anti-Defection Law.

(C) Give reasons to justify why the Lok Sabha is considered to be more powerful than the Rajya Sabha. **[ICSE 2016]**

Ans. (A) The speaker of the Lok Sabha is elected from among its members by a simple majority of members present and voting. He is elected soon after the newly elected House meet for the first time.

The disciplinary functions of the Speaker are:

(1) The speaker is responsible for maintaining order in the House.
(2) The speaker decides whether there is a valid case for any matter regarding breach of privilege or contempt of the House.

(B) The conditions under which a member of Parliament can be disqualified under Anti Defection Law are:

(1) He/she has voluntarily given up membership of such political party.
(2) He/she abstains from voting in such House contrary to any direction issued by the political party to which he/she belongs.
(3) If he joins any political party after his elections.

(C) Lok Sabha is considered more powerful than the Rajya Sabha because of following reasons:

(1) Motion of No Confidence against the government can only be introduced and passed in the Lok Sabha.
(2) Money Bills are introduced only in the Lok Sabha. The Rajya Sabha cannot make amendments in a Money Bill passed by the Lok Sabha and transmitted to it.
(3) In case of deadlock, the opinion of Lok Sabha prevails due its bigger numerical strength.

(A) The Speaker is elected from the members of the House i.e. Lok Sabha. He should be one amongst them.
Functions:
(1) Receive all petitions and documents in the House.
(2) He communicates the decisions of the House to the concerned authorities.
(3) He regulates the admission of visitors and Press Correspondents to the galleries of the House.
[Any two]

(B) (1) If he voluntarily gives up his membership of such political party or votes or abstains from voting in the House contrary to any direction of such party.

(2) If he voluntarily gives up his membership of the party or votes or abstains from voting in the House contrary to any direction of such party.
(3) If he joins any political party after the expiry of the said period of six months.
(4) If he joins any political party after his elections.
(5) However, where a member claims that he belongs to a group representing a faction arising from a split and the group consists of not less than one-third of the members of the legislative party.

[Any three]

(C) (1) Members of the Lok Sabha are directly elected by the people.
(2) Money Bills originate in the Lok Sabha.
(3) Non-Money Bills originate in either House on a disagreement a joint session is held where numerical strength of the Lok Sabha is more.
(4) Lok Sabha can pass the No-Confidence Motion.
(5) Lok Sabha has a greater say in the election of the President and the Vice-President of India, impeachment of the President, judges of the high courts & supreme Court because of its numerical strength. [Any four]

[Marking Scheme]

What Examiners Say

→ (A) *Most candidates answered the first part of the question correctly but were unable to mention the Disciplinary functions of the Speaker. Many candidates wrote the general functions too.*

→ (B) *Very few candidates were able to explain the Anti-Defection Law. Only the definition of the law was written.*

→ (C) *Answered correctly by most candidates.*

49. Discuss the relationship between the two Houses of a State Legislature with reference to the following:
(A) Money Bills.
(B) Non-Money Bills.
(C) Control over the Executive.

Ans. (A) **Money Bills:** In Case of Money Bills, the Rajya Sabha has virtually no powers. It cannot reject a Money Bill nor amend it by virtue of its own powers. It must, within the stipulated period of 14 days, return Bill to the Lok Sabha, which may there upon either accept or reject all or any of the recommendations of the Rajya Sabha.

(B) **Non-Money Bills/ Ordinary Bills:** Ordinary Bills may originate in either House. If there is disagreement between the two Houses, the Bill is referred to a Joint sitting of both the Houses are placed on an equal footing. However, the Rajya Sabha is in a weaker position, since the total membership of Rajya Sabha is less than even half of the total strength of the Lok Sabha. Besides, the Joint session is presided over by the Speaker of the Lok Sabha.

(C) **Control over the Executive:** Members of both the Houses can put questions to ministers about the work of their departments. But the Lok Sabha is more powerful than the Rajya Sabha. The Council of Ministers is responsible only to the Lok Sabha. Rajya Sabha cannot pass a motion expressing No-Confidence is the Council of Ministers. Adjournments motion, indicating a strong disapproval of the policy of government is moved only in Lok Sabha.

50. With reference to the Union Parliament, answer the following questions:
(A) How many members may be nominatd to the Lok Sabha and the Rajya Sabha? Give one reason as to why they may be nominated to the Lok Sabha.
(B) Mention any three qualifications required for a member to be elected to the Lok Sabha.
(C) What is meant by the term 'Session'? Name the three Sessions of the Union Parliament. [HOTS]

Ans. (A) Two members in the Lok Sabha and twelve members in the Rajya Sabha may be nominated by the President of India. The two members from the Anglo-Indian community may be appointed to the Lok Sabha by the President of India in case he feels that the community is not adequately respresented.

(B) **The qualifications required for a member to be elected to the Lok Sabha are:**
(1) He/she should be a citizen of India.
(2) He/she should be at least 25 years of age.
(3) He/she should have his/her name on the electoral rolls in some part of the country.
(4) There should be no criminal procedures pending against him/her.

The Union Legislature

(5) He/she should not hold any office of profit directly under the central or State Governments.

(6) He/she should not be of unsound mind.

(7) The candidate should not be insolvent and should be able to meet his/her financial commitments.

[Any three]

(C) **'Session'** is the period during which houses of Parliament meet to conduct its business.

The three sessions of Union Parliament are:

(1) Budget session;

(2) Monsoon session;

(3) Winter session.

2 The President and the Vice-President

The President is the Head of the State and the Supreme Commander of the Defence Forces of India. The executive power of the Indian Union is vested in the President. He is the first citizen of India and acts as the symbol of unity, integrity and solidarity of the nation.
The Vice-President of India occupies second highest office in the country.

Chapter Notes

- The President of India
- The Vice-President

TOPIC 1

THE PRESIDENT OF INDIA

The President is the executive head of the Indian Republic and the Supreme Commander of the defence forces of India. All the Executive Powers are vested in the president. But he/she exercises his or her powers on the advice of the Prime Minister and the Council of Ministers. The Constitution provides that 'there shall be a Council of Ministers with the Prime Minister as the head, to aid and advice the President, in the exercise of his/her functions.' The 42nd Amendment Act made it obligatory for the President to exercise his/her functions in accordance with the advice of the Council of Ministers.

Qualifications for Elections

(1) The candidates should be an Indian citizen.
(2) He/She should have completed 35 years of age.
(3) He/she should be qualified for election as a member of the Lok Sabha.

A person shall not be eligible for election as President if he/she holds an 'Office of Profit' under the Central or State government.

A person who holds, or who has held, office as President shall be eligible for re-election to that office– subject to other provisions of the Constitution.

⚠ Caution

➥ The President is elected by indirect elections and not by direct elections.

➥ The normal term of office of President is five years and not six years.

➥ The minimum age for contesting election for President is 35 years and not 25 years, as in the case of Member of Lok Sabha.

➥ Electoral College for the elections of the President does not include the nominated members of the Rajya Sabha.

Term of Office

The President is elected for a term of five years. He/she is eligible for re-election. During the term of office, the President can only be removed from his/her position in case of violation of the Constitution or proved misbehaviour or incapacity.

Oath of Office

The oath of office to the President is administered by the Chief Justice of India.

Vacation of Office

The Presidential office may fall vacant because of the following reasons:
(1) On expiry of his/her term
(2) In case of his/her death
(3) The President may submit his/her resignation letter to the Vice-President, in order to resign from his office. Such resignation will be communicated by the Vice-President to the Speaker of the Lok Sabha.
(4) The President may, for the violation of the Constitution, be removed from the office by the process of impeachment.

The President will hold his/her office until his/her successor enters upon the office. If the Presidential office falls vacant due to other reasons, a new President must be elected within six months.

Example 1: To whom does the President submit his/her resignation?

Ans. The President may submit his resignation letter to the vice-president in order to resign from his/her office.

Process of Impeachment

(1) The President can be removed from the office for violation of the Constitution through the process of impeachment. The charges for the purpose may be framed by either house of the Parliament.
(2) The resolution to impeach the president must be passed by two-thirds majority of the total membership of the House.
(3) A 14 days notice, signed by at least one-fourth of the total number of members, has to be given.
(4) Then the charges imposed against the President are investigated by the other House.
(5) The President has the right to appear in person, in order to answer the charges. He/she also has the right to be defended by a counsel.
(6) If the charges are established by the two-thirds majority of the total membership of both the Houses; the President is impeached and removed from his/her office.
(7) The President may resign before the expiry of his/her full term by writing a letter addressed to the Vice-President of India. The Vice-President will communicate the decision to the speaker of the Lok Sabha. A new President must be elected within six months. Till then, the Vice-President will act as the President.

Example 2. How can the President be removed from his/her office?

Ans. The President may, for the violation of the Constitution, be removed from the office by the process of impeachment.

Election of the President

The President is elected indirectly by the members of an Electoral College consisting of:

(1) The elected members of both Houses of Parliament.
(2) The elected members of the Legislative Assemblies of the States including NCT of Delhi and Union Territory of Puducherry.

At least 50 members of Electoral College (MPs or MLAs) must propose the name of the President and 50 electors should second the nominations.

The election of the president is held in accordance with the system of proportional representation by means of the single transferable vote and the voting at such election is done by secret ballot.

Example 3. Who elects the President of India?

Ans. The President of India is elected indirectly by the members of the electoral college.

Example 4. Why is the President elected indirectly?

Ans. The President is the executive head and the real power is vested in the council of ministers. If the President is elected directly by the people, he/she would become a rival centre to the council of ministers.

Example 5. What is single transferable vote?

Ans. The single transferable vote is an electoral system of proportional representation in which a person's vote is transferred to second or other competing candidates, in case no candidate is able to get absolute majority or 50 percent votes in the first preference.

 **Important**

→ All doubts and disputes arising in connection with the election of the President can be enquired into and decided only by the Supreme Court of India whose decision stays final.

Reasons for Indirect Election of the President

(1) If the President was to be elected directly by the people, he/she would become a rival centre of power to the Council of Ministers. This would be against the Parliamentary System with ministerial responsibility.
(2) Since the membership in the two Houses of Parliament is likely to be dominated by one party, election of the President merely by a majority of members of the Union Parliament can make him a nominee of the ruling party like the Prime Minister. Such a President cannot represent the Constituent States of the Union.
(3) The President is elected by an Electoral College. In India, this electoral college consists of the elected members of the two Houses of Parliament and Legislative assemblies of the States (Article 54). Such an electoral college would make the president, the elected representative of the whole nation with a clear voice given to the States as well.

Powers of the President of India

(A) Executive Powers

(1) The President is the executive head of the country and executive authority rests within him/her.
(2) He/she appoints the Prime Minister. And, on his advice, appoints the Council of Ministers, the Governors of the States, the Judges of the Supreme Court and the High Courts, the Chairman of the UPSC, the Comptroller and Auditor General of India and the Chiefs of all the armed forces.
(3) Union Territories and Border Areas administration is the responsibility of the President.

Example 6. Who administers the Union territories?

Ans. The President directly administers the Union territories through administrators appointed by him/her.

(B) Legislative Powers

(1) The President, after the General elections, addresses the Joint Sessions of new Parliament and the first sessions of it every year and outlines the Government's national and international Policies.
(2) The President can summon, prorogue the Parliament and dissolve the Lok Sabha or even call a Joint Session of the Parliament.
(3) Money Bills are introduced with the prior consent of the President, so he/she has to give his/her assent when these are presented to him/her.
(4) A bill becomes a law after it gets the assent from the President, he/she may send it back with some recommendations. But, the second time, the President has to give his/her assent.
(5) The President issues ordinance during the recess of the Parliament, Ordinances are like temporary laws which have to be ratified by the Parliament.
(6) The President nominates 12 members to the Rajya Sabha from among persons having special knowledge or practical experience in the field of literature, science, art or social service.
(7) A Bill for the formation of new States or alteration of areas of the existing States cannot be introduced except on the President's recommendation.
(8) The President has the power to send messages to either House of Parliament with regard to any pending Bill or any other matter.

(C) Discretionary Powers

(1) When no party gains majority in the Lok Sabha, the President, using his/her discretionary Power, appoints the Prime Minister.
(2) After the vote of no-confidence is passed against the prevailing Government, the President may dissolve the Parliament or ask the leader of another party to prove its majority on the floor of the House.

The President and the Vice-President 25

(3) He/She can also dismiss Ministers in case the Council of Ministers loses the confidence of the House but refuses to resign.

(D) Emergency Powers

The President can proclaim a State of Emergency in the following cases:

(A) National Emergency (Article 352)

(1) The President, if satisfied, that the security of the nation is threatened by War or external aggression, or an armed rebellion, can issue the proclamation of National Emergency.

(2) Every such proclamation must be approved by the Parliament within 1 month by a special majority. Once passed, it remains operational for 6 months. Beyond that, it has to be passed again by the Parliament.

(3) During the proclamation, Fundamental rights are suspended (except those under Article 20 and 21). The Constitution assumes unitary role and grants Parliament the powers to make laws on 66 subjects of State List. And many of the powers of the States are curtailed.

(4) Also, the country has to lose its federal spirit, as the States, under an emergency, are obliged to carry out the instructions of the Centre.

(5) The financial provisions of the Constitution are also suspended.

(6) The Lok Sabha, under such circumstances, can be extended for a period of one year.

(B) President Rule (Article 356)

(1) President's Rule or Emergency in a State due to constitutional breakdown is proclaimed either on the advice of the governor or otherwise.

(2) If approved by both the Houses, President's rule can continue for six months. It can be extended for a maximum period of 3 years with the approval of the Parliament every 6 months.

(3) The Governor acts in accordance with the direction of the President during the President's rule.

(4) The State Council of Ministers and the Vidhan Sabha may be dissolved.

(5) The annual State budget is passed by the Parliament.

(C) Financial Emergency (Article 360)

(1) If a situation has arisen whereby the financial stability or credibility of the nation is threatened, the President can declare financial Emergency.

(2) The president may appoint a Finance Commission to suggest methods to get out of the financial crisis, he/she may reduce salaries and allowances of all or any class of persons including the Judges of the Supreme Court and the High Courts.

(3) He/She can also issue instructions to the states in regard to the utilization of funds in the manner he/she may deem fit or may order the State to submit money Bills to him/her for his/her assent.

(4) Position of the President as a Nominal Head – The President has all the powers listed above but the Constitution has clearly stated that the president shall act in accordance with the advice given by the Prime Minister and the Council of ministers.

Important

→ The President exercises his/her functions in accordance with the advice of the Council of Ministers.

THE VICE-PRESIDENT

Article 63 stipulates that there shall be a Vice-President of India.

Qualifications for Election

A person standing for election to the Vice-president must:

(1) be a citizen of India
(2) should not be less than 35 years of age.
(3) should be qualified for election as a member of the Council of States. (Rajya Sabha)
(4) A person shall not be eligible for election as Vice-President if he/she holds any office of profit under the Government of India or government of any State or under any local or other authority subject to the control of any of the said Governments.

Term of Office: Normal term of office of the Vice-President is five years. He/she may resign before the expiry of his/her term of office by writing to the President. For the violation of the Constitution, he/she would be removed from the office by a resolution passed by majority in the Rajya Sabha and accepted by the Lok Sabha.

Oath of Office

He takes his oath in front of the President (or person appointed by the President).

Elections

The Vice-President is elected indirectly by an electoral college which includes the elected as well as nominated members of both Houses of the Parliament. The election is held by the method of proportional representation with single transferable vote. Each nomination paper should be proposed by atleast twenty electors and should be seconded by another twenty electors.

Powers and Functions

As Chairman of the Rajya Sabha :

(1) The Vice President is the ex-officio Chairman of the Rajya Sabha and presides over the meetings of the House.
(2) He/she regulates the debates and proceedings of the House and decides the order of speeches.
(3) Decides the admissibility of a resolution or of the questions in Rajya Sabha.
(4) He/she may suspend or adjourn the business of the House when it becomes chaotic.
(5) He/she issues directions to the chairman of various committees in all matters related to their working.

By taking over as the President : The Vice-President under the following situations, takes over the office of the President:
(1) death of the president
(2) resignation by the president
(3) removal of the president
(4) when the president has gone abroad
(5) when the president, owing to absence, illness or any other cause, is unable to discharge his/her duties.

Caution
→ The vice president is not a member of either of the House of Parliament.
→ The term of office of the Vice-President is five years whereas the term of office of a Rajya Sabha member is six years.

Important
→ The Vice President is the Ex-officio chairman of the Rajya Sabha.

In case of the President's death, removal or resignation, the Vice President acts as the President till the new President is elected and takes charge of his/her office.

ICSE Suggestions
→ Identify technical terms such as Electoral College, etc. to be used in Civics and understand the meaning of these terms in detail.
→ Understand the term 'impeachment' and the procedure of impeachment of the President.
→ Draw a flow chart to explain the executive powers and legislative powers of the President. Emphasize that the power of appointments is included in the executive powers while legislative powers include the law-making powers or powers concerning the Parliament.

Glossary

(1) **Proportional representation:** An electoral system in which parties gain seats in proportion to the number of votes cast for them.
(2) **Seconder:** A person who backs a politician or a team, etc.
(3) **Electoral College:** A body of electors, who elect the President and Vice-President of India.
(4) **Prorogue:** Discontinue a session without dissolving it.
(5) **Money Bill:** A bill having financial bearing is called a money bill.
(6) **Ordinance:** The laws promulgated by the President on the advice of the Union Cabinet. They can be issued only when the Parliament is not in session.
(7) **Impeachment:** A special procedure to remove the President before the expiry of his term.
(8) **Emergency:** A sudden situation which needs immediate action to control it.
(9) **Office of Profit:** An office whose holder is entitled to certain powers such as executive, administrative, financial or judicial.
(10) **Ex-officio:** By virtue of holding an office.
(11) **Presidential Address:** A formal speech or written statement by the president directed to a particular group of persons.

OBJECTIVE Type Questions

Multiple Choice Questions
[1 mark each]

1. The executive power of the Indian Union is vested in the ....
   (a) President
   (b) Vice President
   (c) Prime Minister
   (d) Council of Ministers   [HOT]

Ans. *(a) President*

Explanation: The executive power of the Indian Union is vested in the President. He/she exercises this power either directly or through all officers of the Union who are his/her subordinates, in accordance with the Constitution.

2. Which of the following is not a part of the Union Executive?
   (a) The President
   (b) The Vice President
   (c) The Council of Ministers
   (d) The Chief Justice

Ans. *(d) The Chief Justice*

Explanation: The Union Executive of the Government of India consists of the President, the Vice-President, the Prime Minister and his/her Council of Ministers.

3. What is the minimum age required to be eligible for the election of President of India?
   (a) 21 years   (b) 25 years
   (c) 30 years   (d) 35 years

Ans. *(d) 35 years*

Explanation: A person is eligible for election as President of India, if he/she:
(1) is a citizen of India; (2) has completed the age of thirty-five years; (3) is qualified for election as a member of the Lok Sabha.

4. Who elects the President of India?
   (a) Members of Lok Sabha
   (b) Members of Rajya Sabha
   (c) Members of State Legislative Assemblies
   (d) Electoral College   [HOT]

Ans. *(d) Electoral College*

Explanation: The President of India is elected indirectly by an electoral college which consists of: (i) elected members of both Houses of the Parliament; (ii) elected members of the legislative assemblies of all States and also of National Capital Territory of Delhi and the Union Territory of Puducherry. Nominated members of either house of Parliament and State Assemblies are not eligible to be included in the Electoral College.

5. Who administers oath of office to the President of India?
   (a) The Vice President
   (b) The Prime Minister
   (c) The Chief Justice
   (d) The Speaker of Lok Sabha   [HOT]

Ans. *(c) The Chief Justice*

Explanation: The Chief Justice of Supreme Court administers the oath of office to the President of India.

6. Which of the following is not the legislative power of the President of India?
   (a) Assent to bills
   (b) Appointment of Governors of States
   (c) Promulgate Ordinances
   (d) Address Sessions of Parliament

Ans. *(b) Appointment of Governors of States*

Explanation: Appointment of Governors of States is the executive power of the President of India.

7. Which of the following is not a necessary qualification for the election of the Vice President of India?
   (a) He/She should be a citizen of India
   (b) He/She must have completed the age of thirty-five years
   (c) He/She must be qualified for election as member of Lok Sabha
   (d) He/She must not hold any office of profit under the Union or State Government

Ans. *(c) He/She must be qualified for election as member of Lok Sabha*

Explanation: To be eligible for election for the office of the Vice President, a person must be qualified for election as member of Rajya Sabha.

8. Who elects the Vice President of India?
   (a) Members of Rajya Sabha
   (b) Members of Lok Sabha
   (c) Both (a) and (b)
   (d) Members of States Legislative Assemblies

Ans. *(c) Both (a) and (b)*

Explanation: The Vice President is elected by an Electoral College consisting of members of both Houses of the Parliament, according to the system of proportional representation, by means of the single transferable vote.

9. A person should have completed the age of .... to be eligible for election as Vice-President.
   (a) 21 years   (b) 30 years
   (c) 35 years   (d) 25 years
                         [ICSE Sem-2, 2022]

Ans. *(c) 35 years*

Explanation : A person shall be eligible for election as Vice-President, if he/she has completed the age of thirty – five years.

10. The President can declare a National/General Emergency when ....

(a) There is a threat to the security of the country.
(b) There is financial instability in the country.
(c) The Governor gives a report recommending Emergency.
(d) The Election Commission recommends its proclamation.
[HOT] [ICSE Sem-2, 2022]

Ans. *(a) There is a threat to the security of the country.*

Explanation : The President can proclaim a state of National/General Emergency where there is a danger of foreign aggression or danger to the peace and security of the country because of a civil war, insurgency or any other such cause (Article 352).

11. The procedure to remove the President is called ....
(a) Impeachment (b) Interpellation
(c) Resolution (d) Prorogation

Ans. *(a) Impeachment*

Explanation: The President can be removed from office by a process of impeachment for violation of the Constitution.

12. The term of office of the Vice President is ....
(a) five years (b) six years
(c) two years (d) ten years [HOT]

Ans. *(a) Five years*

Explanation: The term of office of the Vice President five years.

 Related Theory

→ The Vice President is not a member of either House of the Parliament. Though he/she is the ex-officio chairman of the Rajya Sabha. His/her term of office is 5 years whereas the term of office of a member of the Rajya Sabha is six years.

13. How many proposers are required for the nomination to the election of the President?
(a) 10 (b) 20
(c) 50 (d) 100

Ans. *(a) 100*

Explanation: Presidential candidate shall have to be proposed by 50 members of the Electoral college as proposer and seconded by another 50 members.

14. Who administers the oath of office to the council of ministers?
(a) The President
(b) The Vice-President
(c) The Prime Minister
(d) The speaker of Lok Sabha

Ans. *(a) The President*

Explanation: The President administers the oath of office to the Prime Minister and his council of ministers.

15. Which of the following is not an executive power of the President?
(a) Issue all executive orders
(b) Appointment of officials of the state
(c) Nomination of members to the Parliament
(d) Administration of union territories

Ans. *(d) Nomination of members to the Parliament*

Explanation: Nomination of members to the parliament is the legislative power of the President. The President nominates 12 members to the Rajya Sabha and 2 members to the Lok Sabha.

16. Who is the Head of State in the Union of India?
(a) President (b) Vice-President
(c) Prime Minister (d) Chief Justice

Ans. *(a) President*

Explanation: The executive power of the Indian Union is vested in the President. He exercises this power either directly or through all officers of the Union who are his/her subordinates, in accordance with the Constitution. The President is the Head of the State and Supreme Commander of the Defence forces of India.

17. Who constitutes the Electoral college for the Election of the Vice-President?
(a) Members of Lok Sabha
(b) Members of Rajya Sabha
(c) Members of the Parliament
(d) Members of the Parliament and State Legislative Assemblies.

Ans. *(c) Members of the Parliament*

Explanation: The electoral college for the election of the Vice-President consists of members of both the Houses of the Parliament but it does not include the members of State Legislative Assemblies.

SUBJECTIVE Type Questions

Short Answer Type Questions

[2 marks each]

18. State any two qualifications necessary for the election of the President of India. **[ICSE 2015]**

Ans. The qualification necessary for the election of the President of India are:
(1) He must be a citizen of India;
(2) He must be at least 35 years of age;
(3) He should be qualified for election as a member of Lok Sabha;
(4) He should not be a member of either House of the Parliament or State Legislature.
(5) He should not be a proclaimed offender.
[Any two]

> A citizen of India.
> Not less than 35 years of age.
> Qualified for election as a member of Lok Sabha.
> Not holding any office of profit under the government.
> Should not be a member of either House of Parliament or State Legislative **[Any two]**
> **[Marking Scheme]**

 What Examiners Say
→ Answered correctly by most candidates. However, a few wrote the incorrect answer.

 Caution
→ Understand all the qualifications necessary for a person to contest the election of the President including the age.

19. How many electors should propose and second the nomination paper of a candidate for the election of the President?

Ans. The nomination paper of a candidate for the election of the President should be subscribed by at least fifty electors as proposers and fifty electors as seconders.

20. State any one reason why the President is elected indirectly. **[ICSE 2018] [Hot]**

Ans. According to the Constitution of India, the President is the nominal head and the real powers vests with the council of ministers headed by the Prime Minister. Direct election of the President would indicate that he/she has a higher status than that of a constitutional head. The President does not exercise any real power and hence is elected indirectly by the electoral college.

Become a rival center of power to the Council of ministers, would be against the parliamentary system, would become a nominee of the ruling party and would not represent the constituent states of the union,

His indirect election by Electoral college makes the President the elected representative of the whole nation.

He is the nominal head. The real power lies in the hands of Prime Minister and the Parliament.

Election to be quiet and dignified affair. Loss of time, energy and money.
[Any one]
[Marking Scheme]

 What Examiners Say
→ A few candidates, misunderstood the question and instead of giving the reason for the President being elected indirectly, wrote on how the President is elected.

 Caution
→ Understand that the President of India is not elected directly by the people since India has a Parliamentary form of Government.

21. What is an Electoral College?

OR

State the composition of the Electoral College in the election of the President of India. **[ICSE 2014] [HOT]**

Ans. The Electoral College consists of:
(1) The elected members of both Houses of Parliament. Nominated members of the Lok Sabha and the Rajya Sabha are not the members of the Electoral College.
(2) The elected members of the legislative assemblies of the states in accordance with the proportional representation by means of single transferable vote including National Capital Territory of Delhi and the Union Territory of Puducherry.

> The Electoral college consists of:
> The elected members of the Vidhan Sabha (Legislative Assembly) of all the states and
> The elected members of the Lok Sabha and the Rajya Sabha. **[Marking Scheme]**

 What Examiners Say
→ Most candidates answered correctly. However, a few mentioned only Member of Parliament, members of the Legislative Assemblies were however excluded.

⚠️ **Caution**
➙ It is an indirect election where our elected representatives in Parliament and State Assemblies elect the President of India.

22. What do you understand by Single Transferable vote?

Ans. The single Transferable vote is an electoral system of proportional representation in which a person's vote is transferred to second or other competing candidates, in case no candidate is able to get absolute majority of 50 percent votes in the first preference.

23. For the election of the President, how is the value of the vote of the elected Members of parliament worked out?

Ans. Each elected Member of Parliament has such number of votes as obtained by dividing the total number of votes assigned to MLAs of the States by the total number of elected Members of Parliament. Thus, the value of the vote of a Member of Parliament is:

Total Number of votes assigned to MLAs/ Total number of elected MPs

24. For the election of the President, how is the value of the vote of the elected Member of State Legislative Assembly worked out?

Ans. Every elected member of the Legislative Assembly of a State has as many votes as there are multiples of thousands in the quotient obtained by dividing the population of the State by the total number of elected members of the Assembly. The voting power of an elected member of a State Legislative Assembly is calculated according to the following formula:

Total population of State/ Number of elected members × 1000

25. Name the official procedure by which the President can be removed. [ICSE 2016]

Ans. The President can be removed through the process of impeachment on account of grave misconduct like violation of the Constitution.

Impeachment
[Marking Scheme]

📝 **What Examiners Say**
➙ Most candidates were specific on the impeachment procedure however they sought to elaborate on it that was not required.

⚠️ **Caution**
➙ Emphasize the need to read the question carefully and write what is required

26. Mention any two important occasion when the President addresses a Joint Session of Parliament. [ICSE 2016]

Ans.

(1) The President addresses the Joint Sitting of the two Houses at the beginning of the first session after each General Election.

(2) The President also addresses both Houses of Parliament at the commencement of the first session of each year, the Budget Session.

(3) If there is a disagreement over a non-money Bill then the President may call for a Joint Sitting of the two Houses.
[Any two]
[Marking Scheme]

📝 **What Examiners Say**
➙ Most candidates wrote the answer correctly. Some were unsure and mentioned that the President addresses joint session during emergency or when there is a deadlock over a Non-Money Bill.

⚠️ **Caution**
➙ Understand that the President is one of the three constituents of Indian Parliament and being the Head addresses the Joint Session after each General Election and the first session of the year, i.e., Budget Session.

27. (A) Who is the Supreme Commander of the Armed forces of India? [ICSE 2020]

(B) Who settles disputes arising in connection with the election of the President of India? [ICSE 2012]

Ans. (A)

President [Marking Scheme]

📝 **What Examiners Say**
➙ This question was well attempted by most of the candidates.

(B) The disputes arising in connection with the election of the President of India are settled by the Supreme Court.

28. Write any two circumstance when the President can declare a National Emergency. [ICSE 2019]

Ans. The President can declare a National Emergency under following circumstances:

(1) When there is a danger of foreign aggression.

(2) Armed rebellion inside the country.

(3) When there is a threat to the peace and security of the country.

(4) When the financial stability or credit of the country is threatened. [Any two]

The President and the Vice-President 31

(1) Danger of foreign aggression or war
(2) Danger to peace and security of the country
(3) Civil war (Internal disturbance) Insurgency
(4) Armed rebellion **[Any two]**
[Marking Scheme]

What Examiners Say
→ A few candidates mentioned natural calamities, floods or earthquakes as the circumstances for declaring the National Emergency.

Caution
→ Understand three types of emergencies that can be declared by the President and the circumstances under which these emergencies can be declared.

29. When can the President use his Discretionary power to appoint the Prime Minister? **[ICSE 2017]**

Ans. The President can use his discretionary power to appoint a Prime Minister if no political party or coalition has a clear majority to form the government. The President has to use his judgement and invite such a leader to head the government as Prime Minister, who in his view can give stable government.

> When no political party has received an absolute majority, when there is a hung Parliament or a coalition government.
> **[Marking Scheme]**

What Examiners Say
→ Some candidates were not clear about the discretionary power of the President related to the appointment of Prime minister. They mentioned wrongly that on the death of the Prime Minister, the President uses this power to appoint the Prime Minister.

Caution
→ Understand the meaning of Discretionary Powers of the President to appoint the Prime Minister.

30. Mention any two discretionary power of the President. **[ICSE 2015]**

Ans.
> (1) The President may withhold assent to a bill or send it back for reconsideration (in case it is not a money bill).
> (2) If no Party gains majority, then President has the freedom to appoint the Prime Minister.
> (3) If the Prime Minister has lost the confidence of the Lok Sabha and asked for the dissolution of the house, then the President is not bound to act on the PM's advice. **(Any two)**
> **[Marking Scheme]**

What Examiners Say
→ Most candidates answered correctly. However, a few were unable to understand the meaning of 'discretionary' and explained the judicial power e.g. The President can pardon a person sentenced to death.

Caution
→ To clear doubts, understand the meaning of the word 'discretionary'. Though the President acts on the advice of the Prime Minister, he can exercise his discretion in the appointment of the Prime Minister or when he has lost the confidence of the Lok Sabha.

31. What is an Ordinance? **[ICSE 2018]**
OR
What is an 'Ordinance'? When can it be passed?  **[ICSE 2014]**

Ans. Ordinance is a law that is promulgated by the President of India on the recommendation of the Union Cabinet, which have the same effect as an Act of Parliament. It can only be issued when Parliament is not in session. It enables the Government to take immediate legislative action.

> When Parliament is not in session or emergency, an Ordinance is used. It is a temporary law/an order issued by the President. **(Any one)**
> **OR**
> An ordinance is a temporary law passed by the President (ii) when the Parliament is not in session or during an emergency.
> **[Marking Scheme]**

What Examiners Say
→ Most candidates wrote the correct answer although a few explained Ordinance vaguely. Some candidates wrote Command, which is more verbal and may not have an authority of law.
Instead of temporary law, many candidates used the words – decree, order or Bill, etc. The phrase 'temporary law' was rarely used and could not be explained as to when it can be passed.

Caution
→ Understand that an ordinance is a law, decree or an order issued by the President during the recess of Parliament.

32. (A) Who elects the Vice President of India?
(B) How long can the Vice-President continue to hold office even after the expiry of his term?

Ans. (A) An Electoral College consisting of the members of both Houses of Parliament elects the Vice President of India.
(B) The Vice-President shall continue to hold office, notwithstanding the expiry of his term, until his successor enters upon his office.

33. **(A)** Who administers the oath of office to the Vice President?

(B) What is the normal term of office of the Vice President of India? **[ICSE 2020]**

Ans. (A) The oath of office to the Vice President is administered by the President.

(B)

| 5 years | **[Marking Scheme]** |

 What Examiners Say

↪ Most of the candidates wrote the correct answer barring a few who mentioned the normal term of office of the Vice President of India is 6 years

 Caution

↪ Apprise that 5 years is the normal term of office of the Vice President of India.

34. How can the Vice-President be removed from his office?

Ans. The Vice-President can be removed from his office by a resolution of the Rajya Sabha passed by a majority of its members and agreed upon by the Lok Sabha through the process of impeachment.

35. Under what circumstances can the President of India declare an emergency in the country? Mention any two. **[ICSE 2012]**

Ans. The President of India can declare an emergency in the country under following circumstances:

(1) **National Emergency:** According to article 352 of the Constitution, if the President feels that there is a threat to the security of the country or any part of the country due to external aggression and armed rebellion, he/she can proclaim emergency for the whole country.

(2) **Emergency due to Failure of Constitutional Machinery in State:** According to Article 356 of the Constitution, if the President is satisfied that a situation has arisen in which the governance of a State cannot be carried in accordance to the provisions of the Constitution, the President may be proclamation, impose President's rule in that State.

(3) **Financial Emergency:** Article 360 of the Constitution empowers the President to proclaim a Financial emergency, if he feels that the financial security or credit worthiness of India is threatened.

[Any two]

 Caution

↪ Learn the difference between the executive and the Legislative powers of the president. Executive Powers pertain to powers of appointments and Legislative Powers involves assent of bills, issuing of Ordinances and nomination of members, etc.

36. Give any two reasons for the indirect election of the President.

Ans. The reasons for the indirect election of the President are:

(1) According to the Constitution of India, the President is the nominal head and the real power vests with the council of ministers. If he is elected directly, he will become a rival centre of power to the council of ministers.

(2) His indirect election makes the President the elected representative of the whole nation.

37. Why is the President referred to as the nominal head?

Ans. The executive power of the Indian Union is vested in the President. According to the 42nd Amendment Act, it is necessary for the President to exercise his/her functions in accordance with the advice of the council of ministers. Hence, he is referred to as the nominal head.

38. Briefly explain President's power in appointment of Prime Minister.

Ans. The President of India enjoys certain discretionary powers. In a situation, where no single party commands the clear support of the majority of the Lok Sabha members and there is a hung Parliament, it is at the discretion of the President to appoint the Prime Minister, whom he thinks can provide a stable government.

Structured Questions

[3+3+4 = **10** marks each]

39. The executive power of the Indian Union is vested in the President of India. In this context, answer the following questions:

(A) Mention any three discretionary powers of the President.

(B) Name the three kinds of emergencies that can be proclaimed by the President.

(C) Mention any four legislative powers of the President.

Ans. (A) The discretionary powers of the President are:

(1) The President can dismiss ministers in case the Council of Ministers loses the confidence of the House but refuses to resign, then the President can use his discretion power.

(2) During Constitutional crisis, it is at the discretion of the President to dissolve the Lok Sabha and explore the possibilities of alternative government.

(3) In case no party attains majority in the Lok Sabha, it is at the discretion of the President to appoint the Prime Minister.

(B) The three kinds of emergencies that can be proclaimed by the President are:
  (1) National or General Emergency
  (2) Breakdown of Constitutional machinery
  (3) Financial Emergency

(C) The legislative powers of the President are:
  (1) He can summon and prorogue both Houses of Parliament and dissolve the Lok Sabha;
  (2) He may summon a joint sitting of both the Houses of the Parliament;
  (3) He can promulgate ordinances when Parliament is not in session.
  (4) He can send the messages to either House of Parliament either in regard to any pending bill or to any other matter.

40. The President represents the nation but does rule the nation. In this context, answer the following questions:
(A) State one reason why the President is elected indirectly.
(B) Explain any three legislative powers of the President.
(C) Explain any four executive powers of the President. **[🔥HOT]**

Ans. (A) The President is the nominal head and the real power lies in the hands of the council of ministers headed by the Prime Minister. Direct election of the President would indicate that he/she has a higher status than that of a constitutional head and become a rival centre of power to the council of ministers, which would be against the Parliamentary system. Hence, the President is elected indirectly.

(B) The legislative powers of the President are:
  (1) He can summon and prorogue both Houses of Parliament and dissolve the Lok Sabha;
  (2) He may summon a joint sitting of both Houses of Parliament;
  (3) Without his assent, no bill passed by the Parliament can become law;
  (4) He has the power to nominate two members of the Anglo-Indian community to the Lok Sabha and 12 members to the Rajya Sabha.
  (5) He can promulgate Ordinances when Parliament is not in session.
  [Any three]

(C) The executive powers of the President are:
  (1) He undertakes all the major executive actions of the Union Government of India;
  (2) He makes rules specifying the manner in which the orders and other instruments made and executed in his name shall be authenticated.
  (3) He appoints the Prime Minister and council of ministers. They hold office during his pleasure.
  (4) The President makes appointments of the officials of the state, the Chief Justice and the Judges of the Supreme Court and the High Courts, the Governors of the states, Attorney General, the Comptroller and Auditor General, etc.
  (5) The President directly administers the Union territories through administrators appointed by him.
  [Any four]

41. The President of India enjoys vast powers. In this context, briefly explain:
(A) Any three of his legislative powers
(B) His emergency powers
(C) Any four of his Executive powers

Ans. (A) The Legislative powers of the President are:
  (1) **Addresses Sessions of Parliament:** The President addresses both Houses of Parliament assembled together for the first session after each General Election to the Lok Sabha and at the commencement of the first session of each year.
  (2) **Summon and Prorogue the Houses:** The President has the power to summon and prorogue the Houses of Parliament. The power to summon Parliament is subject to the condition that there should not be a gap of more than six months between two sessions of each House.
  (3) **Promulgate Ordinances:** Under Article 123, the President can promulgate an Ordinance, which has the same status as an Act of Parliament. The President may withdraw the Ordinance at any time.

(B) The President can proclaim a state of Emergency in the following cases:
  (1) **National or General Emergency:** There is a danger of foreign aggression or danger to the peace and security of the country because of a civil war, insurgency or any other such cause
  (2) **Breakdown of Constitutional Machinery:** The Constitutional machinery in a State has broken down or there is deadlock because of political uncertainties.

(3) **Financial Emergency:** A set back to the financial stability or credit feasibility of the country is likely to occur or has occurred.

(C) The executive powers of the President include:

(1) Head of the Union Administration: All executive orders are issued in the name of the President. All the Union officials are his subordinates.

(2) Appointment of officials of the State: The President makes appointments to key posts to run the government's administration. He appoints:

(i) The Prime Minister, and the Council of Ministers on the Prime Minister's advice. He summons the leader of the majority group in the Parliament and asks him to form the government.

(ii) The Chief Justice and Judges of the Supreme Court and the High Courts

(iii) The Governors of the States

(iv) The Lt. Governor and Chief Commissioners of the Union territories

(v) The Attorney General of India

(vi) The Comptroller and Auditor General of India

(vii) The Chairman and members of Union Public Service Commission

(viii) The Chairman and members of the Planning Commission

(3) Control over State Governments: The Union Government may give necessary direction to a State. During President's rule, the Union Government has complete control over the State.

(4) Union Territories and Border Areas: The administration of the Union Territories and the Border Areas, is the responsibility of the President.

42. **The President of India is the Head of the Indian Union. In this context, explain briefly the following:**

(A) Oath taken by the President

(B) How can the President be removed from his office?

(C) Qualifications required for contesting elections to the office of President

Ans. (A) Before entering upon his office, the President takes an oath in the presence of the Chief Justice of India, to:

(1) Discharge the functions of the President of India

(2) Preserve, protect, and defend the Constitution and the Law, and

(3) Devote himself to the service and well-being of the people of India.

(B) The President can be removed from office for violation of the Constitution by the process of impeachment.

Either House of the Parliament can frame charges against the President. The charges must be filed after a notice of 14 days in writing. The notice must be signed by at least one-fourth of the total number of members of that House. Furthermore, a resolution along with the charges against the President has to be passed by a majority of at least two-thirds of the total membership of the House.

The charges levelled against the President are then investigated by the other House. If the charges are confirmed by a two-thirds majority in the second House, the President stands removed from office with effect from the date on which a resolution has been passed. Except the impeachment, no other punishment can be given to the President for violation of the Constitution.

(C) In order to contest elections to the office of the President of India, a candidate should fulfill the following qualifications:

(1) He or she should be a citizen of India;

(2) He or she should have completed 35 years of age at the time of elections;

(3) He or she should not hold any office of profit under the union government, state government, a local body or any other authority.

(4) He or she should be qualified for election as a member of the Lok Sabha;

(5) He should not be a proclaimed offender.

[Any four]

43. **The Executive Power of the Indian Union is vested in the President. In this context, answer the following:**

(A) How is the President of India elected? State the composition of the Electoral College that elects him.

(B) Explain any three Discretionary Powers of the President.

(C) Mention any four Executive Powers of the President. **[ICSE 2020]**

Ans. (A) The President of India is elected indirectly by the members of an electoral college, in accordance with the system of proportional representation by means of a single transferable vote. Electoral College consists of elected members of both the houses of the Parliament i.e., Lok Sabha and Rajya Sabha, and the elected members of the legislative assemblies of the states including the National Capital Territory of Delhi and the Union Territory of Puducherry.

(B) The discretionary powers of the President are:
 (1) During constitutional crises, it is at the discretion of the president to dissolve the Lok Sabha or explore possibilities of alternative government.
 (2) It is at the discretion of the President to withhold the assent to an ordinary bill. He can refuse his assent and send it back for reconsideration.
 (3) In case no party attains majority in the Lok Sabha, it is at the discretion of the President to appoint the Prime Minister.

(C) The executive powers of the President are:
 (1) The President is the head of the Union administration and all executive orders are issued in his name.
 (2) The President appoints the Prime Minister, and on his advice, appoints the Council of Ministers.
 (3) The President makes appointments of the officials of the state, the Chief Justice and the Judges of the Supreme Court and the High Courts, the Governors of the State, Attorney general, Auditor General etc.
 (4) The President is responsible for the administration of the Union Territories.

(A)
1. President is elected indirectly by the members of an electoral college/ single transferable vote/proportional representation.
2. Composition of Electoral college:
 (i) Elected members of both Houses [LS and RS] of Parliament.
 (ii) Elected members of the Legislative Assemblies of the states including the national capital Territory of Delhi and the Union Territory of Puducherry.
 (iii) OR MPs and MLAs

(B) **The discretionary powers:**
 (1) Where he uses his wisdom and judgement.
 (2) Dissolution of Lok Sabha during Constitutional crisis
 (3) Explore possibilities of alternative government at the centre

 (4) Dismissal of ministers when the government collapses due to No confidence
 (5) Appointment of the PM where no single party commands
 (6) Appointment of PM in case of death
 (7) May withhold assent to an ordinary bill or send it back for reconsideration.
 (8) No time limit within which he is to declare his assent/refusal of bill.
 [Any three]

(C) **The Executive powers:**
 (1) Head of the Union administration/ administration of the country runs in his house/All orders are issued in his name.
 (2) Appointment of officials of the state
 Appoints the:
 (i) Attorney General
 (ii) Auditor General
 (iii) Ambassador
 (iv) Members of UPSC
 (v) Judges of High Court and Supreme Court
 (vi) Members of the Planning Commission
 (vii) Election Commissioner
 (viii) Governor of State
 (ix) PM and the Council of Ministers
 (3) Control over state governments during emergency
 (4) And Union territories and border areas/exercises power through an administrator appointed by the President.
 [Any four]
 [Marking Scheme]

What Examiners Say

→ (A) This subpart was attempted well by most candidates. Some wrote that the President of India is elected by Direct elections. Some candidates did not give the composition of the Electoral College correctly.

→ (B) Many candidates did not write the Discretionary Powers of the President correctly.

→ (C) A large number of candidates answered this part correctly. However, some candidates mixed up the Legislative and the Executive powers. A few candidates confused the Executive powers with the Emergency powers of the President.

⚠ Caution

→ Students should identify technical terms such as Electoral College etc to be used in Civics and know their meanings.

→ *Before learning Discretionary Powers of the President, students should know the meaning of word 'Discretion'. Instances should be explained with discretionary powers of the President.*

→ *Clarify the distinction between the Executive Powers and Legislative Powers of the President.*

44. **The President and the Vice-President are part of the Union Executive.**

In this context, answer the following questions:

(A) State any three qualifications required for a candidate to be elected as the Vice-President of India.

(B) State the three functions of Vice-President.

(C) Explain briefly any two Legislative and any two Executive powers of the President. [ICSE 2018]

Ans. (A) The qualifications required by a candidate to be elected as the Vice-President of India are:
(1) He/she should be a citizen of India.
(2) He/she should have completed 35 years of age.
(3) He/she should not hold any office of profit under the Union Government or any State Government or any local authority or any other public authority.
(4) He/she should be qualified for election as a member of the Rajya Sabha.

(B) The functions of the Vice-President are:
(1) The Vice-President shall be the ex-officio Chairman of the Rajya Sabha. Thus, primarily he/she performs the functions of the Chairman of the Rajya Sabha.

[Any three]

(2) He/she may travel to the foreign countries as the representatives of the President to represent India on matter of neighbourly relations.
(3) The Vice-President assumes the duties of the President whenever he/she takes over the office of the President for the period of six months at best when the office falls vacant by reason of death, resignation or impeachment of the President.

(C) **The legislative powers of the President are:**
(1) He/she can summon and prorogue both Houses of Parliament and dissolve the Lok Sabha.
(2) He/she may summon a joint sitting of both Houses of Parliament.
(3) Without his/her assent, no bill passed by the Parliament can become law.
(4) He/she has the power to nominate two members of the Anglo-Indian community to the Lok Sabha and 12 members to the Rajya Sabha.

(5) He/she can promulgate Ordinances when Parliament is not in session.

[Any two]

The executive powers of the President are:
(1) He/she undertakes all the major executive actions of the Union Government of India;
(2) He/she makes rules specifying the manner in which the orders and other instruments made and executed in his/her name shall be authenticated.
(3) He/she appoints the Prime Minister and Council of ministers. They hold office during his/her pleasure.
(4) The President makes appointments of the officials of the state, the Chief Justice and the Judge of the Supreme Court and the High Courts, the Governors of the states, Attorney General, the Comptroller and Auditor General, etc.
(5) The President directly administers the union territories through administrators appointed by him. **[Any two]**

(A) **A person is eligible for election as Vice-President if he/she:**
(1) is a citizen of India
(2) is not less than 35 years of age
(3) is qualified for election as a member of the Rajya Sabha
(4) must not hold any office of profit either under Union Government or under State Government.

[Any three]

(B) (1) Chairman of the Rajya Sabha, acts as the Ex-Officio Chairman of the Rajya Sabha, he regulates debates and proceedings of the house.
(2) Decides the orders of speech admissibility of resolution or of question suspend or adjourn the house in case of grave disorder.
(3) Takes over the office of the President in case of the president's death, resignation or removal.

[Any three]

(C) **Legislative power:** Addresses Sessions of Parliament, Message to Parliament, summons and prorogue the house, dissolve the Lok Sabha, Nomination of Members (2 Lok Sabha, 12 Rajya Sabha.) Assent to Bills, Issue Ordinances, assent to state bills, Formation of New States.

[Any two]

Executive Powers: Head of the union Administration, Appointment of officials of the State- Appoints Prime minister,

Council of Ministers, Chief Justice and Judges of Supreme Court and the High Courts, Governors of the States, The Lt. Governors and the Chief Commissioners of the Union territories, The Attorney General of India, The Comptroller and Auditor General of India, The Chairman and Members of Planning Commissions and economic Commission, Chief Election Commissioners, control over the state (President's rule) Administration of Union Territories and Border Areas.

[Any four]
[Marking Scheme]

What Examiners Say

→ (A) Most of the candidates answered the question correctly. However, a few candidates, instead of writing the qualifications of the Vice-President wrote the qualifications required for membership of the Lok Sabha.

→ (B) Most candidates wrote the three functions of the Vice-President correctly.

→ (C) A number of candidates muddled up the executive and the legislative powers of the President.

45. The President of India is the Constitutional Head of the Indian Republic. In this context, answer the following questions:

(A) How is the President elected?

(B) Mention three types of emergencies that the President is empowered to proclaim.

(c) Explain briefly any four 'Executive Powers' of the President. [ICSE 2016]

Ans. (A) Refer Answer 43(A)

(B) The emergencies that a President is empowered to proclaim are:

(1) **National Emergency:** According to Article 352 of the Constitution, if the President feels that there is a threat to the security of the country or any part of the country due to external aggression or armed rebellion, he/she can proclaim emergency for the whole country. The proclamation of emergency has to be approved by both the Houses of Parliament within one month from the date of its issue.

(2) **Emergency Due to Failure of Constitutional Machinery in a State:** This is popularly known as 'President's Rule' or 'State Emergency' or 'Constitutional Emergency'. According to Article 356 of the Constitution, if the President is satisfied that a situation has arisen in which the governance of a state cannot be carried in accordance to the provisions of the Constitution, the President, by proclamation, may impose President's Rule in that state.

(3) **Financial Emergency:** Article 360 of the Constitution empowers the President to proclaim a Financial security or credit worthiness of India is threatened. The proclamation of Financial Emergency has to be laid before both the Houses of Parliament and is valid for two months, unless approved by resolution of both Houses of Parliament.

(C) Refer Answer 48(C)

(A)
(1) He is elected indirectly by the elected members of an Electoral College consisting of:
(2) the elected members of both Houses of Parliament.
(3) the elected members of the Legislative Assemblies of the States.

(B) The President may declare emergency in the following cases:
(1) National or General Emergency: There is a danger of foreign aggression or danger to the peace & security of the country.
(2) Breakdown of Constitutional Machinery in the State.
(3) Financial Emergency: In case of a setback to the financial stability in the country.

(C) **Executive Powers:**
(1) He is the Executive head of the State.
(2) Makes all important appointments like Prime Minister, Cabinet and Council of Ministers, Chief Justice and the Judges of the Supreme Court and the High Courts, the Attorney General, Comptroller and Auditor General, Chairman of various communities.
(3) Administers Union Territories.
(4) Function of the Government of the State when the state is put under President's Rule.

[Marking Scheme]

What Examiners Say

→ (A) Answered correctly by most candidates. Only a few candidates described the procedure of the election of the President in detail rather than the composition of the Electoral College.

→ (B) Most candidates answered correctly but some mentioned only two types of emergencies.

→ (C) Generally answered correctly by most candidates however a few wrote the Legislative Powers instead of the Executive Powers.

3. Prime Minister and the Council of Ministers

According to Article 74 of the Constitution of India, the President of India is only a nominal head of the country. But the Prime Minister along with his Council of Minister is the real or active head of the country, who is appointed by the President of India and an advice of the Prime Minister, the other ministers are also appointed by the President. That is why, the Prime Minister is also called the pillar of the cabinet.

Chapter Notes

- *Prime Minister and Council of Ministers*

TOPIC 1

PRIME MINISTER AND COUNCIL OF MINISTERS

The Prime Minister of India

Our Constitution has followed the British Structure of Parliamentary or Cabinet System of Government. Thus, the President of India is a nominal Head and the Prime Minister of India is the real or active Head. The Prime Minister is the Pillar of the Cabinet. Thus, the Council of Ministers, headed by the Prime Minister, is the most powerful institution in the Indian Polity.

Appointment of the Prime Minister

The President appoints the Prime Minister of India.

The President invites the leader of the majority party or group in the Lok Sabha to form the government. The members of the majority party or group elect their leader to be appointed as the Prime Minister. The President then appoints him/her as the Prime Minister. The Council of Ministers is appointed by the President on the advice of the Prime Minister. The President has to accept the choice of the Prime Minister in the matter of appointment and dismissal of Ministers. In case a non-member is appointed as a minister, he must be elected or nominated to the Parliament within six months from the date of his appointment.

Example 1. Who is the real executive of the government?

Ans. The President is the nominal executive and the Prime Minister is the real executive of the government.

Council of Ministers

In the formation of the council of Ministers, the Constitution has not laid down any fixed rule for the appointment of the Ministers. Therefore, it is the duty of the Prime Minister to choose various categories of Ministers. The president, on the advice of the Prime Minister, appoints the Ministers and allocates their portfolios.

There are three categories of the Council of Ministers:

(1) **Cabinet Ministers**

They are the most important members of the council of ministers and hold important portfolios. They together determine the policy and programme of the government.

(2) **Ministers of State**

They are second category of ministers. They do not participate in cabinet meetings but sometimes they are invited to discuss matters related to their departments.

(3) **Deputy Ministers**

They are third category of ministers who assist the Cabinet Ministers and the Council of Ministers.

They take no part in cabinet deliberations.

The Cabinet

Formation

The cabinet is composed of a small but important body of senior leaders of the ruling party, who are included in the Council of Ministers. They hold important portfolios and decide major policies of the government. The cabinet is the pivot round which the whole administration revolves.

Appointment

The Prime Minister selects his senior and trustworthy colleagues and advises the President to appoint them as cabinet ministers. The President then appoints them as Ministers as per the advice of the Prime Minister.

Term of Office

(1) The ministers hold office during the pleasure of the President. But, the President has little power even in this regard because, the Prime Minister and the Council of Ministers are directly responsible to the Lok Sabha and can remain in office so long as they enjoy the majority support in the Lok Sabha.

(2) The Council of Ministers are collectively responsible to the Lok Sabha.

(3) Every minister must be a member of either House of Parliament or must become one within six months of his appointment, failing which, he will have to vacate his office.

(4) The salaries and allowances of Ministers are such as Parliament from time to time by law determines.

Example 2. Who administers the oath of office to the Council of Ministers?

Ans. The President of India administeres the oath of office to the council of ministers.

 **Important**

→ *The maximum term for which a ministry can reamain in office is 5 years i.e one full term of Lok Sabha.*

Features of the Cabinet System

(1) President as Nominal Head
(2) Coordination between Ministers and Parliament
(3) Leadership of the Prime Minister
(4) Control of Parliament over the Executive

 **Important**

→ *The Cabinet decides the major policies of the government.*

Powers and Functions of the Cabinet

The Cabinet has been given vast powers which can be summed up under the following heads :

Policy Making

(1) The Cabinet formulates the external and internal policies of the government.
(2) It takes decisions on matters like–defence, electoral reforms, president's rule in the State, formation of the new states, housing, energy requirements and health projects, etc.
(3) The Ministers have enough freedom of action but they have to consult the cabinet on all major matters.

Administrative Functions

The Cabinet is basically a policy making body.

(1) Once a decision regardiung a particular policy is taken by the Cabinet, the concerned Ministry must execute it.
(2) Each Ministry or Department should sincerely follow the instructions of the Cabinet.
(3) **Appointments:** All appointments are made by the President after consulting the Cabinet. Such appointments include the appointment of the Governors of the State, the Attorney General of India, the Chief Election Commissioner, the Election Commissioners and other high dignitaries.

While appointing the Judges of the Supreme Court and High Courts; the President consults the Ministers as well as others.

The Cabinet chooses our ambassadors to other nations.

(4) **Coordination between various government departments:** The Cabinet coordinates the working of different departments for the smooth functioning of the government. The formulation and implementation of a policy involves the participation of a number of departments.

Legislative Functions

The Cabinet prepares the President's address to the Parliament. Thus, the Cabinet puts forward its legislative programme, at the Commencement of the First session of the Lok Sabha after every general election, and the commencement of the first session of the Parliament every year.

(1) The President issues ordinances on the advice of the Ministers.
(2) The Cabinet is instrumental in moving the Amendment of the Constitution.
(3) The Houses of the parliament are summoned by the President and initiative in this matter is taken by the Cabinet More than ninety five percent of the Bills are government Bills prepared by the Ministers. They are introduced, explained and defended in the Parliament by the Ministers.

Position and Powers of the Prime Minister

While the President is the nominal head of State, the Prime Minister is the real head of the nation. He is the head of the government and is answerable to the people of the country.

Prime Minister and the President

(1) All authority vested in the President is exercised by the Prime Minister. He is the principal advisor to the President. Thus, the President is the nominal head and the Prime Minister is the real executive head of the Indian Union.
(2) It is on the advice of the Prime Minister that the President summons and prorogues the Parliament and dissolves the Lok Sabha.
(3) The Prime Minister chooses the ministers and, on his advice, the President appoints them. The ministers may be dismissed on the advice of the Prime Minister.
(4) The Prime Minister advises the President on various appointments to important posts such as the Judges of the Supreme Court, the Governors and the Ambassadors.
(5) The Prime Minister is the link between the President and the Council of Ministers.

Prime Minister and the Cabinet

(1) Prime Minister is the leader of the Cabinet.
(2) He/She has the power to allocate portfolios and to reshuffle the Council of Ministers.
(3) He/She has the power to select and dismiss Ministers.
(4) He/She has the power to direct and coordinate policy.

Prime Minister Inside the Parliament

(1) Prime Minister is the leader of the Lok Sabha.
(2) He/She is the Spokesperson of the Government.
(3) He/She is the defender of Government policies.
(4) He/She intervenes in case of controversial issues.

Example 3. Who is the chief spokesperson of the Union government?

Ans. The Prime Minister is the chief spokesperson of the government.

Prime Minister as Leader of the Nation

(1) The Prime Minister represents the nation. When he speaks, the whole nation is supposed to be speaking through him.
(2) During national crisis like war, even the opposition parties support the Prime Minister.
(3) The Prime Minister tries to protect the interests of the country in international forums.
(4) The Prime Minister decides what kind of relations India would have with other countries.
(5) The Prime is also the ex-officio chairman of NITI Aayog and Atomic Energy Commission.

Prime Minister and the Council of Ministers

Check on the Authority of the Prime Minister

(1) Though the Prime Minister is the leader of the majority party, he has to ensure the support of his ministers as well as the party.
(2) In case of coalitions, when the Prime Minister does not enjoy an absolute majority in the Lok Sabha, his position becomes most vulnerable.
(3) Opposition parties always look for a chance to criticize the Prime Minister.
(4) The press and public opinion act as effective checks on Prime Minister's authority.

Responsibility of the Cabinet

Collective Responsibility

(1) Under Article 75(3) of the Constitution "the Council of Ministers shall be collectively responsible to the House of the People".
(2) The decisions taken in the meetings of the Cabinet are equally applicable to all the Ministers even though they may differ among themselves on a particular policy.
(3) All Ministers jointly share the responsibility for the government's policies and performance.
(4) A Vote of No-Confidence against one minister is a vote against the whole Ministry and the whole Ministry has to resign.

Individual Responsibility

(1) The Ministers are individually responsible to the President, i.e., they hold office during the pleasure of the President.
(2) Each Minister is answerable to Parliament for the department under his control.
(3) Every Minister is responsible for matters such as, personal lapse, departure from official policy by him or his department, breach of oath of secrecy or so on.

Distinction Between the Cabinet and the Council of Ministers

	Cabinet	Council of Ministers
1.	The Cabinet is a smaller group consisting of Senior Ministers, holding important portfolios. The cabinet meets periodically as a body to shape national policies and programmes of the government.	The Council of Ministers consists of all three categories of Ministers- Cabinet Ministers, Ministers of state and deputy ministers.
2.	The Prime Minister consults the Cabinet before taking any important decisions.	The Prime Minister may or may not consult the other Ministers below the rank of Cabinet Ministers.
3.	The cabinet takes over the functions assigned by the Constitution to the Council of Ministers. The Cabinet advises the President, through the Prime Minister.	The Council of Ministers does not have this authority.

⚠ Caution

→ The Prime Minister is appointed by the President. He is elected by the majority party as its leader.
→ The President is the nominal head and the Prime Minister is the real executive head of the country.
→ The Cabinet comprises of senior ministers and is a part of Council of Ministers.

ICSE Suggestions

→ Student should understand the power, position and functions of the Prime Minister and that he is the real head of the nation and has an important role as the leader of the nation.

→ Understand the difference between the cabinet and the council of ministers. Emphasize on the meaning of terms like portfolio of ministers and the reasons for the importance of the cabinet ministers.
→ Read and understand the question and answer as per its requirement.
→ Give importance to the facts of the answer, rather than on its length.
→ Be brief and to the point. Repetition of points must be avoided.
→ Present answers neatly in legible writing.

 Glossary

(1) **Council of Ministers:** Official name for the body of Political Party which includes all the Ministers.
(2) **Cabinet:** The committee of top-level leaders in-charge of Ministers. They form the inner-ring of the Council of Ministers, who are given important portfolios in holding government.
(3) **Collective responsibility:** Responsibility of the Cabinet to the Parliament for administration.
(4) **Individual Responsibility:** Responsibility of a minister who takes decisions independently in the last interest of the department. He is individually responsible to the President and each Ministers is answerable to Parliament for the department under his control.

OBJECTIVE Type Questions

Multiple Choice Questions

[1 mark each]

1. Who appoints the Prime Minister of India?
   (a) The President
   (b) The Vice President
   (c) The President of the majority party
   (d) The Speaker of the Lok Sabha

   Ans. (a) The President

   Explanation: The Prime Minister is appointed by the President. According to convention, the President invites the leader of the majority party or group in the Lok Sabha to form the government. The members of the majority party or the group elect their leader to be appointed as the Prime Minister.

2. The .... is considered to be the leader of the Lok Sabha.
   (a) President   (b) Speaker
   (c) Vice President   (d) Prime Minister
   [HOT]

   Ans. (d) Prime Minister

   Explanation: The leader of the Lok Sabha is the parliamentary chairperson of the majority party in the Lok Sabha, viz. the Prime Minister.

3. The .... formulates the foreign policy of India.
   (a) President
   (b) Cabinet
   (c) Members of Lok Sabha
   (d) Members of Rajya Sabha

   Ans. (b) cabinet

   Explanation: The cabinet formulates the foreign and all other important policies of India.

4. What is the maximum strength of Council of Minister?
   (a) 50
   (b) 10% of strength of Lok Sabha
   (c) 15% of strength of Lok Sabha
   (d) 10% of strength of Rajya Sabha

   Ans. (c) 15% of Strength of Lok Sabha

   Explanation: The Constitution (91st amendment) Act. 2003, has put a ceiling on the size of the Council of Ministers at the Centre and in the states to 15 percent of the strength of the Lok Sabha and State Legislatures.

5. Who administers the oath of office to the Council of Ministers?
   (a) Prime Minister
   (b) President
   (c) Speaker of Lok Sabha
   (d) Chief Justice [HOT]

   Ans. (b) President

   Explanation: Before a Minister enters upon his/her office, the President administers him/her the oath of office and of secrecy.

6. Which article of the Constitution states the collective responsibility of the Council of Ministers.
   (a) Article 72   (b) Article 75
   (c) Article 352   (d) Article 356

   Ans. (b) Article 75

   Explanation: Article 75 of the Constitution states that "The Prime Minister shall be appointed by the President and the other Ministers shall be appointed by the President on the advice of the Prime Ministers".

7. Complete the analogy:
   President : Nominal Head : : Prime Minister:?
   (a) Real Head
   (b) Supreme Head
   (c) Offcially Head
   (d) Legally Head [HOT]

   Ans. (a) Real Head

   Explanation: The Constitution of India has provided for a Parliamentary form of government. Consequently, the president has been made only a Nominal Executive (de jure executive) and the Real Executive (De facto executive) being the Council of Ministers headed by the Prime Ministers.

    Related Theory
   → All authority vested in the President is exercised by the Prime Minister. He/she is the principal advisor of the President.

8. Choose the correct option to match the following:

	Column I		Column II
(I)	Council of Ministers	(i)	Nominal Head
(II)	President	(ii)	Deputy Ministers
(III)	Prime Minister	(iii)	Senior Ministers
(IV)	Cabinet	(iv)	Real Head

   (a) I- (iv), II- (iii), III- (i), IV- (ii)
   (b) I- (i), II- (iv), III- (iii), IV- (ii)

(c) I- (ii), II- (i), III- (iv), IV- (iii)
(d) I- (iii), II- (ii), III- (i), IV- (iv)

Ans. (c) I- (ii), II- (i), III- (iv), IV- (iii)

Explanation: Council of Ministers consists of Deputy Ministers, President is the Nominal Head of the Indian Constitution, Prime Minister is the Real Head of the Indian Constitution and Cabinet consists of Senior Ministers.

9. The .... Amendment Acts provides that the President shall not issue a proclamation of National Emergency.
(a) 42ⁿᵈ (b) 43rd
(c) 45ᵗʰ (d) 44ᵗʰ

Ans. (d) 44ᵗʰ

Explanation: The 44ᵗʰ Amendment Act provides that the President shall not issue a proclamation of National Emergency unless the decision of the Union cabinet has been communicated to him/her in writing.

10. A Cabinet Ministers are .... category of ministers.
(a) first (b) second
(c) third (d) fourth

Ans. (a) first

Explanation: Cabinet Ministers are the most important members of the Council of Ministers. They are first category of Ministers who hold important portfolios like Home, Defence, etc.

Related Theory
→ Ministers of State are second category and Deputy Ministers are Third category of Ministers.

11. Which of the point is NOT correct about the Cabinet?
(a) They hold important portfolios and decide major policies of the government.
(b) The Prime Minister may or may not consult them.
(c) They are trusted colleagues of the Prime Minister.
(d) The Cabinet takes important decisions.

Ans. (b) The Prime Minister may or may not consult them.

Explanation: The Cabinet is composed of a small but important body of senior leaders of the party, who are included in the Council of Ministers. They are most trustworthy colleagues of the Prime Minister. They hold important portfolios and decide major policies of the government, and they take important decisions. The Prime Minister is always in touch with them, because they form nucleus of the administration. They are the pivot round which the whole administration revolves.

Related Theory
→ The Prime Minister selects his/her senior and trustworthy colleagues and advises President to appoint them as Cabinet Ministers.

12. Every Minister must be a member of .... House of the Parliament.
(a) either (b) neither
(c) one (d) both

Ans. (a) either

Explanation: To become a member of the Cabinet, every Minister must be a member of either House of the Parliament or must become one within six months of his/her appointment.

Caution
→ Students should understand 'either' means any, they should choose 'either'.

13. The business of the government is managed jointly by the .... and the civil servants concerned.
(a) State Ministers
(b) Deputy Ministers
(c) Cabinet Ministers
(d) Council of Ministers

Ans. (d) Council of Ministers

Explanation: Once a Policy decision is taken by the Cabinet on any subject, it is conveyed to the Minister of the State and the Deputy Minister of the concerned Ministry. They work out the details and pass it to the Civil Servants under the ministry to implement the decision. In this way, the business of the Government is managed jointly by the Council of Ministers and the Civil Servants concerned.

Caution
→ This question is very tricky, read question two times before answering.

14. The .... is the spokesperson of the Government.
(a) President
(b) Prime-Minister
(c) Speaker
(d) Chief Minister

Ans. (b) Prime-Minister

Explanation: The Prime Minister is the Chief Spokesperson of the government in the Parliament. He/she makes all important announcements on national Policies on the floor of the House.

Caution
→ Speaker is not the spokesperson of the government. He is the Presiding Officer of the Lok Sabha.

15. The Prime Minister represents the ....
(a) nation (b) parliament
(c) party (d) president [🔥HOT]
Ans. *(a) Nation*

Explanation: The Prime minister as a leader represents the Nation. When the speaker, the whole nation is supposed to be speaking through him.

SUBJECTIVE Type Questions

Short Answer Type Questions
[**2** marks each]

16. Who is the real executive head in India? [🔥HOT]

Ans. Ours is a Parliamentary form of government. The Prime Minister is the real executive head in the Parliamentary form of government.

17. (A) Who appoints the Prime Minister of India? [ICSE 2020]
(B) Who administers the Oath of Office to the Council of Ministers? [ICSE 2018, 14]

Ans. (A)
> President [Marking Scheme]

 What Examiners Say
→ Majority of the candidates wrote the correct answer. However, a few candidates gave the answer as, 'citizens of the country' or 'the party he belongs to' or 'the Chief Justice of India'.

⚠️ **Caution**
→ Understand the appointment procedure of the Prime Minister of India in detail.

(B)
> President [Marking Scheme]

 What Examiners Say
→ Majority of the candidates answered this question correctly. However, a few candidates, instead of writing the President of India, wrote either the Prime Minister or the Chief Justice of the Supreme Court

⚠️ **Caution**
→ Understand the different powers of the President like. He appoints the Prime Minister and the Council of Ministers, also administers oath to them.

18. (A) How is the Prime Minister elected?
(B) What is the term of office of the Prime Minister?

Ans. (A) The Prime Minister is the leader of the party securing majority in the Lok Sabha.
(B) The normal term of office of the Prime Minister is 5 years. But he can remain in office so long as he enjoys the majority support in the Lok Sabha.

19. On whose advice can the President appoint the Council of Ministers? [ICSE 2019]

OR

By whom and on whose advice are the Council of Ministers appointed? [ICSE 2016]

Ans. The Council of Ministers is appointed by the President on advice of the Prime Minister.

> Prime Minister advises President in appointment of Council of Ministers
> [Marking Scheme]

 What Examiners Say
→ Majority of the candidates were able to write the correct answer.

⚠️ **Caution**
→ Understand that the leader of the majority party i.e., the Prime Minister suggests the names of his Council of Ministers and they are then appointed by the President on his advice.

20. Under what condition can a non-member of Parliament be made a Minister? [ICSE 2017]

Ans. In case a non-member of Parliament is made a minister, he must be elected or nominated to either House of Parliament within six months from the date of his appointment as a minister.

> If the Prime Minister so desires, however he/she must be elected / nominated to either house before six months.
> [Marking Scheme]

 What Examiners Say
→ This part was generally answered correct but a few mentioned 'six weeks' instead of 'six months'

⚠️ **Caution**
→ Understand that there are exceptions in choosing the ministers. It need not always be elected member of the Parliament.

21. Mention the different categories of ministers in the Union Council of ministers. [ICSE 2013]

Ans. The different categories of ministers in the Union Council of Ministers are:
(1) The Cabinet Ministers;
(2) The Minister of State;
(3) The Deputy Ministers.

22. (A) Are the ministers responsible to the Parliament?
(B) To which House of the Parliament is the Council of Ministers responsible?

Prime Minister and the Council of Ministers

Ans. (A) Yes, the ministers are individually as well as collectively responsible to the Parliament.
(B) The Council of Ministers is collectively responsible to the Lok Sabha.

23. What is meant by 'Collective Responsibility' of the Cabinet? [ICSE 2017, 13]

Ans. Article 75 (3) of the Constitution provides for the collective responsibility of Council of Ministers, including the Cabinet members, to the Lok Sabha. It means that they enjoy the majority support of the Lok Sabha. The Cabinet members have to resign, if any decision is defeated in the Lok Sabha.

> The Cabinet is collectively responsible to the Parliament and has to resign if it loses the confidence of the Lok Sabha. (Team/Joint Work Responsibility/Swim & Sink together) **[Marking Scheme]**

What Examiners Say
→ This part was well understood and attempted well by majority of the candidates.

⚠ Caution
→ Understand the meaning of collective responsibility of the Cabinet for their acts thoroughly.

24. What is understood by the term 'Individual Responsibility' in a Parliamentary Democracy? [ICSE 2014]

Ans. In a Parliamentary Democracy, the Council of Ministers, including the Cabinet Ministers, are collectively responsible to the Lok Sabha. Individual responsibility means that the ministers are also individually responsible to the Parliament and can be removed by the President on the advice of the Prime Minister.

> Individual responsibility means that each minister is:
> (1) Answerable to the Parliament regarding his department.
> (2) It is obligatory for the particular minister to reply to the questions asked by the Members of Parliament
> (3) If there are personal lapses on his part If he or his department goes against the official policy laid down
> (4) If there is a breach in the oath of secrecy.
> **[Any two]**
> **[Mod. Marking Scheme]**

What Examiners Say
→ Instead of individual responsibility, a few candidates explained collective responsibility.

⚠ Caution
→ Clearly understand the difference between the individual responsibility and the collective responsibility during the course of studies.

25. What happens when a motion of 'No-Confidence' is passed against a minister? [ICSE 2019]

OR

What happens if a Vote of No-Confidence is passed against a minister in the Lok Sabha? [ICSE 2015]

Ans. If a motion of 'No confidence' is passed against a minister, the Prime Minister along with his Council of Ministers has to resign.

> The entire Ministry resigns en-bloc (the government will resign).
> **[Marking Scheme]**

What Examiners Say
→ Majority of the candidates were able to answer this question correctly. However, a few candidates, instead of resign wrote removed.

26. Mention two ways by which the authority of the Prime Minister can be checked? [ICSE 2014]

Ans. The authority of the Prime Minister can be checked by:
(1) The Prime Minister has to ensure that his party as well as his Council of ministers support him all times. They should not be perceived to be pulling in different directions:
(2) An independent press and public opinion act as effective checks on the Prime Minister's working;
(3) A vociferous and strong opposition in Parliament is always on the lookout for chances to be critical of Prime Minister and his way of working. **[Any two]**

> The authority of the Prime Minister can be checked by many ways:
> (1) There may be dissensions within the ruling party itself. He needs to get the support of his party.
> (2) The members of the opposition parties can criticize his policies, so also the mass media and the general public opinion.
> (3) In case of a coalition party, he has to satisfy the leaders of the various parties. Interpolation.
> (4) Vote of No-confidence. **[Any two]**
> **[Mod. Marking Scheme]**

What Examiners Say
→ Most candidates answered this question correctly.

27. What is a Cabinet?

Ans. The Cabinet is a small but important body of senior ministers. They hold important portfolios and decides major policies of the government.

28. State any one administrative function of the Cabinet. **[ICSE 2018]**

Ans. The Cabinet is the chief policy making organ of the government. All decisions on issues relating to the peace keeping requirements, economic policies, electoral reforms, defence and internal security are taken in the Cabinet.

> The Cabinet is a policy framing body, after it determines on a policy, the appropriate Ministry like Ministry of Agriculture or Civil Aviation and others carries it out. Each Ministry or Department faithfully follows the directives of the Cabinet.
> The President makes all major appointments with the aid and advice of the Ministers. Appointment of the Attorney-General of India, the Governor of a State, the Chief Election Commissioner, the Election Commissioners.
> Implementation and coordination policy
> **[Any one]**
> **[Marking Scheme]**

What Examiners Say
→ Quite a few candidates stated the relations of the Cabinet with the President and the Prime Minister instead of stating any one administrative function of the Cabinet.

29. (A) On whose recommendation can the National Emergency be proclaimed in the country?
(B) State the body that decides the major policies of the government. **[ICSE 2020]**

Ans. (A) The National Emergency can only be proclaimed by the President on the recommendation of the Cabinet.
(B) The Cabinet decides the major policies of the government.

> Cabinet/senior ministers/senior members of the Council of Ministers.
> **[Marking Scheme]**

What Examiners Say
→ Most candidates wrote correct answers; however, a few wrote 'Council of Ministers'.

30. Under what circumstances can the President use his discretion to appoint the Prime Minister? On whose advice does he appoint the Council of Ministers?

Ans. The President uses his discretion power (that is without the advice of the Ministers) in the appointment of Prime Minister. Firstly, where no single party commands the clear support of the majority of the Lok Sabha members and there is a hang Parliament or Secondly, when the Prime ministers in office dies suddenly and there is no obvious successor.

31. What qualification should a person possess to be eligible for appointment as a minister?

Ans. To be eligible for appointment as a minister, a person must be the Member of Parliament but sometimes a non-member may be appointed as a minister. Such minister must get elected or nominated to the Parliament within six months from the date of his/her appointment, failing which he/she will have to resign from his/her post as a minister.

Structured Questions

[3+3+4= **10** marks each]

32. The Prime Minister and his Council of Ministers formulate and implement the policies which govern the country. In this context, answer the following questions:
(A) What is meant by the term Collective Responsibility of ministers?
(B) Name the three categories of the Council of Ministers.
(C) Mention any four powers of the Prime Minister with reference to the President.
[ICSE Sem-2, 2022]

Ans. (A) The Parliamentary form of government is based on the principle of Collective Responsibility of the Council of Ministers. The principle of collective responsibility means that the Council of Ministers, as a single body, is responsible to the Lok Sabha for the general conduct of affairs of the Government. Since, all the important policy decisions are taken by the Cabinet which are binding upon all the ministers, thus, the decisions of the Cabinet become the decisions of all the ministers, who have to support such decision at all costs. If a minister does not support the decisions of the cabinet, he has to resign.

Our Constitution, by providing for Collective responsibility of the ministers to the Lok Sabha, has established the principle that all ministers work as a team. If a vote of no-confidence or a censure motion is passed against one minister, the whole ministerial team has to resign all together. Similarly, the resignation of the Prime Minister implies the resignation of the entire ministry.

(B) **The three categories of the Council of Ministers are :**
(1) **Cabinet Ministers:** They are the most important members of the Council of Ministers. They hold important portfolios like Home, Defence, Finance, External Affairs, Railways, etc.

A Cabinet Minister is in charge of a Ministry and sometimes of more than one ministry. Only Cabinet Ministers have a right to attend meetings of the Cabinet. They together determine the policy and programme of the government.

(2) **Ministers of State:** They are the second category of ministers. They may or may not hold an independently charge of any portfolio. The Prime Minister may or may not consult them. They do not participated in the Cabinet meetings. But they may be invited to attend meetings when matters concerning their departments are being considered.

(3) **Deputy Ministers:** They are the third category of ministers who assist the Cabinet Ministers and the Council of Ministers. They are junior ministers and are placed under senior ministers whom they have to assist. They take no part in the Cabinet deliberations.

(C) The powers of the Prime Minister with reference to the President are:

(1) All authority vested in the President is exercised by the Prime Minister. He/She is the principal advisor of the President. Thus, the President is the nominal head and the Prime Minister is the real executive of the Indian Union.

(2) It is on the advice of the Prime Minister that the President summons and Prorogues the Parliament and dissolves the Lok Sabha.

(3) He/She advises the President on various appointments to important posts such as the Judges of the Supreme Court, the Governors and Ambassadors.

(4) The Prime Ministers chooses the ministers and, on his/her advice, the President appoints them. The ministers may be dismissed on the advice of the Prime Ministers.

(5) He/She is a link between the President and the Council of Ministers. Our Constitution lays down that it shall be the duty of the Prime Minister to communicate to the President all decisions of the Council of Ministers relating to the administration of the Union and the proposals for legislation. A minister cannot discuss any matter of National Policy with the President on his her own.

(6) The President can ask the Council of Ministers to reconsider any matter, which has not been considered by the Cabinet and on which a decision has been taken by a minister. The President may call for information regarding the affairs of the Union and the Prime Minister has to furnish such information. **[Any four]**

33. The makers of our Constitution adopted the Parliamentary and the Cabinet form of the government. With reference to this, answer the following questions.

(A) State two points of difference between the Cabinet and the Council of Ministers with reference to their responsibilities to the government.

(B) Mention any three ways by which the authority of the Prime Minister can be checked.

(C) What is understand by the term 'Individual Responsibility', in a Parliamentary Democracy?

Ans. (A) (1) The Cabinet is a group of senior-most ministers which mainly formulates policy while the Council of Ministers is a large group responsible for the implementation of the policies.

(2) The 'Cabinet' is a smaller group consisting of senior ministers holding important portfolios such as Defence, Finance, Home, etc. whereas the Council of Ministers consists of all categories of Ministers – Cabinet Ministers, Ministers of State and Deputy Ministers.

(B) The authority of the Prime Minister can be checked by many ways:

(1) There may be dissensions within the Ruling Party itself. He needs to get the support of his/her party.

(2) The members of the opposition parties can criticize his/her policies, so does the Mass Media and the general public opinion.

(3) In case of a coalition government, he/she has to satisfy the leaders of the various parties.

(4) Interpolation

(5) Vote of no-confidence **[Any three]**

(C) 'Individual Responsibility' means that each minister is:

(1) Answerable to the Parliament regarding his/her department.

(2) It is obligatory for the minister to reply to the questions asked by the Members of the Parliament.

(3) If there are personal lapses on his/her part.
(4) If he/she or his/her department goes against the official policy laid down.
(5) If there is a breach in the oath of secrecy. **[Any four]**

⚠️ **Caution**
➜ *Students should clearly understand the difference between the 'Individual Responsibility' and the 'Collective Responsibility' during the course of learning*

34. The Council of Ministers headed by the Prime Minister, is the most powerful institution in the Indian Polity. In this context, answer the following questions:
(A) State briefly the position of the Prime Minister in the Parliamentary system of Government. State any two powers the Prime Minister has as a leader of a nation.
(B) Distinguish between the Council of Ministers and the Cabinet.
(C) Write any four functions of the 'Cabinet'.
[ICSE 2019]

Ans. (A) The Prime Minister is the head of the Council of Ministers. He advises the President on behalf of the Council of Ministers. He is the leader of the Lok Sabha and Chief Spokesperson and defender of the government in the Parliament.

The powers of the Prime Minister as a leader of opposition are:
(1) The Prime Minister is the leader of the nation. He/she is the Chief spokesperson of the government policies in the Parliament.
(2) Being the Chief spokesperson for the country, he/she decides India's internal and foreign policies.
(3) As a leader of the nation, the Prime Minister represent India at all international conferences.
(4) He/she can sign treaties and is empowered to commit the nation to certain international obligations.
[Any two]

(B)

Council of Ministers	Cabinet
(1) The Council of Ministers consists all categories of ministers i.e., Cabinet Ministers, Ministers of state and Deputy Ministers.	The Cabinet consists senior Cabinet ministers holding important portfolios.
(2) The Council of Ministers is a large group of ministers which meet occasionally.	The Cabinet is a small group of senior ministers which meet regularly.
(3) The Prime Minister may not consult the Council of Ministers on every important issues.	The Prime Ministers consults the Cabinet on all important issues.
(4) It has no collective functions.	It functions collectively.
(5) It implements decisions taken by the Cabinet.	It supervises decisions taken by the Council of Ministers.

[Any three]

(C) The functions of the Cabinet are:
(1) The Cabinet formulates the government policies, both at national and international level.
(2) The Cabinet takes decisions on major issues relating to defence, finance, development, security, planning, *etc*.
(3) The Cabinet coordinates the working of all the ministries and departments, so that the whole government runs smoothly and set goals are achieved.
(4) The Cabinet finalizes different bills and introduces them for necessary amendments in the legislation of the country.
(5) The Cabinet legislates with the advice and consent of Parliament. The time of summoning and prorogation of Parliament is decided by the Cabinet.
(6) The President can declare Emergency of three types, under Articles 352, 356 and 360. But any such Emergency cannot be declared by the President of India on his own, without the same being recommended by the Union Cabinet, led by the Prime Minister. It is the Cabinet which determines the grounds, duration and termination of any emergency.
(7) All financial decisions and related issues cannot be taken without the approval of the Cabinet. Also, a Money Bill can only be introduced in the Lok Sabha by the Cabinet.
(8) The President makes a large number of appointments. Most of these appointments are actually made on the recommendation of the Cabinet.
[Any four]

(A) **Position:** The Prime Minister is the factor or the real leader of the nation.
 (1) He is the Leader of the Lok Sabha.
 (2) He is the chief spokesperson of the Government.
 (3) He is the defender of Government policies.
 (4) He intervenes in case of controversial issues.
 (5) Addresses nation during emergency or on important occasions.
 (6) Represents and visits countries – for economic and social issues of the nation.
 (7) Chairman of NITI Ayog and Atomic Energy Commission.
 (8) Decides what kind of relations India would have with other countries.
 (9) Keeps President informed of the decision of the Cabinet. **[Any two]**

(B)

S. No.	Council of Ministers	Cabinet
(1)	Consists of all the three categories of ministers	Is a group of senior ministers holding Important portfolios.
(2)	The PM may or may not consult them	The PM always consults them.
(3)	Rarely meets as a whole	Meets as frequently as possible
(4)	Does not advise the President	Advises the President through the PM
(5)	Larger Group	Smaller Group
(6)	May or may not hold important portfolios	Holds important portfolios.

[Any three]

(C) **Powers of the Cabinet:**
 (1) Formulates policies and implements them.
 (2) Coordinates the functioning of various Ministers.
 (3) Introduce Bills.
 (4) Amends the Constitution.
 (5) Advises the President to summon the House of Parliament.
 (6) Prepares President's Special; address.
 (7) Advices the President's to issues Ordinances
 (8) Prepare Money and Non-Money Bills (This is a separate point)
 (9) Recommends proclamation of Emergency to the President.
 (10) Decides all major appointments made by the President.
 (11) Preparation of annual budget.
 (12) Acts as source of information.
 [Any four]
 [Marking Scheme]

What Examiners Say
↪ (A) Most of the candidates were able to write the correct answer. However, some candidates were not clear regarding the powers of the Prime Minister as a leader of the Nation. A few candidates mentioned his functions in relation with the Council of Ministers and the President.

↪ (B) A few candidates could not distinguish between the Cabinet and the Council of Ministers and explained the three categories of ministers.

↪ (C) While many candidates scored well in this question. However, a few candidates were confused between the features and the functions of the Cabinet.

⚠ Caution
↪ (A) Students should understand the power, position and functions of the Prime Minister and that he is the Real Head of the Nation and has an important role as the leader of the nation.

↪ (B) Students should be able to differentiate between the Cabinet and Council of Ministers. They should know the meaning of terms like Portfolio of Ministers and the reasons for the importance of the Cabinet Ministers.

↪ (C) They should know the difference between the functions of the Cabinet and its features.

35. The Union Executive which consists of the President, Prime Minister and the Council of Ministers is a powerful body in a Parliamentary Democracy. In this context, answer the following questions:
 (A) State the position of the Prime Minister and state any two of his powers in relation to the President.
 (B) Mention the three categories of Ministers in order of their rank and status.
 (C) Mention any four legislative powers of the cabinet.

Ans. (A) In the Parliamentary system of government provided by the Constitution, the Prime Minister is head of the government and is answerable to the people of India. The Prime Minister enjoys tremendous power and influences both in the executive and legislative sphere. Though he is invited by the President in Parliament as leader of the majority party to form a government known as Central or Union Government in India but in practice, all the powers vested with the President under the Constitution are exercised by the Prime Minister.

The powers of the Prime Minister in relation to the President are:

(1) The Prime Minister is the real executive authority (de facto executive) while the President is the nominal executive authority (de jure executive).

(2) The Prime Minister is the main advisor to the President. He advises the President with regard to the appointment of important officials like Attorney General, chairman and members of the UPSC, election commissioners, *etc.*

(3) The decision for when to summon or prorogue the two Houses of Parliament and dissolution of Lok Sabha is advised by the Prime Minister to the President.

[Any two]

(B) The categories of Ministers in order of their rank and status are:

(1) **Cabinet Ministers:** The Cabinet Ministers are at the top of the hierarchy of ministers. They hold important portfolios like Home, Defence, External affairs, Finance, *etc.* The Cabinet Ministers determine the policies and directions of the government.

(2) **Ministers of State:** Below the Cabinet Minister in the hierarchy are the Ministers of State (MoS). Their activities involve day to-day functioning of ministry and taking care of the state-centric functioning of a ministry. Ministers of State with independent charge do not come under any Cabinet Minister yet they are of lower rank than Cabinet minister.

(3) **Deputy Ministers:** At the third level of the Council of Ministers are the deputy ministers who assist their respective Cabinet ministers in performance of their duties and responsibilities. They neither participate in the meetings of the Cabinet nor are they given independent charge of any department.

(C) The legislative powers of the cabinet are:

(1) **Bills:** The Cabinet forms an integral part of the legislative system. It is in the Cabinet that all the important government bills are drafted. The Cabinet Ministers formulate policies, makes decisions and draft bills on all significant matters which in their judgement require legislative attention.

(2) **Amendments:** Although Parliament is the supreme law making body of the nation, in practice, legislation is essentially the handi-work of the Cabinet. It removes outdated laws from the statute book and makes necessary amendments in the Constitution.

(3) **Ordinance:** The Cabinet is responsible for the approval of ordinances issued by the President.

(4) **Summoning the Houses of the Parliament:** The Cabinet legislates with the advice and consent of Parliament, the time of summoning and prorogation of Parliament is decided by the Cabinet.

(A) The Prime Minister enjoys a unique position in the Indian political set up.

All the powers listed under the President of India are actually exercised by the Prime Minister. As the Executive head of the Indian State, the following are his powers and functions:

(1) He is the real leader of the Nation.

(2) He is the leader of the Council of Ministers.

(3) He is the presiding officer of the Cabinet meetings.

(4) He is the link between the Cabinet and the President.

(5) He is the leader of the House (Lok Sabha).

(6) Ministers are appointed by the President on the advice of the Prime Minister.

(7) President summon & prorogues Parliament on the advice of P.M.

(8) Issue Ordinances on the advice of P.M.

[Any two]

(B) The categories in order of their rank and status are:

(1) **Cabinet Ministers:** Most important and senior members of the Council of Ministers and they hold important portfolios.

(2) **Ministers of State:** They may or may not hold independent charge of any portfolios. Neither does the Prime Minister consult them on regular basis.

(3) **Deputy Ministers:** They normally assist the first two categories of ministers.

Prime Minister and the Council of Ministers

(C) **Legislative Powers:**
   (1) Introduction of Bills.
   (2) Source of Information.
   (3) Amendment to the Constitution.
   (4) Summoning the House of Parliament.
   (5) President's Special; Address
   (6) Issuing Ordinances
   [Any four]
   [Marking Scheme]

What Examiners Say

↪ (A) The candidates were generally able to write the answer correctly but some were not clear regarding the powers of the Prime Minister in relation to the President. Some were confused with the powers in relation to the Council of Ministers.

↪ (B) This part was generally answered well. A few candidates were unable to write the correct rank and status of the three categories of ministers.

↪ (C) Candidates were unsure of the legislative powers of the Cabinet. Some wrote the functions of the Cabinet and other powers of the Cabinet.

36. The makers of our Constitution adopted the Parliamentary and the Cabinet form of Government. With reference to this, answer the following questions:

(A) (a) Who is the Constitutional Head of the Union Government?
   (b) What is meant by the collective and Individual responsibility of the members of the Cabinet?

(B) Explain briefly the position and powers of the Prime Minister in relation to the Cabinet.

(C) Distinguish between the Cabinet and the Council of Ministers. [ICSE 2015]

Ans. (A) (a) The President is the constitutional head of the Union Government.

(b) **Collective Responsibility:** Article 75(3) of the Constitution provides for the collective responsibility of Council of Minister, including the Cabinet members, to the Lok Sabha. It means that they enjoy the majority support of Lok Sabha. These include:

(1) The Cabinet has to resign if any decision, even if related to a ministry, is defeated in the Lok Sabha;

(2) Every decision taken by the government needs to be collectively approved by the Cabinet members and the same needs to be promulgated and defended by the members within and outside the Parliament;

(3) Once the Cabinet ministers have come to a collective decisions, overcoming number of differences of opinions at the time of deliberation of a policy, and the same is endorsed collectively by the Cabinet ministers, none is allowed to express his/her individual opinion on the matter within and outside the Parliament;

(4) If a minister has a contrary view to such a collective decision then he has to change his view and support the collective decision or resign. He is not allowed to oppose the collective decision and at the same time retain his position as minister.

Individual Responsibility: As per Article 75(2) of the Constitution, ministers are also individually responsible to the President and can be removed by the President on the advice of the Prime Minister. Individual responsibility is essential to enforce collective responsibility. A minister disapproving collective decision may refuse to resign. In this case, the Prime Minister may advice the President to remove the minister so as to attain the collective consent of the ministers.

(B) The position and powers of the Prime Minister in relation to the Cabinet are:

(1) The Prime Minister recommends the persons to who can be appointed as the Cabinet ministers by the President;

(2) The Prime Minister allocates various portfolios among the ministers.

(3) In case of difference of opinion, the Prime Minister can ask a minister to resign;

(4) The Prime Minister presides over all the meetings of the Cabinet. He guides, directs, controls and coordinates the activities of all the ministers for the smooth functioning of the government.

(5) The Cabinet cannot function if Prime Minister dies or resigns.

(C) Refer, Answer 34 (B).

(A) (a) President.
   (b) Cabinet jointly shares the responsibility for the government's policies and performance. Every minister is responsible for matters such as personal lapse, departure from official policy, breach of oath of secrecy. They swim and sink together.

(B) The Prime Minister recommends his trusted senior colleagues in the Parliament as members of his Cabinet. The President then appoints them as minister. P.M. has power to allocate portfolios to the Cabinet and dismiss them. He has the power to direct and coordinate policy.

(C) The Cabinet means the Council consisting of the Prime Minister and the other senior Ministers/ all Cabinet members are ministers but the other ministers are not Cabinet members. The Cabinet ministers meet frequently. They decide the program and policy of the government. The Ministers of State and deputy Ministers rarely meet. While Cabinet Ministers attend meetings of the Cabinet in their own right, ministers of State can attend only if invited to. A Deputy Minister is a junior minister and can attend Cabinet meetings in very extraordinary situation. The President acts on the advice of the Cabinet in all matters. Since, the Council of ministers rarely meets it is the Cabinet ministers who are consulted by the Prime Ministers for information and advice. Cabinet is an inner body within the Council of Ministers. It acts in the name of the Council of Ministers and exercises all powers on its behalf.

[Marking Scheme]

What Examiners Say

↪ (A) *Answered correctly by most candidates. A few were unsure and mentioned the Prime Minister as the Constitutional Head. This reflected there was no conceptual understanding on the collective and individual responsibility.*

↪ (B) *Most candidates answered correctly. Few candidates were unable to explain the powers of the Prime Minister in relation to the Cabinet and were unable to write the three points required in the question.*

↪ (C) *Majority of candidates wrote the correct answer. Few however explained the Cabinet only and were unable to differentiate with the Council of Ministers.*

37. The Cabinet holds a pivotal position in the working of the Indian Parliamentary Government. In this context, discuss the following:

(A) Discuss the formation of the Cabinet.

(B) Any two administrative powers of the Cabinet.

(C) Any two legislative powers of the Cabinet. **(ICSE 2014)**

Ans. (A) The Cabinet is an informal body of senior ministers who form the inner circle of the Council of Ministers. It is like a wheel within a wheel. The Council of Ministers, seldom meets as a body. It is the Cabinet which meets as and when summoned by the Prime Minister. As heads of their respective departments, the Cabinet ministers are at the top of the hierarchy of ministers. They hold important portfolios like Home, Defence, External Affairs, Communications, Railways, etc. The Cabinet determine the policy and decisions of the government.

(B) The administrative powers of the Cabinet are:

(1) **Prime Policy Maker:** The Cabinet is the chief policy making organ of the government. It is the highest decision making authority in Indian Politics Administrative system which frames both the external and domestic policies of the government. All decisions on issues relating to peace keeping requirements, economic policies, electoral reforms, defence and internal security, imports and trade etc. are taken in the Cabinet.

(2) **Policy implementation:** Once the policy is formulated, the Cabinet looks after the exectution of the policy. The policies framed by the Cabinet are communicated to the entire Council of Ministers which remains collectively responsible towards the implementation of the policies.

(C) The legislating powers of the Cabinet are:

(1) **Bill:** The Cabinet forms the integral part of the legislative system. It is in the Cabinet that all the government bills are drafted.

(2) **Ordinance and Amendments:** Although, Parliament is the supreme law making body of the nation, in practice, legislation is essentially the handiwork of the Cabinet.

It removes outdated laws from the statute book and make necessary amendments in the existing laws. It also approves the ordinances and proposals for amendment to the Constitution when required.

(A) The Prime Minister will choose his Cabinet and advise the President accordingly. They are the most important members of the Council of Ministers.

(1) The Cabinet holds an important pivotal position in the working of the Government. The Cabinet is a body consisting of important senior leaders of the party.

(2) They hold important portfolios like Defence, Railways and decide major policies of the Government

(3) They are the trusted men and form the nucleus of the administration

(4) They take important decisions which are communicated to the other ministers who have to follow them.

(B) Administrative functions of the Cabinet are:
  (1) **Policy making:** The Cabinet formulates both external and domestic policies of the government. It takes decisions on matters like defence, economic policies. Formation of new states, etc. individual ministers have to consult the Cabinet on all major matters.
  (2) **Implementation of policies:** When the Cabinet takes a certain decision on any subject it is conveyed to the Ministers of State and deputy ministers of the concerned ministry. They will work out the details and pas it to the civil servants for implementation. In this way the business of the government is managed by the Council of ministers and the Civil servants.
  (3) **Co-ordinate the working of various ministers:** The Cabinet coordinates the working of various departments for the smooth implementation of government policies. Any policy like improving public health services, increase in government revenue, etc. requires involvement of several departments for its formulation and implementation.
  (4) **Appointments:** All major appointments made by the Presidents are decided upon by the Cabinet eg. appointment of Judges, Governors of State, Ambassadors and other dignitaries.
  [Any two]
(C) **Legislative Powers:**
  (1) **Introduction of bills:** The Cabinet and the departments of administration take initiative in introducing almost 95% of the bills. These Official bills are given priority and preference over Private bills. It involves preparing the draft proposals and presenting them before the Parliament for approval; which approves these legislative proposals and bills become laws.
  (2) **Sources of Information:** The ministers of the concerned department answer questions put to them by the members and thus provide information to the public.
  (3) **Amendment to the Constitution:** The Cabinet is instrumental in planning and moving amendment to the Constitution.
  (4) **Summoning the Houses of the Parliament:** Although the Houses are summoned by the President but the initiatives are taken by the Ministry of Parliamentary affairs.
  (5) **Presidents' Special address:** The President's address which contains the legislative programmes of the year is prepared by the Cabinet.
  (6) **Issuing Ordinances:** The Cabinet advises the President to issue ordinances when the Parliament is not in session. **[Any two]**
  [Marking Scheme]

What Examiners Say

→ (A) Most candidates were unable to analyse and write the answer correctly. Only a few wrote relevant points except the point – appointed by the President of India.

→ (B) A few candidates were unable to comprehend the word : administrative' and mentioned the Legislative Powers instead. Even though some had a clue of the Cabinet as 'policy makers', they could not specify the points required in the answer.

→ (C) Distinction between the administrative, legislative and executive powers was not clear. Candidates were unsure of the correct facts and answered in a general manner.

Caution

→ Highlight the difference between the Council of Ministers and the Senior Cabinet Ministers. The Prime Ministers selects them and on his advice the President appoints them.

→ Remember that legislative powers deal with the preparing of bills and getting them passed in the Parliament. While administrative functions include formulating of national policies.

→ Students should learn the basic terms and to analyse the question properly. Enlist the various powers under each heading and revise the points well.

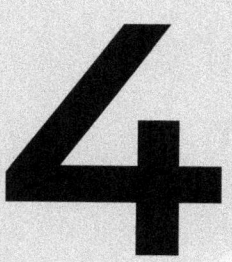

4 The Judiciary

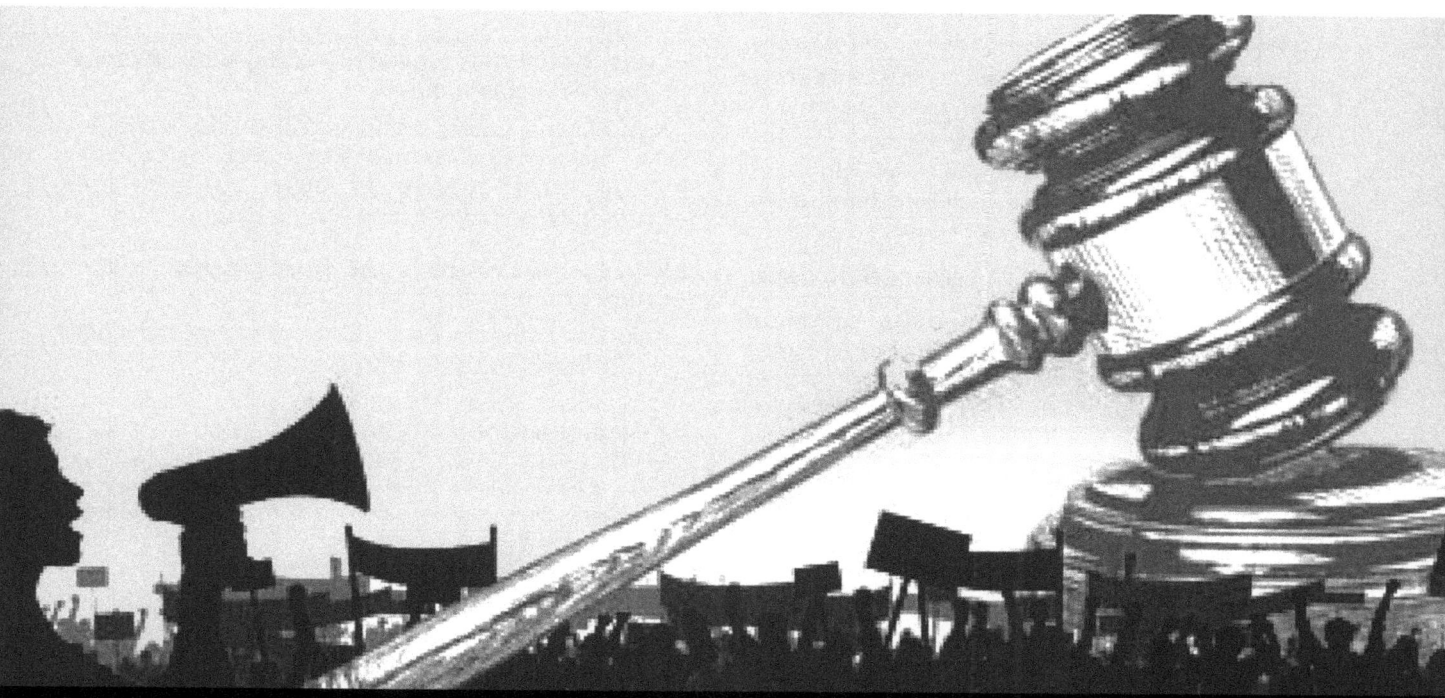

The Judiciary is the third organ of the government. It has the responsibility to apply the laws to specific cases and settled all disputes. It caters as the protector against the possible excesses of legislative and executive organs.

Chapter Notes

- *Single Independent Judiciary*
- *The Supreme Court*

TOPIC 1

SINGLE INDEPENDENT JUDICIARY

Under the Constitution of India, the Judiciary is a single integrated system of courts for the Union and States with the Supreme Court at the apex.

Single Integrated system

The Supreme Court is the head of the entire system and not only supervises but also exercises control over the functioning of other courts.

There are no separate sets of laws and a single system operates throughout the country.

All cases coming from the lower courts can be taken to the High Court and ultimately to the Supreme Court, by way of appeal.

Below the Supreme Court stand the High Courts of different States and under each High Court there is a hierarchy of other subordinate courts.

Need for a Single Integrated Judiciary

(1) In a representative democracy, administration of justice need protection against executive or legislative interference. This protection is given by making the judiciary independent of the two other organs of the government.

(2) An independent and supreme judiciary is also an essential requirement of a federal governance.

(3) An independent and impartial judiciary is an essential requisite for ensuring human rights and protecting democracy.

Example 1. What is single integrated Judicial system?
Ans. A single integrated judicial system means Supreme Court is the apex court and all other courts are below it.

Example 2. Which is the supreme law in India?
Ans. The Constitution of India is the supreme law in India.

Example 3. What type of hierarchy is constituted by the courts in India?
Ans. All the courts in India constitute a single hierarchy which means that each lower court is subordinate to its higher one with the Supreme Court at the top.

Example 4. Which is the final tribunal in the country?
Ans. The Supreme Court is the highest and final tribunal in the country.

📢 Important

→ Though the Indian Constitution is of federal type, yet there is no double chain of courts, i.e., one to administer the Union laws and the other to administer the States laws.

TOPIC 2

THE SUPREME COURT

The Supreme Court is the apex court of the country. It is the supreme judicial body of India and the highest court of the Republic of India, under Constitution.

Composition

The Supreme Court of India consists of a Chief Justice of India and not more than 33 judges, until the Parliament by law prescribes a larger number of judges. The judges of the Supreme Court were increased from 30 to 33 vide The Supreme Court (Number of Judges) Amendment Act, 2019, which received assent of the President on 9th August, 2019.

Qualifications for Appointment as Judge of Supreme Court

(1) He/she should be citizen of India;
(2) He/she has been for at least five years a judge of a High Court or of two or more such courts in succession;
(3) He/she has been for at least ten years an advocate of a High Court or of two or more such courts in succession;
(4) He/she is, in the opinion of the President, a distinguished jurist.

Appointment

Every Judge of the Supreme Court is appointed by the President of India in consultation with the judges of Supreme Court and of High Courts, besides the Council of Ministers.

In case of appointment of a judge other than the Chief Justice, the Chief Justice of India shall be consulted. The consultation would generally mean concurrence.

In case of the Chief Justice, usually the senior most judge of the Supreme Court is appointed.

Example 5. Who appoints the Chief Justice of India?

Ans. The Chief Justice of the Supreme Court is the Chief Justice of India. He/she is appointed by the President.

⚠ Caution
↪ Learn the Executive powers of the President thoroughly to understand that all major appointments, including the appointments of the judges of the Supreme Court and High Courts are made by the President.

Term of Office

A Judge of the Supreme Court shall hold office until he attains the age of 65 years.

A Judge may resign his office, by submitting his resignation letter to the President.

Example 6. What is the tenure of the Judge of the Supreme Court?

Ans. The Constitution of India has not provided for a fix term for the judges of the Supreme Court. However, they continue to hold office till the age of 65 years.

Removal of Judges

A Judge of the Supreme Court cannot be removed from the office except by an order of the President on the ground of proved misbehaviour or incapacity.

An order for the removal of the Judge of Supreme Court is passed by each House of Parliament supported by a majority of the total membership of that House and by a majority of not less than two-thirds of the members of the House present and voting for such a removal. This procedure is known as impeachment.

📢 Important
↪ The first ever move in the history of India to impeach a judge of the Supreme Court was the motion to impeach Justice V. Ramaswamy in May, 1993.
↪ The Supreme Court shall sit in Delhi or in any other place as the Chief Justice may decide with the approval of the President.

Example 7. How can the number of Judges in the Supreme Court be increased?

Ans. The number of Judges in the Supreme Court can be increased by the Parliament by amendment in the Constitution.

Independence of Judiciary From the Control of Executive and Legislature

Independence of the judiciary is ensured by the following provisions:

(1) Appointment of Judges by the President after the consultation with the cabinet as well as the judges of the Supreme Court and High Court.
(2) The judges of Supreme Court cannot be removed from office by any authority through a normal simple procedure. A judge can be removed by the President only for proved misbehaviour and incapacity, by process of impeachment.
(3) A judge can remain in office till he has attained the age of 65. He can be removed by the President on the ground of "misbehaviour or incapacity".
(4) Security of salaries and service conditions.
(5) Freedom to announce decisions and decrees without any danger to their person.
(6) Property or fame.
(7) The Supreme Court can punish for the contempt of court if a person or authority makes an attempt to lower its authority.
(8) Full control over its procedure of work and its establishment as well as conditions of service of its employees.
(9) No discussion in the legislature on the conduct of Judges.
(10) Prohibition of practice after retirement.

Example 8. What is meant by freedom to recruit its staff?

Ans. According to the Constitution of India, the Chief Justice is authorized to recruit its staff and servants of the Supreme Court without any interference from the executive.

Jurisdiction and Powers of the Supreme Court

Jurisdiction is the power that the court of law exercises to carry out judgements and enforce laws.

Original Jurisdiction

Original Jurisdiction means the power to hear and determine a dispute in first instance, i.e., those cases which cannot be moved in other court than the Supreme Court. It includes:

(1) Any dispute between Union Government and one or more States, or between Government of India and one or more States on one side and one or more States on the other; or between two or more States.
(2) Protection of Fundamental rights
(3) Transfer of cases from lower courts.
(4) Interpretation of Constitution.

Appellate Jurisdiction

Appellate Jurisdiction means the powers to grant special leave to appeal against judgement delivered by any court in the Country. It is a court of appeal which may change the decision or reduce the sentence passed by the lower courts. The Supreme Court is the final court of appeal. Few types of cases that can be appealed in the Supreme Court are:

(1) **Constitutional cases:** All matters irrespective of the nature, where a certificate is issued by a High Court that it involves an important point of law and needs interpretation of the Constitution, can be brought before the Supreme Court. If the High Court refuses to give a certificate on such a case, the Supreme Court can grant a special leave of appeal.

(2) **Civil cases:** Appeals in civil matters lie to the Supreme Court, if the High Court certifies that the case involves a substantial question of law of general importance, and that question need to be decided by the Supreme Court.

(3) **Criminal cases:** The types of appeals in criminal cases that lie in the Supreme Court are the cases without the certificate of the High Court, and cases with the certificate of the High Court. The certificate of a High Court is not required in a case where the High Court has reversed the judgment of acquittal given by the lower court and punished the accused with a death sentence, and a case which is withdrawn by High Court from the subordinate court and sentenced the accused to death sentence. In all other criminal cases, a High Court certification that the case involves a substantial point of law and interpretation of the Constitution is required for appealing to the Supreme Court.

Example 9. Who is the protector and final interpreter of the Constitution?

Ans. The Supreme Court is the protector and final interpreter of the Constitution.

Advisory Jurisdiction

The Supreme Court has advisory jurisdiction, to give its opinion, on any question of law or fact of public importance as may be referred to it for consideration by the President. The Supreme Court may be required to express its opinion, in an advisory capacity in matters of any question of law if the President considers that the question is of public importance and it is necessary to obtain the opinion of the Supreme Court. The Advisory jurisdiction of the Supreme Court also includes disputes arising out of pre-Constitution treaties and agreements which are excluded from Original Jurisdiction by Article 131.

 **Important**

→ The opinion of the Supreme Court, in Advisory Jurisdiction, is advisory and not binding on the government nor is it executable as a judgment of the Supreme Court.

Revisory Jurisdiction

The Supreme Court under Article 137 is empowered to review any judgment or order made by it with a view to removing any mistake or error that might have crept in the judgment or order. This is because the Supreme Court is a court of record and its decisions are of evidentiary value and cannot be questioned in any court.

Judicial Review

The Supreme Court is the interpreter of the Constitution and its decision is final. It has the power to reviews laws passed by the Union or State legislatures. The Supreme Court can declare a law ultra vires or null and void, if it is against the letter and spirit of the Constitution or contravenes any provisions of the Constitution. This power is referred to as the power of judicial review.

Need for Judicial Review

The Constitution has provided for a balance of powers between the Centre and the States. Judicial Review is necessary for following reasons:

(1) In a written Constitution a law may be ambiguously worked. The question of interpretation of the Constitution is bound to arise and the Supreme Court only has the power of original jurisdiction.

(2) The legislature may not possess the wisdom, experience and impartiability which are needed to explain what the law means. This function can be best performed by the Supreme Court.

⚠ **Caution**

→ Read out the meaning of the term 'Judicial Review' and understand how this power of the Judiciary can invalidate both the Executive and the Legislature when they go against the Constitution.

 **Important**

→ The minimum number of judges to hear and decide a case involving interpretation of the Constitution shall be five.

Court of Record

A Court of Record is a court whose judgments are recorded for evidence and testimony. They are not to be questioned when they are produced before any subordinate court. The Court of Record has two implications:

(1) Its judgments and orders are preserved as records. These can be produced in any court as precedents.

(2) If a person commits a contempt of court, the court has the authority to punish him.

⚠ **Caution**

→ Emphasize that a complete answer, including the statement that the record of cases is kept for future references and precedents by the lower courts, is imperative in a question on Court of Records. Simply writing that the court keeps the record of all cases, is insufficient.

→ While explaining Supreme Court as a Court of Record, lay stress on the keywords as 'records' and 'future reference'.

Functions of Supreme Court

(1) Settlement of disputes
(2) Enforcement of Fundamental Rights
(3) Appointments of officers and staff of the Supreme Court
(4) Make rules regarding the conduct of advocates and other persons appearing before it.
(5) Simplified procedures in the areas of Public Interest Litigation.

Enforcement of Fundamental Rights

Any citizen whose rights are violated may move the Supreme Court for the enforcement of the rights. The Supreme Court has power to issue orders or writs, in the nature of habeas corpus, mandamus, prohibition, quo warranto and certiorari for the enforcement of any of the Fundamental Rights. The Constitution prohibits the State from making any law which takes away or abridges the Fundamental Rights. If it does so, the law shall be declared null and void by the Supreme Court.

Writs

Habeas Corpus: It means to have a body. By issuing such a writ, the Supreme Court can get any person released if he has been unlawfully detained by any person or group of persons or by the State. This writ is, thus, a safeguard for the personal freedom of a citizen.

Mandamus: The word means we order. It is a command or an order from the Supreme Court to a lower or an administrative authority to perform certain duty.

Writ of Prohibition: The Writ of Prohibition is an order issued by a superior court to the lower court to stop proceedings in case which might be in excess of the jurisdiction of the lower court.

Writ of Certiorari: The writ is issued by the superior court to a judicial authority desiring to be informed of what is going on.

Quo-warranto: It means by what order. It is issued when a person has usurped any office. This writ, thus, prevent public officers from forcibly or wrongly holding a high public office.

⚠ Caution

↪ Familiarise with the names of the Courts that are empowered to issue Writs for the enforcement of the Fundamental Rights.

↪ Learn the examples of writs emphasising on the correct spellings of all the writs.

📢 Important

↪ The word appellate has been derived from the word appeal. It means if a person is not satisfied with judgement of the High Court, he can file an appeal in the Supreme Court against the judgement of the High Court.

ℹ ICSE Suggestions

↪ Teach students the meaning of the Original Jurisdiction of the Supreme court.

↪ Spell out the meaning of the term 'Judicial Review' and explain how this power of the Judiciary can invalidate both the Executive and the Legislative when they go against the Constitution.

↪ While explaining Supreme Court as a Court of record, lay stress on the keywords as 'records' and 'future reference'

↪ Lay emphasis on the key words and explain their meaning with concrete examples. Stress on the word original while explaining Original Jurisdiction of the Supreme Court so that students are clear on the type of cases under it.

↪ Explain to the students how and why the independence of Supreme Court is essential for the functioning of democracy. To prove the independent status of the Supreme Court, give examples like security of tenure and appointment of judges.

↪ Clarify to the students, the differences between the terms Revise and Review with reference to the powers of the Supreme Court.

Glossary

(1) **Impeachment:** Removal from office by a special trial conducted by the Parliament for violation of the Constitution.
(2) **Single Integrated Judicial System:** It means Supreme court is the apex court. Below it, there are High Courts in each State and below High Courts are Sub-ordinate District Courts.
(3) **Infringe:** actively break the terms of a law agreement etc.
(4) **Contempt of Court:** an act of deliberate disobedience or disregard for the lower, regulation or decorum of a public authority, such as a court or legislative body.
(5) **Writ:** A writ is an order from a judicial authority asking a person to perform some act or refrain from performing an act.
(6) **Court of Record:** The decisions and the decrees of the court are kept as precedents for future reference in the dispensation of justice.
(7) **Jurisdiction:** The territorial limits within which court's authority may be exercised.
(8) **Independent Judiciary:** The Judges of the court's function free from the influence or interference of either the Executive or Legislature.

(9) **Judicial Review:** The Power of the court to interpret the Constitution and determine the validity of a law passed by legislative or an act of the Executive.

(10) **Civil Cases:** Cases related to Property, taxes or contracts, etc are called Civil Cases.

(11) **Criminal Cases:** Criminal Cases are those cases in which a violation of the Penal law is involved.

OBJECTIVE Type Questions

Multiple Choice Questions

[1 mark each]

1. Who is the final interpreter of our Constitution?
   (a) Judiciary (b) Government
   (c) Executive (b) Legislative

   Ans. (a) Judiciary
   Explanation: The Supreme Court is the final interpreter of the Constitution.

2. What is the tenure of a Judge of the Supreme Court?
   (a) 5 years
   (b) 6 years
   (c) Till age of 65 years
   (d) Till age of 62 years

   Ans. (c) Till age of 65 years
   Explanation: A Judge of the Supreme Court shall hold office until he attains the age of 65 years.

3. The courts that are empowered to issue writs for the enforcement of Fundamental Rights:
   (a) Supreme Court (b) High Courts
   (c) District Courts (d) (a) and (b)

   Ans. (d) (a) and (b)
   Explanation: The Supreme Court and the High Courts are empowered to issue writs for the enforcement of fundamental rights against any authority of the State

4. Who appoints the Chief Justice of the Supreme Court?
   (a) The President
   (b) The Vice-President
   (c) The Prime Minister
   (d) None of the above

   Ans. (a) The President
   Explanation: The President appoints the Chief Justice of India. Usually, he/she is the senior most judge of the Supreme Court.

5. The Writ issued by the Supreme Court for Enforcement of Fundamental Rights:
   (a) Habeas Corpus (b) Mandamus
   (c) Writ of Prohibition (d) Quo-warranto

   Ans. (a) Habeas Corpus
   Explanation: Habeas Corpus means to have a body. By issuing such a writ, the Supreme Court can get any person released if he has been unlawfully detained by any person or group of persons or by the State. This writ is, thus, a safeguard for the personal freedom of a citizen and issued for Enforcement of Fundamental Rights.

6. Which court is said to be the guardian of the Constitution?
   (a) Supreme Court
   (b) High Court
   (c) District Court
   (d) Lok Adalat

   Ans. (a) Supreme Court
   Explanation: The Supreme Court is said to be the guardian of the Constitution as it can issue writs for the Enforcement of Fundamental Rights.

7. The composition of the Supreme Court is ....
   (a) 31 judges and 1 Chief Justice
   (b) 30 judges and 1 Chief Justice
   (c) 33 judges and 1 Chief Justice
   (d) 22 judges and 1 Chief Justice

   Ans. (c) 33 Judges and 1 Chief Justice
   Explanation: The Supreme Court of India consists of a Chief Justice of India and not more than 33 other judges. The Supreme Court (Number of Judges) Amendment Act, 2019, increased the number of judges of Supreme Court from 30 to 33.

8. The power of the Supreme Court to review laws passed by Union Legislature is ....
   (a) Revisory Jurisdiction
   (b) Advisory Jurisdiction
   (c) Original Jurisdiction
   (d) Judicial Review

   Ans. (d) Judicial review
   Explanation: The Supreme Court is the supreme interpreter of the Constitution. It has the judicial power to review any laws passed by the Union or State legislatures.

 **Important**

→ Word Review in a question, could be used as a 'Revisory' in answer.

9. Which writ of the Supreme Court is an order to a lower court to stop proceedings in a case which might be excess of the jurisdiction of the lower court?
   (a) Habeas Corpus
   (b) Mandamus
   (c) Writ of Prohibition
   (d) Writ of Certiorari

Ans. *(c) Writ of prohibition*

Explanation: The writ of prohibition means to forbid. It is issued by the higher court to a lotter court to prevent the later from exceeding its jurisdiction.

10. The Procedure of Impeachment of a Judge is:
   (i) When an order of the President is on the ground of proved misbehaviour or incapacity of a Judge
   (ii) Such an order is passed after an address by each House of Parliament supported by a majority of the total membership of that House.
   (iii) By a majority of not less than two-thirds of the members of the House present and voting for such a removal.
   (iv) He can resign anytime.
   (a) (i), (ii) & (iii)
   (b) (ii), (iii) & (iv)
   (c) (i), (iii) & (iv)
   (d) (i), (ii) & (iv)

Ans. *(a) (i), (ii) & (iii)*

Explanation: A Judge of the Supreme Court cannot be removed from office except by an order of the President on the ground of proved misbehaviour or incapacity. Such an order is passed after an address by each House of the Parliament supported by majority of the total membership of that House and by a majority of not less than two-thirds of the members of the House present and voting for such a removal. This Procedure is known as impeachment.

11. All cases coming from the Lower Courts can be taken to .... , by way of appeal.
   (a) the High Court
   (b) the Supreme Court
   (c) Supreme Court than High Court
   (d) High Court than Supreme Court

Ans. *(d) High Court than Supreme Court*

Explanation: All cases coming from the lower courts can be taken to the High Court and ultimately to the Supreme Court, by way of appeal.

12. Every Judge of the Supreme Court is appointed by the President of India in consultation with ....
   (a) Judges of Supreme Court
   (b) Judges of High Court
   (c) Council of Ministers
   (d) All of the above

Ans. *(d) All of the above*

Explanation: Every Judge of the Supreme Court is appointed by the President of India in Consultation with the Judges of the Supreme court and of High Courts, besides the Council of Ministers.

⚠ **Caution**

→ Consultation of President is a must with all. Judges of Supreme Court, High Court's and Council of Ministers. Just don't write any one or any two names.

13. .... types of appeals in criminal cases lie in the Supreme Court.
   (a) Three   (b) Two
   (c) Four   (d) Six

Ans. *(b) Two*

Explanation: Two types of appeals in criminal cases lie in the Supreme Court.
   (1) Cases without the certificate of the High Court.
   (2) Cases with the certificate of the High Court.

14. The Supreme Court can review any judgement or order under Article ....
   (a) 137   (b) 139
   (c) 138   (d) 136

Ans. *(a) 137*

Explanation: The Supreme Court under Article 137 is empowered to review any judgement or order made by it with a view to removing any mistake or error that might have crept in the Judgement or order.

⚠ **Caution**

→ Remember the correct Article 137, because in our constitution there are many numbered Articles which mean different in different situations.

SUBJECTIVE Type Questions

Short Answer Type Questions
[2 marks each]

15. (A) What is the composition of the Supreme Court?
(B) Who appoints the Chief Justice of India?

Ans. (A) The Supreme Court consists of one Chief Justice and 33 other judges.
(B) The President appoints the Chief Justice of India. Usually, the senior most judge of the Supreme Court is appointed as the Chief Justice.

16. (A) Who appoints the judges of the Supreme Court?
(B) What is the tenure of a Judge of the Supreme Court? [ICSE 2012]

Ans. (A) The President appoints the judges of the Supreme Court in consultation with the Chief Justice and the Council of Ministers.
(B) The Judge of the Supreme Court shall hold office till he attains the age of 65 years.

17. (A) Name the highest judicial tribunal in India.
(B) Mention the term of office of a Judge of Supreme Court.

Ans. (A) The Supreme Court is the highest judicial tribunal in India.
(B) A judge of Supreme Court continues in his office till he/she attains the age of 65 years.

18. On what grounds can a Supreme Court Judge be removed from office. [ICSE 2019]

Ans. A Supreme Court Judge can be removed from office by the order of the President on the grounds of proven misbehaviour or incapacity to act as a Judge.

Charges of proven misbehaviour
Incapacity
Violation of constitution/grave misconduct
[Any two]
[Marking Scheme]

 **What Examiners Say**
→ A few candidates explained Impeachment (Process) for the removal of a judge of Supreme Court instead of giving specific grounds like, grave misconduct etc. for the removal.

19. Why is the Supreme Court said to be the guardian of the Constitution?

Ans. The Supreme Court is said to be the guardian of the Constitution because if any Fundamental Right of the citizen is violated then he/she can seek the protection of the Supreme Court.

20. Name the cases in which the Appellate Jurisdiction of the Supreme Court can be divided.

Ans. Appellate Jurisdiction of the Supreme Court extends to Constitutional, Civil and Criminal cases.

21. What is meant by a 'Single Integrated Judicial System' as provided in the Indian Constitution? [ICSE 2014]

Ans. The Constitution states, "The law declared by the Supreme Court shall be binding on all courts within the territory of India."
This means that under the Constitution, we have 'Single Intergrated Judicial System'.
The Judiciary is an integrated system in which the courts from the apex level to the lowest level are integrated in a heierarchical pattern. All the courts in the country have the responsibility to interpret and enforce the laws of the state as well as the union. The legal causes initiated at the lower level may be taken up to the highest levels in the form of appeals. The decision of the Supreme Court is binding on the High Courts and the other lower courts.

The single integrated judicial system means
(1) the Supreme Court is at the apex of the entire Judicial system
(2) The Supreme Court supervises and controls the functioning of the other courts
(3) a single civil and criminal system operates throughout the country
(4) there are no separate laws for the states
(5) the Supreme Court is the highest court of appeal -its decisions are final. [Any two]
[Marking Scheme]

 **What Examiners Say**
→ Most candidates answered incorrectly as they were unable to understand the meaning of the word 'integrated'. They explained it as independence of judiciary from the executive control or mentioned the features of the Federal Structure of Government instead.

22. When can the President issue the removal order of the judges of the Supreme Court?

Ans. The President can issue the removal order of the Judges of the Supreme Court only after an address by the Parliament has been presented in the same session.

23. Mention any one condition, that leads to the independence of the Judiciary from the control of the executive and legislature.

Ans. The salaries, allowances and pensions of judges are charged on the Consolidated Fund of India. Thus, they are non-votable by the Parliament.

24. What ensures that the Judges of the Supreme Court does not favour anyone in future?

Ans. A judge of the Supreme Court is prohibited from practice after the retirement. It means that he shall not plead in any court or before any authority within the territory of India. This ensures that the Judges of the Supreme Court does not favour anyone in the future.

25. What is the Original Jurisdiction of the Supreme Court of India?

Ans. Original Jurisdiction means the power of the Supreme Court to hear and determine a dispute in the first instance, *i.e.* those cases which cannot be moved in any court other than the Supreme Court.

26. Mention any two exceptions of the Original Jurisdiction of the Supreme Court.

Ans. The Original Jurisdiction of the Supreme Court does not extend to (1) a dispute arising out of a treaty, agreement, *etc.* which is in operation. (2) adjustment of certain expenses and pensions between the union and the States.

27. Mention any two power of the Supreme Court not enjoyed by the other courts.

Ans. (1) The power of the Supreme Court not enjoyed by the other courts is that only the Supreme Court has the right to revise its earlier decisions.
(2) It has the original jurisdiction to settle disputes between the Central Government and one or more States and Union Territories as well as between different States and UTs.

28. What is meant by Appellate Jurisdiction of the Supreme Court? [ICSE 2019, 14]

Ans. The Supreme Court is the apex court of the country and is the highest court of appeal. The Appellate Jurisdiction of the Supreme Court means it is primarily the court of appeal and has the powers to hear appeals against the orders of High Courts and other lower courts.

> (1) Hears Appeals from a person/ organisation when they are not satisfied.
> (2) Special Leave of Appeal
> (3) Appeals from the judgements of High Court or lower court can be filed in the Supreme Court **[Any two]**
> **[Marking Scheme]**

What Examiners Say
➥ Most of the candidates did not have a clear concept of the term Appellate Jurisdiction. A few candidates mixed it with the original jurisdiction of the Supreme Court.

29. What is the Advisory Jurisdiction of the Supreme Court?

Ans. Under Advisory Jurisdiction of the Supreme Court, the President can seek opinion of the Supreme Court on any question of law or public importance. The Supreme Court is not bound to give its advice on all the cases referred to it.

30. What is meant by the term Judicial Review?

Ans. Judicial review means, the Supreme Court examine the constitutionality of legislative enactments and executive orders of both the Central and State Governments.

31. Name any two writs issued by the Supreme Court. [HOT] [ICSE 2018]

Ans. The writs issued by the Supreme Court are:
(1) Writ of Habeus Corpus
(2) Writ of Mandamus
(3) Writ of Prohibition
(4) Writ of Certiorari
(5) Writ of Quo warranto. **[Any two]**

> Habeas corpus, Mandamus, Prohibition, Certiorari, Quo- warranto. **[Any two]**
> **[Marking Scheme]**

What Examiners say
➥ Some candidates instead of naming two writs issued by the Supreme Court explained the Fundamental Rights. There were spelling errors in a few answer scripts.

32. Name the courts that are empowered to issue Writs for the enforcement of Fundamental Rights. [ICSE 2020, 13]

Ans.
> Supreme Court & High Court
> **[Marking Scheme]**

What Examiners Say
➥ This was a well attempted question.

⚠ Caution
➥ One should be familiar with the names of the Courts that are empowered to issue Writs for the enforcement of the Fundamental Rights

Structured Questions
[3+3+4= **10** marks each]

33. The Supreme Court is the head of the entire system of judiciary. In this context, answer the following questions:

(A) Mention any three cases which come under the Original Jurisdiction of the Supreme Court.
(B) Why is the Supreme Court called the Court of Record?
(C) Mention any four qualifications required by a person to be the judge of the Supreme Court.

Ans. (A) The cases that comes under the Original Jurisdiction of Supreme Court are:
(1) A dispute between Government of India and one or more states;
(2) Disputes between two or more states.
(3) A dispute between the Union and any state on one side and other states on the other side.

(B) The Supreme Court is a court of Record. It implies:
(1) The Judgements, proceeding and acts of the Supreme Court are recorded for perpetual remembdrance and testimony. These records cannot be questioned before any court.
(2) It has the power to punish for the contempt of court.

(C) The qualifications required by a person to be the Judge of the Supreme Court are:
(1) He/She should be citizen of India.
(2) He/She should have been a Judge of a High Court in succession for at least five years.
(3) He/She should have been an advocate of a High Court in succession for at least ten years.
(4) He/She should be a distinguished Jurist in the opinion of the President.

34. The Supreme Court is the apex court in the entire Judicial set up in India. In this context answer the following questions:
(A) What is meant by the term single Integrated Judicial System.
(B) Name three types of Jurisdictions of the Supreme Court.
(C) Discuss any four writs issued by the Supreme Court.

Ans. (A) Under our constitution, the judiciary is a single integrated system of courts for the union and the states with the supreme court at the apex. By the single integrated system, we mean:
(1) The Supreme Court is the head of the entire system and not only supervises but also exercises control over the functioning of other courts.
(2) There are no separate sets of laws and a single civil and criminal system operates throughout the country.
(3) All cases coming from the Lower Courts can be taken to the High Courts and ultimately to the Supreme Court, by way of appeal.
(4) Below the Supreme Court stand the High Courts of different States and under each High Court there is a hierarchy of other subordinate courts.

(B) The different types of jurisdictions of Supreme Court are:
(1) **Original Jurisdiction:** It means the power to hear and determine a dispute in the first instance, *i.e.*, those cases which cannot be moved in any court other them the Supreme Court.
(2) **Appellate Jurisdiction:** It means the powers to grant special leave to appeal against the judgement delivered by any court in the country.
(3) **Advisory Jurisdiction:** The Supreme Court has advisory jurisdiction, to give its opinion, on any question of law or fact of public importance as may be referred to it for consideration by the President.

(C) The writs issued by the Supreme Court are:
(1) **Habeas Corpus:** It means "to have the body". By issuing such a writ, the Supreme Court can get the body of any person released if it has been detained by any person or a group of persons or by the state. This writ is, thus, a great safeguard for the personal freedom of a citizen.
(2) **Mandamus:** It means "we order". It is a command or an order from a Superior Court to a lower or an administrative authority to perform certain duty.
(3) **Writ of Prohibition:** The writ of prohibition is an order issued by a superior court to a lower court to stop proceedings in a case which might be in excess of the jurisdiction of the lower court.
(4) **Writ of Certiorari:** This writ is issued by a superior court to a judicial authority desiring "to be informed of what is going on". The writ of certiorari is issued after the order has already been passed by the lower court.

(5) **Quo-warranto:** It means "by what order." This writ prevents public officers from forcibly or wrongly holding a high public office.

[Any four]

35. With reference to the Supreme Court as the Apex Court in our Indian Judiciary, explain the following:
(A) Any three cases that come under the Original Jurisdiction of the Supreme Court.
(B) Power of Judicial Review.
(C) Supreme Court as a Court of Record.

[🔥HOT] [ICSE 2020]

Ans. (A) The cases that come under the original jurisdiction of the Supreme Court are:
(1) The cases related to disputes between the Government of India and one or more states.
(2) The cases related to disputes between two or more states on which the existence of legal right depends.
(3) The cases related to the enforcement of Fundamental Rights.

(B) Judicial review is a process through which the Supreme Court examines whether a law enacted by a legislative or an action of the executive is in accordance with the Constitution or not. The Supreme Court is the interpreter of the Constitution and it may declare a law 'ultra vires' or null and void if it is against the letter and spirit of the constitution or infringes any provision of the Constitution. The power of Judicial review is an important guarantee of the rights of the people.

(C) The Supreme Court is a Court of Record whose judgements are recorded for evidence and testimony. All its decisions and judgements are cited as precedents in all courts of the country. They have the force of law and are binding on all the lower courts, and even on the High Courts. As a Court of Record, the Supreme Court can even send a person to jail who may have committed contempt of court.

(A) **Original Jurisdiction**
(1) Centre state
(2) Inter-State disputes
(3) Union and State on one side and other states on the other side
(4) Protection of Fundamental Rights
(5) Transfer of cases from lower courts
(6) Interpretation of Constitution

[Any three]

(B) **Power of Judicial Review**
(1) The Supreme Court is the interpreter of the Constitution
(2) It has the power to review law passed by the Union or State legislatures or executive
(3) The Supreme Court can declare a law ultra vires or null and void, if it is against the letter and spirit of the Constitution or contravenes any provision of the constitution.

[Any two]

(C) **The court of record has two implications:**
(1) Its judgement and orders are preserved as a record.
(2) This can be produced in any court as precedents.
(3) Future references
(4) Testimony
(5) If a person commits a contempt of court, the court has the authority to punish contempt.
(6) The supreme Court acts as the Guardian of the Constitution.

[Marking Scheme]

What Examiners Say

➡ *(A) Most candidates attempted this part of the question well. However, a few got confused with the Appellate and other jurisdictions.*

➡ *(B) Many candidates confused Judicial Review with Revisory Jurisdiction and hence could not explain the 'Power of Judicial Review'.*

➡ *(C) This was a well attempted question.*

36. Our Judicial system has a Supreme Court as its Apex, followed by the High Court and other Subordinate Courts. In the light of this statement, explain the following:
(A) Any three types of cases in which the Supreme Court exercises its original jurisdiction.
(B) Any three ways by which the Constitution ensures the Independence of the Judiciary.
(C) 'Advisory' and 'Revisory' Jurisdiction of the Supreme Court. [ICSE 2018]

Ans. (A) According to Article 131 of the Constitution of India, Original Jurisdiction of the Supreme Court means the authority to hear and determine those cases and disputes which can be initiated, in the first instance, only at the Supreme Court. The cases in which the Supreme Court exercises its original jurisdiction are:

(1) The disputes between the Government of India and one or more states;
(2) The disputes between the Government of India and any state on the one side and one or more other states on the other side;
(3) The disputes between two or more states that involves any question or on which the existence of legal rights depends.
(4) The cases regarding the enforcement of fundamental rights. **[Any three]**

(B) The ways by which the Constitution ensures the independence of the Judiciary are:
(1) The appointment and removal of the Judges is done by the President;
(2) The decisions and actions of Judges cannot be open to criticism. The Constitution clearly states that the conduct of the judges of the Supreme Court should not be a subject of discussion in Parliament except in the case of impeachment of any such judge.
(3) The courts have the right to determine their judicial procedure.
(4) A Judge can remain in his office till he attains the age of 65 years. He can only be removed by the President through process of impeachment. **[Any three]**

(C) **Advisory Jurisdiction:** According to Article 143 of the Constitution of India, the Supreme Court of India enjoys Advisory Jurisdiction on the matters referred to the court for legal advice by the President. If it appears to the President that any question of law of public importance has arisen, he/she may refer the question to the Supreme Court to seek its legal opinion on such question. The Supreme Court may after due consideration, report to the President its opinion on that matter. The matters where Supreme Court exercises its advisory jurisdiction are:
(1) Disputes arising out of any treaty or agreement, executed before the commencement of the Constitution;
(2) If President refers that a case or question of law is of public importance, then the Supreme Court is bound to give its legal opinion as it enables the President to receive an authoritative opinion about the subject.

Revisory Jurisdiction: According to Article 137 of the Constitution of India, the Supreme Court is empowered to review any judgement or order made by it with a view to removing any mistake or error that might have crept in the judgement or order. This provision reflects that the Supreme Court may rectify something that was misjudged. It means that it can review the rulings of the lower courts to determine the law not followed the due process.

(A) **Original Jurisdiction**
(1) The Supreme Court has original jurisdiction in all disputes between the Union and States as well as between the states.
(2) Protection of Fundamental Rights.
(3) Final Interpretation of the Constitution.
(4) Transfer of cases from lower courts.
(5) In a dispute between the union and state on none side and any other state on the other side.
[Any three]

(B) (1) Appointment of Judges: Neither political bias nor personal favouritism would play any part in the appointment of Judges. It has enhanced independence of the judiciary.
(2) Security of Tenure: A Judge can remain in office till he has attained the age of 65 years. He can be removed by the President on the ground of 'proven misbehaviour or incapacity. It means that an Address can only be presented after an allegation has been thoroughly examined by some impartial tribunal.
(3) Salaries are charged on the Consolidated Fund of India: Judge's salaries and allowances shall not be varied to their disadvantages during their term of offce.
(4) No discussion shall take place in Parliament with respect to the conduct of any Judge: in the discharge of his duties.
(5) Genuine criticism of a Judgement is allowed, but nothing should be done to lower the authority or dignity of the Court.

(6) **Prohibition of practice after Retirement:** A retired judge of the Supreme Court cannot be placed in any court or tribunal in India.

[Any three]

(C) The President may obtain the opinion / advice of the Supreme Court on a question of law or fact, which is of public importance. Questions must be specific and not general or vague.

The Supreme Court may report its opinion, after such hearing as it thinks fit.

First, the Supreme Court is not bound to express any opinion on the question submitted to it.

Second, the advisory opinion of the Supreme Court is not binding on the President or any other courts, because it is not a 'judicial decision'.

[Any two]

The Supreme Court has power to review any judgement pronounced by it. This provision reflects that human judgement is fallible and the Court may rectify something that was misjudged. The Supreme Court cannot allow errors to continue indefinitely. It causes harm or damage to the general welfare of the public. [Any two]

[Marking Scheme]

What Examiners Say

→ (A) Most of the candidates answered this question correctly. However, a few candidates, instead of writing on the cases in which the Supreme Court exercises its Original Jurisdiction, wrote on cases which come under other jurisdictions of the Supreme Court.

→ (B) Most of the candidates answered three ways by which the Constitution ensures the Independence of the Judiciary correctly.

→ (C) Some candidates got confused between the Advisory and Revisory Jurisdiction of the Supreme Court.

37. The Supreme Court has an extensive jurisdiction. In the light of this statement, answer the following questions:

(A) What are the qualifications of the Judges of the Supreme Court?

(B) (a) Explain the composition of the Supreme Court.

(b) How are the Judges of the Supreme Court appointed?

(C) Explain the cases in which the Supreme Court enjoys Original Jurisdiction.

[🔥HOT] [ICSE 2016]

Ans. (A) The qualifications of the Judges of the Supreme Court are:

(1) He/she must be a citizen of India;

(2) He/she has been a judge of a High Court or two such courts in succession for a period of at least five years or has been an advocate of High Court for at last ten years.

(3) In the view of the President, the person must be a distinguished person in the field of law.

(B) (a) Article 124 of the Constitution states that there shall be a Supreme Court of India consisting of a Chief Justice of India and other judges constituting a number that is prescribed by Parliament through laws passed from time to time. At present the Supreme Court of India consists of one Chief Justice and 30 other judges, taking the total strength to 31.

(b) The Chief Justice and other judges of the Supreme Court are appointed by the President of India after consulting as many judges of the Supreme Court and the High Courts as the President may deem necessary. This system of taking the advice a bench of judges for the appointment of Judges is known as the 'Collegium system'(Judges—selecting—Judges).

(C) The cases that come under the original jurisdiction of the Supreme Court are:

(1) The cases related to disputes between the Government of India and one or more States.

(2) The cases related to disputes between two or more States on which the existence of legal right depends.

(3) The cases related to the enforcement of Fundamental Rights.

(4) All civil and criminal cases at the first instance.

(A) **Qualification of the Judges of Supreme Court:**

(1) Must be a citizen of India

(2) A distinguished jurist or a High Court Judge for at least five years.
(3) An advocate of the High Court for at least 10 years in succession.

(B) (a) The Supreme Court consists of a Chief Justice and 25 Judges (may vary) as decided by the Union Legislature from time to time.
(b) They are appointed by the President in consultation with the Judges of Supreme Court and of the High Court besides the cabinet.

(C) **Original Jurisdiction:**
(1) A dispute between the Government of India and one or more States.
(2) Disputes between two or more States.
(4) Disputes between the Union and any State on one side and other States on the other.
(5) The Supreme Court entertains cases for the enforcement of Fundamental Rights.
(6) Final Interpreter of the Constitution.
(7) All civil and criminal cases at the first instance. **[Any four]**
[Marking Scheme]

What Examiners Say

→ (A) A majority of candidates answered correctly. A few wrote the minimum age (35 years) and maximum age (65 years) which is not required in the qualification of judges.

→ (B) (i) Candidates were confused with the number of judges in the Supreme Court since it has changed from time to time. However, many candidates answered correctly.

(ii) This part of the question was answered correctly by majority of candidates.

→ (C) Some candidates wrote the meaning of Original Jurisdiction which was not asked. Some of the important points like enforcements of Fundamental Rights and Interpretation of the constitution were missing from the answers.

⚠ Caution

→ Qualifications of judges of Supreme Court are different from the qualifications required for a political post. Age and office of profit are not the qualifications for the judges.

→ Be specific on the number of judges in the Supreme Court. Instruct students to mention separately one Chief Justice and 30 other judges. Explain that while appointing a judge the President takes the advice of the Chief Justice of the Supreme Court and the High Court.

→ Students should write correct examples to secure marks. Guess work must be avoided.

38. With reference to the Supreme Court, explain its function stated below:
(A) Original Jurisdiction
(B) Advisory Function
(C) As a guardian of Fundamental Rights
[ICSE 2014]

Ans. (A) According to Article 131 of the Constitution, Original Jurisdiction means the authority to hear and determine those cases/disputes which can be initiated, in the first instance, only at the Supreme Court. This Jurisdiction primarily deals with disputes which cannot be moved in any other court other than the Supreme Court. Under the original jurisdiction the disputes covered are:
(1) Disputes between the Government of India and one or more states;
(2) Disputes between the Government of India and any state on one side and one or more states on the other;
(3) Between two or more states that involves any question or on which the existence of a legal right depends.
(4) Cases regarding enforcement of fundamental rights.

(B) According to Article 143 of the Constitution, the Supreme Court enjoys Advisory jurisdiction on the matters referred to the court for legal advice by the President. If it appears to the President that any question of law of public importance has arisen, he/she may refer the questions to the Supreme Court to seek its legal opinion or such question. The matters where Supreme Court exercises its advisory jurisdiction are:
(1) Disputes arising out of any treaty or agreement, executed before the commencement of the Constitution;
(2) If the President refers that a case or question of law is of public importance, then the Supreme Court is bound to give its legal opinion as it enables the President to receive an authoritative opinion about the subject.

(C) The Supreme Court acts as a true guardian of the Constitution. It protects the fundamental rights of Indian citizens through various types of writs. The Constitution has assigned the responsibility to the Supreme

Court for the protection of the Fundamental Rights. The Supreme Court can declare any law null and void if it violates the exercise of Fundamental Rights. The court also protect these rights if they are infringed by the actions of the executive.

(A) **Guardian of Fundamental Rights:**
(1) The constitution guarantees the citizen the right to move the court for the enforcement of fundamental Rights.
(2) It can issue orders or writes like Habeas Corpus for the enforcements of Fundamental Rights.
(3) Any law passed by the Parliament which abridges or takes away the Fundamental Right will be declared null and void by the Supreme Court.

(B) **Advisory Jurisdiction:** The President of India may seek advice of the Supreme Court on important questions of law or facts of public importance and it is necessary to obtain the opinion of the Supreme Court. The Supreme Court is not bound to express any opinion and its advisory opinion is not binding on the President.

(C) The Supreme Court performs various functions:
In cases which are brought before it in the first instance i.e., those cases which cannot be moved in any court other than the Supreme Court.
Centre-State or inter-State disputes
(1) Between Governments of India and one or more states.
(2) Between Government of India and any State or States on one side and one or more States on the other.
(3) Disputes between two or more States. **[Marking Scheme]**

What Examiners Say

↦ (A) This question was correctly answered by most candidates though a few mistook it for Appellate Jurisdiction.

↦ (B) Most candidates answered the question correctly. However, a few could not understand it and explained judicial review or the revisory jurisdiction instead.

↦ (C) Most candidates answered the question correctly, mentioning the various writs to safeguard the Fundamental Rights. Writs were explained which can be citied as examples but incomplete answers were however written.

⚠ Caution

↦ Students should need to cite examples correctly to score marks. Guess work does not help. They also need to differentiate between the Union Government and the Union Legislature while giving examples regarding the disputes.

↦ Remember that the President may seek the advice of the Supreme Court on important issues. However, the opinion of the Supreme Court is not binding on the President. It is only on advice.

↦ Highlight the importance of the Fundamental Rights and with this in mind explain the various ways by which the Supreme Court plays an important role in guarding the Fundamental Rights.

39. The country's Judicial System has a Supreme Court at its apex. In his context, discuss the following:
(A) Manner of appointment of judges
(B) Term of office and removal of Judges
(C) Its power of 'Judicial Review'.
[ICSE 2013]

Ans. (A) The Chief Justice and other judges of the Supreme Court are appointed by the President of India after consulting as many judges of the Supreme Court as the President may deem necessary. However, a while appointing a judge other than the Chief Justice, it is necessary for the President to consult the Chief Justice of the Supreme Court. The Chief Justice, in his turn, must consult the four senior-most judges of the Supreme Court before forwarding his recommendations to the President in this regard. This system of taking advice of a bench of judges for the appointment of judges is known as 'Collegium system'.

(B) The Chief Justice and any other Judge of the Supreme Court shall hold office till they attain the age of 65 years. However, a Judge may resign voluntarily before his/her term of office is completed by submitting his letter of resignation to the President. Before completion of tenure, a Judge of Supreme Court can only be removed on the ground of proven misbehaviour or incapacity, through the process of impeachment. This procedure of removal of a judge of the Supreme Court involves an order of the President passed by each House of Parliament supported by a majority of the total membership of that

House and by a majority of not less than two-thirds of the members present and voting in the House.

(C) Judicial review is a process through which the Supreme Court examines whether a law enacted by a legislative or an action of the executive is in accordance with the Constitution or not. The Supreme Court is the interpreter of the constitution and it may declare a law 'ultra vires' or null and void if it is against the letter and spirit of the Constitution or infringes any provision of the Constitution. The power of Judicial review is an important guarantee of the rights of the people.

5 The High Courts and Subordinate Courts

The Constitution of India provides for a High Court for each State. There are 25 High Courts in India, including those having jurisdiction over more than one state. Below High Courts there are Subordinate Courts, which function at the district level and below. And also there are Lok Adalats, which are alternative dispute redressal mechanism where disputes/cases pending in the court of law are settled amicably.

Chapter Notes

- The High Court
- Subordinate Courts
- Lok Adalats

TOPIC 1
THE HIGH COURTS

Article 214 of the Constitution of India provides for a High Court for each State. But the Parliament under Article 231 of the Constitution can establish a common High Court for two or more States or Union territories. There are 24 High Courts in India, including those having jurisdiction over more than one State.

Composition

Each High Court consists of a Chief Justice and such other judges as the President of India appoints from time to time. Besides, the President has the power to appoint:

(1) Additional judges for a temporary period not exceeding two years, for the clearance of work in a High Court.
(2) An acting Judge, when a permanent Judge other than the Chief Justice, is temporarily absent or is appointed to act temporarily as Chief Justice. The acting Judge holds office until the permanent Judge resumes his office.

Example 1. Who determines the strength of Judges of a High Court?

Ans. The President determines the strength of the Judges of a High Court.

Qualifications

According to the Constitution, a person shall be qualified for appointment as a Judge of a High Court under the following conditions:

(1) He/she should be citizen of India;
(2) He/she should not be over 62 years of age;
(3) He/she has held a judicial office in the territory of India for at least ten years;

Or

He/she has been an advocate of a High Court for at least ten years.

Important

→ The qualification "He should have been a distinguished Jurist" has been omitted by the 44th Amendment Act (1978).

Appointment of Judges

The Chief Justice of a High Court is appointed by the President of India in consultation with the Chief Justice of the Supreme Court and the Governor of the concerned State.

Other Judges of a High Court are appointed by the President in consultation with the Chief Justice of India, the Governor of the State and the Chief Justice of the High Court of that State.

Example 2. What is the maximum age of retirement of a High Court Judge?

Ans. The maximum age of retirement of a High Court Judge is 62 years.

Important

→ The High Court is at the head of the judicial hierarchy of the State.

Powers and Jurisdiction of High Court

The Jurisdiction of a High Court of a State extends to the territorial limits of that State. If there is a common High Court for two or more States or Union Territories then the jurisdication of such a court extends to the territorial limits of the States or the Union Territories. High Court has extensive and effective powers like Supreme Court. It is the highest court of appeal in the State. It is the protector of the Fundamental Rights of the citizens as well as the interpreter of the Constitution.

Original Jurisdiction

High Court has original jurisdiction which means that it has power to hear disputes in the first instance, not by way of appeal. Its power extends to the following:

(1) Disputes relating to the election of members of the Parliament and State Legislatures.
(2) Regarding revenue matter or an act ordered or done regarding revenue collection relating to State.
(3) Enforcement of Fundamental rights of citizens.
(4) Cases ordered to be transferred from a Subordinate Court, involving the interpretation of the Constitution to its own file.
(5) Matter on morality, will, marriage, divorce, company laws and Contempt of Court may be referred or brought before the High Court directly.

Appellate Jurisdiction

Appellate Jurisdiction of the High Court means that the High Court has the power to accept appeals against the decisions of District Courts, in Civil as well as Criminal matters.

Civil Cases

Only those civil cases which are decided by the District courts, come under the jurisdiction of the High Court by any appeal. Appeals can be brought to the High Court:

(1) In matters concerning land revenue and
(2) In cases where a blatant injustice has been committed by any Tribunal. In such cases, the High Court may quash the order of Tribunals.

Criminal Cases

In criminal case appellate jurisdiction consists of appeals:

(1) Against the judgement of a Sessions Judge or an Additional Sessions Judge, where the sentence of imprisonment exceeds seven years.
(2) Against the judgements of an Assistant Sessions Judge, the chief Metropolitan Magistrate or other Judicial Magistrates, where the sentence of imprisonment exceeds four years.
(3) Against the State, when the order of acquittal is passed by a Sessions Judge.
(4) A sentence of death must be confirmed by the High Court before it can be carried out.

⚠️ **Caution**

→ Students are advised to learn the differences between Original Jurisdiction and Appellate Jurisdiction. They should not mix the points.

TOPIC 2

SUBORDINATE COURTS

Subordinate Courts are the courts, which function at the district level and below. Therefore, all the courts in India except the Supreme Court and the High Courts, are Subordinate Courts. The organization and structure of the Subordinate Courts are generally uniform throughout the country. For the purpose of judicial administration every State is divided into a number of districts, each under the Jurisdiction of a District Judge. Every district has Civil courts, Criminal courts and Courts of Revenue.

The Court of the District Judge

It is the principal or the highest court of the district. It decides both civil and criminal cases. When a Judge decides civil cases, he is called the District Judge and when he decides criminal cases, he is called the Sessions Judge. The District Judge also acts as a Deputy Commissioner and District Collector.

Distinction Between Court of the District Judge and Sessions Court

	Court of the District Judge	Sessions Court
(1)	It is highest civil court of the district.	It is highest criminal court of the district.
(2)	It is presided over by a District Judge.	It is presided over by a Sessions Judge.
(3)	The District Judge decides civil cases related to land, property, money transactions, arbitration, guardianship, marriage, divorce and will.	The Sessions Judge decides criminal cases like murders, theft, dacoity, pick-pocketing, etc.
(4)	The District Judge acts as a Deputy Commissioner and District Collector and in this capacity he maintains law and order and supervises the collection of revenues and taxes in the district.	The Sessions Judge does not perform any administrative functions.
(5)	The District Judge and the additional District Judges are appointed by the Governor in consultation with the chief Justice of the High Court of the concerned State.	The Sessions Judge and the Additional Sessions Judges are appointed by the Governor in consultation with the Chief Justice of the High Court of the concerned State.

Example 3. Name the highest criminal court in a district.

Ans. The highest criminal court in a district is Sessions Court.

⚠️ **Caution**

→ Make a table to understand the powers and functions of a District Judge and Session Judge and the types of cases they are supposed to deal.

📢 **Important**

→ The District Judge is the highest Judicial authority in the district.
→ The Subordinate courts are also known as lower courts.

TOPIC 3
LOK ADALATS

Meaning

Lok Adalat means "People's Court". It is an alternate dispute redressal mechanism where disputes/cases pending in the court of law or at pre-litigation stage are settled amicably. On the recommendation of Justice P.N. Bhagwati, Lok Adalats were set up by Legal Services Authorities Act, 1987 as a legal forum to provide legal aid and quick justice to those who are not in a position to engage lawyers or bear the expenses of legal proceedings. The Legal Services Authorities Act, 1987 provides that State shall organize Lok Adalats from time to time. All decisions of the Lok Adalats shall be deemed to be decrees of a Civil Court and shall be binding on the parties to the dispute. Main condition of the Lok Adalat is that both parties in a dispute shall agree for a settlement.

Purpose

(1) To provide legal aid and quick justice to those who are not in a position to engage lawyers;
(2) To relieve the courts of heavy backlog of cases;
(3) To eliminate high costs and delays in imparting justice.

Example 4. Mention one reason why the system of Lok Adalat has become popular.

Ans. The system has become popular because the disputes between the parties are settled amicably and hence both the parties feel satisfied.

Example 5. Which types of cases are settled in the Lok Adalat?

Ans. The Lok Adalat mainly settles small civil cases, settlement of family feuds, minor cases of assault and injury which can be settled amicably.

Important

→ There is no court fee payable when a matter is filed in Lok Adalat.
→ The parties to a dispute should agree for a settlement.

Advantages

(1) Lok Adalats play important role in the settlement of family feuds, disputes between the neighbours and minor cases of assault and injury by settling the disputes through compromise.
(2) Lok Adalats deliver fast and inexpensive justice.
(3) Lok Adalats work in the spirit of compromise and understanding and as such both the parties feel satisfied.
(4) Lok Adalats reduce the workload of other courts enabling them to deal with more serious matters.
(5) Lok Adalats promote social justice by providing legal aid to weaker section of society.

ICSE Suggestions

→ Study the power of Judicial Review and the Revisory Power of the Supreme Court.
→ While studying Supreme Court as a Court of Record, lay stress on the keywords as 'records' and 'future reference'.
→ Mark and underline the key words and key points in your textbook/s for retention of relevant points and to write the answers specifically to questions.
→ Do not miss regular tests and after assessment, take the help of your teacher to resolve your problems.
→ Always appear in school assessment tests to improve learning and to be familiar with the pattern of questions.
→ Follow the Scope of Syllabus and adjust your learning accordingly.
→ Do not write unwanted details in an answer.

Glossary

(1) **Revenue:** A State's annual income from which public expenses are met.
(2) **Interpretation:** The action of explaining the meaning of something.
(3) **Arbitrary:** Based on random choice or personal whim, rather than any reason or system.
(4) **Flagrant:** An action considered as wrong or immoral
(5) **Perpetual:** Never ending or changing.
(6) **Appellate Jurisdiction of a High Court:** Appellate Jurisdiction means that the High Court has the power to accept appeals against the decision of District Court in civil as well as criminal matters.
(7) **Lok Adalats:** A Lok Adalat means "People's Court" It encourages the settlement of disputes through compromise between two parties.

OBJECTIVE Type Questions

Multiple Choice Questions

[**1** mark each]

1. **The Sessions Court deals with .... cases.**
   (a) Civil
   (b) Criminal
   (c) Constitutional
   (d) Revenue   [ICSE Sem-2, 2022]

   Ans. *(b) Criminal*

   Explanation : A court of session is the highest criminal court in a district and the court of first instance for trying serious offences those carrying punishment of imprisonment of more than seven years, life imprisonment, or death.

2. **Which is the highest civil court in a district?**
   (a) District Court
   (b) Sessions Court
   (c) Chief Metropolitan Court
   (d) District Magistrate

   Ans. *(a) District Court*

   Explanation: The District Court, presided by the District Judge is the highest civil court in a district.

3. **The High Court judge can remain in office till he/she attains the age of ....**
   (a) 60 years
   (b) 65 years
   (c) 62 years
   (d) 55 years   [ICSE Sem-2, 2022]

   Ans. *(c) 62 years*

   Explanation : A Judge of a High Court enjoys security of tenure and can remain in office till he/she has attained the age of 62 years.

4. **There are .... High Courts in India.**
   (a) 22   (b) 24
   (c) 28   (d) 32

   Ans. *(b) 24*

   Explanation: There are 24 High Courts in India, including those having jurisdiction over more than one State.

   Related Theory
   → *Among the Union Territories, only Delhi has a High Court of its own.*

5. **Which of the following statements does NOT apply to the Lok Adalat?**
   (a) It reduces the burden on High Courts
   (b) Works on the spirit of Compromise
   (c) The cases take a long time to get resolved
   (d) It involves very less expenses
                                  [ICSE Sem-2, 2022]

   Ans. *(c) The cases take a long time to get resolved*

   Explanation : Lok Adalats deliver fast and inexpensive Justice. They work in the spirit of Compromise and understanding, both the Parties feel satisfied. And they reduce the workload of other courts enabling them to deal with more serious matter.

   Related Theory
   → *It provides legal aid and quick justice to those who are not in a position to engage lawyers.*

6. **Who Presides over the highest criminal court in a district?**
   (a) District Judge
   (b) Sessions Judge
   (c) Chief Metropolitan Magistrate
   (d) Chief Justice of High Court

   Ans. *(b) Session Judge*

   Explanation: The Sessions Judge presides over the highest criminal court in a district, i.e. Sessions Court.

7. **The High Court judges are appointed by the ....**
   (a) President
   (b) Prime Minister
   (c) Governor
   (d) Chief Justice of India

   Ans. *(b) President*

   Explanation : The High Court Judges are appointed by the President in Consultation with the Chief Justice of the Supreme Court and the Governor of the concerned State.

   Related Theory
   → *Other Judges of a High Court are appointed by the President. The President shall consult the Chief Justice of India, the Governor of the State and the Chief Justice of the High Court in the matter of appointment of a Judge to the High Court.*

8. **The .... acts as a deputy commissioner to maintain law and order in the district.**
   (a) Chief Justice of High Court
   (b) District Judge
   (c) Sessions Judge
   (d) Chief Metropolitan Magistrate

   Ans. *(b) District Judge*

The High Courts and Subordinate Courts

Explanation : The District Judge acts as a Deputy Commissioner and District Collector and in this capacity, he maintains law and order and supervises the collection of revenues and taxes in the district.

9. Which Court is known as the People's Court?
   (a) Supreme Court
   (b) High Court
   (c) District Court
   (d) Lok Adalat

Ans. *(d) Lok Adalat*

Explanation : Lok Adalat means 'People's Court'. It is an alternative dispute redressal mechanism where disputes/cases pending in the court of Law or at Pre-litigation stage are settled amicably.

10. Every District has ....
    (a) Civil Courts
    (b) Criminal Courts
    (c) Courts of Revenue
    (d) All of the above

Ans. *(d) All of the above*

Explanation : Every district has civil courts, criminal courts and courts of Revenue.

11. Complete the analogy:
    Court of the District Judge : Highest Civil Court of the district
    Sessions Court : : _____ .
    (a) Highest Criminal Court
    (b) Highest Law Court
    (c) Highest Public Court
    (d) Highest Popular Court

Ans. *(a) Highest Criminal Court*

Explanation : Court of the District Judge is the highest court of the district and is Presided over by a District Judge. Whereas the Sessions Court is the highest criminal court of the district which is presided over by a Sessions Judge.

12. According to the code of Criminal Procedure (1973) in every State there shall be criminal courts of .... classes.
    (a) two   (b) three
    (c) four   (d) five

Ans. *(c) four*

Explanation : According to the code of Criminal Procedure (19730 in every State there should be criminal courts of four classes.
(i) Courts of Sessions
(ii) Judicial Magistrates of the First Class and in any Metropolitan area Metropolitan Magistrates
(iii) Judicial Magistrates of the Second Class
(iv) Executive Magistrates

 Related Theory
Criminal Courts exercise Jurisdiction in cases related to Murder, Robbery, Theft, Assault, etc.

SUBJECTIVE Type Questions

Short Answer Type Questions
[**2** marks each]

13. What is the composition of a High Court?
Ans. The composition of High Court varies in different High Courts according to their workload. There is no fixed number of Judges for a High Court.

14. Who appoints the Chief Justice of a High Court?
Ans. The Chief Justice of the High Court is appointed by the President in consultation with the Chief Justice of the Supreme Court and the Governor of the State.

15. (A) Apart from being citizen of India, mention one qualification for the appointment as a Judge of a High Court.
    (B) What is the term of office of a Judge of High Court?

Ans. (A) He/she should have held a judicial office in a territory of India for at least ten years.
    (B) A Judge of a High Court continues in his office till he attains the age of 62 years.

16. Mention two types of subordinate courts in a district.
Ans. The two types of subordinate courts in a district are:
    (1) District Court   (2) Sessions Court

17. (A) Name the highest Civil Court in a District. **[ICSE 2016]**
    (B) Name the highest criminal court in a district. **[ICSE 2018, 13]**

Ans. (A)   Court of the District Judge.
    [Marking Scheme]

📝 **What Examiners Say**
→ *Most candidates answered the question correctly. Few however were confused with criminal or Sessions court.*

(B) Sessions Court/Court of Session Judge
[Marking Scheme]

What Examiners Say
→ Majority of the candidates were able to answer this question correctly. However, a few candidates, instead of writing Session Court mentioned either District Court or Civil Court.

18. State two point of distinction between a District and a Sessions. **[Mod. ICSE 2019, 14]**

Ans.

S. No.	District Judge	Session Judge
1	A district judge decides civil cases.	A session judge decides criminal cases.
2	A district Judge possesses administrative power in addition to his judicial power.	The sessions judge does not perform any administrative functions.

(1) Sessions Court- Criminal cases (robbery, dacoities and murder). Court of the District Judge- Civil Cases (Land and Property disputes and money transactions)

(2) District Judge presides over District Court and Sessions Judge presides over Session Courts.

(3) Sessions Judge has no administrative power but District Judge has.
[Any two]
[Mod. Marking Scheme]

What Examiners Say
→ Most of the candidates wrote the correct answer. However, a few candidates got confused and wrote the functions of a District Judge as that of a Sessions Judge and vice-versa.

19. What is meant by Lok Adalats?
[HOT] [ICSE 2018, 16]

Ans. Lok Adalat means People's court. 'Lok' stands for people and the word 'Adalat' means court. It is a legal forum for the friendly compromise of legal disputes among the contending parties.

People's Court **[Marking Scheme]**

What Examiners Say
→ Many candidates, instead of writing the meaning of Lok Adalat, explained its advantages.

20. Mention any two advantages of the Lok Adalat. **[Mod. ICSE 2020, 15]**

Ans.
Advantages of the Lok Adalat:
(1) Saves time/speedy justice/fast/quick.
(2) Saves money/inexpensive/cheap/economical/no court fee / the fee will be refunded if case is settled.
(3) Lessens the burdens on the other courts/reduces backlog.
(4) Works on a spirit of compromise/no ill feeling/decision is binding on both the parties.
(5) Can move application on a plain paper/can pass awards regarding those cases which are at pre litigation stage.
(6) Decisions are final and binding/No appeal in any court against decision / Promotes social justice or justice for weaker sections. **[Any two]**
[Marking Scheme]

What Examiners Say
→ This question was attempted well by most candidates.

21. Mention two reasons to state that the Lok Adalat has its own advantage.
[Mod. ICSE 2017]

Ans. The Lok Adalats has its own advantages as these adalats work with an essence of compromise and to finish the disputes and also, they are less expensive for common man.

(1) Speedy justice/ (Reduces Delay/ Save Time)
(2) Is affordable /(inexpensive, cheap, economical)
(3) Caters to the weaker sections of society
(4) No compromise/ (settle disputes through compromise, understanding)
(5) Reduces the workload of other courts.
(6) Awards passed by Lok Adalat are final and binding on the parties. / (No appeal) **[Any two]**
[Mod. Marking Scheme]

What Examiners Say
→ Most candidates could attempt this question correctly.

22. State two other qualification required to become a judge of the High Court, apart from Indian citizenship. [Mod. ICSE 2017]

Ans. The qualification required to become a Judge of a High Court are:

(1) He/she should not be over 62 years of age

(2) He/she should have held a judicial office in the territory of India for 10 years or more or should have been an advocate of a High Court for minimum 10 years.

> He should have held a judicial office for at least ten years.
>
> He must have been an advocate of a High Court for at least ten years.
>
> [Marking Scheme]

What Examiners say

➡ Most of the candidates wrote the correct answer although a few failed to mention the time period– 10 years and some mentioned the age as 62 years, which is not correct.

23. (A) Who administers the oath of office to the judges of the High Court?

(B) Mention the process of removal of a Judge of a High Court. [🔥HOT]

Ans. (A) The Governor of the State administer the oath of office to the judges of the High Court.

(B) A judge of a High Court can be removed from his/her office by the President on the recommendation of the Parliament.

24. What do you understand by the Subordinate Court?

Ans. The Subordinate courts are so called because of their subordination to the State High Court. They function under the High Court at district and lower levels.

25. Which body is the highest judicial authority in both civil as well as criminal matters at the district level?

Ans. The District Judge is the highest judicial authority in civil matters at the district level. As a Sessions Judge, he is the highest judicial authority in criminal matters at the district level.

26. Mention the different courts at the district level.

Ans. There are usually three types of courts at the district level:

(1) Civil Courts

(2) Session Courts

(3) Court of Revenue

27. Name the different types of civil courts in a district.

Ans. (1) Court of District Judge

(2) Court of Civil Judge

(3) Munsif Court

(4) Court of Small cases

Structured Questions

[3+3+4= **10** marks each]

28. The constitution of India provides for a High Court for each state. In this context, answer the following questions:

(A) State three qualification for appointment as Judge of the High Court.

(B) State any three functions of High Court.

(C) How are the Chief Justice and other Judge of the High Court appointed?

Ans. (A) According to the constitution, a person shall be qualified for appointment as a Judge of a High Court under the following conditions:

(1) He/she should be citizen of India.

(2) He/she should not be over 62 years of age.

(3) He has held a Judicial office in the territory of India for at least ten years.

or

He/she has been an advocate of High Court for at least ten years.

(B) The functions of High Court are:

(1) Settlement of disputes

(2) Enforcement of Fundamental Rights

(3) Power of superintendence over all courts and tribunals throughout the territories under its Jurisdiction.

(C) The Chief Justice of a High Court is appointed by the President of India in consultation with the Chief Justice of the Supreme Court and the Governor of the concerned state. Other Judges of a High Court are appointed by the President. The President shall consult the Chief Justice of India, the Governor of the State and the Chief Justice of the High Court in the matter of appointment of a Judge to the High Court.

29. Lok Adalat means 'People's Court'. In this context answer the following questions:

(A) What is the meaning of Lok Adalat and what is its scope?

Edu*art* ICSE History and Civics Class X

(B) State any three advantages of the Lok Adalat.

(C) Mention any four functions of Lok Adalat.

Ans. (A) Lok Adalats are the 'People's Court' which try and bring around settlement through negotiations and compromise. It is an alternative dispute/cases pending in the court of law or at pre-litigation stage are settled amicably.

The system of Lok Adalats has now become so popular that various government departments like the Telephone Department, Traffic and the Electricity Boards have begun to hold Lok Adalats solving hundreds of cases in a day.

(B) Advantages of Lok Adalats are as follows :

(1) Lok Adalats play important role in the settlement of family feuds, disputes between the neighbours and minor cases of assault and injury by settling the disputes through compromise. Since, the Lok Adalat work in the spirit of compromise and understanding, both the parties feel satisfied.

(2) Lok Adalats deliver fast and inexpensive justice. Any person can move Lok Adalat by an application on a plain paper or using the format available with Legal Service Authorities and expect speedy justice.

(3) The Lok Adalats reduce the workload of other courts enabling them to deal with more serious matters. This reduces delays in higher courts.

(4) Lok Adalats promote social justice by providing legal aid to weaker sections of society. **[Any three]**

(C) **Functions of the Lok Adalat are:**

(1) It is an alternative dispute redressal mechanism where disputes/ cases pending in the court of law or at pre-litigation stage are settled amicably.

(2) All decisions of the Lok Adalats are deemed to be decrees of a Civil court and should be binding on the Parties to the dispute.

(3) Main Condition of the Lok Adalat is that both parties in a dispute should agree for a settlement.

(4) Voluntary Organisations organise such courts in places like factories, forms, commercial complexes and neighbourhood of the litigants to settle disputes in a spirit of harmony and compromise.

(5) Cases are settled informally and cordially with the involvement of conflicting parties.

(6) Lok Adalats also resolve cases which have not yet gone to any Court.

[Any four]

30. India has a single integrated judicial system that is independent and Supreme. With reference to the Judiciary, answer the following:

(A) (a) Who appoints the Judges of the High Court?

(b) State any two qualifications required for a person to be appointed as a High Court Judge. **[ICSE 2019]**

(B) Why is the Judiciary kept independent of the control of the Executive and the Legislature? **[ICSE 2015]**

(C) Explain the Appellate Jurisdiction of High Court. **[ICSE 2017]**

Ans. (A) (a) The Judges of the High Court are appointed by the President of India in consultation with the Chief Justice of the Supreme Court, Chief Justice of the High Court and the Governor of the concerned State.

(b) The qualifications required for appointment as a High Court Judge are:

(1) He should be a citizen of India.

(2) He should have held a Judicial office for not less than 10 years in India or should be an advocate in High Court for minimum 10 years.

(3) He should not be over 62 years of age. **[Any two]**

(A) (a) President

(b) (1) One should be a citizen of India.

(2) One should have held a judicial office in India for at least 10 years.

(3) One should have been advocate of a High Court for at least 10 years.

(4) He should not be over 62 years of age. **[Any two]**

[Marking Scheme]

(B) In a democracy like India, the timely administration of justice is of paramount importance since, the fundamental rights of the citizens have to be protected from the Executive or Legislature's interference. This protection is ensured by having a Judiciary that is independent from the two organs of the government. An impartial and independent judiciary is a vital pre-requisite for ensuring non-violation of human rights and preserving the true spirit of democracy. Also, in a federal setup like India, there is a Constitutional division of powers between the Executive, Legislature and Judiciary.

(B) Judiciary's independence is essential for the functioning of a democratic constitution. An independent judiciary is said to be the first condition of liberty. The Supreme Court and the High Courts are the guardians of peoples' fundamental rights. The Supreme Court and the High Courts administer justice not only between citizen and citizen but also between State and a citizen.

[Marking Scheme]

(C) A High Court is primarily a Court of Appeal. It hears appeals against the judgements of the subordinate courts functioning in its territorial jurisdiction.

It has appellate jurisdiction in both civil and criminal matters.

Only those civil cases can be brought to the High Court which have been decided by the District Courts under the jurisdiction of that High Court. Such appeals can be in matters concerning land revenue and in cases where blatant injustice has been committed by a Tribunal. The High Court may squash the order of such a Tribunal.

While in criminal cases, appellate jurisdiction consists of appeals against the judgement of Sessions Court where sentence exceeds seven years, against the judgement of an Assistant Sessions Judge or Chief Metropolitan Magistrate or Judicial Magistrate where the sentence exceeds 4 years imprisonment, where the order of acquittal is passed by a Sessions Judge; a sentence of death must be confirmed by a High Court before execution can be carried out.

(C) **Appellate Jurisdiction:**
The High Court has the powers to accept appeals against the decisions of District Courts, in Civil as well as Criminal matters.

Civil Cases:
(1) In matter concerning land revenue
(2) In cases where blatant injunctions been committed by the Tribunal.

Criminal Cases:
(1) Against the judgement of a Session judge or an additional judge where the sentence of imprisonment exceeds 7 years.
(2) Against the judgement of an Assistant Session Judge, the Chief Metropolitan Magistrate, where the sentence of imprisonment exceeds 4 years.

[Marking Scheme]

What Examiners Say

→ (A) (a) Most of the candidates were able to answer this question correctly. However, a few candidates instead of the President mentioned the Governor.

  (b) A number of candidates gave the correct qualifications of a High Court Judge.

→ (B) Only a few candidates answered this question correctly. The question 'why' is the judiciary kept independent was interpreted as 'how' it is kept independent. Candidates wrote about judges, appointments, security of tenure and contempt of court, etc that was not required.

→ (C) Most candidates answered incorrectly as they failed to comprehend the meaning of Appellate Jurisdiction and the various cases that comes under it. A few confused it with the original jurisdiction.

⚠ Caution

→ (A) (i) Explain the Executive powers of the President clearly.

  (ii) Students should learn all major appointments, including the appointments of the judges of the supreme Court and High Courts are made by the President.

  (iii) Highlight the major qualifications required for the appointment of judges.

→ (B) Students should read the question carefully. Explain explicitly as to why the judiciary has been kept independent of the executive and legislature.

1 HISTORY

The First War of Independence, 1857

The spark of Mutiny started at Meerut on 26th February, 1857 and took a form of huge Revolt to achieve independence finally from British rule in India.

Chapter Topics

- Causes and Events of the First War of Independence/Revolt of 1857
- Consequences of the First War of Independence

TOPIC 1

CAUSES AND EVENTS OF THE FIRST WAR OF INDEPENDENCE/REVOLT OF 1857

In the year 1857, during the governor-generalship of Lord Canning, a Revolt occurred against the British which spread over a large part of India. Though, it started as a "Mutiny of the Indian Sepoys" in the Company's Army, but it soon turned into a large scale civilian uprising. Several factors were responsible for the uprising.

Example 1. What is Mutiny?

Ans. Mutiny is an act of a group of people (e.g. soldiers) refusing to obey the person who is in command.

Uprising of 1857

It was a massive rebellion against East India Company. It started at Barrackpore in Meerut, when most of the Indian soldiers refused to use the cartridges which were rumoured to have been greased with the fat of pig and cow.

As a result, a Brahmin soldier named Mangal Pandey, led an attack on the officer of the 34th native Infantry on 29th March, 1857. It ended Company's rule and beginning of the Crown's direct rule. Major figures like Mangal Pandey, Rani Laxmi Bai, Tantia Tope, Khan Bahadur Khan, Nana Sahib, Begum Hazart Mahal and Bahadur Shah, etc.

The major centres of Revolt were Meerut, Delhi, Lucknow, Bareilly, Jhansi and Gwalior. It was referred to as 'Mutiny' by the British and 'First War of Independence' by Veer Savarkar and Netaji Subhash Chandra Bose.

Causes of Revolt

Political Causes

(1) Lord Dalhousie's Policy of Annexation and Doctrine of lapse made British very unpopular.

(2) Refusal of pension to Nana Sahib, as he was the adopted son of Peshwa Baji Rao II.

(2) Discourtesy to the Mughal Emperor Bahadur Shah Zafar. In 1849, Lord Dalhousie announced that after Bahadur Shah, his successors would not be permitted to use the Red Fort as their palace. In 1856, Lord Canning announced that Bahadur Shah's successors would not be allowed to use the Imperial titles with their names.

(4) The annexation of Oudh was done on the theory that it was misruled by Nawab Wajid Ali Shah.

(5) Unpopular administration of British became highly unpopular, the British officials looked down upon the Indians.

(6) The British expended their territorial power in India and to safeguard their economic and political interest, they waged many wars against the Indian rulers of different states. e.g. The Battle of Buxar, Anglo–Mysore War, Anglo–Moratha War, Anglo–Sikh War, etc.

Example 2. What is Subsidiary Alliance?

Ans. Subsidiary Alliance was an agreement between the British East India Company and the Indian Princely States by virtue of which these states lost their sovereignty (the Power of a Ruler to rule independently without any interference) to the British.

Example 3. Which kingdom of India was the first to enter into Alliance and how?

Ans. The Kingdom of Awadh (Oudh) was the first to enter into an alliance through the Treaty of Allahabad in 1765.

Example 4. Which other states accepted Subsidiary Alliance besides Awadh?

Ans. The Other states which accepted the Subsidiary Alliance were the Nizam of Hyderabad, the ruler of Mysore, the Raja of Tanjore, the Sindhia and the Rajput States of Jodhpur, Jaipur, Macheri, Bundi and the ruler of Bharatpur.

Social and Religious Causes

(1) Taxing Religious Places hurt the sentiments of the Indians. Taxes were imposed on Temples and Mosques.

(2) The work of the Missionaries, who were spreading Education and Christianity, had upset the masses.

(3) The British Government's attempts to interfere in the social and religious life of the Indians led to wide spread of fear among the masses. The reforms like the Abolition of Sati (1829), the introduction of the Widow remarriage Act (1856) and the opening of western education to the girls were not welcomed by the masses.

(4) People were suspicious of introduction of modern innovations like railways and telegraph. They believed that British had introduced such practices to defy their caste and religion.

(5) The British were rude and arrogant towards the Indians. They believed that they were superior to Indians and followed a policy of contempt towards the Indians. Some European officers ill-treated and insulted Indians. Such acts alienated the British from the Indian masses.

(6) The Importance of traditional educational institutions like Madrasas and Gurukuls was reduced due to the establishment of the English Schools. Thus, Indians felt hurt.

Example 5. Name any two states that felt victim of the Doctrine of Lapse.

Ans. Jhansi and Nagpur are the two states that fell victim of the Doctrine of Lapse.

⚠ Caution

→ Doctrine of Lapse and subsidiary Alliance are two different policies of British East India Company they are not the same. Some children get confused between the two.

📣 Important

→ Rani Laxmibai and Nana Sahib were the two leaders who were the major victims, who lost their kingdoms because of 'Doctrine of Lapse' Policy.

Economic Causes

(1) The Resources from India were exploited for the benefit of the British people and growth of industries in Britain. Raw material was exported and finished goods were imported, which ruined the Indian industries and Handicrafts. It deprived the artisans of their income and reduced the avenues of employment for labour.

(2) Indian Handicrafts declined and Cottage Industries were shut down. Because machine-made British cloth was cheaper than Indian products. Heavy duties on Indian silk and cotton textiles in Britain destroyed the Indian Industries.

(3) Till the Battle of Plassey (1757) the European traders used to bring gold into India to buy Indian cotton and silk. However, after the conquest of Bengal, the British stopped getting gold into India. They began to purchase raw material for their Industries in England from the surplus revenues of Bengal and profits from duty-free inland-trade. They started plundering India's raw materials, resource and wealth and this was called 'Drain of Wealth'.

(4) People moved to cities to find employment, which was very difficult to get. Peasants were forced to pay tax in cash, which pushed them into the hands of the moneylenders, as tax was collected even during the famines.

(5) Tea, Cotton, Indigo, Jute and Opium were crops which the British wanted the Indians to grow for them. If the peasants planted something else besides these crops, then their crops were destroyed. The food shortage arose. People suffered through the ever-increasing and spreading famine. And India was made Agricultural Colony for their needs of crops.

(6) Because of the high taxes, famines, fewer job opportunities, etc. poverty was at its peak and this motivated the masses to join the revolt.

Military Causes

Several factors contributed to the change in the attitude of the Indian soldiers towards the company. These included the following:

(1) Ill-treatment to Indian soldiers was given by their British military authorities. They forbade the sepoys from bearing caste or sectarian marks, beard or turbans, they showed disregard for the sentiments of the sepoys. On top of that they were ill-fed, poorly paid and badly housed.

(2) According to the General Service Enlistment Act of 1856, the Indian soldiers could be sent overseas on duty. But the Indian soldiers dreaded the sea voyage and considered it against their customs. This led to a feeling of resentment among them.

(3) The Indian and the British soldiers were not treated equally. The salary of the Indian soldiers was too meagre to support their families, while the duties of both the British and the Indian soldiers were more or less similar.

(4) All higher positions in employment was reserved for the British. The Indian soldiers could only rise to the position of Subedar. The future of Indian soldiers was bleak without any chance of promotion.

(5) The number of British troops in India was never very large with the British in the British in the ratio as low as one in four thousand. This made it easier for the large number of Indian soldiers to take up arms against the British.

(6) Poor performance of British Troops in the First Afghan War (1838–1842), Punjab War (1845–49) and Crimean War (1853–56) revealed to the Indian soldiers that the British Army could be defeated by the determined Indian Army.

Immediate Cause (Introduction of the Enfield Rifle)

In 1856, the British authorities decided to replace the old fashioned musket by the new 'Enfield Rifle'. The loading process of the Enfield rifle involved bringing the cartridge to the mouth and biting off the top greased paper with the teeth. In January 1857, there was a rumour in the Bengal regiment that the greased cartridge had the fat of cow or pig. The Sepoys were now convinced that the introduction of greased cartridges was a deliberate move to defile Hindu and Muslim religions as the cow is sacred to Hindus and the pig is a taboo to the Muslims. So, both the Hindus and Muslim soldiers refused to use these Cartridges and staged an uprising when they were forced to use them.

Main Events Related to the Revolt of 1857

(1) On 29th March, 1857 Mangal Pandey, a sepoy led an attack on the Adjustment of the 34th Native

Infantry at Barrackpore, in protest of using Enfield Rifle.

(2) Trouble which started in Barrackpore, soon spread to Meerut where 85 sepoys disobeyed orders to use the new greased cartridges. They were stripped of their uniforms and awarded 10 years of imprisonment.

(3) These sepoys were freed by their colleagues. They killed the British soldiers, burnt their houses and marched to Delhi. They seized the city and proclaimed the Mughal Emperor Bahadur Shah Zafar as their Emperor of India.

(4) Loss of Delhi lowered the respect of the British Army, to this Sir John Nicholson, with the help of loyal Sikh soldiers, besieged Delhi. In the end, the British Army defeated Bahadur Shah Zafar's army and killed his sons. And exiled Bahadur Shah Zafar and his wife to Rangoon.

(5) Begum Hazrat Mahal, wife of Nawab of Awadh, led the uprising at Lucknow on 30th May, 1857. The city was recaptured by the British in March 1858. Begum Hazrat Mahal fled towards the Nepal Frontier.

(6) In Jhansi, rebellion as led by Rani Laxmibai, who brought against Sir Hugh Rose. After leaving Jhansi, she met Tantia Tope at Kalpi. She fought courageously, but died while fighting.

(7) In Kanpur, rebellion was led by Nana Sahib with his Commander Tantia Tope.

(8) There were uprisings in other parts of India as well. At Bareilly Khan Bahadur took Command of the Movement. By the end of 1858 all the rebellions had been completely controlled.

⚠ Caution
→ Students are not clear about the causes, they got confused by mixing the points of several causes in one single answer.

📢 Important
→ Students should study all four causes of the war of Independence carefully and they should make summary of the points under each cause separately to memorize easily.

TOPIC 2

CONSEQUENCES OF THE FIRST WAR OF INDEPENDENCE

The British tried to suppress the uprising of 1857, but it shook their foundation. It brought about far reaching effects on Indian socio – political life.

Consequences of the First War of Independence

(1) End of the Company's Rule in India

The most significant result of the Revolt of 1857 was that it brought the end of the rule of the East India Company in India. India came under the rule of Queen Victoria and the British Parliament. This was done by the Government of India Act of 1858.

Example 6. What was the importance of the Government of India Act of 1858?

Ans. This Act abolished the Board of Directors of the Company and the responsibility of the Government of India was passed on to a separate minister, who was known as the Secretary of State for India, who would be advised by a Council consisting of 15 members.

Example 7. Who was made Viceroy and what was his role in this Act?

Ans. The Governor General was made the Viceroy, who dealt with the Nawabs, the Rajas and other native Princes.

(2) Queen Victorias' Proclamation

The Queen's Proclamation regarding the transfer of governance from the East India Company to the British Crown was announced on 1st November, 1858 publicly at Allahabad by Lord Canning, the first Viceroy of India. The Proclamation promised the following:

(i) To follow a policy of non-intervention in social and religious matters of India.

(ii) To treat all Indian and Europeans subject equal (Education and ability would be the basis of all appointments).

(iii) It will do its best to advance the Industries in India.

(iv) It will grant a general pardon to all those who had taken part in the war except those who were found guilty of murder of British Subjects.

(v) To promote works of public utility in India so as to ensure the material as well as the moral progress of the people.

(3) Relations with Princely States

The policy of Annexation and the Doctrine of Lapse were abandoned.

(4) End of Mughals and Peshwas

With the death of Bahadur Shah Zafar, the Mughal Dynasty came to an end – Nana Sahib, the last Peshwa fled to Nepal after the failure of the uprising and with him the office of Peshwa also came to an end.

(5) Religious Freedom

After the Revolt of 1857, the British ruler declared their policy of non-interference in the religious affairs, customs and traditions of the Indians.

(6) Divide and Rule Policy

After 1858, The British continued to follow their 'Divide and Rule' Policy by turning the province against province, group against group, caste against caste and above all Hindus against Muslims. This policy of 'Divide and Rule' ultimately encouraged the partition of India.

(7) Change in the Army

(i) The whole army was reorganized. This was done to prevent the reoccurrence of another uprising. The strength of the European troops in India was increased. In Bengal Army the ratio was 1 : 2 and in Madras and Bombay Armies the ratio was 2 : 5.

(ii) Artillery and other effective weapons of war were exclusively under the charge of the Europeans.

(iii) Discrimination on the basis of caste, region and religion was practiced in the recruitment of the army.

(iv) Newspapers, Journals and Nationalist Publications were not provided to the soldiers to keep the Indian Army separated from the life of the rest of the population.

(8) Economic Exploitation

The era of territorial expansion ended with the uprising of 1857, and the economic exploitation began in the following manner:

(i) India was turned into a typical colonial economy. When raw material was exported and finished goods were imported.

(ii) The salary and allowances of the members of the Indian Council and Secretary of State, The Civil Servants and the Military Officers were a large drain on the country's resources.

(iii) Rural Artisan Industries such as handicrafts, spinning and weaving collapsed.

(iv) The Indians had to pay heavy interests and dividends on the British capital invested in India like railways, coalmines, plantations, shipping, jute mills, etc.

Rise of Nationalism

The uprising of 1857 was the first struggle of Indians for the freedom from British Imperialism. It raised national feelings and paved the way for the rise of National Movement. The sacrifices made by Rani Laxmi Bai, Nana Sahib and Mangal Pandey served as a source of inspiration for the future freedom fighters and also became a symbol of challenge for the Indians.

Drawbacks of the First War of Independence

The following were the drawbacks of the Revolt of 1857:

(1) The Indians had no common specific goal before it except for the anti-foreign sentiments like Rani Laxmi Bai fought for Doctrine of Lapse, Nana Sahib fought for pension, Nawab of Awadh for Subsidiary Alliance, etc.

(2) The Revolts were not planned and co-ordinated. It lacked in planning, organization and leadership.

(3) The British Empire had for superior resources in terms of men, money, latest guns and ammunition to finance their efforts, while the Indians did not have enough guns and hardly some money to finance themselves.

(4) The British Army had experienced services of their Military Generals like Lawrence Nicholson, Havelock, Outram and Campbell, etc. Even though the Indian leaders were brave, but very few were expert in Military Planning.

(5) Some of the rulers of the Indian states and big zamindars refused to join the movement.

(6) There was lack of spirit of nationalism. Some Sections of the Indian society were hostile to the uprising. Some big merchants, moneylenders and zamindars were loyal to the British.

(7) The uprising was supposed to begin on May 31, 1857. But it began much before the fixed date, due to the incident of grease cartridges. So, the whole plan remained disorganised.

(8) Main centres of revolt were Delhi, Jhansi, Agra, Lucknow, Kanpur centres were far from each other so there was a communication gap between each other.

(9) Rebels were weaker than British Army in weapons and finance.

⚠ Caution

➥ When immediate cause of the Great Revolt is asked, few students wrote the immediate cause of the First World War instead of the Great Revolt of 1857.

➥ Students should perticular while answering the questions

ℹ ICSE Suggestions

➥ The policy of Expansion, Doctrine of Lapse, Subsidiary Alliance should be studied separately because All Policies of annexation were counted as one point by the students.

Glossary

(1) **The First War of Independence:** It was fought in 1857 against the British Government. Its main aim was to push the Britishers out of India.

(2) **Doctrine of Lapse:** According to the Doctrine of Lappse, if an Indian ruler died without a male heir, his kingdom would 'lapse', that is, it would come under the company's territory in India.

(3) **Drain of Wealth:** The transfer of wealth from India to England for which India got no proportionate economic return, is called the 'Drain of wealth'.

(4) **General Service Enlistment Act:** The British passed the General Service Enlistment Act in 1856. As per this Act, Indian soldiers could be sent overseas on duty but according to traditional belief, it was a taboo for a brahmin to cross the seas. The Brahmin soldiers saw in this a danger of their caste.

Who's Who?

(1) **Lord Wellesley:** Introduced the Doctrine of Subsidiary Alliance.
(2) **Lord Dalhousie:** He was the Governor – General of India, he annexed many Indian states to the Company using the Doctrine of Lapse.
(3) **Zeenat Mahal:** She was the wife of Bahadur Shah Zafar.
(4) **Baji Rao II:** The last Peshwa; he was Nana Sahib's father. (who adopted Nana Sahib as his son).
(5) **Lord Canning:** In 1856, he announced that after the death of Bahadur Shah, his successors would not be allowed to use the imperial titles with their names and would be known as mere Princes.
(6) **Sir John Nicholson:** He surrounded and captured Delhi back for the East India Company.
(7) **Begum Hazrat Mahal:** She was the wife of the Nawab of Awadh "Wajid Ali Shah".
(8) **Sir Hugh Rose:** He laid siege to the fortress of Jhansi in March 1858 against Rani Laxmi Bai.
(9) **Khan Bahadur:** A descendent of the former ruler of Rohikhand.
(10) **Kunwar Singh:** He was the zamindar of Jagdishpur, Bihar.
(11) **Maulvi Ahmadullah:** He took the leadership at Faizabad and answered the Muslim Community against the British rule.
(12) **Empress of India:** In 1876, Queen Victoria assumed the title of the "Empress of India".
(13) **Vinayak Damodar Savarkar:** He was also known as Veer Savarkar, He was an Indian politician, activist and writer. He wrote a book called "The Indian War of Independence".

Chronology

1757: Battle of Plassey
1764: The Battle of Buxar
1765: Treaty of Allahabad
1767 to 1799: Anglo–Mysore Wars
1817 to 1818: Third Anglo–Maratha War
1829: Abolition of Sati System
1838 – 1842: First Afghan War
1845 – 1849: The Punjab Wars
1853 – 1856: The Crimean War
1856: Awadh was annexed
1856: Widow Remarriage Act
1856: General Service Enlistment Act
February 26, 1857: Unrest among the soldiers at Berhampur, Bengal against greased Cartridges.
February 29, 1857: Resentment by Mangal Pandey at Barrackpore.
May 9, 1857: Resentment by 85 sepoys of the Third Cavalry at Meerut.

May 10, 1857: The Sepoys at Meerut out openly against the British and headed towards Delhi.
May 30, 1857: Uprisng at Lucknow by Hazrat Mahal (wife of Nawab of Awadh)
June, 1857: Battle began at Jhansi.
June 17, 1858: Rani Laxmi Bai died at Gwalior.
April 18, 1859: Tantia Tope was hanged.
November 1, 1858: Queen Victorias Proclamation was read by Lord Canning, the first Viceroy of India.
1876: Queen Victoria assumed the title of "Empress of India".

OBJECTIVE Type Questions

Multiple Choice Questions-I

[1 mark each]

1. The General Service Enlistment Act implied that soldiers:
   (a) would not be given promotions.
   (b) would have to travel overseas to fight.
   (c) would be given less salaries.
   (d) would not be given extra allowance

   [ICSE Specimen Paper Sem-1, 2021]

   Ans. (b) would have to travel overseas to fight.

   Explanation: The General Service Enlistment Act was passed by the British Parliament in 1856. It required every Indian soldier to go overseas for deployment if required. The Act was brought just before the Anglo-Persian War.

2. Which of the following states was the first to be annexed by the Doctrine of Lapse?
   (a) Nagpur   (b) Satara
   (c) Jhansi   (d) Udaipur   [HOT]

   Ans. (b) Satara

   Explanation: The Doctrine of Lapse was an annexation policy introduced by Lord Dalhousie. According to this Doctrine, if an Indian ruler died without a male heir his kingdom would lapse, i.e. it would come under company's territory in India. The first State annexed by Lord Dalhousie by Doctrine of Lapse was Satara. The other prominent states which were annexed by applying this doctrine were Jaitpur, Jhansi, Sambalpur, Udaipur and Nagpur.

   ⚠ **Caution**
   → Read the question carefully first state annexed by Doctrine of lapse is asked not the first stated annexed by Subsidiary Alliance.

3. Who was the author of the book 'The Indian War of Independence'?
   (a) Gopal Krishna Gokhale
   (b) Bal Gangadhar Tilak
   (c) Rabindranath Tagore
   (d) Veer Savarkar   [HOT]

   Ans. (d) Veer Savarkar

   Explanation: The Indian War of Independence is an Indian national history of the revolt of 1857 which was written by Vinayak Damodar Savarkar, also known as Veer Savarkar and was first published in 1909.

4. In 1857, the Hindu and Muslim soldiers refused to use the new cartridges because:
   (a) they were greased with cow and pig fat
   (b) they were paid less salaries.
   (c) they were forced to go abroad on duty.
   (d) they were ill fed.

   Ans. (a) They were greased with cow and pig fat.

   Explanation: In 1856, the Brithish authorities decided to replace the old fashioned musket, called the 'Brown Bess', by the new Enfield Rifle. The loading process of the Enfield Rifle involved bringing the cartridge to the mouth and biting of the top greased paper with the teeth. It was believed that the greased cartridge had the fat of cow and pig.

5. .... was denied pension under the Doctrine of Lapse.
   (a) Zeenat Mahal
   (b) Baji Rao II
   (c) Bahadhur Shah Zafar
   (d) Nana Sahib

   [ICSE Specimen Paper Sem-1, 2021]

   Ans. (d) Nana Sahib

   Explanation: Nana Sahib was the adopted son of Baji Rao II, the last Peshwa. The British refused to grant Nana Sahib pension they were paying to Baji Rao. Nana Sahib was forced to live at Kanpur far away from his family seat at Poona.

   💡 **Related Theory**
   → Nana Sahib was the adopted son of Baji Rao II, the last Peshwa.

6. Begum Hazrat Mahal, led the uprising at ....

The First War of Independence, 1857

(a) Kanpur (b) Lucknow
(c) Meerut (d) Jhansi

Ans. *(b) Lucknow*

Explanation: Begum Hazrat Mahal, the wife of the Nawab of Awadh led the uprising at Lucknow on 30th May, 1857.

⚠️ **Caution**
↪ Don't be confused with this name of Zeenat Mahal (wife of Bahadhur Shah Zafar).

7. Bahadur Shah II was deported to ....
   (a) Nepal (b) Malaysia
   (c) Yangon (d) Singapore

Ans. *(c) Yangon*

Explanation: Bahadur Shah II was found guilty of aiding the revolutionary movement. As a punishment, he was sentenced to life imprisonment and deported to Yangon in Myanmar, where he died in 1862.

8. Which statement does not apply to the Subsidiary Alliance?
   (a) The kings virtually lost their powers.
   (b) It was introduced by Lord Dalhousie.
   (c) The kings had to maintain the British army at their cost.
   (d) They had a British resident in their Court.
   [ICSE Specimen Paper Sem-1, 2021, 19]

Ans. *(b) It was introduced by Lord Dalhousie.*

Explanation: Subsidiary Alliance was introduced by Lord Wellesley. Subsidiary Alliance was an agreement between the British East India Company and the Indian Princely States by virtue of which these states lost their sovereignty to the British. Under this system, the Indian rulers, who agreed to the Subsidiary Alliance:
(1) Accepted the British as the Supreme Power;
(2) Surrendered their foreign relations to the East India Company and agreed that they would not enter into any alliance with any other power and would not wage any wars;
(3) Accepted a British Resident at their headquarters and agreed not to employ any European in their services without consulting the company;
(4) Agreed to maintain British troops at their own cost;
(5) Virtually lost their Independence.

⚠️ **Caution**
↪ Some students have marked (b) Statement Correct. Because they are confused between Lord Dalhousie and Lord Wellesley. Infact (b) statement is wrong. Because Subsidiary Alliance was introduced by Lord Wellesley not Lord Dalhousie. So read the question properly.

9. Which was the correct allegation put on Awadh for being annexed by the Britishers?
   (a) Because the Nawab of Awadh refused to pay taxes.
   (b) Because the Nawab had insulted British Officers.
   (c) Because it rebelled against the company.
   (d) Because it was misruled.

Ans. *(d) Because it was misruled.*

Explanation: The Nawab of Awadh Wajid Ali Shah was very loyal to the British. But Lord Dalhousie annexed Awadh to the British territory under the pretext that the State of Awadh was not properly governed by the Nawab and he was removed on this basis.

💡 **Related Theory**
↪ Lord Dalhousie justified the annexation of Awadh on the pretext of "the good of the governed". On the countrary the people of Awadh, had to face more hardship.

10. Which was the State that was not annexed on the basis of Doctrine of Lapse Policy?
    (a) Nagpur (b) Raipur
    (c) Sambalpur (d) Udaipur [HOT]

Ans. *(b) Raipur*

Explanation: Raipur was not annexed by applying Doctrine of Lapse Policy. Whereas Nagpur, Sambalpur and Udaipur were annexed on the policy of Doctrine of Lapse.

11. Who led the rebels at Bareilly during the revolt of 1857?
    (a) Nana Sahib
    (b) Khan Bahadur Khan
    (c) Kunwar Singh
    (d) Tantia Tope

Ans. *(b) Khan Bahadur Khan*

Explanation: At Bareilly, Khan Bahadur Khan, a descendent of the former ruler of Rohilkhand, took command of the Movement.

12. Choose the correct option to match the following:

	Column I	Column II
(A)	Abolition of Sati System	(i) 1856
(B)	Ruler of Jhansi died	(ii) 1764
(C)	Widow Remarriage Act	(iii) 1829
(D)	The Battle of Buxar	(iv) 1853

Options:
(a) (A) – (ii); (B) – (iii); (C) – (i); (D) – (iv)
(b) (A) – (iii); (B) – (iv); (C) – (i); (D) – (ii)
(c) (A) – (iv); (B) – (ii); (C) – (i); (D) – (iii)
(d) (A) – (i); (B) – (iii); (C) – (iv); (D) – (ii)

Ans. (b) (A) – (iii); (B) – (iv); (C) – (i); (D) – (ii)

Explanation: Sati System was stopped by British in 1829.

The Ruler of Jhansi (Rani Laxmi Bai's husband) died in 1853. The Widow Remarriage Act started in 1856 and the Battle of Buxar was fought in 1764.

13. Arrange the following wars in Chronological order.
(A) Anglo – Mysore War
(B) Battle of Buxar
(C) Anglo – Maratha War
(D) Battle of Plassey

Options:
(a) (A), (C), (B), (D)
(b) (D), (B), (A), (C)
(c) (D), (B), (C), (A)
(d) (B), (D), (C), (A)

Ans. (b) (D), (B), (A), (C)

Explanation: Battle of Plassey – 1757
Battle of Buxar – 1764
Anglo – Mysore War – 1767 to 1799
Anglo – Maratha War – 1817 to 1818

 Caution
→ Learn the dates carefully, most of the students have not answered this chronological order correct because they are not familiar with dates and events also.

14. Choose the correct option to match the following:

Column I	Column II
(A) Queen Victorias' Proclamation	(i) 1852
(B) Inam commission	(ii) 1876
(C) "Empress of India"	(iii) 1757
(D) Battle of Plassey	(iv) 1858

Options:
(a) (A) – (iv); (B) – (i); (C) – (ii); (D) – (iii)
(b) (A) – (iii); (B) – (ii); (C) – (iv); (D) – (i)
(c) (A) – (iii); (B) – (ii); (C) – (i); (D) – (iv)
(d) (A) – (i); (B) – (iii); (C) – (iv); (D) – (ii)

Ans. (a) (A) – (iv); (B) – (i); (C) – (ii); (D) – (iii)

Explanation: Queen Victorias' Proclamation was read by Lord Canning on 1st November, 1858 at Allahabad. Inam Commission was a provision set up in 1852. Queen Victoria assumed the title of "Empress of India" in 1876. The Battle of Plassey was fought in 1757.

15. Which is the incorrect information about Mangal Pandey?
(a) Mangal Pandey was a Brahmin Sepoy.
(b) On 29th March, 1857 he led an attack on the Adjutant of the 19th Native Infantry at Bengal.
(c) He refused to use the grease Cartridge.
(d) Mangal Pandey was executed after Court – Martial.

Ans. (b) On 29th March, 1857 he led an attack on the Adjutant of the 19th Native Infantry at Bengal.

Explanation: Mangal Pandey led an attack on the Adjutant of the 34th Native Infantry at Barrackpore on 29th March, 1857.

 Related Theory
→ A commemorative postage stamp of Mangal Pandey on it was issued by the Indian Government in 1984.

16. Which was not the promise made by Queen Victoria in her Proclamation?
(a) Treat all Indian and European Subjects equal.
(b) Follow a policy of non-intervention in social and religious matters of Indians.
(c) To return back whole wealth to India.
(d) To grant a general pardon to all those who had taken part in the war except who were found guilty to murder British Subjects.

Ans. (c) To return back whole wealth to India.

Explanation: The Queen made all three promises (a), (b) & (d) except (c) to return back whole wealth to India. The Britishers plundered India's raw material, resources and wealth to England by Drain of Wealth. The drain included the salaries, incomes and savings of Englishmen, purchase of military goods, etc.

17. In context of the Revolt of 1857, Mangal Pandey belonged to which Bengal Native Infantry?
(a) 32
(b) 34
(c) 36
(d) 38

Ans. (b) 34

Explanation: The first Martyr of the Revolt of 1857, Mangal Pandey belonged to an Indian Sepoy of 34 Bengal Native Infantry Unit. He refused to use the Grease Cartridges and single-handedly attacked and killed British

The First War of Independence, 1857

Officers on Parade at Barrackpore. Later, he was arrested and hanged on 8th April, 1857 at Barrackpore. The regiment to which he belonged was disbanded and sepoys guilty of rebellion punished.

18. Choose the correct option to match the following:

Column I	Column II
(A) Poverty and Famines	(i) Socio – Religious Cause
(B) Low Salaries	(ii) Political Cause
(C) Taxing Religious Places	(iii) Economic Cause
(D) Disrespect shown to Bahadur Shah	(iv) Military cause

Options:
(a) (A) – (ii); (B) – (i); (C) – (iii); (D) – (iv)
(b) (A) – (iv); (B) – (iii); (C) – (ii); (D) – (i)
(c) (A) – (i); (B) – (ii); (C) – (i); (D) – (iii)
(d) (A) – (iii); (B) – (iv); (C) – (i); (D) – (ii)

Ans. (d) (A) – (iii); (B) – (iv); (C) – (i); (D) – (ii)

Explanation: Poverty and Famines falls under Economic Cause. Low Salaries given to the Sepoy is related to the Military Cause. The British taxing the religious place was a Socio–Religious Cause and disrespect shown to Bahadur Shah was a Political cause of the uprising of 1857.

Multiple Choice Questions-II
(Other Question Types, for Extra Practice)

[**4** marks each]

Read the passages given below and answer the questions that follow:

19. India's First War of Independence, better known as the Indian Rebellion 1857, began on May 10th in the year 1857. The First Martyr of the Revolt was Mangal Pandey and the War was the result of accumulation of many factors over time. The Rebellion of 1857 is considered the first blow that came to shatter the British rule in India. Some epicenters of the revolt were Kanpur, Lucknow, Aligarh, Agra, Delhi, and Jhansi. Due to all the epicenters being far from each other, there was a communication gap between the leaders of different parts of India. Due to the rebellion having no Central leadership, it got limited to some parts of India only. Rebels did not have enough weapons and finance whereas British people had advanced weapons and enough finance.

(A) Identify the immediate cause of the above revolt.
(a) The General Service Enlistment Act.
(b) The inhuman treatment of Indigo Cultivators.
(c) The Subsidiary Alliance.
(d) The incident of Greased Cartridges.

(B) Which Policy of expansion led to the Annexation of Awadh?
(a) Subsidiary Alliance
(b) Doctrine of Lapse
(c) Pretext of Alleged Misrule
(d) Outright Wars

(C) Which of these is a Socio-Religious Cause of the revolt?
(a) Taxing religious places
(b) Decay of Cottage Industries
(c) Drain of Wealth
(d) Exploitation of economic resources

(D) The British showed total disregard towards the soldiers. In this context, which of the following statements is not True?
(a) They were deprived of allowances.
(b) They were forced to go overseas on duty.
(c) They were given the same salaries as that of the British soldiers.
(d) The chances of promotion were very bleak. [ICSE Sem-1, 2021]

Ans. (A) *(d) The incident of Greased Cartridges.*

Explanation: In January 1857, there was a rumour in the Bengal Regiment that the Greased Cartridges had the fat of cow or pig. So, both the Hindu and Muslims refused to use these Cartridges and staged an uprising when they were forced to use them.

(B) *(a) Subsidiary Alliance*

Explanation: The kingdom of Awadh was the first to enter into Subsidiary Alliance Policy. Awadh was annexed on the basis of Misrule in 1856.

(C) *(a) Taxing religious places*

Explanation: Only Taxing religious places is a socio-religious cause rest all are economic causes.

(D) *(c) They were given the same salaries as that of the British soldiers.*

Explanation: The British soldiers received more than eight times the salary of the Indian soldiers.

20. By June 27, 1857 the First War of Independence had spread to Cawnpore (Kanpur, as it is known today). Cawnpore was an important garrison town for the East India Company forces. It was ideally located on the Grand Trunk Road. Initially, the sepoys at Cawnpore were not a part of the war. The British General at Cawnpore, at that time, was Hugh Wheeler.

He knew the local language, had adopted local customs, and to top it all was married to an Indian woman. So confident was he that his sepoys would not join the fight, he despatched two British companies to besieged Lucknow.

The British in Cawnpore numbered 900, including military men, women and children, merchants, business people, salesmen and engineers. The war was coming closer, and although there was no trouble in Cawnpore, the European families were afraid. They began to shift into the entrenchment (a military position fortified by trenches). The Indian sepoys were asked to collect their pay one by one, to avoid an armed mob.

The sepoys on their part felt threatened by the fortifications and the prepared artillery guns. There was a minor skirmish when a Lieutenant fired on his Indian guard when drunk, and was jailed for a night. The next day, however, he was released. There were also rumours that the Indian troops had been summoned to a parade, where they were to be massacred. The sepoys joined the war against the East India Company on June 5.

The besieged Company forces and the civilians were not prepared for such a long siege. After almost three weeks, they surrendered to Nana Sahib, in return for a safe passage to Allahabad. Nana Sahib was the adopted heir to Baji Rao II, the ex-Peshwa of the Maratha Confederacy.

—*The Hindu*

(A) From where did the revolt of 1857 start?
 (a) Delhi (b) Lucknow
 (c) Meerut (d) Jhansi

(B) During the First War of Independence in 1857, who led the rebels at Lucknow?
 (a) Nawab of Awadh
 (b) Rani Laxmi Bai
 (c) Begum Hazrat Mahal
 (d) Nana Sahib

(C) Which were the results of the revolt of 1857?
 (I) The rule of East India Company came to an end in India.
 (II) The British rule discontinued the use of Enfield Rifle.
 (III) The annexed Princely states were returned by the British.
 (IV) End of Mughal rule.
 (a) (I) and (II) (b) (I), (II) and (III)
 (c) (I), (III) and (IV) (d) (I) and (IV)

(D) Which of the following was not a cause of revolt of 1857?
 (a) Respect shown to Bahadur Shah
 (b) Absentee sovereignty of the British
 (c) Interference with social customs
 (d) Introduction of Enfield Rifle

Ans. (A) (c) Meerut

Explanation: The Revolt of 1857 started on 10 May 1857 at Meerut, as a mutiny of sepoys of the British East India Company's army. It is also called the First War of Independence.

(B) (c) Begum Hazrat Mahal

Explanation: Begum Hazarat Mahal, the wife of the Nawab of Awadh led the uprising at Lucknow on 30 May 1857.

(C) (c) (I), (III) and (IV)

Explanation: The most significant result of the uprising of 1857 was the end of the rule of East India Company and the assumption of the Government of India directly by the Crown. This was done by the Government of India Act of 1858.

The revolt of 1857 also brought an end to Mughal rule in India. With the death of Bahadur Shah II, who was deported to Yangon, the Mughal dynasty came to an end.

(D) (a) Respect shown to Bahadur Shah

Explanation: The British never showed any respect to Bahadur Shah-II. It was disrespect shown to him, which was one of the causes of revolt of 1857.

21. The Revolt of 1857 was a prolonged period of armed uprising as well as rebellions in Northern and Central India against British occupation of that part of the subcontinent. Small precursors of brewing discontent involving incidences of arson in cantonment areas began to manifest themselves in January. Later, a large-scale rebellion broke out in May and turned into what may be called a full-fledged war in the affected region. This war brought about the end of the British East India Company's rule in India, and led to the direct rule by the British Government (British Raj) of much of the Indian Subcontinent for the next 90 years.

(A) Who among the following led the rebels during the revolt at Cawnpore?
 (a) Nana Sahib
 (b) Peshwa Bajirao II
 (c) Begum Hazrat Mahal
 (d) Khan Bahadur Khan

(B) Whom did the rebel sepoys proclaimed the Emperor of India?
 (a) Bahadur Shah I
 (b) Bhadur Shah II
 (c) Nawab of Awadh
 (d) Nana Sahib

The First War of Independence, 1857

(C) Which Governor General introduced the Doctrine of Lapse?
  (a) Lord Dalhousie
  (b) Lord Curzon
  (c) Lord Mountabatteb
  (d) Lord Minto

(D) Which sepoy of 34th Native Infantry at Barrackpore led an attack on the Adjutant?
  (a) Bhagat Singh
  (b) Mangal Pandey
  (c) Tantia Tope
  (d) Kunwar Singh

Ans. (A) *(a) Nana Sahib*
Explanation: Siege of Cawnpore happened between 5-25 June, 1857. The rebels besieged the company forces and civilians in Cawnpore (Kanpur). The British needed to surrender to the rebels for a safe passage to Allahabad but their evacuation turned into a massacre, resulting into death of around 120 Britishers. The British forces from Allahabad recaptured Kanpur and then engaged into widespread retaliation with rebel soldiers and civilians. The leader in Siege of Cawnpore was Nana Sahib, adopted son of Peshwa Baji Rao II.

(B) *(b) Bahadur Shah II*
Explanation: 85 sepoys of the Native Infantry were sentenced to 10 years of rigorous imprisonment. The next day all the sepoys at Meerut rushed to the jail and set free their comrades and other convicts and reached Delhi next morning. They were joined by the local infantry. They seized the city and proclaimed the aged Mughal Emperor Bahadur Shah II the emperor of India.

(C) *(a) Lord Dalhousie*
Explanation: Lord Dalhousie introduced the Doctrine of Lapse.

(D) *(a) Mangal Pandey*
Explanation: The sepoys feared loss of their caste and religion if they accepted the Greased Cartridges of the Enfield Cartridges. As a result, Mangal Pandey, a sepoy, led an attack on the Adjutant of the 34th Native Infantry at Barrackpore on March 29, 1857.

22. As regards to the revolt of 1857, answer the following questions:

(A) Who introduced the Subsidiary Alliance System in India?
  (a) Lord Canning   (b) Lord Dalhousie
  (c) Lord Wellesely (d) Lord Curzon

(B) Who among the following led the rebels during the "Siege of Cawnpore"?
  (a) Nana Sahib
  (b) Peshwa Bajirao II
  (c) Begum Hazrat Mahal
  (d) Khan Bahadur Khan

(C) Arrange the following states chronologically as per their annexation by the Doctrine of Lapse?
  (I) Satara
  (II) Udaipur
  (III) Nagpur
  (IV) Sambalpur
  Choose the correct option from the codes given below:
  (a) (I), (II), (III), (IV)
  (b) (I), (IV), (II), (III)
  (c) (II), (I), (IV), (III)
  (d) (I), (III), (IV), (II)

(D) Identify the Socio-Religious Cause of Revolt of 1857:
  (a) Corruption in Administration
  (b) Drain of Wealth
  (c) Absentee Sovereignty of the British
  (d) Introduction of Enfield Rifle.

Ans. (A) *(c) Lord Wellesely*
Explanation: Some Indian States were brought under the British Control without actually annexing them. This was done by following the Subsidiary Alliance, introduced by Lord Wellesley.

(B) *(a) Nana Sahib*
Explanation: The leader in siege of Cawnpore was Nana Sahib, adopted son of Baji Rao II.

(C) *(b) (i), (iv), (ii), (iii)*
Explanation: Chronological order of the states as per their annexation by Doctrine of Lapse– Satara (1848), Sambalpur (1849), Udaipur (1852), Nagpur (1854).

(D) *(a) Corruption in Administration*
Explanation: There was corruption in Administration because the Police and Petty officials were corrupt During those days, the rich got away with the crime but the common man was looted, oppressed and tortured.

23. With regard to First War of Independence, answer the following questions:

(A) Which of the following states was the first to be annexed by the Doctrine of Lapse?
  (a) Nagpur   (b) Satara
  (c) Jhansi   (d) Udaipur

(B) Who introduced the Subsidiary Alliance System in India?
   (a) Lord Canning   (b) Lord Dalhousie
   (c) Lord Wellesely (d) Lord Curzon
(C) Which Governor General introduced the General Service Enlistment Act, 1856?
   (a) Lord Canning   (b) Lord Dalhousie
   (c) Lord Curzon   (d) Lord Rippon
(D) .... led the uprising at Lucknow.
   (a) Hazrat Mahal
   (b) Nana Sahib
   (c) Khan Bahadur Khan
   (d) Kunwar Singh

Ans. (A) *(b) Satara*

Explanation: The first state annexed by Lord Dalhousie by Doctrine of Lapse was Satara.

(B) *(c) Lord Wellesely*

Explanation: Some Indian States were brought under the British Control without actually annexing them. This was done by following the Subsidiary Alliance, introduced by Lord Wellesley.

(C) *(a) Lord Canning*

Explanation: Lord Canning introduced the General Service Enlistment Act, 1856 which required every Indian soldier to go overseas for deployment if required. It was one of the main causes of the uprising of 1857, as it was a taboo for Brahmins in those days to cross the sea.

(D) *(a) Hazrat Mahal*

Explanation: Begum Hazrat Mahal, the wife of Nawab of Awadh led the uprising at Lucknow on 30th May, 1857. The city was recaptured by the British in March 1858. Begum Hazrat Mahal fled towards the Nepal Frontier.

SUBJECTIVE Type Questions

Short Answer Type Questions

[2 marks each]

24. What was the General Service Enlistment Act?

[HOT] [ICSE 2019, 13]

Ans. The General Service Enlistment Act was intorduced by Charles Canning in 1856. it mandated all soldiers of the Indian Army to go overseas, if required.

> (1) Passed in 1856.
> (2) According to this act, the Indian soldier in the East India Company could be sent overseas on duty.
> (3) It was a taboo for Indian soldiers, especially the Brahmins to go overseas.
> (4) To go overseas went against their religious sentiments.
>
> [Marking Scheme]

What Examiners Say

→ Majority of the candidates answered the question correctly. A few candidates mentioned other acts also passed by the British.

⚠ Caution

→ Topic of General Service Enlistment Act should be understood clearly by the student along with its consequences and the reaction of the Indian soldiers to it.

25. Why did the Doctrine of Lapse become a political cause for the Revolt of 1857?

Ans. The Prominent states who become the victims to the Doctrine of Lapse were Jhansi, Sambalpur, Satara, Nagpur, Udaipur and Jaitpur. According to the Doctrine of Lapse, if king died and he did not have male heir, so his kindgom would be lapsed even if he adoped a son. His kingdom would be Company's Territory.

 Related Theory

→ Noted historian S.N. sen believes that the uprising of 1857 was a war of independence.

26. Mention any two causes of the failure of the Revolt of 1857.

Ans. The two Causes were:
   (1) There was lack of planning and co-ordination among the rebels.
   (2) The resources of the British were superior to those of revolutionaries.

27. What is meant by the Doctrine of Lapse?

Ans. According to the Doctrine of Lapse, if ruler died without any heir to succeed him, his adopted son could neither inherit the throne, nor the title, and in such cases, the state was to be annexed to the British Empire.

28. What impact did the uprising of 1857 have on the Mughal rule? [ICSE 2016]

Ans. After the rebellion of 1857 was unsuccessful the Mughal rulers were demid of using royal titles with their names. Bahadur Shah Zafar was deported to Rangoon and Mughal rule officially came to an end.

> Ended the rule of Mughals and the end of their titles viz Emperor.
>
> [Marking Scheme]

What Examiners Say
→ A majority of candidates answered correctly. A few committed errors like disrespect shown to Bahadur thah or end of Company's rule in India.

Caution
→ Students should read the question carefully during the allotted reading time and answer accordingly.

29. What was Nana Sahib's grievance against the British? **[HOT♨]**

Ans. The pension of ₹ 8 lakhs due to Nana Sahib was rejected by the Governor General on the grounds that he was merely the adopted son of Peshwa Baji Rao II. The British did not recognise him as the ruler of Marathas and he was forced to live far away from Peshwa's Headquarters at Poona.

Structured Questions
[3+3+4= **10** marks each]

30. With reference to the First World War, answer the following questions:

(A) Mention three administrative changes that the British Government brought about regarding the East India Company's rule in India.

(B) Give three causes for the resentment of the Sepoys against the British.

(C) State any four political causes responsible for the First War of Independence.

[ICSE 2014]

Ans. (A) The administrative changes brought about by the British Government regarding the East India's company rule in India were:

(1) The British Parliament passed an "Act for the Better Government of India", whereby the responsibility of Indian administration was passed into the hands of the British Queen and her Parliament. With this, the company rule came to an end.

(2) The Board of Control was abolished and the Board of Directors had no powers left.

(3) A Secretary of State for India was to take the place of the President of the Board of Control. He was to be advised by a Board of fifteen members.

(4) The designation of Governor General of India was changed. He was given the additional title of Viceroy and was made responsible to the Secretary of State for India, who in turn was made a member of the Cabinet and was responsible to the British Parliament.

[Any three]

(B) Three causes for the resentment of the Sepoys against the British were :

(1) The Sepoys of the Bengal Army belonged to high castes of Oudh and the North – Western Province. Although, the Sepoys had fought and won many wars for the Company with determined devotion in the most difficult and dangerous circumstances, yet they did not get a fair deal. Their emoluments were very low in comparison with those of the British soldiers and their chances of promotion were negligible.

(2) The loyalty of the Sepoys were further undetermined by certain military reforms which outraged their religious feelings.

(3) They had an aversion to overseas services, as travel across the seas meant loss of caste for them.

(C) The political causes responsible for the First War of Independence were:

(1) **Doctrine of Lapse:** In order to annex more and more states, Lord Dalhousie introduced 'Doctrine of Lapse'. By this doctrine, if any ruler died without a natural heir to succeed him, his kingdom would automatically lapse to the care of the East India Company. The adopted son was declared ineligible for succession. This policy of Dalhousie caused on uproar amongst the people of India;

(2) **Annexation of Awadh:** Dalhousie, on the pretext of badministration, annexed Avadh and dispossessed its Nawab, Wajid Ali Shah in 1856. The Nawab was always loyal to the company and yet, the Governor General showed utter discourtesy to him. The company's sepoys, 75000 of whom were from Awadh, reacted angrily to the annexation of the homeland by the British.

(3) **Discourtesy shown to Bahadur Shah Zafar :** Even the Mughal Emperor, Bahadur Shah Zafar was humiliated by the Britishers. In 1849, Dalhousie announced that Bahadur Shah would not be allowed to stay in the historic Red Fort any more. Further, in 1856 Lord Canning announced that after Bahadur Shah Zafar, his successors would not be allowed to use royal titles with their names. This decision

to put an end to Mughal sovereignty led to anxiety among the Muslim community and hatred for the British.

(4) **Absentee Rule of the British:** Absentee sovereignty of the British was unacceptable to the Indians and a cause of deep resentment amongst them. The British ruled India from England, thousand miles away and the Indians felt that their country's wealth was being drained to England instead of being recycled within the country and being put to use for the welfare of the local people.

> (1) Many states like Jhansi, Satara, Nagpur were annexed under the Doctrine of lapse introduced by Lord Dalhousie. According to this heirs adopted without the consent of the Company could inherit the private property of the deceased ruler but the kingdom would come directly under the Company's rule.
> (2) Awadh ws annexed by Lord Dalhousie on the pretext of alleged misrule.
> (3) The disrespect shown to Bahadur Shah, the Mughal ruler. Dalhousie announced that Bahadur Shah's successors could not use the Red Fort as their palace and were to shift to Qutub Minar. Later Lord Canning announced that after the death of Bahadur Shah his successors will not be allowed to use the imperial titles with their names and would be known as mere princes.
> (4) Treatment given to Nana Sahib, the adopted son of Baji Rao II resented as the British refused to give the pension they were paying to Baji Rao II. Rani Laxmi Bai of Jhansi was a bitter enemy of the British as she was adversely affected by the Doctrine of lapse.
> (5) The rule of the British was resented by the Indians as they felt that they were being ruled from England and India's wealth was not being sued for their welfare.
> [Any four]
> [Marking Scheme]

 What Examiners Say
→ Most candidates answered the question correctly. However, a few mentioned the economic causes or the causes of the First World War.

31. With reference to the First World War, answer the following questions:

(A) When and why was Oudh annexed by Lord Dalhousie? **[ICSE 2018]**

(B) Describe the Contribution of Rani Laxmibai to the Revolt of 1857.

(C) What was 'Divide and Rule' Policy of the British after the First War of Independence ? **[HOT🔥]**

Ans. (A) The Nawab of Awadh "Nawab Wajid Ali Shah" was very loyal to the British. But Lord Dalhousie annexed Awadh on 7th February, 1856 to the British territory under the pretext that the state of Awadh was not properly governed by Nawab Wajid Ali Shah and he was removed on this ground. This annexation left many nobles, officers and soldiers unemployed. The British also confiscated the estates of the Zamindars and Taluqdars. This created dissatisfaction among the people and annoyed them and when the Revolt broke out they rallied with the Sepoys.

(B) Rani Laxmibai was the queen of Jhansi. When the ruler of Jhansi died in 1853, leaving no natural heir, the widowed Rani was pensioned and their adopted son, Anand Rao, was not recognized as a lawful successor to the throne. After the annexation of Jhansi, she became a rebel and joined in the uprising of 1857. She was considered the bravest and best military leader of the rebels. She with the help of Tantia Tope occupied Gwalior. Sir Hugh Rose advanced towards Gwalior defeated the Indian troops.

Rani Laxmibai fought like a hero and died in the battlefield. Her courage and military skill inspired her countrymen. She is still remembered by Indians for her great sacrifice.

(C) The British followed the policy of 'Divide and Rule' . After 1858, they continued to follow their rule by promoting their policy of 'Divide and Rule'. In this policy they turned the Princes against their subjects, Province against Province, caste against caste , group against group and above all, Hindus against Muslims. During the War both Hindus and Muslims fought together, but the British first victimised the Muslims and favoured the Hindus. And after some time they reversed the policy of treatment. They alienated the people from their rulers by giving them special protection and concessions.

The Government cleverly used the attractions of government service to create a split along religious lines among the educated Indians. The British also encouraged hatred and ill-feeling among the Hindus and the Muslims so that they could never challenge the British Empire in India.

32. By 1857, conditions were ripe for a mass uprising in the form of the Great Revolt of 1857. In this context, explain the following:

(A) Any three economic causes for the revolt of 1857.

(B) Any three military causes.

(C) Any four political causes of the revolt.

[ICSE 2016, 20]

Ans. (A) The economic causes of Revolt of 1857 were:

(1) **Capitalising Indian Economic Resources:** Indian economic resources were utilized to meet the needs of the British and not the requirements of the Indians. India was confined to producing raw materials like cotton and jute for the textile industry in Britain, which was processed into finished products and exported back to India to be sold in Indian markets. The British traders made massive profits through this two way trade and it proved death knell for the age-old Indian Cottage Industries.

(2) **Unemployment:** Handicraft and Cottage Industries died out as the poor Indian weavers could not compete with the machine made goods imported from Britain and were driven to bankruptcy. As a result, thousand of artisans were left jobless which infuriated the common artisans and resulted in resentment among workers against the British rule.

(3) **New Land Policies:** The British East India Company introduced several forms of revenue administration like Zamindari system, Ryotwari and Mahalwari systems, etc. These were used by the British to collect revenues from the cultivators and aimed at maximizing the income for the government and not to help the peasants. The peasants became the worst sufferers due to the new land policies.

(4) **Coniscation of Land and Properties:** The British confiscated the land and properties of many landlords and Talukdars, especially those of Awadh. Many retainers and native soldiers under the employment of the native states became jobless with the annexation of the native states to the British dominion.

(5) **Famine:** Several changes took place in the agraian scene in India under the rule of the British. Landless agricultural population grew in the country. Large tracts of land were converted to raise only commerical crops like cotton, jute and indigo. Food grains production was thus, reduced. Landlords, merchants and money lenders started to hoard grains and thus severe famines occurred frequently in many parts of the country. The government took little or no interest in resolving such issues.

[Any three]

(B) The military causes for the Revolt of 1857 were:

(1) **Prejudices Against Indian Soldiers:** The British army was divided into two sections, the Indian soldiers were called 'Sepoys' and the European army men were called 'Soldiers'. The Indians were undermined and humiliated. All the high ranks were reserved for white men irrespective of their capacity to perform. Their salaries were low, promotions slow and the service conditions were poor.

(2) **General Service Enlistment Act:** In 1856, Lord Canning passed the General Service Enlistment Act which stated that the Indian sepoys were bound to go and fight in whichever place in the world they were asked to. The Bengal sepoys hated this regulation since they were unwilling to cross the seas as it was their belief that they would lose their religious identity if they went outside the country.

(3) **Religious Jeopardy:** The sepoys also resented the British interference in their religious beliefs. The Hindu sepoys were unhappy as they were mostly ordered to fight overseas, which was not desirable to them at all. The Muslim sepoys were forced to shave off their beards in the name of uniformity.

(C) The political causes for the Revolt of 1857 were:

(1) **Doctrine of Lapse:** In order to annex more and more native states, Lord Dalhousie introduced the policy of 'Doctrine of Lapse'. By this doctrine, if any native ruler died without a natural heir to succeed him, his kingdom would lapse to the care of the East

India Company. The adopted son was declared ineligible for succession. By applying this doctrine. Dalhousie annexed kingdoms like Satara, Sambalpur, Jhansi, Nagpur, Jaitpur, Bhagat and Udiapur. This policy of Lord Dalhousie caused an uproar amongst the people of India.

(2) **Annexation of Avadh:** Dalhousie, on the pretext of badministration, annexed Avadh (Oudh) and dispossessed its Nawab, Wajid Ali Shah. The Nawab was kept under custody in Calcutta with a meager pension. Avadh, reacted angrily to the annexation of their homeland by the British, even though they had played a major role in helping the British to conquer large parts of India. Hence, Avadh played an important role during the Revolt of 1857.

(3) **Discourtesy shown to Bahadur Shah Zafar:** Even the Mughal Emperor, Bahadur Shah Zafar, was humiliated by the Britishers. In 1849, Dalhousie announced that Bahadur Shah would not be allowed to stay in historic Red Fort any more. He, along with his natives, was forced to move to a humbler residence at the Qutub Minar, in the outskirts of Delhi. Further, Lord Canning announced that after Bahadur Shah Zafar, his successors would not be allowed to use royal titles with their names. This decision to put an end to Mughal sovereignty led to anxiety among the Muslim community and hatred for the British.

(4) **Absentee Rule of the British:** Absentee sovereignty of the British was unacceptable to the Indians and cause of deep resentment amongst them. The British ruled India from England, thousand miles away and the Indians felt that their country's wealth was being drained to England instead of being recycled within the country and being put to use for the welfare of the local people.

33. Severals factors led to the Revolt of 1857. With reference to this, explain each of the following:
(A) Resentment of the rulers of the native states against the British.
(B) Unhappiness of the Indian Artisans and Craftmen.
(C) Discontentment of Sepoys.

Ans. (A) **Resentment of the rulers of the natives states against the British:** A tricky method was adopted by the British to gain control over the rulers of the native states as they struck at the very root of their existence by the Doctrine of Lapse. According to the policy, if a ruler died without his natural heir, his adopted son could neither get the throne nor the title and the State would be annexed to the British Empire using the Doctrine.

Lord Dalhousie annexed Satara, Jhansi, Nagpur, Sambalpur, Jaitpur and Udaipur. The Principle of Lapse was also applied to take away the titles and pensions of the rulers of some states. Royal titles of the Nawabs of Carnatic and Tanjore were taken away. This caused discontent among the rulers as well as among the people in general.

(B) **Unhappiness of the Indian Artisans and Craftsmen:** Heavy duties imposed on the Indian Cotton and Silk Textiles in Britain destroyed the Indian Industries on the other hand, British goods were imported into India at a nominal duty. As a result of the British policy of making India merely a raw material producing country. Indian handicrafts and cottage industries were ruined.

Thousand of Craftmen and Artisans were thrown out of employment. The manufacturers of silk and cotton goods get no profits from their work and began to look for other means of livelihood. The miserable condition of the workmen became a potent cause of resentment against the British rule.

(C) **Discontentment of Sepoys:** Several factors were responsible for the discontentment of the Indian soldiers (sepoys). These are as follows :

(1) Indian and British soldiers were not treated equally. Indian soldiers were ill-fed, poorly paid and were provided poor accommodation. British Military Authorities forbade the Sepoys from wearing caste or sectarian marks, beards or turbans; and they showed disregard for the sentiment of the Sepoys.

(2) The General service Enlistment Act of 1856 made it compulsory for Indian soldiers to go overseas on duty, this was strictly objected by Indians on religious grounds.

(3) On one hand, the wages of Indian soldiers were inadequate to support

their families, while on the other hand, the British soldiers received more than eight times the salary than the Indian Sepoys.

(4) All higher positions in employment were reserved for the British, irrespective of their performance. Even the Indian soldiers formerly occupying high positions in the armies of native princes could not rise above the rank of Subedar. The feature of the Indian soldiers was bleak without chances of promotion.

(5) The Enfield Rifles used Greased Cartridges which were to be loaded by the soldier by biting all the greased paper. In January 1857, there was a rumour in the Bengal Regiment that the Greased Cartridges had the fat of cow or pig. So, both the Hindus and the Muslims soldiers refused to use these cartridges and staged an uprising when they were forced to use them.

(6) The extension of British Dominion in India adversely affected the service conditions of the Sepoys.

34. Numerous causes gave rise to the First War of Independence and its consequences led to several changes in the British Government in India. In this context, answer the following:

(A) Explain any three political causes of the Revolt of 1857.

(B) Briefly explain the immediate cause of the Great Revolt.

(C) State any four changes in the administration of the British Government as a consequence of the revolt.

Ans. (A) The political causes for the Revolt of 1857 were:

(1) **Doctrine of Lapse:** In order to annex more and more native states, Lord Dalhousie introduced the policy of 'Doctrine of Lapse'. By this doctrine, if any native ruler died without a natural heir to succeed him, his kingdom would lapse to the care of the East India Company. The adopted son was declared ineligible for succession. By applying this doctrine. Dalhousie annexed kingdoms like Satara, Sambalpur, Jhansi, Nagpur, Jaitpur, Bhagat and Udiapur. This policy of Lord Dalhousie caused an uproar amongst the people of India.

(2) **Annexation of Avadh:** Dalhousie, on the pretext of maladministration, annexed Avadh (Oudh) and dispossessed its Nawab, Wajid Ali Shah. The Nawab was kept under custody in Calcutta with a meager pension. Avadh, reacted angrily to the annexation of their homeland by the British, even though they had played a major role in helping the British to conquer large parts of India. Hence, Avadh played an important role during the Revolt of 1857.

(3) **Discourtesy shown to Bahadur Shah Zafar:** Even the Mughal Emperor, Bahadur Shah Zafar, was humiliated by the Britishers. In 1849, Dalhousie announced that Bahadur Shah would not be allowed to stay in historic Red Fort any more. He, along with his natives, was forced to move to a humble residence at the Qutub Minar, in the outskirts of Delhi. Further, Lord Canning announced that after Bahadur Shah Zafar, his successors would not be allowed to use royal titles with their names. This decision to put an end to mughal sovereignty led to anxiety among the Muslim community and hatred for the British.

(4) **Absentee Rule of the British:** Absentee sovereignty of the British was unacceptable to the Indians and cause of deep resentment amongst them. The British ruled India from England, thousand miles away and the Indians felt that their country's wealth was being drained to England instead of being recycled within the country and being put to use for the welfare of the local people. **[Any three]**

(B) The introduction of the new Enfield Rifle by Lord Canning and the greased cartridge became the immediate cause for the Great Revolt of 1857. The loading process of the Enfield Rifle involved biting the cartridge's seal off with the teeth, which would mean getting some of the grease in the mouth. Both the Hindus and the Muslims found it objectionable as they were greased with the fat of cows and pigs. The sepoys refused to use them as they felt that the British were deliberately trying to hurt their religious sentiments. This refusal by the sepoys and consequent British reaction resulted in disobedience of orders and the sepoys rose in revolt.

(C) The changes in the administration of the British Government as a consequence of the revolt were:

(1) The rule of East India Company came to an end;

(2) The British Parliament passed an "Act for the better Government of India"

whereby the responsibility of Indian administration was passed into the hands of the British Crown and her Parliament. It came to be known as Queen's Proclamation.

(3) The administration was given in the hands of secretary of State for India and he was to be advised by a Board of fifteen members.

(4) The designation of the Governor General was changed and he was given the additional title of Viceroy and made responsible to the Secretary of State for India.

35. The Great uprising of 1857 was an important event which produced for reaching results. Explain the following with reference to the great uprising:

(A) The changes introduced in the administrative set up of the British territory in India.

(B) Right granted to Indian Princes.

(C) Rise of Nationalism

Ans. (A) (1) The most significant result of the uprising of 1857 was the end of the rule of East India Company and assumption of the Government of India directly by the Crown. This was done by the Government of India Act of 1858. It transferred the power to govern India from the East India Company to the British Crown.

(2) Appointments to the Civil Service were to be made by open competition under rule made by the Secretary of State.

(3) Actual governance was to be carried on, as before, by the Governor-General who was also given the title of Viceroy, that is, a personal representative of the Crown. Lord Canning was appointed as the first Viceroy under this Act.

(B) (1) In Rights granted to Indian Princes, the Policy of Annexation and the Doctrine of Lapse were abandoned.

(2) All the treaties entered by the Indian rulers with the East India Company were to be honoured.

(3) Their rights of adoption and succession were also recognized.

(C) (1) The uprising of 1857 was the first struggle of the Indian people for freedom from British Imperialism.

(2) It paved the way for the rise of the National Movement.

(3) The sacrifices made by great Indian leaders like Rani Laxmi Bai, Nana Sahib and Mangal Pandey served as a source of inspiration for the future freedom fighters.

(4) The heroic struggle also established valuable traditions of resistance to the British rule.

36. (A) Answer the following questions based on the picture given below :

(a) Name the lady shown in the picture and where does she belong from?

(b) Which Proclamation was passed by her? By whom and where was this proclamation made public.

(c) According to the Proclamation, what promise was made on equality of subjects?

(B) (a) Identify the person shown in the picture.

(b) Who was responsible for the beginning of the uprising of Revolt, 1857?

(c) When was he hanged and what was its result?

Ans. (A) (a) The lady shown in the picture is Queen Victoria from England.

(b) She passed the Queen's Proclamation incorporating the transfer of governance from East India Company to the British Crown. It was made public at Allahabad on 1st November, 1858 by Lord Canning the first Viceroy of India.

(c) The Proclamation promised to treat all subjects equal, whether they were

Europeans or Indians. And it further said education and ability would be basis of all appointments done in employment.

(B) (a) The person shown is Mangal Pandey.
 (b) A Brahmin soldier of the 34th native infantry at Barrackpore, named Mangal Pandey strated the Revolt on 29th March, 1857. He led an attack on the military officer and was arrested and hanged.
 (c) Mangal Pandey was hanged on 8th April, 1857. After this the uprising began in Meerut and spread in other parts of country like Delhi, Kanpur, Lucknow, Jhansi, etc.

37. Answer the following questions based on the picture given below:

(A) Identify the person shown in picture. What was her real name? And what is her nickname?
(B) Under which British Policy was her State annexed and Why?
(C) Why is she still an inspiration to her countrymen?

Ans. (A) The person shown in the picture is Rani Laxmi Bai. Her real name was Manikarnika Tambe. Her nickname is Jhansi ki Rani.

(B) Her State Jhansi was annexed under British Policy of Doctrine of Lapse. Because when her husband, the ruler of Jhansi died in 1853, he left no natural heir.

The widowed Rani was pensioned and their adopted son, Anand Rao was not recognised as a lawful successor to the throne. According to the Doctrine of Lapse, if a kingdom will 'lapse' and would come under the company's territory in India.

(C) She was the leader of revolutionaries in Jhansi, who fought against British Rule. She is considered the bravest and the best military leader of the rebels. She fought like a true heroine. Her courage and military skill inspired her countrymen. The great sacrifice of Rani is still remembered by all Indians.

2 Growth of Nationalism

The growth of Nationalism in India in the second half of 19th century, brought out socio-religious movement in India, which started uprooting the British rule from India and led to the formation of Indian National Congress in 1885.

Chapter Notes

- Factors Leading to the Growth of Nationalism
- Precursors of the Indian National Congress
- Formation of the Indian National Congress

TOPIC 1

FACTORS LEADING TO THE GROWTH OF NATIONALISM

What is Nationalism?

Nationalism is the desire of a group of people who share the same race, culture, language, etc. to form an independent country. It is also a feeling of love or pride for our own country, it is a feeling that our country is better than any other. Nationalism in India was inspired by the French Revolution of 1789. From the second half of the 19th Century the idea of Nationalism started to originate in India and it gave birth to national awakening in India.

Nationalism emerged in India during the British rule mainly as a reaction to the British rule and the clash of interests of the Indian people with those of the British.

Factors Leading to the Growth of Nationalism

There were many factors which contributed to the growth of Nationalism in India they were:

Economic Exploitation

The British adopted and followed their exploitative policies in India. India being an agricultural land was converted an economic colony to serve the interests of the Industries of England. The Indian cottage and handicrafts Industries were shut down and ruined. Millions of artisans and craftsmen became jobless and unemployed. The Britishers invested huge capitals in Indian markets which helped British Industries in serving them raw material and huge profits like railways, shipping, mining, oil exploitation, tea, coffee plantations, etc. The heavy taxes and land revenue collected from the Indians was not spent in India for the welfare of the Indian people. It was drained away to Britain in the form of their profits, salaries, savings and pensions. All the weaker and stronger sections of the Indian society like zamindars, peasants, craftsmen felt the effect of the economic exploitation of the British and realized that some measures had to be taken to improve the situation. And this urge automatically led to an upsurge in a nationalist favour.

Example 1. Who was Dadabhai Naoroji and what did he proclaimed?

Ans. Dadabhai Naoroji was famous Indian Economists. Dadabhai Naoroji wrote a book "Drain of Wealth" and he proclaimed that the Britishers in India were draining all its wealth from India to their country in the form of their savings, salaries, profits and pensions, without knowledge of Indian people.

Repressive Colonial Policies

The British had conquered India to promote their own interests and they made many repressive policies, which became a major barrier to India's economic, social, cultural, intellectual and political development. Viceroys like Lord Lytton (1876 – 1880) and Lord Curzon (1899 – 1905) took many repressive policies. They were as follows:

(1) Lord Lytton organised a Grand Delhi Durbar in 1877 to Proclaim Queen Victoria as the Empress of India.

(2) Lord Lytton introduced the Vernacular Press Act on 14th March, 1878 to suppress the freedom of native Press.

(3) Lord Curzon passed the Calcutta Corporation Act in 1899 which rejucel the strength of elected members from India giving the British majority.

(4) Lord Curzon partitioned Bengal on communalines into East and West Bengal. This fuelled national sentiments in the country.

Example 2. What was Vernacular Press act?

Ans. The Vernacular Press Act forbade or censored reports published in vernacular news papers to publish any material that might incite feelings of dissatisfaction against the British Government. This law was not applicable to English newspapers. In 1882 this Act was replaced by Lord Ripon.

(5) Lord Lytton also passed the Indian Arms Act in 1878, it made a criminal offence for Indians to carry arms without licence. This Act was also not applicable to the British.

(6) To appear in the Indian Civil Service Examination the maximum age limit was reduced from 21 to 19 years, thus making it difficult for the Indians to compete for it.

(7) The Import Duties on British textiles were removed. It proved harmful for the Indian Industry.

(8) The Ilbert Bill of 1883 abolished judicial disqualification on the basis of racial discrimination. Earlier Indian Judges were racially discriminated for sentencing Europeans. But this Bill provided for the trial of British or European persons by Indians. By this Act, the British tried to introduce equality between Indian and British Judges in India. This was resented by the British and they started a Defence Association to defend their special privileges. Ultimately, the Bill was amended.

Development of Transport and the Means of Communications.

The British built a network of Roads and Railways in order to promote their own commercial interest. It made easier for the people to travel from one part of India to another part and means of transport made it possible the basic unity of the Indians to mobilise their public opinion on a national scale.

The development of modern postal and telegraph system brought a radical change in social, intellectual and political life of Indians.

Important

→ The First Railway Line connecting Bombay with Thane was laid down in 1853.

→ By 1869, more than 600 km of railways had been built and by 1905 it extended to nearly 45,000 km.

Influence of Western Education

The British introduced Western education in India through the maximum of English to serve their own interests. They wanted to train Indian people as clerks for their administration. The impact of Western Education led to a rational, humanitarian and scientific approach to life. It made the educated Indians realise the need to reform their religion and society. The Indians felt that the progress of a nation laid in the acceptance of the best of both East and west. The result was the birth of socio-religious reform movements covering all segments of Indian society.

Socio-Religious Reform Movements

The Second half of the 19th century witnessed the rise of many social reformers in India. In the social sphere, these movements worked for the following:

(1) Abolition of Caste System
(2) Child Marriage System
(3) Dowry System
(4) Pardah System
(5) Sati System
(6) Widow Remarriage
(7) Infanticide

Prominent Reform Movements were started by Raja Ram Mohan Roy, Swami Dayanand Saraswati, Swami Vivekanand and Jyotiba Phule.

Contributions of Raja Ram Mohan Roy

Raja Ram Mohan Roy found Brahmo Samaj in 1828. He was the great socio-religious reformer of the 19th century. He is known as "The Father of modern Indian renaissance:" Brahmo Samaj was formerly named Brahmo Sabha. It supported the monotheism or the worship of one supreme God. It condemned idol worship and laid emphasis on prayers, mediation, charity, morality and strengthening the bonds of unity between men of all religious and creeds.

Raja Ram Mohan Roy was against the rigidity of caste system, untouchability, polygamy, child marriage, female infanticide. He started a campaign for the abolition of Sati System. It was because of his efforts, that the Governor-General of India William Bentinck, passed a law in 1829 making the practice of sati illegal and punishable by law. He also favoured widow remarriage (which was legalised in 1856) and inter-caste marriage, Raja Ram Mohan Roy was a loyal nationalist and pioneer of Indian journalism. He wrote journals in Bengali, English, Hindi and Persian languages. He started a Bengali weekly called 'Samwad Kaumudi' and a news paper in Persian called 'Mirat-ul- Akhbar".

Contributions of Jyotiba Phule

He was born in an affluent farmer family of low caste. He did a great work for the upliftment of the depressed classes. He laid the foundation of 'Satyashodhak Samaj' in 1873 to work continuously for the betterment of depressed classes. Jyotiba Phule worked for the upliftment of women. In 1851, Jyotiba Phule along with his wife, Savitribai Phule started one of the first girls school in Pune. In 1854, he established a school for untouchables and started a private orphanage for the widows. He pioneered the widow remarriage movement in Maharashtra and worked for the education for women.

He opened many schools for the upliftment of the down-trodden people. He wanted to liberate the depressed classes and make them aware of their rights by educating them. He raised his voice against the caste system. In his book 'Gulamgiri' he focused on the Brahmin domination and the poverty of the lower castes. And he wrote another book on this caste system. 'Tales of the untouchables' . He had the aim of securing social justice for the weaker sections of society.

Other Socio-Religious Reform Movements

Swami Vivekananda in 1897 had set up the Ramakrishna Mission while Dayanand Saraswati had set up the Arya Samaj in 1875.

The unique features of all these movements were that they did not ignore the political aspect of men. They all instilled confidence in the minds of the Indians and made Indians proud of their culture. Swami Dayanand was the first to use the word 'Swaraj' and to raise the slogan 'India for Indians'. The reformers condemned untouchability and the caste system. The reform movements created a consciousness of a new society devoid of privileges based on caste, creed or religion.

Role of Press and Indian Literature

The Press played an important role in fostering national unity and creating consciousness among the Indians. A large number of newspapers were started in the later half of the 18th Century, nationalism was spread greatly by the contribution of both English and Vernacular Press.

(1) Some of the prominent newspapers were the Amrit Bazor Patrika, The Bengali, The Tribune, The Pioneer, The Times of India, The Hindu and the Statesman in English.
(2) Indian books written at this time inspired the Indians.
(3) Bankim Chandra's 'Anand Math' and the play 'Bharat Durdarsha' inspired countless Indians.
(4) It was through the Press that the message of patriotism and modern liberal ideals of liberty, freedom, equality, home rule and independence spread among the people.
(5) The Press carried on daily criticism of the unjust policies of the British Government in India and exposed the true nature of British rule in India.

📢 Important
→ Bankim Chandra Chatterji's Bengali novel 'Anand Math' become the Bible of modern Bengali Patriotism. It contained the national Song "Vande Matram" which greatly inspired the people.

⚠ Caution
→ Most students could not explain the contributions of Jyotiba Phule. They even didn't know whether Jyotiba Phule was a man or a woman.

TOPIC 2

PRECURSORS OF THE INDIAN NATIONAL CONGRESS

The seeds of 'modern political consciousness' were sown by Raja Rammohan Roy in the first half of the nineteenth century. But the second half of the century witnessed the consciousness among the Indians that the British were exercising control over the resources of India and the lives of its people and until this control was ended, India could not be a sovereign nation. During this period various political associations were founded in various parts of India, but they had common goals for all the people of India. They did not work for any one religion, community or class.

In 1838, the first political association started in India was the landholder's Society in Kolkata by Dwarkanath Tagore. It safeguarded the interests of the Landlord's of Bengal, Bihar and Orissa (New Odisha). The Bengal British India Society was formed in 1843. Other Organisations like British Indian Association (1851), Bombay presidency Association (1871), Madras Native Association (1852), Poona Sarvajanik Sabha (1870) and Indian League (1875) were formed.

The London India Society was an Indian Organisation founded in London in March 1865 under the leadership of Dadabhai Naoroji and W.C. Bannerjee. All these associations served as a base for the formation of the Congress. They played an important role in the foundation of the Indian National Congress in December 1885. They are called the forerunners of the Congress.

East India Association (1866)

The East India Association was founded by Dadabhai Naoroji in London in 1866. The Association provided information on all the Indian subjects to the British Citizens and the Members of the Parliament. The Association had its branches in Bombay, Calcutta and Madras. It soon become popular and recommended the abolition of cotton duties and withdrawl of the Vernacular Press Act.

Example 1. Who was The Grand Old Man of India and what was his opinion regarding British Nation?

Ans. Dadabhai Naoroji was called 'The Grand Old Man' of India. He had the opinion that the British Nation was just and good. He wanted to place the true state of affairs in India before the people of England so that the grievances of the Indians may be removed.

Related Theory
→ On the sugestion of Dadabhai Naoroji the name of Union was changed to Indian National Congress.

East India Association (1876)

The Indian Association was founded in 1876 by Surendranath Banerjee. It was meant as an Association for All India Movement. The Association had Lawyers, Professionals and educated middle class as its Members. It had branches in Bengal as well as in towns outside Bengal. It was also called 'Indian Association of Calcutta'.

The objectives of Indian association were:

(1) Integration of Indian People on the basis of common political interests
(2) To create Public opinion on Political Matters
(3) To Promote friendly relations between Hindus and Muslims
(4) Mass Participation in Public Movements

Acheivements of Indian association were:

(1) It launched agitations against oppressive Licence Act, the Arms Acts and the Vernacular Press act.
(2) It demanded reform in the Indian Civil Service Exmaination by lowering the age limit from 21 to 19 years.
(3) It also took up the cause of the workers on the British owned Plantations and also protection of the rights of tenants against Landlords.

(4) But, the association failed to become an All-India body.

Indian National Conference (1883)

In 1883, Surendranath Banerjee convened the All India National Conference at Kolkata.

Example 2. Who presided over the Conference?

Ans. Ananda Mohan Bose presided over the Conference. It was attended by more than a hundred delegates from all over India.

 Related Theory

→ Indian National Conference was a provincial organisation.

Example 3. Why did Indian National Conference merged with the Indian National Congress?

Ans. Since, both these bodies were formed on the same line and they served the same purpose, that is, to work for the welfare of Indians, it merged with the Indian National Congress in December 1886.

 Important

→ The Landholder's society (1838) and the Bengal British Indian Society (1843) merged to form the British India Association of Bengal.

 Caution

→ The Word 'precursors' was misinterpreted by some candidates as 'personalities'. Here 'precursor' means 'forerunner'

TOPIC 3

FORMATION OF THE INDIAN NATIONAL CONGRESS

It was founded by an Englishman and a retired Civil Servant, Allan Octavian Hume in association with various Indian national leaders. In 1884 Hume, in consultation with the Indian leaders, laid the foundation of Indian National Union.

The Conference of the representatives of different parts of India was convened by the Union at Pune on 25th December, 1885. The first Secretary of the Indian National Congress was Mr. A.O. Hume.

On suggestions of Dadabhai Naoroji the name of the Union was changed to the Indian National Congress.

Its aim was to provide a 'Safety Valve' for the British Empire against the growing discontent among the Indians.

Many prominent Indian leaders such as Surendranath Banerjee, Dadabhai Naoroji, Pherozshah Mehta, Badruddin Tyabji, Womesh Chandra Banerjee and Justice Ranade also played an important role in the formation of INC.

Objectives of the Indian National Congress

W.C. Banerjee Presided the first session of the Indian National Congress and declared the following aims:

(1) Uniting the people of India's irrespective of caste, Religion or province.

(2) To train and organise public opinion in the country.

(3) To formulate popular demands and present them before the British Government

(4) To promote friendly relations between Nationalist Political Workers from different parts of the country

Session of the Congress

The First Session of the Congress under the Presidentship of W.C. Banerjee was attended by 72 delegates from all parts of India, including such eminent persons as Dadabhai Naoroji, K.T. Telang, Pherozshah Mehta, Badruddin Tyabji, G. Subramania Iyer, Ananda Charlu, N.G. Chandavarkar and Justice Ranade.

The Second Session of 1886 was held at Kolkata under the presidentship of Dadabhai Naoroji.

Thereafter, the National Congress held its sessions every year in December in different parts of the country and the number of its delegates soon increased to thousands.

The Surat Session (23rd Session) of the Congress was held in 1907 under the Presidentship of Rash Behari Ghosh. There was a dispute between the Early Nationalists and the Assertive Nationalists of the Congress regarding the methods of agitation in Bengal after its partition. There was a split in the Congress and it was called Surat split of 1907.

The Assertive group was excluded from Congress for nearly a decade. But in 1916 both wings of Congress reunited at Lucknow Session.

 Important

→ The first Session of INC was to be held in Pune on 25th December, 1885. But Plague broke out in Pune. So the Conference was shifted to Bombay at Gokuldas Tejpal Sanskrit College from 20th December to 31st December, 1885.

 Caution

→ INC was split into two groups at the surat session in 1907. The Moderates and the Radiculs.

Growth of Nationalism

Example 4. Who is called the 'Father of the Indian National Congress'?

Ans. Allan Octavian Hume (A.O. Hume) was called the 'Father of the Indian National Congress'.

Example 5. Which Viceroy of England favoured the foundation of Indian National Congress and why?

Ans. The Viceroy, Lord Dufferin favoured the foundation of the Congress because he wanted it to act as a safety valve for popular rule and its interests in India.

Related Theory
→ A.O. Hume had written a book called 'Allan Octavian Hume : Father of the Indian National Congress.'

ICSE Suggestions
→ Study the factors responsible for the growth of Nationalism by making a flow chart, with separate headings – economic, social, religious and political, etc. This will aid in conceptual clarity.

→ Important dates of historical events must be emphatically learnt with the ability to retain because incorrect dates can result in the loss of marks.

→ The first two sessions of the Indian National Congress, years and names of the Prsidents who presided the sessions should be emphasized.

Glossary

(1) **Aggressive or Radicals:** They were the Congress leaders who did not believe in the British sense of Justice.

Who's Who?

(1) **Lord Lytton :** He was an English statesman and poet. He served as Viceroy of India between 1876 to 1880, during which time Queen Victoria was Proclaimed Empress of India. He is largely responsible for economic distress in India.

(2) **Mahadeo Govind Ranade:** A distinguished Indian scholar, social reformer and author, he was one of the most ardent supporters of women's rights and liberation. He was also one of the following members of Indian National Congress.

Who Said What?

(1) 'Raja Rammohan Roy inaugurated the modern age in India. He was the 'Father of Indian Renaissance' and the 'Prophet of Indian Nationalism'. —*Rabindranath Tagore.*

[Raja Ram Mohan is called the 'Father of the Modern Indian Renaissance' due to the remarkable changes instituted in 18th and 19th century in India.]

Chronology

1828: Brahmo Samaj was set up by Raja Ram Mohan Roy.
1838: The Landholders Society was started in Kolkata.
1839: British India Society was founded in London.
1851: British Indian Association was formed.
1852: Madras Native Association was founded by Gazulu Lakshminorasu Chetty.
1866: East India Association was formed by Dadabhai Naoroji.
1870: Poona Sarvajanik Sabha
1873: Jyotiba phule founded the Satya Shodhak Samraj.
1875: The Indian League
1875: Arya Samaj was set-up by Dayanand Saraswati.
1876: Indian Association of Calcutta was founded.
1877: Grand Delhi Durbar was organised.
1878: Vernacular Press Act, and Indian Arms Act were introduced.
1882: Vernacular Press Act was replaced by Lord Ripon.
1883: Ilbert Bill was prepared.
1883: First session of Indian National Conference was held in Kolkata.
1885: Foundation of Indian National Congress

OBJECTIVE Type Questions

Multiple Choice Questions-I

[**1** mark each]

1. Who was the founder of the Indian National Congress?
   (a) A.O. Hume
   (b) W.C. Banerjee
   (c) Dadabhai Naoroji
   (d) Gopla Krishna Gokhale   [ICSE 2021]

Ans. *(a) A.O. Hume*

Explanation: In 1884, Hume in consultation with Indian leaders, laid the foundation of Indian National Union. On the suggestion of Dadabhai Naoroji, the name of union was changed to the Indian National Congress.

2. Which of these statements is NOT associated with Jyotiba Phule?
   (a) He established school for girls.
   (b) He established the Brahmo Samaj.
   (c) He established the Satya Shodak Samaj.
   (d) He was against the Caste System.
   [HOT]

Ans. *(b) He established the Brahmo Samaj.*

Explanation: Raja Ram Mohan Roy established the Brahmo Samaj not Jyotiba Phule.

⚠️ **Caution**
→ Students should read question carefully word 'NOT' is important.

3. Replace the underlined word and correct the statement:
   Surendranath Banerjee presided over the second session of the Indian National Congress.
   (a) Dadabhai Naoroji
   (b) W.C. Bannerjee
   (c) Rashbehari Ghosh
   (d) Badruddin Tyabji   [ICSE 2021]

⚠️ **Caution**
→ Don't be confused with Surname 'Banerjee'. Many student may select 'W.C. Banerjee' which is wrong answer.

Ans. *(a) Dadabhai Naoroji*

Explanation: The Second Session of 1886 was held at Kolkata under the Presidentship of Dadabhai Naoroji.

4. The year in which the Congress was established:
   (a) 1885   (b) 1856
   (c) 1898   (d) 1886

Ans. *(a) 1885*

Explanation: The Indian National Congress was found on 28th December, 1885 by A.O. Hume, an Englishman and retired civil servant.

⚠️ **Caution**
→ Dates and events should be memorized carefully in history by students.

💡 **Related Theory**
→ Establishment of Congress marked the formal beginning of the organized national movement in India.

5. Choose the correct option to match the following:

Column I	Column II
(A) Jyothiba Phule	(i) Indian National Congress
(B) Raja Ram Mohan Roy	(ii) Forward Bloc
(C) Subash Chandra Bose	(iii) Brahmo Samaj
(D) A. O. Hume	(iv) Satya Shodak Samaj

(a) (A) (i) (B) (ii) (C) (iii) (D) (iv)
(b) (A) (ii) (B) (i) (C) (iv) (D) (iii)
(c) (A) (iii) (B) (iv) (C) (i) (D) (ii)
(d) (A) (iv) (B) (iii) (C) (ii) (D) (i)

Ans. *(d) (A) (iv) (B) (iii) (C) (ii) (D) (i)*

Explanation:
(A) Jyotiba Phule founded Satya Shodhak Samaj in 1873.
(B) Raja Rammohan Roy founded Brahmo Sabhi in 1828 which was later renamed, Brahmo Samaj.
(C) Subhash Chandra Bose founded Forward Block in 1939.
(D) A.O Hume founded Indian National Congress in 1885.

6. Complete the following anology:
   Raja Rammohan Roy : Brahmo Samaj : Jyotiba Phule : ?
   (a) Atmiya Sabha
   (b) Arya Samaj
   (c) Ramakrishna Mission
   (d) Satya Shodhak Samaj   [HOT]

Ans. *(d) Satya Shodhak Samaj*

Growth of Nationalism

Explanation: Raja Rammohan Roy founded Brahmo Sabha in 1828 which was later renamed Brahmo Samaj. The Brahmo Samaj believed in monotheism or worship of one God. Jyotiba Phule founded the Satya Shodhak Samaj in 1873 with the aim of securing social justice for the weaker sections of the society.

Atmiya Sabha was founded by Raja Rammohan Roy, Arya Samaj was founded by Swami Dayanand Saraswati and Ramakrishna Mission was founded by Swami Vivekananda.

 Related Theory
→ The famous book 'Gulam giri' is authored by Jyotiba Phule.

7. Who was the first President of Indian National Congress?
(a) A.O. Hume
(b) Surendra Nath Banerjee
(c) W.C. Banerjee
(d) Dadabhai Naoroji

Ans. *(c) W.C. Banerjee*

Explanation: A.O. Hume, a retired civil servant, laid the foundation of Indian National League in 1884. On the suggestion of Dadabhai Naraoji the name of the League was changed to Indian National Congress. The first session of the Indian National Congress was held at Bombay from December 28 to 31, 1885 under the presidentship of Womesh Chandra Banerjee.

8. Which among the following is not a correct statement regarding Jyotiba Phule?
(a) He used dalit word for the first time in nineteenth century.
(b) He was the staunch supporter of Mahatma Gandhi's Harijan Sevak Sangh.
(c) He is known as the author of Gulamgiri.
(d) He formed Satya Shodhak Samaj in 1873.

Ans. *(b) He was the staunch supporter of Mahatma Gandhi's Harijan Sevak Sangh.*

Explanation: Jyotiba Phule was an urban educated member of a so called low caste. In his famous book 'Ghulamgiri', he described the hardships and distress felt by the lower castes. He founded the Satya Sodhak Samaj in 1873 with the aim of securing social justice for the weaker sections of society. He was an active social reformer in Pre Gandhian era.

⚠ **Caution**
→ Since Jyotiba Phule was of low caste, few students have written (a) option as their answer instead of (b).

9. With which of the following Raja Ram Mohan Roy cannot be associated?
(a) Sanskrit Education
(b) Brahmo Sabha
(c) Widow remarriage
(d) Abolition of Sati

Ans. *(a) Sanskrit Education*

Explanation: Raja Rammohan Roy started a campaign for the abolition of sati and purdah system and advocated the right of widows to remarry. He founded the Brahmo Sabha in 1828.

 Related Theory
→ Brahmo Sabha was later renamed. Brahmo Samaj, which believed in monotheism or worship of one God.

10. Which of the following was not a precursor of the Indian National Congress?
(a) Indian National Army
(b) East India Association
(c) Indian Association
(d) Indian National Conference

Ans. *(a) Indian National Army*

Explanation: The precursors of Indian National Congress were :
(1) East India Association (1866)
(2) Indian Association (1976)
(3) Indian National Conference (1883)
(4) Indian National Army (INA) was founded in 1941.

⚠ **Caution**
→ Most of the children were confused between INA and INC, so they have written Indian National Conference as their answer.

Multiple Choice Questions-II
(Other Question Types, for Extra Practice)

[**4** marks each]

11.

(A) This is the picture of a greatest social and religious reformer of 19th century. Identify the person.

(a) Jyotiba Phule
(b) Raja Rammohan Roy
(c) Dadabhai Naoroji
(d) Surendranath Banerjee

(B) The leader in the picture founded the ....
(a) Brahmo Samaj
(b) Satya Shodhak Samaj
(c) Arya Samaj
(d) Ramakrishna Mission

(C) Which were the reforms demanded by the leader in the picture?
(I) Abolition of sati and purdah system
(II) Right of widows to remarry
(III) Right of inheritance and property to women
(IV) Abolition of East India Company's trading rights
(a) Only (I)   (b) (I) and (II)
(c) II and III   (d) All of these

(D) This leader started .... in 1814 and carried on a persistent struggle against worship of idols and meaningless religious riuals.
(a) Atmiya Sabha
(b) Satya Sodhak Samaj
(c) Ram Krishna Mission
(d) Arya Samaj

Ans. (A) (b) *Raja Rammohan Roy*
Explanation: Raja Rammohan Roy was one of the greatest social and religious reformers of 19th century. He wanted to do away with the religious and social evils which were prevalent in Bengal at that time.

(B) (a) Brahmo Samaj
(C) (d) All of these
(D) (a) *Atmiya Sabha*
Explanation: Raja Rammohan Roy strongly held the view that all the principal ancient texts of the Hindus preached monotheism, i.e. worship of one God. In 1814, he started the Atmiya Sabha and carried on a persistent struggle against worship of idols and meaningless religious rituals.

SUBJECTIVE Type Questions

Short Answer Type Questions
[**2** marks each]

12. Name the two Presidents under the first two sessions of the Indian National Congress were held? **[ICSE 2018]**

Ans. (1) W.C. Banerjee
(2) Dadabhai Naoroji

 Caution
↪ Few candidates have mentioned Surendranath Banerjee instead of W.C. Banerjee.

13. Mention any two Repressive Colonial Policies of Lord Lytton. **[HOT** **] [ICSE 2017]**

Ans. The repressive colonial policies of Lord Lytton were:
(1) He abolished taxes on the import of British textiles, a measure meant to discourage Indian monufacturers.
(2) He held on Imperial Darbar in Delhi in 1877 to proclaim Queen Victoria as the Empress of India when the entire country was reeling under a severe famine.
(3) He passed the Venracular Press Act in 1878 which imposed restrictions on the notive press.

(4) He introduced the Arms Act of 1878, which prevented Indians from possessing arms without licence, while the Europeans never required such licences.
(5) The minimum age for Indians to compete at the Civil Services Examination was reduced from 21 to 19 years. **[Any two]**

> Arms Act (1878) and Vernacular Press act (1878). The Imperial Darbar at Delhi/The age limit for the ICS Exam reduced/Import duties on Indian Textile. **[Any two]**
> **[Marking Scheme]**

What Examiners Say
↪ Majority of the candidates answered well but a few of them were confused with the repressive policies of Lord Curzon and mentioned Partitioning of Bengal, Calcutta Corporation Act and Universities Act, etc.

 Caution
↪ Students should read the question carefully, because the question clearly asked for the Repressive Policies of Lord Lytton and not of Lord Curzon.

14. Name the two main associations that were the precursors of the India National Congress. **[ICSE 2017]**

Ans. Indian National Association, the East India Association, Indian National Conference.
[Any two]

Growth of Nationalism   109

15. What was the Indian Arms Act 1878?

Ans. Lord Lytton had passed an Indian Arms Act in 1878, which forced the Indians to acquire a licence to keep, purchase or sell arms. But this law did not imply on English, Anglo-Indians and government servants of some particular categories.

16. How did English language played a leading role in 'spreading of Nationalism in India'?

Ans. The spread and popularity of English language gave the educated Indians a common language i.e. a 'lingua franca' through which they could communicable and exchange their views worldwide. And in doing so Press and Newspaper played important role, in spreading nationalism in India and outside world.

Structured Questions

[3+3+4 = **10** marks each]

17. With reference to the Growth of Nationalism, answer the following questions:
   (A) Mention any three contributions of Jyotiba Phule in preparing the ground for the National Movement. [ICSE 2015]
   (B) Give three factors that gave rise to Nationalism in India in the 19th Century. [ICSE 2018]
   (C) Explain any four points on the foundation of the Indian National Congress.

Ans. (A) Jyotiba Phule was an educated activist from Maharashtra, belonging to a so called lower caste.

His contributions in preparing the ground for national movement were:
   (1) He revolted for the rights of peasants and people belonging to the lower castes. In 1873, he formed Satyasodhak Samaj for the liberation of Shudras and Atishudras and to prevent their exploitation by the upper castes like Brahmins.
   (2) He was a pioneer of the widow remarriage movement in Maharashtra and worked for the education of women and the people belonging to the lower castes.
   (3) Jyotiba Phule along with his wife, Savitribai started one of the first girls school in Pune.

Up-liftment of lower castes/advocated education for the dalits to end their misery/founded schools for girls and lower casts/set up an orphanage in 1854 to provide shelter to poor widows and their children/founded Satya-Shodhak Samaj to mitigate the distress and sufferings of women, dalits and common people/conceived of a society based on the principles of justice, equality and fraternity/got water tank constructed outside his house for the use of dalits/wrote 'Ghulam Giri' which focused on the domination of the upper cast and the plight of peasants.

[Any Three]
[Marking Scheme]

(B) Following were the two factors that gave rise to the Nationalism in India in the 19th Century:
   (1) **Corruption in Administration:** The police and petty officials were corrupt. The rich got away with crime but the common man was lotted, oppressed and tortured.
   (2) **British Imperalism :** The British Imperalism was the most important factor, which contributed to the rise of Nationalism in India. It helped in the geographical unification of the country possible. Before the arrival of British, the people of the South were separated from the rest of India. The British Imperalism made people to think about India as one large nation.
   (3) **Influence of the Western Civilisation:** The establishment of the British rule in India made closer relations with the Western world possible. Thus, the contacts with the European countries influenced the Indians immensely. The Nationalism Century in Europe was the Century of Nationalism and Liberalism. In this way Indians learnt their lessons from the Europeans on these both ideologies.

(C) (1) The foundation of the Indian National Congress (INC) in 1885 by A.O. Hume was the most remarkable event in the history of India.
   (2) Lord Dufferin favoured the foundation of INC because he wanted it to act as a 'Safety valve' for popular discontentment to safeguard the British rule and its interest in India but soon however, the Congress became a revolutionary organization leading the Indian people to independence in 1947.
   (3) It was the INC which helped in uniting the people of different religions, provinces and castes. So, it was a secular movement in which all Indians participated.
   (4) INC was the first organization which wanted to promote friendly relations between Nationalist Political Workers from different parts of the country.

(5) INC helped to train and organize the public opinion in the country.

[Any four]

18. With reference to the Growth of Nationalism, answer the following questions:

(A) **What was the role of the press in promoting nationalistic sentiments amongst the Indians?**

(B) **Mention any three objectives of Indian National Congress.**

(C) **What were the causes of economic exploitation? Discuss any four points.**

Ans. (A) The press played an important role as it:

(1) spread the message of patriotism and modern liberal ideals of liberty, freedom, equality among the people.

(2) it criticized daily the unjust policy of the British Government in India and exposed the true nature of the British rule in India.

(3) it made exchange of views possible among different social groups from different parts of the country and in organizing political movements.

(4) it made the Indians aware of what was happening in the world and it helped them to shape their own policies and programmes. **[Any Three]**

(B) **The three objectives of Indian National Congress were :**

(1) To promote friendly relations between nationalists political workers from different parts of the country.

(2) To develop and consolidate the feelings of national unity irrespective of caste, religion or province.

(3) To formulate popular demands and present them before the government.

(4) To train and organise public opinion in the country. **[Any three]**

(C) (1) **Poor condition of village Economy:** Before the arrival of Britishers, Indian villages were independent. But later on the different villages and regions became interdependent. Under the zamindari system the peasants were left absolutely at the mercy of landlords, who could drive them off their land at any time. After the Industrial Revolution, farmers were forced to grow only those crops which could be used as a raw material in the British Industry and even they purchased at very low rates. This forced the peasants to revolt and forced them to unite.

(2) **Poor Condition of Handicrafts:** The British rule had a very devastating effect on the Indian Handicrafts. Heavy duties were imposed on goods exported to England from India and British goods were forced upon India. This ruined the Indian Handicrafts.

(3) **Unemployment and under employment:** Because of the introduction of English education, number of educated youth were increasing but job opportunities were limited. Even higher jobs were reserved for the European youth. This forced the Indian youth to join the Indian National Movement.

(4) **Attitude of the Government:** The burden of taxes was constantly on increase, but the government did very little to promote the welfare of the people. This forced the people to unite and join the National Movement.

(5) **Poor condition of Indian industries and workers:** The economic policies of the Britishers were hampering the growth of Indian Industries. British Industrialists were encouraged to set up industries instead of encouraging native capitalists to raise industries. The Indian labour was fully exploited. The workers had no right and they were made to work on low wages.

[Any four]

19. With reference to the rise of 'National Consciousness' in India, explain the following:

(A) **The influence of Western Education**

(B) **Any three contributions of Raja Rammohan Roy**

(C) **The development of modern means of transport and communication**

[ICSE 2017]

Ans. (A) **The influence of Western education:**

(1) It provided opportunities for assimilating ideas of democracy and nationalism.

(2) Educated Indians had access to ideals of liberty, equality, nationality, rule of law and self-Government.

(3) The English language too served as a link language, uniting people and developing a sense of National consciousness.

(4) People in India drew inspiration from the American War of Independence and the French Revolution.

[Any Three]

(B) **Contributions of Raja Rammohan Roy**
  (1) Advocated Monotheism
  (2) Liberty Rights and a free press
  (3) Started his Anti-Sati crusade
  (4) Woman's emancipation
  (5) Uplifted the cause of the poor peasants who were exploited by the zamindars.
  (6) Impressed upon the government to make the English language the medium of Education.
  (7) Literature – he started 'Samvad Kaumudi'/ Mirat –ul-Akhbar'
  (8) Wanted the Military Budget to be reduced.
  (9) Founded Brahmo Samaj.
  (10) He was against caste system/child marriage. **[Any Three]**

(C) **Development of modern means of Transport and Communication :**
  (1) The development of the postal system, telegraph, railways and roads helped to unify the country.
  (2) There was speedy transmission of messages and communication.
  (3) This enabled the Indians to come in contact with one another and discuss the problems facing one another.
  (4) Besides encouraging Trade and Commerce, the railway facilitated the growth of Nationalism.

What Examiners Say

→ (A) Most of the candidates answered correctly. A few candidates wrote about the negative impact of western education as a cause of the Revolt of 1857.

→ (B) This part was generally answered correctly by most of the candidates. A few mentioned 'Arya Samaj' instead of 'Brahmo Samaj'.

→ (C) Some candidates misunderstood the question and gave negative points rather than positive points of development, like, "telegraph poles were erected to hang Indians" and "Railway was introduced to break the social order".

Caution

→ (A) Students should be specific in their answers, and they should write on what the question is asked about.

→ (B) Reform Movements and the contributions made by the leaders mentioned in the syllabus should be understood well.

→ (C) Modern means of Transport and Communication in relevance to its contribution to the rise of nationalism in the country should be discussed in details.

3 First Phase of the Indian National Movement

People loving Moderate leaders of India, who dreamt for constitutional and other reforms within the framework of British rule, hoped for self-government just within British rule. Their demands were very nominal and moderate in nature. The three famous moderates were Dadabhai Naoroji, Gopal Krishna Gokhle and Surendranath Banerjee.

Chapter Topics

- Objectives and Methods of the Early Nationalists
- Contributions of Dadabhai Naoroji, Gopal Krishna Gokhale and Surendranath Banerjee.

TOPIC 1

OBJECTIVES AND METHODS OF THE EARLY NATIONALISTS

The history of the Indian national movements is broadly categorized in three phases:
(1) The Early Nationalist (Moderates) from (1885 – 1907)
(2) The Assertive (Radicals) Phase from (1907 – 1916)
(3) The Gandhian Era from (1915 – 1947)

The Early Nationalist

In the early years (1885 – 1907) the Congress was led by a group of leaders, who were called 'Early Nationalists' or 'Moderates'.

The main moderate leaders were:

W.C. Banerjee, Rashbehari Ghosh, Surendranath Banerjee, R.C. Dutt. They all were from Bengal.

Dadabhai Naoroji, Gopal Krishna Gokhale, Pherozeshah Mehta and Justice Ranade from Maharashtra and Gujarat.

Pandit Madan Mohan Malviya from Uttar Pradesh

Liberal Englishmen like Hume and Wedderburn

Beliefs of the Early Nationalists

They were staunch believers in open-minded and 'Moderate Politics'.

(1) They believed in the loyalty to the British Crown. They had faith in the British sense of justice, fair play, honesty and integrity of the British.
(2) It was their hope that the British would grant 'Home Rule' to Indians. They wanted that Indians should have their proper and legitimate share in the government.
(3) They believed that the British rule had many benefits. For example, it aided in cleansing social ills like untouchability, sati system, child marriage, etc. They concerned themselves with the demands for reforms.
(4) They were of the opinion that Britain would help Indians govern themselves according to Western Standards.
(5) They believed that the main obstacle in India's progress was social and economic backwardness of Indians and not the British Colonial Rule. They believed that continuation of the British connection with India was in the interest of both England and India.
(6) They relied on Constitutional and peaceful methods to achieve their aims. They believed in patience and reconciliation rather than in violence and confrontation.

Objectives or Demands of the Early Nationalists

Constitutional Demands

(1) The Moderates wanted a large share in the government of their country. They also demanded.
(2) Expansion of Legislative Councils
(3) Abolition of Indian Council
(4) Increase in the membership of the Councils
(5) Increase in greater powers of the legislative Councils
(6) Demand for Swaraj and self-government
(7) Adequate representation of Indians in the Executive Council of the Viceroys and those of Governors

Administrative Demands

(1) Demand for Indianisation of services
(2) Simultaneous holding of ICS examination in England and India
(3) Complete separation of the executive and the judiciary
(4) Increase in the powers of the local bodies (Municipal)
(5) Repeal of the Arms Act and Licence Act
(6) Wider employment of Indians at high ranks in administrative services
(7) Spread of Primary Education among the masses
(8) Improvement of the Police System to make it popular, honest and efficient

Economic Reforms

(1) Reduction in land revenue and protection of peasants
(2) Reduction in expenditure on the Army and to spent on welfare activities such as health and education.
(3) An enquiry into Indians growing poverty and famines
(4) Availability of cheap credit to peasants
(5) Development of banking, irrigation, medical and health facilities for the people
(6) Industrial growth through trade Protection
(7) Total abolition of salt-tax and the duty on sugar.

Defence of Civil Rights

(1) Removal of the restrictions imposed by the British Government on the freedom of speech and freedom of the press
(2) Abolition of the Preventive Act and restoration of individual liberties
(3) Restoration of right to assemble and form associations

Methods of the Early Nationalists

Early Moderates were very practical; they wanted to win freedom by a gradual process. They did not aim at high demands because they wanted to work on the lines of least resistance. But, they did not want to arouse serious oppositions.

The methods adopted by the Early Nationalists had two objectives:

(1) **First Objective** was to educate people in India in modern politics, to arouse national political consciousness and to create a united public opinion.
   (i) They held meetings where speeches were made and resolutions for popular demands were passed.
   (ii) They used Press to criticise government policies
   (iii) They sent memorandums and petitions to the government officials and the British Parliament.

(2) **Second Objective** was to influence the British Government and the British Public, they followed the following methods.
   (i) They made use of three P's *i.e.* Petitions, Prayers, and Protests.
   (ii) A British Committee of the Indian National Congress was set up in London in 1889.
   (iii) Deputations of Indian leaders were sent to Britain, who carried on active propaganda in Britain.

Example 1. Why did Early Nationalists followed the Constitutional Agitation Method?

Ans. The Early Nationalists believed in the Policy of Constitutional agitation within the legal framework, and slow orderly political progress so they followed the Constitutional Agitation Method.

Achievements of the Early Nationalists

(1) They created national awakening among people that they belonged to one common country – India.
(2) The Early Nationalists trained people in politics by popularising the ideas of democracy, civil Liberties, secularism and nationalism.
(3) They did pioneering work by exposing the true nature of the British Rule in India.
(4) Their political and economic programmes established the truth that India must be ruled in the interest of the Indians.

The efforts of the Early Nationalists led to the following reforms:

(1) The appointment of a Public Service Commission in 1886.
(2) A resolution of the House of Commons (1893) for simulataneous examination for the ICS in London and India.
(3) Appointment of the Welby Commission on Indian expenditure (1895)
(4) The Indian Councils Act of 1892.
(5) They managed to give a strong base for the National Movement in later years.

Criticism of the Early Nationalists

The methods used by moderates of passing resolution and sending petitions were criticized as inadequate.

They failed to realise that British and Indian interests clashed with each other. Britain was using Indian resources to increase its wealth.

The Early Nationalists failed to draw the masses into the mainstream of the National Movement. Their area of influence was confined to urban educated Indians.

Example 2. What was the official attitude of Britishers towards the Congress?

Ans. In the beginning, the British Government looked upon the Congress movement with favour. By 1890, realisisng that the growing unity of the Indians. Pushed further the policy of 'Divide and Rule'. They sowed seeds of Communalism between the Hindus and Muslims on the one hand and between the Indian masses and their leaders on the other.

Example 3. Name two Pro-British individuals to start an Anti–Congress Movement?

Ans. The Britishers encouraged Sayyid Ahmad Khan and Raja Shiva Prasad of Banaras (Varanasi) and other Pro-British individuals to start an Anti-Congress Movement.

 Related Theory

→ Sir Sayyid Ahmad Khan established Mohammedan Anglo-Oriental College (MAO) College in Aligarh during 1875, which became Aligarh Muslim University in 1920. He was an Indian Muslim pragmatist, Islamic Reformer, philosopher and educationist in nineteenth – century British India.

 Caution

→ Students should study each topic separately like methods and acheivements of Early Nationalists. They should not get confused between the two. Because this is common error done by them while writing answers in examination.

First Phase of the Indian National Movement

TOPIC 2

CONTRIBUTIONS OF DADABHAI NAOROJI, GOPAL KRISHNA GOKHALE AND SURENDRANATH BANERJEE

Dadabhai Naoroji (1825-1917)

Dadabhai Naoroji was born in a Parsi family of Bomaby in 1825 on September 4th. He worked as a professor of mathematics in Elpinstone College at Mumbai for 10 years. He took an active part in the National Movement of India. His name ranks highest among the leaders of the National Movement. Dadabhai was elected as the president of the Indian National Congress thrice (1886, 1893 and 1906). He was one of the founder members of the Indian National Congress. He also founded the Bombay Association. He edited the newspaper "Rast Goftar" (speaker of Truth). He started a magazine 'Dharma Marg Darshak'.

He started movements against the Vernacular Press Act and atrocious treatment of poor peasants by zamindars. He was known as the 'Grand Old Man of India' and was looked upon as Indian's unofficial ambassador in England.

He formed the East India Association to bring the Indians and British close to each other. He was in favour of appointing the educated Indians to high posts. It was done to his efforts that in 1893 the House of Commons passed a resolution in favour of holding the Imperial Civil Service (I.C.S.) Examination in England and India simulatneously.

The credit for demanding 'Swaraj', from the Congress platform in (1906) for the first time goes to him. Swaraj was the key-note of his Presidential address at Calcutta Session in 1906. Four resolutions of self-government, boycott, swadeshi and national education were passed by the Congress under his Presidentship.

Dadabhai Naoroji was also a great Economist and Economic thinker. In his book 'Poverty and un-British Rule in India', he had discussed about the 'Drain theory'. Dadabhai passed away in 1917, leaving behind a lesson of selfless service to the Nation.

Example 4. What is 'Drain Theory'?

Ans. 'Drain Theory' was revealed by Dadabhai Naoroji in his book 'Poverty and un-British Rule in India'; in which he asserted how the British rule and its costly administration was a heavy drain on the poor resources of India. He also revealed what was the basic cause of India's poverty. In the book he exposed the exploitation of the Indian people through British. And how all the wealth of India was being drained away from India in the form of profits, salaries, pensions and savings and how the Indian economy was being ruined through this 'Drain theory' of British through various ways.

Gopal Krishna Gokhale (1866–1915)

Gopal Krishna Gokhale was born at Kolhapur in Maharashtra in 1866. He was a professor of History and Economics at Fergusson College in Pune. He is often called the political Guru of Gandhiji. He was a mentor to Mahatma Gandhi. In 1912 he visited South Africa at Gandhi's invitation. As a young Barrister, Gandhi returned from his struggles against the Empire in South Africa and received personal guidance from Gokhale, including knowledge about understanding of India and the issues confronting common Indians. He was a Moderate with faith in the British sense of Justice. He was awarded the title of 'Companion of the Indian Empire'. He was influenced by the ideals of Justice M.G. Ranade. He joined the Deccan Education founded by Justice Ranade. He was keen to set up local self-governing units and organize state protection for Indian industries. He stressed the need for separation of the executive from the Judiciary. As a member of the Central Legislative Assembly, he moved a resolution for reduction in excise duty on cotton goods, relief to the bonded labour in Natal (South Africa) and revival of Village Panchayats. His efforts led to the reduction in Toll Tax. He wanted to work for the betterment of Indian peasants. In 1905, Gokhale became the President of the Indian National Congress. He founded the 'Servants of India Society' in 1905, to take up the cause of the expansion of Indian education. Being an Economist, he demanded radical changes in the fiscal policy and better jobs for the educated middle class Indians. He was instrumental in bringing in Minto-Morley reforms of 1909. He stressed on training Indians to dedicate their lives to the cause of the country in a religious spirit and to promote national interests. He advocated the use of Constitutional means to achieve nationalist ends. Gokhale died at an early age of 49 on 19th February, 1915.

Surendranath Banerjee (1848–1925)

Surendranath was born in Bengal on 10th November, 1848. He was a Nationalist leader, popular journalist and dedicated educationist. He was the first Indian to qualify for the Indian Civil Service Examination.

 Related Theory

→ Surendranath Banerjee had cleared the Indian Civil Service Examination in 1869, but he was barred owing to a dispute over his exact age. Banerjee cleared the Exam again in 1871 and was posted as Assistant Magistrate in Sylhet. However, he was dismissed soon from his job owing to racial discrimination.

He formed the Indian Association in 1876. Later he formed the Indian National Conference in 1883 which merged with the Indian National Congress. He was leader of the Moderates. Through the paper, 'The Bengali', he had spread his views. He wrote a book 'A Nation in Making' in which he wrote his views about self-government. He firmly opposed the partition of Bengal. He was an important figure in the Swadeshi Movement and advocated the manufacture of goods in India against foreign products. He openly stressed the use of Swadeshi goods and Constitutional methods to deal with the British. He supported Representative Institutions. He believed in 'opposition where necessary and co-operation where possible,' which was his famous saying.

Banerjee was popularly known as the 'Father of Indian Nationalism' and 'Rashtraguru'. Surendranath was elected to the Calcutta Corporation and remained its member for nearly twenty years. He was elected to the Bengal Legislative Council four times. In 1921 he was appointed as Minister of self-government and Health by the Governor of Bengal. He was the first Indian to hold that position. He breathed his last on 6th August, 1925.

ICSE Suggestions

→ Students should understand the meaning of the terms 'beliefs', 'aims', and 'methods' thoroughly to avoid committing errors. Learn the factors responsible for the growth of Nationalism by making a flow chart, with separate headings—economic, social, religious and political, etc. this will aid in conceptual clarity.

→ Students should study contributions of the three leaders by making short summary of the points. Atleast five points of each leader should be written in the answer.

→ The name of the associations and formation year should not be mixed with other leaders. Student should be very careful in this concept.

Glossary

(1) **Self-Government:** A government under which, people themselves participate in the governing process
(2) **Nationalist:** A person who wants his country to become free and independent
(3) **Moderates:** Early leaders of Congress who believed in Constitutional Agitation
(4) **Repeal:** To stop or abolish something by a government or a person with authority
(5) **Political Rights:** The rights to elect and right to be elected to form the government.
(6) **Restoration:** To bring back a situation that existed before
(7) **Deputation:** A small group of people who are asked to act or speak for others
(8) **Indianisation of the Services:** Inclusion and employment of more Indians in Government Services
(9) **The Indian National Association:** The Association formed by Surendranath Banerjee in 1876 to integrate the Indian people on the basis of common political interest

Who Said What?

(1) "I am loyal to the British Government because with me loyalty to the British Government is identical with loyalty to my own people and my own country." —Bipin Chandra Pal

(B.C. Pal, then a moderate leader said it in 1887, just because he loved self-government in India under British rule).

(2) "The Congress wanted Self-government or Swaraj like that of the United Kingdom on the Colonies". —Dadabhai Naoroji

(The credit for demanding Swaraj from the platform for the first time 1906 goes to Dadabhai Naoroji, he said these lines in his Presendential address).

(3) "The Public life of India had been adorned by a galaxy of brilliant intellects and selfless patriots, but there has been in our time none comparable with Dadabhai Naoroji". —C.Y. Chintamani

(In 1917, when Dadabhai passed away leaving behind a lesson of selfless service to the Nation C.Y. Chintamani said these lines in remembrance of Dadabhai Naoroji).

(4) "The goal of the Congress should be the attainment of a form of government similar to that which existed in the self- governing Colonies of the British Empire". —Gopal Krishna Gokhale

(Gokhale, the most popular leader of the Indian National Congress said these lines, when he presided over the Varanasi session of the Congress in 1905.)

(5) "Opposition where necessary, co-operation where possible". —Surendranath Banerjee.

(Surendranath Banerjee advocated the use of constitutional methods for the attainment of India's goals. The above said lines were his famous saying).

 **Chronology**

1825: Dadabhai Naoroji was born.
1848: Surendranath Banerjee was born.
1866: Gopal Krishna Gokhale was born.
1876: Surendranath Banerjee founded Indian Association of Calcutta.
1879: 'The Bengali' newspaper was launched by Surendranath Banerjee.
1885: The Indian National Congress was led by the Early Nationalists (Moderates).
1885: Indian National Congress was formed.
1886: Public Service Commission was established.
1889: Gopal Krishna Gokhale became a member of the Congress.
1892: The Indian Council Act/ Dadabhai Naoroji was elected to the British House of Common as Liberal Party candidate.
1895: Introduction of the Welby Commission on Indian expenditure.
1897: Gokhale became the General – Secreatary of the Congress.
1905: Gokhale became the President of the Congress and formed the 'Servants of India Society'.
1906: Dadabhai Naoroji was elected as President of Indian National Congress.
1915: Gopal Krishna died.
1917: Dadabhai Naoroji died.
1921-1924: Surendranath Banerjee held office as Minister for local Self–Government.
1925: Surendranath Banerjee died.

OBJECTIVE Type Questions

Multiple Choice Questions-I

[**1** mark each]

1. Which of the following statements about Early Nationalists is false?
   (a) Their leaders were Dadabhai Naoroji and Gopal Krishna Gokhale.
   (b) They believed in Constitutional means of Protest.
   (c) They wanted Self – Government under British rule.
   (d) They wanted to launch violent agitations against the British.

   Ans. (d) They wanted to launch violent agitations against the British.
   Explanation: The Early Nationalists relied on the Constitutional and Peaceful methods to achieve their aims. They believed in patience and reconciliation rather than a violence and confrontation.

   Related Theory
   → The Early Nationalists believed in loyalty to the British Crown.

2. Who was the person during the 19th century to write a book on the economic drain of India caused by the British rule?
   (a) Jawaharlal Nehru
   (b) Subhash Chandra Bose
   (c) Dadabhai Naoroji
   (d) Gopal Krishna Gokhale

   Ans. (c) Dadabhai Naoroji
   Explanation: Dadabhai Naoroji, as a economic thinker, in his famous 'Drain Theory' explained how India's wealth was being drained to England through varius ways.

3. Which of the leaders set up the Servants of India Society in 1905?
   (a) Gopal Krishna Gokhale
   (b) Dadabhai Naoroji
   (c) Surendranath Banerjee
   (d) Mahatma Gandhi   [HOT]

   Ans. (a) Gopal Krishna Gokhale
   Explanation: Gopal Krishna Gokhale set up the Servants of Indian Society in 1905. The main aim of the Society was to train national leaders who would dedicate themselves to the service of India. Some of the important members of the society were Srinivas Shastri and Hridaynath Kunzru.

4. Which of the following was Early Nationalist Leader?
   (a) Dadabhai Naoroji
   (b) Bal Gangadhar Tilak
   (c) Lala Lajpat Rai
   (d) Bipin Chandra Pal

Ans. *(a) Dadabhai Naoroji*

Explanation: Only Dadabhai Naoroji was Early Nationalist, rest all three leaders were Assertive leaders.

5. Complete the given analogy:
Dadhabhai Naoroji : East India Association :: Gokhale : ?
   (a) Servants of India Society
   (b) Indian National Congress
   (c) Indian National Conference
   (d) Indian Association   [HOT]

Ans. *(a) Servants of Indian Society*

Explanation: Gokhale had set up the servants of India Society in 1905.

 Caution
→ Many students had written Indian National Congress. Gokhale had set up servants of the Indian Society.

6. The early Nationalists wanted a .... share in the government of their country.
   (a) smaller   (b) largest
   (c) smallest   (d) larger

Ans. *(d) larger*

Explanation: The Early Nationalists wanted a larger share in the government of their country. They believed that eventually India should make towards democratic Self-Government.

 Related Theory
→ The Nationalists aimed at winning freedom through a gradual process.

7. Identify the three P's of Early Nationalists:
   (i) Press   (ii) Petitions
   (iii) Prayers   (iv) Protests
   (a) (i), (ii) and (iii)
   (b) (ii), (iii) and (iv)
   (c) (i), (iii) and (iv)
   (d) (i), (ii) and (iv)

Ans. *(b) (ii), (iii) and (iv)*

Explanation: The three P's of Early Nationalists were Petitions, Prayers and Protests. They sent petitions, requests and letters of protest to the British Government to look into the problems of the Indians.

 Caution
→ Protests were done by assertives, students should remember this point.

8. Choose the correct option to Match the following: :-

Column I	Column II
(A) Raja Rammohan Roy	(i) Nation in the making
(B) Dadhabhai Naroji	(ii) Ghulamgiri
(C) Surendranath banerjee	(iii) Samwad Kaumudi
(D) Jyotiba Phule	(iv) Poverty and un-British Rule in India

   (a) (A)-(iii), (B)-(i), (C)-(iv), (D)-(ii)
   (b) (A)-(iv), (B)-(iii), (C)-(ii), (D)-(i)
   (c) (A)-(ii), (B)-(i), (C)-(iii), (D)-(iv)
   (d) (A)-(iii), (B)-(iv), (C)-(i), (D)-(ii)

Ans. *(d) A-(iii), B-(iv), C-(i), D-(ii).*

Explanation: Raja Rammohan Roy wrote 'Samwad Kaumudi' weekly in Bengali. Dadabhai Naoroji views are written in the book Poverty and un-British rule in India explaining 'Drain Theory'. Surendranath Banerjee book Nation in the making, gives an account of his political concern and his views about Self-Government. Jyotiba Phule has described the hardships and distress felt by lower castes in his book 'Ghulamgiri'.

9. Gokhale went to .... and helped Gandhiji against racial discrimination.
   (a) Russia   (b) England
   (c) South Africa (d) Germany

Ans. *(c) South Africa*

Explanation: Gokhale met Gandhiji in South Africa in the year 1914, where he helped him to fight against racism of racial discrimination.

 Related Theory
→ Gokhle set up the Servants of Indian Society in 1905.

10. Resolutions on Self-Government, Boycott, Swadeshi and National Education were passed by Congress under Presidentship of:
   (a) Gopal Krishna Gokhale
   (b) Dadabhai Naoroji
   (c) Surendranath Banerjee
   (d) W.C. Banerjee

Ans. *(b) Dadabhai Naoroji*

Explaination: Dadabhai Naoroji was President of Indian National Congress in 1906, when the resolution of Self-Government, Boycott, Swadeshi and National Education were passed.

 Caution
→ Many children have written Gopal Krishna Gokhle as answer.

First Phase of the Indian National Movement

Multiple Choice Questions-II
(Other Question Types, for Extra Practice)

[**4** marks each]

11.

(A) This is a picture of a great social reformer of 19th Century. Identify the person.
   (a) Gopal Krishna Gokhale
   (b) Jyotiba Phule
   (c) Lala Lajpat Rai
   (d) Raja Rammohan Roy

(B) Which organization was found by the above social reformer?
   (a) Brahmo Samaj
   (b) Satya Sodhak Samaj
   (c) Servants of India Society
   (d) Indian National Conference

(C) When was the social reformer in the picture elected as the President of the India National Congress?
   (a) 1905
   (b) 1907
   (c) 1912
   (d) 1915

(D) Identify the incorrect statement from the following:
   (a) This leader became the member of the Imperial Legislative Council in 1902
   (b) Gandhi ji accepted this leader as his 'political mentor'.
   (c) This leader founded the Brahmo Samaj
   (d) This leader impressed upon the government to reduce the land revenue.

Ans. (A) *(a) Gopal Krishna Gokhale*
   Explanation: Gopal Krishna Gokhale was a liberal political leader and social reformer of 19th century.

(B) *(c) Servants of India Society*
   Explanation: Gopal Krishna founded the Servants of India Society to train men prepared to devote their lives to the cause of country in a religious spirit.

(C) *(a) 1905*
   Explanation: Gopal Krishna Gokhale was elected as the President of Indian National Congress in 1905.

(D) *(c) This leader founded the Brahmo Samaj.*
   Explanation: Gopal Krishna Gokhle was the founder of Servants of India Society in 1905.

SUBJECTIVE Type Questions

Short Answer Type Questions
[**2** marks each]

12. State, any two methods adopted by the Early Nationalists in the National Movement.
   [ICSE 2020]

Ans. The methods adopted by the Early Nationalists in the National Movement were:
   (1) They held meetings, discussions and processions, and made speeches to arose Nationalism among the people.
   (2) They criticised government policies through Press and Newspapers and sent memorandum and petitions to the Government Officials and the British Parliament.

   (1) Held meetings
   (2) Speeches were made
   (3) Made use of the Press, Newspapers and journals
   (4) Criticized government policies.
   (5) Sent memorandums
   (6) Sent petitions to government officials and the British Parliament.
   (7) Petitions, Prayers and Protest through Constitutional methods. / 3Ps
   (8) Peaceful propaganda
   (9) Adopted Constitutional means
   (10) Held discussions
   (11) Held processions
   (12) Passed resolutions
   (13) United public opinion
   (14) Sent deputations and delegations
   (15) distribution of leaflets and pamphlets.
   [Any two]
   [Marking Scheme]

What Examiners Say
→ This question was well attempted by most candidates. However, a few wrote 'objectives' or got confused with the methods adopted by the Aggressive Nationalists instead of methods adopted by Early Nationalists.

Caution
→ Students should make out the distribution between the Early Nationalists and Assertive Nationalists in their methods, objectives and belief to avoid writing wrong answers.

13. Name the two books that Dadabhai Naoroji authored explaining the "Drain of India's Wealth". **[ICSE 2019]**

Ans. The book authored by Dadabhai Naoroji explaining the 'Drain of India's wealth' were :
(1) Poverty and un-British rule in India.
(2) Poverty of India.

What Examiners Say
→ Most of the candidates wrote the name of only one book which was Poverty and un-British Rule in India.

Caution
→ Students should read the names of famous books written by leaders as mentioned in the scope of syllabus to avoid writing wrong names and not attempting to answer the question.

14. Why was the session of 1906 important? **[HOT]**

Ans. The session of 1906 was important because four resolutions were passed by the Congress under the Presidentship of Dadabhai Naoroji. They were :
(1) Self-government (2) Swadeshi
(3) Boycott (4) National Education

Structured Questions
[3+3+4= 10 marks each]

15. With reference to the Early Nationalists, answer the following questions:
(A) What were the three-fold objectives of the Early Nationalists leaders? Write any three. **[3]**
(B) Why were the Early Nationalists called 'Moderates'? **[3]**
(C) Mention any four Constitutional Reforms required by Early Nationalists. **[4]**
[HOT]

Ans. (A) (1) To arouse national and political consciousness among the people.
(2) To create a United Public opinion on political questions.
(3) To educate people in modern politics.

(B) The Early Nationalists were called 'Moderates' because:
(1) They believed in loyalty to the British Crown.
(2) They had faith in the British Sense of justice and fair play. Their attitude was not Anti-British.
(3) They believed that the British rule had many benefits, for example, it aided in cleansing social ills like untouchability, sati system and child marriage.

(C) (1) Abolition of the Indian Council.
(2) They laid stress on 'Colonial form of Self – government', which was prevalent in the dominions of Canada and Australia.
(3) The Congress asked for the expansion of the Legislative Councils created by the Act of 1861 and making them representative by including some members elected by the Local Bodies, Chambers of Commerce, Universities etc..
(4) Complete separation of Executive and Judicial functions.
(5) They demanded that all legislative measures and all financial questions, including budgets, should be submitted to these Councils. **[Any four]**

16. With reference to the Early Nationalists, answer the following questions:
(A) Mention three reasons of the Moderate's faith in the British Sense of Justice. **[ICSE 2012]**
(B) Mention any three achievements made by the Moderates.
(C) Mention four Economic demands made by Early Nationalists.

Ans. (A) The reasons for the moderates faith in the British sense of justice were:
(1) They were influenced by western education, literature, history and culture.
(2) They had a belief that the moment the British understood the problems of the Indian, they would solve them.
(3) The moderates simply wanted certain reforms and they even felt to an extent the Indians had benefitted from the British administration e.g. introduction of English language and modern means of communication;
(4) They acknowledged British rule and considered their association as a boon

First Phase of the Indian National Movement 121

as it cleansed Indian society of its ills such as sati pratha, untouchability and child marriage. **(Any three)**

(B) **The three achievements of Moderates were as follows :**

(1) They created National awakening among the people that they belonged to one common country–India. They made Indian conscious of the bonds of common political, economic and cultural interests that united them.

(2) The Early Nationalists trained people in politics by popularizing the ideas of Democracy, Civil Liberties, Secularism and nationalism.

(3) Their political and economic programmes established the truth that India must be ruled in the interest of the Indians

(C) (1) They wanted more funds for technical education to promote Indian industries.

(2) They wanted abolition of Salttax.

(3) There should be reduction in Land Revenue and Expenditure on Military.

(4) There should be improvement in the working conditions of plantation workers.

(5) They wanted an end in unfair, tariffs and excise duties. **[Any four]**

17. With reference to the role of the Moderates in arousing National awakening in India, answer the following questions:

(A) Who was known as 'The Grand Old Man of India'? When and Why did he form East India Association?

(B) Name the Moderate leader who was known as "The Indian Burke" and Why ? What was his famous saying?

(C) Name four moderate leaders and why were they called so?

Ans. (A) Dadabhai Naoroji was known as the "The Grand Old Man of India". He formed the East India Association in London in 1866 to let the British in England know the Plight of the Indians under the British Rule.

(B) Surendranath Banerjee was the Moderate leader who was known as the "Indian Burke". Because his one year stay in England he studied the works of Edmund Burke and these works guided him in his protests against the British.

His famous saying was "Opposition where necessary and co-operation where possible."

(C) Dadabhai Naoroji, W.C. Banerjee, Gopal Krishna Gokhale, Madan Mohan Malviya, Pherozshah Mehta and Justice Ranade were some major Moderate leaders. They were called Moderate leaders because the nature of their demands were moderate along with their methods, which were constitutional as well.

4. Second Phase of the Indian National Movement

The second phase of Indian National Movement witnessed Swadeshi Movement, demand for Swaraj, rise of Militant Nationalism and the Home Rule Movement, contributions of leaders like Bal Gangadhar Tilak, Lala Lajpat Rai and Bipin Chandra Pal, partition of Bengal and Split of Indian National Congress at Surat.

Chapter Notes

- Rise of the Assertive/Radical Nationalism
- Causes of the Partition of Bengal and its Perspective by the Nationalists
- Surat Split of 1907
- Contributions of Bal Gangadhar Tilak, Lala Lajpat Rai and Bipin Chandra Pal.

TOPIC 1

RISE OF THE ASSERTIVE/RADICAL NATIONALISM

By the end of the 19th Century, young radical nationalists emerged within the Congress. They were not satisfied by the methods used by Moderates. They blamed the British for gradual impoverishment of masses and stagnation of agriculture and industries. By now the Indians were aware of their ill-treatment by the British and discrimination in South Africa. Social reformers reminded the Indians of their glorious past. Anti-Indians Acts passed by Lord Curzon further ignited the radical Indians. Mass support was mobilized and self-confidence, self-reliance and national pride acquired the prime position. Demand for self-rule provided the base for the mass movement.

Bal Gangadhar Tilak revived many Hindu festivals to arouse nationalist sentiments.

Swadeshi and Boycott Movements were launched against the repressive policies of the Britishers.

Steps were taken to develop indigenous industries. Demand for self-rule provided the base for the mass movement.

Example 1. Who were the members of Lal-Bal-Pal trio?

Ans. Three prominent leaders of this group were Bal Gangadhar Tilak, Lala Lajpat Rai and Bipin Chnadra Pal. They are famous as Lal-Bal-Pal trio.

Causes for the Rise of Assertive Nationalism

The main causes were:
(1) Restrictions on the Indians for their own natural rights.
(2) Failure of the Early Nationalists
(3) Worsening Economic Conditions
(4) Growing Consciousness among Indians
(5) Need for Mass Action
(6) Influence of International Events
(7) Growth of Education and Unemployment
(8) Ill – treatment of Indians Abroad
(9) Existence of a Nationalist school of Thought
  (i) Repressive Policies of Lord Curzon
  (ii) Partition of Bengal

Belief of Radicals

(1) They did not believe in the 'Politics of Prayers'.
(2) They had no faith in the fair judgement of the British.
(3) They realized that British Imperialism would not let India grow economically.
(4) They believed in mobilizing the masses to put pressure on the government and make them yield to the demands of the Nationalists.

Main Objective of Assertive Nationalists

The main objective of the Assertive Nationalists was the immediate attainment of 'swaraj'. This means complete independence and not just self – government as in the colonies of Australia, New Zealand, etc.

Methods of Assertive Nationalists

(1) National Education scheme
(2) Swadeshi
(3) Boycott
(4) Passive Resistance
(5) Revivalism
(6) Personal Sacrifices
(7) Mass Involvement

Achievements of Assertive Nationalists

(1) These leaders were able to inculcate national pride by extolling India's past. Tilak revived the Ganpati and Shivaji festivals to arouse national sentiments. Through his writings in *Mahratta* and the *Kesari* Tilak preached nationalism.
(2) They gave new slogans to the Indian nationalist movement like 'Non–Cooperation', passive resistance, mass agitation and self–reliance'.
(3) They spoke, wrote and edited newspapers in Vernacular languages and succeeded in conveying their message to a large number of people.
(4) Through their writings and speeches they infused in the Indians, the spirit of Active Nationalism. They exposed the hollowness of the belief in the sense of Justice and fair play of the British rulers.
(5) Self-reliance was promoted by setting up Swadeshi stores, that sold Indian made goods. Jamshedji Tata established Iron and Steel industry. Bengal Chemical works was set up during this phase. Even Rabindranath Tagore had set up a Swadeshi Bhandar. They declared that what Indian needed was total freedom from foreign rule.
(6) Many new Educational Institutions were set up during the Swadeshi Movement. The National Council of Education was set up in 1906. National College was set up at Kolkata with Sri Aurobindo Ghosh as its Principal.
(7) The Movement which had started from Bengal, soon spread to other parts of the country. Swadeshi and Boycott of foreign goods assumed an All – India character.

(8) It was because of their efforts and sacrifices that the partition of Bengal was annulled in 1911. This enchanced the self-confidence of the Indian Nationalists.

Related Theory
→ The D.A.V. Movement in Punjab tried to spread education through various schools and Colleges. However, the contents of the National Education included.
(1) Secular Education
(2) Political Education
(3) Moral Education
(4) Vocational Education

Important
→ The 'Bande Mataram' Slogan was shouted during the bonfire. The Swadeshi idea was popularized by occasional bonfires of foreign sugar, salt and cloth.

Caution
→ The main Objective of Radicals was the immediate attainment of 'Swaraj', students should remember this objective, they should not mix it with methods or achievements of Radicals.

TOPIC 2

CAUSES OF THE PARTITION OF BENGAL AND ITS PERSPECTIVE BY THE NATIONALIST

On 20th July, 1905, Lord Curzon, the British Viceroy, announced the division of the Province of Bengal as that time 'Bengal' included present five states of India- Bengal, Bihar, Odisha, Chota Nagpur Plateau and Part of Assam. Finally, the scheme of Partition of Bengal was implemented on 16th October, 1905.

Example 2. Which city was the capital of 'Bengal' then?

Ans. Calcutta (Kolkata) was made the capital of 'Bengal' then.

Example 3. Which city was the capital of 'Eastern Bengal and Assam'?

Ans. Dacca was made the capital of the new province of Eastern Bengal and Assam.

Lord Curzons motive Behind the Partition:

(1) To Curb Bengali influence by not only placing Bengalis under two administrations, but by reducing them to a minority in Bengali itself.
(2) To drive a wedge between the Hindus and the Muslims.
(3) To break the solidarity of Bengali Nationalism.
(4) To foster divisions on the basis of religion. East Bengal would predominately be a Muslim majority state and West Bengal would have a Hindu majority.

The Indian nationalists clearly saw the intention behind the partition and condemned it. They saw that it was a deliberate attempt to divide the Bengalis on religious and territorial grounds and thereby, disrupt and weaken nationalism in Bengal.

The Anti-Partition Movement

The Partition of Bengal was opposed by the Indian National Congress and the day of Partition was observed as a day of mourning. After a dip in the river Ganga people tied 'rakhi' to each other symbolizing brotherhood. It was observed as a day of fasting.

The streets of Kolkata were full of the cries of 'Bande Mataram' which become the theme song of the national movement. Rabindranath Tagore composed the Patriotic song, 'Amar Sonar Bangla' (My Golden Bengal), for the occasion which was sung by huge crowds parading the streets.

A new phase of Nationalism had started. The Anti-Partition Movement was initiated in the Town Hall of Calcutta, the Veteran leader Ananda Mohan Bose laid the foundation of a Federation Hall to mark the indestructible unity of Bengal. All gathered there took the vow to follow Swadeshi.

Impact of the Anti-Partition Movement

(1) The Partition of Bengal along with the Anti – Partition Movement accelerated the Nationalists Movement by spreading it among the general masses. The people rose in unity to resist, to suffer and to sacrifice.

(2) The ideas of Swadeshi and Boycott were used as weapons of political agitation and training of self-sufficiency for the attainment of Swaraj. British goods were burnt at public places and shops selling them were picketed.

The spirit of Swadeshi spread to every walk of life industries, education, culture, literature, etc.

(3) The people lost their faith in the fair play and Justice of the British. Lord Curzon refused to concede to the demands of annulling the partition.

(4) The Anti–Partition agitation backfired the places of Lord Curzon. It gave added strength to the National Movement.

(5) The Methods adopted by the Early Nationalists lost their appeal and gave an opportunity to

the Assertive Nationalists to lead the National Movement.
(6) The Partition of Bengal was revoked in 1911. A new scheme of partition of Bengal was implemented on linguistic rather than a religious grounds. Hindu, Oriya and Assamese speaking areas were separated from Bengal and to form separate administrative units.
(7) The administrative capital of British India was shifted from Kolkata to Delhi in 1911.

Related Theory
→ Curzon followed the policy of 'Divide and Rule' while partitioning Bengal. Salimullah, the Nawab of Dacca, become the favourite of Curzon by his backing for the partition and he was granted a heavy loan at normal interests. Thus, Curzon's purpose was to create enmity between the Hindus and the Muslims of Bengal.

TOPIC 3

SURAT SPLIT OF 1907

In the year 1907, Annual session of the Congress was held in Surat. The Moderates were quite reluctant to pass the motion on the demand for Swaraj. The notion of Swaraj and Swadeshi was the hallmark of the programme of the Extremists. A group of nationalists openly showed their anger against the British. This brought about a clash within the Congress which was dominated by Moderates.

The Proposal by the Assertive Nationalists of Lala Lajpat Rai as President was countered by the proposal of Ras Behari Ghosh as the President of the Moderates in 1907. This resulted in the final split in the Congress at the Surat Session with the Assertive Nationalists walking out.

The Extremists were led by Bal Gangadhar Tilak, Lala Lajpat Rai and Bipin Chandra Pal and the moderates were led by Gopal Krishna Gokhale.

The Surat split was a big jolt to the Indian National Congress. In fact, the differences between the Moderates and the Extremists presented an opportunity to the British.

Example 4. Who became the president, of Indian National Congress in 1906?

Ans. Dadabhai Naoroji, one of the founding members of Indian National Congress (INC) became the president of the organisation in 1906.

Important
→ The 'Swaraj Split' need to be called a 'Split', as the Extremists merely remained indifferent to the Indian National Congress and did not form a Seperate Organisation. In 1916, they runited with the Congress in the Lucknow session, thus there was only an ideological difference between the Extremists and the Moderates and not a division or split as such. They reunited after 9 years.

Related Theory
→ The Surat split was a dream come true of Curzon, who had already conceived about the split between the Moderates and the Extremists. Lord Curzon had made the Statement 'Congress was tottering to its fall and one of the biggest ambitions in my life is to give it a peaceful demise.'

Caution
→ Students should remember the exact names of leaders and also know which leader belonged to Moderates and which belonged to the Extremists, to avoid writing wrong names in their answers.

TOPIC 4

CONTRIBUTIONS OF BAL GANGADHAR TILAK, LALA LAJPAT RAI AND BIPIN CHANDRA PAL

Bal Gangadhar Tilak (1856 – 1920)

Bal Gangadhar Tilak, was born in a brahmin family of Maharashtra in 1856. He is known as the 'Father of the Assertive Nationalism'. Also 'The Father of the Indian Unrest'.

He played a leading role in popularizing the cult of Patriotism and making the Congress Movement broad-based.

After taking his degree in Law he founded the Poona New English School. The Deccan Education was founded by him under Justice Ranade's guidance in 1884.

Tilak started two newspapers to spread his ideas *Mehratta* (English) and *Kesari* (Marathi) and he reached nationalism and taught the people to be courageous and self-reliant. He wrote two well-known books–The *Gita Rahasya* and The *Arctic Home of the Vedas*.

He organised the *Swadeshi* and the *Boycott* movements to pressurise the British. The British sentenced him to six years imprisonment.

Tilak organized the celebration of Ganpati and Shivaji festivals to arouse feelings of pride, discipline and nationalism. *Akharas* which involved the youth were set up in Maharashtra.

Along with Annie Besant, Tilak set up the Home Rule League. He was responsible for the League in Maharshtra. He also helped to spread the anti-Partition of Bengal movements outside Bengal.

He declared–'Swaraj is my birthright and I shall have it". Tilak was the forerunner of Mahatma Gandhi.

Example 5. When and why was Home Rule League set up by Tilak?

Ans. Tilak had set up the Home Rule League at Pune in 1916 to attain self-government within the British Empire by Constitutional means.

Lala Lajpat Rai (1865-1928)

Lalaji was born in Jagraon in Ludhiana district of Punjab in 1865. He was known as *'Punjab Kesari'* means 'The Lion of Punjab'. He was influenced by the Arya Samaj Movement.

He started his career as a Lawyer in Hissar, but later he shifted to Lahore.

Being an eminent educationist, he was associated with the DAV College Lahore. He also wrote a book on 'National Education'. He started the magazine 'Youth India' in U.S.A. to publicize the right of the Indians to attain Swaraj. When he went to America in 1914, he joined the Ghadar Party there. In U.S.A. he started the Indian Home Rule League. He used the anti-partition Bengal Movement to generate Patriotism in the hearts of the Indian youth. He favoured the Swadeshi and specially the Boycott Movements as these undermined the very prestige of the British and dampened their spirits.

In 1920 he was elected President of the Indian National Congress. He became a member of the servants of India society. The Congress adopted the 'Non – Co-operation' resolution under him. When this movement was suspended, he was disappointed, he was part of the Congress group which formed the Swaraj Party. He fought and won the elections to the Central Legislative Assembly.

He formed the Nationalist Party with the help of Madan Mohan Malviya.

He founded the 'Servants of the People Society' which worked for the welfare of the downtrodden and outcasts and Freedom Movement.

His other Publications included "The Call to Young India", "England Debt to India" and "The Political Future of India". He also founded 'Punjab', 'Vande Mataram' (Urdu Daily) and 'People' (English Weekly).

In 1928 while leading a procession at Lahore against the Simon Commission he was injured in a lathi charge. He was gravely injured and died. His death was a great loss for India.

Bipin Chandra Pal (1858-1932)

Bipin Chandra Pal was born in Sylhet (Bangladesh) in the year 1858. He is known as the 'Father of the Revolutionary thought in India'. He was a teacher and a headmaster of a high school at Cuttack.

He started his Political career as a social reformer and was attached to the Brahmo Samaj from 1876. In 1898, he was sent to Oxford by Brahmo Samaj to study Theology. In his later life, he left Brahmo Samaj and became a total convert to orthodox Hinduism.

In the beginning, he supported the Early Nationalists (Moderates) but during anti – Partition Movement, he took active role in popularising Extremist ideals. He travelled to different parts of India spreading the message of Swaraj or Freedom. He condemned the 'Arms Act' like other Extremists leaders, and he stressed on self – reliance and national Pride.

Bipin Chandra wanted to remove social and economic evils from the society. He opposed the caste system, he advocated widow remarriage, educating women for elevating their position, he stressed the need to develop indigenous industries in the country, he emphasized on the use of Swadeshi and Boycott of foreign goods to eradicate poverty and unemployment.

As a Journalist he worked for Bengal Public opinion, The Tribune and New India to propagate his brand nationalism. The British Government found his writing seditious. Further, he was required to give testimony against Aurbindo Ghosh which he refused. On his refusal, he was arrested and sentenced to six months imprisonment. Bipin Chandra died in 1932.

 Related Theory

→ Tilak had set up the Home Rule League at Pune in Maharashtra in 1916. He along with Mrs. Annie Besant launched the Home Rule Movement within the British Empire by Constitutional means. This movement infused new spirit within the masses and people adored Tilak and he was called 'Lokmanya' means "accepted by the people as their leader".

 Important

→ Tilak was forerunner of Gandhiji in a number of ways :
(1) Tilak's idea of Swaraj was similar to Gandhiji's concept of Complete independence.
(2) Tilak relied on the strength of masses, Gandhiji also involved the masses in politics.
(3) Tilak had preached Swadeshi, Boycott and Prohibition, which Gandhiji later followed these as his ideals.

 ICSE Suggestions

→ Students should make a table of differentiation between Assertive and Early Nationalists and learn about their methods and achievements separately.

→ Students should remember the dates and name of leaders, name of magazines and Books of Bengal carefully. And it should be studied as a memorable event in Indian history.

→ Make a rough flow chart of all three Prominent leaders—Bal Gangadhar Tilak, Lala Lajpat Rai and Bipin Chandra Pal and study it as comparative study of them under headings like Birth, Profession, beliefs, their contribution, etc.

Second Phase of the Indian National Movement

Glossary

(1) **Extremist:** A person who has extreme political opinions.
(2) **Radicals:** Group of younger leaders within the Congress, who did not agree with the methods and ideologies of the Moderates. They were Assertive Nationalists.
(3) **Swadeshi and Boycott Movement:** It was the Movement which was launched by the Indian people after the Partition of Bengal. Under this Movement, it was decided to use products which were made in India and to boycott the foreign goods.
(4) **Morley–Minto Reforms:** Reforms introduced in 1909, which expanded the Legislative Assembly, introduced communal Electorate.
(5) **Revolutionaries:** The freedom fighters who wanted to obtain 'Swaraj' by terrorizing the Britishers.

Who's Who?

(1) **Lord Curzon:** He was the viceroy of India. He was an Imperialist and deadly opposed to Indian Nationalism. His most unpopular act was the Partition of Bengal into two provinces – Eastern Bengal (a Muslim dominated area) and Western Bengal (a Hindu dominated area) in 1905
(2) **Bankim Chandra Chatterjee :** Composer of National Song 'Bande–Mataram'.

Who Said What?

(1) "Bengal united is a power. Bengal divided will pull in several different ways..........one of our main objects is to split up and thereby to weaker a solid body of opponents to other rule". —Risley
[Risley, the Home Secretary to the Government of Britain said these words, explaining the Political purpose behind the Partition of Bengal.]

(2) "Partition of Bengal is a settled fact and what is settled cannot be unsettled". —Lord Curzon
[Lord Curzon said these words by refusing to concede the demands of annulling the Partition of Bengal to the people of India.]

(3) "Self–help and Self–Sacrifice is the real force in the field of nationalism" —Bipin Chandra Pal
[Bipin Chandra Pal reminded the people of India to rely on their abilities.]

(4) "The only hope of India is from the masses. The upper classes are physically and morally dead" —Swami Vivekanand
[There was the realization that only masses could make the immense sacrifices needed to win freedom.]

(5) "When you accept Swadeshi, you must boycott foreign goods". —Lokmanya Tilak
[Lokmanya Tilak said these words because Swadeshi and Boycott are two sides of the same coin.]

(6) "We desire to turn our faces away from government house and turn them to lots of people. This is the spiritual significance of the Boycott Movement". —Lala Lajpat Rai
[Lala Lajpat Rai said these words in favour of boycotting foreign goods and encouraging indigenous industries of India."

(7) "Swaraj is my birth right, and I shall have it" —Lokmanya Tilak
[Bal Gangadhar Tilak said these words because he was convinced that Political rights could be achieved aggresively demanding them.]

(8) "Lathi blows inflicted on me would prove some day as nails in the coffin of the British Empire". —Lala Lajpat Rai
[Lala Lajpat Rai said these words on the day when he was wounded in 1928, while leading the procession at Lahore. In a lathi charge.]

Chronology

1899-1905: Tenure of Lord Curzon
20th July, 1905: The Partition of Bengal was announced.

16ᵗʰ October, 1905: The Partition of Bengal was implemented.
1907: Surat split
1909: Morley – Minto Reforms
1916: Bal Gangadhar Tilak started Home League in Maharashtra.
1928: Lala Lajpat Rai was severely wounded while leading a peaceful procession against the Simon Commission at Lahore by lathi charge.
1928: Lala Lajpat Rai died.

OBJECTIVE Type Questions

Multiple Choice Questions-I

[1 mark each]

1. When was Bengal Partitioned?
   (a) 1905
   (b) 1907
   (c) 1906
   (d) 1911
   [ICSE Sem-1, 2021]

Ans. (a) 1905
   Explanation: The Partition of Bengal came into effect on 16ᵗʰ October, 1905.

2. Which of the following was a Nationalists perspective of the Partition of Bengal?
   (a) There were only Hindus in West Bengal.
   (b) To divide the Hindus and Muslims.
   (c) There were many riots in Bengal.
   (d) It was an administrative necessity as Bengal was a large territory
   [ICSE Sem-1, 2021]

Ans. (b) To divide the Hindus and Muslims.
   Explanation: The Nationalists believed that Bengal was Partitioned by the British to break the unity among the Hindus and the Muslims.

3. Which of the following is a method of the Assertive Nationalists?
   (A) Swadeshi
   (B) Boycott
   (C) Passive Resistance
   (D) Revivalism
   (a) (A), (B), (C)
   (b) Only (D)
   (c) Only (B) and (C)
   (d) All of the above   [HOT🔥]

Ans. (d) All of the above
   Explanation: The method adopted by Assertive Nationalists are:
   (1) Swadeshi
   (2) Boycott
   (3) National Education
   (4) Possitive Resistance
   (5) Revivalism
   (6) Personal sacrifices
   (7) Mass involvement

4. Choose the correct option to match the following:

Column I	Column II
(A) W. C. Banerjee	(i) Political mentor of Gandhiji
(B) Lala Lajpat Rai	(ii) Home Rule League
(C) Gopal Krishna Gokhale	(iii) Indian National Congress
(D) Bal Gangadhar Tilak	(iv) Punjab Kesri

   (a) (A) (i), (B) (iii), (C) (iv), (D) (ii)
   (b) (A) (ii), (B) (iv), (C) (iii), (D) (i)
   (c) (A) (iii), (B) (iv), (C) (i), (D) (ii)
   (d) (A) (iv), (B) (ii), (C) (i), (D) (iii)   [HOT🔥]

Ans. (c) (A) (iii), (B) (iv), (C) (i), (D) (ii)
   Explanation: W.C. Banerjee was the first President of Indian National Congress in 1885. Lala Lajpat Rai was popularly known as 'Punjab Kesri' or 'Sher-e-Punjab'. Gopal Krishna Gokhale went to South Africa where he helped Gandhiji in his fight against racial discrimination. Gandhiji accepted Gokhale as his 'political mentor'. Bal Gangadhar Tilak founded the Home Rule League in 1916 at Pune.

5. Which of the following were Assertive Nationalist Leaders?
   (A) Dadabhai Naoroji
   (B) Bal Gangadhar Tilak
   (C) Lala Lajpat Rai
   (D) Gopal Krishna Gokhale
   (a) (A) and (B)
   (b) (B) and (C)
   (c) (B) and (D)
   (d) (A) and (D)

Ans. (b) (II) and (iii)
   Explanation: In the second phase of the national movement, there emerged a new and a younger group of leaders within the Congress who did not agree with the methods and ideology of the Early Nationalist Leaders. These 'angry young men' stood for complete Swaraj to be achieved by more reliant methods. These group of leaders

Second Phase of the Indian National Movement

came to be known as Assertive Nationalists. Three prominent leaders of this group were Bal Gangadhar Tilak, Lala Lajpat Rai and Bipin Chand Pal, popularly known as Lal-Bal-Pal trio.

Related Theory
→ In its initial years, the Congress was led by a group of leaders known as Early Nationalists. Some prominent Early Nationalist Leaders were Dadabhai Naoroji, Rashbehari Ghosh, W.C. Banerjee, Gopal Krishna Gokhale, Pandit Madan Mohan Malaviya, etc.

Caution
→ Students should remember the names of Assertive leaders and Moderate leaders carefully. Most of the students mix with the names.

6. Complete the given analogy:
   Early Nationlists : Self government Within the British Regime :: Assertive Nationlists :?
   (a) Loyalty to British Crown
   (b) Total Independence
   (c) Consitutional Agitation
   (d) Patience and Reconciliation

Ans. (b) Total Independence

Explanation: The Early Nationalist group of Indian National Congress adopted the path of prayer and petition to oppose the British rule in India. They did not want to overthrow British rule by violence. Their chief demand was self government within the British regime. They expressed loyalty to the British Crown. They believed in patience and reconciliation rather than the confrontation and violence. The main objective of the Assertive Nationalists was to gain total indpendence for India.

7. "Swaraj is my birth right and I will have it" Statement was given by Lala Lajpat Rai.
   Replace the underlined words to correct the statement.
   (a) Bal Gangadhar Tilak
   (b) Bipin Chandra Pal
   (c) Subhash Chandra Bose
   (d) Mahatma Gandhiji

Ans. (a) Bal Gangadhar Tilak

Explanation: Bal Ganghadhar Tilak was the leader of Assertive Nationalist section in the Congress. He insisted that the aim of the Congress should be Swaraj. His famous slogan "Swaraj is my birth right and I shall have it," went on to become the battle cry of the new aggressive nationalists.

Related Theory
→ 'Vande Mataram' became the theme song of the National Movement.

Caution
→ Few students have written answer as Mahatma Gandhi. This is famous slogan of Bal Gangadhar Tilak.

8. The Partition of Bengal was announced by ....
   (a) Lord Dalhousie
   (b) Lord Curzon
   (c) Lord Mountbatten
   (d) Lord Minto   [HOT]

Ans. (b) Lord Curzon

Explanation: Lord Curzon announced the Partition of Bengal in July 1905, which became effective on 16th October 1905.

Related Theory
→ Lord curzon announced the division of the province of Bengal into two provinces. (1) Bengal and (2) Eastern Bengal and Assam.

9. Consider the following statements with reference to the extremists and the moderates within the Congress during the years 1905-07.
   (A) The extremists believed in Constitutional methods and worked within the framework of the Law.
   (B) The moderates aimed at nothing short of Swaraj.
   Which of the statements given above is/are correct?
   (a) Only (A)
   (b) Only (B)
   (c) Both (A) and (B)
   (d) Neither (A) nor (B)

Ans. (d) Neither (A) nor (B)

Explanation: The Early Nationalists or Moderates wanted to achieve self government and they strove for autonomy within the Empire and not for full independence. The extremists were assertive in their approach and aimed at nothing short of Swaraj.

Caution
→ Many students are confused between the aims of Early Nationalists and Assertive Nationalists, students are advised to study both topics in comparative table.

10. In the 1907 Session of the Congress at Surat, whose name was proposed by extremists group as the next President of the Congress?
    (a) Aurobindo Ghosh
    (b) Bal Gangadhar Tilak
    (c) Lala Lajpat Rai
    (d) Bipin Chandra Pal

Ans. (c) Lala Lajpat Rai

Explanation: At the Surat Session of Indian Congress in 1907, the extremists group proposed the name of Lala Lajpat Rai as President. The early nationalists proposed the name of Rasbehari Ghosh. This led to the split in the Congress.

11. Choose the correct option to match the following:

Column I	Column II
(A) Gopal Krishna Gokhale	(i) Home Rule League
(B) Bal Gangadhar Tilak	(ii) Bharamo Samaj
(C) Jyotiba Phule	(iii) Servants of India Society
(D) Raja Rammohan Roy	(iv) Satya Sodhak Sama

   (a) (A)-(i), (B)-(ii), (C)-(iii), (D)-(iv)
   (b) (A)-(iii), (B)-(iii), (C)-(iv), (D)-(ii)
   (c) (A)-(iv), (B)-(iv), (C)-(iv), (D)-(iii)
   (d) (A)-(ii), (B)-(i), (C)-(ii), (D)-(i)

Ans. (a) (A)-(i), (B)-(ii), (C)-(iii), (D)-(iv)

12. Complete the following anology:
    Gopal Krishna Gokhale : Servants of India Society :: BalGangadharTilak : ?
    (a) Home Rule League
    (b) Arya Samaj
    (c) Ramakrishna Mission
    (d) Satya Shodhak Samaj

Ans. (a) Home Rule League

Explanation: Tilak had set up the Home Rule League at Pune in 1916 to attain Self Government within the British Empire by Constitutional means.

13. The Partition of Bengal came into effect on ....
    (a) 4th September 1825
    (b) 16th October, 1905
    (c) 14th April, 1908
    (d) 13th April, 1919

Ans. (b) 16th October, 1905

Multiple Choice Questions-II
(Other Question Types, for Extra Practice)
[4 marks each]

14. Look at the Picture given below and answer the questions that follow :

   (A) Identify the leaders in the Picture.
      (a) Surendranath Banerjee, Dadabhai Naoroji, Gopal Krishna Gokhale
      (b) Dadabhai Naoroji, Lala Lajpat Rai, Bipin Chandra Pal
      (c) Gopal Krishna Gokhale, Bal Gangadhar Tilak, Dadabhai Naoroji
      (d) Lala Lajpat Rai, Bal Gangadhar Tilak, Bipin Chandra Pal

   (B) Which group of Congress did they belong to ?
      (a) Early Nationalists
      (b) Assertive Nationalists
      (c) Revolutionaries
      (d) Swarajists

   (C) What was their main objective?
      (a) attainment of Poorna Swaraj
      (b) Self-Government under British Rule
      (c) abolition of India Council
      (d) demand for Provincial Governments for Indians.

   (D) What are the methods associated with them?
      (a) prayers and Protests
      (b) swadeshi and Boycott
      (c) sending deputations of Indian leaders to Britain.
      (d) sending petitions to the British Government.

Ans. (A) (d) Lala Lajpat Rai, Bal Gangadhar Tilak, Bipin Chandra Pal

Explanation: They were the three prominent leaders of one group and they were called as Lal – Bal – Pal Trio.

(B) (b) Assertive Nationalists

Explanation: They belonged to the second phase, of the national movement, who did not agree with the methods and Ideology of the Early Nationalists leaders.

(C) (a) attainment of Poorna Swaraj

Explanation: The main objectives of the Assertive Nationalists was the immediate attainment of 'Swaraj'. A complete independence and not just self-government as in the colonies of Australia, New Zealand, etc.

(D) (b) Swadeshi and Boycott

Explanation: They adopted Swadeshi and Boycott methods because Tilak said, "When you accept Swadeshi, you must boycott foreign goods".

OR

(A) Who among the following is not present in the picture?
   (a) Subhash Chandra Bose
   (b) Lala Lajpat Rai
   (c) Bal Gangadhar Tilak
   (d) Bipin Chandra Pal

(B) Which of the following leaders died due lathi charge during a protest?
   (a) Subhash Chandra Bose
   (b) Lala Lajpat Rai
   (c) Bal Gangadhar Tilak
   (d) Bipin Chandra Pal

(C) Which leader gave the slogan, "Swaraj is my Birthright and I shall have it"?
   (a) Subhash Chandra Bose
   (b) Lala Lajpat Rai
   (c) Bal Gangadhar Tilak
   (d) Bipin Chandra Pal

(D) Who among these leaders established the Home Rule League?
   (a) Subhash Chandra Bose
   (b) Bal Gangadhar Tilak
   (c) Bipin Chandra Pal
   (d) Lala Lajpat Rai

Ans. (A) (a) Subhash Chandra Bose

Explanation: The picture is of the famous trio of Bal Gangadhar Tilak, Lala Lajpat Rai and Bipin Chandra Pal, popularly known as Lal-Bal-Pal trio.

(B) (b) Lala Lajpat Rai

Explanation: Lala Lajpat Rai played a pivotal role in the Indian Independence movement. In 1928, the British Government appointed Simon Commission, headed by Sir John Simon, to report on the political situation in India and need for further constitutional reforms. The Commission was opposed by all the sections of society and leaders. On October 30, 1928 while leading a demonstration against the Simon Commission at Lahore Railway Station, Lala Lajpat Rai lost his life as a result of lathi blows from the police.

(C) (c) Bal Gangadhar Tilak

Explanation: Balgangadhar Tilak gave the slogan "Swaraj is my bisthright and I shall have it."

(D) (b) Bal Gangadhar Tilak

Explanation: Bal Gangadhar Tilak set up a Home Rule League at Pune in 1916 to attain self government within the British Empire by constitutional means.

SUBJECTIVE Type Questions

Short Answer Type Questions
[**2** marks each]

15. Mention any two contributions of Bipin Chandra Pal in promoting Nationalism.
[ICSE 2020]

Ans. The two contributions of Bipin Chandra Pal in promoting Nationalism were :
(1) He encouraged the use of Swadeshi and boycott of foreign goods.
(2) He wrote 'Spirit of Indian Nationalism' and advocated National Education.

Contributions of Bipin Chandra Pal
(1) Role of journalist
(2) worked for Bengal Public Opinion.
(3) The Tribune/New India to propagate nationalism.
(4) Founder of Vande Mataram.
(5) Wrote New Economic Menace to India.
(6) Wrote Spirit of Indian Nationalism.
(7) Advocated National Education.
(8) Aroused nationalistic passions or patriotism.
(9) Wanted National Education to be the basis of the freedom movement.
(10) Opposed the Caste system/worked for social progress.
(11) Advocated widow remarriage.
(12) Educated women.
(13) Participated in several Congress Sessions.
(14) Pleaded for Arms Act to be repealed.
(15) Contributed to promote National Consciousness.
(16) Played an active role in anti-partition movement.
(17) participated in Swadeshi Movement.
(18) proposed remedies to eradicate poverty.
(19) wanted Swadeshi and Boycott to become means of freedom.

(20) was against only Non-Cooperation Movement/wanted more action or aggressive measures.

(21) was called The Father of Revolutionary thought in India. **[Any two]**
[Marking Scheme]

What Examiners Say

→ Majority of the candidates mentioned the contributions of Bipin Chandra Pal in promoting Nationalism correctly. However, a few got confused with the points of contributions of other Nationalists.

16. Why is October 16, 1905 regarded as an important day in the history of the Indian National Movement? [HOT]

Ans. On October 16, 1905, Partition of Bengal formally came into force, which was announced by the Viceroy of India, Lord Curzon. It separated the largely Muslim eastern areas of Bengal from the rest of Bengal. It was observed as Day of Mourning throughout Bengal.

Caution

→ The Partition of Bengal should be learnt as a chronological event.

17. What were the two basic reasons responsible for the Surat Split in 1907 between the Early Nationalists and the Assertive Nationalists?
[ICSE 2014]

Ans. The basic reasons for the Surat Split in 1907 between the Early Nationalists and the Assertive Nationalists were:

(1) There was a row over the election of the President. At Surat Session, the Assertive Nationalists tried to push the candidature of Lala Lajpat Rai for Presidentship of Congress while Early Nationalists nominated Dr. Ras Bihari Bose for the Presidentship.

(2) The Early Nationalists tried to repudiate the resolution on Boycott, Swadeshi and National Education which had been adopted in 1906. The Early Nationalists withdrew their support from Swadeshi and Boycott Movements as they were afraid that these Movements would make the British refuse to give them more political rights, so, they did not want to continue with these movements.

The two basic reasons for the Surat split in 1907 were:
(1) the Early Nationalists did not want to extend the Swadeshi and the Boycott to the rest of India but confine it only in Bengal. The Assertive Nationalists wanted to extend the Boycott and Swadeshi movement and make it a full-fledged mass struggle to achieve Swaraj

(2) there was a disagreement over who would be the next President of the Congress – the Early Nationalist proposed the name of Ras Behari Bose and the Assertive Nationalists proposed the name of Lala Lajpat Rai. **[Any two]**
[Marking Scheme]

What Examiners Say

→ One factor responsible for the Surat split i.e. the difference of opinion with regard to Swadeshi and Boycott movements was mentioned correctly however the second factor–the election of the President was not mentioned by majority of candidates.

18. State two reasons given by Lord Curzon to justify the Partition of Bengal. **[ICSE 2016]**

Ans. The reasons given by Lord Curzon to justify the partition of Bengal were:

(1) The province of Bengal was too large to be administered efficiently;

(2) According to Lord Curzon, it was mere readjustment of the administrative boundaries.

Lord Curzon's Reasons:

(1) That the province of Bengal was too big to be efficiently administered by a single provincial government. It was a mere readjustment of administrative boundaries to protect pockets of minorities both in West Bengal as well as East Bengal.

(2) To fetch more revenue through trade outlets.

(3) To protect pockets of minorities in East and West Bengal. **[Any two]**
[Marking Scheme]

What Examiners Say

→ Most candidates were unable to differentiate between the reason of Partition of Bengal and the real motives behind the partition. Some candidates wrote the reason as 'population' which is incorrect.

Caution

→ Students should read the question carefully, because the question pertains to Curzon's Justification of Partition of Bengal and not the Nationalists views as mentioned by some students.

19. Who founded the Home Rule Leagues in India? What was its objective? **[ICSE 2015]**

Ans. There were two Home Rule Leagues founded in India. Bal Gangadhar Tilak founded the Indian Home Rule League in April in 1916 at Belgaum and Annie Besant founded the Home Rule League in September 1916 at Madras.

Second Phase of the Indian National Movement

The main objective of both the leagues was achieving self-government in India.

Tilak, Annie Besant, self-governing Institutions from the grassroots to the Central legislature.

[Marking Scheme]

What Examiners Say

→ *The first part of the question was answered correctly by most candidates. In the second part however a few candidates mentioned 'Swaraj' as the main objectives instead of writing 'Swaraj' within the British Empire.*

Caution

→ *Terms such as 'Dominion Status', 'Self – Government' and 'Swaraj' should be understood and used thoroughly.*

20. Mention any two causes for the Rise of Assertive Nationalism. **[ICSE 2015]**

Ans. The causes for the rise of Assertive Nationalism were:

(1) **Failure of the Early Nationalists:** The early nationalists leaders failed to secure any political reforms from the government and their movement lacked mass involvement. Their polity was confined to the upper strata of society and failed to penetrate to the grass root level. Being dissatisfied with the methods and ideology of Early Nationalists, the Assertive Nationalists advocated the need for a more vigorous and uncompromising movement to achieve swaraj.

(2) **Famine and Plague:** In 1896-97, the entire nation was gripped by famine and plague resulting in great economic distress to the masses. While the people were suffering from severe hardships, the British Government failed to start a 'Famine Relief Fund' to alleviate their sufferings. This negligence on the part of British rulers further fuelled the anger and disgust of the common people. All this sent a wave of resentment throughout India and contributed to the rise of Assertive Nationalism.

(3) **Continued Economic Exploitation:** Due to prolonged effects of drought and famine, the Indian peasants became increasingly impoverished. The Congress demanded relief from the Government for the salt duty, excise duty and other taxes but there was no relief forthcoming from the British. The Early Nationalist leaders failed to make any dent on the British exploitation and plunder of the Indian economy.

(4) **Growth of Education and Unemployment:** The 19th century saw a quantum jump in the numbers of educated Indians, many of whom either remained unemployed or found employment in the British administration at very low salaries. These educated and often exploited youth became ready followers of Assertive Nationalism since it was easy for them to see through the charade of British rule. **[Any Two]**

(1) Famine and plague of 1896 affected crores of people and caused death. The British Government provided slow relief.

(2) Economic exploitation: prolonged drought and famine increased the misery of the peasants/Indian traders and manufacturers lost confidence in the British Government/India's gold reserves were transferred to London/India was starved of its own resources.

(3) Ill treatment of Indian's in South Africa/Indians were subjected to racial discrimination.

(4) International events: boers fight against the mighty British empire, Home Rule agitation in Ireland, Italy's defeat in Ethopia, Japan's victory over Russia shattered the myth of European superiority.

(5) Lord Curzon's repressive policies: Calcutta Corporations Act, Universities Act, Sedation and Official Secrets Act, Partition of Bengal. **[Any two]**
[Marking Scheme]

Structured Questions

[3+3+4= **10** marks each]

21. With reference to the Assertive Nationalist, answer the following questions:

(A) Mention three important contributions of Lala Lajpat Rai. **[ICSE 2014]**

(B) Name of the Nationalist who said, 'Swaraj is my birthright and I shall have it.' State any two of his contributions to the National Movement. **[ICSE 2018]**

(C) What were the achievements of the Assertive Nationalists?

Ans. (A) The contributions of Lala Lajpat Rai were:

(1) He was a fearless freedom fighter who called on the people for direct action aganist the British rule instead of adopting Constitutional methods

of prayers and petitions. His fiery speeches instilled the people with feelings of patriotism and taught the people to fight for swaraj with courage in the face of immense hardships.

(2) He was not only a good orator but also a social reformer and educationist. He founded the 'Servants of the People Society', which worked for the freedom movement as well as for social reform movement in the country.

(3) He led a non-violent procession in Lahore to demonstrate against the Simon Commission. During this procession he was brutally lathi charged by the British police and later on died due to several head injuries sustained during this lathi charge. His death during the Simon Commission agitation did not go in vain as this fuelled anti British protest and produced several revolutionaries.

(4) He actively participated in the Swadeshi Movement in the wave of the partition of Bengal and strongly protested against the policies of the government.

(5) He went to America in 1914 to garner support for India and joined the 'Ghadar Party' there. He founded the Indian Home League Society of America and wrote a book called Young India in which he criticized the British rule in India. **[Any three]**

Lala Lajpat Rai
(1) started a monthly magazine 'Young India' to spread the message of the right of India to attain Swaraj.
(2) He wrote a book on National Education as he wanted to reform the existing education system.
(3) he was associated with the Arya Samaj Movement
(4) He helped in the expansion of D.A.V. College at Lahore
(5) he set up the Servants of the Peoples Society for the welfare of the down trodden and outcastes.
(6) he opened orphanages, hospitals and schools
(7) he went abroad to mobilize opinion in favour of India's struggle for freedom.
(8) he joined the Ghadar party in America
(9) he founded 'Punjabi' , 'Vande Mataram'. (Urdu Daily) and 'People' (English weekly)
[Any three] [Marking Scheme]

 What Examiners Say
→ Most candidates wrote general answers, and appeared confused between Tilak and Lajpat Rai. Specific contributions were missing.

 Caution
→ Students should be very specific in explaining the contributions of prominent leaders.

(B) (a) "Swaraj is my birth right and I shall have it." was said by Bal Gangadhar Tilak.
He was one of the first and strongest advocates of 'Swaraj' or self rule which became the guiding principle of the Indian National Movement. (b) He ignited the spark of patriotism among Indians and successfully mobilised people from all sections of society. (c) He revived Ganpati and Shivaji Festivals to promote national feeling among Indians.

> Bal Gangadhar Tilak Close contact with masses, demand for swaraj inculcate courage, self-defence, patriotism by organizing Akharas and lathi clubs, started Ganapati and Shivaji festivals, two newspapers – Maratha and Kesari, two books – Gita Rahasya and the artic Home of the Vedas, Establishted Home Rule league in 1916, forerunner of Mahatma Gandhi, preached the idea of Swadeshi, Boycott and Prohibition. His role in the anti-partition movement.
> **[Any two]**
> **[Marking Scheme]**

 What Examiners Say
→ Most of the candidates identified the Nationalists correctly but were confused between his contributions with that of the other leaders.

(C) **The achievements of the Assertive Nationalists were as follows:**
(1) They were able to inculcate national pride by extolling India's past. Tilak revived the Ganpati and Shivaji festivals to arouse national sentiments and spread the message of Nationalism through his writings in Maratha and Kesari.
(2) They gave new slogans to the Indian Nationalists Movement like Non-Cooperation, Passive resistance, Mass agitation and self – reliance.
(3) They spoke, wrote and edited newspapers in Vernacular languages for conveying their message to a large number of people.
(4) They exposed the hollowness of the belief in the sense of justice and fair play of the British.

(5) They declared what India needed was total freedom from foreign rule.
(6) New Educational Institutions were set up during the Swadeshi Movement.
(7) Self-reliance was promoted by setting up Swadeshi stores that sold Indian made goods. Jamshedji Tata established Iron and Steel Industry despite the fact that the Industry had a long gestation period. Bengal works was set up during this phase.

[Any four]

22. With reference to the Radicals, answer the following questions:
    (A) State any three repressive policies of Lord Curzon.
    (B) Name three acts enacted by the government to suppress the Anti-Partition Movement.
    (C) Explain any four contribution of Bipin Chandra Pal. [ICSE 2008]

Ans. (A) The repressive policies of Lord Curzon were:
    (1) Seditious Meeting Act preventing political meeting against the government;
    (2) Explosive Substances Act with the provision to imprison without trial;
    (3) Official Secret Act of 1923;
    (4) Indian Universities Act, 1904.

[Any three]

(B) The acts enacted by the government to suppress the Anti-Partition Movement were:
    (1) Prevention of Seditious Meeting Act, 1907
    (2) Explosive Substances Act, 1908
    (3) Newspaper Act, 1908
    (4) Criminal Law Amendment act, 1908

[Any three]

(C) **Contribution of Bipin Chandra Pal (1858–1932)**
    (1) He was an eminent leader of aggressive Nationalists and a great orator, who spread the message of Swadeshi and Swaraj.
    (2) He joined the Congress in 1886 and made a forceful speech to repeal the Arms Act.
    (3) In the role of a Journalist, he worked for 'Bengal Public Opinion', 'The Tribune' and 'New India' to propagate his brand of Nationalism.
    (4) He felt that the spread of National Education could be used to arouse the Indian youth involve them in the struggle of Swaraj.

(5) He also urged Nationalists to work for the removal of the poverty.
(6) He felt that Swadeshi and Boycott would be the best route for both economic as well as political freedom.

[Any four]

23. One of Lord Curzon's administrative measures that resulted in a strong resentment from the masses was the Partition of Bengal in 1905. In this context, answer the following questions:
    (A) What was Lord Curzon's argument in favour of the Partition of Bengal?
    How did the Nationalists interpret Lord Curzon's motives?
    (B) How did the people react to the Partition of Bengal?
    (C) What was the impact of the *Swadeshi* Movement on Indian Industries?

Ans. (A) Lord Curzon advocated that area of Bengal was too large and it was difficult for the British to administer efficiently. Hence, Partition of Bengal was a administrative necessity.

The Nationalists interpreted Lord Curzon's motives as follows:
    (1) The Nationalists understood that due to rising Nationalism, the British hoped to stop the rising tide by partitioning Bengal.
    (2) It was a plan of the British to spread comnunal disharmony because while West Bengal had Hindus in majority, Muslims were in majority in East Bengal.
    (3) It was an attempt by the British to divide Bengal on communal lines and break the Nationalist forces in Bengal.

(B) (1) 16 October 1905, the day Bengal was partitioned, write pointwise was observed as the day of mourning. Right from the morning thousands of people began taking a dip in the Ganges.
    (2) Hindus and Muslims tied Rakhi to each other to show their indestructible unity. People in Calcutta walked barefoot in the streets, shouting the slogans 'Vande Mataram'.
    (3) Rabindranath Tagore composed the famous Bengali patriotic song, 'Amar Sonar Bangla Amei Tomay Bholabhashi' for the occasion and it was sung by the crowds of thousands of delirious patriots parading the streets. Such was the impact of the slogan that the British were forced to prohibit its use in Bengal.

(4) The Assertive Nationalists who were dissatisfied with the methods of 'Prayers, Petitions and Protests' now decided to take an uncompromising stand against the division of Bengal.

(5) They were on a look out for a strong weapon to strike at and undermine the British authority in India. These leaders knew that British authority in India revolved around the economic gains they made from sale of British made goods in India. Therefore, they proclaimed 'Swadeshi and Boycott' as their programme of action.

[Any three]

(C) Swadeshi Movement involved boycotting British goods and promoting Indian goods. People from all walks of life participated in the movement and it resulted in significant decline in the foreign imports during 1905-1908. It led to building of self reliance or Atmashakti asserting on national dignity, honor and confidence. The explicit influence on self reliance gave a much needed stimulus to the cottage industries and also to large scale enterprises. Many textile mills, handloom and weaving factories were established. This improved the demand for swadeshi goods and gave boost to production.

24. **The Second half of the 19th century witnessed the growth of a strong feeling of Nationalism. With reference to the statement, answer the following:**

(A) Write *any three* repressive Colonial policies of the British.

(B) State *any three* ways in which the Press played an important role in developing nationalism amongst Indians.

(C) Explain briefly *any four* differences in the methods adopted between the Early Nationalists and Radicals, in the National Movement. [ICSE 2019]

Ans. (A) The repressive Colonial policies of the British were:

(1) **The Vernacular Press Act (1878):** This Act forbade vernacular papers to publish any material that might excite feelings of dissatisfaction against the British Government. This Act was not applicable to English newspapers.

(2) **The Indian Arms Act (1879):** This Act made it a criminal offence for Indians to carry arms without a license. This Act was not applicable to the Britishers.

(3) **Age limit for Civil Services:** The maximum age limit for the Indian Civil Service Examination was reduced from 21 years to 19 years, thus, making it difficult for Indians to compete for it.

(4) **Removal of Import Duties:** The import duties on British textiles was removed which proved harmful for the Indian industry

(5) **Ibert Bill Controversy:** Lord Ripon tried to pass a law enabling the Indian judges to try even European offenders in criminal cases with a purpose to reduce judicial inequalities. But the Europeans did not like this and organized a vociferous agitation against this bill which was known as the Ibert Bill. In the end, the European lobby was successful and the Bill was withdrawn. The Ibert Bill controversy showed how strong the racial bitterness among the British for the Indians was. Indians decided to get united to fight for their rightful causes.

(6) **Imperial Durbar in Delhi:** In 1877, Lord Lytton held an Imperial Durbar in Delhi to proclaim Queen Victoria as the Empress of India when the entire country was reeling under a severe famine. A huge amount of money was spent on this Durbar, that time when people were dying of famine in various parts of India. [Any Three]

(B) The Press played a vital role in developing nationalism among Indians during the British period. Some important role played by the press include:

(1) It played a vital role in spreading the message of patriotism and modern ideas of liberty and justice

(2) It played an important role in campaigns of social reforms

(3) It played an important role in criticizing the unjust and repressive policies of the British Government.

(C)

S.No.	Early Nationalists	Radicals
(1)	The Early Nationalists followed a peaceful method of opposing through petitions, resolutions and meetings.	The Radicals followed revolutionary methods by launching vigorous political agitations, making people self reliant and bringing national awakening.

(2)	The Early Nationalists had full faith in the British Government and wanted to follow the policy of cooperation.	The Radicals believed in non-cooperation and adopted the programme of boycott against foreign goods, propagation of Swadeshi, a system of national education, etc.
(3)	The Early Nationalists agitated only for certain administrative and economic reforms and wanted that the Indians should have some say in the government.	The Radicals demanded "Purna Swaraj' i.e. self-government.
(4)	They were inspired by the ideas of western philosophers.	They draw their inspiration from India's past.

(A) (1) Organised the Grand Delhi Durbar.
  (2) Introduced the Vernacular Press Act.
  (3) Introduced the Indian Arms Act.
  (4) Reduced the maximum age to take up the ICS examination from 21 to 19 years.
  (5) Removed the import duties on the British goods and harmed the Indian industry.
  (6) Ilbert Bill Controversy.
  [Any three]

(B) The press
  (1) Spread the message of patriotism.
  (2) Spread the ideals of liberty, freedom and equality.
  (3) Popularised the ideas of Home Rule and Independence.
  (4) Carried on daily criticism of the British policies.
  (5) Exposed the true nature of British rule in India.
  (6) Helped in the exchange of views among people from different parts of the country.
  (7) Made the Indians aware of what was happening in the world.
  (8) Aroused public opinion in the country.
  [Any four]

(C) **Early Nationalists**
  (1) They believed in the policy of Constitutional agitation within the legal framework, and slow order political progress.
  (2) They held meetings where speeches were made and resolutions for popular demands were passed.
  (3) They made use of the press to criticize government policies,
  (4) They sent memorandums and petitions.
  (5) They made use of three P's – Petitions, Prayers and Protests.
  (6) A British Committee of the Indian National Congress was set up in London in 1889, which published a weekly journal, India to present India's case before the British public.
  (7) Deputations of Indian leaders were sent to Britain. These political leaders carried an active propaganda in Britain.
  [Any three]

Radicals Methods
  (1) Swadeshi
  (2) Boycott
  (3) National Education
  (4) Passive Resistance
  (5) Revivalism
  (6) Personal Sacrifices
  (7) Mass Movement
  (8) Aggressive or assertive method
  (Any four)
  [Marking Scheme]

What Examiners Say

→ (A) Most of the candidates were able to attempt this question quite well. However, some candidates were not sure whether to write the repressive policies of Lord Curzon or Lord Lytton. The Universities Act and Partition of Bengal were also given as examples of this policy in a few answer scripts.

→ (B) Most of the candidates were able to answer this question correctly. A few candidates, however, only mentioned the names of the books and the newspapers.

→ (C) Majority of the candidates mentioned the beliefs and aims of the Early Nationalists and Radicals rather than mentioning the methods adopted by them in the national Movement. Most of the candidates were not clear regarding the objectives beliefs and methods of both the groups.

⚠ Caution

→ Students should clarify, the time frame of repressive policies during the early part and later part of the 19th Century. The student should be able to recall that Lord Curzon belonged to the early part of the 20th century.

→ Understand the rule of books and newspapers in developing nationalism amongst Indians.

➥ *Students should read and understand the question carefully, The demand of the question must be understood before writing its answer.*

25. With reference to the growth of National Consciousness in India, explain each of the following:

(A) The immediate objectives of the Indian National Congress.

(B) *Two* contributions of Dadabhai Naoroji.

(C) The impact of the Swadeshi and the Boycott Movement. **[ICSE 2015]**

Ans. (A) **The immediate objectives of the Indian National Congress were:**

(1) The promotion of friendly relations amongst nationalist political workers in different parts of the country;

(2) To remove all prejudices regarding race, caste, creed or provinces among the people and to develop the sentiment of national unity;

(3) To take heed of the opinions of educated classes on vital social issues and to present these forcefully before the government;

(4) To formulate popular demands and present them to the government;

(5) To determine the political tasks to be commenced;

(6) To train people and organise public opinion in the country. **[Any three]**

(B) **The contributions of Dadabhai Naoroji:**

(1) He prevented a split between the Early Nationalists and Assertive Nationalists in the Congress and declared 'Swaraj' to be the national goal in his presidential address in 1906;

(2) He exposed the exploitation of India's economy by the British Government through his Drain theory.

(C) **The impact of Swadeshi and Boycott Movement were:**

(1) **Promotion of Indigenous Industries:** The Swadeshi and Boycott Movements were insistent on economic self reliance, which meant an assertion of self confidence. It aimed at the promotion of indigenous industries for strengthening the country. This explicit influence on self reliance gave a much needed stimulus to the cottage industries and also to large scale enterprises;

(2) **Inculcation of National Spirit:** The Swadeshi and Boycott were used as weapons of agitation aganist the British rule. Since these ideas had direct relevance for the welfare of people, they drew diverse sections of society into active participation in the Freedom Movement. Associations of different classes of people were formed which infused the feeling of nationalism among the Indians.

(3) **Making India Self reliant:** The Swadesh and Boycott Movement laid emphasis on self reliance, 'Atmashakti' and aimed at the promotion of indigenous industries for strengthening the country.

(4) **Contribution to Nationalist Literature:** The Swadeshi and the Boycott Movement led to the emergence of a new type of nationalist poetry, prose and journalism, infused with the spirit of patriotism and nationalism. The nationalist literature had the literary quality of permanent value. The newspapers and journals inspired by the Swadeshi and Boycott, published classic articles on freedom, liberty and self-reliance.

(A) **Immediate objectives of the Congress:**

(1) To enable national workers from all parts of India to become personally known to each other.

(2) To end all racial, religious and provincial prejudices and to promote feeling of National unity among all countrymen.

(3) The formulation of popular demands on vital Indian problems and their presentation before the government.

(4) To train and organize public opinion in the country.

(5) To decide upon the political task to be undertaken during the ensuring year. **[Any three]**

(B) Dadabhai founded the East India Foundation in London to inform the British of the true state of affairs in India/ as the member of the British Parliament, he rendered admirable services to the cause of India and to the people of Indian origin in South Africa/ it was due to his efforts that a resolution recommending the ICS examinations to be held simultaneously in England and India was passed/he was one of the founder members of the Congress/ he passed the resolutions on Swaraj, Swadeshi, Boycott and National Education./ he condemned the partition of Bengal/he edited Rast-goftar/started a magazine Dharam marg Darshak/wrote poverty and un –British rule in India/ through his Drain theory he explained how India's wealth was being taken away to England/he advocated a just political system. **[Any Two]**

(C) All the people took the vow of Swadeshi. Rabindra Nath Tagore wrote his famous patriotic song Amaar Sonar Bangla. Vande Mataram was adopted as the war cry of the agitation. Amrit Bazaar Patrika vehemently criticized the partition. Bengali papers like Sanjeevani and Hitaishi took lead in spreading anti-British feelings. Brought into politics, new classes of people encouraged orientation in vernacular needs. Taught Press to be out spoken. **[Marking Scheme]**

What Examiners Say

→ (A) Most of the candidates answered correctly. A few however wrote the demands of the Congress instead of its objectives.

→ (B) Most candidates wrote the contribution of Dadabhai Naoroji correctly. Few wrote the contribution of other moderate leaders too that was not required.

→ (C) Most candidates wrote the correct answer. A few instead of writing the impact of the Swadesh and Boycott Movements wrote on the people's reaction against the Partition of Bengal.

⚠ Caution

→ Students should learn the difference between the objectives and demands of the Congress to avoid confusion.

→ Students should be very specific in writing the contribution of prominent leaders.

→ Learn the meaning of the term 'impact and significance and differentiate it with the reaction or the cause of the Movement.

26. The early Congressmen were liberal in their views and programmes. This led to the rise of Assertive Nationalists who demanded more forceful action against the British. In this context, discuss the following:

(A) Reasons why the early Congressmen were called Moderates?

(B) How did Moderates differ from the Assertive Nationalists in realizing their objectives?

(C) How did Tilak bring a new wave in Indian politics that was distinct from the early Congressmen? **[ICSE 2015]**

Ans. (A) The early Congressmen were called moderates as by and large they followed the methods of "Prayers, Petition and Protest." They believed in working within the Constitutional framework. They asked only for reforms, not swaraj. They expressed confidence in the wisdom of the British. They had great faith in the democratic liberal traditions of their British rulers. The early Congressmen sought only to mitigate the evils of British rule but not to eliminate it completely. They were of the firm belief that only Constitutional and lawful agitation could lead to the administrative and political reforms that they sought to achieve.

(B)

	Moderates	Assertive Nationalists
(1)	The Moderates aimed at administrative and constitutional reforms.	The Assertive Nationalists aimed at nothing less than swaraj.
(2)	Most of the Moderates had great faith in the British sense of justice and fair play. They were loyal to the British and considered British rule a boon for India.	The Assertive Nationalists had no faith in the British rule and denounced it. They wanted to uproot it from India.
(3)	The Moderates received support from the intelligent and urban middle class. They had a narrow social base.	The Assertive Nationalists had mass appeal and drew their support from all sections of society, hence had a wider social base.
(4)	The Moderates believed in Constitutional and peaceful methods to acheive their objectives.	The Assertive Nationalists generated vigorous nationalism by adopting revolutionary methods.

[Any three]

(C) Bal Gangadhar Tilak, also known as Lokmanya Tilak, was perhaps the most learned among the country's political leaders. He started two newspapers, the Kesari and the Mahratta in order to highlight the sufferings of the people and to teach people to become courageous and fearless fighters for the freedom of their country. He organised Akharas and Lathi Clubs to make the youth brave and infuse in them the spirit of Nationalism in order to attain Swaraj. Through celebrations of the Ganpati Festival and Shivaji's birthday, he organised people to spread the spirit of oneness. Realising that Constitutional agitation by itself was futile against the British, he opposed the Moderate view of the early Congressmen and exclaimed "Militancy not Mendicancy" should be the policy of the Congress.

Tilak was the first to enunciate the historic words, "Swaraj is my birth right and I shall have it." He was a great proponent of Prohibition, Swadeshi and Swaraj.

27. The conflict between the two sections of the Congress came to surface in its Session in 1906 at Calcutta. In this context, explain the following:

(A) The Split in the Congress in 1907.

(B) With reference to the picture given below, answer the following:

(a) What were the *three* personalities popularly known as?
(b) Which section of the Congress did they represent?
(c) Mention *two* of their popular beliefs.

(C) State *any four* methods that they advocated for the achievement of their aims. [ICSE 2017]

Ans. (A) The early nationalists regarded British rule as a beneficial necessity. The progressive thinkers among them, otherwise called Radical Nationalists, criticized this policy and believed that any foreign rule, however just and benevolent was a curse. The Radicals wanted to extend the Swadeshi and Boycott Movement from Bengal to the rest of the country and extend boycott to every form of association with the Colonial Government. The debate and disagreement between the Early Nationalists over the methods of agitation in Bengal came into the open during the anti-partition movement which led to the dispute in Indian National Congress.

In 1907, at the Surat session, the confrontation came to the head. There was row over the election of the President.

At Surat session, the Radicals tried to push the candidature of Lala Lajpat Rai for Presidentship of Congress while Early Nationalists nominated Dr. Rash Bihari Ghosh to be the President. The situation was saved by Lala Lajpat Rai by stepping down and Dr. Rash Bihari Ghosh became the President. Gopal Krishna Gokhale and rest of the Early Nationalists withdrew their support from Swadeshi and Boycott Movements as they were afraid that these movements would make the British refuse to give them more political rights so they did not want to continue with these movements. This was not acceptable to the Radicals. As a result, open clashes took place and session was suspended thereafter. Early Nationalists held a separate convention from which the Radicals Nationalists were excluded. This marked a complete split in the Congress and is known as Surat split.

(B) (a) The three personalities were popularly known as Bal-Lal-Pal.
(b) They represented the Assertive Radical Nationalists.
(c) The popular beliefs of Bal-Lal-Pal were:
(1) They declared Poorna Swarajya as their decisive goal. Tilak declared, "Swaraj is my birth right and I shall have it."
(2) They replaced the constitutional methods of agitation with 'Passive Resistance to British Imperialism". Their programme comprised of Boycott, Swadeshi and National Education.

(C) The methods advocated by them for the achievement of their aims were:
(1) **Swadeshi:** The use of swadeshi or home made goods was aimed at encouraging the growth of indigenous industry. It was aimed at providing employment to the rural population.
(2) **Boycott Foreign Goods:** Lala Lajpat Rai pointed out the reason for the boycott of foreign goods. It aimed to strike at the roots of British economy. It also included boycott of government services, honours and titles. Anyone found buying or selling foreign goods was subjected to social boycott. It proved to be an effective weapon for hitting out at British interests in India.
(3) **National Education:** The Radicals desired that a National scheme of

Education be put in place to replace the government controlled schools, colleges and universities. Several new colleges were established with a view to further National education.

(4) **Revivalism:** The Radical Nationalists tried to use religious sentiments to evoke the sentiments of the people. Tilak revived the Ganpathi and Shivaji festivals. The greatness of Rana Pratap, Shivaji and Ashoka were highlighted to inspire the masses and instill them with self confidence and pride about India's glorious past.

(A) The Assertive Nationalists wanted to extend *Swadeshi* and boycott to the rest of India. The Early Nationalists however wanted to confine it to Bengal only. They also were opposed to openly supporting boycott. There were differences regarding the election of the INC President too.

(B) (a) The trio – Bal – Lal – Pal
 (b) Assertive Nationalists
 (c) Supremacy of Indian Culture. No faith in the goodness of the British.

(C) The methods advocated by the Assertive Nationalists to achieve their aims were:
 (1) They propagated boycott of foreign goods and the use of Swadeshi.
 (2) These leaders inculcated national pride by extolling India's past.
 (3) They introduced new methods of waging political struggle like non-cooperation, passive resistance, mass agitation and self-reliance.
 (4) Many educational institutions were set up during the Swadeshi movement.
 (5) Revived Shivaji festival and presented Rana Pratap and Shivaji as National Heroes. **[Any Four]**
 [Marking Scheme]

What Examiners Say

→ (A) Most candidates answered this part correctly. A few however, were unsure of the correct facts and wrote general answers.
→ (B) (a) Most candidates identified the personalities correctly.
 (b) While most candidates answered correctly, a few candidates were unsure of the answer and wrote "Moderates" or "Early Nationalists".
 (c) A few answered incorrectly as they wrote on the beliefs of the Moderates.
→ (C) Some candidates were confused with methods and beliefs and wrote their achievements too.

⚠ Caution

→ Lay stress on ideological differences and the tussle in the session.
→ Students should identify pictures properly.
→ Students should understand the meaning of the terms–methods, beliefs, aims and achievements to avoid any confusion.

The Muslim League

The British started sowing the seeds of Communalism between the Hindus and Muslims just after the Revolt of 1857. The idea was prolong their rule in India and also to check the rising tide of Nationalism, which gave birth to the formation of the Muslim League in India.

Chapter Notes

- *Factors Leading to the Formation of the Muslim League and its Objectives*
- *Lucknow Pact-1916*

TOPIC 1

FACTORS LEADING TO THE FORMATION OF THE MUSLIM LEAGUE AND ITS OBJECTIVES

Factors Leading to the Formation of The Muslim League

The British Policy of 'Divide and Rule'

The Hindus and Muslims had lived together in India for centuries. Both the communities were exploited by British, they fought together during the First War of Independence in 1857. Such a unity between the two communities posed a danger to British Imperialism.

After the Revolt of 1857, the British started discriminating between the Hindus and the Muslims, because their unity proved a threat to their Empire. So, they applied 'Divide and Rule Policy' and encouraged separatist and Communal politics in India. Their frame of mind was:

(1) They started favouring Muslims over Hindus.
(2) They branded the Congress as a Hindu organisation.
(3) They talked of Bengali domination and encouraged Provincialism.
(4) They even encouraged the upper class Muslims to start their own organization.
(5) They tried to create hatred among the Hindus and Muslims by portraying Muslim rulers as plunderers and Hindu rulers as cruel kings to their Muslim subjects.
(6) In 1871, Lord Mayo's government adopted a resolution which made Urdu the medium of instructions for the Muslims in Primary and Secondary schools and increased government aid to educational institutions run by the Muslims.
(7) They tried to spread Communal hatered through press, posters, literature and public platform.
(8) They tried to utilize the caste structure to turn the Non-Brahmins and the lower caste against high castes. They treated Hindus, Muslims and Sikhs as separate communities and accepted their Communal leaders as authentic representatives of all their co-religionists.

Loss of Sovereignty by Mughal Rulers

The British became rulers in India after defeating Mughal rulers, who were followers of Islam. This resented the Muslim community against the British rulers, who became the bitter enemies of the British. They participated in the Wahabi Movement, aimed at ending British domination in India. They also took part in the uprising of 1857. This made the British view them with suspicion. After the Revolt of 1857, the British thought that Muslim community could take revenge at any time, so they adopted a policy of indifference towards Muslims and started to appease the Hindus.

Backwardness of the Muslim Community in Education, Trade and Industry

(1) The upper Class Muslims comprising zamindars and aristocrats during the first 70 years of the 19th century were anti-British. They were conservative and hostile to Western education. For this reason, they remained economically and educationally backward.
(2) After 1858, the British Government in India had consciously discriminated against the Muslims, holding them responsible for the uprising of 1857. They were discriminated in the recruitment to Civil and Military services.
(3) The Muslim community was not much involved in the growth of any organised industry. Here too they were lagging in trade and industry.
(4) Some members of the Muslim community did not keep up with the modern trends in social and cultural spheres. They were stuck to their own literature and culture, as they were proud of it and they did not adapt to the Western system of Education. Many Hindus, on the other hand, who adapted to the Western system of Education got entry into Government services. Thus, Muslims had disadvantage in this respect also. In these situations, the British officials easily incited the Muslims against the Hindus.

Role of Sir Sayyid Ahmad Khan

Sir Sayyid Ahmad Khan was a great Educationist and Social reformer. Initially, he regarded Hindus and Muslims as one Quam (notion). He founded Mohammedan Anglo-Oriented College (MAO College) at Aligarh, which had both Hindu and Muslim patrons. Under the influence of Mr. Theodore Beck, (the British Principal his College), he gave up his earlier views and in 1880 declared that the political interest of Hindus and Muslims were different.

Sir Sayyid Khan opposed the Indian National Congress, when it was founded. In its competition, he founded the United Indian Patriotic Association in 1888, mainly with a view to oppose the Congress. In this effort Mr. Beck supported him. Beck's idea was that Anglo – Muslim Unity was possible, but Hindu – Muslim unity was impossible.

Sir Sayyid believed that the continuance of British rule was a "guarantee for the welfare and progress of the community", otherwise the Hindus who formed the majority of Indian population, would dominate the Muslim community. Therefore, he declared that if the educated Muslims support the British, then the latter would reward them with government jobs and other special favours

Rise of Assertive Nationalism

Even though Assertive Nationalists played an important role in the National Movement, but some of their actions marked a step back in respect of the growth of national unity. The speeches and actions of some leaders like Bal Gangadhar Tilak and Aurobindo Ghosh's concept of India as mother and nationalism as religion, propagation of Shivaji and Ganpati festivals, Anti – Partition of Bengal agitation with dips in the Ganga did not appeal to some of the Muslims.

Wrong Interpretation of History

The manner in which Indian History was interpreted in those days contributed to the growth of Communal thinking among the Hindus and the Muslims.

Economic Backwardness of the Country

Due to the British Colonial Policies, India lacked in modern Industrial development ; and there was acute unemployment among the educated youth. As a consequence, there was a fierce competition among the youth to secure the few available jobs. This led the people to demand reservation in jobs on the basis of castes, creed or religion.

Events leading to the formation of the Muslim League

The Hindu-Urdu Controversy

Before 1900 in the United Provinces (present Uttar Pradesh), Urdu was the Court language and all the petitions to the offices and courts were submitted in Urdu. But, some sections of the society protested against this practice. On 8th April, 1900, the Government instructed that all petitions were to be submitted in Hindi in Devnagri script. And the court summons and official announcements to be issued in Hindi as well as in Urdu. The Muslims resented this. The Controversy continued for months and relations between the communities became worse.

Foundation of Mohammedan Anglo – Oriental Association (1893)

The British were concerned about the growing influence and popularity of the Congress. The British encouraged the formation of Mohammedan Anglo-Oriente (M.A.O.) Association in order to counter the growing influence of the Congress. Principal Beck of the M.A.O. College Aligarh, was its secretary. The motive of the British in setting up the Association was to promote loyalty to the British and to prevent Muslims from participating in any Political Movement.

Sir Antony MacDonald, the then Governor of Uttar Pradesh, removed Urdu from Public Offices which was supported by the Congress. Thus, the need for the formation of a Muslim Political Party was felt severely.

Partition of Bengal (1905)

Lord Curzon had partitioned Bengal into two provinces on the ground of easy administration. However, the real purpose of partition of, Bengal was to create differences between the Hindus and the Muslims; and also to check the rising tide of nationalism. The British got the support of the Muslims on the ground that the new province would be a Muslim majority province , which was East Bengal, led by Nawab Salimullah of Dhaka.

The Aligarh Politics

Nawab Mohsin–ul–Mulk led the Aligarh Movement after the death of Sir Sayyid in 1898. The new Principal of MAO College, Mr. Archibald chalked out a plan to forge Communalism in India. He invited Nawab Mohsin – ul – Mulk to Shimla and advised him to put forward a demand for separate electorate for the Muslims as the government wanted to introduce reforms along these lines. He also helped him to prepare a Memorandum to Lord Minto, who agreed to receive the deputation of the Muslim leaders under the leadership of Agha Khan on 1st October, 1906.

Muslim Deputation to Lord Minto

Their Chief demands were:

(1) Representation of Muslims in elected bodies on the basis of their political importance and not on their numerical strength.

(2) Separate electoral constituencies for the Muslims in the Provincial Council and the Imperial Legislative Council.

(3) Preference to be given to the Muslims while nominating members of the Viceroy's Council.

(4) Reservation of seats for Muslims in the State Services.

(5) More State aid for promoting new Muslim Universities.

The Viceroy Minto received the deputation and expressed his sympathy with their aspirations. He assured them that their political rights and interests as a community would be safeguarded

Formation of the Muslim League

In December 1906, Muslim representatives from various provinces gathered for a Muslim Educational Conference at Dhaka. Nawab Salimullah suggested a setting up of an organization to represent Muslims.

The Muslim League was formed in Dhaka on 30th December, 1906. Under the Presidentship of Nawab Salimullah. Agha Khan was elected as permanent President of the Muslim League.

Its first regular session was held in December, 1908 at Amritsar under the Chairmanship of Sayyid Ali Immam.

Its Headquarters was in Aligarh but its Central Office was shifted to Lucknow in 1910.

Aims and Objectives of the Muslim League

(1) Promotion of the feelings of loyalty to the British Government.
(2) Protection and advancement of the Political rights and interests of the Muslims of India by checking the growing influence of the Congress, and
(3) Prevention of the rise of hostility towards other communities.

Impact of the Muslim League on the National Movement

Initially, the British welcomed the formation of the Muslim League. The League stood apart from the National Movement, it opposed the Anti-Partition Movement and the Swadeshi and Boycott Movements. The League was a Political organization of the Muslims, which tried to cut off the Muslim masses from the National Movement. Thus, the policies of the Muslims League had weakened Nationalists sentiments.

League's role in the beginning was greater representation of Muslims in all services. As regards to representation in Assemblies, it wanted more seats than its numerical representation warranted.

With the help of Lord Minto, the Muslim League secured the demand for separate electorates i.e. the system of election to legislatures which divides voters on the basis of religion, castes or occupation. The provision for separate electorate in the Morley– Minto Reforms was intentionally incorporated to please the Muslim League and create a rift between the Muslim League and the Congress.

From 1910 to 1913, new forces emerged in Muslim League politics and some of its leaders realized that reapproachment with the Congress was desirable. Inspite of these differences, a group of educated men among the Muslims promoted the Radical and Nationalist ideas among them. The most prominent leaders were Maulana Abdul Kalam Azad, Habib-ur-Rahman, Hakim Ajmal Khan and Muzhar – ul – Haq. In 1913, the Muslim League adopted the goal of self – government for India. And in the same year Muhammad Ali Jinnah joined the Muslim League. He also supported the progressive and national aims of the Congress.

When the British Government acted against the Turkish interests and supported the cause of the Balkan countries in the First World War, Indians reacted and Anti-British sentiments started to grow among the Muslims. As a result, many more Radical young Muslims joined the nationalists towards the common cause. Muslims stood up and launched the Khilafat Movement against the British. Even the Congress joined them and the Khilafat issue was included as one of the demands of the Non-Cooperation Movement. As a result, a Pact, which is known as the Lucknow Pact, was signed.

📢 Important
➡ In December 1915, the Extremists under Tilak and Moderates under Gokhale met at Bombay where Muslim League joined them to draft a set of minimum Constitutional demands through mutual consultations.

Example 1. When was the Muslim League formally founded ? Who Presided over its session at Dhaka?

Ans. The Muslim League was formally founded on 30th December, 1906 at Dhaka. The League was founded under the leadership of Aga Khan, Nawab Salimullah of Dhaka and Nawab Mohsin-ul-Mulk.

The Dhaka session of the Muslim League was presided over by Viqar-ul-Mulk.

⚠ Caution
➡ Be careful in learning the names of all Muslim leaders involved in the formation of the Muslim League, some students get confused with the names of some leaders and their surnames.

LUCKNOW PACT – 1916

The Lucknow Pact refers to the joint scheme of political reforms agreed to by both the Congress and the Muslim League in 1916 regarding the structure of government in India and the relationship between the Hindus and the Muslims. The period of the First World War (1914 – 1919) was of intense Nationalists Political activities. The events during the War and the prevalent sentiments were responsible for the signing of the Lucknow Pact between the Congress and the Muslim League.

Circumstances leading to the Lucknow Pact

International Events

During 1912 and 1913, Turkey's Ottoman Empire had to fight the Balkan Powers. The British policy during the Balkan Wars was not sympathetic to Turkey. The Sultan of Turkey was regarded as the Caliph or the religious head of the Muslims. Moreover, all the Muslims holy places of the Muslims were situated within the Turkish

Empire. In the First World War, Britain was fighting against Turkey. This caused a wave of Pro-Turkey and Pro-Caliph or Khilafat sentiments amongst the Muslims.

National Events

(1) The Partition of Bengal was annulled in 1911
(2) Nationalist Muslims like Abdul Kalam Azad and Ali Brothers (Mohammad Ali, Shaukat Ali) made use of this opportunity to spread nationalist ideas among Muslims for mobilizing public opinion in favour of self – government.
(3) Tilak was released from jail in 1914, after six years. Under 'Seditious Meetings Act', some prominent Muslim leaders were arrested. This brought Congress and Muslim League closer.

Changes in the Objectives of the Muslim League

In 1913, the League had amended its Constitution to include 'a system of self-government under the umbrella of British crown' as the ideal of the Muslim League. Therefore, it agreed with the Congress to have a political goal for India. Their renewed cooperation opened the doors of unity of interests and objectives between them. Annie Besant and Bal Gangadhar Tilak too played a significant role in bringing (Home League) the two organisations together.

A Compromise between the two fractions of the Congress

Annie Besant tried to unite the two wings of the Congress, the Early Nationalists and the Assertive Nationalists. Tilak rejoined the Congress in 1916 and played a significant role in resolving differences between the Congress and the League.

Terms of the Lucknow Pact

Efforts were made to bring the Congress and the Muslim League to reach an agreement on the scheme of political reforms in India. In 1915, both the Congress and the League held their sessions at Bombay. The Bombay sessions of the League was attended by the Congress leaders. The leaders of both the parties forged a joint plan of Post War Constitutional reforms.

In 1916, the Congress and the League again held simultaneous sessions at Lucknow. The Joint Scheme of Political reforms was put forward and adopted by both parties in 1916. This agreement signed by the two parties is known as the Lucknow Pact.

Main Features of the Lucknow Pact

Some of the main features were as follows:

(1) The Council of the Secretary of State for India operated from England shall be abolished. The Secretary of State was to be assisted by two Under Secretaries, of whom one should be Indian.
(2) Four-fifths of the members of the Provincial Legislatures were to be directly elected and one-fifth to be nominated. The number of members in the Provinces was laid down in the scheme. 50% in Punjab, 40% in Bengal and 30% in U.P., on the whole, the proportion of Muslim members was large. And they were to be elected through separate electorates.
(3) The Imperial Legislative Council shall have 150 members. Four-fifth members of the Imperial Legislative Council shall be elected, but one-third of these shall be Muslims elected on the principle of separate electorates.
(4) The Minorities should have adequate representation in elected bodies.
(5) Defence, Foreign Affairs and political relation of India, i.e. declaration of War, or signing of Peace treaties, were excluded from the control of the Imperial Legislature.
(6) All Bills passed by the Legislature were to be operative unless vetoed by the Governor – General in the Council. If the same Bill was passed again by the Legislative Council within a year, the government was obliged to pass it. Extensive power was to be given to the Legislature for control over financial matters.
(7) The Provincial Legislative Council shall have full control over the Provincial Government.
(8) No Legislative Council shall proceed with a Bill or Resolution if ¾th members of any community opposed to it on the ground that it adversely affected their interests.
(9) Half of the members of the Viceroy's Executive Council were to be Indians, elected by the elected Members of the Imperial Legislative Council.
(10) The Judiciary in every province shall be placed under the Highest Court of the Province.

Significance of the Lucknow Pact

Hindu–Muslim Unity

The joint scheme symbolised Hindu – Muslim unity. Both the Communities agreed to compromise for the common goal. The Muslim League accepted the principles of election and majority rule, whereas, the Congress compromised on its secular character by accepting the scheme of separate electorates for Muslims. As a result of the Pact, both Hindus and Muslims mutually worked together from 1916 to 1922.

Unity within the Congress

The Assertive Nationalists and the Early Nationalists united during the Lucknow session and the signing of the Lucknow Pact. After the Surat session of 1907, both the wings of the Congress had moved in different directions. But they came together in 1916 and as a result, the Congress was strengthened. Mr. Ambica Charan Majumdar was the President of the Lucknow session in 1916.

Pressure on the Government

The unity between the Congress and the Muslim League and between the Early Nationalists and

Assertive Nationalists became a threat to the British Government in India. Until now, the Government had been repressing the Nationalists Movements by using force. But, now the Government had no excuse for delaying Political or Constitutional reforms.

Necessity to Pacify Indians

As the First World War continued, the leaders of the Congress and the League impressed upon the British Government that their demands for Constitutional Reforms should not be rejected if they wished Indians to be loyal to the British.

The British Government, therefore, felt it necessary to pacify the Indians by the Declaration of August 20, 1917, which promised a policy of gradual development of self – government institutions in India.

Drawbacks of the Lucknow Pact

(1) The Lucknow Pact was confined only to educated and rich Hindus and Muslims. Therefore, it did not involve the masses.

(2) The Lucknow Pact had seemed to lay stress on the separate interests of the Hindus and Muslims and their separate political existence. But the Congress made this apparent compromise for the sake of political unity. They thought that unity with the League would put more pressure on the British Government to grant political concessions.

(3) The Pact provided for Muslim representation in the Council in excess of their total proportion in the total population.

(4) By accepting separate electorates for Muslim, the Congress lost its secular character and proved the way for future communal tension.

(5) The Pact provided for a 'Communal veto' in legislation, because no Legislative could proceed with any Bill if three – fourths of the members of a particular community opposed it.

(6) The Lucknow Pact was a temporary patch up between the Congress and the Muslim League. The Muslim League still remained a separate entity, with a Communal outlook, advocating separate political interests from those of the Hindus.

Example 2. What was the impact of the first world war on India or on the National Movement?

Ans. (1) The war was indirectly responsible for changing the aims and objectives of the Muslim League. After the war, both the Congress and the Muslim League decided to work together.

(2) The war period was of intense nationalist political activities.

Important

→ Muhammad Ali Jinnah, then member of the Congress as well as League, made both the parties reach an agreement to pressurize the British Government to adopt a more liberal approach towards India and give Indians more authority to run their country, besides safeguarding basic Muslim demands.

Caution

→ Clauses of Lucknow Pact means main features of the Lucknow Pact, it should not be confused with the circumstances leading to Lucknow Pact. Students are required to relate to meaning of the term used in question.

ICSE Suggestions

→ Objectives of the Muslim League are different from impact of the Muslim League. Students should remember impacts are the consequences of the League which were met after the formation of League. So, they should be clear in their understanding of question properly.

Glossary

(1) **Muslim League:** It was an organization which was formed in 1906 by Nawab Salimullah of Dacca with the aim to promote, among the Muslims of India, a feeling of loyalty to the British Government.

(2) **MAO College:** Mohammedan Anglo Oriental College. It was formed by Sir Sayyid Ahmad Khan in 1885 to spread education among the Muslims.

(3) **Muslim Deputation to Lord Minto (1906):** A depuation led by Agha Khan, who met the Viceroy Lord Minto, and submitted some demands, such as separate electorates, weightage in representation, separate representation in the municipal and university bodies, greater representation in Civil, Military and Judicial Services and the founding of a Muslim University. Lord Minto gave a favourable reply to delegation.

(4) **Communalism:** It is referred to as an ideology of a particular community, which are only for its narrow interests, disregarding the interests of the whole society. It creates division between the people on religious lines, which often leads to tension and riots in the society.

(5) **Separate Electorate:** It meant that the Muslims would choose their separate leader by separate elections for Muslim Community. The Morley-Minto Reforms of 1909 introduced the principle of Communal representation in the legislatures.

(6) **Seditious:** The use of words or actions that are intended to encourage people to oppose a government.

(7) **Separatist:** A group of people within a country who wanted to become separate from the rest of the country and form their own government.

(8) **Appease:** To make somebody calmer by giving them, what they want.

(9) **Delegation:** A group of people who represents the views of an organization.

(10) **Electorate:** The people in a country or an area who have the right to vote.

Who's Who?

(1) **Agha Khan:** Title given to the religious head of Khoja Muslims. Khojas are a wealthy section of Muslim Community.

(2) **Sayyid Ahmad Khan:** He was an educator, politician, an Islamic Reformer and a progressive nationalist. He popularized Scientific and Western learning worked for the social and economic development of the Indian Muslims. He founded the Mohammedan Anglo – Oriental College.

(3) **Mohammad Ali Jinnah:** He was a barrister, politician and the founder of Pakistan. He served as the leader of the All India Muslim League from 1913 until the inception of 14th August, 1947 and then as the Dominion of Pakistan's first Governor General until his death.

Who Said What?

(1) *"If the United Congress was buried at Surat, it is reborn at Lucknow".* —Ambica Charan Majumdar

Mr. Ambica Charan Majumdar rightly remarked these words in Lucknow session in 1916 when Congress leaders, both (Assertive and Moderates) united in Lucknow session after the split of Surat in 1907. Ambica Charan was the President of Congress during Lucknow session then.

Chronology

1905: Partition of Bengal
1906: Formation of the Muslim League
1907: The Surat Split
1909: Morley–Minto Reforms
1913: Mohammad Jinnah joined the Muslim League. The Muslim League adopted a resolution of self–government.
1914-1918:– First World War
1916: The Lucknow Pact between the Congress and Muslim League, Home Rule Movement.

OBJECTIVE Type Questions

Multiple Choice Questions
[1 mark each]

1. From the given list, identify the objective of the Muslim League:
   (a) To train and organize public opinion in the country
   (b) To promote friendly relations between Nationalist political workers
   (c) To promote among the Muslims of India, support for the British Government
   (d) To agitate through Constitutional means
   [ICSE Sem-1, 2021]

   Ans. (c) *To promote among the Muslims of India, support for the British Government.*

   Explanation: The objective of the Muslim league was to promote among the Muslims of India, support for the British Government and to remove any misconceptions regarding the intention of the government in relation to Indian Muslims.

   ⚠ **Caution**
   → *The Aims and Objectives are same thing.*

2. Which of the following is not the aim of the Muslim League?
   (a) To develop and consolidate the feelings of national unity among the Muslims.
   (b) To protect and advance the political rights of the Muslims.

The Muslim League 149

(c) To promote among Muslims of India, support for the British Government.
(d) To prevent hostilities between the Muslims and other communities.

Ans. *(a) To develop and consolidate the feelings of national unity among the Muslims.*

Explanation: The objectives of Muslim League were laid down as follows:
(1) To promote, among the Muslims of India, support for the British Government;
(2) To protect and advance the political rights and interests of the Muslims;
(3) To prevent the rise of feelings of hostility between the Muslims of India and the other communities.

 Related Theory
The events during the First World War and the prevalent sentiments were responsible for signing of the Lucknow Pact between the Congress and the Muslims League.

3. The Lucknow Pact was signed between the Congress and ....
   (a) The British East India Company
   (b) Lord Curzon
   (c) The Muslim League
   (d) The British Crown [HOT🔥]

Ans. *(c) Muslim League*

Explanation: The Lucknow Pact was signed between the Congress and the Muslim League in 1916 to bring about Hindu Muslim Unity after the First World War.

4. The All India Muslim League was formed in ....
   (a) 1906   (b) 1920
   (c) 1885   (d) 1942   [HOT🔥]

Ans. *(a) 1906*

Explanation: The All India Muslim League was formed at Dacca in 1906.

5. In which year did the Muslim League pass a resolution demanding the partition of the country?
   (a) 1935   (b) 1940
   (c) 1942   (d) 1946

Ans. *(b) 1940*

Explanation: In 1937, M.A. Jinnah and other leaders of the Muslim League proclaimed that they cannot expect any justice at the hands of the Congress. In 1940, the Muslim League passed a resolution demanding the partition of the country and the creation of a State called Pakistan.

 Related Theory
Despite a severe opposition from Ghandhiji, the country drifted towards the partition. The communal riots broke out in the country and in 1947, a seperate country, Pakistan came into existence.

6. In which year, the Congress recognized the Muslim League as the political party representing the Muslims for the first time?
   (a) 1912   (b) 1914
   (c) 1916   (d) 1923

Ans. *(c) 1916*

Explanation: During the Lucknow session of the Indian National Congress in 1916, the Congress and the Muslim League together started demanding common reforms rom the government. Since the year 1906, Muslim league had been demanding separate electorate for them. Through the Lucknow Pact, the Congress and the Muslim League agreed to allow representation of religious minorities in the Provincial Legislatures.

SUBJECTIVE Type Questions

Short Answer Type Questions
[2 marks each]

7. Name two Muslim leaders linked with the Muslim League.

Ans. Maulana Mohammad Ali and Mohammad Ali Jinnah.

8. What is the importance of the Lucknow session of 1916 of the Indian National Congress?

Ans. In December 1916, the Congress and the League held their sessionss at Lucknow. In the session, both the parties decided to work together and signed a joint scheme of Reforms, that later came to be known as the Lucknow Pact.

9. What did the British do to foster the Policy of 'Divide and Rule', which gave rise to the formation of the Muslim League?

Ans. (1) They encouraged the Muslims to start separate organisations.
(2) The system of Separate Communal Electorates sowed the seeds of communalism and widened the gap between the Hindus and the Muslims.

10. Give the name of the two leaders who led the Home Rule Movement in India. [HOT🔥]

Ans. Bal Gangadhar Tilak and Annie Besant led the Home Rule Movement in India.

11. Name the famous Pact that demostrated the Unity between the Congress and the Muslim League. When was its signed? [ICSE 2016]

Ans. The unity between the Congress and the Muslim League was demonstrated by Lucknow Pact. It was signed in 1916.

> Lucknow Pact, 1916
> **[Marking Scheme]**

 What Examiners Say

→ Answered correctly by most candidates however some wrote the year of the Pact incorrectly.

 Caution

→ Emphasis on learning facts thoroughly, learn timeline of all important dates.

Structured Questions

[3+3+4= **10** marks each]

12. With reference to the Muslim League and Lucknow Pact, answer the following questions:

(A) What were the main features of the Lucknow Pact of 1916?

(B) Why was the Lucknow Pact important? Write 3 points.

(C) What were the terms of Lucknow Pact. Write any four.

Ans. (A) The Lucknow Pact of 1916 was an important step towards achieving Hindu-Muslim Unity. In 1913, a new group of Muslims leader, under Muhammed Ali Jinnah, entered the folds of the Muslim League with the aim of bridging the gulf between the Muslims and the Hindus. The Muslim League changed its major objective of establishing friendly relations with the Crown and decided to join hands with the Congress in order to put pressure on the British Government. The principal leaders of both the parties addressed a memorandum to the Viceroy on the subject of reforms in October 1916. The agreement was confirmed by the Congress and the League in their annual session held at Lucknow in December 1916, which came to be known as the Lucknow Pact.

(B) **Importance of the Pact**

(1) **Unity:** It brought about the Hindu – Muslim unity, which was the need of the hour. It also brought Assertive and Early Nationalists together on the same platform.

(2) **Strengthening of the National Movement:** The unity between the Congress and the League and between the Moderates and the Extremists upset the Government of India. Now, the Government was under pressure for Constitutional Reforms. This helped in the strengthening the National Movement.

(3) **Constitutional Reforms:** At that time, the Home Rule League was also gaining momentum. Both the leaders of the Congress and the League made it clear to the government that their demands for Constitutional Reforms could not be easily ignored, if they wished Indians to be loyal to the British. In the phase of overwhelming odds, the government announced on 20th August, 1917, that their policy in India was "The gradual development of self-government institutions".

(C) **Terms of the Lucknow Pact:**

(1) **Independent Unit:** India was to be treated as an independent unit of Empire in the form of a self-autonomous state with equal rights and responsibility.

(2) **Provincial Legislatures:** Four-fifth of the members of the Provincial Legislatures were to be elected and one-fifth to be nominated. One-third of the elected members were to be from Muslim Community.

(3) **Separation of Judiciary from Executive:** Judiciary should be separated from Executive. Members of the Judiciary in each province should be placed under the control of the highest Court of that Province.

(4) **Bills related to Religion interests:** No bill could be introduced in the Legislative Council if it influenced the interests of any community and such a bill could not be passed if it was opposed by three-fourth of that Community.

13. With reference to the Muslim League and Lucknow Pact, answer the following questions:

(A) State any three objectives of the Muslim League. [ICSE 2018]

(B) How did the Hindi – Urdu Controversy became an important factor in the formation of the Muslim League?

(C) Write four demands made by the Muslims Deputation in 1906 to the Viceroy Lord Minto.

Ans. **(A) Objectives of the Muslim League:**
(1) To promote among the Muslims of India, feelings of loyalty to the British Government and remove any misconception that may arise as to the intention of government with regard to any of its measures pertaining to Indian Muslims;
(2) To protect and advance the political rights and interests of Muslims of India and to respectfully represent their needs and aspirations to the government.
(3) To prevent the rise of feelings of hostility between Muslims of India and other communities.

> To promote among the Indian Muslims support for British rule, to remove misconceptions between the British Government in relation to Indian Muslims, to protect and advance the political rights and interests of the Muslims, to represent the needs and aspirations to the government in mild and moderate way. To prevent the rise of feelings of hostility between the Muslims and other communities.
> **[Any three]**
> **[Marking Scheme]**

 What Examiners Say

→ *Majority of the candidates were unable to write the objectives of the Muslim League. Instead of writing its objectives in 1906, they wrote about the demands made by it later for Pakistan and for the introduction of the Urdu language.*

⚠ **Caution**

→ *Students should clearly differentiate between the objectives of Muslim League at the time of its formation in 1906 and the demands made by it later on.*

(B) The Hindi–Urdu Controversy in United provinces in 1900 was due to the British accepting the petition made by Hindus in government Courts and offices in Devnagri Script. This made the Muslims upset as this lowered the importance of Urdu. The Muslims now began feeling that it was time to form an organization that could safeguard their interests.

(C) **The main demands of Muslims deputation were:**
(1) Representation of Muslims in legislatures should not be according to their members but according to their Status.
(2) the setting up of separate electorate.

(3) They wanted assured and greater representation in the **Military Civil Educational** and even Municipal bodies.
(4) They wanted to set up their own educational centres where they would develop Muslim culture.

14. The Partition of Bengal and the formation of the Muslim League were two important events that had their impact on the National Struggle for Independence. In this context, explain the following:
(A) Impact of Swadeshi and Boycott Movements as part of the Anti-Partition Movement.
(B) Objectives of the Muslim League.
(C) *Any three* factors leading to the formation of the Muslim League.
[HOT🔥] [ICSE 2016]

Ans. (A) (1) The Swadeshi and Boycott Movements were the greatest mass struggle as all classes and communities took active part in these movements. A large number of people went to jail but refused to capitulate under British pressure. The movements served as light house for freedom fighters as they could now understand the concept of non-violence.
(2) The Movements popularized the use of Swadeshi goods to give stimulus to Indian Cottage industries by boycotting the use of imported foreign goods. It became a strong weapon against the British and affected the sale of British products adversely.
(3) These Movements brought several regions and sections of the people together.
(4) These Movements gave a bigger economical setback to British interests in India. Imported goods from Britain declined by fifty percent. **[Any three]**

(B) **The objectives of Muslim League were:**
(1) To promote among the Muslims of India, feelings of loyalty to the British Government and remove any misconception that may arise as to the intention of government with regard to any of its measures pertaining to Indian Muslims.
(2) To protect and advance the political rights and interests of Muslims of India and respectfully represent their needs and aspirations to the government.

(3) To prevent the rise, among the Muslims of India, of any feeling of hostility towards other communities without prejudice to the objects of the league.

(C) **The factors leading to the formation of the Muslim League were:**

(1) **British Policy of Divide and Rule:** After the revolt of 1857, the British adopted a vindictive attitude towards Indian Muslims. They were looked upon with suspicion. The British tried to appease the Muslims and tried the 'Divide and Rule' policy to counter the National Movement carried on by the Congress leaders. The British rulers even helped the Muslim leaders to come together and form a separate organization so as to keep the Muslims away from the Congress and its National Movement. Thus, by the beginning of the 20th century, there was a gradual growth of communalism among the Muslims.

(2) **Economic and Educational Backwardness:** The Muslims felt that the British were responsible for the end of the Mughal rule. They rejected western education and values in a bid to retain their own identity. Thus, neither modern thought with the emphasis on Science, Democracy and Nationalism take root nor spread among the Muslim intellectuals. As a result, the number of educated Muslims remained small and many of them remained traditional and backward. The Muslims remained backward even in trade and industry, as there was no support and encouragement from the government. This led to the relative backwardness of Muslims in education, trade and industry, resulting in economic setback. These factors sowed the seeds of discontent among the Muslims and Hindu and further widened the gulf between the two communities.

(3) **Communalism in Writing of Indian History:** The manner in which the history was taught in schools and colleges also contributed to the growth of communal feelings among the Hindus and the Muslims. The Muslims were depicted as cruel invaders who were intolerant and oppressed their Hindu subjects. Such communal representation of history spread suspicion among the two communities which poisoned the minds and political life of the nation.

(4) **Religious Tinge to Nationalism by the Radicals:** The emergence of Radical Nationalism after the Surat session of Congress in 1907 gave a great fillip to the Indian National Movement. The Radical Nationalists drew their inspiration from traditional Hinduism. However, this was misinterpreted by some people and instilled fear in the Muslims that India was being identified with Hindu culture and religion.

(5) **Role of Sir Sayyid Ahmad Khan and Aligarh Movement:** The suppression of the Muslims after the Revolt of 1857 convinced Sir Sayyid Ahmad Khan that the Muslims must remain loyal to the British in order to obtain concessions and privileges from them. He exorted the Muslims to receive western education and established Aligarh Muslim University which was open orly to Muslims and Britishers. The purpose of this association was to prevent Muslims from entering the National Movement and to strengthen British r343512ule in India. **[Any four]**

(A) **Impact:**

(1) Brought into politics new classes of people.
(2) Taught the Press to be outspoken, youth power demonstrated.
(3) Encouraged native industries.
(4) Gave impetus to Nationalist poetry, prose and journalism.
(5) Gave ecucation a National Orientation.
(6) Created confidence of patriotism.
[Any three]

(B) **Objectives of the League:**

(1) To promote among the Indian Muslims feelings of loyalty towards the British Government.
(2) The League would also remove misconception that may arise as to the intentions of government in relation to Indian Muslims.
(3) To protect the political and other rights of the Muslims and to place their needs and aspirations before the Government in mild and moderate language.
(4) To prevent the rise of any feeling of hostility between the Muslims and other communities without adversely affecting the aforesaid objectives of the League. **[Any three]**

(C) (1) Mohemmedan Anglo-Oriental Association (1893)? to promote support for the British to prevent Muslims from participating in any Political Movement.

(2) Bengali Bengal partitioned in 1905 to create division between the Hindus and the Muslims.

(3) Lord Minto received a deputation of Muslims at Shimla in October 1906 and assured Muslims that their political rights would be protected.

(4) Mohammedan Educational Conference was held at Dacca in December 1906 and it accepted the proposal form a Central Organisation for the Muslims. Muslim League was established on December 30, 1906 under the Presidentship of Nawab Salimullah.

[Marking Scheme]

What Examiners Say

- (A) Explanation of the terms 'Swadeshi' and 'Boycott' were mentioned but not their impact. Impact of the Movement was confused with that of the impact of the Non-cooperation Movement.
- (B) Some candidates were unable to write all four objectives of the Muslim League. A few wrote the demand for Pakistan which was not objective of the Muslim League.
- (C) Answered correctly by most candidates. A few wrote vague points not connected with the questions.

Caution

- (A) The Impact of Swadeshi and Boycott highlighting the relevant points should be explained well and supported with various examples.
- (B) Practice writing assignments which will help in the preparation of the topic.
- (C) Stress on the importance of learning facts carefully so that correct answers may be written

6. Mahatma Gandhi and the National Movement

Mahatma Gandhi steered the Indian National Movement during the period from 1919 to 1947 and this period of the National Movement was known as Gandhian Era in the Indian History. He adopted Satyagraha, Ahimsa, Boycott, Swadeshi, Non-Cooperation Movement and Civil Disobedience methods to achieve independence for our country from the British rule in India.

Chapter Notes

- *Gandhiji's Early Life, His Methods and Directions*
- *Non-Cooperation Movement*
- *Civil Disobedience Movement*

TOPIC 1

GANDHIJI'S EARLY LIFE, HIS METHODS AND DIRECTIONS

Gandhiji was born on 2nd October, 1869 at Porbandar, Gujarat. After gaining his legal education in Britian, he went to South Africa for practicing Law. He revolted against the policy of racial discrimination in South Africa. From 1893 to 1914, he stayed at South Africa and practiced his law there.

Once, while travelling from Durban to Pretoria in South Africa by train, the British passengers asked him to shift to the compartment meant for Non-Europeans. They threw his luggage on the platform and he was forcibly pushed out. This incident proved to be a turning point in Mahatma Gandhi's life and he vowed to fight against social injustice.

Methods Adapted by Gandhiji

Satyagraha—The term Satyagraha is made up of two Sanskrit words-Satya (truth) and Agraha (insistence to hold fast). To Gandhiji, Satyagraha was a moral force born of truth and non-violence.

Doctrine of Non-Violence—Non-Violence of Ahimsa means non-killing or avoiding injury. But for Gandhiji, it meant avoiding injury to anything by thought, word or deed.

Swadeshi—Swadeshi means producing necessary items of utility in one's own country and using them for one's use without depending on imported goods. He emphasized on wearing khadi by manufacturing on Charkha.

Mass Movement—The South African train experience gave Gandhiji the experience of leading Indians belonging to different religions, regions and social class. South Africa built his faith in the ability of the Indian masses to particpate in the freedom movement. Gandhiji returned to India in January 1915 and spent the next four years in studying the Indian situation. During the course of 1917 and early 1918, he was involved in three significant struggles in Champaran (Bihar) in Ahmedabad and in Kheda (Gujarat).

Example 1. What is mass involvement in Gandhi's methods?

Ans. The mass involvement means people of all castes, creeds and professions should participate in the Movement. Gandhiji realised the power of the organised masses.

Champaran Satyagraha (1917)

Gandhiji's first great experiment in Satyagraha was accomplished in 1917 in Champaran (Bihar). The Indigo cultivators of Champaran were greatly exploited by European planters. They were bound by law to grow indigo 3/20th of their land and sell it to the British planters at prices fixed by them. They invited Gandhiji to take up their cause, but the British banned his entry to the district. He offered Satyagraha, as a result of which, inquiry was conducted into condition of the peasants. This helped in giving the indigo cultivators some relief.

Ahmedabad Satyagraha (1918)

Gandhiji led the mill-workers of Ahmedabad in a strike against the mill-owners who had refused to pay them higher wages. When the workers seemed to weaken, he provided support to them by undertaking a fast (hunger strike). The mill-workers were afraid of the consequences, on the fourth day of the Satyagraha, they agreed to give a 35 percent increase in wages.

Kheda Satyagraha (1918)—Crops failed in Kheda and the peasants were not in the position to pay land revenue. The British Government refused to forgo the land revenue. To this, Gandhiji asked peasants to offer Satyagraha. The peasants refused to pay the revenue and ultimately, the government was forced to arrive at a settlement with the peasants. Sardar Vallabhbhai Patel became Gandhiji's follower during this struggle. These three experiments in Satyagraha brought Gandhiji close to the masses and the peasants in rural areas and workers in the urban areas.

Related Theory
→ His literary works were Harijan, young India (Newspapers); My experiments with truth and Hind Swaraj (Books).

Important
→ He introduced a comprehensive constructive programme which included removal of untounchability, upliftment of women, village development, basic education and communal harmony, etc.

TOPIC 2

NON-COOPERATION MOVEMENT

Major Causes of Non-Cooperation

Major causes of the Non-Cooperation movement were:

(1) The Rowlatt Act, 1919
(2) Jallianwala Bagh Massacre 1919
(3) Khilafat Movement.

The Rowlatt Act, 1919

In 1919, Gandhiji decided to launch a nation wide Satyagraha against the Rowlatt Act, 1919. This act had been hurriedly passed through the Imperial Legislative Council. It gave the government immense powers to:

(1) Repress political activities
(2) Detain political prisoners without a trial for 2 years. An all-India strike was observed on 8th April, 1919. Rallies were organised at various cities, shops were closed down and workers went on strike. Alarmed by the popular upsurge, the British Government decided to suppress the Nationalists. On 10th April, 1919, Police in Amritsar fired upon a peaceful procession. Martial law was imposed.

Example 2. **Which provision of the Rowlatt Act caused widespread popular indignation?**

Ans. The provision of No Dalil, No Vakil, No appeal, *i.e.* No plea, No lawyer caused widespread popular indignation.

Jallianwala Bagh Massacre

On 13th April, 1919, a massive unarmed crowd gathered in Jallianwala Bagh in Amritsar protest against the government's new repressive policies. It was a very peaceful gathering, it was against the arrest of leaders like Dr. Saifuddin Kitchlu and Dr. Satya Pal. The British Government was determined to suppress the mass agitation. It repeatedly lathi-charged and fixed upon unarmed demonstrators before. But on that day General Dyer took the command of the area. Jallianwala Bagh had only one exit, its other three sides were enclosed by buildings, General Dyer surrounded the bagh with his soldiers. After closing the exist by his troops, he ordered them to shoot the crowd by open fire. The troops kept on firing till their ammunition was exhausted. About one thousand innocent demonstrators were killed and many more wounded. The conscience of the nation was shaken at the massacre of innocent people. As the news of the Jallianwala Bagh massacre spread, crowds took to the streets. There were strikes and clashes all around. The government responded with brutal repression. Noticing the violence spread, Mahatma Gandhi called off the movement.

Khilafat Movement

In the First World War Turkey was defeated and the Ottoman Empire was divided. The Sultan of Turkey, who was the Caliph, was deprived of all authority. In those days, the Caliph was looked upon by large sections of Mulsims as their religious head. They felt that weakening of Caliph's position would adversely affect the position of the Muslims. In the First World War, Britain was in favour of Ottoman Empire and fought against Turkey. At the end of the War, Turkey stood defeated. British and its allies divided the territories of the Turkish Empire among themselves and abolished the office of the Khalifa – the spiritual head of the Islamic World. This led to Anti – British feelings among the Muslim Community.

The Muslim population in India started a powerful agitation known as the Khilafat Movement, under the leadership of the Ali Brothers – Mohammad Ali and Shaukat Ali, Maulana Azad, Hakim Ajmal Khan and Hasrat Mohani. Gandhiji saw in the Khilafat Movement an opportunity for uniting Hindus and Mulsims. He was elected as President of the All – India Khilafat Conference in November 1919. He advised the Khilafat Committee to adopt a policy of Non-Cooperation with the Government.

By August 31, 1920, the Khilafat Non-Cooperation Movement started. People resigned from Government services, shops selling foreign goods were picketed. Students boycotted schools and colleges and 'hartals' and demonstrations were held. By the end of 1920, the Khilafat Movement and the Congress Non-Cooperation Movement merged into one nationwide Movement.

Non-Cooperation Movement

In 1909, Gandhiji wrote in his famous book 'Hind Swaraj' that British rule in India was set up in co-operation with the Indians. If the Indians refused to cooperate, the British rule in India would collapse within a year and Swaraj would be attained. In 1920, at the Nagpur Session of the Indian National Congress, the programme of Non-Cooperation was adopted.

Objectives or Aims of the Non-Cooperation Movement

(1) To attain Swaraj or Self – Government within the British Empire if possible and outside if necessary.
(2) Annulment of the Rowlatt Act and to punish those responsible for brutalities in Punjab (Amritsar).
(3) To get back the proper position for the Caliph of Turkey.

Programmes of Non-Cooperation

It was decided that the Movement should unfold in stages:

(1) To begin with, surrender of titles awarded by the British Government.

(2) Boycott of Civil Services, Army, Police, Courts, Legislative Councils, Schools and foreign goods.

(3) If government used repressive action, then full scale Civil Disobedience will be launched.

(4) Extensive tour to mobilize popular support for the Movement.

(5) Adoption of Swadeshi Khadi by reviving hand – spinning and hand weaving.

(6) Establishment of national schools and colleges and private arbitration courts known as Panchayats all over India.

Positive aspects of the Movement

(1) National Educational Institutions such as the Jamia Millia Islamia was established as a National Univeristy. The Bihar Vidhyapith, Kashi Vidhyapith and the Gujarat Vidhyapith were the other National Universities that were established with teachers like Acharya Narendra Dev, Dr. Zakir Hussain and Lala Lajpat Rai.

(2) Lawyers like Deshbandhu Chittaranjan Das, Motilal Nehru, C. Rajagopalachari, Dr. Rajendra Prasad and many others gave up their legal practice.

(3) The Congress boycotted the elections to the Legislatures by not putting up candidates for the first elections to the Councils.

(4) Rabindranath Tagore and many other distinguished citizens of India renounced their titles and awards. Gandhiji returned the medals that were awarded for his work in South Africa.

(5) Students left schools and colleges.

(6) Charkhas were manufactured for the people to spin cloth.

(7) Shops selling foreign goods and liquor were picketed. Foreign cloth was burnt in market places.

Repression by the Government

The Government took severe measures to suppress the Movement. Under Gandhiji's inspiration many important leaders except Gandhiji were arrested and sent to jail. Processions and Public meetings were banned. The Khilafat and the Congress volunteer organizations were declared illegal.

Suspension of the Non-Cooperation Movement

Unfortunately, the whole Non-Cooperation Movement was called off on 12th February, 1922 by Gandhiji, after the incident of Chauri Chaura.

Chauri-Chaura Incident

The tragedy occurred on 5th February, 1922 at Chauri Chaura, a village in Gorakhpur (Uttar Pradesh). A procession of about 3,000 peasants marched to the Police Station to protest against the Police Officer, who had beaten some volunteers picketing a liquor shop. The Police fired at the peasants. A violent crowd burnt the Police Station on 5th February, 1922 where twenty-two policemen were burnt alive, who were inside the Police Station. Gandhiji immediately withdrew the Non-Cooperation on 12th February, 1922 as he was against violence (Ahimsa).

Gandhiji was arrested for propogating sedition on 10th March, 1922. He was sentenced to six years imprisonment. But, he was released after two years because of his ill health.

Impact of the Non-Cooperation Movement

The Non-Cooperation Movement failed to achieve any of its three main demands. Even Gandhiji's promise to achieve Swaraj within one year of launching the movement was not fulfilled. But it helped in the Indian National Movement in the following ways:

(1) The National Movement became a mass movement with the participation of different sections of Indian society such as peasants, workers, students, teachers, men, women and children joined the movement to make it a great success.

(2) It generated a desire for freedom and inspired people to challenge the colonial rule by instilling confidence among them.

(3) It transformed the Indian National Congress from a deliberative assembly into an organization for action. It became the organizer and leader of the masses in their national struggle. Thus, the Congress became a force to reckon with.

(4) It fostered Hindu-Muslim unity which could be seen in the merger of the Khilafat issue with this Movement. It provided an opportunity to the Congress to bring the urban Muslims into the National Movement by convincing them that the nation was equally concerned with the problems affecting them.

(5) As a consequence of the Non-Cooperation Movement, several steps were taken in the direction of prohibition and removal of untouchability. Many national schools and colleges were set up in different parts of the country. The Boycott of the foreign goods led to the promotion of Indian handicrafts and industries. 'Khadi' became the symbol of the National Movement.

(6) The Movement gave a new boost to nationalism in India. At its annual session at Nagpur in December 1920, changes were made in the Constitution of the Congress. The Congress organization was able to reach down to villages. Its membership fee was reduced to four annas per year to enable the rural and urban poor to become its members.

(7) The goal of the Non-Cooperation was to attain Swaraj. The Congress realized the nature and value of the popular support. Though the Movement failed immediately to attain Swaraj, it definitely came nearer to it. The 'Swaraj Party was formed in March 1923 by Motilal Nehru and C.R. Das (known as Pro-Changers).

Related Theory

→ After the Jallianwala Bagh shootings the government formed a Committee of enquiry to investigate the issue. On October 14, 1919, Hunter Commission was set up. In the final report submitted in March 1920, the Committee unanimously condemned General Dyer's actions but it did not impose any disciplinary action against him.

Important

→ In September, 1920 the special Calcutta Session of the National Congress approved Gandhiji's proposal of Non-Cooperation Movement and supported the Khilafat Cause.

TOPIC 3

CIVIL DISOBEDIENCE MOVEMENT

Factors Leading Upto Civil Disobedience Movement

After Suspension of Non – Cooperation Movement on 12th February, 1922, Mahatma Gandhi gave the call for a Civil Disobedience Movement in 1930. But this Movement was different from the Non-Cooperation Movement. The Non–Cooperation (1921 – 22) had sought to bring the working of the government to a standstill by not Cooperating with the administration of British Government. Whereas the Civil Disobedience Movement was an attempt of paralysing the administration by breaking some specific rules and regulations. Following were the causes that led to the Civil Disobedience Movement:

Simon Commission

To Investigate the need for further Constitutional reform, the British Government appointed the Indian Statutory Commission called as Simon Commission in November, 1927. The Commission was composed of seven British members of Parliament but it had no Indian member. This was seen as a violation of the principle of Self determination and a deliberate insult to the self respect of the Indians. Wherever this Commission went, it met with protests. On 3rd February, when the Commission reached Bombay, an All India *hartal* was organised. Wherever the Commission went, it was greeted with *hartals* and black flag demonstrations under the Slogan "Simon go back". The Government used brutal suppressions and police attacks to break the opposition. On 30th October, 1928, while leading a demonstration at Lahore railway station, Lala Lajpat Rai was grievously charged with lathi and was brutally injured. He lost his life in this incident. Inspite, of all the protests, the Simon Commission travelled to different parts of the country, met people and made recommendations.

Recommendations of the Simon Commission

(1) Enlargement of provincialLegislatures councils.
(2) Setting up a Federation of Princely States and British Provinces.
(3) Continuation of Communal or Separate Electorates.
(4) Removal of Dyarchy or dual form of government
(5) Governor General should select and appoint his cabinet members.
(6) British troops and British officers should stay on in Indian regiments for many more years.
(7) High Courts should be under the administrative control of the Government of India.

The British had explained that there were no Indians in the Simon Commission because with the Indians around, no such, 'Programme for reforms' or Constitution could be marked out which would be acceptable to all the political parties.

Nehru Report (1928)

The challenge of forming a Constitution acceptable to all the political parties was accepted and all parties meeting was held in Bombay, which appointed Motilal Nehru to head a Committee and to draft a Constitution for India. The draft or report of this Committee is known as Nehru Report. Motilal Nehru was made Chairman of the Committee with Sir Tej Bahadur Sapru and N.C. Kelkar as his Principal associates.

The Nehru Report proposed:

(1) Dominion Status for India;
(2) That the Parliament of India should consist of (i) the Senate elected for 7 years containing 200 members elected by the Provincial Councils and (ii) the House of Representatives with 500 members elected for five years through Adult Franchise;
(3) Joint electorates with reservation of seats for minorities (except in Punjab and Bengal) on population basis with the right to consent additional seats;
(4) Creation of 'New Provinces' on linguistic basis;
(5) 'Nineteen Fundamental Rights' including the right to vote, freedom from arbitrary arrest, searches and seizures and freedom of conscience.

(2) Declaration of Poorna Swaraj

The Congress demanded the implementation of the Nehru Report by 31st December, 1929. When this was not granted, then in December 1929, during the Lahore Session of the Congress, under the Presidentship of Jawaharlal Nehru, the Congress declared their aim of achieving Poorna Swaraj. 26th January, 1930 was celebrated as the Poorna Swaraj Day. From then onwards, on every 26th January, people took the Independence pledge. On the midnight of December 31, 1929, Jawaharlal Nehru led a procession to the banks of the river Ravi at Lahore and hoisted the tricolour flag. The Congress Working Committee met in January 1930, and decided the following programme :-

(i) Preparation for Civil Disobedience.
(ii) As per the Poorna Swaraj resolution, the word Swaraj in the Congress Constitution, would thenceforth mean Complete Independence or Poorna Swaraj which was set forth as the goal of the National Movement.
(iii) Resignation by members of the legislatures.
(iv) Observance of 26th January as the 'Poorna Swaraj' day, all over the country with the hoisting of the tricolour flag.
(v) Withdrawl from all possible association with the British Government.

Civil Disobedience Movement (1930 – 1934)

The Congress Working Committee met in February 1930 at Sabarmati Ashram and vested in Gandhiji, powers to launch the Civil Disobedience Movement.

Dandi March

Gandhiji now decided to launch a 'Civil Disobedience Movement' and informed the British about his decision.

Gandhiji started this Movement from the Sabarmati Ashram on 12th March, 1930. It was a historic March from Sabarmati Ashram to Dandi (a village on the sea coast of Gujarat). 78 people followed him, many more joined him on the way to Dandi. Gandhiji broke the salt law on 6th April, 1930 by making or actually picking up salt from the seashore. He also advised people to break the unjust laws of the British.

He started the Disobedience Movement by breaking salt laws. As salt was the basic need used by everyone i.e., rich, poor, rural and urban people.

Soon people started breaking other British laws. Some refused to pay tax, others broke different British laws. People organised mass movements in various ways. Women joined in large numbers. People were prevented from buying foreign goods.

The Important leaders of this movement were Jawaharlal Nehru, Madan Mohan Malviya, Abdul Gaffar Khan and Baddrudin Tyabji.

The Programme of the Movement

Civil Disobedience Movement involved:

(1) Defiance of Salt Laws
(2) Boycott of Liquor
(3) Boycott of foreign cloth and British goods of all kinds
(4) Non-Payment of taxes and revenues.

Civil Disobedience Movement was different from the Non-Cooperation Movement. The former involved non-payment of taxes and land – revenue as well as violation of laws of different kinds in addition to Non-Cooperation activities.

Repression by the Government

The Government restored to firing, lathi charges and large scale imprisonment. Over 90,000 Satyagrahis including Congress leaders and Gandhiji were imprisoned. The Congress was declared illegal and severe restrictions were imposed on the nationalist Press. Protest meetings were held everywhere. The Textile and Railway workers of Mumbai went on strike. There were instances of firing at Delhi and Kolkata.

Round Table Conference

The Indian Round Table Conference held three Sessions which are also referred to as the First, Second and Third Round Table Conferences.

First Round Table Conference (November 12, 1930 to January 19, 1931)

It was held in London in 1930. Main Agenda was to discuss the Constitutional Progress. Congress boycotted the Conference. British were unwilling to grant Dominion Status.

Second Round Table Conference (September 7, 1931 to December 1, 1931)

Held in London in 1931. Mahatma Gandhi attended it. It failed due to different demands of different Political Parties.

Third Round Table Conference (November 17, 1932 to December 24, 1932)

It was held in 1932 in London. It was attended by 46 delegates only. The Congress did not participate in it.

Example 3. What do you mean by Gandhi – Irwin Pact and when was it signed?

Ans. Since the Satyagraha could not be suppressed, the Government through Tej Bahadur Sapru and Jayakar, started negotiations with Gandhiji in Jail. This resulted in the signing of a Pact by Gandhiji and Lord Irwin (who was the Viceroy) in March 1931. And this is known as Gandhi – Irwin Pact.

Terms Agreed by the Government in This Pact

(1) It would withdraw all ordinances and end prosecutions.

(2) Release all political prisoners, except those guilty of violence.
(3) Permit peaceful picketing of liquor and foreign cloth shops.
(4) Restore the confiscated properties of the Satyagrahis
(5) Permit the free collection or manufacture of salt by persons near the seacoast.

The Congress Consented to the Following Conditions

(1) To suspend the Civil Disobedience Movement.
(2) To participate in the Second Session of the Round Table Conference. (It was attended by Gandhiji as sole representative of the Congress, according to the terms of the Gandhi- Irwin Pact of 1931).
(3) Not to press for investigation into police excesses.

Poona Pact (1932)

Example 4. What was the demand of B.R. Ambedkar in the Third Round Table Conference?

Ans. In Third Round Table Conference, the Indian National Congress refused to attend the Conference. Taking advantage of the situation B.R. Ambedkar, who attended the Conference demanded separate electorate for the Depressed Classes there.

Example 5. What was Communal Award and who all were awarded?

Ans. The Prime Minister of Britain, Ramsay Macdonald announced an award known as the Communal Award. This award provided separate representation of the Muslims, Buddhists, Sikhs, Indian Christians, Anglo-Indians, European and the Depressed Classes.

Mahatma Gandhi strongly opposed this award on the grounds that it would disintegrate Indian society and started a fast in protest against it.

Example 6. By whom was Poona Pact signed and what did it contain?

Ans. On 25th September, 1932, the agreement known as Poona Pact was signed between B.R. Ambedkar and the Congress.

The agreement provided reservation of seats for the Depressed Classes in the Provisional Legislatures, Within the general electorate and not by creating a separate electorate. Due to the Pact, the Depressed classes received 148 seats in the legislatures, instead of the 71 as allocated in the Communal Award earlier proposed by the British Prime Minister, Ramsay Macdonald.

Renewal of Civil Disobedience Movement

While attending the Second Round Table Conference, Gandhiji realized that emphasis was being laid on the Communal problems rather than political solutions. With no clear solution Gandhiji returned 'empty handed' and gave a call to revive the Civil Disobedience Movement. The Government again adopted strict measures and Congress was declared illegal. Thousands of leaders including Gandhiji were again arrested. Prisoners were illtreated and brutalities started. Cruel methods were used to subdue crowds In 1934, Gandhiji suspended the Civil Disobedience Movement and he withdrew himself from active politics for a year.

Impact of the Civil Disobedience Movement

(1) It shattered people's faith in the British Government.
(2) It revived the will to fight the elections.
(3) It deepened the social roots for the Freedom Struggle.
(4) It popularized new methods of propoganda like the prabhat pheris, pamphlets, etc.
(5) It made people understand the significance of the Principles of Non-violence, people could resist violence with tolerance and courage.
(6) These political Movements were always accompanied by social Movements. Removal of untouchability, improving the status of women and spreading education, were important aspects of the Movement.
(7) It brought women out of their homes to participate in politics and to make them equal partners in the freedom struggle.

Related Theory

↪ The Salt March is also known as the Salt Satyagraha, Dandi March and the Dandi Satyagraha. It was a twenty-four day March (from 12th March 1930 – 6th April 1930). It was a direct action campaign of tax resistance and Non-violent protest against the British monopoly. The March spanned 239 miles (385 km) from Sabarmati Ashram to Dandi . Gandhiji broke the British Raj Salt law at 8 : 30 am on 6th April 1930, by picking up lumps of salt from Seashore this act was symbolic.

Important

↪ From all the Three Round Table Conferences only 2nd Round Table Conference was attended by the Congress.

ICSE Suggestions

↪ The role of Gandhiji in the National Movement is very important and the Non-Cooperation Movement and Civil Disobedience are very significant movements, it should be studied event wise in details, by the students.
↪ Students should write all Historical facts / clauses/ provisions correctly because they cannot be diluted or misquoted. Students should present their answers in factual manner.

Caution

↪ Students should remember that Non-Cooperation Movement came prior to Civil Disobedience Movement. They feel both movements were same and quote wrong movements in their answers.

Mahatma Gandhi and the National Movement

Glossary

(1) **Martial law :** It was an imposition of direct military control over the civilians on Jallianwala Bagh used by General Dyer.

(2) **Dominion Status :** It is a status enjoyed by other dominions of British Commonwealth, such as Australia or Canada.

Who's Who?

(1) **John Simon:** He was the Chairman of Seven – member Commission appointed by the British called 'Simon Commission', named after him.

(2) **Khan Abdul Ghaffar Khan:** He was the leader of the North-West Frontier Province, he was popularly known as the 'Frontier Gandhi'.

Who Said What?

(1) "Non – Cooperation with evil is as much a duty as is co-operation with good". —Mahatma Gandhi

Gandhiji said these words to Indians in order not to assist the foreign government to rule over them.

(2) "The Congress plea for Hindu – Muslim unity would be an empty phrase of the Hindus held aloof from the Muslims when their vital interests are at stake". —Mahatma Gandhi

Gandhiji saw in the Khilafat Movement an opportunity for uniting Hindus and Muslims and said these words.

(3) "If the thing had not been suspended we would have been leading not a non–violent struggle but essentially a violent struggle. The cause will prosper by this retreat". —Mahatma Gandhi

These words were said by Gandhiji to assure Jawaharlal Nehru, when Gandhiji against the agitation of suspending Non–Cooperation Movement after Chauri Chura incident.

(4) "Out of the experience of this attempt to defy openly the foreign rulers and the government they had set up, was born a sense of self-confidence and self-esteem". —Bipin Chandra Pal

Bipin Chandra Pal said these words, when confidence started instilling among the people and a desire for freedom was generated and it also inspired people to challenge the Colonial rule during Non-Cooperation Movement.

Chronology

1915: Mahatma Gandhi returned to India.
1917: Champaran Satyagraha accomplished
1918: Ahmedabad Mill workers' Satyagraha
1918: Kheda Satyagraha
1919: Rowlatt Act was introduced
13th April, 1919: Jallianwala Bagh Massacre
1919: Khilafat Committee was formed in Bombay.
1920: Non-Cooperation Movement started.
5th February, 1922: Incident of Chauri–Chaura
12th February, 1922: Withdrawl of Non-Cooperation Movement
10th March, 1922: Gandhiji was arrested for the first time.
1922: Formation of Swaraj Party
1928: Nehru Report/Simon Commission came to India.
1929: Demand for Poorna Swaraj
1930: Dandi March / First Round Table Conference

1930: Launch of Civil Disobedience Movement
1931: Gandhi–Irwin Pact/Second Round Table Conference/Suspension of Civil Disobedience Movement
1932: Third Round Table Conference / Renewal of Civil Disobedience Movement / Poona Pact signed
1934: End of Civil Disobedience Movement

OBJECTIVE Type Questions

Multiple Choice Questions-I

[**1** mark each]

1. Complete the analogy:
Non Cooperation Movement : 1920 : : Civil Disobedience Movement : ....
[ICSE Sem-1, 2021]
(a) 1919 (b) 1932
(c) 1931 (d) 1930

Ans. *(d)* 1930

Explanation : The Congress Working Committee met in February 1930 at Sabarmati Ashram and vested in Gandhiji, powers to launch the Civil Disobedience Movement.

2. Complete the given analogy:
Simon Commission : Civil Disobedience Movement :: Cripps Mission : ?
(a) Non Cooperation Movement
(b) Anti Partition Movement
(c) Quit India Movement
(d) Khilafat Movement [HOT🔥]

Ans. *(c)* Quit India Movement

Explanation: In 1930, Mahatma Ghandhi gave a call for Civil Disodience Movement. The major cause for this movement was Simon Commission. The Commission was composed of Seven British members of Parliament and had no Indian member. This was seen as a violation of the principle of self determination and a deliberate insult to the self respect of the Indians. In March 1942, the Cripps' Mission proposed certain Constitutional reforms. Almost all the parties and sections of the people rejected the proposals. The failure of the Cripps' Mission left no further meeting ground between the British and the Congress. The Congress started Quit India Movement in August 1942 under the leadership of Mahatma Gandhi.

3. Which of these statements is NOT associated with the Jallianwala Bagh Massacre?
(a) It happened in the year 1919.
(b) General Dyer was responsible for this Massacre.
(c) It became a cause for the Non-Cooperation Movement.
(d) It became a cause for the Civil Disobedience Movement.
[ICSE Sem-1, 2021]

Ans. *(d)* It became a cause for the Civil Disobedience Movement.

Explanation: It was a cause for the Civil Disobedience Movement is wrong because it was related to Non-Cooperation Movement.

⚠️ **Caution**
Some children have written as Non-Cooperation movements Read question properly to avoid mistakes.

4. The Khilafat Movement was started under the leadership of ....
(a) Ali Brothers
(b) Dr. Saifuddin Kitchlu
(c) Khan Abdul Ghaffar Khan
(d) Sir Sayyid Ahmed Khan
[ICSE Sem-1, 2021]

Ans. *(a)* Ali Brothers

Explanation: The Khilafat Movement in India started under the leadership of Ali Brothers – Mohammad Ali and Shaukat Ali.

5. Identify the clauses of the Rowlatt Act
(a) in camera trial
(b) arrest people with a warrant
(c) vernacular Press must not publish anything against the British.
(d) compulsory License for arms

Ans. *(a)* In camera trial

Explanation: The Rowlatt Act, passed in 1919, implied:
(1) Arrest of a person without warrant;
(2) In camera trial (trial in seclusion);
(3) Restrictions on movements of individuals
(4) Suspension of the Right of Haebas corpus.

 Related Theory
Offically it was known as the Anarchical and Revolutionary Crimes Act, 1919. It was passed by the Imperial Legislative Council in March, 1919.

6. Gandhiji started the Civil Disobedience Movement in 1930 by ....
   (a) Ahmedabad Satyagraha
   (b) Dandi March
   (c) Khilafat Movement
   (d) Champaran Satyagraha   [HOT🔥]

Ans. (b) Dandi March

   Explanation: On 12th March 1930, Mahatma Gandhi began the historic march from Sabarmati Ashram to Dandi, a village on the Gujarat Sea coast. On the morning of 6th April, Gandhiji violated the Salt Law at Dandi by picking up some salt left by the sea waves. According to Salt Law, the government had the monopoly to manufacture and sell the salt. Gandhiji's breaking of the salt law marked the beginning of the Civil Disobedience Movement.

7. Jallianwala Bagh Tragedy took place at Amritsar on ....
   (a) 13th April, 1919
   (b) 31st August, 1920
   (c) 6th June, 1919
   (d) 17th October, 1919   [HOT🔥]

Ans. (a) 13th April, 1919

   Explanation: A large but peaceful crowd gathered at the Jallianwala Bagh in Amritsar on 13th April, 1919 to protest against the arrest of leaders like Dr. Saifuddin Kitchlu and Dr. Satya Pal. General Dyer, the military commander of Amritsar, surrounded the Bagh with his soldiers and ordered them to shoot at the crowd. About one thousand innocent demonstrators were killed and several were wounded.

8. What was the cause for the sudden suspension of the Non-Cooperation Movement?
   (a) repressive measures of the British
   (b) the Chauri-Chaura Incident
   (c) the Gandhi – Irwin Pact
   (d) the Jallianwala Bagh Massacre
   [ICSE Sem-1, 2021]

Ans. (b) The Chauri-Chaura Incident

   Explanation: After Chauri–Chaura Incident Gandhiji was greatly shocked and he withdew the Non-Cooperation Movement on February 12, 1922.

9. How did the Lahore Session of 1929 lead to the Civil Disobedience Movement?
   (a) The Declaration of Poorna Swaraj was passed.
   (b) Subhash Chandra Bose was made the President of the Congress.
   (c) Simon Commission recommendations were accepted.
   (d) Congress passed a resolution to begin the Civil Disobedience Movement.
   [ICSE Sem-1, 2021]

Ans. (a) The Declaration of Poorna Swaraj was passed.

   Explanation: In the Lahore Session of 1929. Jawahar Lal Nehru, the President of the Session, declared Poorna Swaraj as the main objective of the Congress.

10. Which of the following was NOT a method adopted by Mahatma Gandhi during freedom struggle?
    (a) Satyagraha
    (b) Doctrine of violence
    (c) Swadeshi
    (d) Mass movement

Ans. (b) Doctrine of violence

   Explanation: During the freedom struggle, Mahatma Gandhi used the Doctrine of non-violence or Ahimsa. His methods included Satyagraha, Doctrine of non-violence, Swadeshi and Mass movement.

11. .... forced Mahatma Gandhi to suspend the Non-Cooperation Movement.
    (a) Jallianwala Bagh Tragedy
    (b) Rowlatt Act
    (c) Chauri Chaura incident
    (d) Boycott programme

Ans. (c) Chauri Chaura incident

   Explanation: The tragedy at Chauri Chaura, a village in Gorakhpur district in Uttar Pradesh occured on 5th February, 1922. A procession of about 3000 peasants set a police station on fire killing 23 policemen who were inside the police station. Gandhiji, a believer in 'Ahimsa' was greatly shocked at this incident and withdrew the Non-Cooperation Movement on 12th February, 1922.

 Caution
→ Some students have opted for Jallianwala Bagh tragedy which was the beginning of the Non-Cooperation Movement, but it was not the cause of suspension.

12. Which of the following was NOT a clause of the Gandhi-Irwin Pact?
    (a) Withdraw all ordinances and end prosecutions by the government
    (b) End of Civil Disobedience Movement by the Congress

(c) Suspension of Subhash Chandra Bose as the President of the Congress

(d) Restore of confiscated properties of the satyagrahis by the government

Ans. (c) *Suspension of Subhash Chandra Bose as the President of the Congress*

Explanation: To end the Civil Disobedience Movement, a pact was signed between Gandhiji and Lord Irwin, Viceroy of India, known as Gandhi-Irwin Pact in March, 1931. In this Pact, the Government agreed to:

(1) Withdraw all ordinances and end prosecutions;

(2) Release all political prisoners, except those guilty of violence;

(3) Permit peaceful picketing of liquor and foreign cloth shops;

(4) Restore the confiscated properties of the Satyagrahis; and

(5) Permit the free collection or manufacture of salt by persons near the sea coast.

The Congress, in its turn, consented to the following:

(1) To suspend the Civil Disobedience Movement;

(2) To participate in the Second Session of Round Table Conference; and

(3) Not to press for investigation into police excesses.

Subhash Chandra Bose was elected as the President of the Congress at Haripura session in 1938. Due to rift with Gandhiji, he resigned from the Presidentship on 29th April, 1939.

13. Which of the following was NOT a cause for Non-Cooperation Movement?

(a) Rowlatt Act, 1919

(b) Sepoy Mutiny, 1857

(c) Jallainwala Bagh Tragedy

(d) Khilafat movement   [HOT🔥]

Ans. (b) *Sepoy Mutiny, 1857*

Explanation: The Sepoy Mutiny was the cause of Revolt of 1857, also known as the First War of Independence.

14. Dandi March by Gandhiji marked the beginning of the Quit India Movement.

Replace the underlined word to correct the statement.

(a) Non-Cooperartion Movement

(b) Civil Disobedience Movement

(c) The First War of Independence

(d) Declaration of Poorna Swaraj

Ans. (b) *Civil Disobedience Movement*

Explanation: On 12th March 1930, Mahatma Gandhi began the historic march from Sabarmati Ashram to Dandi, a village on the Gujarat Sea coast. On the morning of 6th April, Gandhiji violated the salt law at Dandi by picking up some salt left by the sea waves. According to Salt Law, the government had the monopoly to manufacture and sell the salt. Gandhiji's breaking of the salt law marked the beginning of the Civil Disobedience Movement.

 Related Theory

→ *The Dandi March was undertaken to launch the Civil Disobedience Movement and to break the Salt Law.*

15. The Act passed by the British which gave them the authority to arrest a person without warrant was?

(a) Rowlatt Act

(b) General Enlistment Act

(c) The Official Secrets Act

(d) The Vernacular Press Act

Ans. (a) *Rowlatt Act*

Explanation: Inspite of opposition from the Indians, the Rowlatt Act was passed by the British Government in 1919. This act authorized the government to imprison any person without trial and convict him in a court.

16. In which session of Indian National Congress the resolution of Poorna Swaraj was passed?

(a) Calcutta session of 1928

(b) Lahore session of 1929

(c) Tripuri session of 1939

(d) Bombay session of 1942

Ans. (b) *Lahore Session of 1929*

Explanation: At the Lahore session of 1929, Jawaharlal Nehru was made the President of the Congress and it passed a resolution declaring Poorna Swaraj as the objective of the Congress. At the Calcutta session of 1928, the Congress had served an ultimatum to the British Government to accept the Nehru Report by the end of 1929 or face a mass movement.

The Tripuri session of the Congress in 1939 saw the widening of the gulf between Gandhiji and Subhash Chandra Bose.

At the Bombay session of 1942, the Congress passed the Quit India Resolution.

Mahatma Gandhi and the National Movement

17. Which of the following events, organised by Gandhiji, was first to happen?
   (a) Champaran Satyagraha
   (b) Ahmedabad Satyagraha
   (c) Kheda Satyagraha
   (d) Non-Cooperation Movement

Ans. *(a) Champaran Sathyagraha*

Explanation: Gandhiji returned to India in 1915 and spent the next four years in studying the Indian situation. During the course of 1917 and 1918, he was involved in three significant struggles in Champaran (Bihar), in Ahmedabad and in Kheda (Gujarat).

Gandhiji's first experiment in Satyagraha was accomplished in 1917 in Champaran, Bihar. Gandhiji organised the Ahmedabad and Kheda Satyagraha in 1918. The Non-cooperation Movement was started by Gandhiji in 1919.

18. From the given list, identify the objectives of Non-Cooperation Movement.
   (a) To attain self govenment within the British Empire
   (b) Abolition of Zamindari System
   (c) Introduction of new monetary and credit system
   (d) Defiance of Salt Laws.

Ans. *(a) To attain self government within the British Empire*

Explanation: The Non-Cooperation Movement sought to acheive the following objectives;
   (1) To attain self government within the British Empire, if necessary and from outside, if necessary;
   (2) Annulment of the Rowlatt Act;
   (3) Remedying the Khilafat wrong.

Abolition of Zamindari system and introduction of new monetary and credit systerm were the objectives of Forward Bloc.

19. The Movement that came to an abrupt end due to the Chauri Chaura incident was the ....
   (a) The Revolt of 1857
   (b) Non-Cooperation Movement
   (c) Civil Disobedience Movement
   (d) Quit India Movement

Ans. *(b) Non-Cooperation Movement*

Explanation: Gandhiji, a strong believer in 'Ahimsa' was greatly shocked by the Chauri Chaura incident and he withdrew the Non-Cooperation Movement on 12th February, 1922.

Caution
➡ Non-Cooperation Movement ended with Chauri-Chaura incident because it was suspended just after that.

20. Lala Lajpat Rai was assaulted by British during ....
   (a) Non-Cooperation Movement
   (b) Civil Disobedience Movement
   (c) protest against Simon Commission
   (d) First War of Independence   [HOT]

Ans. *(c) protest against Simon Commission*

Explanation: Lala Lajpat Rai played a pivotal role in the Indian Independence movement. In 1928, the British Government appointed Simon Commission, headed by Sir John Simon, to report on the political situation in India and need for further constitutional reforms. The Commission was opposed by all the sections of society and leaders. On October 30, 1928 while leading a demonstration against the Simon Commission at Lahore Railway Station, Lala Lajpat Rai lost his life as a result of lathi blows from the police.

21. Who of the following presided over the Lahore Session of Indian National Congress in 1929 in which resolution for Poorna Swaraj was passed?
   (a) Surendra Nath Banerjee
   (b) Subhash Chandra Bose
   (c) Mahatma Gandhi
   (d) Jawahar Lal Nehru

Ans. *(d) Jawahar Lal Nehru*

Explanation: The resolution of Poorna Swaraj was passed at the Lahore Session of Indian National Congress. Jawaharlal Nehru presided over the session. He hoisted the flag of India on 31st December, 1929 on the banks of Rabi river.

22. Which of the following were included by Mahatma Gandhi towards Non-Cooperation Movement?
   (A) Surrender of titles and honors bestowed by the British
   (B) Development of unity between Hindus and Muslims
   (C) Non payment of taxes and revenues
   (D) Defiance of Salt Laws
   (a) (A) and (B)   (b) (A) and (C)
   (c) (A), (B) and (C)   (d) (B), (C) and (D)

Ans. *(a) (A) and (B)*

Explanation: Gandhiji's Non Cooperation Movement included boycott of foreign goods, boycott of government schools, colleges and courts, surrender of titles and honorary offices, development of unity between Hindus and Muslims, removal of untouchability and emancipation and upliftment of women. Non payment of taxes and revenues and defiance of salt laws were included in Civil Disobedience Movement.

Multiple Choice Questions-II

(Other Question Types, for Extra Practice)

[**4** marks each]

Read the passages given below and answer the questions that follow:

23. On February 4, 1922, a large group of nationalist volunteers had gathered on the streets of a small, obscure hamlet. More than a year had passed since Mahatma Gandhi had launched the movement with the aim of attaining 'Poorna Swaraj' (full independence). The volunteers marched through the streets shouting slogans of Gandhi and the Khilafat. Soon they walked into the police. Sticks and stones were thrown from one end in return for bullets from the other. As the crowd grew larger and fiercer, the cops retreated inside the police station. The protestors doused the building in kerosene and set it on fire. Twenty-three policemen perished. A total of 228 people were brought to trial in the incident, out of which 19 were sentenced to death.

—*The Indian Express*

(A) Where did this incident take place?
   (a) Lahore   (b) Chauri Chaura
   (c) Dandi   (d) Awadh

(B) Which movement did Gandhiji withdrw because of this incident?
   (a) Non-Cooperation Movement
   (b) Civil Disobedience Movement
   (c) Quit India Movement
   (d) Anti Partition Movement

(C) Identify the programmes that were adopted during this movement.
   (a) Swadeshi and Boycott
   (b) Violent agitations
   (c) Walked barefoot and bathed in the Ganga
   (d) Established many British schools

(D) Identify any two impacts of the movement that was suspended due to this event.
   (a) Instilled confidence in people
   (b) Led to large scale communal riots
   (c) Promoted Social reforms
   (d) Led to the First Round table Conference

Ans. (A) (b) *Chauri Chaura*

Explanation: The tragedy at Chauri Chaura, village in Gorakhpur district in Uttar Pradesh, occurred on February 4, 1922. A procession of about 3000 peasants marched to the police station to protest against the police officer who had beaten some volunteers picketing a liquor shop. The police fired at the peasants. This infuriated the demonstrators and they set the nearby police station on fire, killing 23 policemen who were inside the police station.

(B) (a) *Non-Cooperation Movement*

Explanation: After the Chauri Chaura incidence, there were few violent incidents in other parts of the country. Gandhiji, a believer in 'Ahimsa' was greatly shocked at these incidents and he withdrew the Non-Cooperation Movement on February 12, 1922.

(C) (a) *Swadeshi and Boycott*

Explanation: The Non-Cooperation Movement included the following programme:
(1) Swadeshi programmes which included popularisation of swadeshi and khadi by reviving hand spinning, removal of untouchability, development of unity between Hindus and Muslims, emancipation and upliftment of women, etc.
(2) Boycott programmes which included boycott of government schools, colleges and courts, boycott of foreign goods, surrender of titles and honorary offices, resignation from nominated seats in local bodies, etc.

(D) (a) *Instilled confidence in people and (c) promoted social reforms*

Explanation: The impact of the Non-Cooperation Movement was as follows:
(1) The National Movement became a mass movement.
(2) Instilled confidence among the people.
(3) The Congress became a revolutionary movement.
(4) Fostered Hindu-Muslim unity.

(5) Promoted social reforms.
(6) Spread nationalism to every part of the country.
(7) Popularised the cult of Swaraj.

24. *This was not the first time that Mohandas Karamchand Gandhi had decided to lead a march.*

   A great column of over 2000 men, women and children had moved in 1913 under his lead from Natal across the Transvaal border to break a ban on Indians travelling from one South African province to another, and to protest against a law that rendered all marriages barring those under Christian aegis as illegal. The result, coming with the Relief of Indians Act, was dramatic.

   His work among the indigo peasants in Champaran, Bihar in 1917 and among Kheda's peasants in Gujarat the following year saw him trudging the dusty trail again. Both those roads led to the removal of the peasants' grievances within some six months.

   The 24 days during which he led a column of 80 Satyagrahis traversing 241 miles from Sabarmati to the Surat coastline to break the salt laws did not yield such results. Though, raw salt was lifted 'illegally' by Gandhiji and his followers and though 'contraband' salt was made and sold, the salt laws stayed and the salt tax was not repealed. And yet the Salt March culminating at Dandi on April 6, 1930 is regarded as the most electrifying of all his satyagrahic campaigns, with Jawaharlal Nehru saying "it seemed as though a spring had been suddenly released." —**The Hindu**

   (A) When did Gandhiji's famous Dandi March begin?
   (a) 12th March, 1930
   (b) 15th March, 1930
   (c) 10th March, 1930
   (d) 6th March, 1930

   (B) The historic Dandi March by Gandhiji marked the beginning of ....
   (a) Non-Cooperation Movement
   (b) Civil Disobedience Movement
   (c) Quit India Movement
   (d) First War of Independence

   (C) Which of the following was not the programme of the Movement followed by historic Dandi March of Gandhiji?

   (a) Defiance of Salt Laws
   (b) Boycott of Liquor and foreign clothes
   (c) Non payment of taxes and revenues
   (d) Boycott of elections to be held for councils as suggested by the reforms of 1919

   (D) The Movement launched Gandhiji by historic Dandi March came to an end after signing a Pact. Who was the Viceroy with whom Gandhiji signed the Pact?
   (a) Lord Curzon
   (b) Lord Irwin
   (c) Lord Mountbatten
   (d) Sir John Simon

Ans. (A) (a) *12th March, 1930*
   Explanation: On 12th March, 1930, Mahatma Gandhi began the historic March from Sabarmati Ashram to Dandi, a village on the Gujarat Sea coast. The March culminated at Dandi on 6th April, 1930.

   (B) (b) *Civil Disobedience Movement*
   Explanation: On 6th April, 1930 Gandhiji violated the Salt Law at Dandi by picking up some salt left by the sea waves. According to the Salt Law, the Government had the monopoly to manufacture and sell the salt. Gandhiji's breaking of the Salt Laws marked the beginning of the Civil Disobedience Movement.

   (C) (d) *Boycott of elections to be held for councils as suggested by the reforms of 1919*
   Explanation: Boycott of elections to be held for councils as suggested by the reforms of 1919 was a programme of Non-Cooperation Movement.

   (D) (b) *Lord Irwin*
   Explanation: The Civil Disobedience Movement came to an end after signing of a pact by Gandhiji and Lord Irwin, the Viceroy, in March 1931. This is known as Gandhi-Irwin Pact.

25. *Civil disobedience becomes a sacred duty when the State has become lawless or corrupt. And a citizen who barters with such a State shares in its corruption and lawlessness.*

   Complete Civil disobedience is a state of peaceful rebellion, a refusal to obey every single state-made law.
   —**Mahatma Gandhi**

(A) With which event did Mahatma Gandhi launched the Civil Disobedience Movement?
  (a) Champaran Satyagraha
  (b) Dandi March
  (c) Chauri Chaura incident
  (d) Protest of Simon Commission

(B) Which of the following was not the programme of the Civil Disobedience Movement?
  (a) Defiance of Salt Laws
  (b) Boycott of Liquor and foreign clothes
  (c) Non payment of taxes and revenues
  (d) Boycott of elections to be held for Councils as suggested by the reforms of 1919

(C) Consider the following statements relating to the Civil Disobedience Movement:
  (A) By the Gandhi-Irwin Pact, the Congress agreed to suspend the Civil Disobedience Movement.
  (B) By the Gandhi-Irwin Pact, the government promised to release all political prisoners not convicted for violence.
  Which of the above statements are correct?
  (a) Only (A)
  (b) Only (B)
  (c) Both (A) and (B)
  (d) Neither (A) nor (B)

(D) Identify the factor leading to Civil Disobedience Movement:
  (a) Simon Commission
  (b) Rowlatt Act
  (c) Cripps' Mission
  (d) Chauri Chaura incident

Ans. (A) (b) *Dandi March*
  Explanation: On 12th March, 1930, Mahatma Gandhi began the historic March from Sabarmati Ashram to Dandi, a village on the Gujarat Sea coast. The March culminated at Dandi on 6th April, 1930. This March was the launching of Civil Disobedience Movement.

(B) (d) *Boycott of elections to be held for councils as suggested by the reforms of 1919*
  Explanation: Boycott of elections to be held for Councils as suggested by the reforms of 1919 was a programme of Non-Cooperation Movement.

(C) (c) Both (A) and (B)
(D) (a) *Simon Commission*
  Explanation: Simon Commission was appointed by the British Government to investigate the need for further constitutional reforms. It was opposed by the Indian National Congress as it has no Indian member. It was a factor that led to Civil Disobedience Movement.

Study the pictures given below and answer the questions that follow:

26.

(A) Which event led by Mahatma Gandhi is depicted in the picture?
  (a) Champaran Satyagraha
  (b) Dandi March
  (c) Revolt of 1857
  (d) August Kranti

(B) The historic event by Gandhiji marked the beginning of ....
  (a) Non-Cooperation Movement
  (b) Civil Disobedience Movement
  (c) Quit India Movement
  (d) First War of Independence

(C) Which of the following was not the programme of the Movement followed by historic event of Gandhiji?
  (a) Defiance of Salt Laws
  (b) Boycott of Liquor and foreign clothes
  (c) Non payment of taxes and revenues
  (d) Boycott of elections to be held for Councils as suggested by the reforms of 1919

(D) Identify the factor leading to the Movement launched by Gandhi ji.
  (a) Rowlatt Act
  (b) Simon Commission
  (c) Cripps' Mission
  (d) Jallianwala Bagh Tragedy

Ans. (A) (b) *Dandi March*
  Explanation: On 12th March, 1930, Mahatma Gandhi began the historic

Mahatma Gandhi and the National Movement

Dandi March from Sabarmati Ashram to Dandi, a village on the Gujarat Sea coast. The March culminated at Dandi on 6th April, 1930.

(B) *(b) Civil Disobedience Movement*

Explanation: On 6th April, 1930 Gandhiji violated the Salt Law at Dandi by picking up some salt left by the sea waves. According to the Salt Law, the Government had the monopoly to manufacture and sell the salt. Gandhiji's breaking of the Salt Laws marked the beginning of the Civil Disobedience Movement.

(C) *(d) Boycott of elections to be held for councils as suggested by the reforms of 1919*

Explanation: Boycott of elections to be held for councils as suggested by the reforms of 1919 was a programme of Non-Cooperation Movement.

(D) *(b) Simon Commission*

Explanation: Simon Commission was appointed by the British Government to investigate the need for further constitutional reforms. It was apposed by the Indian National Congress as it had no Indian member. It was a factor that led to Civil Disobedience Movement.

27.

(A) Gandhiji signed a Pact with Lord Irwin to bring an end to a Movement. When was this Pact signed?
  (a) March, 1931
  (b) July, 1932
  (c) March, 1933
  (d) March, 1934

(B) Which Movement was suspended by Gandhiji as a result of signing of this Pact?
  (a) Non-Cooperation Movement
  (b) Civil Disobedience Movement
  (c) Quit India Movement
  (d) Khilafat Movement

(C) Mahatma Gandhi launched the Movement with a famous event. What was the event?
  (a) Champaran Satyagraha
  (b) Kheda Satyagraha
  (c) Dandi March
  (d) Ahmedabad Satyagraha

(D) Which of the following was not a programme of the Movement launched by Gandhiji in 1930?
  (a) Defiance of Salt Laws
  (b) Do or Die
  (c) Boycott of foreign goods
  (d) Non payment of taxes and revenues

Ans. (A) *(a) March, 1931*

Explanation: Gandhiji signed a Pact with Lord Irwin, the Viceroy, in March, 1931. This is known as Gandhi-Irwin Pact.

(B) *(b) Civil Disobedience Movement*

Explanation: As a result of Gandhi-Irwin Pact, the Congress consented to suspend the Civil Disobedience Movement.

(C) *(c) Dandi March*

Explanation: On 12th March, 1930, Mahatma Gandhi began the historic Dandi March from Sabarmati Ashram to Dandi to mark the beginning of the Civil Disobedience Movement.

(D) *(b) Do or Die*

Explanation: The Movement launched by Gandhiji in 1930 was Civil Disobedience Movement. The call for 'Do or Die' was given by Gandhiji during Quit India Movement in 1942.

SUBJECTIVE Type Questions

Short Answer Type Questions
[2 marks each]

28. **State any two causes that led to the Civil Disobedience Movement in 1930.** [ICSE 2018]

Ans. The causes that led to the Civil Disobedience Movement in 1930 were:

(1) There was not a single Indian in the Simon Commission, appointed to propose reforms for further constitutional development. It was an 'All White' Commission.

(2) Simon Commission refused to accept the demand for Swaraj.

Simon Commission, Declaration of Poorna Swaraj at Lahore session (1929), Nehru Report, Viceroys Declaration, Gandhi's Eleven demands, Salt satyagraha.

[Marking Scheme]

 What Examiners Say

→ Most of the candidates could write the causes that led to the Civil Disobedience Movement in 1930 correctly. However, a few candidates mentioned the causes that led to the launching of Non-Cooperation Movement.

⚠️ **Caution**

→ Students should know the difference between the Civil Disobedience Movement and Non-Cooperation Movement.

29. Why was the Congress Session, held at Lahore in 1929, significant to the National Movement? [ICSE 2016]

Ans. The Congress session held at Lahore in 1929 was significant to the National Movement because under the Presidentship of Jawahar Lal Nehru, a resolution for Poorna Swaraj was passed in this session. The session marked the start of a serious and dedicated struggle towards freedom from British rule and launch of Civil Disobedience Movement.

It declared Poorna Swaraj (Complete Independence) as its goal and took steps to launch a programme of Civil Disobedience.
[Marking Scheme]

 What Examiners Say

→ Answered correctly by most candidates which was 'Poorna Swaraj', however few candidates wrote Hindu-Muslim Unity as the significance of the Congress session held at Lahore.

30. Why did Mahatma Gandhi start the historic March to Dandi? [HOT]

Ans. Under the leadership of Gandhi, the Civil Disobedience Movement was launched in the year 1930. The movement was aimed at openly resisting British Laws and it began with the historic 'Dandi March'. This historic march was undertaken by Gandhi to observe and exhibit Civil Disobedience. He chose salt for the purpose.

On 12th March 1930, Gandhi with some of his followers left the Sabarmati Ashram at Ahmedabad and made his way towards Dandi, a village on the west coast of India. Here, Gandhi protested against the Salt Law by making salt himself. He threw up a challenge to the British government as salt was a monopoly of the government and no one was allowed to make salt himself.

31. Why was the Simon Commission rejected by the Congress?

Ans. In 1927, the British government appointed a six men Commission under the Chairmanship of John Simon for the purpose of enquiring into the working of the Rowlatt Act of 1919 and to propose reforms for further constitutional development. It was called the Simon Commission. The Commission disappointed people and was seen as an insult to the self-respect of the Indians due to the following reasons:

(1) There was not a single Indian in the commission. It was an 'All-White' commission.

(2) It refused to accept the demand for Swaraj. At its Madras session in 1927, presided over by Dr. Ansari, the Indian National Congress decided to boycott the Simon Commission. A resolution was passed calling for the total boycott of the Commission.

32. Mention any two provisions of the Gandhi-Irwin Pact signed in 1931. [ICSE 2014]

Ans. The provisions of Gandhi-Irwin Pact signed in 1931 were:

(1) The Congress would suspend the Civil Disobedience Movement and Gandhi agreed to take part in the proceedings of the Second Round Table Conference;

(2) The government would release all political prisoners, except those convicted of violence and killing, and withdraw all ordinances issued to curb the Congress.

The Gandhi Irwin pact agreed to by the Congress and the Government.

The Congress agreed to suspend the civil disobedience movement. (ii) They agreed to participate in the Second Round Table conference (iii) that they would not press for investigation into police excesses. The Government agreed to (i) withdrawl all ordinances and end prosecution. (ii) release all political prisoners except those guilty of violence (iii) permit peaceful picketing of liquor and foreign clothes. (iv) restore the confiscated properties of the Satyagrahis (v) permit the free collection or manufacture of salt by persons near the sea coast.
[Any two]
Marking Scheme]

Structured Questions

[3+3+4= **10** marks each]

33. With reference to Mahatma Gandhi and the National Movement, answer the following questions:
   (A) State any three provisions of the Rowlatt Act passed by the Government in 1919. **[ICSE 2017]**
   (B) State any two causes for the Non-Cooperation Movement.
   (C) Mention features of the Montague – Chelmsford Reforms.

Ans. (A) The provisions of the Rowlatt Act, passed by the Government in 1919, were:
   (1) According to the Act, the government could arrest anyone without warrant and imprison them indefinitely without a trial.
   (2) Possession of seditious pamphlets was declared a punishable offence.
   (3) Restrictions on movements of individuals.

   Rowlatt Act:
   (1) Arrest of a person without warrant.
   (2) In camera trial (trial in seclusion).
   (3) Restrictions on movements of individuals
   (4) Suspension of the Right of Habe Corpus.
   (No dalil No vakil No appeal)
   [Any three] Marking Scheme]

   (B) The two main causes for Non-Cooperation Movement were:
   (1) The more important cause of the Non-Cooperation Movement was the Khilafat Movement which began in 1919, brought the Muslims and the Hindus, on a common platform against the British rule.
   (2) It was launched against the Rowlatt Act and the Jallianwala Bagh massacre.

 Caution
➡ *Students should emphasise on the causes, course and consequences of three important Gandhian events.*

   (C) Montague – Chelmsford Reforms (1919) is also known as the Government of India Act, 1919. Its main features were:
   (1) Government of India still remained under British Parliament.
   (2) System of Dyarchy.
   (3) Provincial Subjects were divided into – Reserved and Transferred subjects. The Governor enjoyed exclusive powers over the administration of these subjects.

The Reforms were considered to be inadequate, unsatisfactory and disappointing by the Indians and thus, they sought more reforms. British government failed to fulfill their promise to introduce a responsible government in India.

34. With reference to Mahatma Gandhi and the National Movement, answer the following questions:
   (A) Name any three leaders of the Khilafat Movement.
   (B) What was the Khilafat Movement? **[ICSE 2017]**
   (C) The Non-Cooperation Movement had two types of programmes namely negative and positive. Name three each.

Ans. (A) The leaders of Khilafat Movement were Mohammad Ali and Shaukat Ali, Maulana Azad, Hakim Ajmal Khan and Hasrat Mohani. **[Any three]**

 Caution
➡ *Khilafat Movement including the names of the two main leaders should be studied in detail.*

   (B) When England waged war against Turkey during the First World War, the sentiments of the Muslims all over the world were hurt. Turkey was defeated and some of its activists were captured by England. Moreover, the British abolished the title of Khilafat, the highest religious head of Islam which added insult to injury. Muslims in India were agitated and started a movement with the idea of forcing the British to restore the power and dignity of the Khalifa. Under the leadership of the Ali brothers, Shaukat and Mohammed Ali, a powerful movement was launched. This movement is called the Khilafat Movement.

   (1) The Caliph of Turkey lost all territories inhabited by people other than Turks.
   (2) The Sultan was deprived of real authority over such territories and this angered the Muslims in India.
   (3) A Khilafat Committee was formed to champion the cause of the Caliph of Turkey by the Ali brothers, Mohammad Ali and Shaukat Ali.
   [Marking Scheme]

   (C) **The Negative aspect of the Programme included:**
   (1) The boycott of government schools and colleges.
   (2) The boycott of British goods.
   (3) The boycott of Legislative Councils
   (4) The Boycott of law Courts
   [Any three]

The Positive aspect of the Programme included:
(1) Hindu-Muslim Unity
(2) Promotion of Swadeshi
(3) Removal of untouchability
(4) The banning of intoxicating drinks (liquor) **[Any three]**

35. With reference to the picture given below, answer the following questions:

(A) (a) Identify the Memorial built for those who were killed in this incident.
   (b) Where did this incident take place?
   (c) Name the movement launched by Gandhi in 1920 as a consequence.
(B) Explain briefly the reason for the suspension of this particular movement by Gandhi in 1922.
(C) State *any four* impacts of the movement.

[HOT] [ICSE 2019]

Ans. (A) (a) The memorial built for those killed in this incident is Jallianwala Bagh Memorial.
(b) This incident took place at Jallianwala Bagh, Amritsar, Punjab.
(c) The movement launched by Gandhji in 1922 as a consequence was Non-Cooperation Movement.

(B) The main reason for the suspension of Non-Cooperation Movement by Gandhiji in 1922 was the violent incident that took place in Chauri Chaura village in Gorakhpur district of Uttar Pradesh in which 22 policemen were burnt alive by a mob. Gandhiji took a serious view of this incident. Non-violence was creed to Gandhiji who could hardly tolerate that his followers should indulge in violence. So he took the step of suspending the movement.

(C) **The impact of the Non-Cooperation Movement was as follows:**
(1) **Unity:** The Non-Cooperation Movement was the first movement in which the Hindus and Muslims participated as one and reflected unity among themselves.
(2) **Mass movement:** The Movement gave rise to the sentiments of nationalism on a wider scale. The National Movement naturally became quite wider in its scope and it was no longer limited to only few educated urban people.
(3) **Change in the approach of Congress:** The Movement had a great impact on the working of the Congress. The Congress decided to use the weapons of Satyagraha and Non-Cooperation or wider scale.
(4) **Desire of freedom among people:** The Non-Cooperation Movement developed a desire of freedom among the people and they had a belief to get independence.

(A)
(1) Jallianwala Bagh Memorial
(2) Jallianwala Bagh in Amritsar
(3) Non-Cooperation Movement.
(B)
(1) The Tragedy at Chauri Chaura, a village in Gorakhpur district in Uttar Pradesh.
(2) A procession of about 3,000 peasants marched to the police station to protest against the police offcer.
(3) Police fired at the peasants.
(4) Peasants reacted and set the police station on fire.
(5) 22 policemen were killed.
(6) Gandhiji, who believed in Ahimsa was greatly shocked and withdrew the movement on February 12, 1922.
(7) A police officer had beaten some farmers picketing a liquor shop.

(Narration of Incident with any of the three points cited in the answer)

(C) **Impact of Non-Cooperation Movement**
(1) The National Movement became a Mass Movement (Gave a national base to the Congress Party)
(2) Instilled confidence, Patriotism among people.
(3) Congress became a revolutionary party.
(4) Undermined the power and prestige of British Government.
(5) Fostered Hindu-Muslim unity.
(6) Promoted social reforms (like removal of untouchability/promotion of khadi/ setting up of national schools)
(7) Promoted the cult of Swaraj.
(8) Showed the true nature of the British.
(9) Spread Nationalism to every part of the country.
(10) Affected British trade
(11) Showed power of passive resistance

[Any four]

What Examiners Say

→ (A) (1) Majority of the candidates could identify the given picture.
(2) Most of the candidates wrote the correct place in which the incident occurred. Some candidates, however, mentioned Punjab instead of Amritsar.
(3) Majority of the candidates named the movement correctly barring a few candidates, who named it as the Civil Disobedience Movement.

(B) The reason for the suspension was explained correctly as the Chauri Chaura incident by almost all the candidates.

(C) The impact of the movement was written correctly by most of the candidates. However, a few candidates got confused with the other movements launched by Mahatma Gandhi and mixed up the points.

Caution

→ (A) Students should identify the pictures of not only monuments, but also the leaders along with their importance.
→ (B) Important events should be connected with the incidents.
→ (C) Students should understand the impact of each movement launched by Mahatma Gandhi clearly.

36. In 1930 Mahatma Gandhi's demands were rejected by the British, as a result of which he launched the Civil Disobedience Movement. In this context, explain the following:

(A) Name the famous march undertaken by Gandhiji. Where did he begin this march? State *two* of its features.
(B) The Gandhi-Irwin Pact as a consequence of this Movement.
(C) Significance of the Second Round Table Conference. [HOT🔥] [ICSE 2015]

Ans. (A) The famous march undertaken by Gandhiji was 'Dandi March'. Gandhi began this march from his Sabarmati Ashram at Ahmedabad on 12th March, 1930 to Dandi, a village on the west coast of India.

The features of the Dandi March were:
(1) The Dandi March signified the start of the Civil Disobedience Movement.
(2) It was a protest against the Salt law as salt was a monopoly of the government and no one was allowed to make salt.

(B) Under the leadership of Gandhi, the Civil Disobedience Movement was launched in the year 1930. The Movement was aimed at openly resisting British laws. The Civil Disobedience Movement resulted in mass strikes and demonstrations. Perturbed by the growing popularity of the Movement, the British Government imprisoned Mahatma Gandhi and Jawahar Lal Nehru in a bid to thwart it. The British Government convened the First Round Table Conference. The Indian National Congress did not attend it because most of the Congress leaders were either in jail or followed the decision of the Congress to boycott the conference. Since, without the participation of the congress in the political negotiations, any settlement was not possible. The decision to hold the Second Round Table Conference was taken on 26 January 1931. Gandhi and all the national leaders were released from prison when the Gandhi-Irwin Pact was signed.

The members of the Round Table Conference met Gandhi and requested him to meet the then Viceroy, Lord Curzon. Gandhi wanted peace but with honour. The government also wanted to end the stalemate. Gandhi-Irwin Pact was signed on 5th March 1931. As per the pact, Gandhi agreed to suspend the Civil Disobedience Movement on agreement to following points:

(1) The government would release all political prisoners except those convicted of violence and killing;
(2) The government would withdraw all ordinances issued to curb the Congress;
(3) The government would allow people residing near the coast to manufacture salt for personal use;
(4) The government would allow restoration of all confiscated land and property;
(5) The government would allow peaceful picketing of liquor shops and drug stores.

As British Government agreed to all these points, the Civil Disobedience Movement was suspended.

(C) The Second Round Table Conference was attended by Gandhiji as the sole representative of the Indian National Congress. The deliberations at the conference were only on communal representation in legislative bodies and not on the question of independence or of a responsible government in India. Gandhi's effort to achieve a communal settlement proved unsuccessful. He returned to India without any positive result. The Gandhi-Irwin Pact was violated and Viceroy, Lord Wellington took to the suppression of the government. Gandhiji was, thus, forced to repudiate the Gandhi-Irwin Pact and Civil Disobedience Movement was resumed.

(A) Dandi March. On 12th March Mahatma Gandhi began this historic march from Sabarmati Ashram to Dandi. 78 persons followed him but as he advanced others followed the crowd. He reached Dandi on 5th April. On the 6th April, after his morning prayers Gandhiji violated the salt laws by picking up salt at the coast. Gandhiji's campaign against the salt laws was a signal to disobey the government laws.

(B) On 5th March 1931, a pact was signed between Gandhiji and the Governor General Lord Irwin.
  (1) To release all political prisoners except those guilty of violence.
  (2) To give back to the Congressmen their confiscated properties.
  (3) To permit peaceful picketing of liquor and foreign cloth shops.
  (4) To permit people living near the sea coast to manufacture salt.

Mahatma Gandhi agreed to suspend the Civil Disobedience Movement and agreed to attend the second round table conference.

(C) Gandhiji was chosen as the sole representative of the Congress for the Second Round Table Conference.

The Conference devoted most of its time to communal question and the representation of minorities in the legislatures both at the centre and the provinces. Gandhiji was disgust to find that most leaders seemed concerned only about their vested interests. The question of independence or of setting up of a responsible government receded into background. Mahatma Gandhi returned to India empty handed.

(Marking Scheme)

What Examiners Say

➡ (A) Most candidates wrote correct answers. Few however wrote general answers and were not specific. They were unable to explain the main features of the Dandi March and failed to mention the violation of the salt laws.

➡ (B) Most candidates wrote the Gandhi-Irwin Pact correctly. Few however, were unable to understand the question and wrote irrelevant points not connected with the pact.

➡ (C) Most candidates wrote correct answers. However a few were confused and could not specify the significance of the Second Round Table Conference.

⚠ Caution

➡ (A) Students should emphasise on specific points rather then general statements.

➡ (B) Students should know meaning of word 'Consequences' etc.

➡ (C) Students are advised to explain the Round Table Conferences and their significance point-wise.

37. Gandhiji introduced new ideas in politics and adopted new methods to give a new direction to the political movement. In this context, explains the following:

  (A) Gandhiji's Doctrine of Satyagraha.
  (B) Gandhiji's Social Ideals.
  (C) Which mass struggle was launched by him on non-violent lines in 1920?

Explain in brief the programmes of such a campaign. **[ICSE 2012]**

Ans. (A) The term Satyagraha was coined and developed by Mahatma Gandhi who practiced Satyagraha in India. In his earlier struggles in South Africa, Gandhi's philosophy was based on non-violence. Gandhi described the form of non-violent struggle that he forged and used as Satyagraha. He defined the two main principles of Satyagraha as insistence on the Truth, holding to the Truth, and dependence on the force inherent on Truth. According to Gandhi, passive resistance was the weapon of the weak while Satyagraha was the weapon of the strong. He laid stress upon peaceful talks, non-cooperation, social boycott, civil disobedience, etc. to realise his aim of Satyagraha.

(B) The whole philosophy of Gandhiji was based on non-violence. Gandhi always used mass movements as weapons of protests. He realised that movement which involved rural, urban, men and women, educated, uneducated are more liable to have an effect. He launched many movements and all of them were non-violent.

(C) Gandhiji launched Non-Cooperation Movement in 1920 on non-violent terms. Non-Cooperation means withdrawal of all support and co-operation. Gandhi realised that for the smooth functioning of any government, the willing co-operation of the people is essential. Gandhi, therefore, resorted not to extend such co-operation to the government.

A two fold programme was launched, for the Non-Cooperation Movement, as follows:

(1) **Constructive Programme:** As part of the Non-cooperation movement, constructive programmes were taken up which dealt purely with constructive work.
   (i) to spin thread from cotton and to promote Khadi;
   (ii) to eradicate untouchability;
   (iii) to prohibit consumption of liquor;
   (iv) to achieve Hindu Muslim unity.

(2) **Boycott Programme:** As a part of Non-Cooperation Movement, Boycott Programmes dealt with the boycott of British Government.
   (i) To surrender the titles and honours conferred by the government;
   (ii) To boycott functions, durbars and celebrations organised by the government;
   (iii) To boycott law courts and to substitute them with local Panchayats and Swadeshi courts;
   (iv) To give up foreign cloth and to wear only swadeshi products.

7. Quit India Movement

The period from 1935 to 1942 saw the widening of rift between the Congress and the Muslim League and the parting of ways between Mahatma Gandhi and Subhash Chandra Bose. It was during this period that the Second World War showed its ugly head in 1939. With the failure of Cripps Mission, the Congress started the Quit India Movement. emphasising the British to quit India.

Chapter Notes

- Quit India Movement (Events Leading to the Movement and its Failure)
- Quit India Resolution and Significance of the Movement

TOPIC 1

QUIT INDIA MOVEMENT
(Events leading to the Movement and its Failure)

Act of 1935

After the Third Round Table Conference in London in 1932, the British Government worked out a set of proposals for reforming the Government of India. Consequently, the Government of India Act got the Royal Assent on 4th August, 1935 and it provided ground for the formation of an All India Federation including eleven British Provinces and the Princely States.

In 1937, election was held and the Congress won 711 out of 1585 Provincial Assembly seats. The Congress formed Ministries in six provinces (Bihar, United Province, Central Province, Orissa, Bombay and Madras).

It formed coalition Ministries in Assam and Sind except Bengal. (NWFP means the North West Frontier Province of Pakistan) was formed by the Congress then along with Assam.

The Muslim League had not done well in the elections.

The Congress Ministers functioned well and stressed on welfare measures like education, local self-government and Fundamental Rights.

Events Leading to the Quit India Movement

On 1st September, 1939, Germany attacked Poland. Britain and France declared war on Germany on 3rd September, 1939 and the Second World War began. India, being a colony of Great Britain, was expected to fight on behalf of the British against the Fascist Powers.

Resignation of the Congress Ministers

The British Government wanted to involve the Indians in the Second World War without consulting the Central Legislatures and the Provincial Governments. The Congress leaders asked how was it possible for an enslaved nation to aid others in their fight for freedom. They therefore, demanded that India must be declared free or atleast have effective power before it could actively participate in the war. They also demanded to know about the war aims of the British.

But, the British Government did not pay any attention to their demands. So, the Congress Ministers in the various Provinces resigned in October, 1939. The Muslim League was elected over the resignation of the Congress Ministers and celebrated the day as the 'Thanks Giving' and the "Day of Deliverance". The League promised to help the British in their war efforts.

In 1940, at the Lahore Session of the Muslim League, Jinnah demanded the creation of Pakistan, a separate Muslim State.

Example 1. When was the 'Deliverance Day' celebrated by the Muslim League?

Ans. 'Deliverance Day' was celebrated by the Muslim League on 22nd December, 1939.

August Offer (1940)

A Change of government took place in Britain in May, 1940. Winston Churchill became Prime Minister and Amery took over as the Secretary of State for India. The situation in Europe had been worsening and therefore, the British Government wanted to have some sort of settlement with the Congress. Hence, on 8th August, 1940, the Viceroy Lord Linlithgow, made a new offer known as 'August Offer'. It proposed that: After the war an Indian representative body would be set up to frame a Constitution for India.

It also proposed that the Executive Council of the Viceroy would be expanded without any delay.

The Minorities were assured that the government would not transfer power to any system of government whose authority was directly denied by large and powerful elements in the Indian National life.

Reaction of the congress and the Mulsim Leage

(1) The Proposals for minorities in the 'August Offer' failed to satisfy the Congress. Moreover, there was no time limit when the Constitution making body would be set up. Hence, the Congress rejected these proposals.

(2) The Muslim League also rejected the 'August Offer', as it did not give a clear Out assurance for the establishment of Pakistan.

Individual Satyagraha

Though the Congress stood for freedom, it did not wish to help the British, as long as the British did not clarify war aims and India's position. At this time, Vinoba Bhave was the first Satyagrahi who launched Individual Civil Disobedience Movement. This Movement soon spread. The British were worried and arrested thousands of people.

Example 2. Name the movement which was launched by the Congress Workers in 1940 to resist the war efforts of the British government.

Ans. 'Individual Satyagraha'.

 Related Theory

➡ The movement started on 7th October, 1940, with an Anti-War speech in Poona. Women leaders like – Sarojini

Naidu, Satyawati and Aruna Asaf Ali were imprisoned. By 1941, nearly 25,000 had offered Individual Satyagraha by defying government orders. Thousands of people courted arrest to prove that India was taking power in the war effort, unwillingly December 1941, all the Satyagrahis were released and the movement continued for a year and a quarter.

The Cripps Mission (1942)

Reason for the Arrival of the Mission

The Japanese aircrafts shattered the American naval base at Pearl Harbour in the Hawaii Island on 7th December, 1941. This event indicated that Japan had joined the War on the side of the Axis Powers. With the Japanese Army rapidly advancing towards India, it became necessary for the British to break the political deadlock in India. Churchill announced in March 1942, that Sir Stafford Cripps, a member of the War Cabinet, would go to India for consultation with parties. He came to Delhi on 22nd March, 1942 and put forward his proposals.

The Cripps proposals

(1) India would be given Dominion Status when the Second World War would be over.
(2) A Constituent Assembly would be set up including the elected members from British India and the representatives of the Princely States nominated by their rulers. It would make a draft of the new Constitution.
(3) The British Government would accept the Constitution prepared by the Constituent Assembly.
(4) If any province was not willing to accept this Constitution, it could make its own Constitution which would be given the same status as that the Indian Union had.
(5) Provisions would be made for the protection of the racial and religious minorities.
(6) Princely States would be free to join the Indian Union or stay out.
(7) During the Second World War, the Viceroy and his Executive Council would be responsible for the defence of the country.
(8) The government wanted the effective participation of the Indian leaders, until the new Constitution was prepared.

Reaction towards the Cripps proposal

The Muslim League rejected the Cripps proposals because there was no concrete announcement for the Partition of India.

They demanded Pakistan as a separate Muslim State, but these proposals did not accept Pakistan. The Congres rejected the proposals on the following grounds:

(1) The people of the Princely States were deprived of their right to elect their representative to the Constituent Assembly. These representatives would be nominated by the rulers of those respective Princely States.
(2) The proposals would involve Partition of India into a number of independent States.
(3) The Congress wanted that defence should be handed over to the National Government.
(4) Attainment of Self-Government or Dominion Status was also quite uncertain. Gandhiji described the Cripps' proposals as a "Post-dated cheque on a failing bank".
(5) The Cripps Mission did not bring with it the promise of independence in the near future.
(6) The Hindu Mahasabha rejected the proposals because it feared the Partition of the country.
(7) The Sikhs, the Anglo-Indians, the Indian Christians and labour–leaders also opposed them because they did not provide sufficient safeguards for their interests.
(8) The Congress insisted on the immediate formation of a National Government with full responsibility. These were all the reasons of the failure of the Cripps Mission.

Possibility of Japanese attack on India

The Japanese army had attacked Burma (Myanmar) and was marching towards Assam. Gandhiji felt that the presence of British in India had been a threat to the security and safety of India. Japan had no enmity with India, but it was fighting in the Second World War against Britain and as India was a British Colony, therefore, Japan might attack India. But, if the British left India, then India could be saved from the possible Japanese attack. Gandhiji remarked that India's safety was dependent on the orderly and timely withdrawl of the British from India. On 8th August, 1942, the All India Congress Committee met at Bombay (Mumbai) and passed the Quit India Resolution. If the demand for immediate and complete independence was not accepted by the British, the Congress would start a non-violent Mass Movement.

 Related Theory

→ The Japanese threat to attack India was so real that Jawaharlal Nehru had advised people to be ready to defend themselves using guerilla tactics, if required.

 **Caution**

→ Students should remember the names of the countries who were in Axis Power and Allied Powers in the Second World War. They should avoid writing countries in their respective powers.

Quit India Movement

TOPIC 2

QUIT INDIA RESOLUTION AND SIGNIFICANCE OF THE MOVEMENT

Quit India Resolution

In 1942, the failure of the Cripps Mission left no further meeting ground between the British Government and the Congress. Mahatma Gandhi felt that the British presence in India was an invitation to Japan to invade India and that their withdrawl would remove the bait. He therefore, asked the British "to leave India in God's hands."

The Congress Working Committee met at Wardha in July, 1942. It adopted a resolution, known as the Quit India Resolution.

Example 6. What did the Quit India Resolution stated?

Ans. The Quit India Resolution stated that the British rule in India must end immediately.

 Related Theory

→ The Quit India Resolution was passed by the Congress Working Committee at Wardha in July, 1942 but this was ratified in the Mumbai Session of the All India Congress Committee on 08th August, 1942.

Quit India Movement

The All-India Congress passed the Quit India Resolution on 08th August, 1942. The Congress proposed to start a non-violent mass struggle under Gandhiji's leadership if this demand of immediate and complete independence was not conceded by the British. In his speech before the All India Congress Committee, Gandhiji declared that it was a decision "To Do or Die".

In the very next morning on 09th August, prominent leaders of the Congress including Gandhiji were arrested.

Isolated and secured people took to violence. Violence was directed towards government buildings.

(1) People attacked police stations, Government buildings, all means of transport and communications.

(2) Jai Prakash Narayan, Ram Manohar Lohia, Aruna Asaf Ali and Nana Patil were among the prominent leaders of the underground movement.

(3) The movement spread in different parts of the country, power houses were attacked, roads were blocked.

 Related Theory

→ The Movement also saw the active participation of women such as Matangini Hazra in Bengal, Kanaklata Barua in Assam and Rama Devi in Odisha.

→ Aruna Asaf Ali hoisted the Indian National Flag at the Gowalia Tank ground, Mumbai on August 09, 1942.

→ She along with Usha Mehta, also broadcasted news through an underground Radio Station.

Government's Repressive Measures

The government restored to severe measures to crush the 1942 Movement.

(1) The Press was completely chocked.

(2) The demonstrating crowds were machine-gunned and even bombed from the air. Prisoners were tortured.

(3) Nearly ten thousand people were killed and 60,000 people were arrested by the end of 1942.

(4) Gandhiji was detained at the Agha Khan Palace in Pune; the other leaders were sent to Jail in Ahmednagar Fort. In the end, the government succeeded in crushing the Movement.

Significance of the Quit India Movement

The Quit India Movement did not get the British to quit India, but it shook the foundation of the British Empire.

The Movement made independence of India as the only agenda of the National Movement. It proved that there could be no retreat and future negotiations could only be on the manner of the transfer of Power.

The Movement had the following impact:

(1) It demonstrated the depth of the nationalists feelings in India and the capacity of Indians for struggle and sacrifice.

(2) It made it clear that the British would no longer find it possible to rule India against the wishes of its people.

(3) People of all sections of society participated in this movement. The Hindus, Muslims, Sikhs, Christians and Parsis and even people from the Princely States participated in it.

(4) The Quit India Movement strengthened the Congress Socialist Party because of its heroic role in the movement. Its leader Jai Prakash Narayan became a legendary figure.

(5) After the suppression of the Quit India Movement, the Constitutional question remained dormant till the close of the War in 1945.

(6) After the suppression of the Quit India Movement of 1942, there was hardly any political activity inside the country till the War ended in 1945. The leaders of the National Movement were in jail, and no new leaders arose to take their place to give a new lead to the country.

Henceforth, the battle for the freedom of India was carried beyond the country's frontiers. It was led by the Indian National Army and its Chief, Subhash Chandra Bose.

Important

→ A number of patriots took to violence. Bhagat Singh, Sukhdev and Rajguru were sentenced to death for their fight using violence against the British. The hanging of these three shook the nation. Chandra Shekhar Azad, Ram Prasad Bismill were also great revoluntionaries.

ICSE Suggestions

→ Students should remember names of maximum leaders who took part in the Quit India Movement, names of leaders who were sent to Jail and also names of women leaders who took part in the Quit India Movement and the role played by them. Also the names of leaders of 'Underground Movement' should be learnt.

Glossary

(1) **Dominion Status:** The power or right of governing
(2) **Two-Nation Theory:** It was given by Jinnah. According to this theory, there should be two separate nations for the Hindus and the Muslims.
(3) **Underground Movement:** It was an important feature of Quit India Movement, led by prominent leaders like Achyut Rao Patwardhan, Jai Prakash Narayan, Ram Manohar Lohia, Aruna Asaf Ali and Nana Patil. They set up the organisation Azad Dasta with its branches all over India.

Who's Who?

(1) **Achyut Rao Patwardhan:** Was an Indian Independence activist and political leader and founder of the Socialist Party of India.
(2) **Aruna Asaf Ali:** Was an Indian educator, political activist, and publisher. She was an active participant in the Indian Independence Movement, she is widely remembered for hoisting the Indian National Flag at the Gowalia Tank Maidan, Bombay during the Quit India Movement in 1942.
(3) **Sucheta Kriplani:** Was an Indian freedom fighter and politician, she was India's first woman Chief Minister, serving as the head of the Uttar Pradesh from 1963 to 1967.
(4) **Jai Prakash Narayan:** Was an Indian Independence activist, Socialist and Political leader. He formed Congress Socialist Party by separating from Congress.
(5) **Vinobha Bhave:** He was a disciple of Mahatma Gandhi and the first Satyagrahi who launched Individual Civil Disobedience Movement. He also started the Bhudan Movement.

Who Said What?

(1) **"We do not seek our independence out of British ruin"** —Mahatma Gandhi
Mahatama Gandhi declared these words on June 1, 1940, during August offer (1940).

(2) **"The presence of British in India is an invitation to Japan to invade India. Their withdrawl removes the bait"** —Mahatma Gandhi
Gandhiji said these words, when the Japanese Army attacked Myanmar and was marching towards Assam.

(3) **"India's safety, and Britains too, lies in the orderly and timely British withdrawl from India".** —Mahatma Gandhi
These words were said by Gandhji before launching the Quit India Movement.

(4) **"To Do or Die"** —Mahatma Gandhi
These words were said by Gandhiji on 08th July, 1942 in his speech before the All India Congress Committee. Gandhiji declared that it was a decision to gain independence at any cost from British rule.

Chronology

1935: Government of India Act of 1935
1937: Formation of Congress Ministries in 6 Provinces
1939: Second World War started.
1940: Jinnah declared Two Nation Theory/August Offer
1942: Cripps Mission/Quit India Movement/Formation of INA
1945: The end of Second World War

OBJECTIVE Type Questions

Multiple Choice Questions

[1 mark each]

1. What were the causes of the Quit India Movement?
   (a) Failure of Simon Commission and Rowlatt Act
   (b) Failure of the Cripps Mission and Declaration of Poorna Swaraj
   (c) Growing unemployment and Jallianwala Bagh Massacre.
   (d) Failure of Cripps Mission and Japanese threat. [ICSE Sem-1, 2021]

Ans. (d) Failure of Cripps Mission and Japanese threat.

   Explanation: In 1942, the failure of Cripps Mission left no further ground between the British Government and the Congress. Mahatma Gandhi felt that the British Presence in India was an invitation to Japan to India and their withdrawl would remove the bait.

2. The Quit India Resolution was passed by the Congress in ....
   (a) 1929   (b) 1936
   (c) 1942   (d) 1947   [HOT🔥]

Ans. (c) 1942

   Explanation: The Congress Working Committee met at Wardha in July, 1942. It adopted a resolution known as the Quit India Resolution at Wardha in July, 1942.

3. Which of the following were the causes of the Quit India Movement?
   (A) Japanese threat
   (B) Jallianwala Tragedy
   (C) Failure of Cripps
   (D) Rowlatt Act Movement
   (a) (A) and (B)
   (b) (A) and (C)
   (c) (B) and (D)
   (d) (B) and (C)

Ans. (b) (A) and (C)

   Explanation: The causes of the Quit India Movement were Japanese threat and failure of Cripps Mission. Jallianwala Bagh and Rowlatt Act were the causes of Non-Cooperation Movement.

4. Identify the causes of the Quit India Movement:
   (A) Gandhi-Irwin Pact
   (B) Failure of Cripps Mission
   (C) Split in Indian National Congress
   (D) Japanese Threat
   (a) (A) and (B)
   (b) (A) and (C)
   (c) (B) and (C)
   (d) (B) and (D)   [HOT🔥]

Ans. (d) (B) and (D)

   Explanation: In 1942, Sir Stafford Cripps introduced certain Constitutional reforms in India. Almost all the parties and sections of the people rejected the proposals. The failure of Cripps Mission left no further meeting ground between the British Government and the Congress. The Congress Working Committee met at Wardha in July, 1942. It adopted a resolution called the 'Quit India Resolution'.

5. When was the Quit India Movement launched by Mahatma Gandhi?
   (a) 1919   (b) 1929
   (c) 1942   (d) 1946

Ans. (c) 1942

   Explanation: Mahatma Gandhi launched the Quit India Movement in 1942.

6. Gandhiji gave the mantra of "Do or Die" on the eve of which mass movement?
   (a) Non-Cooperation Movement
   (b) Civil Disobedience Movement
   (c) Champaran Satyagraha
   (d) Quit India Movement

Ans. (d) Quit India Movement

   Explanation: The Quit India Movement was started on 8 Aug, 1942 in Bombay under the leadership of Mahatma Gandhi. In this movement he gave a slogan "Do or Die".

Multiple Choice Questions-II

(Other Question Types, for Extra Practice)

[4 marks each]

7. Read the following passage carefully and answer the questions that follow :

   "Here is a mantra, a short one that I give you. You may imprint it on your hearts and let every breath of yours give expression to it. The mantra is: 'Do or Die'. We shall either free India or die in the attempt; we shall not live to see the perpetuation of our slavery."

   "In Satyagraha, there is no place for fraud or falsehood, or any kind of untruth. Fraud and untruth today are stalking the world. I cannot be a helpless witness to such a situation."

"Ours is not a drive for power, but purely a nonviolent fight for India's independence."

"A non-violent soldier of freedom will covet nothing for himself, he fights only for the freedom of his country."

"Truth alone will endure, all the rest will be swept always in the tide of Time."

—Mahatma Gandhi

(A) Which movement did Mahatma Gandhi launch in 1942?
 (a) Non Cooperation Movement
 (b) Civil Disobedience Movement
 (c) Champaran Satyagraha
 (d) Quit India Movement

(B) Which movement was known as the August Revolution?
 (a) Non Cooperation Movement
 (b) The First War of Independence
 (c) Quit India Movement
 (d) Civil Disobedience Movement

(C) What among the following were the reasons of the Movement launched by Gandhiji?
 (I) Failure of Cripps Mission
 (II) Rowlatt Act
 (III) Jallianwala Bagh Massacre
 (IV) Japanese threat
 (a) (I) and (II)   (b) (II) and (III)
 (c) (I) and (IV)   (d) (II) and (IV)

(D) When was this Movement launched?
 (a) 1919   (b) 1930
 (c) 1942   (d) 1946

Ans. (A) *(d) Quit India Movement*
 Explanation: Mahatma Gandhi launched the Quit India Movement in 1942.

(B) *(c) Quit India Movement*
 Explanation: Quit India Movement was also known as August Kranti.

(C) *(c) (I) and (IV)*
 Explanation: The causes of the Quit India Movement were Japanese threat and failure of Cripps Mission. Jallianwala Bagh Tragedy and Rowlatt Act were the causes of Non-Cooperation Movement.

(D) *(c) 1942*
 Explanation: The All India Congress Committee met at Bombay on August 8, 1942 and passed the Quit India Resolution adopted at Wardha in July 1942. The Quit India Movement was launched in 1942 under the leadership of Mahatma Gandhi.

SUBJECTIVE Type Questions

Short Answer Type Questions
[2 marks each]

8. **Which proposal of the August Offer was welcomed by the Muslim League?**
Ans. The Muslim League welcomed that part of the offer which gave an assurance to the minorities.

9. **Name the 'Mantra' which was given by Gandhiji during Quit India Movement. [HOT]**
Ans. "Do or Die"

10. **What was the proposal of Cripps Mission regarding the Defence of India?**
Ans. The 'Defence of India' would remain under the control of the British Government.

11. **When were the elections held as an outcome of the Government of India act, 1935 ?**
Ans. The elections were held in 1937.

12. **When and in which session did the Muslim League demand formation of Pakistan ?**
Ans. The Muslim League demanded formation of Pakistan in 1940, during the Lahore Session.

Structured Questions
[3+3+4= 10 marks each]

13. **With reference to the Quit India Movement answer the following questions:**

(A) What was the cause of the rift in the Congress in 1939 ?
(B) Why was Quit India Movement launched ?
(C) What was the British Government's reaction to the 'Quit India Movement' ?

Ans. (A) By 1937, Subhash Chandra Bose became a prominent leader of the Indian National Congress. He differed with Gandhiji in his policies and methods of dealing with the government. In 1939, Subhash Chandra Bose resigned from the Congress Presidentship over the issue of the formation of the Congress Working Committee and formed a separate party within the Congress known as Forward Bloc.

(B) Quit India Movement was launched for the following reasons :
 (1) The failure of the Cripps Mission had dis-illusioned Indian leaders who were now looking at other points.
 (2) Communal tension by now had worsened and there was unrest in the country.
 (3) The Japanese threat to attack India was so real that to defend themselves using guerilla tactics if required.

Quit India Movement   183

(C) The British government reacted very harshly to the Quit India Movement. They used their full might to surpress this movement. Prominent leaders of the Congress including Gandhiji were arrested. Martial Law was imposed in many places. More than 10,000 people were killed. Although the official figure showed much less, many people were arrested. But inspite of all this the movement spread and soon the British realized that they couldn't stay in India for much longer.

14. With reference to the Quit India Movement and Second World War answer the following questions:
    (A) What were the circumstances during the Second World War which forced the national leaders to launch the 'Quit India Movement'?
    (B) Where were the Congress Ministries formed after the 1937 elections?
    (C) Why did the Congress Ministries resign in 1939?

Ans. (A) During the Second World War, there was a growing threat of Japanese invasion on India. The Congress leaders were of the opinion that to save India from the Japanese attack it was necessary that the British withdrew from India, this forced the national leaders to launch the 'Quit India Movement'.
(B) The Congress Ministries were first formed in six Provinces – UP, Bihar, Orissa (Odisha), The Central Provinces, Madras (Chennai) and Bombay (Mumbai). Later they were formed in North West Frontier Province (NWFP) and in Assam.
(C) (1) The British Government implicated India in the Second World War without the consent of the Indians.
    (2) The Congress wanted a definite assurance from the British Government regarding independence but that assurance never came.
    (3) The British Government tried to put the religious minorities and Princess against the Congress.
    (4) Consequently, the Congress Ministries resigned in November, 1939.

15. With reference to the Mass Phase of the National Movement under the leadership of Gandhi, answer the following:
    (A) Briefly explain the Dandi March of 1930.
    (B) State *any three* reasons for the launching of the Quit India Movement.
    (C) Explain *any four* significant effects of the Quit India Movement. [HOT🔥]
    [ICSE 2020]

Ans. (A) Under the leadership of Gandhi, the Civil Disobedience Movement was launched in the year 1930. The Movement was aimed at openly resisting Salt Laws and it began with the historic 'Dandi March'.

On 12th March 1930, Gandhi with some of his followers left the Sabarmati Ashram at Ahmedabad and made its way towards Dandi, a village on the west coast of India. After travelling for 25 days and covering a distance of 385 kilometres, the group reached Dandi on 5th April 1930. On the morning of 6th April, 1930, Gandhi protested against the Salt Law, as salt was a monopoly of the government and no one was allowed to make salt, by picking up the salt from the shore and making salt himself and throwing up a challenge to the British Government. The Dandi March signified the start of the Civil Disobedience Movement.

(B) **The reasons for the launching of the Quit India Movement were:**
(1) **Failure of the Cripps Mission:** Through the Cripps Mission, the British Government for the first time recognized the 'Right of Dominion' for India. Not only the Congress and the Muslim League, but every party picked holes in the Cripps proposal and it was rejected by all.
(2) **The Japanese Threat:** After bombing Shanghai and Philippines, the Japanese attacked Burma and then began marching towards Assam. Gandhiji became convinced that the presence of British in India is only tempting the Japanese to invade the country. According to Gandhiji and his associates, for the sake of India's safety as well as that of Britain, it would be wise for the British to leave the country.
(3) **Increasing Communal Problems:** The communal situation was growing out of control as the Muslim League had also made a definite demand for the formation of a separate Pakistan.

(C) **The significant effects of Quit India Movement were:**
(1) It gave utterance to India's anger against imperialism and her determination to achieve independence.
(2) The movement revealed that the depth of nationalism had permeated deep into Indian society as people from all religious communities such as Hindus,

Muslims, Sikhs, Christians, Parsis and even the Princely states participated.

(3) The capacity for struggle and readiness for sacrifices revealed to the British that Indians were no long afraid of British attrocities.

(4) The movement was not completely non-violent and it clearly revealed that the patience of the Indian public to follow only non-violent methods was on the wane that they became impatient to drive the British away.

(A)
(1) On 2nd March 1930, Gandhi wrote a letter to the Viceroy.
(2) Communicating his decision to start the Civil Disobedience Movement.
(3) On 12th March began Mahatma Gandhi's historic march from Sabarmati Ashram to Dandi, a village on the Gujarat seacoast.
(4) 78 persons followed him.
(5) He reached Dandi on 5th April.
(6) On the Morning of 6th of April, Gandhi violated the Salt-Laws by picking up some salt left by the sea-waves.
(7) Gandhi's signal to disobey the government law.

(B) **Reasons for launching the Quit India Movement:**
(1) Failure of the Cripps Mission
(2) Worsening of Communal problem
(3) Japan posed a serious threat to India.

(C) **Significant consequences of the Quit India Movement**
(1) Important landmark – it saw disturbances practically all over India.
(2) It warned the British that they were not wanted in India/days were limited/collapse of authority.
(3) Demand from Indians that they could have nothing short of Independence.
(4) Quit India Movement strengthened the Congress Socialist Party.
(5) In the Quit India Movement, the Indian Revolution reached its climax.
(6) Led to political awakening.
(7) Indian problem attracted the attention of the world especially USA.
(8) Symbolic of new confidence among Indians.
(9) Demonstrated nationalistic feelings/Mass movement/last mass movement.
(10) United young and old and people of different religions and regions.
(11) No political activity till the war ended in 1945.   **[Any four]**

 What Examiners Say

→ (A) Most candidates were able to narrate the Dandi March of 1930 well
→ (B) Several candidates wrote the reasons for the launching of the Quit India Movement such as 'economic distress', while some wrote the causes of other mass movements led by Gandhi such as the Non-Cooperation Movement and the Civil Disobedience Movement.
→ (C) Most of the candidates answered this question correctly. However, a few jumbled up the parts with the impact of the Non-Cooperation Movement and the Civil Disobedience Movement. Some candidates wrote that the British quit India and we gained independence as the effect of the Quit India Movement.

⚠ **Caution**

→ (A) Students should be able to narrate the event of the historic Dandi March from Sabarmati to Dandi and the subsequent violation of the Salt Law point wise as it was an important day that marked the beginning of a non-violent Civil Disobedience Movement.
→ (B) The political reasons in India as well as in the International arena during 1942 study will help the students understand and comprehend the reasons for the passing of Quit India Resolution and its significant effects.
→ (C) Students should understand the three major Gandhian Movements–Causes, Course and Consequences.

16. The Congress Working Committee passed the famous 'Quit India' resolution at Wardha in July 1942. With reference to this, answer the following questions:

(A) What were the reasons for the passing of this resolution?
(B) What was the British Government's reaction to the 'Quit India Movement'?
(C) What was the impact and significance of this movement?

Ans. (A) The reasons for passing 'Quit India' resolution at Wardha in July 1942 were:

(1) **Failure of Cripps Mission:** Through the Cripps Mission, the British government for the first time accepted "Right of Dominion" for India. Not only the Congress and the League, but every party picked holes in the Cripps proposals for varied reasons and it was rejected by all. Gandhi wanted an undivided India, the Muslim League wanted a seperate Pakistan and Congress demanded full control over defence. Thus, Cripps Mission did not bring satisfaction to all Indians for various reasons.

(2) **Japanese Threat:** After bombing Shanghai and Philippines, the

Quit India Movement 185

Japanese attacked Burma and then began marching towards Assam. The Indian Congress became worried that the Japanese might now attack India as well. Gandhiji become convinced that the presence of British in India is only tempting Japanese to invade the country.

(3) **Communal Situation:** The communal situation was growing out of control as the Muslim League had also made a definite demand for the formation of a separate Pakistan.

(B) The British Government's response to Quit India Movement was quick. In the early hours, of 9th August, 1942, Gandhi, Maulana Azad, Jawahar Lal Nehru and most of the leaders of the Congress Working Committee were arrested. The government took severe repressive measures to suppress the movement. Public processions, meetings and the Indian Press were banned. Lathi charges and tear gas shells were used by the police to disperse the crowds. Collective fines were imposed on those who participated in the movement. The movemnet was thus, crushed ruthlessly by the government using all the machinery of modern warfare at its disposal.

(C) Though, the Quit India Movement was put down ruthlessly by the government, it gave utterance to India's anger aganist imperialisim and her determination to achieve independence. It was this mass movement which revealed that the depth of nationalism had permeated deep into Indian society as people from all religious communities such as Hindu, Muslims, Sikhs, Christians, Parsis, and even the Princely states participated. The capacity for struggle and the readiness for sacrifices revealed to the British that India were no longer afraid of British attrocities. They would go to any length and even lay down their lives for the freedom of their motherland. The movement was not completely non-violent and it clearly revealed that the patience of the Indian public to follow only non-violent methods was on the wane that they were becoming impatient to drive the British away.

8 Forward Bloc and the INA

Subhash Chandra Bose popularly called Netaji was a man of action, believed in agitation and restored to revolutionary methods for the attainment of Swaraj. He was also the founder of Forward Bloc within the Indian National Congress and he independently created Indian National Army (INA) outside India, to help in achieving independence from the British rule in India.

Chapter Notes

- Subhash Chandra Bose
- Forward Bloc and the INA

TOPIC 1

SUBHASH CHANDRA BOSE

Subhash Chandra Bose was born on 23rd January, 1897 at Cuttack in Orissa. He graduated from the Calcutta University in 1919 and went to England to appear in the ICS Examination and passed it. But he resigned from the Civil Services because he did not want to work under the British Crown. He responded to Gandhiji's call for Non-Cooperation against the British. He joined politics after returning to India in 1921. He entered active politics at the age of twenty-four and became a 'Swarajist', because he did not agree with the Gandhain thought. Bose was a man of action. He believed in agitation and restored to revolutionary methods for the attainment of Swaraj. Bose became the Chief Executive Officer of Calcutta corporation and discharged his duties sincerely.

Related Theory

→ Subhash Chandra Bose stood fourth in the merit list of ICS Examination, but he did not complete his period of probabtion as he was highly disturbed by the British action at Jallianwala Bagh and he resigned from his job.

Bose and the Congress

Bose was a man of action. He was a bold fighter of Swaraj. He did not agree with the decision of Gandhiji. When Gandhiji suspended the Non-Cooperation Movement in 1922, Bose advocated complete independence and was opposed to Motilal Nehru's concept of Dominion Status. He participated in the Civil Disobedience Movement of 1930. By 1930's, Bose emerged as the most dynamic and radical leader of the Congress. He was unanimously elected the President of the Congress in the Haripura Session of the Congress in 1938. His election indicated that a section of the Party workers had been drawn to Subhash Chandra Bose's radical and dynamic policies. At the same time, his difference with Gandhiji had also become evident.

Bose's Rift with Gandhiji and Congress

In 1939, Subhash was re-elected as the President of the Tripuri Session of the Congress defeating the veteran right wing leader, Pattabhi Sitaramayya – the nominee of Gandhiji by 95 votes.

After Subhash's re-election, the crisis came regarding the formation of the Congress Working Committee. Leaders like G.B. Pant and Sardar Patel, wanted Bose to constitute with the Working Committee, with members approved by consequently, Bose resigned on 29th April, 1939 and the next day Dr. Rajendra Prasad was elected as the President of the Congress.

Bose's views were totally different from those of Gandhiji

(1) Subhash believed in socialism and was convinced that the masses were ready for a revolution. Bose did not hesitate to go for war against the enemy. He was aggressive in his approach. But Gandhiji believed that the time was not ripe enough for a mass struggle. Besides, Gandhiji always preferred non-violent and peaceful methods.

(2) Subhash believed that freedom could not be attained without outside support. As Britain was facing problem in Europe due to the German threat, Bose wanted to take advantage of the situation for winning freedom for India. But Gandhiji wanted to follow a compromising attitude towards the British.

(3) Bose favoured in employing tact and diplomacy while dealing with the British. He did not like the way Gandhiji behaved highlighting his demands at the time of the Second Round Table Conference at London.

(4) Bose favoured the policy of large-scale Industrialisation. On the other hand, Gandhiji favoured the idea of small-scale industries to make the villages self-suffcient.

Example 1. Who was the mentor and guide of Subhash Chandra Bose in India in 1921 ?

Ans. C.R. Das became Boses' mentor and guide, when he joined politics after returning to India in 1921.

⚠ Caution

→ Topic 1 Subhash Chandra Bose shall be studied carefully to answer questions based on the Contributions of Subhash Chandra Bose, which is important.

TOPIC 2

FORWARD BLOC AND THE INA

Forward Bloc

Bose felt the urgent need for an organised left-wing party in the Congress. After resigning from the Presidentship of the Congress in 1939, he laid the foundation of a new party within the Congress, to bring the entire left-wing under one banner. This party, was known as Forward Bloc and it was formed on 3rd May, 1939.

Objectives of the Forward Bloc

The immediate objective of the Forward Bloc was liberation of India with the support of workers, peasants, youths and all radical organizations. After attaining independence, Forward Bloc would work for the establishment of a Socialist State through :

(1) Abolition of Zamindari System.
(2) Introduction of a new monetary and Credit System.
(3) Reorganization of agriculture and industry on socialist lines.
(4) Providing several kinds of benefits to the workers.

Netaji's Arrest and Escape

In July 1940, Bose was arrested by the British Government for his anti-government activities. While he was in prison, he decided to go on a hunger strike. But his health declined rapidly and the government released him. He was placed under house arrest in Kolkata. But in January, 1941, Subhash managed to escape disguising himself as a Pathan.

He crossed Indian border and reached Afghanistan. First he went to Russia. Then on 26th March, 1941 he flew from Moscow to Berlin in Germany, where with the help of the enemies of the British; he organized 'Free India Centres' in Rome and Paris, to launch Anti-Imperialist Propoganda against government. From this centre with the help and co-operation of the German, 'Azad Hindus' Radio was set up. From these Centre he carried on regular propaganda in support of India's freedom. As the Second World War was going on, he approached Hitler for help, but later he realized that Far East would be a better place to launch his struggle with the help of Japan.

Example 2. How was the slogan 'Jai Hind' associated with Subhash Chandra Bose?

Ans. When Netaji had reached Berlin, the Indian Community in Germany welcomed him as their leader-Netaji and greeted him with "Jai Hind".

Events in South-East Asia

The outbreak of the War in South- East Asia in 1941 caused a great stir among the Indians in those regions. Indians, living in territories captured by Japan, organised themselves into associations with the objective of contributing to the liberation of India and serving the interests of the overseas Indians during the critical period. Out of these associations was born the idea of an Indian Independence League. A definite shape was given to this idea by Rashbehari Bose who lived in Singapore after escaping from India.

The Indian Independence League

The Second World War was going on and on 7th December, 1941 Japan declared war against the Allies. After the fall of Singapore in Japanese attack on 15th February, 1942, a large number of Indian soldiers of the British Army were captured by Japan as Indian Prisoners of War (POW'S). These Prisoners of War were handed over to Captain Mohan Singh, who inducted them into the INA.

Example 3. Who was Mohan Singh in INA ?

Ans. Mohan Singh was an Indian Military Officer and member of the Indian Independence Movement best known for organizing and leading the Indian National Army in South-East Asia during World War II.

Mohan Singh was from the 14th Punjab Regiment, who earlier had surrendered to Japan in Malaya. The Indian Prisoners of the Second World War renounced their allegiance to the British and agreed to fight for India's freedom. The number soon rose to 40,000. By the end of 1942, forty thousand men expressed their willingness to join the INA. It was made clear at meetings of leaders of the Indian Community and of the Indian Army Officers that the INA would go into action only on the invitation of the Indian National Congress and the people of India.

The Tokyo Conference

This conference was held at Tokyo in March 1942 under the initiative of Rash Behari Bose. The Indian Officers, both Civil and Military, met the Japanese High Command and the following decisions were taken at the Tokyo Conference (28th March to 31st March, 1942) :

(1) to expand and strengthen the Indian Independence League.
(2) to form an Indian National Army under the command of the Independence League.
(3) to hold a Conference at Bangkok to endorse these decisions.

Bangkok Conference and the Establishment of the INA

The Bangkok Conference was attended by more than 150 delegates of East Asian Countries (Like Java, Malaya, Singapore, Thailand, Hong Kong, Burma and Manila). It was held from 15th June to 23rd June 1942. It passed the following resolutions:

(1) Subhash Chandra Bose should be invited to come from Europe to lead this Movement.
(2) A Council of Action to be established for carrying out all necessary actions of the Independence Movement.
(3) The Indian National Army was formally set up under the command of Captain Mohan Singh on 1st September, 1942.
(4) Rash Behari Bose to be appointed as the President of the Indian National Army (INA).

The Japanese Government agreed to supply the arms, ships, aeroplanes to the INA and made arrangements for the training of the INA soldiers. All the Indian Prisoners of the Second World War and many East-Asian Indians joined the INA.

Subhash Chandra Bose and INA

Subhash Chandra Bose accepted the invitation of Rash Behari Bose and reached Tokyo on 13th June, 1943. He was cordially received by the Japanese Premier Tojo. Boses' arrival had created unprecendented enthusiasm among the Indians living in South-East Asia.

Rash Behari Bose handed over the leadership of the Indian Independence League to Subhash Chandra Bose and he became the Supreme Commander of INA. On 5th July, 1943, he took the salute of INA and was popularly known as Netaji – the Great Leader. He set up the INA headquarters in Yangon (Burma) and in Singapore and began to reorganize the INA. Recruits were made from civilians. A women's regiment called the Rani Jhansi Regiment was led by Dr. Laxmi Swaminathan. Recruitment and training camps were opened in large numbers to cope with the rush of volunteers offering themselves for the INA.

Objectives of the INA

The main objectives of the INA were the following:

(1) To organize an armed revolution and to fight the British Army with modern arms.
(2) Since it was not possible for the Indians to organize an armed revolution from their homeland, the task to be assigned to the Indians living abroad, particularly on Indians living in East Asia.
(3) To organize a provisional government of Free India in order to mobilise all the forces effectively.
(4) Total mobilization of Indian Non-Power and money for a total War.
(5) The Motto of the INA was 'Unity, Faith and Sacrifice'.

Provisional Government of Free India

Netaji Subhash Chandra Bose founded the Provisional or Interim Government of free India at Singapore on 21st October, 1943. The government was reorganized by nine World Powers including Germany, Italy, Japan and Burma. As the head of the Provisional Government, Bose declared War against Britain. Netaji's Provisional Government got its first independent territory when Japan handed over Andaman and Nicobar Islands to Bose on 6th November, 1943. He re-named them 'Shaheed' and 'Swaraj' islands respectively.

Acheivements of the INA and Netaji

The INA made preparations to launch its fight for the liberation of India and went into action in February, 1944. INA captured Mowdok, an outpost situated south-east of Chittagong and advanced upto the frontier of India. They captured the strong military post of Klang Klang. The INA gave a tough fight to the British forces in the Assam Hills and succeeded in capturing Ukhral and Kohima. They raised the Tricolour Flag for the first time on the liberated soil on 19th March, 1944.

Fate of the INA and Netaji

The INA's victories were short-lived. The INA backed by the Japanese force, captured Kohima and reached Imphal. Monsoon started and Japan was forced to surrender after the bombing of Hiroshima and Nagasaki. INA's fate was sealed. Bose left from Rangoon to Bangkok and from there flew to Tokyo. It is said that while travelling, he died in an air-crash in Taipei in Taiwan on 18th August, 1945, but its authenticity still lies in mystery.

Impact of the INA

The INA's victories gave moral support to the National Movement. The slogans "Jai Hind", "Dilli Challo" of the INA and their patriotic marches and songs enthused the Indians to fight for their country. The INA inspired uprisings in the armed forces of the country. The new struggle took the form of a massive movement against the trials of the soldiers and officers of the INA. The INA set an inspiring example of Patriotism. The heroic deeds and sacrifices of the soldiers of INA led to political consciousness among the Indian Forces. The British now realized that they could not rely on the Indian Forces to continue their rule in India.

 Caution

→ *Objectives of INA are different from Objectives of Forward Bloc, both topics should be studied separately.*

 ICSE Suggestions

→ *Students should understand the fact that the Forward Bloc was a party formed within the Congress by Subhash Chandra Bose whereas INA refers to the army.*

→ *Students should stress on the contributions and achievements of the INA in detail.*

→ *Students should highlight the important points and learn the facts well.*

→ *Write answers precisely and to the point.*

 **Glossary**

(1) **Forward Bloc:** A Party formed by Subhash Chandra Bose to carry on the freedom struggle.
(2) **Disarmament:** Reducing the number of weapons by a country for the cause of establishment of Peace.
(3) **Convicted:** Declare someone to be guilty of a criminal offence by the verdict of a Jury or the decision of a Judge.

(4) **Mercenaries:** Professional soldiers hired to serve in a foreign army.
(5) **Socialist:** Believes in or supports socialism.
(6) **Battle Cry:** A shout that soldiers used to give in battle to encourage their own army or to frighten the enemy.
(7) **Treason:** It is the action of betraying one's own country.

Who's Who?

(1) **Adolf Hitler**—The Dictator of Germany

Who Said What?

(1) *"I do not think that one could be loyal to the British Raj and yet serve India honestly, heart and soul"*
—Subhash Chandra Bose

Subhash Chandra Bose said these words, when he resigned from the Civil Service because he did not want to work under the British Crown.

(2) *"Give me blood and I shall give you freedom"* —Subhash Chandra Bose

Bose gave the call to his soldiers, and he encouraged them to fight for the freedom of the country.

Chronology

23rd January, 1897: Subhash Chandra Bose was born.
1920: Subhash Chandra passed Indian Civil Service Examination.
1938: Bose was elected as the President of the Congress at Haripura Session.
1939: Bose was elected as the President of the Congress at Tripuri Session.
3rd May, 1939: Forward Bloc was formed by Netaji.
1940: Bose was arrested under the Defence of Indian Rules.
17th January, 1941: Subhash Chandra escaped from house arrest and went to Peshawar, Afghanistan.
1942: Tokyo Conference
15th to 28th January, 1942: Bangkok Conference was held.
1st September, 1942: Indian National Army was established.
18th August, 1945: Netaji was killed in a plane crash.

OBJECTIVE Type Questions

Multiple Choice Questions-I
[1 mark each]

⚠️ **Caution**
→ Students should learn the slogans of famous leaders to avoid writing wrong answers.

1. Identify the famous slogan of Subhash Chandra Bose:
   (a) Give me blood and I shall give you freedom.
   (b) Swaraj is my birthright and I shall have it.
   (c) Do or Die
   (d) Vande Mataram   [ICSE Sem-1, 2021]

   Ans. *(a) Give me blood and I shall give you freedom.*
   Explanation: Subhash Chandra Bose gave the call to his soldiers, "Give me blood and I shall give you freedom".

2. Which of the following was an Objective of the Indian National Army?
   (a) To formulate and present the demands of the government.
   (b) To make the world aware of the true nature of British rule in India.
   (c) Total mobilization of Indian manpower and money for a total War.
   (d) To establish Home Rule in India.
   [ICSE Sem-1, 2021]

   Ans. *(c) Total mobilization of Indian manpower and money for a total War.*

Forward Bloc and the INA 191

Explanation: The only objective of the INA from the above statements is Total mobilization of Indian man-power and money for a total War.

3. The Supreme Commander of the Indian National Army:
   (a) Subash Chandra Bose
   (b) Ras Behari Bose
   (c) Jawaharlal Nehru
   (d) Lord Wavell   [HOT🔥]

Ans. *(a) Subash Chandra Bose*

Explanation: Due to Rashbehari's efforts a conference was held at Tokyo from 28th March to 30th March, 1942. It was decided to form an Indian National Army (INA), i.e. an army for Indian liberation. In August 1943, Subhash Chandra Bose took the charge of the Indian National Army and became its Supreme Commander. He set up the INA headquarters in Yangon and in Singapore.

 Related Theory

→ *Rash Behari Bose, an old revolutionary leader along with Captain Mohan Singh formed the 'Independence League'. The League aimed at mobilizing the members of the Indian Community for the purpose of securing Indian Independence.*

4. Unity, Faith, Sacrifice was the motto of the Forward Bloc.
   Replace the underlined word to correct the statement.
   (a) Indian National Congress
   (b) Indian National Army
   (c) East India Association
   (d) The Muslim League

Ans. *(d) Indian National Army*

Explanation: The motto of the Indian National Army (INA) was 'Unity, Faith, Sacrifice'.

⚠ **Caution**

→ *Most of the students have written Indian National Army, but few have written Indian National Congress. There was no motto for Indian National Congress as such.*

5. "Give me blood and I shall give you freedom" slogan was given by Bipin Chand Pal.
   Replace the underlined word to correct the statement.
   (a) Bal Gangadhar Tilak
   (b) Jyotiba Phule
   (c) Lala Lajpat Rai
   (d) Subhash Chandra Bose   [HOT🔥]

Ans. *(d) Subhash Chandra Bose*

Explanation: Netaji Subhash Chandra Bose founded the Indian Army and gave a call to his soldiers, "Give me blood and I shall give you freedom. His battle cries were "Delhi Chalo" and "Jai Hind".

6. From the given list, identify the objectives of the Indian National Army (INA):
   (a) To provide relief to indigo cultivators
   (b) To develop unity between Hindus and Muslims
   (c) Boycott of foreign goods
   (d) To organize an armed rebellion and fight the British Army with modern arms

Ans. *(d) To organize an armed rebellion and fight the British Army with modern arms.*

Explanation: To provide relief to indigo cultivators was the objective of Gandhiji's Champaran Satyagraha in 1917. To develop unity between Hindus and Muslims was one of the objectives of Swadeshi programme of Non-Cooperation Movement in 1920 and boycott of foreign goods was a objective of Boycott Programme of Non-Coperation Movement in 1920.

The main objectives of Indian National Army (INA) were:

(1) To organize an armed rebellion and fight the British Army with modern arms.

(2) To organize a Provisional Government of Free India in order to mobilise all the forces effectively.

(3) Total mobilization of Indian man power and money for a total war.

(4) The motto of the INA was "Unity, Faith, sacrifice".

7. Whom did Subhash Chandra Bose defeated at Tripuri Session of 1939, to be re-elected as the President of the Indian National Congress?
   (a) Jawaharlal Nehru
   (b) Mahatma Gandhi
   (c) Pattabhi Sitaramayya
   (d) Dr. Laxmi Swaminathan

Ans. *(c) Pattabhi Sitaramayya*

Explanation: At the Tripuri (Madhya Pradesh) Session of the Indian National Congress in 1939, Gandhiji tried to dissuade Subhash Chandra Bose from standing for re-election as President of the Congress for a second term. Bose, however, decided to contest and Gandhiji's choice fell on Pattabhi Sitaramayya for the Presidential candidate. Bose won by majority of votes.

Related Theory

→ When Bose won the elections of President at Tripuri Session defeating the nominee of Gandhiji Pattabhi Sitaramayya by 95 votes, Gandhiji declared that the defeat of Sitaramayya was 'more mine than him'. Because he had put his full weight in nominee's favour during the contest.

Multiple Choice Question-II

(Other Question Types, for Extra Practice)

[**4** marks each]

8.

(A) Identify the leader in the picture.
 (a) Bal Gangadhar Tilak
 (b) Subhash Chandra Bose
 (c) Lala Lajpat Rai
 (d) Gopal Krishna Gokhale

(B) Which party did he forme?
 (a) Indian National Congress
 (b) Gadar Party
 (c) Forward Bloc
 (d) Muslim League

(C) Identify from the list, the objectives of the organization formed by the leader.
 (I) Organized an armed revolution
 (II) Abolition of Zamindari system
 (III) Introduction of new monetary and credit system
 (IV) Organized a Provisional Government of Free India
 (a) (I) and (II)   (b) (I) and (III)
 (c) (I), (II) and (III)   (d) (II) and (IV)

(D) The leader in the picture was the Supreme Commander of an organization. Identify the orgnization.
 (a) Indian National Congress
 (b) Indian National Army
 (c) Forward Bloc
 (d) Indian National Conference

Ans. (A) *(b) Subhash Chandra Bose*

Explanation: Subhash Chandra Bose was born on 23rd January, 1897 at Cuttack in Orissa. He passed the Civil Service Examination but resigned because he did not want to work under the British Crown. Bose entered politics at the age of twenty four and became a Swarajist, because he did not agree with Gandhian thought. He believed in agitation and resorted to revolutionary methods for the attainment of Swaraj.

(B) *(c) Forward Bloc*

Explanation: Due to his rift with Gandhiji, Bose resigned from the Presidentship of Indian National Congress. After resigning, he laid the foundation of a new party within the Congress. This party known as Forward Bloc, was formed on 3rd May, 1939.

(C) *(b) (I) and (III)*

Explanation: The objectives of the Forward Bloc, formed by Subhash Chandra Bose were:
(1) reorganization of agriculture and industry on socialist lines;
(2) abolition of Zamindari system; and
(3) introduction of new monetary and credit system.

(D) *(b) Indian National Army*

Explanation: The idea of Indian National Army (INA) was conceived by Mohan Singh, an Indian officer in the British Indian Army. In August 1943, Subhash Chandra Bose took the charge of the Indian National Army and became its Supreme Commander.

SUBJECTIVE Type Questions

Short Answer Type Questions

[**2** marks each]

9. Mention any two objectives of the Indian National Army. **[ICSE 2017]**
 OR
 State two important objectives of the Indian National Army. **[HOT♨] [ICSE 2014]**

Ans. The Objectives of Indian National Army (INA) were:
(1) To launch an armed fight against British from outside India.
(2) Formation of Provisional Government of Independent India.
(3) To develop Patriotism among Indian Prisoners of War;
(4) To overthrow the British rule in India.

Forward Bloc and the INA 193

Objectives of the INA:

(1) To organize an armed revolution and to fight the British army with modern arms.
(2) Since it was possible for the Indians to organize an armed revolution from their homeland, this task must be assigned to Indians living abroad, particularly to Indians living in East Asia.
(3) To organize a Provisional Government of Free India in order to mobilize all the forces effectively.
(4) Total mobilization of Indian man-power and money for a total war.
(5) The motto of the INA was Unity, Faith, Sacrifice.
(6) To lead the Indian people to regain their lost freedom.
(7) To liberate India from the British Rule.
[Any two]
[Marking Scheme]

What Examiners Say

→ Many candidates confused the objectives of INA with the objectives of forward Bloc. A few mentioned only one objective.

10. Who founded the Forward Bloc? Mention any one of its objectives. [ICSE 2015]

Ans. After resigning from the Presidentship of the Congress in April 1939, Subhash Chandra Bose laid the foundation of a new party within the Congress known as Forward Bloc.

The objectives of Forward Bloc were:
(1) The establishment of a rival government.
(2) It aimed to work for the liberation of India with the help of workers, peasants, youth and all radical organisations.
(3) It aimed to establish socialism in the country after attaining independence.
(4) Abolition of Zamindari System.
(5) Introduction of a new monetry and credit system. [Any one]

Subhash Chandra Bose
Objective: Liberation of India from Foreign rule/establishment of a socialist society.
[Marking Scheme]

What Examiners Say

→ Most candidates wrote the correct answer. Few however were confused with the 'INA'.

Caution

→ Students should know the fact that the Forward Bloc was a party formed within the Congress by Subhash Chandra Bose whereas INA refers to the Army.

11. Name the Party formed by Subhash Chandra Bose. What was its immediate objective?
[ICSE 2012][HOT]

Ans. The party formed by Subhash Chandra Bose was Forward Bloc.

The immediate objectives of the Forward Bloc was the establishment of a rival government.

12. How was the Indian Independence League formed? Who was its President?

Ans. From the different associations of South-East Asia, who were sympathetic about India's freedom struggle, the Indian Independence League was formed. Rash Bihari Bose was its President.

13. Where and when the Provisional Government of free India was set-up?

Ans. The Provisional Government of free India was set-up at Singapore on 21st October 1943 by Netaji Subhash Chandra Bose.

14. Name any four countries which accorded recognition to the Provisional Government.

Ans. Japan, Germany, Italy and Burma (Myanmar).

Structured Questions
[3+3+4= **10** marks each]

15. With reference to the Forward Bloc and the INA, answer the following questions:
(A) Mention any three objectives of the Forward Bloc. [ICSE 2020]
(B) Mention any three contributions of the INA to the National Movement.
[ICSE 2016]
(C) Explain any four contributions of Subhash Chandra Bose to the National Movement.

Ans. (A) The two Objectives of Forward Bloc were:
(1) Freedom of India.
(2) Abolition of Zamindari System and introduction of new Monetary and Credit System.
(3) Reorganisation of agriculture and industries on socialist lines.

What Examiners Say

→ Many candidates confused the objectives of the Forward Bloc with the objectives of the INA. A few mentioned only one objective.

Caution

→ The Objectives of INA and Forward Bloc should be well explained and student should clearly distinguish between the two.

(B) (1) INA inspired uprising in the armed forces in the country.

(2) Indian Naval ratings in Mumbai rose in revolt in February 1946.

(3) INA undermined the very security of the British in India.

What Examiners Say

→ Few candidates wrote the objectives of INA and not its contributions.

⚠ Caution

→ Students should buy stress on the contributions/achievements of INA and also they should identify its objectives and contributions separately.

(C) Subhash Chandra Bose has a place of great honour in India's national struggle for independence. He and the INA under him, gave moral support to the National Movement. The slogans popularized under him, 'Jai Hind', "Dilli Chalo' and many patriotic marches enthused the Indian youth.

Bose managed to internationalise India's national struggle for independence. Netaji made it clear to the British that their days in India were numbered. Now, it was clear to the British that they could not rely on the Indian soldiers to maintain their hold on India.

16. With reference to the Forward Bloc and the INA, answer the following questions:

(A) Who was the first Commander-in-Chief of the INA?

By which name was Subhash Chandra Bose popularly known and what was its meaning?

(B) How the Indian National League and Indian National Army was formed?

(C) What were the three decisions taken at the Tokyo Conference?

Ans. (A) The First Commander-in-Chief of the INA was Captain Mohan Singh.

Subhash Chandra Bose was popularly known as 'Netaji' . Netaji means 'respected leader'. Due to his fearless spirit and endeavour to liberate India, people called him 'Netaji'.

(B) People living in the South-Asian territories were free from European domination and sympathetic about Indian National Movement. They started some associations with the objective of working for the liberation of India. From the associations, the Indian Independence League (IIL) was born, Rash Behari Bose was its leader.

It aimed to fight for the attainment of complete and immediate independence of India. In the Tokyo Conference (28th and 31st March, 1942) of the Indian Independence League decision about the formation of an Indian National Army (INA) or Azad Hind Fauj was formed by Indian Nationalists on 1st September, 1942 in South-East Asia during the Second World War. It became the Military Army of the Indian Independence League.

(C) The Tokyo Conference was held to basically discuss political issues. It passed a resolution to form an Indian National Army. Rash Behari Bose was unanimously elected as the President of the Conference.

The Conference formally inaugurated the Indian Independence League. The Conference also passed a resolution that an Indian National Army be formed comprising the citizens of Indian towns and civilians of East Asia. Captain Mohan Singh would be its Commander-in-Chief. A Council of Action would be established to carry out actions with regards to the War of Independence.

17. Study the picture given below and answer the following questions:

(A) (a) Identify the leader given in the picture.

(b) Name the Political Party and Military Organization that he formed.

(B) State *any three* objectives of the Political party that he founded.

(C) Mention *any four* objectives of the Military Organization that he formed.

[ICSE 2018]

Ans

(A) (a) The leader given in the picture is Netaji Subash Chandra Bose.

(b) The political party formed by Netaji Subash Chandra Bose was 'Forward Bloc' and the military organization formed by him was 'Indian National Army' (INA).

(B) **The objectives of 'Forward Bloc' formed by Netaji Subash Chandra Bose were:**

(1) The establishment of a rival government;

(2) It aimed to work for the liberation of India

with the help of workers, peasants, youth and all radical organizations;

(3) It aimed to establish socialism in the country after attaining independence by abolition of landlords *i.e.*, zamindari system, and introduction of a new monetary and credit system.

(C) **The objectives of Indian National Army (INA) were:**

(1) To launch an armed fight against British from outside India;

(2) Formation of Provisional Government of Independent India;

(3) To develop patriotism among Indian Prisoners of War;

(4) To overthrow the British rule in India.

(A) (a) Subhash Chandra Bose
 (b) Forward Bloc
    Indian National Army

(B) Forward Bloc:
 Objectives:
 (1) Reorganization of agriculture and industry on socialist lines.
 (2) Abolition of the zamindari system.
 (3) Introduction of a new monetary and credit system.
 (4) Liberation of India.
 (5) Making Right to work as Fundamental.
 (6) Providing workers several kinds of benefits. **[Any three points]**

(C) (1) To organize an armed resolution and to fight the British army with modern arms.

(2) To use the Indians living abroad in East Asia and then to confront the British.

(3) To organize a Provisional Government of free India.

(4) Total mobilization of Indian manpower and money for a total-war.

(5) The motto of the INA was 'Unity, Faith, Sacrifice'.

(6) To train people for armed struggle inside and outside the country.

(7) To throw the British out of the country. **[Any four]**
[Making Scheme]

What Examiners Say

→ (A) All the candidates were able to identify the leader given in the picture. They were also able to name the political party and the Military Organization founded by Subhash Chandra Bose.

→ (B) Majority of the candidates, instead of stating the objectives of the Forward Bloc, mentioned the objectives of the Indian National Army.

→ (C) Many candidates, instead of mentioning the objectives of the Indian National Army either mentioned the objectives of the Forward Bloc or a mix of the objectives of both Forward Bloc and the Indian National army.

Caution

→ Students should be able to identify the pictures of important leaders and learn about the contributions of these leaders in the freedom struggle.

→ They should know how to differentiate between the objectives of Forward Bloc and the Indian National Army.

Independence and Partition of India

India's unique struggle for freedom, set an example for the other colonial countries of Asia and Africa to follow. This was followed by tragic and bloody partition of the country, causing for more grave problems of national reconstruction.

Chapter Notes

- *Mountbatten Plan*
- *The Indian Independence Act, 1947*

TOPIC 1

THE MOUNTBATTEN PLAN

Lord Mountbatten ultimately assumed that partition of India was inevitable. He therefore, wanted to transfer the Power without delay. He personally went to England to inform the British Government about the Political deadlock prevailing in India and get his Plan approved. On 3rd June, 1947 Lord Mountbatten announced his Plan.

Main Clauses of Mountbatten Plan

(1) **Partition of India:** The country would be divided into two Dominions, i.e., India and Pakistan.
(2) **Bengal and Punjab:** The Partition of Bengal and Punjab was proposed; provided that the Legislative Assemblies of the two provinces decided in favour of Partition.
(3) **The District of Sylhet:** The Muslim majority of Sylhet was to decide by referendum whether it would join East Bengal or remain in Assam.
(4) **Sindh:** The Legislative Assembly of Sindh was to take its own decision at a special meeting.
(5) **The North-West Frontier Province:** In the NWFP, a referendum was to be held to decide the future of the Province.
(6) **The Princely State:** The treaties with the Princely States would come to an end. They would be free to join either of the two dominions.
(7) **A Boundary Commission:** The Plan provided for the creation of a 'Boundary Commission' to settle the boundaries of the two dominions.
(8) **Relations Between the Two New Dominions:** The two dominions would decide what relations they would have with each other and with the British Commonwealth.
(9) **The Constituent Assembly:** The existing Constituent Assembly would continue its work, but the Constitution framed by it would not be applicable to Pakistan. A separate Constituent Assembly would be formed for those areas of India which accepted Partition.
(10) **Transfer of Power Before 1948:** The Plan ended with a declaration that the transfer of power would take place earlier than June, 1948.

Acceptance of the Mountbatten Plan

The historic pronouncement was received with mix feelings by the public. The Nationalists deplored the Partition of India, while the Muslims of the League were not fully satisfied with the way Pakistan was divided, but they accepted the Plan for Partition. The All-India Congress Committee accepted the Mountbatten Plan because according to Maulana Azad, the Congress had no other alternative.

The reasons for finally accepting the Mountbatten Plan may be summarized as follows:

(1) The large-scale communal rights that engulfed the whole country convinced all that the only solution to the communal problem lay in the Partition of India.
(2) The League had joined the Interim Government to obstruct and not to cooperate.
(3) The only alternative to Partition was a Federation with a weak centre. A smaller India with a strong central authority was better than a bigger state with a weak Centre.
(4) Any further continuation of British rule would mean a greater calamity for India. The British were instigating the rulers of the Indian States to remain independent. Hence, Partition was the price for immediate independence.
(5) The leaders felt that further delay in the transfer of power could find India in the midst of a Civil War.
(6) The leaders felt that Partition would rid the Constitution of separate electorates and other undemocratic procedures. India could then evolve a truly secular and democratic policy.

 Related Theory

↪ *Finally the Congress had to accept Mountbatten Plan and East Bengal, West Punjab, Sindh and NWFP all voted for Pakistan. The district of Sylhet joined East Bengal.*

Example 1. When did Lord Wavell leave India and who assumed his Office?

Ans. Lord Wavell left India on 23rd March, 1947 and Lord Mountbatten assumed his office on 24th March, 1947 as the new Viceroy of India.

Example 2. Why did Lord Mountbatten came to India?

Ans. Lord Mountbatten was there in India to restore peace between the Congress and the League and among the Hindus and Muslims of India.

TOPIC 2

THE INDIAN INDEPENDENCE ACT, 1947

The British Prime Minister introduced the Indian Independence Bill in the House of Commons on 4th July, 1947 and it was passed by both the Houses of the British Parliament on 15th July, 1947. It received the Royal Assent on 18th July, 1947.

The main Provisions of the Act were as follows:

(1) **Creation of Two Dominions:** India would be partitioned and two independent dominions namely India and Pakistan would be formed on 15th August, 1947. The Act provided the legislative supremacy of both the dominions.

Pakistan would comprise Sindh, Baluchistan, North-West Frontier Province, the West Punjab, East Bengal and the district of Sylhet in Assam. And India would include all the remaining territories of British India.

(2) **Constituent Assemblies:** The Constituent Assemblies of the two dominions were to act as the Central Legislatures and would have power to make laws for the respective Dominion. They would act as Sovereign bodies for the legislative purposes.

(3) **Governor-General:** There would be a Governor-General for each Dominion who would function as a Constitutional Head. He had to act upon the advice of the Minister.

(4) **The Office of the Secretary of State:** The Office of the Secretary of State for India was to be abolished.

(5) **Princely States:** All agreements between the British Governments and the rulers of the Indian States would lapse. They became independent.

Arrangements concerning customs, transit and communications were to continue until they were denounced by the two dominions.

(6) **Division of Indian Army and Sharing of Assets:** Provision was made for the division of the Indian Army between the two dominions and steps were taken to share the assets and liabilities between the two dominions.

(7) **To Safeguard the interest of the Existing Officer:** Provisions were made for safeguarding the interests of the existing officers appointed by the Secretary of the State however, lost his power for future appointments.

(8) **End of Jurisdiction of the British Parliament:**
(i) The Legislative authority of the British Parliament would cease from 15th August, 1947.
(ii) Abolition of the use of the title, 'Emperor of India' by the British Monarch.
(iii) Till the new Constitution was framed, each of the dominions and all Provinces were to be governed in accordance with the Act of 1935.
(iv) The Governor General was given the powers to modify or adopt the Government of India Act 1935 by 31st March, 1938.
(v) The right of the king to veto laws was given up. This right was given to the Governor General.

(9) **Treaties and Agreements:** With effect from 15th August, 1947, His Majesty's government would cease to have any responsibility for the Government of India. All treaties between the British Government and the rulers of the Indian States or any authority in tribal areas would lapse Frontier Province were to be negotiated by the dominion concerned.

(10) **Bringing the Act into operation:** The Governor General was vested with necessary powers for bringing the Indian Independence into effective operation.

India's Independence

Lord Mountbatten continued as Governor General of the dominion of India upto June, 1948 and Mohammad Ali Jinnah became the Governor General of the dominion of Pakistan.

C. Rajagopalachari was the only Indian and the last Governor General of India.

The independent nations of India and Pakistan came into existence on 15th August, 1947.

Jawaharlal Nehru became the First Prime Minister of India.

India became a Republic on 26th January, 1950.

Dr. Rajendra Prasad took over as the First President of India.

📢 Important

➜ The special session of the Indian Constituent Assembly was held in the midnight of 14-15 August, 1947. Lord Mountbatten was the first Governor-General of Independent India and Jawaharlal took the oath as the First Prime Minister of India.

💡 Related Theory

➜ After the departure of Lord Mountbatten from India, Chakravarti Rajagopalachari became the first and last Indian Governor-General of Independent India.

⚠ Caution

➜ Students should learn about the issues of how Lord Mountbatten had discussion with both the Congress and the Muslim League and found that Partition of India was the only solution to the Communal problem existing in the country.

Independence and Partition of India

ICSE Suggestions

→ Students are advised to explain the Cabinet Mission Plan, Mountbatten Plan and the Indian Independence Act separately. Written assignments will benefit them immensely.

→ Students should be acknowledged about the Cabinet Mission Plan, Mountbatten plan and the Indian Independence Act.

→ It is important to know that the country was divided according to Mountbatten's plan and finally the British parliament passed the Indian Independence Act which provided the basis for the creation of India and Pakistan.

Glossary

(1) **Deadlock :** A complete failure to reach to an agreement or settle an argument.
(2) **Vest :** to give somebody the legal rights or power to do something.
(3) **Plebiscite :** A vote by the people of a country or a region on an issue that is very important.
(4) **Direct Action Day :** The Working Committee of the Muslim League met on 30th July and fixed August 16th as the 'Direct Action Day' throughout the country. Under this the Muslim League decided to say good bye to Constitutional methods and prepared for self-defence and self-preservation by restoring to Direct Action.
(5) **Sepratist :** A person who supports the separation of a particular group of people from a larger body on the basis of ethnicity, religion or gender.
(6) **Surrender :** Stop resisting to opponents and submit to their authority.
(7) **Veto :** A Constitutional right to reject a decision or proposal made by law making body.
(8) **Interim :** Provisional or temporary.
(9) **Pledge :** A promise or an oath to do or not to do something.

Who's Who?

(1) "I repeat that the division of India can only do harm to the countrys' future" —Mahatma Gandhi
Mahatma Gandhi said these words on the same day i.e. 3rd June, 1947 when Mountbatten put his plan for the Partition of India before the 'big Seven Leaders – Nehru, Patel, Kriplani, Jinnah, Liaquat, Nishtar and Baldev Singh.

(2) "Refusal of the demand for Pakistan will amount to dividing the country into so many Pakistans.
—Sardar Vallabhbhai Patel
Sardar Patel said these words because the large-scale Communal riots had engulfed the whole country and convinced all that the only solution to the communal problem lay in the Partition of India.

(3) "At the stroke of midnight hour, when the world sleeps, India will awake to life and freedom"
—Nehruji
These words were said in his memorable speech in the Constituent Assembly on 14th August, 1947 on the eve of India's Independence.

Chronology

May, 1945: Second World War ended
1945: The Wavell Plan
26th July, 1945: Clement Atlee became the Prime Minister of Britain.
24th March, 1946: The Cabinet Mission arrived at India
16th May, 1946: The Cabinet Mission submitted the Cabinet Mission Plan.
July, 1946: Elections of Constituent Assembly were held.
16th August, 1946: Direct Action Day
24th March, 1947: Lord Mountbatten became the Viceroy of India.
15th June, 1947: The Congress accepted the Mountbatten Plan.
4th July, 1947: Atlee introduced the Indian Independence Act in the House of Commons.
18th July, 1947: The Indian Independence Act was passed by both the Houses of the British Parliament.
15th August, 1947: Country was divided into two independent nations.
15th August, 1947: India became independent.
26th January, 1950: New Constitution was adopted and India became Republic.

OBJECTIVE Type Questions

Multiple Choice Questions-I

[**1** mark each]

1. Which of the following is NOT a Clause of the Indian Independence Act of 1947?
   (a) All treaties made with the British would lapse.
   (b) The Army and assets would belong only to India.
   (c) The Constituent Assemblies would serve as Central Legislatures.
   (d) The Princely States were free to associate themselves with their dominion.
   [ICSE Sem-1, 2021]

Ans. *(b) The Army and assets would belong only to India.*

   Explanation: The provisions were made for the division of the Indian Army between the two dominions and share the assets and liabilities between the two.

2. Which of the following was a reason for the acceptance of the Mountbatten Plan?
   (a) The British forced the Congress to accept the Plan.
   (b) The Muslim League would cooperate in the governance.
   (c) The only alternative to Partition was a Federation with a weak Centre.
   (d) The Princely States wanted to accept the Plan. [ICSE Sem-1, 2021]

Ans. *(a) The British forced the Congress to accept the Plan.*

   Explanation: All-India Congress Committee accepted the Mountbatten Plan, because according to Maulana Azad, the Congress had no better alternative.

 Related Theory

→ By applying the 'Divide and Rule Policy' the Britishers not only divided Hindu and Muslim Community in our Country, but they instigated the native rulers of the Indian States to remain independent. So, the Congress leaders accepted Partition of our country for the sake of betterment of our people.

3. "Refusal of the demand for Pakistan will amount to dividing the country into so many Pakistans".
   Which leader gave this Statement?
   (a) M.A. Jinnah
   (b) Sardar Patel
   (c) Jawahar lal Nehru
   (d) Subhash Chandra Bose [HOT]

Ans. *(b) Sardar Patel*

   Explanation: The large-scale communal riots that engulfed the country convinced all that the only solution to the communal problem lay in the Partition of India. In the words of Sardar Patel, "Refusal for the demand of Pakistan will amount to dividing the country into so many Pakistans."

⚠️ **Caution**

→ Students should study 'who said what' in this book, which will help them in writing correct answers.

4. Complete the given anology:
   Quit India : 1942
   Indian Independence Act : ?
   (a) 1926
   (b) 1930
   (c) 1942
   (d) 1947

Ans. *(d) 1947*

   Explanation: Mahatma Gandhi launched the Quit India Movement in 1942 and the Indian Independence Act was passed by the British Government in 1947 to transfer the powers.

Multiple Choice Question-II

(Other Question Types, for Extra Practice)

[**4** marks each]

5. Look at the picture and answer the questions that follow:

   (A) Identify the man with Mahatma.
      (a) Lord Mountbatten
      (b) Lord Curzon
      (c) Lord Wavell
      (d) Lord Dalhousie

   (B) He was deputed to India for the following reason:
      (a) to implement Lord Wavell Plan
      (b) for effective administration

Independence and Partition of India

(c) for peaceful transfer of power
(d) to delay the Partition of India

(C) Identify from the list, two proposals of the Plan formulated by him.
   (a) The country would be divided into two Dominions
   (b) Formation of a Constituent Assembly
   (c) There would be grouping of Provinces
   (d) Setting up of a Boundary Commission

(D) Which of the following clauses about the Princely states was not part of the Plan proposed by him?
   (a) Princely States had to join only India.
   (b) All treaties with the Princely States would come to an end.
   (c) Princely States could remain independent.
   (d) The States could join either India or Pakistan.

Ans. (A) *(a) Lord Mountbatten*

Explanation: Lord Mountbatten was the Viceroy and Governor General of India, who assumed office in 1947.

(B) *(c) for peaceful transfer of power.*

Explanation: For the purpose of taking necessary steps for the transfer of power to the Indians, Lord Wavell was recalled and Lord Mountbatten was appointed the new Viceroy.

(C) *(a) and (d)*

Explanation: The main points of Lord Mountabatten plan included:
(1) The country would be divided into two dominions.
(2) The plan provided for the creation for a Boundary Commission to settle the boundaries of the two dominions case partition was decided upon.
(3) As regards the Princely States, the treaties with them would come to an end. They would be free to associate themselves with either of the dominions or to remain independent.
(4) The partition of Bengal and Punjab was proposed.
(5) The Legislative Assembly of Sindh was to take its own decision.
(6) A plebiscite was to be held in the North West Forntier Province (NWFP) to ascertain whether the people wanted to join India or Pakistan.
(7) The Muslim majority district of Sylhet was to decide by refrendum whether it would form East Bengal or remain in Assam.
(8) The existing Constituent Assembly would continue to work, but the Constitution framed by it would not apply to Pakistan.
(9) The plan ended with o declaration that the transfer to power would take place before August 15, 1947.

(D) (a) *Princely states had to join only India.*

Explanation: As per Mountbattlen Plan, all treaties with Princely States would come to an end and they would be free to associate themselves with either of the dominions, India or Pakistan or to remain Independent.

6. (A) Identify the causes of Quit India Movement:
   (I) Gandhi-Irwin Pact
   (II) Failure of Cripps Mission
   (III) Split in Indian National Congress
   (IV) Japanese Threat
   (a) (I) and (II)   (b) (I) and (III)
   (c) (II) and (III)   (d) (II) and (IV)

(B) Which of the following was not a clause of Indian Independence Act, 1947?
   (a) Two new dominions
   (b) Princely States were to join India
   (c) Constituent Assemblies to serve as Central Legislatures
   (d) Division of the Army

(C) The plan on which Indian Independence Act was based was framed by:
   (a) Lord Mountbatten
   (b) Sir Stafford Cripps
   (c) Sir John Simon
   (d) Clement Atlee

(D) When was Quit India Movement launched by Gandhiji?
   (a) 1919   (b) 1930
   (c) 1942   (d) 1946

Ans. (A) *(d) (ii) and (iv)*

Explanation : In 1942, Sir Safford Cripps introduced certain Constitutional reforms in India. Almost all the parties and section of the people rejected the proposals. The failure of Cripps' Mission left no further meeting ground between the British Government and the Congress. The Congress Working Committee met at Wardha in July, 1942. It adopted a resolution called 'Quit India Resolution'.

(B) *(b) Princely States were to join India.*

Explanation: The Princely States would become independent and all the powers exercised by the British authority were to be terminated was the real Clause. It was not that Princely States were to join India. They would be free to associate themselves with either dominion or to remain independent after August 15, 1947.

(C) *(a) Lord Mountbatten*

Explanation: Mountbatten put his Plan for the Partition of India. The Plan was announced on June 3, 1947. It was known as the 3rd June Plan or Mountbatten Plan. The Plan was acceptable to Congress and Jinnah. The Congress accepted the Plan and Jinnah undertook to do his utmost to make the Plan work.

(D) *(c) 1942*

Explanation : Mahatma Gandhi launched the Quit India Movement in 1942.

SUBJECTIVE Type Questions

Short Answer Type Questions
[**2** marks each]

7. State any two provisions of the Indian Independence Act of 1947 that was to decide the fate of the Princely States ? [ICSE 2019]

Ans. The provisions of the Indian Independence Act of 1947, regarding the fate of the Princely States were:

(1) The Princely States would become independent from the British and the powers earlier wielded by the British colonial government would be terminated. From August 15, 1947, all treaties and agreements made by the British with the Princely States would stand cancelled.

(2) These states could decide to remain independent or join either India or Pakistan.

(1) The Princely States would become Independent from the British authority.
(2) All treaties and agreements made by the British with reference to the States would lapse.
(3) States could remain independent or
(4) Join either India or Pakistan   **[Any two]**
[Marking Scheme]

What Examiners Say
→ Some candidates mentioned the provisions of the Indian Independence Act other than the ones deciding the fate of the Princely States, as asked for in the question. A few candidates mixed up the provisions of the Indian Independence Act with the provisions of the Cabinet Mission or the Mountbatten Plan.

⚠ Caution
→ Students should explain the Provisions of the Independent Act point-wise and separate headings for each point.

8. Write any two reasons for the acceptance of the Mountbatten Plan by the Congress.
[ICSE 2019]

Ans. The reasons for the acceptance of the Mountbatten Plan by the Congress were:

(1) The Congress was convinced that it was impossible to work with the Muslim League, after experiencing the working with it, in the Interim Government.

(2) The large scale communal violence that engulfed the country convinced the political leadership that the partition was inevitable.

(3) The only alternative to partition was to have a federation with a weak center. It was better to have a strong but smaller India than to have a bigger State with weak Centre.

(4) The leaders felt that delay in transfer of power could lead to Civil War. **[Any two]**

(1) It was the only solution to the communal problem/no other option.
(2) The League had joined the Interim Government to obstruct and not to cooperate.
(3) The only alternative was a federation with a weak Centre.
(4) Any further continuation of the British rule would mean greater calamity.
(5) Further delay would cause a Civil War.
(6) Partition would rid the Constitution of separate electorates.
(7) A smaller India with a strong Central authority was better than a bigger State with a weak Centre.

[Any two]
[Marking Scheme]

Independence and Partition of India   203

What Examiners Say

→ Instead of mentioning the reasons for the acceptance of the Mountbatten Plan, a few candidates explained the provisions of the Plan.

Caution

→ Students should clearly explain the reasons for the Congress to accept the Mountbatten Plan.

9. What were the two proposals related to the Princely States in the Mountbatten Plan?

Ans. The proposals related to Princely States in Mountbatten Plan were:
(1) All Indian Princely States shall be released from their official commitments and treaty relationships with the British Empire;
(2) The Princely States were given liberty to join either dominion, India or Pakistan or remain independent.

Structured Questions

[3+3+4= **10** marks each]

10. With reference to the Cabinet Mission Plan and Lord Mountbatten's Plan, answer the following questions:

(A) **Name the last Vicerory of India. State any two of the provisions of the Indian Independence Act, 1947.** [ICSE 2018]
(B) **Why did the Congress accept the Mountbatten Plan?** [ICSE 2015]
(C) **Mention any four clauses of the India Independence Act, 1947.** [ICSE 2015]

Ans. (A) Lord Mountbatten was the last Viceroy of India.
(1) The important provision of Indian Independence Act 1947 was that India would be partitioned and two independent dominions, India and Pakistan would be created. The Act provided for the legislative supremacy of both dominions.
(2) There would be a Governor-General who would be appointed by the British king on the advice of the cabinet of the concerned dominion. This arrangement would work till the framing of the constitutions.

Lord Mountbatten
1. Two new dominions.
2. Provisions of Partition
3. Governor General for each dominion
4. Constituent Assemblies to serve as Central legislatives.
5. End of jurisdiction of the Pre-Parliament.

6. Princely States
7. Treaties and Agreements
8. Division of the Army and the Assets
9. Bringing the act into operation.
10. Office of Secretary of State of interests of existing offcers. [Any two]
[Marking Scheme]

What Examiners Say

→ Answered correctly by majority of the candidates. However, a few candidates mentioned the name of C. Rajagopalachari who was the last Governor-General of India.

Caution

→ Students should clarify the difference between the Indian Independence Act, 1947 and the Mountbatten Plan.

(B) The Mountbatten Plan evoked a mixed response. No Congress leader favoured the idea of partition but there was no alternative either. The reasons for accepting the Plan were:
(1) There were communal riots in several places as a declaration of the 'Direct action' by the Muslim League. Partition seemed to be the only option.
(2) The attempts made by the Muslim League to obstruct the function of the Interim Government convinced the Congress leaders like Patel and others that it was not possible to work together with the League.
(3) The leaders felt that delay in transfer of power may lead to Civil War.

(C) The clauses of the Indian Independence Act, 1947 were:
(1) **Two New Dominions:** India would be partitioned and two independent dominions, India and Pakistan would be created on 15 August 1947. The Act provided for the legislative supremacy of both dominions. Pakistan would comprise Sindh, British Baluchistan, North West Frontier Province, West Punjab and East Bengal.
(2) **Two Boundary Commissions:** The two Boundary Commissions were set up, one for the partition of Bengal and the separation of Sylhet from Assam and other for the partition of Punjab. The boundaries were to be decided by the Boundary Commission.
(3) **The Governor General:** For each of the two dominions there would be a Governor General who would be appointed by his Majesty. He would function as a constitutional head and

represent his Majesty for the purposes of the government of the dominion.

(4) **Central Legislation for the New Dominions:** The Constituent Assemblies of both the dominions would act as the Central Legislatures with full powers to make laws for the dominions.

(5) **End of Jurisdiction of the British Parliament:** With effect from 15 August, 1947, his Majesty's Government would cease to have any responsibility for Government of India and all treaties and agreements with the British Government and the rulers of Indian States would come to an end.

[Any four]

(B) (1) Communal riots had taken a serious turn as a result of the Direct Action of the Muslim. The League had joined the Interim Government to obstruct and not to cooperate.

(2) It was felt that a smaller India with a strong Central authority was better than a bigger State with a weak Center.

(3) The leaders felt that the partition would rid the Constitution of separate electorates and India could evolve as a truly secular and democratic polity.

(4) The leaders felt that further delay in the transfer of power would find India the midst of a Civil War.

[Any three]

(C) (1) The Act provided for the creation of two independent dominions from 15th August 1947, to be known as India and Pakistan

(2) Each dominion was to have a Governor General who would function as a Constitutional Head.

(3) Both would have separate Constituent Assemblies which would even serve as central legislatures.

(4) Princely States would become independent and all powers and authority exercisable by his Majesty would be terminated.

(5) The office of the Secretary of State would be abolished.

(6) Provision made for the division could evolve as a truly secular and democratic polity. [Any three]

[Marking Scheme]

What Examiners Say

→ (A) Though most candidates wrote the correct answer some mixed the points of Indian Independence Act of 1947.

→ (B) Answered correctly by most candidates. Few however wrote answers based on guess work.

→ (C) Most candidates wrote correct answers. Few candidates mixed up the India Independence Act with the Mountbatten proposals.

11. **With reference to the Partition Plan, answer the following:**

(A) (a) Name the last Viceroy of India.
(b) State *any two* reasons for him to come to India.

(B) Mention *any three* proposals under his Plan.

(C) State *any four* reasons for the Congress to finally accept the Plan. [ICSE 2020]

Ans. (A) (a) Lord Mountbatten was the last Viceroy of India.

(b) Lord Mountbatten came to India for the following reasons:

(1) To present the plan of transfer to power from British to the Indians.

(2) To restore peace among the Congress and the Muslim League.

(B) The proposals of Mountbatten Plan were as follows:

(1) The country would be divided into two dominions, India and Pakistan.

(2) The provinces of Bengal, Assam and Punjab were to be divided. A Boundary Commission was to be set up to determine the boundaries of these states. Boundary Commission was also supposed to demarcate the boundaries of the two countries.

(3) Princely States were given the liberty to join either of the dominion, India or Pakistan, or remain independent.

(C) The reasons for the Congress to finally accept the plan were:

(1) There were communal riots in several places as a declaration of the 'Direct action' by the Muslim League.

(2) The attempts made by the Muslim League to obstruct the functioning of the Interim Government convinced the Congress leaders like Patel and others that it was not possible to work together with the League.

(3) The only alternative to partition was to have a federation with a weak Centre. It was better to have a strong but smaller India than to have a bigger State with a weak Centre.

(4) The leaders felt that delay in transfer of power could lead to Civil War.

(A) (a) Lord Mountbatten
(b) He came to India for the purpose of taking necessary steps for the transfer of power to the Indians. / To restore peace among the two sections of Congress and the League. / To present a Plan for the Partition.

(B) **Three proposals under his Plan :**
(1) **Partition**—In two dominions
(2) **Relations between the two new Dominions**—To decide what relation to have between each other and the commonwealth
(3) **A Boundary Commission**—To settle the boundaries
(4) **Princely States**—Treaties would end, and they could decide to join either of the dominions or remain independent.
(5) **Bengal and Punjab**—Legislative Assemblies to decide
(6) **Sindh**—Legislative Assembly to decide
(7) **N.W. Frontier Province**—To decide by a referendum
(8) **District of Sylhet**—To decide by a referendum
(9) **Constituent Assembly**—Separate Constituent Assembly for both parties
(10) **Transfer of Power**—Would take place before 1948. **[Any three]**

(C) **Acceptance of Plan :**
(1) Large scale communal riots
(2) League joined Interim Government to obstruct and not to cooperate.
(3) Only alternative to Partition was a Federation with a weak Centre.
(4) Any further continuation of British rule would mean a greater calamity for India. /People and leaders were fed up with their rule in India/wanted to get rid of the British rule by paying any price.
(5) Further delay could find India in a Civil War.
(6) Leaders felt that partition would aid the Constitutions of separate electorates/and other undemocratic procedures. **[Any four]**
[Marking Scheme]

What Examiners Say

→ (A) *This question was well attempted by the candidates.*
→ (B) *Some candidates found it difficult to write four reasons why the Congress finally accepted the Plan.*

Caution

→ (A) *Each and every event related to the Partition Plan of India should be studied in detail.*
→ (B) *Students should understand the Mountbatten Plan and the Provisions of the Indian Independence Act of 1947.*
→ (C) *Students should study the clauses of above – mentioned Plans / Act thoroughly and present them in a factual manner.*

12. The Quit India Resolution in 1942 was one of the final calls given by Gandhi for the Britishers to leave India. Moving towards Independence, Lord Mountbatten's Plan was significant. In this context, answer the following:

(A) State *three reasons* for the launching of the Quit India Movement.

(B) Give *any three* effects of the Quit India Movement launched by Gandhi in 1942 that was significant to the last phase of the National Movement of India.

(C) Give *any four* clauses of the Mountbatten Plan of 1947. [HOT] [ICSE 2018]

Ans. (A) The reasons for the launching of the Quit India Movement were:

(1) **Failure of the Cripps Mission:** Through the Cripps mission, the British government for the first time recognized the 'Right of Dominion' for India. Not only the Congress and the Muslim League, but every party picked holes in the Cripps proposal and it was rejected by all.

(2) **The Japanese Threat:** After bombing Shanghai and Philippines, the Japanese attacked Burma and then began marching towards Assam. Gandhiji became convinced that the presence of British in India is only tempting the Japanese to invade the country. According to Gandhiji and his associates, for the sake of India's safety as well as that of Britain, it would be wise for the British to leave the country.

(3) **Increasing Communal Problems:** The communal situation was growing out of control as the Muslim League had also made a definite demand for the formation of a separate Pakistan.

(B) The significant effects of the Quit India Movement were:

(1) It gave utterance to India's anger against imperialism and her determination to achieve independence.

(2) The movement revealed that the depth of nationalism had permeated deep

into Indian Society as people from all religious communities such as Hindus, Muslims, Sikhs, Christians, Parsis and even the Princely states participated.

(3) The capacity for struggle and readiness for sacrifices revealed to the British that Indians were no long afraid of British atrocities.

(4) The movement was not completely non-violent and it clearly revealed that the patience of the Indian public to follow only non-violent methods was on the wane that and become impatient to drive the British away.

[Any three]

(C) The clauses of the Mountbatten Plan were:
(1) The country would be divided into two domimons, India and Pakistan;
(2) The provinces of Bengal, Assam and Punjab were to be divided. A Boundary Commission was to be set up to determine the boundaries of these States;
(3) Princely States were given liberty to join either of the dominion, India or Pakistan or remain independent;
(4) The existing Constituent Assembly would continue to work and draft the Constitution of free India;
(5) A referendum was to be held in the case of North West Frontier Province (NWFP) to determine the people's decision to join either India or Pakistan;
(6) A separate Constituent Assembly will be formed for Pakistan;
(7) The Muslim majority of Sylhet was to decide through referendum whether it would join East Bengal or remain as part of Assam;
(8) The date of British withdrawal from India was to be advanced to 15 August 1947, and the British Parliament would pass an Act for the transfer of power before this date. [Any four]

(A) (1) Failure of the Cripps Mission
(2) Japanese Threat
(3) Worsening of Communal problem.
(4) The movement hastened the British decision to quit India. [Any three]

(B) (1) It demonstrated the depth of the nationalist feelings in India and the capacity of Indians for struggle of sacrifice.
(2) Undermined the strength of the British in India.

(3) It once again became a mass movement.
(4) The movement was symbolic.
[Any three]

(C) **Mountbatten's Plan**
(1) Two new dominions
(2) Provisions of Partition (Sindh, NWFP, Sylhet, Bengal and Punjab)
(3) Governor General for each dominion
(4) Constituent Assemblies to serve as Central Legislatives
(5) End of British Parliament
(6) Princely States
(7) Treaties and Agreements
(8) Divisions of the army and assets
(9) Bringing the act into operation
(10) Office of Secretary of State of interest of existing officers.
(11) Creation of a Boundary Commission
(12) Transfer of Power
(13) Relations with Commonwealth
[Any four]
[Marking Scheme]

What Examiners Say

→ (A) Several candidates, instead of stating the reasons for the launching of the Quit India Movement, wrote the reasons for launching the other movements like Civil Disobedience Movement and Non-Cooperation Movement.

→ (B) Most of the candidates were able to write the correct answer. Some candidates wrote only two effects and repeated the same points in different forms.

→ (C) Most of the candidates wrote the correct clauses of the Mountbatten Plan of 1947. A few candidates got confused between the Mountbatten Plan and the Indian Independence Act.

Caution

→ (A) Students should know clearly the causes and consequences of all the movements launched by Mahatma Gandhi.

→ (B) Study carefully the Mountbatten Plan and the Indian Independence Act.

→ (C) Students should have clear idea that the country was divided according to the Mountbatten Plan and finally the British Parliament passed the Indian Independence Act which provided the basis for the creation of India and Pakistan.

13.

Independence and Partition of India

With reference to the picture given above answer the following:

(A) Identify the Viceroy in the picture. Why was he sent to India?

(B) How did he plan to solve the communal problem existing in India?

(C) Why did the Congress accept the Plan? State three reasons to justify its acceptance. [HOT🔥]

Ans. (A) The Viceroy in the picture is Lord Mountbatten.

The Muslim League demanded a separate and fully independent sovereign State of Pakistan. The situation was explosive as riots were taking place on large scale. It appeared that maintaining the unity of India was impossible and its partition was inevitable. Lord Mountbatten was sent to India as Viceroy as Britain prepared to transfer its power over India to some responsible hands.

(B) Lord Mountbatten had discussions with the Indian leaders and finally came up with his plan, popularly known as "The Mountbatten Plan". The Plan was approved by the British Cabinet and accepted by the Congress, the Muslim League and the Sikhs. To solve the communal problems, Lord Mountbatten proposed the following provisions in his plan:

(1) The country would be divided into two dominions, India and Pakistan;

(2) A seperate Constituent Assembly will be formed for Pakistan;

(3) The Provinces of Bengal, Assam and Punjab were to be divided. A Boundary Commission was to be set up to determine the boundaries of the state;

(4) A referendum was to be held in the case of North West Frontier Province to determine the people's decision to join either India or Pakistan;

(5) The Muslim majority region of Sylhet was to decide through referendum whether it would join East Bengal or remain as part of Assam.

(C) Refer Answer 10(B)

10 The First World War

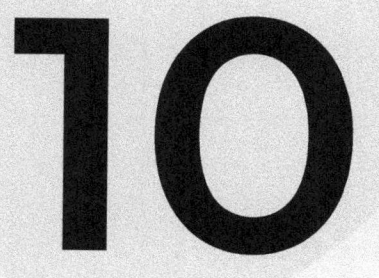

In 1914, there broke out a war which soon engulfed the whole of the world in its vicious circle. This in history is called the First World War. It was fought worldwide on land, in the air, on the sea and under the sea. New methods of destruction and defence were used in it. It displaced many people, ruined many lives and damaged the property of millions. Hence, it is named as the First World War.

Chapter Notes

- ☐ Causes of the First World War
- ☐ Results/Consequences of the First World War

The **First World War** broke out in the year 1914. It was the first major Warfare involving almost all the countries of Europe and parts of Asia and Africa. It displaced many people, ruined many lives and damaged the property of millions. Hence, it is termed as the First World War. During this War new methods of defence and destruction were used.

TOPIC 1

CAUSES OF THE FIRST WORLD WAR

The following causes were responsible for the First World War:

Nationalism and Imperialism

Nationalism refers to the sense of unity felt by the people, who share a common history, language and culture. In the latter half of the nineteenth century, this feeling of unity turned into extreme pride, which made the people of many countries believe that their country was superior to other countries, and this led to aggressive nationalism in Europe.

Aggressive nationalism meant love for one's own country and hatred of other countries. Each nation thought about its own national interests and did not care for the interests of other nations. For example, France wanted to get back its province of Alsace and Lorraine from Germany. Similarly, Italy wanted to get back the territory of Trieste from Austria and Balkan States like Serbia wanted that their fellow nationals (slavs) who lived in other states should come together to form a greater Balkan State. Every country began to increase its military power in the name of expansionist policies.

 Related Theory

→ Example of militant nationalism was German Emperor, Kaiser William II, he wanted to make Germany the most powerful country of the World. He was an expansionist ruler and wanted to set by a huge Empire. After the Franco-Prussian War, Germany had captured the provinces of Alsace and Lorraine that were rich in mineral deposits. The French were dissatisfied and desired to regain their lost territories.

Example 1. Explain how aggressive nationalism led to the rise of Imperialism?

Ans. Imperialism refers to the State Policy or practice by which a powerful nation establishes its control over another country, either by direct territorial acquisition or conquered, this country was claimed as a colony. Then these colonies were governed and administered by the Imperial Nation through its representatives or a Puppet Government.

The Imperial Nations exploited the resources of these colonies for their own economic interests. The colonies provided raw material, cheap labour, agricultural land and ports of trade to the Imperial Nations. By the end of the 19th century, England and France had built up a huge Colonial Empire in Asia and Africa.

Example 2. Which all British Colonies helped England in expanding its trade by exploiting resources from them?

Ans. India, Sri Lanka, Myanmar, Egypt, South Africa, Caribbean Islands and many parts of Africa.

Example 3. How was Britain's Imperial Power reinforced?

Ans. Britain's Imperial Power was reinforced by her powerful and world's largest Navy.

Example 4. Beside Britain which other countries wanted to create their colonies in Asia and Africa?

Ans. Germany, Italy, Russia and Japan.

 Caution

→ Learn four names properly, to avoid writing wrong names.

These colonies were essential for the following reasons to imperial powers:

(1) For their progress as they would provide them raw materials for their Industries.
(2) They would provide markets for their finished products.
(3) Besides, acquiring colonies, it would add to the power and prestige of these Imperial Countries.

Thus, aggressive nationalism and fierce economic competition filled the atmosphere with fear, apprehension, mutual hatred and international tension.

Division of Europe into Two Rival Camps

France was defeated very badly in the France – Prussian War of 1870-71, After 1871, the German Chancellor, Bismarck, adopted such a policy so as to keep France isolated and prevented her from establishing friendly relations with any other European country. He himself, however, formed a Dual Alliance with Austria-Hungary in 1879. Italy joined it later on and in 1882, it was converted into a **'Triple Alliance'**, including **Germany – Austria –Hungary and Italy**. As long as Bismarck was alive, he by his diplomacy did not allow any country to make friendship with France. It was only after his fall that France established friendly relations with Russia and England. To counter the Triple Alliance, **Britain-France and Russia** entered into **Triple Entente** in 1907. This agreement was a reply to the Triple Alliance, and they agreed to help each other to check German expansion.

Later on, Japan joined the Triple Entente while Turkey joined the Triple Alliance.

Thus, Europe was divided into two distinct rival camps. On one side, there had been Germany - Austria – Hungary, Italy and Turkey. And on the other hand there was Britain – France and Russia. The emergence of two opposing groups led to the First World War.

Immediate Cause

The Sarajevo Crisis: The gun – Powder of the War in Europe was getting ready since long time but the Murder of Austrian Archduke, the heir to the throne of Austria-Hungary was assassinated at Sarajevo, capital of Bosnia on 28 June, 1914. The murderer was a Serbian. The assassination was organised by a secret society called 'Black Hand' or 'Union of Death' formed by extremists Serbian nationalists whose aim was to unite all Serbians into a single Serbian State. Austria had put the blame on the Serbian Government for their Crime and sent an ultimatum on July 23. As Serbia refused to comply with some of the conditions related to the loss of her sovereignty.

Austria declared War on Serbia on July 28, 1914. Russia started Preparation of War to support Serbia on August 1, 1914 Germany declared War on Russia; and on August 3, on France. German troops marched into Belgium to press on to France on August 4 and on the same day Britain declared War on Germany.

Within no time this War culminated in the First World War. England and Germany tried to make this War a local affair but they could not succeed. France and Russia come to the help of Serbia. At this Germany declared War against Russia. England wanted to keep aloof but when Germany attacked Belgium, then England was compelled to join the War in order to safeguard the Belgian neutrality and her own political interests.

On one side there were Serbia – Russia – France, England – Japan – Italy – America, etc. They were called **'The Allies'**. On the other side were Germany– Austria – Turkey – Bulgaria, etc and they were known as **'The Centeral Powers'**.

📢 Important
➝ The major Cause of tension between Serbia and Austria was Balkan region. The Balkan States of Serbia and Bulgaria wanted that all the Slavonic people of the Balkan region must unite under one State and this was known as Pan-Slav Movement.

⚠ Caution
➝ The immediate cause of the First World War the assassination of Austrian Archduke, immediately after his murder the First world War began, it should not be misunderstood with the other causes of World War I.

TOPIC 2

RESULTS/CONSEQUENCES OF THE FIRST WORLD WAR

The Treaty of Versailles (June 28, 1919)

The First World War came to an end by the Treaty of Versailles which was the main treaty, though some sub – treaties were signed with other defeated nations other than Germany, like Austria – Hungary, Turkey, etc.

The treaty of Versailles was concluded on 28th June, 1919, in the Hall of Mirrors at Versailles in France. Though representatives of 27 countries were present at the Conference, the terms of the Treaty had been dictated by certain eminent persons – they were – The British Prime Minister – David Lloyd George, President of the United States of America – Woodrow Wilson, The French Prime Minister – M. Clemenceau and V.E. Orlando of Italy.

Terms of the Treaty or Consequences of the First World War on Germany.

Germany was forced to accept the following terms which are comparatively very harsh:

(1) Germany and her Alliance were held guilty for aggression and hence she was forced to pay for the loss and damages suffered by the Allies during the War. The amount of the reparations was fixed at 33 billion Dollars. Germany had to cede her merchant ships to the Allies as compensation and had to supply huge quantities of coal to France, Italy and Belgium for ten years.

(2) The area of the Rhine Valley was to be demilitarized and the German territory West of Rhine was to be occupied by the allied Troops for 15 years.

(3) Germany lost Alsace Lorraine to France, Eupen – et- Malmedy to Belgium, Schleswig to Denmark. Danzing became a free port in the Polish territory.

(4) Germany ceded parts of her pre – war territory to Denmark, Belgium, Poland, Czechoslovakia and France.

(5) The coal mines in the German area called Saar were ceded to France for 15 years and the area was to be governed by the League of Nations.

(6) Germany lost all her colonies to the Victorious Allies-Britain, Belgium, South Africa and Portugal.

(7) German Colonies in the Pacific and the areas under her control in China were given to Japan. China was aligned with the Allies during the War

but her areas under German Control were given away to Japan.

(8) The German Army was restricted to a force of 1,00,000 soldiers and the Navy was limited to 15,000 men and 24 ships. The Air Force and Submarines were banned.

(9) The Treaty affirmed the complete independence of Belgium, Poland, Czechoslovakia and Yugoslavia.

(10) The Covenant (the Pact) of the League of nations was added to the Treaty of Versailles.

Thus, the Treaty of Versailles was a 'dictated Peace' which was imposed on the Germans. They were only told to sign it under the threat of invasion. Thus, the Treaty of Versailles was very humiliating for Germany. It led to the rise of Nazism in Germany. Its leader, violated all the terms of this humiliating treaty (of Versailles) and plunged the world into another World War. (Second World War).

*Formation of the League of Nations

One of the most significant consequences of the war was the creation of the League of Nations. The Death and destruction caused by the First World war convinced the leaders of the world that there must be international Organ for the maintenance of Peace and Security in the World. The American president, Sir Woodrow Wilsons' 14 Points emphasized the creation of the International Organisation, to preserve the peace and to promote the spirit of cooperation.

*Example 5. When and why was the League of Nations formed ?

Ans. The League of Nations came into being on 10th January, 1920. It was set up to promote international co-operation and to achieve Peace and Security.

 **Caution**
→ Some children have answered only first Part of the question. Read both the parts of the question properly before answering.

*Example 6. Where was its headquarters?

Ans. Its headquarters was at Geneva in Switzerland.

 **Caution**
→ Spelling of 'Switzerland' is written wrong by some students.

Aims and Objectives of the League of Nations:

(1) The main aim of the League was to maintain international Peace and Security and to promote international cooperation.

(2) The member– states were to respect each other's sovereignty.

(3) The member states were not supposed to maintain huge armies, dangerous weapons and warships.

(4) All the states of the world were prohibited from entering into any secret treaties and alliances.

(5) The member–states were to take necessary action as directed by the League against any State which tried to disturb World Peace and Order.

Membership: Initially the League had 42 members. The USA did not join the League. Germany was not allowed to become its member until 1926. Russia became its member in 1934. While India, which was not independent, was made a member. The United States which had played an important part in the setting up of the League ultimately decided not to join it.

Organs of the League of Nations:

Main Organs of the League of Nations were as follows:

(1) The General Assembly
(2) The Council
(3) The Secretariat
(4) The Permanent Court of International Justice.

There were a number of Commissions and Committees for international labour, health, child welfare, economic and financial Organisations and women's rights.

League's Failure:

The League failed to maintain Peace in the World and prevent the Second World War for the following reasons:

(1) The rise of dictatorship in Italy and Germany.
(2) The USA decided not to join it as she believed in the policy of isolation and tried to avoid political dispute with other states as well as the signing of the treaties.
(3) The members were not sincere enough. Many of them signed secret treaties and did not resort to collective action.
(4) The League did not have any standing army.
(5) The League tried to apply economic sanction against an aggressor but it was not fruitful.
(6) When any country behaved aggressively, the League either ignored it or defied it.
(7) The League seemed to be an Organisation for the benefit of the Victorious Power.
(8) The Policy of Appeasement followed by Britain and France emboldened the aggressors like Hitler who flouted the League. He committed aggression on Poland which began the World War II (1939-1945).

 **Caution**
→ Most of the candidates were unsure of the facts and they have answered questions incorrectly that reflected inadequate preparation.

ICSE Suggestions
→ Students should learn all the causes of the First World War and should learn and understand the facts well before writing any answer related to them.

* This topic is not included in syllabus now, given for Information only

→ Students should study aims and objectives of the League of Nations carefully.

→ Students to be specific. They should learn and understand the facts well.

→ Students should be able to comprehend the question to answer specifically rather than writing vague and irrelevant answers.

→ Analyze the question correctly as to what specific facts are expected from the question.

 **Glossary**

(1) **Imperator**: A German ship, built in 1912. It was the largest ship in the world.
(2) **Lusitania**: A British ship which was sunk by the German boats in 1915.
(3) **Versailles**: A suburb of Paris where the first conference of all the allies was held.
(4) **Ramonav**: The ruling dynasty in Russia.
(5) **Hohenzollern**: The ruling dynasty in Germany.
(6) **Habsburg**: The ruling dynasty of Austria–Hungary.
(7) **Allies**: The name given to the Victorious Powers of the First World War.
(8) **Treaty of Brest-Litovsk**: The treaty of Brest-Litovsk ended the War between Russia and Germany.
(9) **First World War**: The War which was fought from 1914 - 1918 in which most of the European Countries were involved.

 **Chronology**

1970–71: France was defeated by Germany and lost Alsace-Lorraine.
1882: Triple Alliance including Germany – Austria – Hungary and Italy was formed.
1907: Triple Entete comprising France – Russia and Britain was formed.
28th June, 1914: Archduke Franz Ferdinand, the heir to the throne of Austria – Hungary was assassinated.
1st August, 1914: Germany declared War on Russia.
3rd August, 1914: Germany declared War on France.
4th August, 1914: Britain declared War on Germany.
1915: Italy joined the War against Austria – Hungary and Germany. German u-boats sank the British ship called Lusitania.
6th April, 1917: US declared War against Germany.
1914–1918: First World War.
1919: Treaty of Versaillies was signed.
1920: Formation of League of Nations.

OBJECTIVE Type Questions

Multiple Choice Questions
[1 mark each]

⚠ **Caution**
→ Students should memorise Dates and Events thoroughly in History.

1. The First World War took place from :
(a) 1814 – 1818
(b) 1914 – 1918
(c) 1939 – 1945
(d) 1919 – 1924   [HOT🔥]

Ans. *(b) 1914 – 1918*

Explanation: The First World War broke immediately after the assassination of Archduke Francis Ferdinand on June 28, 1914 and lasted on 11th November, 1918 on Germany signing an armistice.

2. What was the immediate cause of the First World War?
(a) Sarajevo Crisis
(b) Japan's invasion of China
(c) Germany's invasion of Poland
(d) Discontentment with Treaty of Versailles

Ans. *(a) Sarajevo crisis*

Explanation: The assassination of Archduke Francis Ferdinand and his wife in Sarajevo, capital of Bosnia was the immediate cause of the First World War.

3. Which of the following countries was NOT a part of Triple Alliance during the First World War?
   (a) Germany
   (b) France
   (c) Austria-Hungary
   (d) Italy [HOT]

Ans. (b) France

Explanation: France was a part of the rival bloc– Triple Entente during the First World War.

4. Which country was blamed for the assassination of the Archduke Francis Ferdinand?
   (a) Austria – Hungary
   (b) Serbia
   (c) Russia
   (d) Germany

Ans. (b) Serbia

Explanation: Serbia was blamed for the assassination of Archduke Francis Ferdinand. Austria declared War on Serbia after that incident immediately on July 28, 1914.

Related Theory
The assassination of Archduke was organised by a Secret Society called 'Black Hand' or 'Union of Death' formed by extremist Serbian nationalists whose aim was to unite all Serbians into a single Serbian State.

5. Match the following by choosing the correct option :

	Column I		Column II
(A)	Allied Powers	(i)	France, Russia and Britain
(B)	Triple Alliance	(ii)	Britain, France, Russia and United States
(C)	Central Powers	(iii)	Germany, Austria – Hungary and Italy
(D)	Triple Entente	(iv)	Germany, Austria – Hungary, Bulgaria and Ottoman empire

   (a) (A)-(ii); (B)-(iii); (C)-(iv); (D)-(i)
   (b) (A)-(i); (B)-(iv); (C)-(ii); (D)-(iii)
   (c) (A)-(iii); (B)-(i); (C)-(iv); (D)-(ii)
   (d) (A)-(iv); (B)-(i); (C)-(ii); (D)-(iii)

Ans. (a) (A)-(ii); (B)-(iii); (C)-(iv); (D)-(i)

6. .... meant love for one's own country and hatred for other countries.
   (a) Nationalism
   (b) Imperialism
   (c) Patriotism
   (d) Aggressive Nationalism

Ans. (d) Aggressive Nationalism

Explanation: In Aggressive Nationalism each nation thought about its own interests and did not care for the interests of the other nations.

Caution
This question was a bit tricky. Many students have written wrong answers. They should know the difference between Nationalism, Patriotism and Aggressive Nationalism Clearly.

7. Imperialism refers to:
   (a) State policy or practice by which a powerful nation establishes its control over another country.
   (b) It either gets direct territorial acquisition.
   (c) Or it gets political and economic control
   (d) All of the above [HOT]

Ans. (d) All of the above

Explanation: Imperialism refers to State Policy or practice by which a powerful nation establishes its control over another country either by direct territorial acquisition or by gaining political and economic control. Once conquered, this country was claimed as colony.

Related Theory
By the end of the 19th century, England and France had built up a huge colonial empire in Asia and Africa.

8. Complete the given analogy :
   France, Holland and Germany : Single Nation States
   Austria – Hungarian Empire and the Russian Empire : : ?
   (a) Double States   (b) Triple States
   (c) Imperial States (d) Multiple States

Ans. (c) Imperial States

Explanation : The Imperial States had different Cultural traditions, and they spoke different languages unlike single Nation States.

9. The treaty of Versailles restricted Germany to an army of .... soldiers.
   (a) Fifty thousand   (b) One lakh
   (c) Two lakhs   (d) Five lakhs

Ans. (b) One lakh

10. The Treaty of Versailles mandated Germany to pay a war reparation of ....
    (a) 35 billion dollars
    (b) 40 billion dollars
    (c) 33 billion dollars
    (d) 50 million pounds

Ans. (c) 33 billion dollars

Explanation : Germany was required to pay 33 billion dollars for the loss and damage suffered by the Allies during the War.

11. Which of the following was not a term of Treaty of Versailles?
   (a) Germany was required to pay an amount of reparations of 33 billion dollars.
   (b) The coal mines in the German area called Saar were ceded to France.
   (c) Germany army was restricted to a force of 1,00,000 soldiers.
   (d) Establishment of United Nations.

Ans. (d) Establishment of United Nations

Explanation: (a), (b) & (c) were all terms of Treaty of Versailles but (d) was not the term of Treaty of Versailles.

12. Year of .... was also called the period of global economic depression.
   (a) 1925 - 1926   (b) 1929 - 1930
   (c) 1935 - 1936   (d) 1928 - 1929

Ans. (b) 1929 - 1930

Explanation : Year 1929 – 1930 was known for global economic depression, which attributed to the I World War. It gave rise to many serious social problems.

13. Apart from political functions, the League of Nations was supposed to promote .... co-operation among the member States.
   (a) social   (b) cultural
   (c) economic   (d) all of the above

Ans. (d) All of the above

Explanation : Apart from Political functions, the League of Nations was supposed to promote cultural, social and economic co-operation among the member – States.

14. When was League of Nations formed?
   (a) 1930   (b) 1940
   (c) 1920   (d) 1910   [HOT🔥]

Ans. (c) 1920

Explanation : The League of Nations was created as a World Organisation of all independent States in 1920.

15. The signatory countries of the Triple Alliance were ....
   (a) Germany, France, Italy
   (b) France, Britain, Russia
   (c) Germany, Italy, Austria-Hungary
   (d) Britain, Russia, Italy   [ICSE Sem-2, 2022]

Ans. (c) Germany, Italy, Austria-Hungary

Explanation : Germany entered into an alliance with Austria-Hungary. In 1882 Italy joined the alliance and it came to be known as Triple Alliance.

SUBJECTIVE Type Questions

Short Answer Type Questions
[2 marks each]

16. Mention two causes of the First World War.
Ans. (1) Imperialism and Economic competition.
(2) Militarism and Armament race.

17. How many major power countries were there at the end of the 19th century?
Ans. England, France, Germany and U.S.A. were the major power countries at the end of 19th century.

18. Name the major powers, which got involved in World War I.
Ans. The major powers were Russia, Germany, Britain, Austria and France.

19. Name the Signatory Countries of the Triple Alliance.
Ans. Germany, Austria-Hungary and Italy were the signatory countries of the Triple Alliance.

20. Name the signatory countries of the Triple Entente.   [HOT🔥]
Ans. England, France and Russia formed the Triple Entente.

21. What was the immediate cause of the First World War?   [HOT🔥]
Ans. The immediate cause of the war was the murder of Archduke Francis Ferdinand on June 28th, 1914.

22. Which country declared war on Serbia and when?
Ans. Austria declared a war on Serbia on 28th July 1914.

23. When did the First World War come to an end?
Ans. The First World War came to an end on November 11th, 1918.

24. Why was the place Sarajevo got highlighted?
Ans. Sarajevo was the capital of Bosnia and the heir prince of the throne of Austria-Hungary, Archduke Francis Ferdinand, came there with his wife. He was assassinated there and the First World War started.

25. How did the division of Europe resulted in the First World War?

The First World War

Ans. Europe was divided into rival blocs known as "Triple Alliance' and 'Triple Entente'. These blocs showed rivalry by initiating arms race and capturing colonies of Asia and Africa that resulted in the First World War.

26. **State any two objections imposed by the Treaty of Versailles on the German military power.** [ICSE 2019]

Ans. The objections imposed by the Treaty of Versailles on the German Military Power were:
(1) The German Army was allowed to keep a force of only one lac soldiers.
(2) Germany was not allowed to have any Air Force or the Sub-marines.

> (1) The army was restricted to a force of 1 lakh soldiers.
> (2) The navy was limited to 15,000 men and 24 ships.
> (3) Air force and submarines were banned.
> (4) Rhine valley was demilitarized.
> [Any two]
> [Marking Scheme]

What Examiners Say
→ Some candidates could not comprehend the question correctly and wrote those provisions of the Treaty of Versailles which were not related to the crippling of the German military power.

27. **Name the Signatory Countries of the Triple Alliance.** [ICSE 2019]

Ans. The signatory countries of the Triple Alliance were Germany, Austria, Hungary and Italy.

> Germany, Austria-Hungary & Italy (All three countries) [Marking Scheme]

What Examiners Say
→ Many candidates, instead of naming the signatory countries of the Triple Alliance, named those of the Triple Entente.

28. **Name the two rival blocs formed in Europe before World War I ?** [HOT] [ICSE 2015]

Ans. (1) Triple Alliance, comprising of Germany, Italy and Austria – Hungary;
(2) Triple Enterte, comprising of Britain, France and Russia.

What Examiners Say
→ Most candidates answered correctly. A few mentioned the blocs of the Second World War – Axis Powers and Allied Powers.

⚠ **Caution**
→ The rival groups of both the wars must be understood clearly.

29. **Mention any two terms of the Treaty of Versailles signed on June 28, 1919.**

Ans. The terms of Treaty of Versailles signed on June 28, 1919 were:
(1) Germany was held guilty of causing the First World War. She had to pay war indemnity of 33 billion dollars to the victor nations.
(2) Germany had to evacuate territories she had captured during the war;
(3) German territory of Rhineland was to be demilitarized. The territory of the Rhine Valley was to be occupied by Allied powers.
(4) Germany was forced to return Alsace and Lorraine to France. Danzing was to be free port under the League of Nations;
(5) Germany had to surrender the areas of Eupen and Malmedy to Belgium. The city of Menel went to Lithiuania;
(6) Germany lost all her colonies and overseas possessions. [Any two]

> The terms of the Treaty of Versailles were:
> (1) It declared Germany guilty of aggressions
> (2) Germany was required to pay 33 billion dollars for the losses and damages suffered by the Allies
> (3) Germany had to cede her merchant ships to the Allies as compensation
> (4) it had to supply huge quantities of coal to France, Italy and Belgium for 10 years
> (5) the area of Rhine Valley was to be de-militarised
> (6) the German territory west of Rhine was to be occupied by the Allied troops for 15 years.
> (7) Germany lost Alsace Lorraine to France, Eupen-et-Malmedy to Belgium, Schleswig to Denmark. Danzing became a free port in the Polish territory. [Any two]
> [Marking Scheme]

30. **State two factors which were responsible for the failure of the League of Nations.** [ICSE 2014]

Ans. The factors responsible for the failure of the League of Nations were :
(1) When Japan occupied Manchuria in China, and when Italy attacked Abyssinia, the League failed to prevent these aggressions.
(2) The membership was not universal. The US did not become a member of the League of Nations.

Reasons for the failure of League were:
(1) the US did not join the League
(2) the members of the League were not interested in the principal of collective security.
(3) the League was not able to help the members in allying the threat of war as it was not strong.
(4) the members defied or ignored the League. eg: Japan seized Manchuria and Italy conquered Ethiopia.
(5) member states were not willing to apply economic sanctions as it affected their economy.
(6) it failed to maintain international peace so the European countries lost faith in the League
(7) it failed to check the rise of dictatorship in Germany and Italy.

[Any two]
[Marking Scheme]

31. Name the two alliances formed in Europe during the First World War.

Ans. The two alliances formed in Europe during the First world War were:
(1) **Triple Alliance:** It consisted of Germany Austria-Hungary and Italy.
(2) **Triple Entente:** It was formed by Britain, France and Russia.

32. Explain briefly the term 'Militant Nationalism'.

Ans. Militant Nationalism meant high degree of love for one's own country and hatred towards other nations. It is an aggressive policy to achieve national goals.

33. Name the signatory countries of the Triple Entente.

Ans. The signatory countries of the Triple Entente were France, England and Russia, which was formed in 1907 to counter the Triple Alliance.

Structured Questions

[3+3+4= **10** marks each]

34. With reference to the First World War, answer the following questions:
(A) Name the two countries which came under dictatorship after the First World War. Name the dictators.
(B) Explain the Sarajevo Crisis.
(C) Mention any four ways in which the Treaty of Versailles benefited France.

Ans. (A) The countries that came under the dictatorship after the First World War were:
(1) **Italy:** Under the dictatorship of Benito Mussolini.
(2) **Germany:** Under Adolf Hitler

(B) The Sarajevo crisis refers to the incidence of assassination of Archduke of Austria, Francis Ferdinand and his wife Sophia during a state visit to Sarajevo. They were assassinated by a 19-year old Gavrilo Princep, a member of terrorist organization 'Black hand'. As a result of this assassination, Austria served an ultimatum on Serbia and declared war on Serbia on 28th July, 1914. This Sarajevo crisis was the immediate cause of the First World War.

(C) The ways in which Treaty of Versailles benefited France were:
(1) Germany lost Alsace Lorraine to France;
(2) The coal mines in the German area called Scar were ceded to France for 15 years;
(3) The Treaty of Versailles got France more colonies as all the German Colonies were taken and given to Britain and France.
(4) Germany had to cede her merchant ships to the Allies as compensation and had to supply huge quantities of coal to France.

35. The assassination of Archduke Francis Ferdinand, the heir to the throne of Austria-Hungary was the immediate cause of the First World War. In this context, describe the following:
(A) Sarajevo crisis
(B) Why did the USA join the First World War?
(C) The role of Nationalism and Imperialism in the First World War.

Ans. (A) Archduke Francis Ferdinand, the heir to the throne of Austria-Hungary was assassinated at Sarajevo, capital of Bosnia on June 28, 1914. The assassination was organised by a secret society called 'Black Hand' or 'Union of Death' formed by extremist Serbian nationalists whose aim was to unite all Serbians into a single Serbian state. Austria served an ultimatum on Serbia making eleven demands. Serbia accepted most of the demands except those that would have led to the loss of her sovereignty. Austria declared war on Serbia on July 28, 1914. Thus, Sarajevo resulted in the immediate cause of First World War.

(B) In 1915, the German U-boats had sink a British Ship *Lusitania*. Among the 1153 passengers killed, 128 were Americans. The Americans were generally sympathetic to Britain, and this incident further roused anti-Germans feelings in the USA.

The Allied powers has raised vast amounts of loans in the USA to pay for the arms and other goods bought by them. Therefore, the USA feared that if Germany won the war, she would become a serious rival to the USA. Thus, USA declared war on Germany.

(C) Nationalism refers to the sense of unity felt by the people who share a common history language and culture. In the latter half of the 19th century, this feeling of unity turned into extreme pride, which made the people of many countries believe that their country is superior to other countries. This led to aggressive nationalism in Europe. This aggressive nationalism also led to the rise of imperialism. Imperialism refers to the state policy by which a powerful nation established its control over another country, either by direct territorial acquistion or by gaining political and economic control.

By the end of the 19th century, England and France had built up a huge colonial empire in Asia and Africa. British imperialism was focussed on maintaining and expanding trade by exploiting the resources of its colonies. Britain's imperial power was reinforced by her powerful and the world' largest navy. Some other countries of the world like Germany, Italy, Russia and Japan also wanted to increase thier sphere of influence and create their colonies in Asia and Africa. This led to a clash among these countries. Thus, aggressive nationalism and fierce economic competition filled the atmosphere with fear apprehension, mutual hatred and international tension resulting in First World War.

36. With reference to the First World War answer the following questions:

(A) What was meant by the term 'Imperialism', as a cause for World War I?
 [ICSE 2020]

(B) Mention any three objectives of the League of Nations.

(C) What do you know about the World Organisation formed after the First World War?

Ans. (A) Imperialism is the state policy, practice or advocacy of extending power or dominion by political pressure, infiltration and annexation or outright wars. The best example of imperialism as a cause of World War I was the annexation of Bosnia and Herzegovina, which were former territories of Ottoman Empire, by Austria-Hungary in 1908.

(1) A system by which a powerful nation used to establish its control over another country
(2) By political pressure
(3) Infiltration and annexation
(4) By outright wars.
(5) Supremacy over weaker countries
(6) Establish colonies
(7) Mad scramble among European nations for new territories in Asia and Africa
(8) Morocco Crisis/Any other example of conquests. **[Any three]**
 [Marking Scheme]

What Examiners Say

→ Many candidates confused 'imperialism' with 'aggressive nationalism'. A large number of candidates gave the meaning as "extreme love for one's country and hatred for other."

(B) **The Objectives of the League of Nations were:**

(1) To encourage international co-operation.
(2) To attempt to reduce War weapons.
(3) To keep a check on War.
(4) All the states should refer their mutual disputes to the League of Nations.
(5) To preserve the territorial integrity and political independence of all its members. **[Any three]**

(C) (1) As there had been no organization to solve the disputes, which led to the First World War, the League of Nations was established 'to promote international co-operation and to achieve Peace and Security'.

(2) It had its headquarters at Geneva, in the beginning and had 42 members.

(3) Its five important organs were the General Assembly, The Council, The Secretariat, The International Court of Justice and The International Labour Organisation.

(4) The important goals of the League of Nations were to promote disarmament, to prevent war through collective security, to settle conflicts through negotiations or diplomacy and to improve quality of life at Global level.

37. The First World War had a devastating effect on the world and caused unprecedented destruction. With reference to the First World War, answer the following questions:

(A) What is meant by the term Imperialism?

(B) Explain the immediate cause of the First World War.

(C) What was the amount of war reparation that Germany had to pay the allies? Mention any two terms of the Treaty of Versailles which affected the German military. **[ICSE Sem-2, 2022]**

Ans. (A) 'Imperialism' refers to the state policy or practice by which a powerful nation establishes its control over another country, either by direct territorial acquisition or by gaining political and economic control.

(B) Archduke Francis Ferdinand, heir to the Austrian throne, went on an official visit to Sarajevo, the capital of Bosnia. He was assassinated at Sarajevo on 28th June, 1914 by a Serbian. Austria held Serbia responsible for the murder and sent an ultimatum. As Serbia refused to comply with some of the conditions, Austria declared war on Serbia and soon most of the powers were involved in the war. Within no time this war was culminated into the First World war, which became the immediate cause of the First World War.

(C) Germany was required to pay for the loss and damages suffered by the Allies during the War. The amount of the reparations was fixed at 33 billion dollars:
The two terms of the Treaty of Versailles which affected the German Military were:
(1) Germany had to cede her merchant ships to the Allies as compensation.
(2) The area of Rhine valley was to be demilitarized and the German territory West of Rhine was to be occupied by the Allied Troops for 15 years.
(3) The German Army was restricted to a force of 1,00,000 soldiers and the Navy was limited to 15,000 men and 24 ships. The Air Force and Submarines were banned.

38. With reference to the First World War, answer the following questions:

(A) Explain briefly the causes of World War–I with reference of Nationalism and Imperialism. **[ICSE 2018]**

(B) Explain the immediate cause of the First World War. **[ICSE 2017]**

(C) Mention any four terms of the Treaty of Versailles which affected Germany after World War–I. **[HOT] [ICSE 2017]**

Ans. (A) The causes for World War-I were:

(1) **Aggressive Nationalism:** The unlimited spirit of nationalism was a major cause of World War-I. There existed strong feeling of hatred between France and Germany, Germany and England and Russia and Balkans. Each nation wanted "National Honour" and the idea of mutual give and take did not exist among the European countries. This narrow nationalism and competitive patriotism led to bitterness and suspicion amongst nations.

(2) **Economic Imperialism:** There was a race for colonial expansion among the European countries. The rapid growth of industrialization brought great demand from the colonies for raw materials and to find new markets for their finished goods. This resulted in colonial conflicts and national rivalries.

(3) **Armament Race:** Germany defeated France in the Franco Prussian war and took away the provinces of Alsace and Lorraine. The French never recovered from the shocks of this defeat and waited to take revenge and recover their lost territories. The intense nationalism and distrust triggered an armament race among European countries.

What Examiners Say

Most of the candidates could not distinguish between Nationalism and Imperialism and hence were unable to write the correct answer. In many answer scripts there was overlapping of points. A few candidates mentioned the other causes of the First World War.

(B) With all countries fully armed, ever ready to go to war, it needed only a little spark to ignite and set off the forces of war into motion. The outbreak of the great war was initiated by an incident that occurred in Bosnia. The Serbian people became independent and Bosnia came to be a part of Serbia. But as Bosnia was ceded to Austria, the Serbians were agitated. Bosnia became the centre of rebellions, only supported by the Serbian Government. The Archduke Francis Ferdinand, the heir apparent to the throne of Austria, was murdered along with his wife, Sophie, at Sarajevo a city in Bosnia while on a visit to Bosnia. As the assassin, Gavrilo Princep, a nineteen-year-old student was a Serbian, Austria blamed Serbia as the conspirator of the crime and gave a stiff ultimatum with eleven severe demands to Serbia. The Serbian government, while accepting most of these demands, refused to accept one of the terms threatening her sovereignty. This refusal by Serbia turned out to be the immediate cause of the First World War.

What Examiners Say
→ This part was answered correctly by most candidates. A few candidates wrote other causes in place of the immediate cause. A few candidates confused it with the immediate cause of the First World War of Independence 1857.

(C) The terms of Treaty of Versailles that affected Germany after World War I were:

(1) Germany was held guilty of causing the First World War. She had to pay war indemnity of 6,600 million pounds to the victor nations.

(2) Germany had to evacuate territories she had captured during the war;

(3) Germany territory of Rhineland was to be demilitarized. The territory west of the Rhine valley was to be occupied by the Allied powers;

(4) Germany was forced to return Alsace and Lorraine to France. Danzing was to be a free port under the League of Nations;

(5) As compensation to France for the destruction of her coal mines by Germany, France was given full control over the rich coal mines in the Saar Valley.

(6) Germany had to surrender the areas of Eupen and Malmedy to Bulgaria;

(7) Estonia, Latvia and Lithiuania earlier seized by Germany were now made independent. **[Any four]**

(A) Causes of World War-I

(1) **Aggressive nationalism:** Military strength became the same with national prestige and every country began to increase her military power e.g. Serbia, France and Italy.

(2) Imperialism was a system by which a powerful nation used to establish its control over another country / dispute over Morocco.

(3) England and France built up a huge colonial empire in Asia and Africa.

(4) Each nation thought about its national interest and did not care for the interest of other nations.

(5) France wanted to get back Alsace-Lorraine.

(6) Unsatisfied nation spirit of Balkans/ discontent among Italians/Franco-Prussian war/Germany wanted to be the leader of the world.
[Any three]

(B) Archduke Francis Ferdinand, the heir to the throne of Austria was assassinated at Sarajevo, the capital of Bosnia. This assassination was carried out by a secret society called "Union of Death" formed by extremist. Serbian Nationalists whose aim was to unite all Serbians into a single state. Austria served an ultimatum to Serbia making 11 demands. Serbia accepted most of them except those that would have led to the loss of sovereignty. On July 28, 1914, Austria declared war on Serbia. This was the beginning of the First World War.

(C) Treaty of Versailles concerning Germany

It was declared guilty of aggression and had to pay war reparation of 33 billion dollars. / The area of the Rhine valley was demilitarized and the German territory, west of Rhine was to be occupied by the Allied troops for 125 years./ Danzing became a free port in Polish territory / Lost Alsace Lorraine to France / The Saar coal mines were given to France. / Lost all her colonies to the allies. The German force was restricted to 1 lakh, the Navy to 15,000 men and 24 ships / The Air force and submarines were banned. **[Any four]**

[Marking Scheme]

What Examiners Say
→ Most candidates answered correctly. However, a few candidates wrote other terms of the Treaty which did not affect Germany.

11 Rise of Dictatorship

The political and economic instability prevailing in countries like Italy and Germany after the First World War led to the rise of 'Dictatorship' in these countries of Europe. The Democracy was destroyed by these dictatorial government: Italy under Benito Mussolini become a Fascist State and Germany under Adolf Hitler was converted into a Nazi Dictatorship.

Chapter Notes

- Rise of Fascism in Italy
- Rise of Nazism in Germany
- Comparative Study in Fascism and Nazism

TOPIC 1

RISE OF FASCISM IN ITALY

When the United States of America entered the First World War it raised the Slogan 'Make the World Safe for Democracy'. In the decade after the First World War (1919 to 1929), democracy made remarkable progress all over the world. After the war monarchical governments were abolished and republics were founded in many European countries. Democracy, however, progressed only for a short period and gave way to totalitarian dictatorships under different names and forms in Russia, Italy, Germany and Spain. They were governments under the rule of one man or a small group of men and the masses had little to say in the administration. Great importance was attached to national interests rather than to individual interests. Everybody lived for the State. The motto of the dictators was "Everything for the State, everything within the State, and nothing outside the State". The dictatorial governments destroyed democracy. Italy under Benito Mussolini become a Fascist State and Germany under Hitler was converted into a Nazi dictatorship.

Fascism

The word 'Fascism' has originated from the term 'fasces' which in Italian language means ' a bundle of rods with protruding axe' that symbolized civic unity and the authority of Roman Officials to punish wrongdoers. Thus 'Fascism' means autocracy or dictatorship where the power of the State is vested in one men only; and it is obligatory for all the others to obey his orders. The fascist allowed cruel treatment to opponents. Military strength and violence played a vital role in the Fascist pattern of government.

Causes for the Rise of Fascism

Soon after the First World War 'Fascism', a dictatorial form of government rose in Italy under Mussolini. Following were the causes of the rise and spread of Fascism in Italy :

Discontentment after the Treaty of Versailles

Italy joined the Allies in the First World War and by the Secret Treaty of London (1915) she hoped to gain Trentino, Trieste, Istria, Fiume, Coastal Regions of Dalmatia, Albania and some parts of Turkey and Germany. But during the Paris Conference her hopes were dashed to the ground by Wilson's opposition and so by the Treaty of Versailles she could get only Southern Tyrol and Trentino and the Coastal Regions of Dalmantia. She could not get the part of the German and Turkish Colonial empire.

The Italians felt as if they had been deceived and thought that their right demands were ignored. Imperialist designs of Italy were completely ignored. This very fact helped in spreading Fascism in Italy.

Economic Crisis

An economic Crisis developed in Italy as a result of the loss of money and life in the War. Many people had been killed in the War and millions of rupees had been spent. The national debt had increased a lot. There was a great shortage of food-grains in the country and unemployment were increasing day-by-day. The industries and trade was ruined. The condition of the middle class people, farmers and the working class became very critical. As a result of the War, Italy suffered a lot and her people became very poor. Such a deteriorated condition unrest in the country.

Political Instability

In 1919, Democracy was introduced in Italy for the first time. Since, no single party could gain clear majority in the elections, there was complete instability between 1919 and 1922 and six coalition governments were formed in Italy. Each government has its own policy and there was no continuity in their policies. As they were not able to solve the problems of unemployment and poverty, the Fascist took advantage of the prevailing political instability under Mussolini.

Threat of Socialism or Communism

The Socialists who included the Anarchists, the Communists and the Social Democrats created conditions conducive to the growth of Fascism in Italy. Inspired by the Russian Revolution, the Communists inflamed the atmosphere with revolutionary ideas. Peasants took away the land from landlords; workmen organised strikes, damaged machines and took hold of the factories. The Communists began to devise new plans of overthrowing the government and capturing power. People wanted a powerful leadership who could establish peace and prosperity by ending lawlessness and insecurity prevalent in Italy. The Industrialists viewed the growing strength of the labour unions with alarm and provided financial support to Fascism.

Class Conflicts

Class conflict increased in many countries after the First World War. The real issue in most parts of Continental Europe was whether control of government and economic systems would continue in the possession of aristocracies or would be in the hands of less privileged majorities. The common man had been promised, during the War, that he would be rewarded by greater attention to his economic needs. These promises were ignored and the common man was embittered.

Failure of the League of Nations

After the First World War, The League of Nations was established to maintain peace in the world and to prevent wars. But it proved weak and failed to achieve its aims. It failed to check the rise of Dictatorships. Had it acted well in time, the ambitious plans of Mussolini and Hitler would not have materialised.

Leadership Provided by Mussolini

Mussolini played an important role of Italy. He had a charismatic personality. His speeches praised the past glories of Italy and won the faith of his countrymen. Mussolini was called 'Duce' which means the Leader.

Principles/Ideology of Fascism

The main principles of fascism were as follows:

(1) Fascism was the antithesis of democracy. Fascist believed that democracy was not suitable for the country because it widens the gulf between the poor and the rich.

(2) Fascism was the supporter of one party and one leader. According to Fascism dictatorship was the best form of government. There was no place for opposition in Fascism and it was in favour of bringing an end to all other forces.

(3) The leader of the party was all in all in the country. None could challenge his authority. He was above law. He had all the military and civil rights and nobody could criticize him.

(4) Fascism was against the individual. It preferred the State to the man or the individual because he gets all the rights from the State. Individuals did exist only for the State. Fascism laid more stress on the duties of the individual and the rights of the State.

(5) Fascism laid stress on nationalism and national institutions.

(6) According to Fascism, Peace should be established in the country and the private property should be maintained.

(7) For the all-round development of the country, Fascism favoured equal control on the capitalists and the poor, labourers, peasants, factory owners, landlords, etc.

(8) Fascism wanted to enhance the power and prestige of the country by making it powerful.

(9) Fascism was the supporter of an imperialist and aggressive policy so that the country should become strong and might gain power and prestige in the international sphere.

Example 1. State two underlying Principles of Fascism.

Ans. (1) Anti-democratic
(2) Opposition not tolerated
(3) One party system, controlled by a dictator.
(4) Supported Imperialistic, Aggressive Policy.
(5) Interests of the State were superior to the rights of the people. **[Any two]**

⚠ **Caution**
➥ *Some students have mixed both the Principles of Fascism and Nazism, they have written mixture of both.*

Fascism in Italy

Italy was reunited under Victor Emmanuel II between 1860 and 1870. At the beginning of the First World War, the country was being ruled by king Victor Emmanuel III, a weak ruler. It bagged behind in the industrial revolution and in the race for Colonial Possessions. However, the Italians were proud of their history and so were willing to listen to anyone who talked of reviving their past glory.

Rise of Mussolini

(1) The Fascist Party was formed in Italy in 1922 under the leadership of Benito Mussolini. It attracted people from all sections of the society. Mussolini started off as a socialist but became anti-socialist when he realized that he could get finance from industrialists.

(2) He formed different groups called "Fascios" (groups of bonds) who were used to organize violence against socialists and communists. They wore a black uniform and were known as Black – Shirts. They adopted 'Fasces' as their symbol. These volunteers believed in violence and took over factories, municipalities and police stations. Later on, Mussolini organised them into the Fascist Party.

(3) In October 1922, a conference of the Fascist Party was held at Naples, which was attended by about 40,000 armed volunteers. In this conference, Mussolini announced that if his demands were not fulfilled, he would attack Rome with his volunteers.

The demands put forward by Mussolini included the following :

(1) Five members of the Fascist party to be included in the Cabinet;
(2) New elections to be announced;
(3) The government should act firmly on its foreign Policy; and
(4) Economic reforms to be implemented as early as possible.
(5) The Italian Government turned down these demands and Mussolini decided to March towards Rome. The March took place in October 1922. The

Government of Italy did not show any signs of resistance. Emperor Victor Emmanuel III invited Mussolini to form a new government, which he did.

(6) Mussolini appointed Fascists as Perfects in provinces and chief officers in the department of Police and Administration. He organised the national army which included the armed youth of the Fascist Party.

(7) The takeover of the government by Fascists was followed by a reign of terror. Within a short time, Mussolini became the absolute master of Italy. Victor Emmanuel was still the king. Mussolini governed by plain orders or decrees.

(8) The Victory of Fascism in Italy was neither the result of a victory in elections nor of a popular uprising. The government of Italy was handed over to the Fascists because the ruling classes of Italy considered democracy and socialism as threats to their power.

(9) Mussolini used to say "Italy must expand or perish". He regained the Islands of Rhodes Dodecanese (which were ceded to Greece) as well as the city of Fiume. He turned Albania into a protectorate of Italy. He entered into commercial and diplomatic treaties with France and Russia. He captured Abyssinia in 1936 and when there was an objection in the League of Nations, Italy left the League of Nations. After that, Italy's relations with England and France deteriorated and she was drawn towards Germany.

End of Fascism in Italy

Italy was defeated in the Second World War. The Career and life of Mussolini ended in disgrace. He was deposed by his own party Council. In April 1945, he was executed ending Fascism in Italy.

Impact of Fascism

Initially, Italy benefitted a lot under the Fascist regime but in longer run, it proved quite disastrous for Italy and her people. The following were the Consequences of Fascism:

(1) Mussolini fully devoted himself to make Italy a powerful nation and he carried out administrative and economic reforms. He devaluated the Italian currency, set up hydroelectric power plants to overcome the shortage of cool. He brought more lands under cultivation and tried to improve and expand the transport system.

(2) All factories and mills were nationalized to reduce unemployment and to improve the lot of workers. Various syndicates were established to improve relations between the capitalists and the workers. He started an impressive public works programme which included the building of roads, bridges, canals, railways, schools, hospitals, etc.

(3) Many new schools, colleges and libraries were set up to eradicate Illiteracy by making provisions for education.

(4) Various steps were taken to increase the Military might of the country. Military training was made compulsory and efforts were made to enhance the Naval Power of Italy to match it with Naval Power of France and Germany.

(5) A Pact (Treaty of Lateran) was made with Pope by Mussolini in 1929. By this Pact the Pope agreed to accept a subordinate position to Mussolini and recognized the Italian Government of Rome. In return Pope was permitted to keep in his possession, the Vatican and the St. Peter's Cathedral under the Pact, the Fascist Government recognized Roman Catholicism religion as the State religion.

(6) Mussolini embarked upon an aggressive Foreign Policy to revive the past glories of the Roman Empire and to make Italy a great nation.

Negative Impacts

Besides all the above positive impacts, there were many negative effects of Fascism in Italy :

(1) All efforts were made to curb political freedom.
(2) After gaining Power, Mussolini become a dictator, and took all the Military and Civil Powers into his own hands.
(3) All parties except the Fascists were banned.
(4) The system of Jury was abolished and special courts were set up where the Fascist Civilian and Military officers were empowered to decide political cases.
(5) Press was censored.
(6) The Freedom of Speech and organising meetings was also prohibited.
(7) Mussolini crushed his opponents brutally.

Example 2. How did Mussolini become the Prime Minister of Italy and when ?

Ans. During March 1922, the king Victor Emmanuel III was forced to invite Mussolini to become the Prime Minister and form his government. The king gradually became a nominal head, while Mussolini become the real ruler of Italy. By 1924, he became all powerful and could govern by just his plain order and decree.

 Caution

➥ *Impact of Fascism should not be mixed with aims of Fascism. Impacts are the consequences left by the Fascism after its rule.*

TOPIC 2

RISE OF NAZISM IN GERMANY

After the First World War, Germany had to face an economic crisis. There was unrest in the country. lawlessness appeared and there were revolts at many places. The weak government could not control the situation. The ruler of Germany Kaiser William II, was compelled to resign and he fled to Holland on November 10, 1918 to save his life. The Communists tried to get Power in their hands, but they failed badly. The Constituent Assembly was formed on January 19, 1919 to frame a new Constitution for Germany. The new Constitution known as 'Weimer Constitution' was introduced on August 10, 1919. It set up a Democratic Republic in Germany. The new Republic had to face many problems. But it could not solve these problems and its failure gave rise to dictatorship (or Nazism) in Germany under the leadership of Adolf Hitler.

Hitler's Rise to Power

Adolf Hitler, an Austrian by birth, had fought in the German army during the First World War and had attained the rank of a corporal. In 1919, he joined a small political group called 'The German Workers Party' which was based in Munich. Soon he became its leader and changed its name to the Nationalist Socialist Party or the Nazi Party.

The Nazi Party had its own army. The army was divided into two groups. One group wore brown shirts and its main function was to save its party members and to break up the meetings of the opposition parties. The other group wore black shirts and its main duty was to save their party leaders. Hitler had planned to capture power through a March on Berlin. He was arrested and jailed, but released long before his term was over, in jail he wrote 'Mein Kampf' (literal meaning 'My Struggle') which expressed some of the most monstrous ideas of the Nazi Movement.

In the elections of 1932, he failed to get a majority in the Reichstag. A coalition government, headed by Von Papen, could not continue for long. President Hindenburg then offered Chancellorship to Hitler who formed his first Nazi Government on January 30, 1933. After President Hindenburg's death, Hitler became President and Chancellor and adopted the designation of 'Fuhrer' (the Leader). Hitler abolished the Constitution and made himself the dictator of Germany.

Fall of Hitler

In the Second World War Germany was totally defeated by the Allied Powers. With Hitler' death in 1945, Nazism came to an end in Germany.

Causes of the Rise of Nazism

The following causes led to the rise of Hitler and the Nazi Party in Germany:

Humiliating Treaty of Versailles

Germany was compelled to sign the Treaty of Versailles by which she had to pay a huge War-indemnity. This treaty was very harsh and humiliating. This created the feeling of dissatisfaction among the people of Germany. They looked down upon the Weiner Republic which had signed such a disgraceful treaty. The Republic was regarded as a symbol of national disgrace. Germany wanted to establish her old prestige. When Hitler assured the Germans about restoring their old prestige, they became his followers.

Economic Crisis

Germany had to face an economic crisis after the First World War. She suffered heavy losses in life and property in the First World War. After the War many soldiers became unemployed. Trade and commerce were also ruined. The workers were thrown out of employment. In 1929, there was a great slump in Europe. It affected Germany also. Germany was in the gap of unemployment and starvation. The Prices rose and value of money declined. The Republic failed to solve the economic crisis. Hitler took advantage of this situation. The Germans believed in Hitler and his promises.

Spread of Communism

Being inspired by the Russian Revolution of 1917, the German Communists also tried to bring about a revolution in Germany. Hitler feared that Germany would become a slave of Russia if Communism spread there. He exposed the destructive results of Communism to his people. He roused the national feeling among the people and instigated them against Communism. Consequently, the workers and the masses joined the Nazi Party in large numbers.

Resurgence of Militant Nationalism

The Germans could not reconcile with the democratic Parliamentary System prevailing in their country. They preferred prestige and glory to liberty and freedom. They felt that only a strong man could restore the past prestige of Germany and check the rising popularity of Communism. When Hitler promised them all glory, they welcomed him with open arms.

Absence of Strong Opposition

The rise of the Nazi Party in Germany was facilitated by the absence of any strong opposition party. As a result, the Nazi Party did not encounter any effective resistance and its popularity achieved great heights.

Personality of Hitler

Hitler possessed a very influential and charming personality. He had all the qualities required for a popular leader. He was a shrewd politician and a brave soldier. He had the art of moulding public opinion in his favour according to the circumstances. He was a first-rate Orator. He was a resourceful person, a tireless worker and an able organizer. His speeches were very effective and had great logic in them. Naturally, the people began to have a blind faith in him and started thinking of him as a great leader. It has been rightly said "of Propaganda he was past master". He told the Germans what they wanted to hear, i.e. the betray of Germany by the Treaty of Versailles and the Jewish – Communist plot to conquer the world.

The Volunteer Corps

German military force had been greatly reduced by the Treaty of Versailles. Many soldiers were rendered surplus and unemployed. Hitler organized the volunteer corps with the help of these soldiers. Hitler crushed the opposition parties with the help of this volunteer corps and later on the greatly organized and strengthened his party with their help.

Anti-Semitic Propaganda

The Anti-Semitic (Anti-Jewish) propaganda carried on by the Nazi Party increased Hitler's popularity. They described the Jews as traitors and blamed them of conspiring with the Allies during the War. They inspired upon the Germans that the cause of their hardships were the Jews who exploited the German economy. As a result, many Germans rallied behind the Nazi Party.

Aims of Nazism

Hitler in his book 'Mein Kampf' (My Struggle) expressed the aims of the Nazi Movement as follows:
(1) To exalt nationalism.
(2) To advocate the rule by a great leader from a single party.
(3) To extol War;
(4) To use force and brutality;
(5) To despise internationalism, peace and democracy.
(6) To uphold the racial supremacy of the Germans and to hate Jews.

Impact of Nazism

(1) Established a Totalitarian State

Hitler had no faith in the Parliamentary system of government. He had set up a strong Central Government with all the Powers concentrated in his hands. The leaders of the Opposition were assassinated or imprisoned. He changed the Federal government into a Unitary government. Various political parties were abolished. A ban was imposed on the Press, Public speeches and writing of articles. A secret police, known as the Gestapo, kept a check on the activities of citizens. Those suspected of disloyalty were arrested or executed without trial.

(2) Economic Reforms

Hitler introduced various reforms to meet the economic crisis after the War. He launched the First Five-Year Plan to have greater production. The economic life of Germany was organised so as to remove unemployment and also become self-sufficient. Workers were given facilities but not the Right to Strike. Hitler freed Germany from the economic crisis and put an end the problem of unemployment. The Industrial Production almost doubled and the Foreign Trade also expanded.

(3) Militarism and Compulsory Military Training

Special efforts were made to increase the military force of the country. Military training was made compulsory which again created more employment. Ships, aeroplanes and other war materials were produced. Treaty of Versailles was violated, by starting rearmament.

(4) Repudiated Peace Treaties

The main objective of Hitler's Foreign Policy was to reject the Treaty of Versailles, which had humiliated Germany. Hitler openly condemned the Treaty of Versailles. He refused to pay the War indemnity as stipulated under the Treaty of Versailles. He even restored to the policy of territorial expansion and fortification of Germany in complete violation of the Treaty.

(5) Acquisition of Territories

Hitler tried to acquire more territories for the Surplus German population. He Hitler reclaimed Saar from France, German troops re-entered the Rhineland and reclaimed from France. Hitler tried to expand in South and East of Europe because that region was economically useful for Germany as it possessed huge potential for wheat, oil and coal. To attain this objective, Hitler made use of force and rejected all compromises. He entered into a non-aggression treaty with Poland for a period of ten years in 1934 for the safety of his eastern frontiers. In 1938, he annexed Austria by force. He concluded a Non-Aggression Pact with Russia. Hitler concluded treaties with Italy and Japan against Communists, helped Gen France (along with Mussolini) to become Dictator in Spain. Germany joined Italy and Japan in an Alliance known as Berlin-Rome-Tokyo Axis. Hitler conquered one country after another like Denmark, Norway, Luxemburg and Belgium. Hitler succeeded in occupying a part of Czechoslovakia in 1938.

(6) Racial Supremacy

Hitler believed in the Doctrine of Racialism, which presented Germans as the "Master race" with the right and destiny to dominate the world. He wanted Germany to cleanse itself from the contamination by Jews, Christians and Communists. Jews were deprived of German Citizenship, removed from government service, prohibited from practising most professions in the beginning. Later plans were executed to exterminate the Jews. Their shops and houses were looted. Jews were sent to concentration camps. Thousands were killed churches were controlled. All Protestors were sent to concentration camps. The Nazi Party considered Germany superior to all other nations and wanted to have her influence all over the world.

(7) Negative Aspects

Hitler put an end to civil liberties. Those who were suspected of opposing him were treated harshly. Strict Censor was imposed on Books, the Press and the Cinema. All Anti-Nazi Books and Magazines were consigned to fire.

(8) Education

Education was given according to principles of Nazism and the minds of children were completely influenced.

Example 3. Mention the two humiliating terms of the Treaty of Versailles towards Germany.

Ans. (1) Germany was forced to pay the cost of War, called War-indemnity of about 33 billion Dollars to the victor nations.
(2) Germany was to evacuate the places she had captured during the War.

 Related Theory
→ The Germans resented the humiliating and insulting behaviour meted out to them by the Allies and wanted to avenge the same. Hitler openly encouraged the Germans to consign the Treaty of Versailles into the waste-paper basket, rebuild the German empire and to recapture the lost colonies. He assured the Germans that if they would abide by the Nazi Ideology their economic misery would come to an end.

 Caution
→ Topic of Treaty of Versailles should be studied carefully because it was the main cause for the Rise of Nazism in Germany.

 Important
→ The name of Hitler's Biography was 'Mein Kampf' which means (My Struggle) was written by Hitler in jail which expressed most monstrous ideas of the Nazi Movement and aims of Nazism.

TOPIC 3

COMPARATIVE STUDY OF FASCISM AND NAZISM

Similarity Between the Causes of Fascism and Nazism

(1) **Treaty of Versailles:** Both were discontented after the treaty.
(2) **Economic Crisis:** There was unemployment and decline in production in agriculture and trade.
(3) **Hatred for democratic principles:** Both had hatred for democratic principles and they preferred for totalitarian system and one-party rule.
(4) **Fear of Communism:** Both had fear of the spread of Communism.
(5) **Political instability:** In both countries there was Political instability and class conflict between the aristocrats and the common people.
(6) Failure of the League of Nation was common issue.
(7) Leadership was provided by Mussolini in Italy and Hitler in Germany.

Similarity Between the Ideologies of fascism and Nazism :

(1) To have faith in the totalitarian rule.
(2) To despise democratic political system.
(3) To hold that the State in supreme and it could suppress the fundamental rights and freedoms of individuals.
(4) To uphold one-party and one leader.
(5) To believe in aggressive nationalism and imperialism.
(6) To regard war as an instrument for furthering national interests.
(7) To uphold intensely nationalistic, anti-communists and anti-democratic rule.

Example 4. Mention any two common factors in Italy and Germany.
Ans. (1) The Peace Treaties after the War were dissatisfactory and humiliating for both the countries.
(2) The Political and economic situations of both the countries were linked and identical like problems of unemployment, price-rise, inflation, etc.

 Caution
→ Common factors are common causes responsible for the Rise of Fascism and Rise of Nazism. Students can quote any two common reasons between two countries.

 ICSE Suggestions
→ Students should know the correct meaning of word 'Facism' because it is related to both the topics like 'Causes

Rise of Dictatorships 227

for the rise of "Fascism' and 'Fascism in Italy'. Students should avoid wrong meaning.

→ Topics of Fascism and Nazism have to be read in details to answer all questions related to them. Students should study them in sub-topics by making short notes of topics.

→ Students are advised to read their text-books carefully and underline important quotes, which will help them in answering these type of questions.

Glossary

(1) **Dictatorship:** Dictatorship is an anti-thesis of democracy. It is a rule by a dictator who has got total power of a country which he rules without popular consent.
(2) **Dasces :** Bundle of rods tied together, signifying unity, strength and authority.
(3) **Fascios :** groups or bonds
(4) **Reichstag :** The Parliament (Lower House of the Legislature building of Germany which was set on fire by the Nazis).
(5) **Gestapo :** A secret Police of Germany which kept a check on the activities of citizens.
(6) **Fuhrer :** the leader
(7) **Chancellors :** Prime Ministers
(8) **Pope :** The head of the Roman Catholic Church.

Who's Who?

(1) **Benito Mussolini :** The Fascist leader belonging to Italy.
(2) **Adolf Hitler :** The Nazi leader of Germany.

Who Said What?

(1) All Parties must end, must fall. I want to see a Panorama of ruins around me, the ruins of the other political forces so that Fascism may stand gigantic and dominant". —Benito Mussolini
(2) "Italy must expand or Perish" —Mussolini
(3) "Germany within her existing frontiers could attain only limited self-sufficiency in raw materials and none at all in foodstuffs. The only remedy lay in the acquisition of greater living space ...."
—Adolf Hitler

Chronology

1921: Elections in Italy
1922: Rise of Mussolini in Italy
28th October, 1922: Mussolini organized a March at Rome.
29th October, 1922: Mussolini was invited by the king of Italy to join the government
April 1945: Mussolini was executed
30th January, 1933: Hitler become the Chancellor of Germany. He formed the Nazi Government in Germany.

OBJECTIVE Type Questions

Multiple Choice Questions-I
[1 mark each]

1. Fascism and Nazism did NOT believe in:
   (a) Democratic political system
   (b) Opposition to the rights and liberties of people
   (c) Rule of one party and one leader
   (d) Totalitarian rule   [HOT]

   Ans. (a) Democratic political system
   Explanation: Both Fascism and Nazism were against democratic political system.

2. Which of the following was not a common ideology of the dictators?
   (a) Faith in totalitarian rule
   (b) One party and One Leader

(c) Faith in Communism
(d) Aggressive Nationalism and Imperialism
[ICSE Sem-2, 2021]

Ans. *(c) Faith in communism*

Explanation: The dictators wanted to uphold anti-communist and anti-democratic rule.

 Related Theory

→ The common ideologies of the dictators were:
(1) Faith in totalitarian rule.
(2) Believed in state supremacy.
(3) One party and one leader.
(4) Aggressive nationalism and imperialism.
(5) Regarded war as instrument of national interests.
(6) Anti-communist and anti-democratic rule.

3. Which of the following was not a similarity between Fascism and Nazism?
   (a) Fundamental Rights and Individual freedom
   (b) Corporatism and Racism
   (c) Aggressive nationalism and imperialism
   (d) Anti-communist and anti-democratic rule

Ans. *(b) Corporatism and Racism*

Explanation: Fascism believed in the 'Corporatism' of all elements in the society to form an organic state, while Nazism emphasised on racism.

4. Totalitarian Dictatorship under different names was formed in Russia, ...
   (a) Italy   (b) Germany
   (c) Spain   (d) All of the above

Ans. *(d) All of the above*

Explanation: Totalitarian Dictatorships were formed under different names in Russia, Italy, Germany and Spain.

 Related Theory

→ The motto of all Totalitarian Dictatorships and their countries were "Everything for the State, everything within the State and nothing outside the State".

5. Which of the following is NOT the meaning of Fascism?
   (a) Union or league
   (b) Bundle of sticks bound to an axe
   (c) Autocracy or dictatorship
   (d) Freedom   [HOT🔥]

Ans. *(d) Freedom*

Explanation: The word 'Fascism' has derived from the Italian word fascio which means union or league. It also refers to the ancient Roman symbol of Power; the fascis was a bundle of sticks bound to an axe that symbolized the unity and authority of Roman officials to punish wrongdoer and also Fascism means autocracy or dictatorship. It does not mean Freedom.

6. Between 1919 and 1922 .... coalition governments were formed in Italy.
   (a) three   (b) five
   (c) six   (d) four

Ans. *(c) six*

Explanation: Democracy was introduced in Italy for the first time in 1919. Elections failed to give a majority to a single party. As a result, there was complete instability in the country and between 1919 and 1922 six coalition governments were formed in Italy.

⚠️ **Caution**

→ A few of students have written wrong answer, they are confused between different terms like socialists, communists, etc, students are advised to know the meanings of all the terms, before their correct usage.

7. The .... began to devise new plans of overthrowing the government and capturing power.
   (a) Socialists   (b) Communists
   (c) Anarchists   (d) Social Democrats

Ans. *(b) Communists*

Explanation: The Communists began to devise new plans of overthrowing the government and capturing power. People wanted a powerful leadership who could establish peace and prosperity by ending lawlessness and insecurity prevalent in Italy.

8. Which were the demands put forward by Mussolini in the Conference?
   (a) Five members of the Fascist Party to be included in the Cabinet.
   (b) New elections to be announced.
   (c) Economic reforms to be implemented as early as possible .
   (d) All of the above

Ans. *(d) All of the above*

Explanation: The demands put forward by Mussolini also included the government should act firmly on its foreign policy besides all above said demands in (a), (b), & (c) points.

9. Who said the following? "Italy must expand or Perish".
   (a) Victor Emmanuel III
   (b) Victor Emmanuel II
   (c) Benito Mussolini
   (d) Adolf Hitler   [HOT🔥]

Ans. *(c) Benito Mussolini*

Explanation: Mussolini believed in regaining territories from neighbouring countries and expanding boundaries of Italy. He regained Islands of Rhodes, Dodecanese, Fiume, etc.

⚠️ **Caution**
→ Many students have answered this question correctly, but few of them have written wrong answers by overlooking 'Who said What' and important quotes of leaders and politicians.

10. What is the Lower House of the Legislative called in Germany?
    (a) Reichstag   (b) Fuhrer
    (c) Duce   (d) Parliament House

Ans. (a) Reichstag

11. Adolf Hitler was .... by birth.
    (a) German   (b) Polish
    (c) Austrian   (d) Jewish

Ans. (c) Austrian
    Explanation: Adolf Hitler was born in Austria, but he fought in the German Army during the First World War and had attained the rank of corporal and by joining. "The German Workers Party" he became famous leader.

12. Complete the following Analogy:
    Brown Shirts : to save its party members ? : : to save their party leaders
    (a) Blue Shirts   (b) Black Shirts
    (c) Green Shirts   (d) Red Shirts   [HOT]

Ans. (b) Black Shirts
    Explanation: The Nazi Party had its own army. The army was divided into two groups. One group were Brown shirts and its main function was to save its party members and to break up the meetings of the opposition parties. The other group wore black shirts and its main duty was to save their party leaders.

13. What were the causes for the Rise of Nazism?
    (i) Humiliating Treaty of Versailles
    (ii) Economic Crisis
    (iii) Growing Fear of Communism
    (iv) Anti-Semitic Propanganda
    Options:
    (a) (i) and (ii)   (b) (ii) and (iii)
    (c) (i), (ii) and (iv) (d) (i), (ii), (iii) and (iv)

Ans. (d) (i), (ii), (iii) and (iv)
    Explanation: Causes for the Rise of Nazism were many, but above said Humiliating Treaty of Versailles, Economic Crisis, Growing fear of Communism and Anti-Semitic Propanganda were also some of the affected factors.

14. Hitler was a charismatic personality, he had qualities of ....
    (a) shrewd politician
    (b) brave soldier
    (c) gifted orator
    (d) All of the above

Ans. (b) Shrewd Politician
    Explanation: Hitler had all the qualities of a popular leader. He was a Shrewd Politician, brave soldier also he was a gifted orator who captivated Germans by his emotional speeches.

15. Hitler believed in the doctrine of racialism, he wanted Germany to cleanse itself of the contamination of:
    (a) Jews
    (b) Jews, Christians
    (c) Jews, Christians and Communists
    (d) None of the above

Ans. (c) Jews, Christians and Communists
    Explanation: Hitler believed in the doctrine of racialism which presented Germans as the "Master Peace" with the right and destiny to dominate the world. For this he wanted Germany to cleanse itself of the contamination by Jews, Christians and Communists.

💡 **Related Theory**
→ Nazi racial ideology was based on Adolf Hittler's antisemitic, racist ideas. In his book 'Mein Kampf (1925), Hitler explained his racist worldview.

Multiple Choice Question-II
(Other Question Types, for Extra Practice)

[**4** marks each]

16. Study the picture carefully and answer the following questions:

(A) Benito Mussolini was a Dictator of:
    (a) France   (b) Italy
    (c) Germany   (d) Spain

(B) Fascist supported:
    (a) One party and one leader
    (b) Many parties and many leaders
    (c) One party and few leaders
    (d) One Party and many leaders

(C) A conference of the Fascist Party was held at .... in October 1922.
    (a) Munich   (b) Venice
    (c) Italy   (d) Naples

(D) Mussolini was also called ....
(a) Emperor   (b) Duce
(c) Fuhrer   (d) Master

Ans. (A) *(b) Italy*

Explanation: Benito Mussolini was an Italian Political leader who become Fascist Dictator of Italy from 1925 to 1945?

(B) *(a) One-party and one leader*

Explanation: They believed that the country could make progress leaders under one party and one leader.

(C) *(d) Naples*

Explanation: A conference of the Fascist Party was held at Naples in October 1922. It was attended by about 40,000 armed volunteers.

(D) *(b) Duce*

Explanation: Mussolini had a charismatic personality. His speeches praised the Past glories of Italy and he won the forth of his countrymen. He was also called 'Duce' which means the Leader.

SUBJECTIVE Type Questions

Short Answer Type Questions

[2 marks each]

17. Mention the dictatorships that emerged in Europe after the First World War. [HOT]

Ans. Nazism in Germany and Fascism in Italy emerged after the First World War.

18. State two cause for the rise of Fascism in Italy.

Ans. The dissatisfaction with the Treaty of Versailles and failure of league of nations two main cause of rise of Fascism in Italy.

19. Which two countries were mainly dissatisfied with the Treaty of Versailles?

Ans. Germany and Italy were mainly dissatisfied with the Treaty of Versailles.

20. What is meant by Nazism?

Ans. Nazism is a set of political beliefs associated with the Nazi party of Germany.

21. Give any two reasons for the rise of Fascism. [ICSE 2020]

Ans. The reasons for the rise of Fascism were:
(1) Discontentment after the Treaty of Versailles.
(2) Political instability and economic crisis in Italy.

> Rise of fascism:
> (1) Discontentment after the Treaty of Versailles/Italy got nothing from the spoils of the war
> (2) Economic crisis
> (3) Political instability/Inefficient government/weak government/failure of democracy
> (4) Class conflicts
> (5) Threat of socialism or communism
> (6) Failure of the league of nations
> (7) Leadership provided by Mussolini.
> [Any two]
> [Marking Scheme]

What Examiners Say
→ Most candidates answer this question correctly. However, a few did not write the reasons for the rise of Fascism

22. Give any two similarities between the ideologies of Nazism and Fascism. [HOT] [ICSE 2018]

Ans. The similarities between Nazims and Fascisms were:
(1) Both were anti-communist and wanted to prevent the spread of communism.
(2) Both laid stress on nationalism and shunned individual institutions. They favoured equal control over all sections of society viz. capitalists, industrialists, labourers, peasants, etc.

> Faith in Totalitarian rule (dictatorship), to despise democracy, communism, socialism, internationalism. One party one leader, Belief in aggressive nationalism, imperialism, war, policy of expansion, believe in supremacy of state rather than individual use of force. Anti-intellectualism, belief in racial supremacy.
> [Any two]
> [Marking Scheme]

What Examiners Say
→ Many candidates mixed up the causes and ideologies of Nazism and Fascism with the causes that led to the rise of dictatorship in Germany and Italy.

23. What is the meaning of 'Fascism'? [ICSE 2015]

Ans. The word 'Fascism' is derived from the Latin word Fascios, which means a "bundle or union of

Rise of Dictatorships

rods". The fascios, which consisted of a bundle of rods tied around an axe, was an ancient Roman symbol which suggested strength through unity; Fascism was an extreme right wing totalitarian nationalist and corporatist ideology which assumed its height under the leadership of Benito Mussolini. Fascism was much influenced by the ideas of thinkers who believed that state is more than a collection of citizens and has an organic life of its own. For a fascist, everything is the state; nothing else exists outside the state. Fascism, therefore, was a right-wing collectivistic ideology in opposition, to socialism, liberalism, and democracy. The fascists believed in having a powerful dictatorship by controlling all aspects of life of the citizens.

24. Give two similarities in the foreign policies of Mussolini and Hitler. [ICSE 2012]

Ans. The similarities in the foreign policies of Mussolini and Hitler were:
(1) Both Mussolini and Hitler aimed to restore the status and past glory of their respective nations.
(2) Both felt that the Treaty of Versailles was unjust to their respective countries and wanted to undo the treaty. They regarded war as a fair instrument for furthering national interests and thus favoured on aggressive foreign policy.

25. Define Dictatorship.

Ans. Dictatorship is an anti-thesis of democracy. It is a rule by a 'dictator' who has got total power of a country which he rules without popular consent. It gives no rights to people, tolerates neither opposition nor criticism. It envisages one party rule, controlled by one leader with complete authority. The individual, his freedom, his thinking one controlled by the state.

26. Mention the two important causes of the rise of Fascism.

Ans. (1) Economic crisis
(2) Dissatisfaction over humiliating peace treaties.

27. What did Mussolini do to restore law and order in Italy? [HOT🔥]

Ans. Mussolini restored law and order by banning all other Political Parties except his own Fascist Party.

28. Name Hitler's autobiography and where did he write it?

Ans. Hitler's autobiography was named Mein Kampf (My Strength). He wrote it in jail when he was arrested in 1923 for 5 years.

29. Why did the League of Nations failed to keep Dictators under control?

Ans. Many nations thought that this institution was framed during the Treaty of Versailles and so was not just. Then they ignored the League of Nations like Italy and Germany.

30. What do you know about the Enabling Laws?

Ans. The Enabling laws allowed the government to make laws without the majority support in the Reichstag. It curbed all the rights of the people.

31. How did Mussolini become the Prime Minister of Italy and When?

Ans. During March 1922, King Victor Emmanuel III was forced to invite Mussolini to become Prime Minister and form his government. The king gradually became a nominal head, while Mussoliuni became the real ruler of Italy. By 1924, he become powerful and control govern Italy by just his Plain order and decree.

Structured Questions

[3+3+4= **10** marks each]

32. With reference to the rise of Hitler in Germany, answer the following questions :
(A) Why did the Nazi Party become very popular in Germany?
(B) What do you know about Germany under the Nazi party?
(C) What are the basic features of Nazism?

Ans. (A) The Nazi Party became popular in Germany as this seemed to be a strong alternative to weak democratic governments which had failed to solve the problems after the First World War.

(B) (1) Under the Nazis, Germany become like a Police State. The media was state controlled. A strong central government, with Hitler as its head, was established. Opposition was completely crushed.

(2) Unemployment was removed, economically Germany did well. It became self-sufficient. But the right to strike was not enjoyed by the workers. Education was also state controlled. Compulsory military service was started. Treaty of Versailles was forgotten and new Germany produced military equipment.

(3) At the same time the Jews were segregated, removed from government employment. They lost their German Citizenship and thousand lost their lives.

Many were sent to concentration camps never to be seen again.
(C) The basic features of Nazism were:
(1) Nazism believed that the state is above all. National interest demanded sacrifice from all classes of people to make Germany a great nation.
(2) All powers should be with the State – end- Parliamentary institutions, control education, Press and Radio.
(3) Hitler believed that the interest and right of individuals were subordinate to the interest of the State. In other words, the State could interfere in the people's lives to discipline them.
(4) Nazism wanted to crush opposition, remove communism, to mobilize efforts to improve agriculture and industry.
(5) They looked at Jews as a cause of economic leaderships of the people and wanted to turn them out of Germany. Betrayal by Jews during the First World War they believed, had made Germany lose the war. Hitler, in fact, believed that Aryans were the most superior race in the world and that Germans were pure Aryans.
(6) Nazis denounced the Treaty of Versailles and wanted to regain the Empire. Hitler believed that a nation became great by defeating other nations. **[Any four]**

33. With the rise of Fascism in Italy, answer the following questions:
(A) What were the two main complaints of the people about the working of the democratic government in Italy?
(B) Why were the Italians dissatisfied with Treaty of Versailles?
(C) What is meant by Mussolini's famous March to Rome in 1922? **[HOT]**

Ans. (A) (1) The government of Italy was not interested in solving the problems of the country and failed to keep the situation under control.
(2) There were frequent strikes. The workers broke the machinery and captured the factories. The Industrialists were sick of these strikes. They wanted a strong leader to handle the crisis.
(B) Italians were dissatisfied with the Treaty of Versailles because they had joined the First World War on the side of Britain and France in 1915. Italy hoped to get large territories such as Trentino, Triesto, Istria, Fiune, Coastal regions of Dalmatia, Albania and some parts of Germany and Turkey after their Victory. But the Paris Peace Treaties gave her nothing from the defeated German and Turkish empires. So, Italians developed a feeling that they "had won the war, but lost the peace".
(C) Seeing the disorder caused by Communists in 9122, Mussolini organised his March to Rome. Thousands of the Fascist armed men, who wore black-uniform and were called as Black-shirts, believing in violence, attacked Rome on October 27, 1922. They took over Police Stations, Municipalities and factories and whatever came their way. King Victor Emmanuel III was forced to invite Mussolini to become Prime Minister and make the government. The king gradually became the nominal head, while Mussolini the Ruler of Italy.

34.

(A) Identify the leader in the picture. Give two examples to state that the leader followed an expansionist policy.
(B) State three factors that led to the rise of Fascism. **[ICSE 2019]**
(C) State four similarities between the ideologies of Nazism and Fascism.
[HOT] [ICSE 2016]

Ans. (A) The leader in the picture is Benito Mussolini. The examples that state that he followed an expansionist policy are:
(1) Military training and service were made mandatory to increase the nation's military power and the navy too received attention and funds to bring it at par with those of France and Germany.
(2) Mussolini annexed Ethiopia in 1936 and Albania in 1939
(B) The reasons for the rise of Fascism in Italy were:
(1) **Dissatisfaction with the Treaty of Versailles:** Italy had joined hands with

France and Britain against Germany and her allies in the First World War as Britain had promised large territorial gains to her, if and when the victory comes. But the Treaty of Versailles only partially fulfilled that promise. Moreover, Italy had lost 7,00,000 soldiers in the war and there was a widespread feeling of disappointment and discontent.

(2) **Economic Crisis:** At the end of the war, thousands of soldiers were discharged from the army and were unemployed. The Italian economy was not only unable to recover from the post war losses but also was unable to provide jobs for the unemployed youth.

(3) **Inefficient and Corrupt Democratic Government:** A full-fledged Parliamentary system of government based on voting rights for adult male citizens was introduced in Italy for the first time in year 1919. Democracy was thus a new experiment in the politics of Italy. No single party got a clear-cut majority and Italy was governed by a series of six coalition governments that functioned only for short durations and were unable to deal effectively with the problems of unemployment, strikes and riots post World War I.

(4) **Rise of Totalitarian Ideologies:** The philosophy of Hegel flourished in Italy. Hegelians justified an authoritarian regime. The success of Russian Revolution of 1917 and the ideas of one-party rule and totalitarian concepts appealed to the masses in Italy.

(5) **Failure of the League of Nations:** The League of Nations, formed at the end of the First World War, for maintaining peace and war amongst nations, failed miserably in its purpose. **[Any three]**

(C) The similarities between the ideologies of Nazism and Fascism were:

(1) Both Nazism and Fascisim did not believe in democracy and personal stated liberty.
(2) Both laid great emphasis on the ruthless organisation of all aspects of the lives of the masses under the Central Government. The State was supreme and the interests of the individual always considered second to the interests of the State.
(3) Both believed in Nationalism as a driving force for the people of their country.
(4) Both propagated the belief that nations become great only be defeating other nations in war.
(5) Both were intensely anti-communist.
[Any four]

(A) Benito Mussolini.
(1) Mussolini used to say "Italy must expand or perish."
(2) He regained the Islands of Rhodes.
(3) Dodecanese (ceded to Greece) as well as the city of Fiume.
(4) He turned Albania into a protectorate of Italy.
(5) Entered into commercial and diplomatic treaties with France and Russia.
(6) Captured Abyssinia in 1936.
(7) Italy was drawn towards Germany. **[Any two]**

(B) Factors:
(1) Discontentment after the Treaty of Versailles.
(2) Economic Crisis.
(3) Political Instability.
(4) Class conflicts.
(5) Threat of Socialism and Communism.
(6) Failure of League of Nations.
(7) Leadership provided by Mussolini. **[Any three]**

(C) Four similarities:
(1) Faith in Totalitarian rule (Dictatorship).
(2) to despise democratic political system.
(3) State is supreme and could suppress Fundamental Rights and freedom of individuals.
(4) to uphold one party-one leader.
(5) Believed in aggressive Nationalism and Imperialism.
(6) Extol war, believed in Aggressives Foreign policy.
(7) Anti-Communist, anti-Socialist, anti-Democratic.
[Any four]
[Marking Scheme]

What Examiners Say

→ (A) Most candidates correctly identified the leader in the picture. Only a few incorrectly identified the leader as Hitler. However, candidates could not explain the expansionist policy of Mussolini.

→ (B) Some candidates mentioned the principles of Fascism and not the factors that led the rise of Fascism as asked in the question.

↳ *(C) Answered correctly by most candidates though some failed to mention all four similarities.*

35.

Study the picture given above and answer the following questions:
(A) Identify the leader in the picture.
(B) State any four factors that led to the rise of dictatorships in Germany and Italy.
(C) Why did he invade Poland? State similarities between Fascism and Nazism. [ICSE 2013]

Ans. (A) The leader in the picture is Adolf Hitler.

(B) The factors that led to the rise of dictatorships in Germany and Italy were:

(1) **Discontentment with the Treaty of Verssailles:** Italy had joined hands with France and Britain against Germany and her allies, in the First World War as Britain has promised large territorial gains to her, if and when the victory comes. But the Treaty of Versailles only partially fulfilled that promise. On the other hand, the Treaty of Versailles had imposed very harsh terms on Germany. She had to pay heavy war indemnity.

(2) **Economic Crisis:** The Italian economy was not only unable to recover from the post war losses but was also unable to provide jobs for the unemployed youth. After the war, Germany suffered from economic anaemia. unemployment, hunger and starvation became the order of the day.

(3) **Political Instability:** A full-fledged parliamentary system of government based on voting rights for adult male citizens was introduced in Italy for the first time in the year 1919. No single party got a clear-cut majority and Italy was governed by a series of six coalition governments. In Germany, there was lack of respect for democratic government and great admiration for the army.

(4) **Rise of Totalitarian Ideologies:** The philosophhy of Hegel flourished in Italy. Hegelians justified an authoritarian regime. In fact, the irrational and anti-intellectualists philosophy of Alfred Rocco also got an upper hand. The ideas of one-party rule and totalitarian concepts appealed to the masses in Italy and Germany.

(C) Hitler was demanding Danzig corridor as the city of Danzig was inhabited mainly by the Germans and secondly by occupying the Danzig corridor, he could link East Prussia with Germany. Poland was accused of committing attrocities against the Germans living there. This is why Hitler invaded Poland.

The similarities between Fascisms and Nazims were:

(1) Both aimed to restore the status and past glory of their respective nations.
(2) Both were anti-communist and wanted to prevent the spread of communism in their respective countries.
(3) Both wanted to solve the post war economic crisis and provide employment to the people.
(4) Both aimed to provide a strong and stable government. According to them, dictatorship was the best form of government and progress could be assured by working under one leader only.
(5) Both Nazism and Fascism did not believe in democracy and personal stated liberty.

36. In the Post-World War I Scenario, Italy and Germany experienced the rise of Dictatorship. In this context, explain:
(A) Any three circumstances that led to the rise of Fascism in Italy.
(B) Any three domestic policies of Hitler.
(C) How the foreign policies of Hitler were responsible for the outbreak of the World War II?

Ans. (A) Circumstances that led to the rise of Fascism in Italy:

(1) **Dissatisfaction with Treaty of Versailles:** Italy had joined the Anglo-French Alliance against Germany and its allies in the First World War, as Britain had promised large parts of territory after their victory. This Promise was not kept as they had only two islands in the Adviatic and Aegean Seas. The Italians were also feeling unhappy. Mussolini, who had supported Italy's fight with the British and French, was very dissatisfied.

Rise of Dictatorships

(2) **Economic Factors:** Thousands of soldiers in Italy became unemployed. Industrialisation had not progressed and unemployment was on the alarming rise. Even the working class felt the blow of inflation with less wages and poor working conditions. There were frequent strikes and agrarian riots. Italy seemed to be heading towards communism. The Industrialised were alarmed and financed the Fascists to stop breakout.

(3) **Inefficient Government:** Democracy was introduced in Italy in 1919. No single Party could win a majority. There were short-unemployment, strikes, riots, etc. the Aristocrats believed that only a strong leader absolute power could restore peace and stability in the society.

(B) **Domestic Policies of Hitler:**

(1) **Aggressive Nationalism:** The State is above all and all powers should vest with the state. All classes of people should make whatever sacrifices required of them to make their country a Great nation.

(2) **Destruction of Democracy:** The Basis of administration was one party, one leader. The common people had no Freedom of Speech and Expression.

(a) They had no right to form associations and trade unions.

(b) Capitalists had all the opportunities to grow and earn profits. The working conditions of workers were miserable.

(c) In Germany, a secret police, known as the Gestapo kept a check on the activities of all the citizens.

(3) **Compulsory Military:** Hitler believed that Nations became great only by defeating other nations in War. He started rearmament in violation of the Treaty of Versailles.

(4) **Hitler's Treatment of Jews:** Hitler deprived the Jews of German Citizenship and removed them from the government services. Their properties were confiscated concentration camps were established by the Nazis in Germany. According to Hitler, the policy of Genocide (mass killing) was the final and only solution to the Jewish problem.

[Any three]

(C) Hitler's Policies were responsible for the outbreak of the World war-II.

(1) Hitler ignored the Treaty of Versailles and occupied the Rhineland that had been demilitarized by the Treaty of Versailles.

(2) There was rearmament and compulsory military service.

(3) When France refused to bring down its own level of military equipment as per the Treaty of Versailles, Hitler also withdrew from the Disarmament Conference.

(4) Hitler and Mussolini came closer to each other.

(5) Tripatite Pact between Japan and Germany became the Rome-Berlin-Tokyo Axis. They entered into an agreement to help each other if a fourth power attacked them. **[Any four]**

12 The Second World War

The unjust clauses of the "Treaty of Versailles" of Germany bred the germs for the Second World War. The League of Nations failed to stop the next war which was more devastating then the First World War. The damage caused by this war surpassed all other wars and brought the world to complete destruction.

Chapter Notes

- *Causes of the Second World War*
- *Consequences of the Second World War*

TOPIC 1

CAUSES OF THE SECOND WORLD WAR

Introduction

The First World War came to an end in 1918. The World heaved a sigh of relief but it was not known that after 20 years there would be another War which would be even more disastrous then the first one. The League of Nations failed to establish peace in the world. When Hitler came to power in Germany, he refused to accept the Treaty of Versailles. He started the expansion of his empire and increased his military power. Soon Europe was divided into two rival groups as a result of his aggressive policy. The cold war began and in 1939 it culminated in the Second World War.

Causes of the Second World War

The following were the chief causes of the Second World War:

Dissatisfaction with the Treaty of Versailles

The Treaty of Versailles, by which the first World War came to an end, was one sided. It was very harsh. It was a dictated peace and Germany was forced to sign it. The defeated nations, especially Germany had to cede many of her territories, and all her colonies were forcibly taken away from her. Germany was divided into two parts for the benefit of Poland. She was burdened with huge War – indemnity which she could never pay. Her military power was considerably reduced. The treatment meted out to her was based on the spirit of revenge. Consequently, that treaty created hatred in the minds of the Germans. It was a black spot for the Germans and they wanted to wash it away. This could never be done without armament and as such war became quite inevitable.

Rise of Fascism and Nazism

The rise of extreme nationalism in Italy and Germany in the form of Fascism and Nazism, respectively contributed to the causes which led to the Second World War. Italy wanted to revive the glory of the old Roman Empire. She joined the Anti-Comintern Pact in 1937 and formed a ten years alliance with Germany in 1939 to strengthen her position. Mussolini established Dictatorship in Italy. He opposed the Treaty of Versailles. Italy demonstrated her imperialistic designs by attacking Abyssinia. The League of Nations failed to take any action against Italy, which exhibited the weakness of the League.

In Germany, Hitler wanted to re-establish the prestige of Germany in the international field. He flouted the military clauses in the Treaty of Versailles and declared re-armament. In 1938, he annexed Austria and dismembered erstwhile Czechoslovakia. Thus, Mussolini and Hitler drove the countries of the World towards another World War.

Japanese Policy of Expansion

Invasion of China: another cause of the War was the Japanese policy of expansion. The ambitions of Japan increased after the First World War. Though, Japan and China fought on the side of the Allies then China. She developed her Navy and by 1930, she greatly increased her strength. In 1931, she attacked China and Seized Manchuria. Again, there was a war between Japan and China in 1937. Many Chinese cities fell into the hands of the Japanese. During the Second world War Japan joined the Rome-Berlin-Tokyo-Axis and entered the War in 1941 to satisfy her hunger for more territories.

Failure of the League of Nations

The League of Nations was created after the First World War to maintain international Peace and security and to prevent any future Wars; but the League became ineffective against the powerful aggressors. The economic sanctions were useless against the aggressor. Besides, the member states were not eager to apply economic sanctions as it affected their economy too. The League's authority was ignored when Italy occupied Ethiopia and Japan captured Manchuria. The League did nothing when Poland, with the backing of France, seized a part of Lithuania in 1920. In 1923 there was a threat of war between Italy and Greece. Italy refused to submit to the League's intervention and the dispute was settled by direct mediation of Great Britain and France. Moreover, the members of the League were not interested in the 'Principle of Collective Security". Different countries of Europe lost faith in the League of Nations as it failed to maintain international Peace.

Hitler's Invasion of Poland (Immediate Cause)

Hitler invaded Poland in September 1939 for the following reasons:

(1) By the Treaty of Versailles, Germany was divided into two parts in order to give a land – route to Poland upto the sea and the port of Danzing was also given to Poland Germany wanted to regain her lost territories.

(2) The city of Danzing was inhabited mainly by the Germans and by occupying Danzing Corridor, Germany could connect with East Prussia.

(3) Germany signed a Non-Aggression Pact with Russia in August 1939, Poland was accused of committing atrocities against Germans living there.

On September 1, 1939, the German armies marched into Poland. France and Britain gave an ultimatum to Germany. In reply, Germany attacked France. On September 3, Britain and France declared War on Germany. Thus, the invasion of Poland marked the beginning of the Second World War. The German armies completed the conquest of Poland in less than three weeks so as to ensure that no aid reached Poland. In spite, of the Declaration of War, there was little actual fighting for many months. Therefore, the war during this period from September 1939 to April 1940 was dormant.

Example 1. Mention two reasons to show the weakness of the League of nations to prevent the Second World War.

Ans. (1) The League of Nations had no power to act on its own, the only weapon that was available with the League, was the economic sanctions.

(2) The USA did not become its members, because the senate of the United States did not ratify the convenant of the League of Nations.

 Related Theory

→ The United States did not officially join the League of Nations due to opposition from isolationists in Congress.

 Caution

→ Most candidates get mixed up with the causes of First World War and Second World War. Study both topics separately.

TOPIC 2

CONSEQUENCES OF THE SECOND WORLD WAR

Following were the consequences of the Second World War:

Defeat of Axis Powers

The Second World war was more destructive than the First World War. Upto the mid-1942, the Axis Powers (Germany, Italy and Japan) met with remarkable success, they captured large territories in Europe, Africa and Asia. But by the end of 1942, the Axis Powers were turned down by the Allied forces (Britain, France, the Soviet Union and the USA) recaptured African territories lost by France, then they had victory over Italy and then Germany. The Allies occupied Germany and it was divided into four zones namely – American Zone, British zone, the French zone and the Russian zone. The American, British and French zones were combined together to form the Federal Republic of Germany (FRG) or commonly known as 'West Germany' Bonn was its capital. It came under the capitalist ideology and was called 'Capitalist Bloc'.

The Russian zone with Berlin as its capital came to be known as 'German– Democratic Republic (GDR) or 'East Germany'. It was influenced by the Communist ideology of Russia. It became 'Eastern Bloc'

After the defeat of Germany, the Allied Powers turned their attention towards Japan. Japan had won and occupied most of South Eastern Asia. The British forces liberated Myanmar, Malaya, Philippines and Singapore. On July 26, 1945, in Potsdam Conference, Japan was asked to surrender, but Japan refused. Consequently, America dropped the atomic bombs on Hiroshima and Nagasaki. After that Japan offered to surrender on the terms of Potsdam declaration and the war came to an end. Japan and Italy also become very weak. Unlike Germany, they were not divided into zones to be governed by conquering forces. The American army was to occupy Japan until 1952. After this period, the Japanese would resume sole control over their own affairs. Emperor Hirohito was left on the throne as a Constitutional Monarch and the Japanese Parliament retained some of its law-making powers. All lands acquired or seized by Japan since 1895 were taken away.

Formation of the UN

After the Second World War was over, people worked a peaceful world devoid of any devastating war. Winston Churchill (The British Prime Minister) Joseph Stalin (premier of the USSR) and Franklin Roosevelt (The American President) met at Yalta Conference in February 1945, and decided to hold a conference again at San Francisco to finalise "The Charter of the United Nations". Thus, the United Nations emerged as a World Peace keeping body on 24th October, 1945. Any peace country, who was ready to obey the UN Charter could become the member of the UNO.

Cold War

After the Second World War, the traditional colonial powers of Europe like England, France, Italy, Germany, Spain and Portugal ; lost their importance in the world politics as they themselves became politically, economically and militarily weak. In their place, two superpowers emerged in international politics namely America (Capitalist Country) and Russia (the Communist Country). There had been ideological differences between them. There had been mutual suspicion, hatred and tension. But this tension did not take the form of an open armed clash. This is known as the 'Politics of Cold War'. But there was a state of tension between countries in which each side adopted policies designed to strengthen itself and weaken the other without armed conflict, which was known as the 'Cold War'.

Example 2. Define Cold War.

Ans. Cold War is defined as an atmosphere when there is no armed struggle, but the rivals continue to maintain their peace time diplomatic relations along with their hostility.

Thus, the USA and the USSR continued to maintain diplomatic relations and did not resort to over clashes, but treated each other with hostility. This led to the division of the world into two power Blocs.

(1) The Democratic and Capitalist Bloc: The bloc led by the USA, called the Western Bloc or the American Bloc believed in liberal democracy based on capitalism. This bloc comprised Britain, France, Belgium, Italy, Canada, Australia, the Netherlands, Greece, Pakistan, Turkey, etc. they collectively formed NATO (North Atlantic Treaty Organisation).

(2) The Communist Bloc: The bloc led by the USSR, called the Eastern Bloc or the Soviet Bloc believed in Communism based on Marxist theory. This bloc comprised of Bulgaria, Cuba, Czechoslovakia, East Germany, Hungary, Poland and Romania. They collectively formed the 'Warsaw Pact'.

 Caution

→ Some students get confused and mixed up with the members of two Blocs and the names of two Blocs, which will result in deduction of marks.

 ICSE Suggestions

→ Students are advised to draw a flow-chart in order to clearly understand the causes of the two World Wars.

→ Students should make notes of Cold War in tabular form and memorize all the names correctly along with correct spellings, to score good marks.

→ Students should prepare flash cards to learn and retain the names of the countries and the alliances formed during the two World Wars.

 **Glossary**

(1) **Turmoil:** A state of great disturbance
(2) **Allied Powers:** The four countries in the Allied Powers were Britain, France, America and Russia.
(3) **Totalitarian:** Relating to a system of government that is centralised and dictatorial.
(4) **Authoritarian:** Favouring complete obedience to authority as opposed to individual freedom.
(5) **Communism:** It is a socio-economic structure based on common ownership of the means of production and property.
(6) **Capitalism:** It is an economic system in which resources are controlled by Private individuals. All the major economic decisions are taken by keeping the market in hand.
(7) **Axis Powers:** Three countries in the Axis Powers were Germany, Italy and Japan who were opposed by Allied Powers.
(8) **United Nations Organisations (UNO):** The United Nations Organisations was established on October 24, 1945 with its headquarters at New York (USA).
(9) **Anti-Comintern Pact:** It was signed between Germany, Italy and Japan to fight communism globally.
(10) **NATO:** The North Atlantic Treaty Organisation, also called the North Atlantic Alliance, is an inter-governmental military alliance formed between USA and many West European 28 States like Canada, Britain, France, Belgium, Holland, Luxembourg, Iceland, Portugal, etc.
(11) **Warsaw Pact:** The Pact was signed by Russia and the socialist countries of East Europe like Poland, Hungary, Bulgaria, Romania and Czechoslovakia to meet the challenges posed by the American sponsored NATO.

 **Chronology**

1937: Anti-Comintern Pact was signed
1st September, 1939: German Invasion of Poland. Beginning of World War-II
3rd September, 1939: Declaration of War by England and France against Germany.
7th May, 1945: Germany surrendered
6th August, 1945: Atom bomb dropped on Hiroshima
9th August, 1945: Atom bomb dropped on Nagasaki
15th August, 1945: Surrender of Japan and end of the Second World War.

OBJECTIVE Type Questions

Multiple Choice Questions

[**1** mark each]

1. Which of the following countries was not a part of Allied powers during the Second world war?
(a) Britain (b) France
(c) Japan (d) Soviet Union

Ans. *(c) Japan*

Explanation: Japan was a part of Axis powers during the Second World War which consisted of Germany, Italy and Japan.

2. Which of these countries was not part of the Berlin-Rome –Tokyo Axis?
(a) Germany (b) Italy
(c) Japan (d) France

Ans. *(d) France*

Explanation: The Rome-Berlin-Tokyo Axis, also known as the Axis powers, was a military coalition that initiated World War II and fought against the Allies. Its principal members were Nazi Germany, the kingdom of Italy, and the Empire of Japan.

3. What was the immediate cause of the Second World War?
(a) Sarajevo Crisis
(b) Treaty of Versailles
(c) Hitler's invasion of Poland
(d) Formation of League of Nations [HOT]

Ans. *(c) Hitler's invasion of Poland*

Explanation: The invasion of Poland by Hitler marked the beginning of the Second World War in 1939.

 Related Theory

→ Sarajevo Crisis was the immediate cause of the First world war.

→ Treaty of Versailles was the result of First World War. Dissatisfaction with the Treaty of Versailles was one of the causes of Second World War but not the immediate cause.

→ Formation of league of Nations was the result of the First World War. The failure of league of Nations was one of the causes of Second World War but not the immediate cause.

4. The Treaty of Versailles demanded annexation of .... territories and creation of many states.
(a) Germany (b) Italy
(c) Austrian (d) French

Ans. *(a) Germany*

Explanation: According to Treaty of Versailles all the German Colonies forcibly taken away from her by the Allies. So demand for annexation of German territories and creation of new States was a must.

5. The .... failed to take any action against Italy, which exhibited its weakness.
(a) United Nations Organisation
(b) League of Nations
(c) Security Council
(d) International Court of Justice

Ans. *(b) League of Nations*

Explanation: Mussolini opposed the Treaty of Versailles. Italy demonstrated her imperialistic designs by attacking Abyssinia. But the League of Nations failed to take any action against Italy, which exhibited the weakness of League.

6. Who drove the countries of World towards another World War?
(a) Hitler (b) Mussolini
(c) Both of them (d) None of them

Ans. *(c) Both of them*

Explanation: Both Dictators i.e. Benito Mussolini in Italy and Adolf Hitler in Germany were equally responsible to drive the countries of the World towards the another World War. Because of the humility Treaty of Versailles and its terms.

7. In .... Japan left the League of Nations.
(a) 1931 (b) 1934
(c) 1933 (d) 1935

Ans. *(c) 1933*

Explanation: In 1933 Japan left the League of Nations and started occupying the British and American properties in China.

8. Causes of the failure of the League of Nations were:
(a) The member states were not willing to apply economic sanctions.
(b) It failed to maintain international Peace
(c) USA did not join the League.
(d) All of the above

Ans. *(d) All of the above*

Explanation: Causes of the Failure of the League of Nations were many. Firstly, the League received an early blow when USA did not join the League of Nations. Secondly, its member states were not willing to apply economic sanctions as it affected their economy as well. So the economic sanctions were of no

The Second World War **241**

use against a determined aggressor. Besides, the League failed to lost faith in its usefulness. Thereafter, they themselves entered into mutual political and military alliances.

9. When was the Second World War fought?
   (a) 1940 - 1945
   (b) 1943 - 1948
   (c) 1942 - 1947
   (d) 1939 - 1945

Ans. (d) 1939 - 1945

   Explanation : It started on 1st September 1939 and losted till 2nd September 1945.

10. Complete the Analogy:
    FRG : Anglo – American and their Allies
    GDR : : ?
    (a) France
    (b) Communist Russia
    (c) Communist China
    (d) Japan   [HOT]

Ans. (b) Communist Russia

   Explanation : The Federal Republic of Germany (FRG) come under the capitalist ideology of Anglo-American and their Allies and became a part of the Capitalist Bloc whereas The German Democratic Republic (GDR) came under the influence of the Political ideologies of Communist Russia and became part of the communist or Eastern Bloc.

⚠️ **Caution**
➡ Students should read both blocs, their full forms, their administrative country names and their capitals carefully in tabular form to avoid confusions.

11. The State of tension between countries in which each side adopt policies designed to strengthen itself and weaken the other without armed conflict is called ....
    (a) Cold War   (b) World War I
    (c) World War II   (d) Guerrilla Warrfare

Ans. (a) Cold War

   Explanation: Cold War is defined as an atmosphere when there is no armed struggle, but the rivals continue to maintain their peace time diplomatic relations along with their hostility.

💡 **Related Theory**
➡ U.S.A. and U.S.S.R continued to maintain their diplomatic relations and did not resort to avert clashes, but treated each other with hostility after the end of Second World War.

SUBJECTIVE Type Questions

Short Answer Type Questions
[**2** marks each]

12. What was the expansion policy of Japan?

Ans. In 1931, Japan attacked China and captured Manchuria. Japan also captured many nations of the South-East regions.

13. What was the immediate cause of the Second World War?   [HOT]

Ans. The invasion of Poland by Germany was the immediate cause of the Second World War.

14. Which all countries formed the Axis powers?

Ans. Germany, Italy and Japan formed the Axis powers.

15. What made Japan surrender to the Allies in August, 1945?

Ans. Bombing at Hiroshima and Nagasaki by the USA made Japan to surrender to Allies in August,1945.

16. When did the Second World War begin?

Ans. The Second World War began on 3rd September, 1939.

17. Name the countries that formed the Axis Bloc during the World War-II.   [ICSE 2018]

Ans. Germany, Italy and Japan formed the Axis Bloc during the World War II.

> Germany, Italy, Japan (Berlin-Rome-Tokyo axis) (Three countries)
> **[Marking Scheme]**

📋 **What Examiners Say**
➡ Some candidates got baffled between Axis and Allied powers. A few candidates mixed up the names of the countries.

18. How did the USA enter the Second World War and why?   [HOT]

Ans. USA remained neutral when the Second World War started. Japan attacked Pearl Harbour through aircrafts, which forced USA to join the war.

19. Give the reason as to why Japan invaded China.   [ICSE 2017]

Ans. Japan's policy of expansionism was the main reason for Japanese invasion of China. Being rich in natural resources, Manchuria, a region of China was taken over by Japan in 1931.

(1) Japan's policy of expansion. (Policy of Imperialism)

(2) Japan was determined to dominate the Far East.

(3) Japan's ambitions for more conquests and for more wealth increased after the First World War, Japan was not satisfied with only Manchuria.

[Any two]

[Marking Scheme]

What Examiners Say

→ *The question was answered vaguely. Candidates wrote about the Japanese invasion on China in general. They failed to mention the policy of expansion or the conquest of Manchuria.*

20. What is meant by the term Cold War?
[ICSE 2013]

Ans. A cold war is a state of conflict between nations that does not involve direct military action but is pursued primarily through economic and Political actions.

21. State two factors which were responsible for the failure of the League of Nations.
[ICSE 2014]

Ans. The two factors which were responsible for the failure of this League are as follows:

(1) Lack of cooperation among the member nations and they used League as grinding their own axis.

(2) The League had no Army to depend upon.

22. Mention any two consequences of Second World War.

Ans. Two consequences of Second World War are the following:

(1) After surrendering of Italy, Germany and Japan, most of the captured nations were liberated by the Allied Powers. Both the Axis and Allied faced economically turmoil, but soon Allied came up through this.

(2) Japan and Italy become very weak, so that the American General MC Arthur was given complete control of Japan. Thus, the Allied Powers maintained the World at Peace.

23.  **Identify the leader in the picture. What was the name given to the form of dictatorship practiced by him?**
[ICSE Sem-2, 2021]

Ans. The leader in this picture is Adolf Hitler. He was Chancellor of Germany from 1933 to 1945. Later he became Dictator of Germany. In 1919 he had joined a small political group called "The German Workers Party' which was based in Munich, after becoming its leader he changed its name to the Nationalist Socialist Party or the Nazi Party And he practiced dictatorship in the name of Nazism in Germany."

24. Dissatisfaction with the Treaty of Versailles.

Ans. Dissatisfaction with the treaty of Versailles: The Treaty of Versailles, by which the First World War came to an end, created more problems than it solved. The treaty was based on the spirit of revenge and Germany was forced to sign the treaty. German colonies were forcibly taken away from her and she was burdened with huge war indemnity which she could never pay. This humiliation gave rise to the spirit of revenge and Germany started looking for an opportunity to do away with the harsh treaty. Hence, war become inevitable.

Structured Questions

[3+3+4= **10** marks each]

25. Answer the questions that follow :

(A) **State any three similar ideologies of the Fascism and Nazism.**

(B) **What was the immediate cause of the Second World War? Mention any three reasons for it.**

(C) **Explain how the Japanese invasion of China became a cause for the Second World War.** [Mod. ICSE Sem-2, 2022]

Ans. (A) Similarity Between the Ideologies of Fascism and Nazism:

(1) To have faith in the Totalitarian rule.

(2) To despite democratic Political Systems.

(3) To hold that State is Supreme and it could suppress the fundamentals rights and freedoms of individuals.

(4) To uphold one-party and one leader.

(5) To believe in aggressive nationalism and Imperialism.

(6) To regard war as an instrument for furthering national interests.

(7) To uphold intensely nationalists, anti-communists and anti-democratic rule.

[Any three]

(B) Hitler's invasion of Poland was the immediate cause of the Second World War.

Hitler invaded Poland in September 1939 for the following reasons:

(1) By the Treaty of Versailles, Germany was divided into two parts in order to give a land – route to Poland upto the sea and the Port of Danzing was also given to Poland. Germany wanted to regain her lost territories.

(2) The City of Danzing was inhabited mainly by the Germans and by occupying Danzing corridor, Germany could connect with East Prussia.

(3) Germany signed a Non- Aggression Pact with Russia in August 1939. Poland was accused of committing atrocities against Germans living there.

On September 1, 1939, the German Armies marched into Poland. France and Britain gave an ultimatum to Germany. In reply, Germany attacked France. On September 3, Britain and France declared War on Germany. Thus, the invasion of Poland marked the beginning of the Second World War.

(C) **Japanese invasion of China**: Japanese Policy of expansion was another cause of the Second World War. Japan's ambitions rose after the First World War. She was determined to dominate the Far East. In 1931, Japan intervened in Manchuria and, in spite of the League's opposition, occupied it and set up a government there. Japan also started an undeclared War against China in 1931. China appealed to the League of Nations to declare sanctions against Japan. Britain and France, the leading members of the League did not pay any attention to the appeal. Japan joined the Berlin – Rome axis to farm the Berlin – Rome – Tokyo Axis to form the Berlin – Rome – Tokyo Axis to its policy of expansion and conquest. In 1933, Japan left the League of Nations and started occupying the British and American Properties in China. Britain and France followed the Policy of appeasement, thinking that the Japanese could be used to weaken China. Thus, a War was inevitable under these circumstances.

26. The real causes for the outbreak of the Second World War were much deeper and varied in character. In this context, explain the following cause of the war.

(A) Rise of Fascism and Nazism.
(B) Japanese Invasion of China.
(C) Failure of the League of Nations. [HOT🔥]

Ans. (A) The rise of extreme nationalism in Italy and Germany, in the form of Fascism and Nazism, respectively contributed to the causes which led to the Second World War. Mussolini established dictatorship in Italy. He opposed the Treaty of Versailles. Italy demonstrated her imperialistic designs by attacking Abyssinia. In Germany, Hitler wanted to re-establish the prestige of Germany in the international field. In 1938, he annexed Austria and dismembered Czechsolovakia. Thus, Mussolini and Hitler drove the countries of the world towards another world war.

(B) Japanese policy of expansion was another cause of the Second World War. Japan started an undeclared war against China in 1931. China appealed to the League of Nations of declare sanctions on Japan. Japan joined the Berlin-Rome Axis to form the Berlin-Rome-Tokyo Axis to further its policy of expansion and conquest. In 1933, Japan left the League of Nations and started occupying the British and American properties in China. Britain and France followed the policy of Appeasement, thinking that the Japanese could be used to weaken China. Thus, a war was inevitable under these circumstances.

(C) The League of Nations was created after the first World War to prevent future wars. However, the league suffered an early blow when the USA did not join the league. The league did nothing when Poland, with the backing of France, siezed a part of Lithiuania in 1920. The authority of the league was flouted by Japan when it seized Manchuria and by Italy when it conquered Ethiopia. The league failed to maintain international peace and countries of Europe lost faith in its usefulness.

27. With reference to the Rise of Dictatorships and the Second World War, answer the following:

(A) State any three reasons for the Rise of Fascism in Italy.
(B) Explain any three consequences of World War II.
(C) Name the two rival blocs that fought against each other during World War II and state its signatory countries.
[ICSE 2019]

Ans. (A) The reasons for the rise of Fascism in Italy were:

(1) **Dissatisfaction with the Treaty of Versailles:** Italy had joined hands with France and Britain against Germany

and her allies in the First World War as Britain had promised large territorial gains to her, if and when the victory comes. But the Treaty of Versailles only partially fulfilled that promise. Moreover, Italy had lost 7,00,000 soldiers in the war and there was a widespread feeling of disappointment and discontent.

(2) **Economic Crisis:** At the end of the war, thousands of soldiers were discharged from the army and were unemployed. The Italian economy was not only unable to recover from the post war losses but also was unable to provide jobs for the unemployed youth.

(3) **Inefficient and Corrupt Democratic Government:** A full-fledged Parliamentary system of government based on voting rights for adult male citizens was introduced in Italy for the first time in year 1919. Democracy was thus a new experiment in the politics of Italy. No single party got a clear-cut majority and Italy was governed by a series of six coalition governments that functioned only for short durations and were unable to deal effectively with the problems of unemployment, strikes and riots post World War I.

(4) **Rise of Totalitarian Ideologies:** The philosophy of Hegel flourished in Italy. Hegelians justified an authoritarian regime. The success of Russian Revolution of 1917 and the ideas of one-party rule and totalitarian concepts appealed to the masses in Italy.

(5) **Failure of the League of Nations:** The League of Nations, formed at the end of the First World War, for maintaining peace and war amongst nations, failed miserably in its purpose. **[Any three]**

(B) The consequences of Second World War were:

(1) Lowering of Status of European Powers: Though England and France were victorious, their status and economic position was lowered.

(2) Rise of U.S.A. as Super Power: By using atom bomb to crush Japan, U.S. emerged as a super military and economic power.

(3) Emergence of Cold War: After the Second World War, US and USSR emerged as two super powers. They divided the world into two rival blocs, the Capitalistic bloc led by USA and the Communist bloc led by USSR. There existed a cold war among the two blocs.

(C) The two rival blocs that fought against each other during World War II were:
(1) Allied Powers
(2) Axis Powers.
The signatory countries were:
(1) Allied Powers: Britain, France, USSR, China and United States of America
(2) Axis Powers: Germany, Italy and Japan.

(A) Rise of Fascism in Italy
Dissatisfaction with the treaty of Versailles
Economic crisis
Political instability (Failure of democracy/corrupt democratic)
Class conflicts
Failure of League of Nations
Leadership provided by Mussolini
Fear of Communism
Rise of Dictatorship (Totalitarianism)
[Any three]

(B) Consequences of Second World War:
Destruction of life and property.
Defeat of the Axis Powers by the Allied Powers.
Many new weapons of mass destruction were invented and used.
Formation of the UN.
The world was divided into two power blocs
the Democratic or Capitalist bloc led by the USA and the Communist bloc led by the erstwhile Soviet Union.

Beginning of Cold War between two power blocs.
Division of Germany
Japan became weak and its emperor reduced to constitutional head.
Imperialism came to an end.
Fall of dictatorship
Decolonisation
USA and the Soviet Union became super powers. **[Any three]**

(C) Axis – Germany Italy & Japan Allies– Britain, France, USSR and later USA joined the Allies. (Any three countries)
[Marking Scheme]

What Examiners Say

→ (A) Many candidates confused the Rise of Fascism with the Rise of Nazism. A few candidates mentioned the causes of the Second World War.

→ (B) Majority of the candidates answered the question correctly. A few candidates mentioned the consequences of the World War I instead of World War II.

→ (C) Some candidates, instead of writing Axis and Allied Powers, mentioned Capitalist and Communist blocs. A few candidates also mixed up the names of the signatory countries.

⚠ **Caution**

→ Rise of Fascism and Nazism should be studied in detail, also definitions of Fascism and Nazism should be learnt properly. The distinction between the consequences of World War I and World War II should be clear. The students should have a clear concept about the rival blocs during the two World Wars and students should correctly remember the names of the member countries of the two rival blocs- students should read and understand the questions before making any attempt to answer it.

28. The 1914 and 1939 wars that engulfed almost the entire world, were known as the World Wars due to its unprecedented impact and damage. In this context, answer the following:

(A) Explain the immediate cause of the First World War.

(B) Explain the consequences of the Second World War with reference to the Cold War.

(C) Mention any four terms of the Treaty of Versailles which affected Germany after World War I. **[ICSE 2017] [HOT🔥]**

Ans. (A) With all countries fully armed, ever ready to go to war, it needed only a little spark to ignite and set off the forces of war into motion. The outbreak of the great war was initiated by an incident that occurred in Bosnia. The Serbian people became independent and Bosnia came to be a part of Serbia. But as Bosnia was ceded to Austria, the Serbians were agitated. Bosnia became the centre of rebellions, only supported by the Serbian Government. The Archduke Francis Ferdinand, the heir apparent to the throne of Austria, was murdered along with his wife, Sophie, at Sarajevo a city in Bosnia while on a visit to Bosnia. As the assassin, Gavrilo Princep, a nineteen-year-old student was a Serbian, Austria blamed Serbia as the conspirator of the crime and gave a stiff ultimatum with eleven severe demands to Serbia. The Serbian Government, while accepting most of these demands, refused to accept one of the terms threatening her sovereignty. This refusal by Serbia turned out to be the immediate cause of the First World War.

(B) The Cold War was one of the most significant consequences of the Second World War that divided the major portion of the world into two blocs. The Cold War continued for almost half a century, till it ended in 1991, with the disintegration of Soviet Russia or USSR.

(C) The terms of Treaty of Versailles that affected Germany after World War I were:

(1) Germany was held guilty of causing the First World War. She had to pay war indemnity of 6,600 million pounds to the victor nations.

(2) Germany had to evacuate territories she had captured during the war;

(3) Germany territory of Rhineland was to be demilitarized. The territory west of the Rhine valley was to be occupied by the Allied powers;

(4) Germany was forced to return Alsace and Lorraine to France. Danzing was to be a free port under the League of Nations;

(5) As compensation to France for the destruction of her coal mines by Germany, France was given full control over the rich coal mines in the Saar Valley.

(6) Germany had to surrender the areas of Eupen and Malmedy to Bulgaria;

(7) Estonia, Latvia and Lithiuania earlier seized by Germany were now made independent. **[Any four]**

29. With reference to the causes of the Second World War, answer the following:

(A) Explain how the ideologies of Fascism and Nazism led to the Second World War.

(B) How did the Japanese invasion of China create conditions for the outbreak of the war?

(C) Explain the consequences of the war with reference to the formation of the United Nations. **[ICSE 2014]**

Ans. (A) The ideologies of Fascism and Nazism that led to the Second World War were:

(1) Both Nazism and Fascism did not believe in democracy and personal stated liberty. Hence, they did not allow any other party to operate.

(2) Like Mussolini, Hitler also believed in 'Nationalism' as a driving force for the people of their country.

(3) Both theories propagated the belief that nations become great only by defeating other nations in war.

(4) Both were intensely anti-communist.

(B) Japan's expanisionism was one of the causes of the Second World War. Being rich in natural resources, Manchuria, a region of China, was taken over by Japan in 1931. The Japanese attack on Manchuria was the direct challenge to the League of Nations.

(C) The Second World War proved to be more destructive than the first. One of the results of the Second World War was the division of some of the major countries into two diameterically apposed ideological blocs: the Communist bloc and the Western bloc. The League of Nations established in 1919 after the First World War with the objective of fostering peace among the nations of the world failed miserably in its objective. With the invention and deployment of sophisticated nuclear weapons, the threat to the survival of modern civilization had intensified even more. Therefore, an organization was required to ensure that such deadly weapons would not be used.

To save the coming generations and the world from the ravaging effects of war, the three big leaders Roosevelt (President of USA), Winston Churchill (Prime Minister of Great Britain) and Joseph Stalin (Premier of USSR) held a conference at Yalta in the Soviet Union on 25 April, 1945. The representatives of 50 nations decided to establish a new peace keeping organization, the United Nations. These nations were determined not to enter into any other alliances and to establish a formed peace keeping organization that would prevent hostilities among member countries.

The United Nations officially came into existence on 24 October, 1945. The principles of the United Nations are to save future generations from war, reaffirm human rights and establish equal rights for all persons. It also aims to promote justice, freedom and social progress for the people of all its member states.

(A) The rise of Fascism and Nazism as a cause to the Second World War:
  (1) Italy wanted to revive the glory of the old empire.
  (2) She joined the Anti-Comintern Pact in 1937 and formed a ten years alliance with Germany to strengthen her position
  (3) Italy demonstrated her imperialistic designs by attacking Abyssinia.

In Germany Hitler
  (1) wanted to re-establish the German empire in the international field.
  (2) He flouted the military causes in the treaty of Versailles and declared re-armament
  (3) In 1938 he annexed Austria and dis-membered Czechoslovakia.

(B) Japanese invasion of China
  (1) Japan was determined to dominate the Far-East.
  (2) It intervened in Manchuria and occupied it and set up a government in spite of League's opposition.
  (3) Japan also started an undeclared war against China in 1931. China appealed to the League to declare sanctions against Japan.
  (4) Japan joined the Berlin-Rome Axis to form the Rome-Berlin-Tokyo Axis to further its policy of expansion and conquest.
  (5) In 1933 Japan left the League and started occupying the British and American properties in China.
  (6) Britain and France followed the policy of appeasement, thinking that Japanese could be used to weaken China.

(C) The consequences of the war with reference to:

The formation of the United Nations:
  (1) The horrors of the two world wars and
  (2) The failure of the League of Nations led to a meeting of the big three– Roosevelt, President of the USA, Churchill, Prime Minister of Britain and Stallin, Premier of the USSR at Yalta in February 1945.
  (3) They resolved to convene a conference of the representatives of all the nations at San Francisco to draw up 'Charter of the United Nations'. The UNO was thus established on October 24, 1945.

Defeat of Axis Powers :
  (1) The allied forces recaptured African territories lost by France.
  (2) This was followed by their victory over Italy. The allied powers forced Italy to make an unconditional surrender and send an armistice.
  (3) In 1945 the allied forced moved across the Rhine and defeated the German forces
  (4) The allied powers turned their attention towards Japan. The British forces liberated Malaya, Myanmar, Singapore and Philippines.

The Second World War

(5) In the Potsdam Conference Japan was asked to surrender, but did not

(6) America dropped the first atomic bomb on Hiroshima and Nagasaki in 1945. Japan offered to surrender and the war came to an end. At the end of the war Germany was divided into four zones. Japan and Italy became weak. The American army was to occupy Japan till 1952.

[Marking Scheme]

What Examiners Say

→ (A) Most candidates did not understand the meaning of the word 'ideologies'. Many wrote the causes for the rise of Fascism and Nazism. Answers were generalized and vague. Candidates were not sure of the various ideologies responsible for the outbreak of the World War II.

→ (B) The question was answered vaguely by replicating the question itself. Instead of invasion of Manchuria and defiance of the League of Nations, candidates mentioned the attack on Pearl Harbour.

→ (C) Most candidates were unable to understand the question 'the consequences of the War with reference to the formation of the UNO.' Some candidates explained both–consequences of the war as well as formation of the UNO

13 United Nations

In order to save the world from the horrors of Wars, the United Nations Organisation was set up. Its Prime Objective was maintenance of international peace and security. It is an international organization including all Sovereign States in the world, and it came into existence on October 24, 1945.

Chapter Notes

- Purposes and Objectives of the United Nations
- Organs of the United Nations

The world went through two disastrous wars between 1914 to 1945, within a span of 25 years. The Second World War was more destructive compared to the First World War. In order to check such destruction, the world leaders realized the importance of establishing an Organisation, which was more powerful than the League of Nations. In an attempt to avoid future war and to promote World Peace, the world leaders held many conferences to discuss the nature and viability of such an Organisation. Their efforts finally took shape at San Francisco an October 24, 1945 in the form of the United Nations Organisation.

United Nations Organisation

The United Organisation is a world organization comprising of a large number of countries of the world. It was set up after the Second World War on October 24, 1945 to bring an end to wars, to establish permanent peace in the World and to bring about an economic and cultural development to mankind. Its headquarters is at New York City in the U.S.A. Almost all countries of the World are its members. At present its total membership is 193.

TOPIC 1

PURPOSES AND OBJECTIVES OF THE UNITED NATIONS

The main purposes and objectives of the United Nations were defined in Article 1 of the UN Charter as:

(1) To maintain international peace and security.
(2) To take effective collective measures for the prevention and removal of threats to the peace for the suppression of acts of aggression or other breaches of the peace.
(3) To bring about by peaceful means in conformity with the principles of justice and international law, adjustment or settlement of international disputes or situations which might lead to a breach of the peace.
(4) To develop friendly relations among nations based on respect for the principle of equal rights and self – determination of peoples.
(5) To take other appropriate measures to strengthen Universe Peace.
(6) To achieve international co-operation in solving international problems of an economic, social, cultural or humanitarian character. Promoting and encouraging respect for human rights and for fundamental freedoms for all without any distinction as in race, sex, language or religion.
(7) To be a centre for harmonizing the actions of nations in the attainment of these common ends.

Important

→ Disarm, decolonize and development are the three new objectives set by the United Nations.

Principles of the United Nations

(1) To respect the sovereign equality of all its members.
(2) All members should fulfill in good faith the obligations assumed by them.
(3) They should settle their international disputes by peaceful means.
(4) They would refrain from the threat or use of force against any State.
(5) They should give the United Nations every assistance in any action it takes.
(6) The Organization should ensure that States which are not members of the United Nations act in accordance with these principles.
(7) The United Nations shall not intervene in the domestic, i.e., internal affairs of any State.

Headquarters

All the organs of the United Nations are based in New York, USA, except the International Court which is located at The Hague in Netherlands.

Flag

The UN flag is light blue in colour and portrayed in white at its centre is the UN Emblem, a polar map of the world embraced by twin olive branches. The United Nations Flag was adopted on October 20, 1947.

Membership

Membership of the UN is open to all peace-loving nations who believe in the principles of the UN and accept the obligations of the UN Charter. Fifty countries who took part in San Francisco Conference, signed and approved the Charter, became original members of the United Nations. Other countries are admitted by the General Assembly upon the recommendation of the Security Council by a two-third majority of votes. By 2021, 193 countries are its members.

Example 1. When and where was the United Nations set up?

Ans. The United Nations was set up at San Francisco on 24th October, 1945.

Example 2. What are the official languages of the United Nations?

Ans. The official languages of the United Nations are Arabic, Chinese, English, French, Russian and Spanish.

TOPIC 2

ORGANS OF THE UNITED NATIONS

The United Nations has six principal Organs:
(1) The General Assembly
(2) The Security Council
(3) The International Court of Justice
(4) The Economic ands Social Council
(5) The Trusteeship Council
(6) The Secretariat

But as per the latest syllabus, we will cover only three organs. These are the– General Assembly, the Security Council and International Court of Justice.

The General Assembly

The General Assembly is the main deliberative organ of the United Nations. The work of the United Nations is determined by the will of the majority of the members as expressed in resolutions adopted by the Assembly.

 Caution

→ The decisions of the General Assembly have no legal binding force for governments, they carry the weight of world opinion on major international issues, as well the moral authority of the world community.

Composition

All members of the United Nations are members of the General Assembly. Each State has five representatives in the General Assembly, but each State has one vote. The regular session of the General Assembly begins each year on the third Tuesday in September and continues usually until the third week of December. At the start of each regular session, the Assembly elects a new President, 21 Vice-Presidents and the Chairmen of the Assembly's six Main Committees. The presidency of the Assembly rotates each year among five groups of States – Africa, Asia, Eastern Europe, Latin America and Caribbean, and Western Europe and other States in order to ensure equitable geographical representation. Decisions on important questions require $2/3^{rd}$ majority, while decisions on ordinary matters are reached by a simple majority of members present and voting. These matters include the election of the non-permanent members of the Security Council, admission of new members, the suspension or expansion of members, Budgetary issues, etc.

Example 3. Who appoints the Secretary General of the United Nations?
Ans. The General Assembly appoints the Secretary General of the United Nations.

 Important

→ Special sessions of the General Assembly are convened by the Secretary-General at the request of the Security Council or by a special request by a majority of members.

Functions

The General Assembly's main functions are:
(1) To consider and make recommendations on the principles of co-operation, in the maintenance of international peace and security.
(2) To discuss any question relating to international peace and security and to make recommendations on it.
(3) To discuss and make recommendations on any question within the scope of the Charter or affecting the powers and functions of any organ of the United Nations.
(4) To initiate studies and make recommendations to promote international political, social and economic co-operation.
(5) To make recommendations for the peaceful settlement of disputes.
(6) To receive and consider reports from the Security Council and other organs of the United Nations.
(7) To consider and approve the budget of the United Nations and to apportion the contributions among members.
(8) To elect the non-permanent members of the Security Council, the Economic and Social Council and the Trusteeship Council, and to elect the judges of the International Court of Justice.
(9) To appoint the Secretary-General on the recommendation of the Security Council.

Important

→ The General Assembly shall not make any recommendation where a dispute or situation is currently discussed by the Security Council.

The Security Council

The Security Council is the executive body of the United Nations. It has the primary responsibility for the maintenance of international peace and security. It functions continuously. A representative of each of its members must be present at all times at the United Nations Headquarters.

Composition

The Council consists of 15 members. It has five permanent members – China, France, Russia, Britain

and the United States of America. The regional representation of the ten non-permanent members is:
(i) Afro-Asian countries – 5
(ii) Latin American countries – 2
(iii) West European and other countries – 2
(iv) East European countries – 1

The ten non-permanent members are elected by the General Assembly by a two-third majority for a term of two years.

The Presidency of the Council rotates monthly, according to the English alphabetical listing of its member States.

Important
➦ *A retiring member of the Security Council is not eligible for immediate re-election.*

Veto Power
Each member of the Security Council has one vote. Decisions on procedural matters are made by an affirmative vote of nine members, including the concurring votes of all five permanent members. The negative vote of a permanent members is called a veto. The Council is powerless to act if any of the five permanent members uses the veto power.

Important
➦ *The abstinence of a permanent member from voting does not amount to a negative vote or veto.*

Functions
(1) To maintain international peace and security in accordance with the principles and purposes of the United Nations.
(2) To investigate any dispute or situation which might lead to international friction and to take military action against an aggressor.
(3) To recommend methods of adjusting such disputes or the terms of settlement.
(4) To formulate plans for the establishment of a system to regulate armaments.
(5) To determine the existence of a threat to the peace or act of aggression and to recommend what action should be taken.
(6) To call on members to apply sanctions and other measures not involving the use of force to stop or prevent aggression.
(7) To take military action against an aggressor.
(8) To recommend the admission of new members.
(9) To exercise the trusteeship functions of the United Nations in 'strategic areas'.
(10) To recommend to the General Assembly the appointment of the Secretary-General and, together with the Assembly, to elect the Judges of the International Court of Justice.

Example 4. Who elects the non-permanent members of the Security Council?

Ans. The non-permanent members of the Security Council are elected by the members of the General Assembly.

Example 5. Which is the executive body or 'Enforcement wing' of the UN?

Ans. The Security Council is the executive body or enforcement wing of the UN.

⚠ Caution
➦ *Few students have written answer 'The General Assembly' to the question. Students are required to go through the content of the notes carefully.*

International Court of Justice
The International Court of Justice is the principal judicial organ of the United Nations. Its seat is at The Hague, Netherlands. It began work in 1946, when it replaced the Permanent Court of International Justice which had functioned in the Peace Palace since 1922.

Composition
The Court is composed of 15 judges elected to nine years term of office by the United Nations General Assembly and Security Council sitting independently of each other. Elections are held every three years for one-third of the seats, and retiring judges may re-elected. The Members of the Court do not represent their governments but are independent judges (Magistrates). The Court elects its President and Vice-President for a three-year term. The Court has the power to appoint its registrar.

Important
➦ *The International Court of Justice may not include more than one judge from any nationality.*

Functions
(1) To settle, in accordance with international law, the legal disputes submitted to it by States.
(2) To give advisory opinions on legal questions referred to it by duly authorized international organs and agencies.
(3) The Court is competent to entertain a dispute if the States concerned agree to take the issue to it.
(4) The Court has compulsory jurisdiction against the background that a large number of treaties provide that disputes are submitted to the Court.

Example 6. What is the importance of International Court of Justice?

Ans. The International Court of Justice plays an important role to settle the legal disputes submitted to it by the States, and to give advisory opinion on legal questions referred to it by duly authorized international organs and agencies

Example 7. What is the term of office of the President of the International Court of Justice?

Ans. The term of Office of the President of the International Court of Justice is three years.

 Related Theory

→ The International Court of Justice appoints or elects even vice-President for a term of three years.

 **ICSE Suggestions**

→ All three organs of UN covered in syllabus should be studied by students separately, by making different headings covering composition and powers, functions of each organ, etc. which will help them to memorize easily.

Glossary

(1) **UNO**—A world body formed to maintain International Peace and security.
(2) **Charter of the UN**—Constitution of the United Nations
(3) **The General Assembly**—The major deliberative organ of the UN.
(4) **The Security Council**—The executive body of the UN, responsible for maintaining International Peace and Security.
(5) **The International Court of Justice**—The Principle judicial organ of UNO.
(6) **Veto Power**—A right granted to a permanent member of the Security Council of the UN to reject a resolution. If only one member uses its Veto Power against the resolution, it cannot be adopted.

Chronology

October 24, 1945—UNO was formed at San Fransico and it offcially came into existence.

OBJECTIVE Type Questions

Multiple Choice Questions
[1 mark each]

1. The .... is the executive body of the United Nations Organisation.
   (a) General Assembly
   (b) Security Council
   (c) International Court of Justice
   (d) Trusteeship Council   [HOT🔥]

Ans. (b) Security Council

Explanation: The Security Council is the executive body of the United Nations. It has the primary responsibility for the maintenance of international peace and security.

 Related Theory

→ The General Assembly is the main deliberative organ of the United Nations.
→ The International Court of Justice is the principal judicial organ of the United Nations.
→ The Trusteeship Council is in charge of all territories which were administered before the second world war under the mandate system of the League of Nations.

2. The non-permanent members of the Security Council are elected for a term of .... years.
   (a) One   (b) Two
   (c) Three   (d) Five

Ans. (b) Two

Explanation: The ten non-permanent members of the Security Council are elected by the General Assembly by a two-third majority for a term of two years.

3. The non-permanent members of the Security Council are elected by the members of ....
   (a) General Assembly
   (b) International Court of Justice
   (c) The Trusteeship Council
   (d) The Secretariat
   [ICSE Sem-2, 2021]

Ans. (a) General Assembly

Explanation: The ten-non permanent members are elected by the United Nations General Assembly for two years terms.

 Related Theory

→ The non permanent members are elected by 2/3rd majority and any retiring member is not eligible to be re-elected.

United Nations 253

4. Which day is celebrated as United Nations, Day?
   (a) 24th September
   (b) 24th October
   (c) 24th June
   (d) 16th December

Ans. (b) 24th October

Explanation: The United Nations formally come into existence on October 24, 1945. Since then, October 24 is celebrated every year throughout the world as the United Nations Day.

5. How many Vice-Presidents are elected at the regular session of General Assembly of United Nations?
   (a) 4
   (b) 10
   (c) 16
   (d) 21   [HOT]

Ans. (d) 21

Explanation: At the start of each regular session, the Assembly elects a new President, 21 Vice-Presidents and the chairmen of the Assembly's six main committees.

6. The Security Council consists of .... non-permanent members.
   (a) Fifteen
   (b) Ten
   (c) Five
   (d) Six
                                      [ICSE Sem-2, 2022]

Ans. (a) Ten

Explanation: The Council consists of 15 members. It has five permanent members– China, France, Russia, Britain and United States of America. Rest ten non-permanent members are Afro-Asian countries–5 members, Latin American countries–2 members, West European and other countries–2 members and East European countries–1 member.

7. Which of the following countries is NOT a permanent member of the Security Council?
   (a) France
   (b) China
   (c) Germany
   (d) Britain
                                      [ICSE Sem-2, 2022]

Ans. (c) Germany

Explanation: France, China and Britain are three permanent members, whereas Germany is not a Permanent member of the Security Council.

8. The Headquarters of the International Court of Justice is situated at:
   (a) Geneva
   (b) Hague
   (c) New York
   (d) Paris

Ans. (b) Hague

Explanation: The International Court of Justice headquarters are in the Hague (Netherlands).

9. Which of the following is NOT main organ of United Nations?
   (a) International Court of Justice
   (b) The Economic and Social Council
   (c) The Secretariat
   (d) International Monetary Fund

Ans. (d) International Monetary Fund

Explanation: The International Monetary Fund is not the organ of United Nations. It is an agency of UN.

10. How many official languages does the United Nations have?
    (a) 5
    (b) 6
    (c) 7
    (d) 4   [HOT]

Ans. (b) 6

Explanation: The official languages of the UN are Arabic, Chinese, French, Russian, English and Spanish.

11. Who is the Present Secretary General of the UNO ?
    (a) Trgve Lie
    (b) Javier Perez De Cuellar
    (c) Antonio Gutterres
    (d) Dr. Boutros Gholi

Ans. (c) Antonio Gutterres

Explanation: (c) Antonio Gutterres is the current Secretary General of United Nations.

Related Theory
→ *He is the ninth Secretary General and he is from United Kingdom, his term began on 1st January, 2017.*

12. The General Assembly's regular session begins each year on the ....
    (a) First Monday in August
    (b) Second Thursday in March
    (c) Fourth Friday in May
    (d) Third Tuesday in September

Ans. (d) Third Tuesday in September

Explanation: The regular session of the General Assembly begins each year on the Third Tuesday in September and continues usually until the third week of September.

13. By 2021, ... countries are the members of UNO.   [HOT]
    (a) 194
    (b) 193
    (c) 190
    (d) 196

Ans. (b) 193

Explanation: Almost all countries of the World are members of the United Nations Organisation. By 2021, 193 countries are its members now.

14. How many member countries did the UNO have on its formation in 1945?
(a) 45 (b) 48
(c) 51 (d) 54 [HOT]

Ans. (c) 51

Explanation: In 1945 the UN charter was signed by 51 founder members (Participating Nations).

Related Theory
At the San Francisco Conference held from 25th April to 26th June 1945, the United Nations Charter was drawn up. It was approved and signed by delegates of 51 countries, representing 80 percent of the World Population on 26th June, 1945.

15. Which of the following countries is NOT a permanent member of the Security Council?
(a) France (b) China
(c) Germany (d) Britain
(ICSE Sem-2, 2022)

Ans. (c) Germany

Explanation: The Security Council consists of five permanent members–China, France, Russia, Britain and the united states of America.

16. The Security Council consists of .... non-permanent members.
(a) Fifteen (b) Ten
(c) Five (d) Six
(ICSE Sem-2, 2022)

Ans. (a) Fifteen

Explanation: The Council consists of 15 members. It has five permanent members (China, France, Russia, Britain and the United States of America) and it has ten non-permanent members.

SUBJECTIVE Type Questions

Short Answer Type Questions
[2 marks each]

17. When and where was the United Nation formed?

Ans. The United Nations was formed at San Francisco in USA on 24th October, 1945.

18. What are the official languages of the United Nations? [HOT]

Ans. Arabic, Chinese, English, French, Russian and Spanish are the official languages of the United Nations.

19. Name the five permanent members of the Security Council. [HOT]

Ans. The five permanent members of the Security Council are Britain, France, Russia, China and the USA.

20. (A) Which organ is known as the Parliament of the United Nations?
(B) Name the executive body of the United Nations.

Ans. (A) The General Assembly is known as the Parliament of the United Nations.
(B) The Security Council is the executive body of the United Nations.

21. What is meant by the term 'Veto' Power? [ICSE 2019]

Ans. The 'Veto Power' refers to the powers of the five permanent members of the UN Security Council. The five permanent members are China, France, Russia, United Kingdoms and United States of America. The negative vote of the permanent member of UN Security Council is called Veto power.

> The Permanent members of Security Council have veto power i.e. a negative vote that is exercised to make strong decisions or raise objections from any of the five members.
> Council is powerless to act if any of the five members uses the Veto Power
> **[Marking Scheme]**

What Examiners Say
Majority of the candidates explained the Veto Power correctly. A few candidates mentioned the names of the permanent members of the Security Council.

Caution
Students should know that a Veto Power is actually a negative vote by any of the permanent members of the Security Council.

Related Theory
Each member of the Security Council has one vote. Decisions on Procedural matters are made by an affirmative vote of nine members, including the concurring votes of all five permanent members. The Council is powerless to act if any of the five permanent members uses the Veto Power.

22. Mention two functions of the General Assembly. [HOT] [ICSE 2014]

Ans. The functions of the General Assembly are:
(1) The General Assembly considers and approves the budget of the UNO.

(2) The General Assembly elects the non-permanent members of the Security Council and the members of Trusteeship, Economic and Social Council. It also elects the Judges of International Court of Justice and to appoint on the recommendations of the Security Council, the Secretary General of the United Nations.
(3) The General Assembly regulates the working of other organs and agencies of the UNO.
(4) The General Assembly makes recommendations to promote international co-operation, human rights and fundamental freedom for all. It also helps in promoting international cooperation and friendship.

[Any two]

The two important functions of the General assembly are:
(1) to consider and make recommendations on the principles of cooperation in the maintenance of international peace and security.
(2) to discuss questions relating to international peace and security and to make recommendations on it.
(3) to discuss and make recommendations on any question within the scope of the charter or affecting the powers and functions of any organ of the United nations.
(4) to initiate studies and make recommendations to promote international political, Social and economic cooperation.
(5) to make recommendations for the peaceful settlement of disputes.
(6) to consider and approve the budget of the United Nations and to apportion the contributions among members.
(7) to elect the non-permanent members of the Security Council, Economic and Social Council and the Trustee ship Council and elect the Judges of the International Court of Justice.
(8) to appoint the Secretary General on the recommendation of the Security Council. **[Any two]**
[Marking Scheme]

What Examiners say
→ Most candidates answered the question correctly. However, some candidates were confused between the functions of the General Assembly and the Security Council.

23. Who appoints the Secretary General of the United Nations ? **[ICSE 2012]**

Ans. The Secretary General of the United Nations is appointed by the General Assembly upon the recommendations of the Security Council for a five-year, renewable term.

24. Write any two principles of the United Nations.

Ans. (1) The United Nations shall not intervene in the domestic, i.e. internal affairs of any state.
(2) The Principle of the Sovereign equality of all its members.

25. Mention any two electoral functions of the Security Council.

Ans. (1) The Secretary General of the UN is appointed by the General Assembly on the recommendation of the Security Council.
(2) It may also participate in the election of the Judges of the International Court of Justice.

26. Look at the picture given and answer the questions that follow:
Which organization does this emblem represent?

Ans. The organization represented by this emblem is United Nations Organization.

27. Mention this Composition of the General Assembly.

Ans. The General assembly consists of all the members of the United Nations. Every member State can send a maximum of five representatives to the General Assembly bit at the time of voting a State is entitled to cast only one vote. It means that all member States have equal Status.

Structured Questions
[3+3+4= **10** marks each]

28. (A) Mention any three objectives of this organization.
(B) Mention any three functions of the General Assembly.
(C) What is the composition of the Security Council?

Ans. (A) The objectives of United Nations are:
(1) To maintain international peace and security;
(2) To take effective and collective measures for the prevention and removal of threats to the peace;
(3) To develop friendly relations among nations based on respect for the principle of equal rights.

(4) To take appropriate measures to strengthen universal peace;
(5) To promote and encourage respect for human rights. **[Any three]**

(B) The functions of United Nations General Assembly are:
(1) The General Assembly considers and approves the budget of the UNO;
(2) The General Assembly elects the non-permanent members of the Security council and the members of Trusteeship Economic and Social Council.
(3) The General Assembly makes recommendations to promote international co-operation, human rights and fundamental freedom for all.

(C) The Security Council of United Nations consists of 15 members. It has five permanent members viz., China, France, Russia, Great Britain and U.S.A. The ten non- permanent members are elected by the General Assembly by a two-third majority for a term of two years. A retriving member is not eligible for re-election. The countries which are not the members of the Security Council but are party to a dispute may participate in its deliberations with no voting right. Each member of the Security Council is its President in turn for a month. Veto power can be exercised only by any permanent member exclusively.

⚠️ **Caution**
➡ Students are advised to write answers with an emphasis on writing the various keywords and points.

29. With reference to the General Assembly, explain the following:
(A) Its role in promotion of International Cooperation.
(B) Main objectives of the United Nations.
(C) Its functions.

Ans. (A) (1) To consider and make recommendations on the Principles of Cooperation, in the maintenance of international Peace and security.
(2) To initiate studies and make recommendations to promote international political, social and economic cooperation.
(3) To make recommendation for the Peaceful settlement of disputes.

(B) The main objectives of the United Nations are:
(1) To maintain international Peace and Security.
(2) To develop friendly relations among nations.
(3) To achieve international cooperation.
(4) To be a centre for harmonizing the actions of nations. **[Any three]**

(C) Functions of the General assembly are:
(1) **Financial Functions:** The General Assembly considers and approves the budget of the UNO and also determines the amount of funds to be contributed by the different members in accordance with their capacities.
(2) **Electoral Functions:** It elects the non-permanent members of the Security Council and the members of Trusteeship Economic and Social Council. It also elects the Judges of International Court of Justice and to appoint on the recommendations of the Security Council, the Secretary General of the United Nations.
(3) **Supervising Functions:** The General Assembly regulates the working of other organs and agencies of the UNO. It can bring changes in the working of any of its agencies, if required.
(4) **Other Functions:** The General assembly makes recommendations to promote international cooperation, human rights and fundamental freedom for all., it also helps in promoting international cooperation and friendship. Under the uniting for peace Resolution, if the Security Council is unable to reach a decision the General Assembly can deal with the problem.

⚠️ **Caution**
➡ Students should learn the functions of each organ and agency of the United Nations, specifying the key points in their functions.

30. The United Nations Organization was established to maintain peace and 'promote social progress and better standards of life in larger freedom'. With reference to this, explain the following:
(A) The composition of the Security Council.
(B) The role of UNESCO in the development of Science and Technology. **[ICSE 2013]**
(C) The functions of the Security Council related to maintaining World Peace.

Ans. (A) The Security Council of United Nations consists of 15 members. It has five permanent members viz. China, France, Russia, Great Britain and U.S.A. The ten non-permanent members are elected by the General Assembly by a two-third majority for the term of two years. A retiring member is not eligible for immediate re-election. The countries which are not the members of the Security Council but are party to a dispute may participate in its deliberations with no voting right. Each member of the Security Council is its President in turn for a month.

(B) The role of UNESCO in the development of Science and Technology is:

(1) It helps in establishing scientific and technological institutions, particularly in the developing countries. It also promotes basic research in subjects like Physics, Mathematics, Geology, Oceanography and Engineering;

(2) It organises seminars and conferences to bring together scientists, technocrats and other specialists to exchange their ideas and views about developments in modern science;

(3) It makes scientific and technological advancement available to all countries by providing information through books, journals, newsletters and exhibitions.

(C) The functions of the Security Council related to world peace are:

(1) To maintain international peace and security in accordance with the principles of the UN charter. The council can take any quick and effective action to prevent an international war.

(2) To investigate international disputes, any threat to peace or act of aggression and recommend appropriate methods of settling and resolving such disputes.

(3) To call for a cease-fire in case of disputes. A UN peace keeping force, consisting of troops from members countries, may be sent to the troubled area if a cease fire is ordered.

(4) To call on member states to apply and enforce economic sanctions against the aggressor and thus to put pressure on the guilty state to stop aggression.

(5) To take military action against the aggressor, if required. **[Any four]**

31.

Study the given picture and answer the questions that follow:

(A) Identify the organization associated with the above emblem.

Mention any three principles of this organization.

(B) Where is the headquarters of this organization located?

Who can become its member?

(C) Name the principal judicial organ of this organization and explain its composition.
[ICSE 2012]

Ans. (A) The organisation associated with the emblem is United Nations Organisation (UNO). The principles of United Nations Organisation are:

(1) To recognise the sovereignty and equality of all member nations;

(2) Every member nation should try to settle disputes, if any, by peaceful means through negotiations;

(3) The member nations should avoid any use of threat or violence in solving international problems;

(4) The member countries to help the UN in its function as per the charter. They should not aid any country against which the UN was taking any action;

(5) The United Nations on its part will not interfere in the internal affairs of the country. **[Any three]**

(B) The United Nations Organisation has its headquarters in New York in USA, with the exception of its European office which is located in Geneva, Switzerland.

The membership is open to all peace loving nations which agree to abide by the principles of the United Nations. Other countries are admitted to the United Nations by the General Assembly upon the recommendation of the Security Council by a two third majority of votes.

(C) The principal Judicial organ of the United Nations is the International Court of Justice. The court consists of 15 judges taken from different countries and are elected by the General Assembly and the Security Council for a nine-year term. No two judges can be citizens of the same country. The members of the court do not represent their governments but are independent Magistrates. Elections are held every three years for election of President and Vice-President, and they may be re-elected when their term of offce expires.

32. With reference to the formation of the UNO explain:

(A) Objectives of the UNO.

(B) Purpose of its formation.

(C) Guiding Principles of the UNO. **[HOT]**

Ans. (A) The Objectives of the UNO are as follows:
  (1) to save the world from any other world war and maintain peace and security.
  (2) to Promote respect for human rights and to co-operate internationally to solve humanitarian, social and cultural problems.
  (3) to develop friendly relations among nations and conditions under which international treaties can be maintained.
  (4) to promote social progress and better standards of life. To coordinate and harmonize the efforts of nations so that the above aims can be achieved.
  [Any three]

(B) The Purpose of the formation of the UNO was:
  (1) The League of Nations had failed to check the acts of aggression of the 1930 so a strong organization was needed.
  (2) The United horrors and widespread destruction caused by the Second World War led to nations wanting to set up an organization which was strong enough to settle disputes and avoid war.
  (3) The Atom Bomb used in the Second World War had made people realize the destructive power of nuclear weapons. A nuclear war could lead to the end of our civilization so they all were keen to set up a worldwide organization.
  (4) Mutual suspicion would eventually lead to an arms race. Thus, leaders wanted to build a durable organization which would bring a feeling of peace and security in the minds of the people.
  [Any three]

(C) **Guiding Principles of the UNO were:**
  In order to fulfill the purposes for which UNO was established, the members shall act in accordance with the following principles:
  (1) The UNO is based on the sovereign equality of all its members.
  (2) All members should settle their international disputes by peaceful means without putting in danger international peace and security.
  (3) All members should provide full co-operation to the UNO in its working.
  (4) No country should assist states against which Uno is taking some action.
  (5) All members should fulfill in good faith the obligations assumed by them.
  (6) The organization should ensure the States which are not members of the United Nations act in accordance with these principles.
  (7) It should not intervene in the domestic affairs of any country. **[Any four]**

33. **The Security Council is the most important organ of the UNO which looks after the security and Peace of the World.**
  In this context, describe the following:
  (A) Its Composition
  (B) Its decision-making procedure
  (C) Its functions

Ans. (A) It is the executive body of the UNO with 15 members. It has five permanent members.
  (a) China (b) France (c) Russia (d) Great Britain (e) The United States of America.
  The 10 non-permanent members are elected by the General Assembly by two-thirds majority for a two-year term. A retiring member is not eligible for immediate re-election. States which are not the members of the Security Council but are party to a dispute may participate in its deliberations with no voting right. Each member of the Security Council is its President in term for a month.

(B) Each member of the Council has one vote. The ordinary matters are decided by an affirmative of 9 members out of 15. Decisions on important matters require nine votes including the votes of all the 5 permanent members. The Permanent members have the right of 'Veto Power'. By exercising this power, any of the permanent members can reject the decision of the Security Council.

(C) The functions of the Security Council are:
  (1) To maintain international peace and security.
  (2) To investigate any dispute or situation which may lead to friction.
  (3) To recommend methods of setting with disputes.
  (4) To formulate plans for the regulation of armaments.
  (5) To determine the existence of a threat to peace or act of aggression and to recommend action against such a threat.
  (6) To call upon members to apply economic sanctions and other measures to stop aggression.
  (7) To take military action against an aggression.
  (8) To recommend admission of new members.
  (9) To exercise trusteeship functions of the United Nations.

(10) To elect Judges of the International Court of Justice.

(11) To recommend to the General Assembly the appointment of the Secretary General. **[Any four]**

34. With reference to the causes of the Second World War, answer the following:

(A) (i) Explain how the ideologies of Fascism and Nazism led to the Second World War.

(ii) How did the Japanese invasion of China create conditions for the outbreak of the war?

(B) Explain the consequences of the war with reference to the formation of the United Nations. **[HOT🔥] [ICSE 2014]**

Ans. (A) (i) The ideologies of Fascism and Nazism that led to the Second World War were:

(1) Both Nazism and Fascism did not believe in democracy and personal stated liberty. Hence, they did not allow any other party to operate.

(2) Like Mussolini, Hitler also believed in 'Nationalism' as a driving force for the people of their country.

(3) Both theories propagated the belief that nations become great only by defeating other nations in war.

(4) Both were intensely anti-communist.

(ii) Japan's expanisionism was one of the causes of the Second World War. Being rich in natural resources, Manchuria, a region of China, was taken over by Japan in 1931. The Japanese attack on Manchuria was the direct challenge to the League of Nations.

(B) The Second World War proved to be more destructive than the first. One of the results of the Second World War was the division of some of the major countries into two diametrically apposed ideological blocs: the Communist Bloc and the Western Bloc. The League of Nations established in 1919 after the First World War with the objective of fostering peace among the nations of the world failed miserably in its objective. With the invention and deployment of sophisticated nuclear weapons, the threat to the survival of modern civilization had intensified even more. Therefore, an organization was required to ensure that such deadly weapons would not be used.

To save the coming generations and the world from the ravaging effects of war, the three big leaders Roosevelt (President of USA), Winston Churchill (Prime Minister of Great Britain) and Joseph Stalin (Premier of USSR) held a conference at Yalta in the Soviet Union on 25 April, 1945. The representatives of 50 nations decided to establish a new Peace Keeping Organization, the United Nations. These nations were determined not to enter into any other alliances and to establish a formed peace keeping organization that would prevent hostilities among member countries.

The United Nations officially came into existence on 24 October, 1945. The principles of the United Nations are to save future generations from war, reaffirm human rights and establish equal rights for all persons. It also aims to promote justice, freedom and social progress for the people of all its member states.

14 Major Agencies of the United Nations

The UN has several specialised Agencies through which it operates. These work for social and economic development of the developing countries. Each agency has a particular agenda. They cover UNICEF, WHO and UNESCO

Chapter Notes

- United Nations International Children's Emergency Fund (UNICEF)
- World Health Organisation (WHO)
- United Nations Educational Scientific and Cultural Organisation (UNESCO)

The Second World War did not cause only loss of life and property but the economic and social structure of most of the countries was upset. Thus, the UNO formed many Special Agencies for the economic and social development of the backward countries. They are working in economic, social, cultural and scientific spheres and are making efforts to make life peaceful and prosperous. They are 16 in number and report annually to the Economic and Social Council.

Here, will study only three agencies of United Nations : UNICEF, WHO and UNESCO

TOPIC 1

UNITED NATIONS INTERNATIONAL CHILDREN'S EMERGENCY FUND (UNICEF)

The United Nations International Children's Emergency Fund (UNICEF) was created by the General Assembly during its first session in 1946 to purposefully help the emergency needs of children in post-war Europe and China. But later on in 1950, its programme was extended to provide long range benefits to children of all developing countries. Later on, its name was changed to United Nations Children's Fund. UNICEF is governed by a 36-member Executive Board, which reviews UNICEF activities and approves its policies, country programs and budgets.

Headquarters

The UNICEF has its headquarters in New York, and has more than 200 offices in developing countries.

Objectives

The main objective of UNICEF is to look after children's welfare especially in developing countries by providing people with low cost community based services in maternal and child health, nutrition and immunization, etc.

Functions

(1) UNICEF works for the Protection of Children in respect of their survival, health and well-being.
(2) It provides funds for training personnel, including health and sanitation workers, teachers and nutritionists.
(3) It provides technical supplies, equipment and other aids.
(4) It assists governments to plan develop and extend community–based services in the fields of maternal and child health, nutrition, clean water and sanitation.
(5) It provides help to children and mothers in emergencies arising from natural calamities, civil strikes and epidemics. **[Any four]**

 Related Theory

→ *Year 1990 was declared as the World Literacy year by UNICEF.*

TOPIC 2

WORLD HEALTH ORGANISATION (WHO)

The WHO or the World Health Organisation came into existence on April 7, 1948 when 26 members of the United Nations notified its Constitution. Till today, this day is celebrated as the "World Health Day" every year. All the countries of the world, which are the members of the U.N.O., are the members of governing body of the WHO, which is called the World Health Assembly. It meets annually to decide the policy, programme and budget of the WHO and to review its work. The executive organ of the World Health Assembly is the Executive Board Comprised of 31 members designated by as many countries.

Headquarters

The World Health Organisation (WHO) has its headquarters at Geneva, Switzerland.

Objectives

The main Objective of WHO is the attainment by all people, of the highest possible level of health.

Example 1. What is health, as per WHO?

Ans. Health is defined in WHO's Constitution as a state of complete well-being and not merely the absence of disease or infirmity.

Functions

(1) It helps countries to improve their health system by building up infrastructure especially man power, institutions and services for the individual and community.
(2) It gives important drugs needed for medical care.
(3) It promotes research to cure and prevent diseases.
(4) It works towards providing safe drinking water and adequate waste disposal.
(5) It organizes conferences, seminars and training for health care personnel from different countries.
(6) It defines standards for the strength and purity of medicines including biological products.

(7) It publishes health journals to create health consciousness among people. **[Any four]**

Example 2. WHO launched a programme to immunize children against which major diseases?

Ans. The WHO launched a programme to immunize children against six major diseases–Measles, Diphtheria, Tetanus, Tuberculosis, Polio and Whooping cough.

Example 3. When is World Health Day celebrated?

Ans. April 7 is celebrated as World Health Day every year.

 **Important**

→ WHO is governed by 194 Member States through the World Health Assembly. The headquarters of WHO are at Geneva in Switzerland.

TOPIC 3

UNITED NATIONS EDUCATIONAL SCIENTIFIC AND CULTURAL ORGANISATION (UNESCO)

This Organisation was founded on 4th November 1946. A Conference was held at London in November 1945, for the establishment of an educational, scientific and cultural organization. This Agency has a General Assembly which holds its meetings in two years to chalk out its policy and Programme. An Executive Board, consisting of 51 members is responsible for implementing its programmes it conducts at least two meetings in a year.

Headquarters

The Headquarters of UNESCO are in Paris.

Objectives

The main Objective of UNESCO is to contribute to Peace and security in the world by promoting collaboration among nations through education, science, culture and communication. This is undertaken to further respect for justice, for the rule of law for the human rights for all human beings.

Functions

The main functions of the UNESCO in the field of education are:

In the Field of Education

(1) Removal of illiteracy by encouragement to adult education, distance–education and the open school system.
(2) Emphasis on education of girls and women.
(3) Financial assistance for the education of disabled children.
(4) Provision of grants and fellowships to teachers and scholars, organisation of library systems and promotion of international understanding through education.
(5) Organisation of Book fairs and festivals at international and national level.
(6) Encouragement of Science education by providing regional training centres.
(7) Promotion of education as an instrument for international understanding.
(8) It aims to protect the World inheritance of books, works of art and rare manuscripts.
(9) It gives encouragement to artistic creations in literature and fine arts.
(10) It pays attention towards the cultural development through the medium of films.
(11) It sends cultural missions of different countries so that there would be development of contacts which may promote peace and prosperity.

Example 4. State the full forms of the following agencies of the United Nations–UNICEF, WHO, UNESCO.

Ans. (1) **UNICEF:** The full form is United Nations International Children's Emergency Fund.
(2) **WHO:** World Health Organisation.
(3) **UNESCO:** United Nations Educational Scientific and Cultural Organisation

In the Field of Science

The Scientific activities are undertaken by the UNESCO are:

(1) UNESCO organizes Seminars and Conferences of Scientists of various countries and circulates information through journals, press and exhibitions.
(2) It promotes basic research in fields like geology, mathematics, physics and oceanography.
(3) It helps in correcting the imbalance in scientific and technological manpower that exists.
(4) It encourages the study of social sciences in order to focus attention on combating all forms of discrimination, improving the status of women and helping the youth in solving their problems.

In the Field of Communication

(1) It has set up regional networks, trained technicians and deals with both hardware and software aspects of informatics.
(2) It improves the quality of the Press, the films and video services.
(3) It assists developing countries to develop communication.

(4) It upholds the freedom of the press and independence of the media.

In the field of Cultural Heritage

(1) It encourages modernization without the loss of cultural identity and diversity.
(2) UNESCO provides technical advice and assistance, equipment and funds for the preservation of monuments and other works of art. It has prepared a World Heritage List to identify the Monuments and Sites which are to be protected.

ICSE Suggestions
→ Students are advised to make flash cards to retain all the functions of the major agencies of the UN.
→ Present facts while answering questions.
→ Make flow charts to make your learning easy and permanent.
→ Write answers emphasising on keywords and points.

Glossary

(1) **UNICEF**—United Nations International Children's Emergency Fund is exclusively dedicated to the cause of children and Women especially in the developing countries.
(2) **WHO**—World Health Organisation works for the improvement of health and prevention of diseases.
(3) **UNESCO**—United Nations Educational Scientific and Cultural Organisation aims at promoting Education, Science and Culture in the member countries.

Chronology

11th December, 1946: UNICEF was formed.
4th November, 1946: UNESCO was formed
7th April, 1948: The World Health Organisation (WHO) was formed.

OBJECTIVE Type Questions

Multiple Choice Questions
[1 mark each]

1. Where is the headquarter of WHO established?
   (a) Paris (b) London
   (c) Chicago (d) Geneva

Ans. (d) Geneva
Explanation: World Health Organization (WHO) was established on 7th April 1948 with its headquarters at Geneva in Switzerland.

2. World Health Day is celebrated on ....
   (a) 7th April
   (b) 7th July
   (c) 24th September
   (d) 24th October [HOT🔥]

Ans. (a) 7th April
Explanation : WHO was established on April 7, 1948. So April 7 is celebrated as World Health Day every year.

3. When was the UNICEF established?
   (a) 1945 (b) 1946
   (c) 1944 (d) 1947

Ans. (b) 1946
Explanation : UNICEF was created by the UN General Assembly during its first session in 1946 to help the emergency needs of children in post-war Europe.

4. The headquarters of UNICEF is located at ....
   (a) San Francisco
   (b) New York
   (c) Geneva
   (d) Canberra [HOT🔥]

Ans. (c) Geneva
Explanation : The UNICEF has its headquarters in New York and has more than 200 offices in developing countries.

5. The headquarters of UNESCO is located at:
   (a) Brussels (b) Paris
   (c) Berlin (d) Melbourne [HOT🔥]

Ans. (b) Paris
Explanation : The headquarters of the UNESCO are in Paris.

6. The UNICEF is governed by a .... Member Executive Board.

(a) 46 (b) 56
(c) 26 (d) 36

Ans. *(d) 36*

Explanation : UNICEF is governed by a 36 Member Executive Board, which reviews UNICEF activities and approves its policies, country programmes and budgets.

7. The Executive Body of WHO consists of:
   (a) 32 members (b) 33 members
   (c) 34 members (d) 35 members

Ans. *(a) 32 members*

Explanation : The Executive Body of WHO consists of 32 members designated by as many countries.

8. The Executive Board of UNESCO consists of:
   (a) 56 members
   (b) 57 members
   (c) 58 members
   (d) 59 members

Ans. *(c) 58 members*

Explanation : The Executive Board of UNESCO consists of 58 members presently.

9. UNICEF was awarded the Nobel Prize for peace in:
   (a) 1964 (b) 1965
   (c) 1966 (d) 1967 [HOT🔥]

Ans. *(b) 1965*

Explanation : UNICEF was awarded the Nobel Prize for Peace in the year 1965.

10. The UNICEF works for the protection of children in respect of their ....
    (a) Survival (b) health
    (c) Well-being (d) All of these

Ans. *(d) All of these*

Explanation : UNICEF works for the protection of children in respect of their survival, health and well-being. This is done in cooperation with individuals, civic groups, governments and private sector.

11. UNICEF does NOT make efforts to prevent diseases like:
    (a) Skin diseases
    (b) Eye diseases
    (c) Cancer
    (d) Tuberculosis (T.B.)

Ans. *(c) Cancer*

Explanation : UNICEF makes effort to prevent diseases like skin diseases, eye diseases, Malaria and Tuberculosis (T.B.) but not in cancer.

12. WHO has achieved to eradicate ....
    (a) Measles (b) Chicken Pox
    (c) Small Pox (d) Cough and Cold

Ans. *(c) Small Pox*

Explanation : WHO has completely eradicated small pox. Since 1980, no cases of naturally occurring small pox have happened since then.

13. When was UNESCO established?
    (a) 4th October, 1948
    (b) 4th December, 1946
    (c) 4th October, 1947
    (d) 4th November, 1946

Ans. *(d) 4th November, 1946*

Explanation : UNESCO was established on 4th November, 1946.

14. WHO launched a programme to immunize children against .... major diseases.
    (a) four (b) six
    (c) five (d) three

Ans. *(b) six*

Explanation : The WHO launched a Programme to immunize children against six major diseases– measles, diphtheria, tetanus, tuberculosis, polio and whooping cough.

 **Caution**

➜ *Correct number of all diseases is a must, otherwise there will be deduction of marks.*

15. .... is the official monthly magazine of UNESCO.
    (a) Courier
    (b) Bulletin of the World Health Organisation
    (c) Public Health Panorama
    (d) The UN Chronicle [HOT🔥]

Ans. *(a) Courier*

Explanation : UNESCO organizes seminars and conferences of scientists of various countries and circulates information through Journals, Press and exhibitions. 'Courier' is the official monthly magazine of UNESCO. Its Hindu and Tamil editions are available in India.

16. "Respect for human rights and for fundamental freedoms for all without distinction of race, sex, languages or religion" is promoted by:
    (a) UNESCO (b) UNICEF
    (c) WHO (d) ILO

Ans. *(a) UNESCO*

Explanation : The work of UNESCO has been praised everywhere for promoting the broadcast of all the above mentioned objectives listed in the UN Charter. "Respect for human rights ...."

SUBJECTIVE Type Questions

Short Answer Type Questions

[**2** marks each]

17. **(A)** How many members are there in the executive board of UNICEF?

(B) Give the full form of UNICEF and WHO. **[ICSE 2020]**

Ans. (A) UNICEF is governed by 36 members of the executive board.

(B)

> **UNICEF:** United Nations International Children's Emergency Fund
> **WHO :** World Health Organisation
> **[Marking Scheme]**

📝 **What Examiners Say**

→ Most candidates attempted this part well. A few candidates misspelled words.

18. **(A)** When was WHO established?

(B) Where are the headquarters of WHO located?

Ans. (A) World Health Organisation (WHO) was established on 7th April, 1948.

(B) The headquarters of WHO are located in Geneva, Switzerland.

📝 **What Examiners Say**

→ Most of the candidates answered well except for a few, who wrote Social instead of Scientific.

19. Mention any two functions of UNESCO in the field of Education. **[ICSE 2017]**

Ans. The functions of UNESCO in the field of Education are:

(1) It works for promoting education among young children as well as adults, especially in the developing countries to eliminate illiteracy all over the world.

(2) It provides financial assistance to expand and guide education in different countries through distance education and open school system.

(3) It provides funds for the construction of schools and for the preparation of course material for study and text books.

(4) To inculcate reading habits amongst the public, it has set up libraries all over the world. **[Any two]**

📝 **What Examiners Say**

→ Common error in this question basically were that candidates mixed up the functions of UNESCO, UNICEF and WHO.

20. State the full forms of the following agencies of the United Nations :

UNICEF and UNESCO **[ICSE 2016]**

Ans. UNICEF – United Nations International Children Emergency Fund.

UNESCO – United Nations Educational, Scientific and Cultural Organisation.

📝 **What Examiners Say**

→ Some candidates wrote incorrect full forms with wrong spellings. For example, Emergency was written in place of Education and Social in place of Scientific.

📢 **Important**

→ It is important to learn the correct full forms of all major agencies of the United Nations.

21. Mention any two scientific activities of UNESCO.

Ans. Two scientific activities of UNESCO are following:

(1) It promotes research in the fields like Geology, Mathematics, Physics and Oceanography.

(2) It helps in correcting the imbalance in scientific and technological manpower, so existing.

Structured Questions

[**3+3+4= 10** marks each]

22. Look at the picture given and answer the questions that follow:

(A) What is the main objective of this organisation.

(B) State any three functions of this organisation.

(C) From where does this organisation gets its finance?

Ans. (A) The main objective of UNICEF is to look after children's welfare especially in developing countries by providing people with low cost community-based services in maternal, child health, nutrition and immunisation, etc.

(B) The main functions of UNICEF are:
(1) UNICEF works for the protection of children in respect of their survival, health and well-being.
(2) It provides funds for training personnel, including health and sanitation workers, teachers and nutritionists.
(3) It provides technical supplies, equipment and other aids, ranging from paper for textbooks, to equipment and medicines to health clinics to pipes and pumps for bringing clean water to villages.

(C) For financing its projects, UNICEF depends on voluntary contributions made by different governments, donations made by private agencies, sale of greeting cards and through various fund raising campaigns. Sale of UNICEF cards is an important source of income. Almost all the resources of UNICEF are diverted to the poorest developing countries with the largest share going to the children upto the age of five.

23. **Look at the picture given and answer the questions that follow:**

(A) What is the main objective of this organisation?
(B) Mention any three programmes of this organisation.
(C) Name any four functions of this organisation.

Ans. (A) WHO's objective is the attainment of the highest possible level of health by all people. Health is defined in WHO's constitution as a state of complete well-being and not merely the absence of disease or infirmity.

(B) (1) It organises conferences, seminars and training for health care personnel from different countries.
(2) It publishes health journals like the "Bulletin of the World Health Organisation" to create health conciousness among people.
(3) It provides help to children and mothers in emergencies arising from natural calamites, civil strifes, epidemics etc.

(C) The functions of WHO are as following:
(1) It helps countries to improve their health system by building up infrastructure especially man power, institutions and services for the individual and community.
(2) It gives important drugs needed for medical care.
(3) It promotes research to cure and prevent diseases.
(4) It works towards providing safe drinking water and adequate waste disposal.

24. **With reference to the United Nations Organisation, answer the following questions:**
(A) **State any three objectives of the United Nations Organisation.**
(B) **Mention any three functions of the General Assembly.**
(C) **What is the full form of WHO? Mention any three of its functions.**
   [Mod. ICSE Sem-2, 2022]

Ans. (A) The objectives of United Nations Organisations (UNO) are:
(1) To maintain international Peace and Security, to take collective measures for the prevention and removal of threats to peace, to suppress acts of aggression or other breaches of peace.
(2) To achieve international cooperation in solving international economic, social, cultural or humanitarian problems and encouraging respect for human rights and for fundamental freedoms.
(3) To develop friendly relationship among nations based on respect for the principle of equal rights and self-determination of people.

(B) Three functions of General Assembly are:
(1) To make recommendations for the peaceful settlement of disputes.
(2) To appoint the Secretary – General on the recommendation of the Security Council.
(3) To consider and approve the budget of the United Nations and to apportion the contributions among members.

(C) The Full form of WHO is World Health Organisation. The two functions of WHO are as follows:
(1) It helps countries to improve their health system by building up infrastructure especially manpower, institutions and services for the individual and community.
(2) It works towards providing safe drinking water and adequate waste disposal. The decade 1981-1990 was declared as the International Drinking Water Supply and Sanitation Decade.

(3) It Organises conferences, seminars and training for health care personnal from different countries.

25.

(A) Name the organization associated with the above Emblem.
Mention any two of its objectives.
(B) Mention any three functions of WHO, as its agency.
(C) Name the Principal Judicial Organ of this organization and explain its composition. **[ICSE 2020]**

Ans. (A) The organization associated with the Emblem is United Nations Organisation (UNO).
The objectives of United Nations Organisation are:
(1) To maintain international peace and security by preventing and removing all threats to peace and suppressing acts of aggression.
(2) To develop friendly relations among nations based on "respect for the principle of equal rights and self-determination of people."

(B) The functions of WHO are:
(1) It helps the member countries to strengthen their health infrastructure, by improving facilities for health, health institutions, manpower and health related services.
(2) It works towards providing safe drinking water to all and proper disposal of waste in developing and under-developed countries.
(3) To bring about improvement in nutrition, mother and child care, mental health, medical care, environmental safety, prevention of accidents, etc.
(4) It provides effective immunization for children against six major communicable diseases—Polio, Measles, Tetanus, Diphtheria, Tuberculosis and Whooping cough.
(5) It sets standards to check the purity and strength of various life-saving drugs, medicines and other biological products.
(6) It promotes research for development of new technologies in the area of medical care to cure and prevent diseases.
[Any three]

(C) The principal Judicial organ of the United Nations is the International Court of Justice.
Note : For rest of answer refer answers given in marking scheme.

(A) **United Nations Objectives:**
(1) Maintain international peace and security.
(2) To develop friendly relations among nations.
(3) To achieve international cooperation among nations
(4) Solving problems of economic, social, cultural & humanitarian character.
(5) To be a centre for harmonizing the actions of nations.
(6) To disarm
(7) Decolonize
(8) Create faith in human rights.
(9) Establish conditions to maintain international law and international treaties.
(10) To save from scourge of war.
[Any three]

(B) **Functions of WHO:**
(1) Direct and coordinate health work on an international scale.
(2) Works in fields of communicable diseases
(3) Maintains child health
(4) Mental health
(5) Cancer – Diabetes – Eradicate scale /smallpox was eradicated by global campaign by WHO.
(6) Promote the provision of good health and living conditions of the people.
(7) To set international standards with regard to food and medicines.
(8) To provide safe drinking water.
(9) Vaccination/immunization against six major diseases like, measles, diphtheria, tetanus, TB, polio & whooping cough/diarrheal deaths have reduced.
(10) Promote research, to cure and prevent diseases.
(11) Organizes conferences, research, seminars, etc.
(12) Publishes health journals/bulletins/magazines.
(13) Set international standards for biological products and pharmaceutical products such as rugs, medicines, vaccines.

Bring about improvement in nutrition
(14) Housing
(15) Sanitation
(16) Work conditions
(17) Hygiene
(18) Built medical sciences library in Geneva
(19) Infant mortality rate has dropped
(20) Organised malaria and polio eradication programmes globally. **[Any three]**

(C) **The International Court of Justice Composition:**
(1) Consists of 15 judges.
(2) Elected for a period of 9 years.
(3) Elected by the General Assembly and the Security Council.
(4) Each judge is from different country.
(5) Elects its President and Vice President for a period of 3 years.
[Marking Scheme]

What Examiners Say
→ (A) Most of the candidates named the organization associated with the Emblem correctly. However, a few candidates confused the emblem with that of the 'WHO'. A few candidates did not mention the two objectives correctly.
→ (B) This part of the question was answered well by most candidates barring a few who mixed up the functions of WHO with the functions of UNICEF, as some health and hygiene related functions are similar.
→ (C) Some candidates confused the Principal Judicial Organ of the United Nations with the General Assembly and the Security Council.

26. The necessity to maintain international peace led to the establishment of the United Nations Organization. With reference to this statement, answer the following:

(A) Write any three functions of UNESCO that preserves our 'Cultural Heritage'.
(B) State the Composition of the Security Council.
(C) Write any four functions of the General Assembly. **[ICSE 2019]**

Ans. (A) The functions of UNESCO that preserves our Cultural Heritage are:
(1) It helps the member countries in the preservation of their cultural heritage and also protects monuments of artistic or historic symbolic interests.
(2) It promotes the free-flow of information, freedom of expression, press-freedom and media-independence. To increase the scope and quality of the press, film and radio-service throughout the world is another objective of the UNESCO.
(3) It encourages cultural interchange. It provides travel grants to writers and artists.

(B) The Security Council of United Nations consists of 15 members. It has five permanent members viz. China, France. Russia, Great Britain and U.S.A. The ten non-permanent members are elected by the General Assembly by a two-third majority for the term of two years. A retiring member is not eligible for immediate re-election. The countries which are not the members of the Security Council but are party to a dispute may participate in its deliberations with no voting right. Each member of the Security Council is its President in turn for a month.

(C) The functions of the General Assembly are:
(1) The General Assembly considers and approves the budget of the UNO.
(2) The General Assembly elects the non-permanent members of the Security Council and the members of Trusteeship, Economic and Social Council. It also elects the Judges of International Court of Justice and to appoint on the recommendations of the Security Council, the Secretary General of the United Nations.
(3) The General Assembly regulates the working of other organs and agencies of the UNO
(4) The General Assembly makes recommendations to promote international co-operation, human rights and fundamental freedom for all. It also helps in promoting international cooperation and friendship.

(A) **Preservation of Cultural Heritage:**
(1) UNESCO provides technical advice and assistance, equipment and funds for the preservation of monuments and other works of art. It has prepared a World Heritage List to identify the monuments and sites which are to be protected.
(2) It aims to protect the world inheritance of books, works of art and rare manuscripts.
(3) It gives encouragement to artistic creations in literature and fine arts.
It sends cultural missions to different countries so that there

would be development of contacts which may promote peace and prosperity.

It helps the member states in the preservation of their cultural heritage.

It encourages translation of rare manuscripts.

It plays a vital role in distributing knowledge about Human Rights.

[Any three]

(B) **Composition:** The Council consists of 15 members.

It has five permanent members– China, France, Russia, Britain and the United States of America.

The regional representation of the ten non-permanent members is:

(1) Afro-Asian Countries - 5
(2) Latin American Countries – 2
(3) West European and other Countries – 2
(4) East European Countries-1– The ten non-permanent members are elected by the General Assembly by a two-third majority for a term of two years.

A retiring member is not eligible for immediate re-election.

The Presidency of the Council rotates monthly, according to the English alphabetical listing of its member states. **[Any three]**

(C) **Functions of General Assembly:**

(1) To make recommendations for the peaceful settlement of disputes
(2) To promote political, social and economic cooperation
(3) To receive and consider reports from the Security Council and other organs of UN.
(4) To consider and approve the budget of the UN.
(5) To regulate the working of other organs and agencies of UN.
(6) To elect the non-permanent members of the Security Council.
(7) To elect judges of the ICJ.
(8) To appoint Secretary General on the recommendation of Security Council.
(9) To amend the UN Charter.
(10) Functions under 'Uniting for Peace Resolution' 1950.
(11) New members are admitted by the General Assembly on the recommendation of Security Council.

[Any four]
Marking Scheme]

What Examiners Say

→ (A) Many candidates instead of writing the functions of the UNESCO which preserve our Cultural Heritage, wrote its general functions relating to education and science.

→ (B) Majority of the candidates stated the composition of the Security Council correctly, barring a few candidates who wrote the composition of the General Assembly.

→ (C) Attempted well by most of the candidates. However, a few candidates mixed up the functions of the General Assembly with that of the Security Council.

27. With reference to the United Nations and its Specialized Agencies, answer the following:

(A) Mention any three functions of the International Court of Justice.
(B) State the composition of the General Assembly.
(C) State any two functions of the UNICEF and any two functions of WHO.

[ICSE 2018]

Ans. (A) The functions of International Court of Justice are:

(1) **Compulsory Jurisdiction:** The jurisdiction extends to disputes pertaining to the inter- pretation of international law, reparation i.e., compensation for breach of international obligation.

(2) **Voluntary Jurisdiction:** This jurisdiction covers all cases which the parties refer to it. If a party refers a dispute, the court may sit for a hearing only if the other party presents itself before the court otherwise the reference is first filed.

(3) **Advisory Role:** The General Assembly or the Security Council may request the International Court of Justice to give its advice or opinion on any legal question. The other organs and other specialized agencies may also make similar requests.

(4) **Codification of International Law:** The International Court of Justice plays an important role in the codification of international law after thoroughly examining international conventions, customs and judicial decisions.

(5) **Peaceful Settlement of Disputes:** The court can recommend appropriate procedures of methods of settlement. The members of the United Nations have an obligation to abide by the decision of the court. **[Any three]**

(B) The General Assembly is the largest legislative organ of the United Nations. It is the only organ in the United Nations which consists of all the members of the United Nations. Each state can send up to five representatives but is entitled to one vote in the assembly. This ensures that all the member states have equal status. The General Assembly meets once a year for three months. At the beginning of every session, the assembly elects a new president.

(C) **The functions of UNICEF are:**
   (1) To extend services those are beneficial to children in consultation with the government concerned and in the light of experience of the member countries;
   (2) To provide children in member states, especially in the developing countries, nutritious food like milk, meat, fish, etc.
   (3) To prevent fatal diseases like measles, diphtheria, tetanus, tuberculosis, polio, whooping cough, etc.
   (4) To extend support to programmes such as suppression of trafficking of women, children and also to prevent juvenile crimes. **[Any two)**

The functions of WHO are:
   (1) It helps the member countries to strengthen their health infrastructure by improving facilities for health, health institutions, main power and health related services.
   (2) To bring about improvement in nutrition. mother and child care, mental health, medical care, environmental safety,

(A) **Three functions of the International Court of Justice:**
   (1) Advisory opinion on legal matters to the organs of special agencies of the UN.
   (2) Decides disputes between member states when referred.
   (3) Disputes concerning interpretation of international law.
   (4) Compensation for breeding international law & treaty/agreements
   (5) Certification of International law
   (6) To suggest methods for peaceful settlement of disputes. **[Any three]**

(B) (1) All members of the United Nations are members of the General Assembly.
   (2) Each state has five representatives in the General Assembly.
   (3) Each state has only one vote.
   (4) It is a kind of Parliament.
   (5) At the starting of each session the assembly elects a new President, 21 vice Presidents. The Presidency rotates each year among five groups of state. **[Any three]**

(C) **Functions of UNICEF**
   (1) To render assistance in providing protective food like milk, meat, fish and fats to the children. It takes care of interests of women and pregnant mothers.
   (2) To provide funds for the training of health and sanitation workers nutritionist and crèche workers.
   (3) Universal Child Immunization against preventable diseases by 1990.
   (4) To extend support to programmes such as suppression of traffic in women and children and prevention of crimes committed by children.
   (5) To provide instant help to children and women when some disaster like earthquake happens or overtaken by an epidemic.
   (6) To supply paper to publish textbooks.
   (7) Technical supplies, equipment and other aids for medicines and pipes and pumps for bringing clean water to villages. **[Any two]**

Functions of WHO
   (1) Direct and coordinate health work on an international scale.
   (2) Eradicate disease
   (3) Promote the provision of good health and living conditions of the people.
   (4) To set international standards for food and medicines.
   (5) To provide safe drinking water.
   (6) Vaccination /immunization against six major diseases.
   (7) It promotes research to cure and prevent disease.
   (8) To organize conferences and seminars.
   (9) It publishes magazines and bulletins. **[Any two]**
[Marking Scheme]

Major Agencies of the United Nations

What Examiners Say

→ (A) Several candidates did not write three functions of the International Court of Justice correctly. They mixed-up the functions of the United Nations and the Security Council.

→ (B) Majority of the candidates stated the composition of the General Assembly correctly. A few candidates, however, wrote the composition of the Security Council.

→ (C) Most of the candidates stated the functions of the UNICEF and WHO correctly. However, some candidates, instead of writing the functions of UNICEF wrote the functions of UNESCO.

15. Non-Aligned Movement

After the Second World War, the concept of Non-Alignment emerged during the Cold War, when the world was divided into two Power blocs. It was during the period that many newly independent countries in Asia and Africa decided not to join any of the two blocs and to remain non-aligned.

Chapter Notes

- Non-Aligned Movement

TOPIC 1

NON-ALIGNED MOVEMENT

After the Second World War, the concept of Non-Alignment emerged during the Cold War, When the world was divided into two Power blocs. It was during the period that many newly independent countries in Asia and Africa decided not to join any of the two blocs and to remain non-aligned.

Meaning of Non-Alignment

The Strategy of the new independent States of Asia, Africa and South America to keep themselves away from the power blocs in order to protect their independence is known as 'Non-Alignment'. The Concept of non-alignment emerged during the Cold War. After the Second World War, the World was divided into two power blocs one led by the USA and other by erstwhile Soviet Union. It was during this period that many newly independent countries in Asia and Africa decided not to join any of the two blocs and to remain non-aligned.

The main features of the NAM are the following:

(1) It is not aligned to any of the Power blocs.
(2) It is opposed to any kind of military alliances like NATO, SEATO, Warsaw Pact, etc.
(3) It retains its freedom to take independent Foreign Policy decisions.
(4) It does not remain aloof from international problems. It actively participates in the politics among nations. So, non-alignment stands for 'action' rather than passivism.
(5) It judges an issue on merit. It upholds the rights of all people for freedom and justice.

Objectives of the Non-Aligned Movement

(1) The main objective of the NAM at the beginning was to keep away the newly independent countries of Asia and Africa from the super rivalry and to protect and preserve their newly acquired independence, because they were militarily weak.
(2) The newly emerged states did not like to be involved in foreign Wars in which they had no interest.
(3) Colonialism and Imperialism had encouraged the spirit of exploitation, so every attempt was made by non-aligned countries to end Colonialism and Imperialism.
(4) The non-aligned countries kept themselves away from Power blocs so that they could do something to defuse the tense atmosphere and if there was any war, they may act as mediators and prevent war and bring peace in the world.
(5) The NAM was against the spirit of welfares. It had full faith in co-operation and peaceful co-existence.
(6) The non-aligned countries had firm faith in the principle of equality. They condemned racial discrimination as negation of humanity in South Africa.
(7) The non-aligned countries kept themselves away from the Power blocs, so as to receive economic and technical assistance from both the blocs.
(8) The non-aligned countries wanted to establish economic relations between the nations based on equality because they were essential for economic and social reconstruction at home.
(9) To oppose the use of force and the use of nuclear weapons because they poisoned the whole atmosphere.
(10) The non-aligned countries had full respect for human rights because they were necessary for the development of the individuals and to protect the environment.

Architects of NAM

The Non-Aligned Movement was formally launched at its first Summit held in September 1961 at Belgrade in Yugoslavia. It was attended by 25 Afro-Asian and one European Country (Cyprus). Three Latin American countries participated as observers.

The Conference was attended by Prime Minister Jawaharlal Nehru of India, President Gamal Abdel Nasser of Egypt and President Joseph Broze Tito of Yugoslavia. These three are considered as the 'Founding fathers' or 'Architects of NAM'.

Example 1. The Belgrade Summit was attended by how many Non-Aligned nations?

Ans. The Belgrade Summit was attended by the leaders of 25 Non-Aligned nations.

Example 2. Who was the Chairperson during First Summit of Non-Aligned Movement?

Ans. Marshal Tito was the Chairperson during First Summit of Non-Aligned Movement.

 Caution
↪ Students should learn the names of three Architects of NAM along with correct spellings, so that they should not loose marks.

ICSE Suggestions
↪ Mark and underline the key words and key points.
↪ Do not write unwanted detail in an answer.
↪ Explain the relevance of the term NAM in the background of the formation of military alliances by the super powers, by not joining the alliance to boost their economic development and to promote world peace.
↪ Instruct students to learn all the facts that can assist in enhancing their performances.

 **Glossary**

(1) **Non-Alignment**—A strategy of not joining either of the two power blocs.
(2) **Belgrade Conference**—The First Summit of NAM was held at Belgrade in Yugoslavia in 1961.
(3) **Third World**—Economically underdeveloped nations.

OBJECTIVE Type Questions

Multiple Choice Questions
[1 mark each]

1. **Which of the following was not a founder member of Non-Aligned Movement?**
   (a) Jawahar Lal Nehru, Prime Minister of India
   (b) Winston Churchill, Prime Minister of United Kingdom
   (c) Joseph Broze Tito, President of Yugoslavia
   (d) Sukarno, President of Indonesia.

   Ans. *(b) Winston Churchill, Prime Minister of United Kingdom.*

   Explanation : The founders of Non-Aligned Movement were Jawaharlal Nehru, Prime Minister of India, President Joseph Broze Tito of Yugoslavia and Sukarno President of Indonesia and not Winston Churchill, Prime Minister of United Kingdom.

2. **Many new independent countries of .... decided not to join any of the two blocs and to remain non-aligned.**
   (a) Asia and North America
   (b) Australia and Asia
   (c) Asia and Africa
   (d) Asia and Europe

   Ans. *(c) Asia and Africa*

   Explanation : After the Second World War many newly countries in Asia and African decided not to join any of the two blocs and to remain non-aligned. Thus, non-alignment was the chief characteristics of awakening in Asia and Africa.

3. **The main features of NAM are the following:**
   (i) It is not aligned to any of the power blocs.
   (ii) It is opposed to any kind of military alliances.
   (iii) It judges an issue on merit.
   (iv) It does not remain aloof from international problems.
   (v) It retains its freedom to take independent foreign policy decisions.

   (a) (i), (ii) & (iii)
   (b) (ii), (iii) & (iv)
   (c) (i), (ii), (iii) & (iv)
   (d) (i), (ii), (iii), (iv) & (v)

   Ans. *(d) (i), (ii), (iii), (iv) & (v)*

   Explanation: Non-Alignment is the international policy of a sovereign state according to which it does not align itself with any of the power blocs at the same time actively peace, harmony and cooperation. The main features of Nam are all of the above.

4. **The Non-Aligned Movement was formally launched at its first Summit held in ....**
   (a) 1961
   (b) 1963
   (c) 1964
   (d) 1966

   Ans. *(a) 1961*

   Explanation: The Non-Aligned Movement was formally launched at its first summit held in September 1961 at Belgrade in Yugoslavia.

5. **Who are called 'founding fathers' of NAM?**
   (i) Prime Minister Nehru of India
   (ii) President Joseph Broze Tito of Yugoslavia
   (iii) President Nasser of Egypt
   (iv) King Mahendru Bir Bikram Shah of Nepal

   (a) (i), (iii) & (iv)
   (b) (i), (ii) & (iii)
   (c) (ii), (iii) & (iv)
   (d) (i), (ii) & (iv)

   Ans. *(b) (i), (ii) & (iii)*

   Explanation: The NAM Conference was attended by Prime Minister Nehru of India, President Joseph Broze Tito of Yugoslavia and President Nasser of Egypt. And these three are considered as the 'founding fathers' of NAM.

6. **One of the Objective of the Non-Aligned Movement was to oppose**
   (i) Colonialism
   (ii) Dictatorship
   (iii) Imperialism
   (iv) Racial discrimination

   (a) (i), (ii) & (iii)

(b) (ii), (iii) & (iv)
(c) (i), (iii) & (iv)
(d) (i), (ii) & (iv)

Ans. (c) (i), (iii) & (iv)

Explanation: The objective of NAM was to oppose against Colonialism, Imperialism and Racial discrimination.

7. The term Non-Alignment means ....
   (a) not to form any new alliance
   (b) not to align with any of the power blocs
   (c) not to participate in the world affairs
   (d) to be part of military alliances.
   [ICSE-2022, 2nd Semester Exam]

Ans. (a) not to align with any of the power blocs

Explanation : The Non-alignment is the international policy of a sovereign state according to which it does not align itself with any of the power blocs and at the same time actively participate in the world affairs to promote international peace, harmony and cooperation.

SUBJECTIVE Type Questions

Short Answer Type Questions
[**2** marks each]

8. **When and where was the First Summit of Non-Aligned Movement held?**

Ans. The First Summit of Non-Aligned Movement was held in September, 1961 at Belgrade in Yugoslavia.

9. **What is meant by the term 'Non-Aligned Movement'?** [ICSE 2015]

Ans. The Non Aligned Movement is an international organization of developing countries that are not formally aligned with or against any major power bloc. A non-aligned country is an independent country that can take a clear stand on various international issues.

10. **Name the two architects of NAM.** [HOT🔥] [ICSE 2015]

Ans. (1) Jawaharlal Nehru (Prime Minister of India).
(2) Garnal Abdel Nasser (President of Eqypt).
(3) Joseph Broz Tito (President of Yogoslavia)
[Any two]

11. **Mention any two factors responsible for the development of the policy of Non-Alignment.**

Ans. (1) Cold War
(2) Struggle against Imperialism, Racial discrimination and Colonialism.

12. **Name any four countries which attended the first summit of NAM.**

Ans. Egypt, Cyprus, India, Nepal, Burma (Myanmar), Indonesia, Ghana, Ethiopia, etc. [Any four]

13. **Name the European countries which attended the first NAM Summit.**

Ans. Cyprus was the only European country which attended first Summit of NAM.

14. **Mention two Objectives of Non-Aligned Movement.**

Ans. (1) To eliminate all the causes which could lead to war.
(2) To advocate sovereign equality of all States.

15. **Explain the term 'Non-Alignment'.** [ICSE 2014]

Ans. The term 'Non-Alignment' does not imply isolation, neutrality or a negative approach to international issues but it is generally used to describe the constructive and positive foreign polices of nations leading to freedom, peace, security and cooperation. This policy to remain neutral was first adopted by countries like India, Burma, Ceylon and Indonesia. A non-aligned country is an independent country that can take a clear stand on various international issues.

16. **Explain two factors responsible for the formation of NAM.** [ICSE 2014]

Ans. The factors that led to the formation of Non-Aligned Movement were:

(1) **Nationalism:** Nationalism was the most important feature of freedom movements in Asian and African countries. Nationalism in the East was movement to obtain freedom after a long struggle. To preserve this freedom, nations were determined to follow a course whereby they may not become tools in the hands of the big powers. They preferred to follow a policy of non-alignment.

(2) **Anti-Colonialism:** Anti-colonial feelings persisted in the countries of Asia and Africa after they attained independence. It largely contributed to the growth of the policy of non-alignment. These powers were afraid as they may again be subjugated by colonial powers. They were determined to keep off these colonial powers by avoiding membership of blocs and adopting an independent course of action, keeping out of all sorts of alliances.

(3) **Underdevelopment and Economic Aid:** The countries of Asia and Africa who gained independence were underdeveloped. They were keen to improve the standard of living of their people and promote systematic

development of their country. They needed capital and financial assistance from the powers of both the blocs to achieve their objectives at a fast rate. Therefore, they thought it proper to keep off from political alliances and pursue the policy of non-alignment.

(4) **Racial and Cultural Aspects:** Since long, colonial powers have fed the Afro-Asian nations with the idea that they were racially as well as culturally backward. The feeling evoked mutual sympathy among people to the newly emerged states of Africa and Asia. Being common victims of economic exploitation and political domination by the European countries, they had a sense of affinity which led them to co-operate with others.

[Any two]

Factors responsible for the formation of Non-Alignment Movement:

(1) **The global tension caused by the cold war:** Most of the newly independent countries of Asia and Africa realized that the division of the world into two power blocs was not in their interest and would endanger world peace. They therefore, wanted to maintain distance from the super powers.

(2) **Struggle against imperialism and neo colonization:** The newly independent nations wanted to enjoy their newly acquired freedom and the power without being under the pressure of bigger nations.

(3) **Right of independent judgement:** The newly independent nations were able to keep their own identity by not aligning with any of the power blocs. They did not want outside interference in solving their own problems.

(4) **Use of moderation in relation to all big powers:** The newly independent nations wanted to promote good will and co-operation among the Asian and African nations to advance their mutual interests by maintaining friendly relations.

(5) **Restructuring international economic order:** The newly independent countries were economically backward. To boost their economic development, they needed both capital and technical know how so they thought it would be worth while to take help from wherever they could without any strings attached with them.

(6) **Formation of a collective force:** These newly independent nations realised

Formation of a collective force: These newly independent nations realised that ever though they did not have the military and economic power to influence international affairs, they had moral force and with their collective reason they could maintain and promote world peace.

[Any two]
[Marking Scheme]

What Examiners Say

→ *Most candidates answered the question correctly with reference to the Cold War and the Super Powers forming the blocks. However, candidates need to explain the other factors which were equally important.*

Structured Questions

[3+3+4= **10** marks each]

17. (A) What is meant by the term Non-Alignment? Name any two founders of the Non-Aligned Movement.

(B) Mention any three objectives of the Non-Aligned Movement.

(C) Mention any four functions of WHO.

Ans. (A) The term Non-Alignment does not imply isolation, neutrality or a negative approach to international issues but it is generally used to describe the constructive and positive foreign policies of nations leading to freedom, peace, security and cooperation. This policy to remain neutral was first adopted by countries like India, Burma, Ceylon and Indonesia. A non-aligned country is an independent country that can take a clear stand on various international issues.

The founders of Non-alignment movement were:

(1) Pandit Jawahar Lal Nehru, Prime Minister of India;
(2) Sukarno, President of Indonesia;
(3) Josph Broze Tito, President of Yugoslavia.
(4) Gamal Abdel Nasser, President of Egypt.
(5) Kwame Nkurmah, President of Ghana.

[Any two]

(B) The objectives of non-aligned movement were:

(1) The newly independent nations should remain non-aligned and preserve their independence;
(2) No participation in foreign conflicts without having any interest involved;
(3) All non-aligned movement led countries should be away from the race of arms and have full faith in co-operation and peaceful existence.

(C) The functions of WHO are:
   (1) It helps the member countries to strengthen their health infrastructure, by improving facilities for health, health institutions, manpower and health related services.
   (2) It works towards providing safe drinking water to all and proper disposal of waste in developing and under-developed countries.
   (3) To bring about improvement in nutrition, mother and child care, mental health, medical care, environmental safety, prevention of accidents, *etc.*
   (4) It provides effective immunization for children against six major communicable diseases Polio, Measles, Tetanus, Diptheria, Tuberculosis and Whooping cough.
   (5) It sets standards to check the purity and strength of various life saving drugs, medicines and other biological products.
   (6) It promotes research for development of new technologies in the area of medical care to cure and prevent diseases. **[Any four]**

18. (A) When did the concept of non-alignment emerge? Why?
   (B) Name three founder members of Non-Aligned Movement.
   (C) What are the functions of the General Assembly of United Nations?

Ans. (A) The concept of Non-alignment emerged during the cold war. The world was divided into two power blocs-one led by the USA and the other by the erstwhile Soviet Union.
   (B) The founder members of Non-Aligned Movement were:
      (1) Pandit Jawahar Lal Nehru, Prime Minister of India.
      (2) Sukarno, President of Indonesia;
      (3) Joseph Broze Tito, President of Yugoslavia.
      (4) Colonel Gamal Abdel Nasser, President of Egypt.
      (v) Kwame Nkurmah, President of Ghana. **[Any three]**
   (C) The functions of the General Assembly are:
      (1) Consider and make recommendations on the principles of cooperation, in the maintenance of international peace and security;
      (2) Discuss any question related to international peace and security and to make recommendations on it;
      (3) Discuss and make recommendations on any questions within the scope of the charter;
      (4) Initiate studies and make recommendations to promote international political, social and economic cooperation.

19. (A) What is meant by Veto power which is enjoyed by the permanent members of the Security Council?
   (B) Explain three objectives of the united Nations.
   (C) What are the basic principles of Non-Aligned Movement?

Ans. (A) Each member of the Security Council has one vote. Decisions on procedural matters are made by an affirmative vote of nine members, including the concurring votes of all five permanent members. The negative vote of a permanent member is called a veto. The council is powerless to act if any of the five permanent members uses the veto power. However, abstinence from voting does not amount to a negative veto or vote.
   (B) The objectives of United Nations are:
      (1) To maintain international peace and security;
      (2) To develop friendly relations among nations based on respect for the principle of equal rights and self determination of people.
      (3) To achieve international cooperation in sowing international economic, social cultural, or humanitariam problems and encouraging respect for human rights and for fundamental freedoms.
   (C) The principles of Non-aligned movement are:
      (1) Mutual non-interference in each other's internal affairs;
      (2) Mutual non-aggression;
      (3) Equality for mutual benefit;
      (4) Mutual respect for each other's territorial integrity and sovereignty; and
      (5) Peaceful co-existence.

20. Which reference to the Second World War and the Non-Aligned Movement, answer the following:
   (A) Explain briefly three reasons for the Dissatisfaction with the Treaty of Versailles.
   (B) State any three consequences of the Second World War.
   (C) Mention any four chief architects of the Non-Aligned Movement. **[ICSE 2020]**

Ans. (A) The reasons for the dissatisfaction with the Treaty of Versailles were:
(1) It demanded disintegration of Germany and creation of many states.
(2) Germany was forcibly divided into two parts for the benefit of Poland.
(3) Germany was burdened with an immense war indemnity and was forced to surrender important territories like Rhineland, Ruhr, Saar and some parts of her foreign colonies as well.

(B) The consequences of the Second World War were:
(1) **Cold war:** The cold war was one of the most significant consequences of the Second World War that divided the major portion of the world into two blocs.
(2) **Defeat of Axis Powers:** The Second World War resulted in the defeat of Axis powers. Germany was defeated and divided into two regions. West Germany was administrated by Britain, France and USA and the East Germany was administered by Soviet Union.
(3) **Formation of the United Nations Organisation (UNO):** To save the coming generations and the world from ravaging effects of war, a conference was held at Yalta in the Soviet, where representatives of 50 nations decided to establish a new world peace keeping organisation, the United Nations.

(C) The architects of Non-Aligned Movement were:
(1) Jawahar Lal Nehru, Prime Minister of India
(2) Gamal Abdel Nasser, President of Egypt
(3) Sukarno, President of Indonesia
(4) Joseph Broze Tito, President of Yugoslavia.

(A)
(1) Demand annexation of German territories and creation of many states. Germans felt humiliated and helpless. Sowed the seeds of bitterness and conflict.
(2) All the German colonies were forcibly taken away and was divided into two parts for the benefit of Poland.
(3) Burdened with huge war indemnity which could never be paid.
(4) This humiliation gave rise to the spirit of revenge and Germany started looking for an opportunity to do away with the Treaty.

(5) Germany had to pay 3 billion dollars. It had to cede large territories to France, Belgium, Poland, and Denmark.
(6) Italians felt they won the war but lost the peace.
(7) Allies deserted her and she received no valuable addition to her territories.
(8) Germany was crippled.
(9) Danzig was internationalized.
[Any three]

(B)
(1) Defeat of the Axis powers.
(2) Formation of the UN.
(3) Cold war/ rise of communism.
(4) Germany was defeated and divided into four zones.
(5) Nazism came to end.
(6) Japan lost all territories acquired or seized by Japan were taken away.
(7) Italy defected and surrendered. France was liberated/Germany army in Paris surrendered.
[Any three]

(C)
(1) The four architects of NAM are:
(2) Jawahar Lal Nehru of India,
(3) Joseph B. Tito of Yugoslavia
(4) Nasser of Egypt
(5) Sukarno of Indonesia
[Marking Scheme]

What Examiners Say
→ (A) Some candidates mentioned all provisions of the Treaty of Versailles instead of the reasons for the dissatisfaction with the Treaty of Versailles.
→ (B) This subpart was attempted well by many candidates. However, some candidates focused only on the details of the defeat of the Axis powers.
→ (C) Most candidates attempted this part well.

⚠ Caution
→ (A) Treaty of Versailles, the causes, main clauses and how it became a cause of World War II should be discussed in detail.
→ (B) Students should point out the consequences of the Second World War.
→ (C) Students should remember the names in History for each Movement and Organisation.

21. The horrors of the two World Wars, led to the formation of the United Nations Organisations, while the formation of the Non-Aligned Movements followed later. In this context, answer the following:

(A) Mention any three aims and objectives of the United Nations Organisations.
(B) Explain any three functions of the Security Council.
(C) Explain any four factors that led to the formation of the Non-Aligned Movement. [HOT🔥] [ICSE 2017]

Ans. (A) The aims and objectives of the United Nations Organization are:
(1) To maintain international peace and security.
(2) To develop friendly relations among nations based on "respect for the principle of equal rights and self-determination of people;
(3) To achieve cooperation in solving international economic, social, cultural and humanitarian problems.
(4) To promote and encourage respect for fundamental human rights for all, irrespective of race, sex, language or religion. **[Any three]**

(B) The functions of Security Council are:
(1) To maintain international peace and security in accordance with the principles of the UN charter.
(2) To formulate plans, submitted to the members of the UN on issues such as regulation of armaments.
(3) To call on member States to apply and enforce economic sanctions against the aggressor and thus to put pressure on the guilty state to stop aggression;
(4) To take military action against the aggressor, if required;
(5) To investigate international disputes, any threat to peace or act of aggression and recommend appropriate methods of settling and resolving such disputes. **[Any three]**

(C) The factors that led to the formation of Non-Aligned Movement were:
(1) **Nationalism:** Nationalism was the most important feature of freedom movements in Asian and African countries. Nationalism in the East was movement to obtain freedom after a long struggle. To preserve this freedom, nations were determined to follow a course whereby they may not become tools in the hands of the big powers. They preferred to follow a policy of non-alignment.
(2) **Anti-Colonialism:** Anti-colonial feelings persisted in the countries of Asia and Africa after they attained independence. It largely contributed to the growth of the policy of non-alignment. These powers were afraid as they may again be subjugated by colonial powers. They were determined to keep off these colonial powers by avoiding membership of blocs and adopting an independent course of action, keeping out of all sorts of alliances.
(3) **Underdevelopment and Economic Aid:** The countries of Asia and Africa who gained independence were underdeveloped. They were keen to improve the standard of living of their people and promote systematic development of their country. They needed capital and financial assistance from the powers of both the blocs to achieve their objectives at a fast rate. Therefore, they thought it proper to keep off from political alliances and pursue the policy of non-alignment.
(4) **Racial and Cultural Aspects:** Since long, colonial powers have fed the Afro-Asian nations with the idea that they were racially as well as culturally backward. The feeling evoked mutual sympathy among people to the newly emerged states of Africa and Asia. Being common victims of economic exploitation and political domination by the European countries, they had a sense of affinity which led them to co-operate with others.

(A) To maintain international peace and security / to develop friendly relations among nations / to achieve international cooperation in solving international economic, social, cultural or humanitarian problems / to be a centre for harmonizing the actions of nations / disarm, decolonise, develop to save succeeding generations from the Scourge of war/to create faith in Human Rights. **[Any three]**

(B) **Functions and Powers:**
(1) To maintain international peace and security in accordance with the principles and purposes of the United Nations
(2) To investigate any dispute or situation which might lead to international friction and to take military action against an aggressor.

(3) To recommend methods of adjusting such disputes or the terms of settlement.

(4) To formulate plans for the establishment of a system to regulate armaments.

(5) To determine the existence of a threat to the peace or act of aggression and to recommend what action should be taken.

(6) To call on members to apply economic sanctions and other measures not involving the use offorce to prevent or stop aggression.

(7) To take military action against an aggressor

(8) To recommend the admission of new members.

(9) To appoint the Secretary General **[Any three]**

(C) **Factors responsible for Non-Alignment:**

(1) Global tension caused by Cold War

(2) Struggle against imperialism and new colonization

(3) Right of independent judgement

(4) Use of moderation in relations to all big powers

(5) Restructuring international economic order

(6) Formation of a collective force.

(7) Reaction against the system of Military Alliances.

(8) Need for Peace. **[Any four]**
[Marking Scheme]

What Examiners Say

➥ (A) *This part was answered correctly by most candidates but a few confused the objectives of the UNO with the functions of UNO.*

➥ (B) *Majority of candidates answered the question correctly. However, a few candidates wrote the composition of the Security Council rather than its functions.*

➥ (C) *Most candidates wrote correct answers. Few however were confused and wrote other factors not related to the Non-Aligned Movement.*

22. **With reference to the Cold War and the Non-Aligned Movement, answer the following questions:**

(A) **Explain Truman's Doctrine.**

(B) **State any three consequences of the Cold War.**

(C) **Mention four major objectives of the Non-Aligned Movement.** **[ICSE 2012]**

Ans. (A) The Trumar Doctrine was an American foreign policy with the primary goal of containing Soviet geo-political expansion during the cold war. It was announced to Congress by President Harry S. Truman in 1947 and further developed in 1948 when he pledged to contain the communist uprisings in Greece and Turkey. Direct American military force was usually not involved but congress appropriated financial aid to support the economies and militaries of Greece and Turkey. The Truman Doctrine implied American support for other nations thought to be threatened by Soviet Communism. The Truman Doctrine became the foundation of American foreign policy and led to the formation of NATO.

(B) The consequences of the cold war were:

(1) It led to an increase in arms race.

(2) Several military alliances were formed.

(3) It led to rise of Non-Aligned nations.

(C) **The objectives of Non-Aligned Movement are:**

(1) To preserve the freedom of newly independent nations from colonial and alien domination;

(2) To establish a just international economic order;

(3) To eliminate all causes and horrors of war and in particular, elimination of nuclear weapons;

(4) To protect and promote human rights;

(5) To condemn all forms of racial discrimination and promote equality among individuals well as among nations;

(6) To preserve the independence of all those nations which have adopted the policy of Non-Alignment and were once under the control of the great powers.

(7) To ensure economic assistance for development from East and West;

(8) To ensure peaceful co-existence and amicable settlement of international disputes. **[Any four]**

Notes

ICSE
SPECIMEN QUESTION PAPER
2023 EXAMINATION
(Released on July 24, 2022)
SOLVED

HISTORY & CIVICS
[H.C.G. PAPER-1]

Time Allowed: Two hours Maximum Marks: 80

General Instructions:
(i) Answers to this Paper must be written on the paper provided separately.
(ii) You will **not** be allowed to write during first 15 minutes. This time is to be spent in reading the question paper.
(iii) The time given at the head of this Paper is the time allowed for writing the answers.
(iv) Attempt **all** questions from **Part I** (Compulsory).
(v) A total of **five** questions are to be attempted from Part II, **two** out of three questions from **Section A** and **three** out of five questions from **Section B**.
(vi) The intended marks for questions or parts of questions are given in brackets [ ].

PART - I
(Attempt all questions from this Part.)

1. Choose the correct option: [16]

(A) The interval between two sessions of the Parliament should not be more than......
 (a) Two months (b) Three months
 (c) Four months (d) Six months

(B) The maximum composition of the Lok Sabha is:
 (a) 530 (b) 540
 (c) 550 (d) 556

(C)
Lok Sabha member term	5 years
Rajya Sabha member term	?

 (a) 1 year (b) 2 years
 (c) 4 years (d) 6 years

(D) The Council of Ministers is collectively responsible to the

 (a) Lok Sabha (b) Rajya Sabha
 (c) Prime Minister (d) President

(E) A house has 350 members. On a given day, 25 members are present. For which of the following reasons does the Speaker adjourn the session for the day?
 (a) Indiscipline in the House
 (b) Lack of quorum
 (c) Business of the day is over
 (d) There are no questions to admit

(F) When a case comes from a Subordinate Court, the High Court deals with it under
 (a) Revisory Jurisdiction
 (b) Advisory Jurisdiction
 (c) Original Jurisdiction
 (d) Appellate Jurisdiction

(G) Which of these was NOT an aim of the Indian National Congress?
  (a) To train and organise public opinion in the country.
  (b) To promote friendly relations between nationalist political workers.
  (c) To make the world aware of the true nature of the British.
  (d) To formulate popular demands and present them before the government.

(H) .... announced that the successors of Bahadhur Shah could not use imperial titles.
  (a) Lord Canning   (b) Lord Wellesley
  (c) Lord Dalhousie   (d) Lord Ripon

(I) Which of these is NOT a repressive policy of Lord Lytton?
  (a) Arms Act
  (b) Ilbert Bill
  (c) Vernacular Press Act
  (d) Grand Delhi Durbar

(J) Jyotiba Phule : Satya Shodak Samaj : : Raja Rammohan Roy : : ....
  (a) Arya Samaj
  (b) Brahmo Samaj
  (c) Satya Shodak Samaj
  (d) Prarthana Samaj

(K) The Khilafat Movement was started in India by ....
  (a) Ali Brothers
  (b) Mahatma Gandhi
  (c) Jinnah
  (d) Sir Sayyid Ahmed Khan

(L) The Non Cooperation Movement was suspended due to the ....
  (a) Gandhi -Irwin pact
  (b) Chauri-Chaura Incident
  (c) Cripps Mission
  (d) Rowlatt Act

(M) Which of the following clauses was NOT part of the Indian Independence Act of 1947?
  (a) There would be a Governor General for each Dominion.
  (b) The country would be divided into two Dominions.
  (c) The British Parliament had legislative control over India.
  (d) There would be a division of army and assets.

(N) Which of the following is a common ideology of Fascism and Nazism?
  (a) To believe in democracy
  (b) To encourage political systems
  (c) To uphold One party and one leader
  (d) To support communism.

(O) Hitler attacked Poland because he wanted to ....
  (a) seize the coal mines
  (b) militarise the Rhine valley
  (c) regain the Danzing port
  (d) control the trade

(P) Identify the founders of Non Aligned Movement.
  (a) Nasser, Tito, Nehru
  (b) Naseer, Nehru, Stalin
  (c) Churchill, Stalin, Tito
  (d) Tito, Sukarno, Roosevelt

2. (A) Mr. Koushal is 26 yrs of age. Which House of Parliament can he be a member of? Why? [2]
   (B) Ms. Anita wants to approach the Lok Adalat regarding a case. Mention *any two* advantages she will have by taking her case to the Lok Adalat. [2]
   (C) Mention any two ways in which the British ill-treated the Indian soldiers. [2]
   (D) State *any two* objectives of the Muslim League. [2]
   (E) What are the causes of the Quit India Movement? [2]
   (F) Mention *any two* objectives of the Indian National Army. [2]
   (G) Mention any two objectives of the United Nations Organisation. [2]

PART - II
SECTION-A

*(Attempt **any two** questions from this **Section**.)*

3. The Legislature makes the laws which govern the country. With reference to the Union Legislature, answer the following questions:

   (A) What is the maximum composition of the Rajya Sabha? Why is it called a Permanent House? [3]
   (B) Mention *any three* exclusive powers of the Rajya Sabha. [3]
   (C) Mention *any four* legislative powers of the Parliament. [4]

4. The President of India is the nominal head of the Union Administration. With reference to the President, answer the following questions:

(A) What is the term of the President? Give *two reasons* for the indirect election of the President. [3]

(B) Name *the three* kinds of emergencies which the President can declare. [3]

(C) State *any four* legislative powers of the President. [4]

5. An independent judiciary is a feature of federal governance. With reference to the Supreme Court, answer the following questions:

(A) Who appoints the judges of the Supreme Court? What is the composition of the Supreme Court? [3]

(B) Mention the three kinds of cases which come under the Appellate jurisdiction of the Supreme Court? [3]

(C) Explain the terms: [4]
 (a) Revisory Jurisdiction.
 (b) Advisory Jurisdiction

SECTION-B

(Attempt any three questions from this Section.)

6. The culmination of discontent against the British rule came with the Great Revolt of 1857. With reference to this, answer the following questions:

(A) What was the Doctrine of Lapse? Name the queen who became a victim of this policy. [3]

(B) Mention *any three* economic causes of the Revolt. [3]

(C) Mention *any four* administrative changes made by the British after the Revolt. [4]

7. With reference to first and second phase of the Indian National Movement, answer the following:

(A) What was the objective of the Assertive Nationalists? Mention *any two* contributions of Bal Gangadhar Tilak. [3]

(B) Who partitioned Bengal? State *any two* actual reasons behind the Partition. [3]

(C) Mention *any four* methods used by the Early Nationalists. [4]

8. The mass phase of the National Movement led to the freedom of India. With reference to this phase, answer the following questions:

(A) What were the causes of the Civil Disobedience Movement? Name the March which marked the beginning of this movement. [3]

(B) Mention *any three* causes of the Non Cooperation Movement. [3]

(C) Mention *any four* clauses of the Mountbatten Plan. [4]

9. Look at the picture given and answer the following questions:

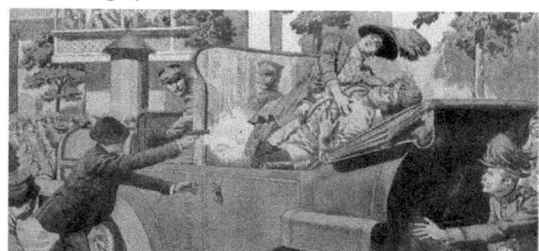

(A) Identify and briefly explain the above incident. [3]

(B) Mention *any four* conditions imposed on Germany in the Treaty of Versailles. [3]

(C) Name the organization established to maintain peace after the First World War. Mention *any three* of its objectives. [4]

10. The United Nations Organisation was established to maintain peace in the world. With reference to this organization, answer the following questions:

(A) What is the composition of the Security Council? [3]

(B) Mention *any three* functions of the International Court of Justice. [3]

(C) What is the full form of UNESCO? Mention *any three* of its functions. [4]

SOLUTION

SPECIMEN QUESTION PAPER

SECTION A

1. (A) *(d) Six months*

Explanation: Each house meets at least twice a year and the interval between two consecutive Sessions has to be less than six months.

(B) *(c) 550*

Explanation: The maximum strength of the lok Sabha, as provided by the Constitution is 550. Out of this, not more than 530 members shall represent the states and 20 members shall represent the Union Territories.

(C) *(d) 6 years*

Explanation: According to the Constitution, the term of the Lok Sabha in five years. And each member of the Rajya Sabha is elected for a period of six years.

(D) *(a) Lok sabha*

Explanation: The Council of Ministers are collectively responsible to the Lok Sabha. If the Lok Sabha passes a vote of No-confidence against the Council of Ministers, they have to resign collectively.

(E) *(b) Lock of quorum*

Explantion: Out of 350 members, if only 25 members are present in a house on a given day, in that case the speaker may adjourn the house. One-tenth of total membership of each house (Lok shabha and Rajya sabha) is required to proceedings and pass Bills and Resolutions.

(F) *(a) Revisory Jurisdiction*

Explanation: Revisory Jurisdiction means that the High Court can call for the record of a case which has been decided by a subordinate court. This is done because the High court feels that the subordinate court has exercised a jurisdiction not vested in it or the latter has not followed proper procedure. Therefore, the High court can review the case and take appropriate action on it.

(G) *(c) To make the world aware of the true notoure of the British.*

Explanation: The aims of the Indian National Congress was **NOT** to make world aware of the true nature of the British. Rest three options (a), (b) and (d) were aims of Indian National Congress.

(H) *(a) Lord Canning*

Explanation: In 1856, Lord Canning announced that after the death of Bahadur Shah, his successors would not be allowed to use the imperial titles with their names and would be known as mere princes.

(I) *(b) Ilbert Bill*

Explanation: Ilbert Bill was not a repressive policy of Lord lytton. It was prepared by Sir C.P. Ilbert, the low member of the Viceroy's Council in 1883. This Bill provided for the trial of British or European persons by Indians. It was popularly known as Ilbert Bill.

(J) *(b) Brahmo Samaj*

Explanation: Arya Samaj was formed by Swami Dayananad Saraswati. *Brahmo Samaj* was formed by Raja Rammohan Roy Satya *Shodak Samaj* was formed by Jyotila Phule *Prarthana Samaj* was formed by Atmaram Pandurang.

(K) *(a) Ali Brothers*

Explanation: The Muslim population in India started a powerful agitation known as the Khilafat movement under the leadership of the Ali Brothers-Mohammed Ali and Shaukat Ali.

(L) *(b) Chauri-Chura Incident*

Explanation: The tragedy at chauri-Chaura in Gorakhpur (U.P.) occurred on February 5, 1922. In which about 3,000 peasants marched to the police station and killed 22 policemen and set the nearby Police station on fire when the Policemen were inside the Police station. This news greatly shocked Gandhiji and he withdrew the Non-Cooperation movement on February 12, 1922.

(M) *(c) The British Parliament had legislative control over India.*

Explanation: Indian Independence Act of 1947 included options (a), (b) and (d) but not option (c) The British parliament had legislative control over India was not part of it. Because the Constituent Assemblies of both the dominions were to act as the Central Legislatures and they would have full powers to make lows for their respective Dominion.

(N) *(c) To uphold One party and one leader.*

Explanation: To uphold one party and one leader was the common ideology of Fascism and Nazism. Because they had hatred for democratize principles, they did not encourage any political systems and they feared Communism.

(O) *(c) regain the Danzing port*

Explanation: By the Treaty of Versailles Germany was divided into two parts in order to give a land-route to Poland upto the sea and the port of Danzing was also given to Poland. Germany wanted to regain her lost territories. And the city of Danzing was inhabited mainly by the Germans and by occupying Danzing corridor, Germany could connect with East Prussia.

(P) *(a) Nasser, Tito, Nehru*

Explanation: Joseph Broze Tito of Yugoslavia, Gamal Abdul Nasser of Egypt and Jawaharlal Nehru of India are the founders of Non-Aligned Movement (NAM).

2. (A) Mr. Koushol could become member of Lok Sabha, because he is elligible for Lok sabha member's age which is 25 and above. But for Rajya Sabha membership, he should be at least 30 years of age.

(B) The two advantages of filing a case in Lok Adalat will be:
 (1) There is no heavy court fee. The lok Adalat eliminates high costs and delays in imparting justice.
 (2) It provides legal aid and quick justice to those who are not in a position to engage lawyers.

(C) East India Company established the British Empire in India with the help of Indian soldiers. They were poorly paid, ill-fed and badly housed. British Military authorities forbade the Sepoys from wearing caste or sectarian marks, beards or turbans; and they showed disregard for the Sentiments of the Sepoys.

(D) The objectives of the Muslim League was:
 (1) To Protect and advance the political rights and interests of the Muslim and represent their needs and aspirations to the government in mild and moderate language.
 (2) To prevent the rise of feelings of hostility between the Muslims of India and other communities.
 (3) To promote, among the Muslims of India, Support for the British government and to remove any misconceptions regarding the intention of the government in relation to Indian Muslims. **[Any two]**

(E) Causes of Quit India Movement
 (1) **Failure if the Cripps Mission:** After the failure of the talks with the Cripps mission (1942), the Congress was left with no alternative but to launch a movement against the British rule. The British government was not ready to give freedom even after their victory in the war.
 (2) **Japanese Threat:** In 1942, Japan had also joined the second world war against England and it reached the borders of India. It was realized by the leaders that presence of Britain in India would invite. Japans attack on India.
 (3) **Command Problems:** In the Lahore Session (1940), The Muslim League put forward the 'Two Nation theory' and thus, a demand for the partition of India was made. The Congress realized that the British were responsible behind this theory. So, the Congress felt that if the British withdraw from India, people would sort out their differences in a very peaceful manner. **[Any two]**

(F) The main objectives of the Indian National Army were:
 (1) To organise an armed revolution and to fight the British army with modern arms.
 (2) Since it was not possible for the Indians to organise an armed revolution from their homeland, this task had to be assigned to the Indians living in East Asia.
 (3) To organise a provisional government of Free India in order to mobilize all the forces effectively.
 (4) Total mobilisation of Indian manpower and money for a total war.
 (5) The motto of the INA was 'Unity, Faith and Sacrifice'. **[Any two]**

(G) Objectives of the United Nations Organisation:
 (1) To maintain international peace and security based on respect for the principle of equal human rights and fundamental freedom.
 (2) To develop friendly relations among the nations.
 (3) To cooperate in solving international problems of an economic, social, cultural or humanitarian nature.
 (4) To be a centre for harmonizing the actions of nations in achieving these aims.
 (5) To protect the environment and to justify the use of natural resources. **[Any two]**

PART-II
SECTION A

3. (A) The maximum strength of the Rajya Sabha is 252 members, out of which 238 members are elected by the States in the Union and 12 members and nominated by the President from among persons having special knowledge or practical experience in matters such as literature, Science, Art and Social Service.

The Rajya Sabha is called a Permanent House, because it cannot be dissolved like the Lok Sabha. Each member of the Rajya Sabha is elected for a period of six years. One-third of the total member of the house retire after every two years.

(B) Three exclusive powers of the Rajya Sabha are:

(1) Motions of No-Confindence against the government can only be introduced and passed in the Lok Sabha. If passed by a majority Vote, the Prime Minister and the Council of Ministers resign collectively. The Rajya Sabha has no power over such a motion, hence, no real power over the escecutive.

(2) Money Bills can only be introduced in the Lok Sabha, and upon being passed, are sent to the Rajya Sabha, Where it can be deliberated on for upto 14 days.

(3) In case of deadlock between the two houses over a non-financial (ordincary bill, the will of the Lok Sabha normolly prevails, as its strength is more than double that of the Rajya Sabha.

(C) Four Legislative Powers of the Parliament are:

(1) Being the low making body at the National level, the Parliament has exclusive Power to make lows on 97 Subjects mentioned in the Union List.

(2) The Parliament can make laws on Residuary Subject- that is, those subjects which are not there in the Union List, State List and even in the Concurrent List.

(3) Emergency Proclamations made by the President must be approved by the Parliament within a month from the date of their proclamation.

(4) The president is empowered to promulgate an ordinance at a time when the parliament is not in session- It has the same effect as an Act. Ordiancers must be put up before both the houses for their approval Ordinances cease to operate after six weak from the re-assembly of Parliament, unless they are approved by the Houses.

4. (A) The President holds office for a term of five years from the date an which he enters upon his office.

Reasons for Indirect Election of the President are:

(1) If the President was to be elected directly by the people, he could become a rival centre of power to the Council of Ministers. This would be against the parliament system with ministerial responsibility.

(2) Since the membership in the two House of Parliament was likely to be dominated by one party, election of the President merely by a majority of members of the Union Parliament could make him a nominee of the ruling party like the Prime Minister. Such a president could not represent the constituent State of the Union.

(3) The president is elected by an Electoral College. In India, the Electoral College consists of the elected memers of the two Houses of Parliament and Legislative Assemblies of the States (Article 54). Such an Electoral College would make the President the elected representative of the whole nation with a clear voice given to the states as well. **[Any two]**

(B) A President can proclaim a state of emergency in the following cases:

(1) **National or General Emergency:** There is danger of foreign aggression or danger to the peace and security of the country because of civil war, insurgency or any other such cause (Article 352).

(2) **Breakdown of constitutional machinery:** The Constitutional machinery in a State has broke down or there is a deadlock because of Political uncertainties or otherwise (Article 356).

(3) **Financial Emergency:** A setback to financial stability on credit feasibility of the country is likely to occur or has occurred (Article 360).

(C) Legislative power of the President are:

(1) The President addresses both houses of Parliament assembled together for the first session after each General Election to the Lok Sabha and at the commandment of the first Sessian of each year. The President has the power to address either House of Parliament on their joint sitting at any time.

(2) He/She has the power to send messages to either House of parliament either in

regard to any pending Bill or to any other matters.

(3) He/She can dissolve the Lok Sabha and order fresh elections. Rajya Sabha is a permanent body, not subject to dissolution.

(4) The President nominates 12 members to the Rajya sabha from among persons having special knowledge or Practical experience in these matters-Literature, Science, Art and Social Science.

(5) No Bill can become a law without the assent and signature of the president.

(6) Under Article 123, the President can promulgate an Ordinance, which has the some status as an Act of Parliament.

(7) The President can refuse his/her assent to some Bills passed by the State legislature or he/She can also send it back for reconsideration. Bill affecting matters such as the powers of the High court are reserved for the consideration of the President.

(8) A Bill for the formation of new states or alteration of areas of the existing states cannot be introduced, except on the President's recommendations. **[Any Four]**

5. (A) Every Judge of the Supreme Court is appointed by the President of India in consultation with the judges of Supreme Court and of High Courts, besides the Council of Ministers. The Superme court of India consists of a Chief Justice of India and not more than 33 other Judges, until Parliament by law prescribes a larger number of Judges.

(B) Appellate Jurisdiction is the power to hear cases which have been heard in the first instance in a lower court and have to come to the Supreme court as an appeal against the judgment given in a lower court.

The Supreme Court has Appellate Jurisdiction regarding all types of cases, *i.e.* Constitutional, Civil and Criminal.

(1) **Constitutional Cases:** An appeal can move to the Supreme court against the High Court decisions about the interpretation of the constitution.

(2) **Cilvil Cases:** Appeals in Civil matters lie to the Supreme court if the High Court certifies either that the case involves a substantial question of low of general importance or that the question needs to be decided by the Superme Court

(3) **Criminal Cases:** An appeal to the Supreme Court with or without a certificate of the High court.
- Where the High Court reverses order of acquittal issued by the Sessions Court and Sentences the accused to death.
- Where the High court withdraws a criminal case from a lower court, convicts the accused person and Sentences him to death.

(C) **Revisory Jurisdiction:** The Supreme court under Article 137 is empowered to review any judgment or order mode by it with a view to removing any mistake or error that might have crept in the judgment or order. This is because the Supreme Court is a court of record and its decisions are of evidentiary value and cannot be questioned in any court.

Advisory Jurisdiction: The Supreme Court has advisory Jurisdiction (to give its opinion) on any question, if law or fact of Public importance as may be referred to it for consideration by the President of India. This Supreme Court may be required to express its opinion in two classes of matters, in an advisory capacity:

(1) Any questions of law may be referred to the Supreme Court if the President considers that the question is of Public importance and it is necessary to obtain the opinion of the Supreme Court. Such opinion of the Supreme Court is advisory and not binding on the government nor is it executable as a judgment of the Supreme Court.

(2) Disputes arising out of Pre-Constitution treaties and agreements which are excluded from original jurisdiction by Article 131.

SECTION B

6. (A) Lord Dalhousie, the Governor-General of India, annexed many states to the company using the Doctrine of lapse.

According to this Doctrine, if an Indian ruler died without a male hair, his Kingdom would 'lapse', that is, it would come under the company's territory in India.

Rani Laxmi Bai of Jhansi became a victim of this policy, when the ruler of Jhansi died in 1853, leaving no natural heir, the widowed Rani was pensioned and their adopted son, Anand Rao, was not recognized as a lawful successors to the throne. And she became a victim of this policy.

(B) Economic causes of the Revolt 1857 were:

(1) The resources from India were exploited for the benefit of the British people and growth of industries in Britain. Raw

material was exported and finished goods were imported. It ruined the Indian industries and handicrafts

(2) The Britishers started plundering India's row material, resources and wealth and transferred it to England, for which India got no proportionate economic return from them, which was called the Drain of Wealth just after the battle of Plassey and their conquest of Bengal.

(3) People moved to cities to find employment, which was very difficult to get. Peasants were forced to pay tax in cash, which pushed them into the hands of the moneylenders, as tax was collected even during the famines.

(4) Indian handicraft slowly declined Machine-made British cloth was cheaper. Therefore, the looms at homes were shut down.

(5) Indigo, tea, jute, cotton and opium were crops which the Britishers wanted the Indians to grow for them if the peasants planted anything else, their crops were destroyed. Thus, there was less food. People suffered through the ever increasing and spreading fornine.

[Any three]

(C) The four changes in the Administration of the British government as a consequences of the Revolt were:

(1) The Control of the Indian Government was finally assumed by the British Crown. The Governor general received a new title of Viceroy. The assumption of the government of India by the Sovereign of Great British was announced by Lord Canning at a Darbar at Allahabad in a Proclamation issued on 1st November, 1858 in the name of Queen Victoria.

(2) The Army which took kart in the outbreak was throughly recognized, and for the next 50 years, 'The idea of division and Counterpoise' dominated the British Military Policy in India.

(3) The British Government now took up a new attitude towards the Indian State. The Act of 1858 ended the dualism in the control of Indian affairs and mode the crown directly responsible for the management of the Indian affairs.

(4) The administrative bodies of the company, namely the Board of Control and Court of Directors were abolished and their Powers were transferred to a British Cabinet Minister known as the Secretary of State. A new body, the Indian council consisting of 15 members was set-up to assist the secretary of the State.

(5) The appointment of the Civil Services was to be made by the Secretary of State in Council by the method of open competition.

(6) The Governor General of India was conferred the additional title of Viceroy and was made the representative of the British Crown in context to Indian Princes.

[Any four]

7. (A) The main objective of the Assertive Nationalists was the immediate attainment of 'Swaraj'. This means complete independence and not just Self-government as in the colonies of Australia, New Zealand etc. They also wanted to achieve a more self-reliant method and to have a mass base for their movement.

Contributions of Bal Gangadhar Tilak :

(1) He started the Home Rule Movement.

(2) He united both wings (Moderates and Extremists) of the Congress Party.

(3) He appealed to the People of India to boycott British Goods, British Courts, Schools and Colleges.

(4) He organised the National movement in Maharashtra in order to bring it into conflict with the British Government.

(5) He infused new spirit of self-sacrifice among the masses.

(6) Tilak was the first to openly declare the demand for Swaraj by saying "Swaraj is my birth right and I shall have it".

[Any two]

(B) Lord Curzon partitioned Bengal on 20th July, 1905, which was considered as a concealed attack on Indian Nationalism.

The two actual reasons behind the Partition of Bengal was:

(1) Bengal was the nerve centre of Indian nationalism at that time. So the British hoped to stop the rising tide of nationalism by Partitioning Bengal.

(2) The Partition of the state was intended to curb Bengali influence by not only placing Bengalis under two administrations but by reducing them to a minority to Bengal itself.

(3) The Partition was meant to foster division on the basis of religion. East Bengal would be prodominantly a Muslim majority State and West Bengal would have a Hindu majority. [Any two]

(C) Methods used by moderates (Early Nationalists):

(1) They had faith in the constitutional or peaceful methods of agitation.

(2) They believed that the British government could be persuaded by agreements. They sent representatives to England to explain India's viewpoints to British Parliamentarians.

(3) They set up a committee of National Congress in England.

(4) They made use of press for criticizing British Policies.

(5) They held meeting and discussions and organized annual sessions with Indian delegates from India. In these sessions, various methods were adopted. They were then forwarded to the British so that, appropriate action could be taken.

(6) They made use of three P's i.e. Petitions, Prayers and Protests. **[Any four]**

8. (A) The cause of the Civil Disobedience Movement were:

(1) **The Simon Commission:** It was an All-British Commission appointed in November 1927 to investigate the need for further constitutional reforms in India. The absence of Indians in the commission was seen as an insult and they decided to boycott the commission at every stage and in every form.

(2) **Demand for Poorna Swaraj:** The British government did not accept the Nehru Report and The Congress passed the Poorna Swaraj resolution at its Lahore Session in 1929. The resolution declared Poorna Swaraj to be the objective of the Congress.

The Dandi March (Salt March) on March 12, 1930 marked the beginning of this movement.

(B) **Causes of the Non-Cooperation Movement:**

(1) **The Rowlatt Act, 1919:** The Act authorized the government to imprison any person without trial and convict him in a court. The Rowlatt Act Implied:

(i) Arrest of a Person without a warrant.

(ii) In Camera trial (trial in Seclusion)

(iii) Restrictions on Movements of individuals

(iv) Suspension of the Right of Habeas Corpus.

(2) **Jullianwala Bagh Incident:** On 13th April, 1919, a peaceful meeting was organised at a small park in Amritsar called Jallianwala Bagh. The meeting was held to protest against the arrest of two popular leaders– Dr. Saifuddin Kitchlew and Dr. Satya Pal.

General Dyer entered the Park with his troops and opened fire on the innocent mob without a warning. This barbaric act shattered the faith of Mahatma Gandhi to never co-operate with the British again.

(3) **Khilafat Movement:** It was started by the Ali Brothers in 1920 for the preservation of the office of khalifa, the religious head of the Muslims. Gandhji combined the Khilafat movement with the Non-Cooperation movement as he saw this as an opportunity to unite the Hindus and Muslims.

(C) **Clauses of Mountbatten Plan:**

(1) **Partition:** The country would be divided into two Dominions, i.e. India an Pakistan.

(2) **Relations between the two new Dominions:** It was for the two Dominions to decide what relations they would have with the British Commonwealth and with each other.

(3) **A Boundary Commission:** The Plan provided for the creation of a Boundary Commission to settle the boundaries of the two Dominions in case partition was decided upon.

(4) **Bengal and Punjab:** The Partition of Bengal and Punjab was proposed provided that the Legislative Assemblies of the two provinces decided in favour of the Partition.

9. (A) **Assassination of Archduke Ferdinand/ Sarajevo Crisis:**

It is also the immediate cause in which Archduke Frances Ferdinand, the heir to the Throne of Austria-Hungory was assassinated at Sarajevo, Capital of Bosnia on June 28, 1914. The assassination was organized by a secret Society called 'Black Hand' or 'Union of Death' formed by extremist Serbian nationalists whose aim was to unite all Serbians, into a single Serbian State.

(B) The Treaty declared Germany guilty of aggression, so they imposed following conditions on Germany through the Treaty of Versailles:

(1) Germany was required to pay for the loss and damages suffered by the Allies during the war. The Amount of reparations was fixed at 33 billion dollars.

(2) Germany had to cede her merchant ships to the Allies as compensation and had to supply huge quantities of coal to France, Italy and Belgium for ten years.

(3) The area of the Rhine Vally was to be demilitarized and the German territory west of Rhine was to be occupied by the Allied troops for 15 years.

(4) Germany lost Alsace Lorraine to France; Eupen-et-malmedy to Belgium, Schleswig to Denmark. Danzig became a Free port in the Polish territory.

(5) The coal mines in the German area called Saar were ceded to France for 15 years and the area was to be governed by the League of Nations.

(6) The German Army was restricted to a force of 1, 00, 000 Soldiers and the Navy was limited to 15, 000 men and 24 ships. The Air force and Submarines were banned.

(7) The Covenant of the league of Nations was added to the Treaty of Versailles.

[Any Four]

(C) The League of Nations was established to maintain peace after the first world war.

Objectives of the league of Nations were as below:

(1) All the states of the world were prohibited from entering into secret treaties and alliances.

(2) All States were to respect each others Independence.

(3) The member-States were not supposed to maintain huge armies, warships and destructive armaments.

(4) All states were to refer their mutual disputers, if any, to the League of Nations for peaceful settlement.

(5) The member-States were to take necessary action as directed by the league against any state which tried to disturb World Peace and Order.

(6) Apart from political functions, the League of Nations was supposed to promote Cultural, Social and Economic cooperation among the member-States. **[Any Three]**

10. (A) The Security Council consists of 15 members. It has five Permanent member-China, France, Russia, Britain and the United States of America. The Regional representation of the ten non-permanent member is Afro-Asian Countries-5 members

Latin American Countries - 2 members

West Europe and other Countries - 2 members

East European Countries – 1 member

All the Permanent members have Veto Power.

(B) Functions of the International Court of Justice.

(1) The International Court of Justice enjoys compulsory jurisdiction in two ways. Firstly, disputes arising under the treaties are dealt by the court. Secondly, disputes regarding interpretation of international law and compensation for violating any international rule or low are also handled by the court.

(2) A country may refer about a dispute to the court if any other country/countries decide to defend itself/themselves, the court accepts it as a consent to the case.

(3) It codifies international law after detailed study of international conventions, customs, judgments of general principle of law.

(4) The Court may advise other UN organs and agencies on any legal issue.

(5) It may suggest suitable methods for solving the matter at any stage of the disputes. **[Any three]**

(C) The full form of UNESCO is united Nations Educational, Scientific and Cultural Organization.

Functions of UNESCO are as follows:

(1) In the sphere of Education:

(i) It tries to eliminate illiteracy by helping to set up educational facilities

(ii) It helps to set up Library System, gives fellowships.

(iii) It advices about production of textbook, Syllabus, teacher training etc. And it has also set up an International Institute of Education Planning.

(2) In the sphere of Science and Technology:

It promotes research and various Science Subjects. It organizes conferences to bring Scientists on one platform. It circulates information through Journals. It encourages the study of Social Sciences, Specially, in order to diagnose the various cause of the world tensions.

(3) In the sphere of Culture and Communication:

(i) It helps its members to preserve their culture and to protect old manuscripts, world of art and ancient monuments.

(ii) It encourages cultural exchanges and promotes original writers.

(iii) It disseminates information about human rights and sets up projects on mass communication.

(iv) UNESCO is helping in providing technical advice and assistance, equipment and funds for the preservation of monuments like Taj Mehal in India.

[Any three]

ICSE SAMPLE PAPER 2023 EXAMINATION SELF ASSESSMENT

HISTORY & CIVICS

[H.C.G. PAPER-1]

Time Allowed: Two hours   Maximum Marks: 80

General Instructions:

(i) Answers to this Paper must be written on the paper provided separately.
(ii) You will not be allowed to write during first 15 minutes. This time is to be spent in reading the question paper.
(iii) The time given at the head of this Paper is the time allowed for writing the answers.
(iv) Attempt **all** questions from **Part I** (Compulsory).
(v) A total of **five** questions are to be attempted from Part II, **two** out of three questions from **Section A** and **three** out of five questions from **Section B**.
(vi) The intended marks for questions or parts of questions are given in brackets [ ].

PART - I

(Attempt all questions from this Part.)

1. Select the correct answers to the questions from the given options. (Do not copy the question. Write the correct answer only): [16]

(A) If the strength of the House is 350 members, the quorum will be ....
  (a) 36 members
  (b) 40 members
  (c) 60 members
  (d) 35 members

(B) Who summons the Budget Session every year?
  (a) The President
  (b) The Vice President
  (c) The Prime Minister
  (d) The Speaker

(C) In case of a tie in the Lok Sabha, who exercises the casting vote?

(a) The President
(b) The Prime Minister
(c) The Speaker
(d) The Leader of the Opposition Party

(D) What happens under President Rule?
  (a) It is proclaimed for six months
  (b) The governor acts in that place
  (c) The Vidhan Sabha may be dissolved
  (d) All of the above

(E) The Vice-President of India performs similar functions in the Rajya Sabha as the .... in the Lok Sabha.
  (a) Cabinet of ministers
  (b) Prime-Minister
  (c) President
  (d) Speaker

Sample Paper 2   293

(F) Who should have held a judicial office within Indian territory for atleast 10 years?
 (a) Supreme Court Judge
 (b) High Court Judge
 (c) Subordinate Court Judge
 (d) Lok Adalat Judges

(G) Who was the first President of Indian National Congress?
 (a) A.O. Hume
 (b) Surendra Nath Banerjee
 (c) W.C. Banerjee
 (d) Dadabhai Naoroji

(H) Who of the following presided over the Lahore Session of Indian National Congress in 1929 in which resolution for Poorna Swaraj was passed?
 (a) Surendra Nath Banerjee
 (b) Subhash Chandra Bose
 (c) Mahatma Gandhi
 (d) Jawahar Lal Nehru

(I) With which of the following, Raja Ram Mohan Roy cannot be associated?
 (a) Sanskrit Education
 (b) Brahmo Sabha
 (c) Widow remarriage
 (d) Abolition of Sati

(J) The administrative consequence of revolt of 1857 was transfer of power from:
 (a) East India Company to Governor General
 (b) East India Company to the British Crown
 (c) British Crown to East India Company
 (d) East India Company to Board of Directors

(K) Gandhiji gave the mantra of "Do or Die" on the eve of which mass movement?
 (a) Non Cooperation Movement
 (b) Civil Disobedience Movement
 (c) Chamaparan Satyagraha
 (d) Quit India Movement

(L) Subhash Chandra Bose was attracted by the .... launched by Mahatma Gandhi.
 (a) Non-cooperation Movement
 (b) Civil Disobedience Movement
 (c) Quit India Movement
 (d) Khilafat Movement

(M) How many kinds of states were there in Europe in the early 20th century?
 (a) four (b) three
 (c) two (d) five

(N) Totalitarian Dictatorships were followed in:
 (a) China, Russia, Italy and Germany
 (b) Spain, Polant, France and Russia
 (c) Germany, Japan, Spain and Austria
 (d) Russia, Italy, Germany and Span

(O) When is United Nations Day celebrated?
 (a) 24 September (b) 24 October
 (c) 24 November (d) 24 December

(P) Which UN agency provides services in primary health-care, nutrition and women's development in developing countries?
 (a) UNO (b) UNESCO
 (c) WHO (d) UNICEF

2. (A) State *any two* federal features of the Indian Constitution. [2]

(B) Why is the Supreme Court said to be the guardian of the Constitution? [2]

(C) Mention *any two* social evils that existed in India during the 19th century. What measures did the British Government take to stop them? [2]

(D) Mention *two reasons* why the Lucknow Pact is considered important int he history of the Indian National Congress. [2]

(E) Name *two leaders* of the Swaraj Party. Why were they said to be pro-changers? [2]

(F) Mention *any two* clauses of the Mountbatten Plan. [2]

(G) State *two* important reasons for the formation of the UNO. [2]

PART - II
SECTION - A

(Attempt *any four* questions from this Section.)

3. The parliament is the body of people's representatives who have supreme power in a democracy. With reference to the Union Legislature, answer the following questions:

(A) How are the upper house members elected? [3]

(B) Why is Rajya Sabha also called a 'Permanent House'? How many members retire at the same time? [3]

(C) Indian Parliament has many powers State *any two* Financial and any two Legislative powers. [4]

4. The President of India is the nominal head of the Indian Union, in context, to this, answer the following questions :

(A) What qualifications are required by a person to contest in elections of the President? [3]

(B) By which process is he elected? Explain briefly. [3]

(C) How could he be removed from his office? [4]

5. With the reference to the Indian Judiciary, answer the following questions :

(A) What is the hierarchial order of the courts? [3]

(B) What do we mean when we refer to the Supreme Court and High Court as a 'Court of Record'? [3]

(C) State any four cases that come under the original jurisdiction of the Supreme Court. [4]

SECTION - B

*(Attempt **any three** questions from this Section.)*

6. The First War of Independence of 1857 was the culmination of people's dissatisfaction with the British Rule. In this context enumerate the following causes:

(A) *Any three* economic causes for the Revolt of 1857. [3]

(B) *Any three* military causes. [3]

(C) *Any four* political causes of the revolt. [4]

7. The conflict between the two sections of the Congress came to surface in its Session in 1906 at Calcutta. In this context, explain the following:

(A) With reference to the Picture given below answer the following: [3]
   (a) What were the three personalities known as?
   (b) Which section of the Congress did they represent?
   (c) Mention two of their popular beliefs.

(B) The split in the congress in 1907. [3]

(C) State *any four* methods that they advocated for the achievement of their aims. [4]

8. From the period between 1930 and 1947 of the Indian National Movement, lot of movements were seen in the country, which were very significant. In this context, answer the following questions:

(A) What was the importance of the Second Round Table Conference? [3]

(B) State *any three* features of the programme of the Civil Disobedience Movement. [3]

(C) State *any four* clauses of the Cabinet Mission Plan. [4]

9. With reference to the causes of the Second World War, answer the following:

(A) Explain how the ideologies of Mussolini and Hitler led to the Second World War. [3]

(B) How did the Japanese invasion of China became one of the cause for the outbreak of the Second World War? [3]

(C) Explain the consequences of the Second World War with reference to the formation of the United Nations.

10. Study the picture given below and answer the questions that follow:

(A) Identify the organization associated with the above emblem.

Mention any three principles of this organization.

(B) Where is the headquarters of this organization located?

Who can become its member?

(C) Name the principal judicial organ of this organization and explain its composition.

ICSE
SAMPLE PAPER
2023 EXAMINATION
SELF ASSESSMENT

HISTORY & CIVICS
[H.C.G. PAPER-1]

Time Allowed: Two hours *Maximum Marks: 80*

General Instructions:

(i) Answers to this Paper must be written on the paper provided separately.
(ii) You will not be allowed to write during first 15 minutes. This time is to be spent in reading the question paper.
(iii) The time given at the head of this Paper is the time allowed for writing the answers.
(iv) Attempt **all** questions from **Part I** (Compulsory).
(v) A total of **five** questions are to be attempted from Part II, **two** out of three questions from **Section A** and **three** out of five questions from **Section B**.
(vi) The intended marks for questions or parts of questions are given in brackets [ ].

PART - I
(Attempt all questions from this Part.)

1. Choose the correct option: [16]

(A)
Lok Sabha	2
Rajya Sabha	?

 (a) 4 (b) 6
 (c) 8 (d) 12

(B) When is Question Hour held in the Lok Sabha?
 (a) Immediately after the Lunch
 (b) At 5 p.m.
 (c) The first hour on every working day
 (d) After Zero hour

(C) Which of the following bills cannot originate in the Rajya Sabha?
 (a) Constitutional Amendment Bill
 (b) Ordinary Bill
 (c) Money Bill
 (d) Special Amendment Bill

(D) What can the President do to the Lok Sabha?
 (a) only dissolve the Lok Sabha
 (b) only summon the Lok Sabha
 (c) only Prorogue the Lok Sabha
 (d) All of the above

(E) The Parliament depends upon the Policy and guidance of:
 (a) Prime Minister
 (b) President
 (c) Home Minister
 (d) Vice President

(F) What is the tenue of a Supreme Court Judge?
(a) 60 years (b) 65 years
(c) 66 years (d) 64 years

(G) Which of the following states was the first to be annexed by the Doctrine of Lapse?
(a) Nagpur (b) Satara
(c) Jhansi (d) Udaipur

(H) The Partition of Bengal came into effect on ....
(a) 4th September 1825
(b) 16th October, 1905
(c) 14th April, 1908
(d) 13th April, 1919

(I) During the First War of Independence in 1857, the British Government found the Mughal Emperor Bahadur Shah II guilty of aiding the movement, and as a punishment, his two sons were shot dead. Which British official was responsible for this incident?
(a) Hugh Rose
(b) Nicholson
(c) Hudson
(d) Campbell

(j) Which of the following is a method of the Assertive Nationalists?
(I) Swadeshi
(II) Boycott
(III) Passive Resistance
(IV) Revivalism
(a) (I), (II), (III)
(b) Only (IV)
(c) Only (II) and (III)
(d) All of the above

(K) Complete the given analogy:
Simon Commission : Civil Disobedience Movement :: Cripps Mission : ?
(a) Non Cooperation Movement
(b) Anti Partition Movement
(c) Quit India Movement
(d) Khilafat movement

(L) In ...., the Muslim League passed a resolution demanding the partition of the country and the creatin of a state called Pakistan.
(a) 1930 (b) 1934
(c) 1940 (d) 1946

(M) From the given list, identify the objectives of the Indian National Army (INA):
(a) To provide relief to indigo cultivators
(b) To develop unity between Hindus and Muslims
(c) Boycott of foreign goods
(d) To organize an armed rebellion and fight the British Army with modern arms

(N) In Treaty of Versailles, the terms of the Peace treaties were mainly decided by:
(a) Woodrow Wilson
(b) Lloyd George
(c) George Clemenceau
(d) All of the above

(O) After the second World War, which two new states emerged as two powerful blocs?
(a) France and Germany
(b) England and USSR
(c) USA and USSR
(d) Italy and USSR

(P) Veto Power of the Security Council can be exercised only by:
(a) All members
(b) Few Members
(c) Permanent members
(d) None of the members

2. (A) An adult Indian Citizen holding an office of profit under the state government wishes to contest for election to the Lok Sabha. Is he/she eligible? Give a reason to justify your answer. [2]

(B) Name the Writ issued by the High Court which provides a remedy to the person who has been unlawfully detained in prison. [2]

(C) What was the immediate cause of the war of 1857? Where did the war have its beginning? [2]

(D) Who founded the 'Landholders' society and when? [2]

(E) Mention atleast *two* proposals given by the Cripps Mission. [2]

(F) What was the composition of Pakistan according to the Indian Independence Act, 1947? [2]

(G) What is meant by the General Assembly of the United Nation? [2]

PART - II
SECTION - A

*(Attempt **any two** questions from this Section.)*

3. With reference to the Indian Parliament, explain the following:

   (A) The tenure of the members of the Lok Sabha and the Rajya Sabha. [3]

   (B) The composition of the Lok Sabha and the Rajya Sabha. [3]

   (C) Its powers to make laws on subjects mentioned in the:
   (a) Union List
   (b) Concurrent List [4]

4. The Executive Power of the Indian Union is vested in the President. In this context, answer the following:

   (A) How is the President of India elected?
   State the composition of the Electoral College that elects him. [3]

   (B) Explain *any three* Discretionary Powers of the President. [3]

   (C) Mention *any four* Executive Powers of the President. [4]

5. The Supreme Court has an extensive jurisdiction. In the light of this statement, answer the following questions:

   (A) What are the qualifications of the Judges of the Supreme Court? [3]

   (B) (a) Explain the composition of the Supreme Court.
   (b) How are the Judges of the Supreme Court appointed? [3]

   (C) Explain the cases in which the Supreme Court enjoys Original Jurisdiction. [4]

6. The Second half of the 19th century witnessed the growth of a strong feeling of Nationalism. With reference to the statement, answer the following:

   (A) State *any three* ways in which the Press played an important role in developing nationalism amongst Indians. [3]

   (B) Explain briefly any *three* differences in the methods adopted between the Early Nationalists and Radicals in the National Movement. [3]

   (C) Write *any four* repressive Colonial policies of the British. [3]

7. With reference to the picture given, answer the following questions:

   (A) (a) Identify the Memorial built for those who were killed in this incident.
   (b) Where did this incident take place?
   (c) Name the movement launched by Gandhi in 1920 as a consequence. [3]

   (B) Explain briefly the reason for the suspension of this particular movement by Gandhi in 1922. [3]

   (C) State *any four* impacts of the movement. [4]

8. With reference to the Partition Plan, answer the following:

   (A) Mention *any two* clauses of the India Independence Act, 1947. [3]

   (B) Why did the Congress accept the Mountbatten Plan? [3]

(C) Explain the Cabinet Mission's proposals regarding the setting up of a Constitution making body. [4]

9. Which reference to the Second World War and the Non-Aligned Movement, answer the following:

(A) Explain briefly three reasons for the dissatisfaction with the Treaty of Versailles. [3]

(B) State *any three* consequences of the Second World War. [3]

(C) Mention *any four* chief architects of the Non-Aligned Movement. [4]

10. (A) Write any three functions of UNESCO that preserve our 'Cultural Heritage'. [3]

(B) State the Composition of the Security Council. [3]

(C) Write *any four* functions of the General Assembly. [4]

ICSE SAMPLE PAPER 2023 EXAMINATION SELF ASSESSMENT

HISTORY & CIVICS

[H.C.G. PAPER-1]

Time Allowed: Two hours Maximum Marks: 80

General Instructions:

(i) Answers to this Paper must be written on the paper provided separately.
(ii) You will not be allowed to write during first 15 minutes. This time is to be spent in reading the question paper.
(iii) The time given at the head of this Paper is the time allowed for writing the answers.
(iv) Attempt **all** questions from **Part I** (Compulsory).
(v) A total of **five** questions are to be attempted from Part II, **two** out of three questions from **Section A** and **three** out of five questions from **Section B**.
(vi) The intended marks for questions or parts of questions are given in brackets [ ].

PART - I

(Attempt all questions from this Part.)

1. Choose the correct option: [16]

(A)

Union List	97
Concurrent List	?

(a) 47 (b) 57
(c) 75 (d) 87

(B) What happens if a vote of No-confidence is passed against a Minister?
(a) The Minister has to resign.
(b) The Prime Minister has to resign.
(c) The Whole Ministry has to resign.
(d) The Lok Sabha is dissolved.

(C) What is meant by Constituency?
(a) Seating arrangement of the members in the Parliament

(b) Territorial area which elects its representatives to the Lok Sabha
(c) Division of work among Council of Ministers
(d) The proportional representation of each State in the Rajya Sabha

(D) Which type of ministers hold important portfolios in the government?
(a) Council of Ministers
(b) Ministers of State
(c) Cabinet Ministers
(d) Deputy Ministers

(E) The Cabinet Ministers act as:
(a) legislators
(b) administrators
(c) supporters
(d) Both 'a' and 'b'

(F) How many types of Lok Adalats are there?
  (a) Two   (b) Three
  (c) Four   (d) Five

(G) .... passed the Vernacular Act in 1878.
  (a) Lord Dalhousie
  (b) Lord Lytton
  (c) Lord Wellesley
  (d) Lord Curzon

(H) Which of the following statements are correct about Simon Commission?
  (i) The Congress boycotted the Simon Commission.
  (ii) The Simon Commission did not have a single Indian member.
  Select the correct option from the codes given below:
  (a) Only (i)
  (b) Only (ii)
  (c) Both (i) and (ii)
  (d) Neither (i) nor (ii)

(I) Which among the following was lady representative from India in the second round table conference?
  (a) Sarojini Naidu
  (b) Aruna Asaf Ali
  (c) Sucheta Kripalani
  (d) Lakshmi Ghosh

(J) The Khilafat Movement was launched to protest against the humiliation of:
  (a) The Turkish caliph
  (b) Aga Khan
  (c) Mohammed Ali Jinnah
  (d) Sir Sayyad Ahmad Khan

(K) "Give me blood and I shall give you freedom" slogan was given by Bipin Chand Pal. Replace the underlined word to correct the statement.
  (a) Bal Gangadhar Tilak
  (b) Jyotiba Phule
  (c) Lala Lajpat Rai
  (d) Subhash Chandra Bose

(L) Under grouping of provinces in Cabinet Mission Plan, which group included Six Hindu Majority Provinces?
  (a) Group A
  (b) Group B
  (c) Group C
  (d) Both Group 'a' and 'c'

(M) What was the immediate cause of the First World War?
  (a) Sarajevo Crisis
  (b) Japan's invasion of China
  (c) Germany's invasion of Poland
  (d) Discontentment with Treaty of Versailles

(N) Fascism and Nazism did not believe in:
  (a) Democratic political system
  (b) Opposition to the rights and liberties of people
  (c) Rule of one party and one leader
  (d) Totalitarian rule

(O) The .... is the executive body of the United Nations Organisation.
  (a) General Assembly
  (b) Security Council
  (c) International Court of Justice
  (d) Trusteeship Council

(P) Where is the headquarter of WHO established?
  (a) Paris   (b) London
  (c) Chicago   (d) Geneva

2. (A) What do you understand by Single Transferable vote? [2]

(B) Mention two types of subordinate courts in a district. [2]

(C) Why was the "War of 1857" hailed as the First War of National Independence? [2]

(D) Name two newspapers started by Bal Gangadhar Tilak in order to spread the idea of notionalism. [2]

(E) Why was the proposal of August offer welcomed by the Muslim League and rejected by the Congress? [2]

(F) How was the outbreak of the Second World War an outcome of the First World War? [2]

(G) Mention *any two* functions of the WHO. [2]

SECTION - B

*(Attempt **any four** questions from this Section.)*

3. With reference to the Union Legislature, answer the following questions:

   (A) How is the Speaker of the Lok Sabha elected? State two Disciplinary Functions of the Speaker. [3]

   (B) Explain *two* conditions under which a member of Parliament can be disqualified under the Anti-Defection Law. [3]

   (C) Give reasons to justify why the Lok Sabha is considered to be more powerful than the Rajya Sabha. [4]

4. The makers of our Constitution adopted the Parliamentary and the Cabinet form of Government. With reference to this, answer the following questions:

   (A) (a) Who is the Constitutional Head of the Union Government?

   (b) What is meant by the Collective and Individual Responsibility of the members of the Cabinet? [3]

   (B) Explain briefly the position and powers of the Prime Minister in relation to the Cabinet. [3]

   (C) Distinguish between the Cabinet and the Council of Ministers. [4]

5. With reference to our Judiciary, discuss the following:

   (A) Why is the Judiciary kept independent of the control of the Executive and the Legislature? [3]

   (B) What do we mean when we refer to the Supreme Court and High Court as a 'Court of record'? [3]

   (C) Name the Writs that the High Courts are empowered to issue. What is meant by the Advisory Jurisdiction of the High Court? [4]

6. The establishment of the Indian National Congress led to the development of the National Movement in India. In this context, answer the following:

   (A) When was the Indian National Congress established? Who presided over its first session? [3]

   (B) What were the *four* aims of the Congress? [3]

   (C) Mention *four* basic beliefs of the Early Nationalists. [4]

7. In 1930, Mahatma Gandhi's demands were rejected by the British, as a result of which, he launched the Civil Disobedience Movement. In this context, explain the following:

   (A) Name the famous March undertaken by Gandhiji. Where did he begin this March? State two of its features. [3]

   (B) The Gandhi-Irwin Pact as a consequence of this Movement. [3]

   (C) Significance of the Second Round Table Conference. [4]

8. The Congress Working Committee passed the famous 'Quit India' resolution at Wardha in July 1942. With reference to this, answer the following questions:

   (A) What were the reasons for the passing of this resolution? [3]

   (B) What was the British Government's reaction to the 'Quit India' Movement? [3]

   (C) What was the impact and significance of this movement? [4]

9. The 1914 and 1939 wars that engulfed almost the entire world, were known as the World Wars due to its unprecedented impact and damage. In this context, answer the following:

   (A) Explain the immediate cause of the First World War. [3]

   (B) Explain the consequences of the Second World War with reference to the Cold War. [3]

(C) Mention *any four* terms of the Treaty of Versailles which affected Germany after World War I. [4]

10. With reference to the United Nations and its Specialized Agencies, answer the following:

(A) Mention *any three* functions of the International Court of Justice. [3]

(B) State the composition of the General Assembly. [3]

(C) State *any two* functions of the UNICEF and *any two* functions of WHO. [4]

ICSE SAMPLE PAPER 2023 EXAMINATION SELF ASSESSMENT

HISTORY & CIVICS
[H.C.G. PAPER-1]

Time Allowed: Two hours
Maximum Marks: 80

General Instructions:

(i) Answers to this Paper must be written on the paper provided separately.
(ii) You will not be allowed to write during first 15 minutes. This time is to be spent in reading the question paper.
(iii) The time given at the head of this Paper is the time allowed for writing the answers.
(iv) Attempt **all** questions from **Part I** (Compulsory).
(v) A total of **five** questions are to be attempted from Part II, **two** out of three questions from **Section A** and **three** out of five questions from **Section B**.
(vi) The intended marks for questions or parts of questions are given in brackets [ ].

SECTION - A
(Attempt all questions from this Section.)

1. Choose the correct option: [16]

(A)

Questions Hour	10 days Notice
Zero Hour	?

(a) 7 days notice
(b) 14 days notice
(c) 30 days notice
(d) No notice

(B) During the Question Hour, what are the starred questions?
(a) Those questions to which a member wishes to have an oral answer on the floor of the House
(b) Those questions to which answers are given in written form
(c) Those questions which relate to a matter of urgent importance
(d) Those questions which are of public interest

(C) "Adjournment of the House means the suspension of the sitting of the House by the Speaker". On which of the following condition the House cannot be Adjourned?
(a) After the business for the day is over
(b) The Prime Minister is absent in the House
(c) For want of Quorum
(d) When the death of a sitting/ex-member of the House occurs

(D) Which of the following is not a necessary qualification for the election of the Vice President of India?

Sample Paper 5   305

(a) He/She should be a citizen of India
(b) He/She must have completed the age of thirty five years
(c) He/She must be qualified for election as member of Lok Sabha
(d) He/She must not hold any office of profit under the Union or State government

(E) Who administers oath of office to the President of India?
(a) The Vice President
(b) The Prime Minister
(c) The Chief Justice
(d) The Speaker of Lok Sabha

(F) The composition of the Supreme Court is ....
(a) 31 judges and 1 Chief Justice
(b) 30 judges and 1 Chief Justice
(c) 33 judges and 1 Chief Justice
(d) 22 judges and 1 Chief Justice

(G) Which statement does not apply to the Subsidiary alliance?
(a) The kings virtually lost their powers
(b) It was introduced by Lord Dalhousie
(c) The kings had to maintain the British army at their cost
(d) They had a British resident in their court

(H) Which of the following were Assertive Nationalist Leaders?
(I) Dadabhai Naoroji
(II) Bal Gangadhar Tilak
(III) Lala Lajpat Rai
(IV) Gopal Krishna Gokhale
(a) (I) and (II)   (b) (II) and (III)
(c) (II) and (IV)   (d) (I) and (IV)

(I) Which of the following was not a cause for Non-Cooperation Movement?
(a) Rowlatt Act, 1919
(b) Sepoy Mutiny, 1857
(c) Jallainwala Bagh Tragedy
(d) Khilafat movement

(J) The Supreme Commander of the Indian National Army:
(a) Subash Chandra Bose
(b) Ras Behari Gosh
(c) Jawaharlal Nehru
(d) Lord Wavell

(K) "Refusal of the demand for Pakistan will amount to dividing the country into so many Pakistans". Which leader gave this Statement?
(a) M.A. Jinnah
(b) Sardar Patel
(c) Jawahar lal Nehru
(d) Subhash Chandra Bose

(L) Britain and France followed the policy of appeasement against ....
(a) Germany   (b) Italy
(c) Russia   (d) Poland

(M) Which of the following countries was not a part of Triple Alliance during the First World War?
(a) Germany   (b) France
(c) Austria-Hungary (d) Italy

(N) Which of the following was not a similarity between Fascism and Nazism.
(a) Fundamental Rights and Individual freedom
(b) Corporatism and Racism
(c) Aggressive nationalism and imperialism
(d) Anti-communist and anti-democratic rule

(O) The non-permanent members of the security council are elected for a term of .... years.
(a) One   (b) Two
(c) Three   (d) Five

(P) .... was awarded the Noble Prize for Peace in the year 1965 and the Indira Gandhi Prize for Peace in 1989:
(a) UNICEF   (b) UNESCO
(c) IMO   (d) WHO

2. (A) What is meant by "Collective Responsibility" of the cabinet? [2]

(B) Which body is the highest judicial authority in both civil as well as criminal matters at the district level? [2]

(C) How was the Army reorganized after the First War of Indian Independence? [2]

(D) Name the moderate leader who explained the economic 'Drain Theory' in the colonial times. [2]

(E) What did the British do to foster the policy of "Divide and Love', which gave rise to the formation of the Muslim League.' [2]

(F) Mention any two contributions of Subhash Chandra Bose in India's Freedom Struggle. [2]

(G) State two underlying principles of Fascism. [2]

(H) What was the Berlin-Rome-Tokyo Axis? Why did Hitler demand the Danzig corridor from Poland? [2]

PART - II

SECTION A

*(Attempt **any two** questions from this Section.)*

3. With reference to the Union Parliament, answer the following questions:

(A) How many members may be nominatd to the Lok Sabha and the Rajya Sabha? Give one reason as to why they may be nominated to the Lok Sabha. [3]

(B) Mention any three qualifications required for a member to be elected to the Lok Sabha. [3]

(C) What is meant by the term 'Session'? Name the three Sessions of the Union Parliament. [4]

4. (A) Identify the person in the picture. Briefly explain his appointment to the post. [3]

(B) What is his position under the Parliamentary system of government? [3]

(C) State the position of the Prime Minister and state any two of his powers in relation to the president. [4]

5. With reference to our Judiciary, discuss the following:

(A) Why is the Judiciary kept independent of the control of the Executive and the Legislature? [3]

(B) What do we mean when we refer to the Supreme Court and High Court as a 'Court of record'? [3]

(C) Name the Writs that the High Courts are empowered to issue. What is meant by the Advisory Jurisdiction of the High Court? [4]

6. With reference to Nationalism and the birth of the Indian National Congress, explain each of the following:

(A) Vernacular Press Act, 1878. [3]

(B) Role of Sir Syed Ahamad Khan in the formation of the Muslim League. [3]

(C) State any four immediate objectives of the Indian National Congress. [4]

7. Through various National Movements, Gandhiji mobilized public support to win freedom for India. In this context, state the following:

(A) Any three causes for Gandhi to launch the Non-Cooperation Movement? [3]

(B) The name given to the uprising of 1942. Two reasons for lauching this mass uprising. [3]

(C) The impact of the Non-Cooperation Movement in India's freedom struggle. [4]

8. (A) Identify the leader in the picture. Give two examples to state that the leader followed an expansionist policy. [3]

(B) State three factors that led to the rise of Fascism. [3]

(C) State four similarities between the ideologies of Nazism and Fascism. [4]

9. With reference to the Cold War and the Non-Aligned Movement, answer the following questions:

(A) Explain Truman's Doctrine. [3]

(B) State any three consequences of the Cold War. [3]

(C) Mention four major objectives of the Non-Aligned Movement. [4]

10. The horrors of the two World Wars, led to the formation of the United Nations Organization, while the formation of the Non-Aligned Movement followed later. In this context, answer the following:

(A) Mention any three aims and objectives of the United Nations Organization. [3]

(B) Explain any three functions of the Security Council. [3]

(C) Explain any four factors that led the the formation of the Non-Aligned Movement. [4]

CPSIA information can be obtained
at www.ICGtesting.com
Printed in the USA
LVHW070841250323
742592LV00017B/1509